'Combining ▓▓▓ with intimacy, and technical grasp with humour and humanity, *The Railways* is by some distance the most ambitious and enriching book I have ever read on this subject. It is destined to become a classic of British social history.' David Kynaston

'Simon Bradley is not an ideal, but *the* ideal railway historian. Yes, he is a buff of buffs, a trainspotter extraordinaire. [T]he joy of Bradley's book is that, by telling the story of the railways, he has told the story of all of us British over the last 150 years. Turning the pages, we will cheer the ingenuity of the Victorians, curse the name of Beeching and Harold Macmillan, and recall the many moments of life in which the railways have played a central role. They made us what we are – both as a nation and as individuals, and this book is the classic, beautifully written, learned exposition of that glorious fact.' A. N. Wilson, *Sunday Times*

'A superbly crafted, lovingly assembled tribute to our railways ... the current, tattered state of our railways should in no way detract from Bradley's narrative. This is a first-class, entertaining analysis of a great, albeit troubled, institution that has now been given a history worthy of its national significance.' Robin McKie, *Observer*

'A magnificent story both intricate and gripping ... Bradley has mastered the detail without losing touch with the romance' Matthew Parris, *The Times*

'The entire book is written with a rare combination of easy-going style and Olympian knowledge ... Bradley is one of that happy band of writers who are interested in everything, and also – rarer still – capable of making everything interesting ... this book concertinas the present and the past, the real and the imagined, and, by doing so, turns what might have been Timothy Potter's trainspotter's guide into something much closer to a work of art' Craig Brown, *Mail on Sunday*

'[A] magnificent homage to railways and their inestimable influence on British society over two centuries. This has to be my railway book of the year.' John Lees, *Railway Magazine*

'A superb and challenging work of railway history, but it is also so much more ... it goes way beyond conventional, introverted, trainspottery literature and deals with some very unexpected themes ... Dr Bradley explodes many myths about the railways ... fascinating ... elegantly written, magisterial and utterly enthralling' Gavin Stamp, *Country Life*

'Bradley's loving tribute to the golden age of the railway is a magnificent achievement ... a gorgeous Christmas pudding of a book ... most eye-catching are the superbly crafted chapters on accidents and murders, yet where his book really shines is in its portraits of the British themselves ... his book is so colourful, so rich and engaging, that even if you don't like railways you should love it' Dominic Sandbrook, *Sunday Times*

'A fascinating, encyclopaedic story of how the railways worked. Bradley's research is astonishing ... [his] tone is witty, elegant and literate ... [a] tour de force' Michael Binyon, *The Times*

'The most enjoyable book I've read this year ... I was totally gripped ... I had more fun reading this book than any book I've read this year ... he writes with such love and enthusiasm, and when you get a writer who brings that degree of enthusiasm it's so infectious' Max Hastings, BBC Radio 4 Front Row

'Bradley has written an authoritative and comprehensive history that entertains and informs in equal measure. This is a celebration of the railways that neither descends into nostalgia nor ventures into trainspotter land ... the reward for Bradley's ambition in writing a comprehensive social history of the railways is that his book will sit happily on the shelves next to railway classics such as Jack Simmons's *The Railway in Town and Country*, probably the nearest equivalent. This is definitely the book to give to that great uncle who you think is interested in trains. But it is also a fitting present for that railway buff who thinks he knows everything there is to know about the railways. This book will show he is mistaken.' Christian Wolmar, *Spectator*

THE
RAILWAYS

SIMON BRADLEY is joint editor of the celebrated Pevsner Architectural Guides, to which he has contributed a number of notable revised volumes. He started trainspotting aged eleven, and his interest in railways has broadened and endured. He is the author of *St Pancras Station* (Profile), and lives in London.

ALSO BY SIMON BRADLEY

St Pancras Station

THE
RAILWAYS

NATION, NETWORK AND PEOPLE

SIMON BRADLEY

P

PROFILE BOOKS

This paperback edition published in 2016

First published in Great Britain in 2015 by
PROFILE BOOKS LTD
3 Holford Yard
Bevin Way
London WC1X 9HD

www.profilebooks.com

Copyright © Simon Bradley, 2015, 2016

3 5 7 9 10 8 6 4 2

Typeset in Garamond by MacGuru Ltd

Printed and bound in Great Britain by Clays, St Ives plc

The moral right of the author has been asserted.

A CIP catalogue record for this book is available from the British Library.

ISBN 978 1 84668 213 1
eISBN 978 1 84765 352 9

FSC
www.fsc.org
MIX
Paper from
responsible sources
FSC® C018072

CONTENTS

INTRODUCTION

Until the age of eleven, I paid almost no attention to railways. The family went everywhere by car. Journeys to school were by bus, or on foot (this was the 1970s). What knowledge I had picked up came mostly from the few pages about trains – trains rather than railways, that is – that cropped up in books of the *Our Amazing World* kind. These introduced George and Robert Stephenson and their *Rocket* and proclaimed the *Mallard*'s world speed record for a steam locomotive in 1938 as another source of legitimate British pride; but this was tame stuff by comparison with atom-smashers, moon shots or Concorde. My great-grandfather had been an engine driver, and his son had briefly followed him on to the footplate, but it was Grandpa's subsequent share in the defeat of the Axis powers that had value in the playground economy of competitive boasting. My father's wistful cries when old footage of steam locomotives appeared on the television woke no echoes within me. I did not even own a Hornby model railway.

All this changed with secondary school. Mine stood on the triangle of land between the tracks leading away from Clapham Junction. Electric commuter trains passed on one side or another every few seconds, and many boys used them to get to school. This profusion had helped to keep the mid-century trainspotting cult alive for successive cohorts of incoming eleven-year-olds. Most gave up after a year or so, but others stayed keen. We could even register as spotters with the school authorities, a bit like more serious cases of addiction in the world outside. Registered spotters were entitled to spend the lunch hour at otherwise out-of-bounds vantage points, including an iron fire escape with a panorama of the main line to Brighton. Here we were safe from harassment by the school's hard lads and free from nosy invigilation by prefects and masters.

All the locomotives and passenger trains that passed had yellow ends for easy visibility and blue or blue-and-white sides: the corporate colours of our own nationalised British Rail, unchanged since the mid 1960s, the same from Penzance to Thurso. Highlights of the passing show were the diesel-hauled freights, especially those with mixed processions of wagons of every shape and size, sometimes with cargoes exposed: National Coal Board fuels, drums of British Steel Corporation wire, British Leyland cars. Their locomotives might come from depots hundreds of miles away, sometimes in obscure localities familiar only to insiders, such as Toton, Bescot or Healey Mills; places more resonant than suburban Wimbledon or Selhurst, where the commuters' electric units were berthed overnight. Trains coasting down the slow incline towards Clapham Junction could be seen half a mile off, prompting competitive displays of recognition skills as the distant yellow blob gradually resolved itself into a distinctive configuration. Trains coming the other way were heard before they were seen, so we tried to memorise the various engine sounds.

We might even wave at the driver in his cab, in the half-ironical spirit with which adolescents carry on with things they fear may appear childish; but we valued the brief transmission of respect when a hand was raised in return. Less exalted in our eyes were the gangs of workers who came regularly to inspect and maintain the four lines of track, retreating to safety every few minutes at a signal from the lookout man; always just too far away for their voices to be overheard, or for their faces to be distinguishable. Driver and ganger alike belonged nonetheless to the world of proper work, visible and practical and comprehensible – a world away from the office-bound lives of most of our own fathers. For all that we dodged the odd fare and cheeked the ticket collectors, we sensed the integrity and purpose of the railway. Encouraged by vague ideas of expressing solidarity with the 'real', there was even a schoolboy fashion for versions of the black donkey jackets worn by the men on the track, the standard working man's apparel of the seventies.

A few summers later, aged sixteen, I spent an entire August day on the end of Platform 4 at Newcastle Central station. The family had returned north to the city of my birth the year before. My new friends there were all mystified by the practice of spotting, and certainly it was hard not to feel self-conscious; surely I was too old for all this now? Dressed in a baggy black V-neck and black corduroys – an almost convincing attempt at post-punk style – I snootily noted the incongruity with the chosen-by-Mum leisure jackets of other teenage spotters. Yet if anyone had challenged us, we would probably have closed ranks and denied being mere trainspotters; we were 'interested in railways', we were 'enthusiasts'.

Besides, there were extenuating circumstances: I was trying to give up. At least, I had decided that this should be the last trainspotting day. There was a target in view, too. In a few months, the most powerful express diesel locomotives on the system – the Deltics, British Rail's Class 55 – were due to be withdrawn after twenty years' service. These were as charismatic as locomotives could get without actually being powered by steam. At once huge and smartly styled, each was equipped with two marine-type engines and made an intense sound quite unlike anything else on the rails. All twenty-two bore names: some of Derby winners, others of Northern or Scottish regiments. With London school friends, I had clambered exultantly into their unattended cabs on weekend visits to the maintenance depot at Finsbury Park in north London, where the indulgent foreman allowed spotters the run of the place, or begged a few moments on board from their drivers on the platform at King's Cross. I had since seen all the Deltics but one: 55 021, *Argyll & Sutherland Highlander*.

That this elusive machine should pull into the station half an hour before I was due to head home, taking the most cinematic approach across the Tyne Bridge and round the sharply curved viaduct towards the platforms, was almost too good to be true. There were even a couple of exposures left on the Kodak to capture the moment. Who cared about looking nerdy now that I had the set? The Deltic numbers printed in my *Locoshed Book* could become a solid block at last, zebra-striped by evenly spaced underlining. Future sightings would produce a sense of conquest and completion.

A year or so later *Argyll & Sutherland Highlander* was so many acetylene-cut chunks ready for the furnace and I was no longer spending days on platforms with notebook in hand. Yet the interest in railways endured, growing broader and deeper. Every public library then had a shelf-load of books by post-war authors such as C. Hamilton Ellis, L. T. C. Rolt and David St John Thomas, lively and engaging writers who leavened technical description with human interest and historical understanding.

They described the railways of their own time, those of their youth and those of bygone generations. I read my way through these shelves.

Any aspect of the railways that was elderly, threatened or declining now assumed an increasing appeal. Those long trains of mixed wagons that had rumbled every day past the school fire escape were among the last of their kind: more than a century and a half after the first locomotive-hauled public railway opened for business, the ordinary general freight train had become hopelessly uneconomic and was disappearing fast. The future looked better for the bulk conveyance of minerals and chemicals, though here too there was change in the air. From the platforms at Newcastle it was still possible to see coal trains running without continuous brakes; when the locomotive stopped, the buffers pushed noisily together as each wagon hit the one in front. This relic of George Stephenson's railways lingered into 1980s Tyneside, sharing the same tracks as the streamlined Inter-City 125s, the fastest diesels in the world. The raw, archaic sound resounded for a few more years over the ancient quays and crumbling warehouses, a rebuke to the shiny consumerism that was taking over the rest of the city.

Much else that was commonplace in the 1980s has since vanished too. Many passenger trains then still included compartments opening off a side corridor, a development of the non-communicating compartment type used on the very first pre-Victorian carriages. The Night Mail in the 1980s was still 'crossing the Border / Bringing the cheque and the postal order'. Some mail trains featured special windowless carriages known as Travelling Post Offices, in which swaying night-shift workers sorted first-class letters into tiers of pigeonholes during the course of the journey. These carriages had slots in their sides, so that last-minute letters could be posted on the platform, subject to a small supplement. British Rail also transported much of the nation's newsprint, and masses of parcels went by train too. This traffic required other specialised vans and carriages, and separate platforms and compounds at the major stations, where a great deal of shunting went on. There were Motorail trains, strange hybrids with carriages at one end and flat wagons or covered vans for the conveyance of passengers' cars at the other. Motorail's advertising stressed modernity and convenience, but the practice had been going on since the 1830s, when private carriages were first mounted on flat trucks.

Such were the joys of train-watching in Mrs Thatcher's first administration. Much of the network is busier now, although in terms of traffic it is much duller and more predictable. But trains are only part of the story. The railways remain a uniquely discrete system: a physically separate domain, its thousands of route-miles fenced off from the rest of the country and ruled by their own mysterious rhythms and laws. Parts of this system are new, other parts very old – some of them the oldest in the world and with buildings and structures intact. For those who have been initiated, a unique allure resides in the fabric and architecture of the railways, rather than in the trains themselves.

Take Newcastle station, an early-Victorian masterpiece, begun in 1846. Its frontage is a mighty display of classical architecture in the local golden sandstone, centred on a round-arched portico as roomy as a concert hall.* Behind, trains still pass through the original curving shelter or train shed of iron and glass, three parallel arched spans following a steady curve, the earliest structure of this form anywhere. Newcastle's street plan was revised in order to align with the station entrance, and the viaducts and bridges approaching it created the modern image of the city. A little way along the line to Carlisle, going west, still older station houses can be found, treated like ornamented lodges to a gentleman's estate. These date from the Newcastle & Carlisle Railway's opening in the mid 1830s: before Victoria and Albert, before postage stamps, electric telegraph companies, ocean-going steamships or photography. By comparison, Clapham Junction station in the 1970s was at a low ebb architecturally – the old booking halls had been shut to save money, and tickets were sold from a prefabricated kiosk. Yet the place inspired awe, both because of its unrelenting traffic flows and for its sheer extent; a quarter of an hour is needed just to walk round the public perimeter of all its running lines and sidings.

The lines themselves – the 'permanent way', in railway terminology – carried a historical charge of their own. Landscapes that had barely altered since Shakespeare's time were suddenly scarred by gigantic embankments, or punctured by tunnels so long that the very survival of the enginemen amid the smoke and fumes was sometimes imperilled. Tens of thousands of bridges and viaducts carried the new routes across roads, rivers and streams, flood plains and estuaries. Some of these – the Forth Bridge, Brunel's bridge over the Tamar at Saltash, the soaring viaduct across Newcastle's Dean Street – still take the breath away; most now carry trains vastly heavier, faster and more frequent than those of their early years.

---

* Spoiled in 2013, when the open arches were glazed.

As teenage interests widened into new historical and literary terrain, I found the railways waiting there too. They had reconfigured many relationships between residence and place of work, and between town and country. They transformed the conventions of tourism and holidays. Regiments no longer marched for days across the land; prisoners handcuffed to their escorts found carriage seats amid the blameless citizenry; the rail-borne dead were smoothly conveyed across the counties to their ancestral parishes for burial. The railways' size and complexity forced the pace of change in insurance, accountancy and management. Railways promulgated mass advertising, both for their own services and for anyone who would pay for display space. They had promoted changes in the national diet, which became at once more varied and less distinctive from region to region. They had fostered new publishing formats, and even new types of literature, easily consumed on the move. The everyday lives of those who wrote so vividly about railways – Dickens, Trollope and Ruskin among them – were in turn subjected to their inexorable discipline.

To travel through Britain equipped with a little knowledge of how its railways were built and operated is therefore to journey in time as well as space. This book attempts to explore further this railway-haunted territory. It does so not by chronicling the growth of the network – that has been ably done elsewhere – nor by turning the spotlight on that old scene-stealer, the locomotive. Instead, it begins by following an imagined journey. The starting point is the carriage itself, a space formed and transformed by ever-shifting force fields in which technological change, safety, social class, gender relations and public health all exerted their pull on travellers' bodies and consciousness. Infrastructure then takes command, from the ballast beneath the track to the grandest achievements of railway architecture and engineering. This leads on to the story of how the railways first fostered the growth of freight traffic and then had to cope with its painful decline. Questions of operation, control, management, communication and labour all come into play. The railway station follows, considered in the broadest terms of form and function and as a place of commerce and image-making. Lastly, the book explores the world of the railway enthusiast, from teenaged spotters to the adult volunteers who have saved entire lines from closure, as well as their forerunners in older generations: the first who came to understand the railways not simply as a force for modernity, but as a place where the present is confronted and enriched by the past.

PART I

IN THE CARRIAGE

THE TIME OF THE RAILWAYS

If you fell asleep on a moving train tomorrow and awoke to find yourself transported back a century and a half in time – say, to 1862 – but still travelling onward, what would the differences be?

For a start, the shape, size, structure and materials of the carriage would be altogether unlike anything on modern commercial rails. Quite different too would be the sounds and smells, the rhythms and jolts, the entire world of the senses. Some aspects of this environment of 1862 would persist into the lifetimes of those still living; other features would be obsolete within less than a generation. But before looking more closely at this mobile enclosure, in which millions of people enjoyed or endured billions of hours – a space of confinement and of liberation, of solitude and of enforced companionship – it is worth sketching some outlines of the British railway network of 150 years ago.

This network had no governing plan. It happened by convergence and individual initiative, joining up the scattering of pioneer lines of the 1830s. Nor was there any consensus at first as to how far the railways might spread. Even after the early lines had shown what they could do, the first rush to invest in extensions and additions soon faltered. More miles of canals than of railways were built in the 1830s, and just one new railway bill passed through the parliamentary sessions of 1840 and 1841. For the *Railway Times*, it was quite good enough that Scotland could be reached after 1840 by fast steamship from the new rail-connected port at Fleetwood, Lancashire ('What more can any reasonable man want?'). But

THE
CHEAPEST AND EASIEST ROUTE
FROM
SCOTLAND
TO
THE SOUTH.

The Public are respectfully informed that a Communication is opened between Carlisle and London, with only Fourteen Miles of Road Travelling.

Passengers leaving Carlisle by the 8·30 a.m. Train, will proceed by the Newcastle and Carlisle and Brandling Junction Railways to Rainton, thence by Superior fast Four-horse Omnibuses through Durham to South Church, afterwards by Rail via Darlington and York, and arrive in London at Five o'clock the following Morning.

A poster of 1841, suggestive of the constant flux in travel
arrangements caused by the opening of new railway routes

the picture changed again as the high dividends on railway shares were noted – so much so that the mid 1840s were remembered for the 'Railway Mania'. This was a textbook boom in which stock was oversubscribed and prices were inflated by speculators who got in early in order to sell up at an immediate profit; hence Karl Marx's description of the phenomenon in *Kapital* as 'the first great railway swindle'. Everything then came down with a crash, so that more than a third of the railway mileage authorised in these years was never built. Even so, the speculative peak of 1844–5 was followed by a mighty wave of construction as the paid-up lines took shape, with the peak of activity in 1847. Investment in railways in that extraordinary year accounted for almost 7 per cent of national income. After which came a period of solemn reflection and abstinence, ending in 1852–3 with a smaller and less well-remembered boom, then another dip, and then a steady rise to a second climax in 1866, by which time the chief investors were institutions rather than individuals.

In the early 1860s there was therefore no sense that the railway adventure had come to an end. The speculative turbulence of the early years left a residue of mistrust, but it was not intrinsic to railways as a *method* of transport. To the contemporary mind, they still represented the essence of modernity. In certain towns bypassed by early main lines, the blame was laid on municipal reactionaries for failing to grasp the chance of a connection when it came. The MP for Abingdon in Berkshire actually managed to kill off the first proposal for a branch line to the town. A similar story is repeated, less fairly, of Northampton. Here the company in question was the London & Birmingham, the world's first long-distance railway, opened in 1837–8; the populace was eager for the line to come that way, and it was the county landowners who led the party of opposition. (Yet the legend of blockheads at the town hall endures: on a train to Northampton an inhabitant was recently overheard repeating it to a visitor, as if to say, *What else can you expect from the folk round here?*) Railway builders around 1860 thus had many goals still to aim at: connecting to bypassed towns, pushing fresh lines into more remote areas, making short cuts for cross-country traffic. Because Britain was served by many independent lines, their companies also increasingly competed for traffic by means of rival or alternative routes.

The last English county to be joined to the national network was Cornwall, into which Isambard Kingdom Brunel's Cornwall Railway began running trains in 1859. Three years later, the Isle of Wight received its first railway, the Cowes & Newport. On 1 July 1862 the inaugural train ran along its four miles of route in less than ten minutes. That was faster than anyone had ever travelled on the Isle of Wight before – simply because the steam railway could routinely go faster than a galloping horse, on which the existing limit on human swiftness depended. Having subjugated the surface of Britain, railways began to probe below it. The Metropolitan Railway's inaugural route was to have opened that same year, had the noxious waters of the Fleet Ditch not burst into its cavernous brick-lined tunnel as the line was under construction through London from Paddington to Farringdon Street. That put back the opening day of the world's pioneer underground railway until the second week of 1863. One year later, the first train steamed into the new station at Aberystwyth, completing the railway route westward through the heart of Welsh-speaking Wales.

In Scotland, where railways spread outwards from the Central Belt anchored by Edinburgh and Glasgow, two great natural barriers had yet to be bridged in 1862, the firths of the Forth and the Tay. The bridges that eventually did the job have both become famous, for rather different reasons; less well-known is that trains had begun crossing these waters by

Railways penetrate beneath the streets of London: King's Cross station
on the Metropolitan Railway, from the *Illustrated London News*, 1868

means of special ferries and floating jetties as early as the 1850s. That these
gaps would one day be filled by something more solid would not have
been doubted by any progressive-minded person in 1862.

The modern-minded traveller in mid-Victorian decades thus kept an
eye on the railway map for new routes and opportunities. The poet and
critic Matthew Arnold (1822–88), who was also a government inspector
of schools, was of this class. His tours of inspection entailed a punishing amount of long- and medium-distance travel, largely by rail. January
1852 – a representative itinerary – began with a train connection from
Windermere to the London & North Western Railway's great junction
at Crewe and continued with appointments at schools in at least fifteen
towns, dotted across eight counties. Windermere was the nearest station
to the inspector-poet's Lake District retreat, Fox Howe at Rydal. Before
setting off for the Monday morning train, Arnold found the time to finish his latest poem, 'The Youth of Nature'. It was an elegy to his recently
deceased neighbour William Wordsworth, a confirmed hater of railways,
who back in 1844–5 had done all he could to prevent the branch line
to Windermere happening at all. To this end, Wordsworth composed a
celebrated anti-railway sonnet, which he posted to Mr Gladstone, then
President of the Board of Trade, and also published as a pamphlet. The
railway company then modified its plans a little, so that the line stopped

a mile short of the Windermere shore. Perhaps the episode came into Arnold's mind that morning as he wrote of the late poet laureate, 'He grew old in an age that he condemn'd ... And, like the Theban seer / Died in his enemies' day'.

Which was true enough: Wordsworth was already sixty years old when the first modern railway opened between Liverpool and Manchester in 1830. Arnold understood all too well that his venerable subject's views on Church, State and Nature were formed in an England that no longer existed. His own father, the headmaster and reformer Dr Thomas Arnold of Rugby (1795–1842), had also realised as much, but had embraced the coming age of change. The railways got to him unusually early: in 1835, to be precise. In that year Dr Arnold received a visit from the engineer Robert Stephenson, who was surveying the London & Birmingham line through Kilsby in Northamptonshire, where the headmaster held some property – this as a consequence of having been turned away from the route through Northampton. Five miles north-west of Kilsby the route passed through Rugby, and before long that town was noted as much for its timetabled stops for visiting the station refreshment rooms as for Dr Arnold's school. Looking down from a bridge at a train running on the completed line, the headmaster made a remark that has become celebrated: 'I rejoice to see it ... and think that feudality is gone forever.' Perhaps Dr Arnold also had in mind some easing of the journey to his country retreat at Rydal, which he had built in 1832 with advice from Wordsworth, his friend. When Matthew Arnold left this house twenty years later, he had an easier journey still.

Arnold's leisure hours, too, were transformed by the growing railway network. From Folkestone on 15 August 1861, Arnold wrote to his mother that he had begged his wife Florence ('Flu') to join him from their home in Belgravia: 'come down today by the new line – London Chatham & Dover – which goes to Victoria'. For Flu it would have been a walk or cab ride of about 500 yards from the Arnolds' residence in Chester Square to the new Victoria terminus, opened only the year before but already familiar enough to be identifiable by the unqualified use of the monarch's name. In 1863 another letter from Arnold to his mother described a pleasant evening party spent with family and friends on Clapham Common: 'by the new rail from Victoria we are only seven minutes from it'. This was the West London Extension Railway, from West Brompton to Clapham Junction, opened three months previously. Its route included a new bridge across the Thames, one of five iron bridges built by railway companies to reach Kensington, Westminster or the City of London in the years 1859– 69. Most of the earlier lines into London had been stopped short of the innermost districts north of the river, so these new bridges made the capital's railways spectacularly visible above ground at the same time that they were beginning to push their way beneath it.

Arnold calls his line to Clapham 'the new rail'. 'I see they have begun our rail,' says Mr Vincent of St Saviour's College in *Loss and Gain*, John Henry Newman's Oxford novel of 1848. Both expressions would have baffled anyone in the 1820s, before the language flexed and compressed itself in the cause of new technology. First, the companies' own terminology became brisker and more businesslike. The ponderous but technically correct 'locomotive engine' was swiftly abbreviated to 'engine' alone, or else, as in writings by Robert Stephenson as early as 1828, to 'locomotive' – a term that was general currency by about 1850. 'Train' is an early contraction of 'train of wagons' or 'train of carriages'. The *Annual Register* for 1830 used both long and short versions, that for 1831 already the short version only. Travellers and customers were quick to catch up, like the frequent flyers who slip into today's airline jargon. Lay British usage gradually gave up the well-established term 'railroad', which now sounds thoroughly North American, but which for several decades was used interchangeably with 'railway', the industry's preferred term.

It is striking also how some usefully terse Victorian railway expressions have lapsed into disuse. To travel by railway was to 'take train for' a destination, or non-specifically, just to 'take train'. In John Galsworthy's *The Man of Property* (1906), George Forsyte 'took train at South Kensington station (for everyone today went Underground)'. The time of departure was 'train-time'; to 'lose the train' was to fail to observe it. 'As lang as ah live, ah winnet forget th' day we lost the train' is the refrain of *Wor Nanny's a Mazer*, by the Tyneside pitman and balladeer Tommy Armstrong, born in 1848 (Nanny and the singer resort to the pub for a quick drink before the next train comes, then another drink, and then one more ...) When Daniel Povey says 'I came by mail from Crewe', in Arnold Bennett's *The Old Wives' Tale* (1908, but set some forty years earlier), he means not some strange self-posting arrangement but an overnight journey on the mail trains, many of which included carriages for fare-paying passengers. Another widely understood convention was the use of 'up' and 'down' to designate trains to and from London, and by extension to other cities and major destinations. The murderous mysteries of timetabling which Miss Marple sets out to unravel in Agatha Christie's *4.50 from Paddington* (1957) are still phrased in these terms. They must be quite opaque to most present-day readers of the Queen of Crime.

Still with us are the railway expressions that have spread into common use: running out of steam, letting off steam, on the right lines, going off the rails, hitting the buffers. Stock phrases now, but smart and vivid in their day, signalling modern-mindedness in speech and in writing. To an author with a genius for extended metaphor, the railways were a golden gift. Here is Dickens, in *Little Dorrit* (1857): 'Mrs General had no opinions. [...] She had a little circular set of mental grooves or rails on which she started little trains of other people's opinions, which never overtook one another, and never got anywhere.'

Metaphors, and vocabulary too: as Dickens's weekly *All The Year Round* asserted in 1863, '"Stoke", "shunt", "siding", &c., are all perfectly legitimate words'. And so we have Mrs Veneering, 'waking Lady Tippins from a snore, by dexterously shunting a train of plates and dishes at her knuckles across the table', in *Our Mutual Friend* (1865).

Dickens had even more fun with one of the early institutions of railway travel, Bradshaw. George Bradshaw (1801–53) was a Manchester Quaker and engraver who had published several well-received maps of canals and early railways. Fame and wealth followed when he spotted a related gap in the market. The railway companies were already advertising the times of trains at stations and by placing notices in the newspapers, and some local railway guides had been published, but there was nothing by way of a compact and portable summary of services across the whole country. Bradshaw therefore set out to provide the first printed *Time Tables* – the term is another railway coinage – beginning in 1839. They were an instant success. This first booklet was tiny, a mere four and a half by three inches and regional in scope. Bradshaw's original intention was that updated sheets could be bought every month, Filofax-fashion, for pasting over those pages that were no longer current. But the network was growing too fast; the following year witnessed the opening of thirteen new lines. Wholly new editions at monthly intervals were the answer. In 1841 came *Bradshaw's Railway Guide*, a somewhat larger object. The September 1845 edition already amounted to eighty-nine pages. Growth continued – 1847 alone added twenty-seven new railway lines – and gradually the essential *Guide* became as thick as a brick. When a time capsule was walled into the foundations of Cleopatra's Needle on the Thames Embankment in 1878, a copy of the latest Bradshaw was included. New editions continued to appear until issue no. 1521 in June 1961, by which time the challenge was to keep up with line closures rather than openings. Passengers and railway staff alike were then left to fumble with the separate volumes produced by British Railways' six separate regions, before an official single-volume compendium at last appeared in 1974.

Many found Bradshaw's ever-expanding book no easier to understand than the network itself. Even now it is difficult to look at its pages without a sense of quiet panic. The timetable columns are confusingly interspersed with bands that indicate arrival times for connections, before the same train resumes (with a later time, referring to departure) at the head of the next band, from the same station. Mysterious little pointing hands appear: in superimposed boxes for cross-references, but also within the columns and indicating up or down. An exhausting variety of exceptions is shown, many according to the day of the week (Mondays and Saturdays especially, but also a marked bias to Wednesdays), others to indicate set-down-only stops. Now and again a threatening black bar intrudes, with the word **Stop** below. Some of the font sizes recall those used for novelty miniature bibles. The paper is bad, the print surprisingly faint. Even the index is harassing: large towns may have references to over a hundred different pages, depending on the line and the direction of travel.

It was easy to get a laugh at Bradshaw's expense. *Punch* put the book in his Tourist's Alphabet: 'B is the *Bradshaw* which leads you to swear'. 'Do not buy a *Bradshaw* unless you want a headache', the sporting novelist R. S. Surtees advised in 1851 (he recommended the companies' timetables instead). The young Charles Dodgson, alias Lewis Carroll, even wrote a comic opera *Guida di Bragia* – a burlesque of Bradshaw – to entertain his sisters.

Dickens conflated the challenges of travel with those of trying to read Bradshaw's guide in the 'Narrative of Extraordinary Suffering', in his magazine *Household Words* for 12 July 1851. As with much of Dickens's best writing on railways – and no literary author wrote better about them in nineteenth-century Britain – the piece straddles the line between journalism and fiction. It was topical, too: July 1851 was the third month of the Great Exhibition in Hyde Park, in a year when railways with a London connection reported rises in passenger traffic of up to 38 per cent.

Dickens imagines among these visiting hordes a Mr Lost, 'of the

Maze, Ware'. Quite unable to master Bradshaw, he gives up on the trains and goes down to London in his own horse-chaise. From there he tries to reach Worcester by rail, but is halted at Tring and again at Leighton. The tone becomes delirious, as Mr Lost's progress is blocked again and again by the 'dreaded black barrier' – the black bar in Bradshaw's columns that indicates when a train goes no further. He finds himself 'listlessly travelling anywhere' on the London & North Western Railway, after which 'He repeatedly found himself in the Isle of Man'. Then Mr Lost goes surreally astray in Bradshaw's back pages, first in the hotel notices, then among the general advertisements. These evoke the same cornucopia of industrial commodities that were displayed in the Crystal Palace, articles that increasingly owed their distribution to the railways themselves: 'the Extract of Sarsaparilla, the Registered Paletot, Rowlands' Kalydor, the Cycloidal Parasol, the Cough Lozenges, the universal night-light, the poncho, Allsopp's pale ale, and the patent knife cleaner'. At last we see Mr Lost, 'a ruin', stranded at the Euston station hotel, 'continually turning over the leaves of a small, dog's-eared quarto volume with a yellow cover, and babbling in a plaintive voice, BRADSHAW, BRADSHAW'.

No matter; railways in the mid-Victorian years were part of normal life for more and more people all the time. As *The Times* put it in 1850, 'Thirty years ago not one countryman in a hundred had seen the metropolis. There is now scarcely one in the same number who has not spent his day there'. An exaggeration, certainly; but even stay-at-homes could *see* the trains, the stations, the new embankments and viaducts, and realise that here was something momentous. As a gauge of this growing familiarity, jokes were told at the expense of those who failed to grasp the new technology. In Essex it was said of the villagers of Coggeshall, by local tradition a slow-witted lot, that they believed the fences along the railway to be there to stop the trains getting out and attacking people. A story from Devon tells of a farmer and his wife who believed London to be a very fine place all spread out under glass, having failed to explore beyond the confines of Paddington station.

In fiction, too, railways changed the conventions. The critic Richard Altick has observed how the mere mention of train or railway in a Victorian novel serves immediately to locate the action in the present, just as a reference to stagecoaches pushed the story back into the past. Novels of the time also remind us that there was then truly no alternative to the train except walking or riding – no cars or taxis, no motorway dashes or helicopters – and that for long and speedy journeys the railway timetable was lord and master. The crucial reading of a will in Anthony Trollope's *The Bertrams* (1859) is arranged for 2 p.m., not to allow for the lunch hour, but to follow the arrival of a particular train precisely fifteen minutes earlier. In *The Warden* (1855), Trollope's gentle Mr Harding knows very well that fierce Archdeacon Grantly cannot be in London until the next train from Barchester arrives at 2 p.m. – though his irrational dread of being tracked down by Grantly at his hotel is so great that he wanders the streets of the capital instead. Like Matthew Arnold, Trollope too was a writer in government employment, a senior Post Office official whose work involved immense amounts of railway travel; we shall be meeting him again.

₪

Trollope modelled his fictional Barchester on Salisbury. A real Mr Harding in London and a real Archdeacon Grantly in Salisbury in the 1850s would have heard the public clocks striking at the same time. Any time-conscious traveller who got out of the train at Basingstoke, roughly half-way between those cities, would (up to 1852 at least) have encountered a puzzling anomaly: the railway kept to standard time, but the town clocks were on the local version, about five minutes faster. This brings up the matter of how the railways transformed the keeping of time itself.

Before Victoria's reign, time was a local responsibility. East Anglian clocks were several minutes ahead of London's, those of the West Country and Wales quite a few minutes behind, all measured in accordance with the twenty-four-hour rotation of the earth. The exactitude of these calculations was a sign of sophistication rather than backwardness, the culmination of centuries of scientific clock-making and astronomical observation. The differences could be substantial – Plymouth time was twenty minutes behind that of London – but the practical difficulties that resulted were few. Those most conscious of the disparities included the guards of mail coaches, who carried watches that could be adjusted to gain or lose the correct number of minutes every twenty-four hours. The time observed on the coach could thus be kept in step with that of the towns it passed through.

In their earliest years the railways also deferred to local time. The first editions of Bradshaw thus seem to show that trains were taking significantly longer to go from west to east than to make the return journey, though in reality the duration was often the same. It was a confusing basis on which to plan and operate a railway timetable, doubly so once lines began to join up. The first companies to adopt London time throughout were those building long lines that ran more east–west than north–south: the Great Western and the London & Southampton. The Great Western main line to Bristol indeed runs almost due west. It opened in full in 1841. Major lines in the north of England, or running towards the north, followed in 1847–8. The change was urged on them by the Railway Clearing House, founded in 1842 chiefly to regularise traffic between subscribing railway companies; in the absence of coherent direction from the State, it often fell to the RCH to bring its members into productive harmony.

Strange anomalies were thrown up as the London standard invaded the realms of local time. At Andover in Hampshire, a sundial set up on the new building of the bankers Messrs Heath in 1846 still reminds the viewer '6 Min Faster for London Time'. In that year the London & Southampton's nearest station to the town was nine miles off, so any miscalculation in meeting the trains risked a serious waste of effort on road travel. The Chester & Holyhead Railway persisted into 1848 in taking its time from the signal gun of Craig-y-Don in Llandudno, sixteen and a half minutes later than the London time observed by the main lines with which it connected. In the same year the Irish Mail began running along this route. Every day, this train took delivery at Euston of a freshly set watch supplied by a messenger from the Admiralty. The watch was carried over to Dublin for checking against the time kept there and brought back by the return ferry and return train, uncontaminated by the lingering North Welsh time zone through which it passed. In Oxford, where the great bell of Tom Tower at Christ Church rang a curfew for undergraduates at 9 p.m., a compromise was reached. The college and cathedral of Christ Church became a sort of rock-pool of local time, so that the curfew sounded as before (as it does still), but the public hours rung out by the clock were adjusted to the London version brought by the Great Western. When the council at Exeter voted to abandon local time the Dean and Chapter refused to make the change, even though their cathedral's clock set the standard for the city.

Elsewhere, the conversion was more straightforward. The two greatest Scottish cities went over to standard time on 29 January 1848, shortly after a request from a railway company. It may have helped assuage national feeling that the line in question was an entirely Scottish outfit, the Edinburgh

& Glasgow. The clocks of Greenock, Perth and Stirling converted on the same day. Thus did London time become Scottish national time.

The London version was derived from the Royal Observatory at Greenwich. In the infancy of the railways its transmission was still managed by visual signals, or by means of a chronometer that was checked daily against the master clock and then carried around from place to place. The process was transformed by the electric telegraph, by which information could be sent almost instantly. Railways, being at once enclosed, secure and wholly owned by the companies themselves, were the perfect conduit for the new technology. The mature apparatus allowed messages to be sent by ringing bells, or by the deflection of an upright needle to left or right on a display dial, in each case mostly in variants of Morse code. It was an easy matter to despatch a regular time signal among the other telegraph messages. All that was missing were direct links between the Royal Observatory and the railways' own network. The first of these was supplied in 1852, by means of a telegraph wire from Greenwich to the South Eastern Railway's station at Lewisham. Thereafter, a single twitch of the telegraph needle at noon and 4 p.m. each day at stations all the way to Dover kept the railway in time with Greenwich to the very second. Time signals to other railways were passed on by wire via the City of London headquarters of the Central Telegraph Company, one of several telegraph firms that grew up symbiotically with the network.

It was one thing to get the railways on to a single time standard, quite another to enforce it universally. In the absence of direction from the government, it fell to the law to decide what the right time was; nor did the law speak until prompted by the case of *Curtis* vs *March*, heard at Dorchester in 1858, when judgment was given in favour of local mean time rather than the Greenwich version. So the standard national time stood exposed as a sort of pragmatic fiction, even as more and more places and persons adhered to it. There matters stood until the Time Act of 1880, which at last made Greenwich time legally binding.

So in the end it was Parliament and not the railways that imposed a standard time on Great Britain. But that is to speak de jure and not de facto. For those who lived through the 1840s and 1850s, it was effectively the railways that brought the change. 'Railway time' entered the Victorian lexicon, at least until all the different local times were in practice quite dead and time came everywhere in just the one version once more. Many companies underscored the point by an extravagant display of giant clocks, presiding from the centre of station façades as at Shrewsbury and Norwich, or raised up high in a clock tower at one end, as at St Pancras in London, at Darlington, and at the lost Scottish stations of Dundee West and Oban. To show the time in this way implied a claim to the kind of authority that had traditionally resided in municipal and communal buildings, guildhall and town hall and church steeple; it was a significant embodiment of the power of capital, and a reminder of the extent to which conditions and standards were to be imposed forthwith from outside the community.

Deeper than any visual display, the railways with their strict timetables also sharpened the sense of how time could be subdivided and refined, so that a minute or less could make a world of difference one way or the other: the 'lost' or missed train that could not be expected to wait, the catastrophic collision when times were muddled by guards or signalmen. Times were increasingly spoken in pure and curt numbers, as written in railway time-tables. Dickens described the habit in his account of a railway district in 1854, where 'The smallest child in the neighbourhood who can tell the clock, is now convinced that it hasn't time to say twenty minutes to twelve, but comes back and jerks out, like a little Bradshaw, "Eleven-Forty"'. Even where older mentalities persisted, at the northern fringes of the kingdom, the habit of timing to the minute took a firm hold. When the Highland Railway attempted to run Sunday fish trains from Strome Ferry in 1883, there was robust resistance from the Sabbatarian population, who fought their way on to the station, the pier and two steam trawlers full of fish. The rebels held their ground for the whole of Sunday 3 June swelling in number to more than 150 men: more than enough to beat off charges by a detachment of police who had joined a special train sent from Inverness to sort things out. But on the minute of midnight the demonstrators slipped away and the fish could at last go off to London, though no longer quite so fresh.

The story of national time is another reminder of how railways achieved a sort of revolution in the head, a sense of the forceful urgency of the present day, before which old customs and attitudes were doomed and impotent. The younger Victorian generations, Dickens's 'little Bradshaws', might be called railway natives; the new era of timetables was the only reality they would ever know. Many of their seniors who had reached adulthood before the railways came were haunted by a sense of loss, of having experienced a world that seemed secure but which had melted away. Here is William Makepeace Thackeray, in a celebrated article for the *Cornhill Magazine*:

Stage-coaches, more or less swift, riding-horses, pack-horses, highway-
men, knights in armour, Norman invaders, Roman legions, Druids,
Ancient Britons painted blue, and so forth – all these belong to the
old period ... We elderly people have lived in that praerailroad world,
which has passed into limbo and vanished from under us. I tell you it
was firm under our feet once, and not long ago. They have raised those
railroad embankments, and shut off the old world that was behind
them. Climb up that bank on which the irons are laid, and try to look
to the other side – it is gone.

Thackeray poses as a fogey, but he was not quite so ancient as he pretended: born in 1811, the novelist was one year older than Dickens, which
made him fifty-one in the year the article was published – which in turn
takes us back once again to 1862, and the imaginary journey with which
this chapter began.

Let us now assume that our traveller has perused his Bradshaw and
has managed to decode it. Before train-time, he will then have 'taken'
or 'booked' a ticket for the journey (to 'buy' a ticket seems to be a post-
Victorian usage). In the first decade of the railway these documents were
hand-written on booklets of printed forms and counterfoils, the inscribed
pages being torn out and handed to the purchaser as required. Such tickets
often served as reservations for specific seats, and might have to be booked
a day ahead. These practices were taken over from the road coaches that
the railways supplanted, on which places usually had to be reserved at the
coaching inn well in advance – a process quite separate from that of payment, which was made to the guard of the coach at the journey's end. The
same early custom explains the not quite obsolete term 'booking office' for
ticket office. The arrangements were slow, unsuitable for the much larger
numbers that could be conveyed by train and open to abuse by dishonest
staff. Other methods were tried: the Leicester & Swannington Railway
favoured stamped octagonal tokens or tallies of brass for its third-class
passengers, to be returned at the end of each journey, but these had the
disadvantage (among others) of having to be ferried back to the point of
issue after use. Season tickets were another early innovation, but applied to
a minority of passengers only.*

---

* The later term 'commuter' derives from the practice of commuting the payments for
individual daily journeys into a lump sum in exchange for a season ticket or pass.

All these shortcomings occupied the mind of another northern Quaker, Thomas Edmondson. After failing to prosper as a cabinet-maker, in 1836 Edmondson began a new life as stationmaster at what is now Brampton station, on the Newcastle & Carlisle Railway. In quieter hours he used his woodworker's tools to contrive a small printing press, capable of producing a strip of card tickets by means of a smart blow with a mallet. The tickets were then individually numbered and the strip cut up and put in a box ready for use. The next refinement was to make a tube in which tickets of the same class and destination could be stacked in numerical order, with a movable plate at the bottom that shifted upwards by means of weighted strings and pulleys every time a ticket was extracted from the top. With the assistance of a Carlisle clock-maker, Edmondson also developed a stout mahogany-framed contraption housing iron jaws that were set with movable type and an inked ribbon, which printed the day of issue on each ticket as it was inserted. Together, these machines comprised a complete system for printing, storing and issuing tickets. By numbering each ticket consecutively by type, Edmondson also guarded against any skimming of the takings, for the total value of tickets issued could be calculated and cross-checked against what was in the cash box. From the passenger's point of view, each ticket doubled as a receipt for the fare paid. Only the more unusual or far-flung journeys required tickets to be made out by hand, using blanks supplied for the purpose.

His employers were slow to appreciate the merits of the completed system, but Edmondson was not deterred. In 1840 he entered into partnership with the Manchester & Leeds Railway, and the following year set up on his own, licensing the system to other companies at the same annual rate of ten shillings per route-mile. That made matters easier for the many new lines then being established, such as the fledgling Sheffield, Ashton-under-Lyne & Manchester, which promptly decided to invest £250 in Edmondson equipment (plus licence fee) and to appoint its own ticket printer on a £50 annual wage.

So we should imagine our traveller of 1862 with one of Edmondson's patent tickets, safely stowed and ready to be brushed reassuringly with the fingertips in wallet, pocket, purse or glove in the course of the journey. The size was a standard two and a quarter by one and three-sixteenths inches, proportions just short of a double square. At once instantly recognisable and universally familiar, the railway ticket thus created its own mental niche, something which could be used down the generations as a rule-of-thumb unit of measurement, like the modern credit card, the old penny, or the postage stamps that first appeared as Penny Black and Tuppenny Blue in 1840. The mathematically minded railway author F. S. Williams had some fun estimating the area that could be covered by the tickets issued annually on the late-Victorian network: 100 acres, he reckoned, allowing for 500 million journeys a year. The stock of the London, Midland & Scottish Railway alone was calculated in 1933 at 300 million, of which 2 million were held at Euston, comprising 90,000 types. This company was the largest of the four giants into which most of the network was amalgamated by statute in 1923, an event known in railway parlance as the Grouping (the others were the London & North Eastern Railway, the Southern Railway, and the venerable Great Western Railway, which was plumped up with a miscellany of regional and local lines). Even the Southern – smallest of the 'Big Four', with hordes of season-ticket holders on its London trains – still required its printing works to turn out some 450,000 tickets every day during the 1940s.

Taking a return ticket – a 'double ticket', as they were sometimes known at first – brought with it an additional challenge for the traveller of forgetful or careless habits. The usual custom was to print tickets with the same information twice over, as it were side by side, so that they could be torn in half at the end of the outward journey. That left the passenger holding a bit of pasteboard not much more than an inch square, its elusiveness greatly enhanced (the loss of a return half was a stock subject for humour). An alternative method, more merciful to the absent-minded or butter-fingered, was to clip or punch a small piece from the ticket to show that it was half-used.

Edmondson tickets also illustrate the conservatism of Britain's railways in the twentieth century, even into the decade of their privatisation. For it was not until February 1990 that the last Edmondson tickets were issued on the national network, as early-Victorian ingenuity finally succumbed to computerised print-on-demand systems. As for the tearing of return tickets in half, the Southern Region of British Rail finally gave this up in favour of clipping as late as 1969; a conservative-minded contributor to *Railway World* magazine wondered whether the queues at the barriers at Waterloo would lengthen as station staff fumbled with the new-fangled technology.

Nor was the electric commuter railway of the 1960s, of John Schlesinger's famous documentary film *Terminus* (1961) or the Kinks' hit

Waterloo Sunset (1966), quite so far in all other respects from the railway of Thackeray's time. Beyond the ticket barriers could still be found carriages by the dozen that were wholly divided into individual compartments – not the side-corridor type with sliding internal doors that lingered until recently in first class, but self-contained spaces separated by wooden partitions of full height, accessible only by a single door on each side. The last of these carriages disappeared from service in the early 1980s, bringing to an end a tradition that began with the Liverpool & Manchester Railway's best carriages a century and a half before.

From this point in the story, matters of class become altogether unavoidable. How the less well-off travelled will be explained later. For the moment, we should imagine a long-distance journey with a first-class ticket, made on a winter's day in 1862.

SEATING, LIGHTING, HEATING, EATING

Trains in 1862 were hauled by steam locomotives. These were received from the first as a prodigious innovation. The first-class railway carriage, in its earliest maturity as achieved around 1830, was not nearly so startling, for it was nothing more or less than a composite of three wooden road-coach-type bodies, mounted on a separately assembled underframe also made of wood and running on four wheels. Access to the compartments was by a single door on each side, just as on a road coach. Passengers sat facing one another, customarily three persons per side in first class. The model underwent detailed refinements and enlargements, but did not change in essence until much later. The compartment rather than the carriage was thus the primary space experienced by the traveller, and lay usage often did not distinguish between them. Evelyn Waugh's Charles Ryder still muddles the two c-words when narrating a journey by troop train in the opening pages of *Brideshead Revisited* (1945): 'My three platoon commanders and myself had a carriage to ourselves.'

Until the railway companies established their own workshops, most carriages were built by the same businesses that manufactured private road conveyances for the rich, as well as the public stages and mail coaches by which the less-than-poor might aspire to travel. English coaches were already the world's epitome of comfort, elegance and finish, so it is not surprising that railway vehicles should have taken over many existing techniques and motifs wholesale, or that images of these early carriages betray their roadway origins immediately. Particularly long lived was the gracefully swept or bellied outline at the bottom of each individual compartment. This refinement of later Hanoverian design appeared on road coaches as the defining edge of the volume enclosed, but on the railway carriage was usually translated into an applied moulding, structurally meaningless but culturally highly charged. Its persistence suggests both a desire to reassure the passengers and a combination of conservatism and proper pride on the part of the builders. The value of reassurance was certainly in the mind of George Stephenson, father of Robert, when he specified black-and-yellow livery for some of the first enclosed carriages built for the opening of the Liverpool & Manchester Railway in 1830. These colours, in this arrangement – yellow below, black above – were familiar on the roads and provided a sort of aesthetic shorthand for smart and fast travel.

A similar visual conservatism appeared in the treatment of the carriage windows. The road-coach model required windows in threes, the central one placed in the compartment door, the side windows corresponding to the seating spaces. Road coaches commonly gave these windows a swept or radiused lower corner, echoing the lower curve of the enclosure itself. Railway coach builders followed suit, even though the shape was harder to make than a plain oblong and allowed less light inside. The fall from favour of these half-lunette windows for new-built carriages was placed around 1858 by the railway author C. Hamilton Ellis, who in 1965 wrote the first full history of the nineteenth-century railway carriage. In 1862 most first-class rolling stock (to use the industry's own term for non-locomotive vehicles) would certainly still have been day-lit in the older fashion, and John Tenniel drew Alice's carriage in *Through the Looking-Glass* with windows of this type as late as 1872.

One other feature of the carriage windows deserves mention. The central opening usually had a separate frame for the window pane or droplight, so that it could be lowered into a void made within the thickness of the door. This was managed by manipulating a leather strap attached to the lower edge of the window frame. To allow the window to be held in place partly open, the strap was pierced at intervals with holes, which engaged belt-fashion with a stubby peg affixed to the door-frame. (Mishandling of the marriage of strap-hole and peg would cause a loud thump as the droplight fell all the way into the door cavity.) Carriages with windows of this type were common up to the middle of the last century, and many will remember them. The design was superseded by a concealed apparatus

Inside Alice's carriage, from *Through the Looking-Glass*, 1872

on the 'lazytongs' principle, allowing windows to stick at any position to which they were pushed or pulled.

The glass in these early windows was not very like the coated, toughened and tinted safety glass of today's carriages. It had the same ripples and watery imperfections that were found in the window glass used in ordinary houses of the time. Flatter plate glass was available, but this was both heavy and expensive to replace (breakages of carriage windows could be expected fairly frequently). So it was through slightly distorting apertures that the first railway travellers viewed the world as it accelerated and decelerated strangely past them.

These carriage interiors were not at all large. Road coaches were likewise far from spacious inside, and while railway compartments were generally somewhat bigger, the difference was not spectacular. A few railways, it is true, built their carriages very small indeed. First-class travellers on the Bodmin & Wadebridge Railway (1834), an isolated Cornish line concerned at least as much with transporting shelly sand for fertiliser as with human traffic, had to put up with compartments that measured just 4ft 6in between the partitions and 5ft 9in to the ceiling. On other lines, a length of at least 5ft 6in could be expected, and a height of around 6ft – which was somewhat more than the height of the door opening. Imagining ourselves making an entry into these carriages, all but the least tall should stoop somewhat, mind any headgear, and draw in the limbs, as when passing through a cottage doorway.

One first-class comfort that could be expected was a good deal of upholstery. Seats and seat-backs were well cushioned, held in place with buttons or quilting. The former colonial administrator Sir Francis Head (1793–1875), whose *Stokers and Pokers* (1849) is one of the first investigative descriptions of a mature railway company, described a carriage receiving attention in the London & North Western Railway's works at Crewe, where the men were 'padding it, and petting it, and stuffing it, as if its object were to fit every bend and hollow in the human frame'. In most cases, sturdy armrests and padded uprights marked the divisions between each place. 'The carriages are very comfortable, like armchairs, for six persons in each'; thus Rachel Whinyates in her diary, 1840, when the Bristol & Gloucester Railway reached her home town of Cheltenham. The carriage sides below the windows were often upholstered too, and sometimes also the insides of the doors. In some cases even the ceiling was quilted, as in the Liverpool & Manchester's second generation of carriages, or the surviving saloon built by the London & Birmingham Railway in 1842 for Queen Adelaide and now on display at the National Railway Museum at York. The saloon's interior is rather a disturbing sight to modern eyes, with its suggestions of a padded cell deluxe, however useful as a means of absorbing the noises of movement. All this padding did no more than keep up with development of the private coach, and also with the increasingly well-stuffed domestic surroundings and social spaces of the upper classes. Sprung seats and seat-backs were later refinements. (The Bodmin & Wadebridge's first class made do with hay stuffing, but it will be clear by now that this was something of a yokel line.)

The apogee of all this quilting and stuffing was reached in early royal saloons. Contemporary descriptions of these often take on something of the gushy fabric-fetishism of the fashion magazine. Here is Richard Mansell, Carriage Superintendent of the South Eastern Railway, on the saloon he designed for Victoria and Albert in the Great Exhibition year:

> The sides and ends are stuffed and covered with damask in shades of
> Amber, White and Drab, decorated ornamental silk tufts, handsome

Gimp of Silk and Stout Silk cord. Draperies of Amber and White Satin are suspended round this Compartment trimmed with cord, gimp and fringe of silk, these are supported by cornices of carved wood richly gilt.

And so on, across the watered lutestring ceiling and over the velvet-pile-carpeted floor. Mansell's interior even featured a painting on the panelling of a door depicting three guardian angels simpering over a sleeping child, as if to guarantee the royal pair the safety of the railway.

Even the most luxurious ordinary first-class carriages fell some way short of all this. However, the first-class passenger of 1862 could expect one further refinement in common with royal saloons and traceable in origin to the road carriage. This was the broad sling-like loop of uphol-stered leather or cloth, sometimes called a cromet, which was fixed to the inside wall of the compartment, often in pairs one above the other. Images of travellers making use of one of these things are rare indeed, and as the years passed there was even some confusion as to their chief purpose: the support of tired arms and wrists has been suggested (although armrests were provided too); or 'to assist passengers in arising from their seats' (a reference in the *Railway Magazine* for 1897); or to grasp tightly when the train was going fast. John Betjeman in 1940 suggested the latter, but admitted never to have seen anyone actually doing so. Yet the Caledonian Railway had thought well enough of the device to extend provision to its better third-class carriages in Edwardian times. In the event of an acci-dent, the carriage strap might be a mixed blessing; a passenger caught in a derailment on the Great Western in 1845 had his arm 'nearly torn from the shoulder socket' by one of them as his carriage toppled over.

If compartments were generally small, where did all the luggage go? Some of it was stowed in luggage vans, an innovation of the 1840s, which usually doubled as accommodation for the guard. But until at least the late 1860s much more was simply manhandled on to the carriage roof, where it was kept from tumbling off by strapping it down within a low railing around the central section. The common practice was to protect these rooftop mounds of luggage by means of a tarpaulin, which between uses was often secured in a roll on the roof. That did not make the task of loading and unloading much less cumbersome, even with the help of movable wooden slides that were sometimes kept on hand at the platform, nor did it simplify the challenge of uncovering and unloading the correct

luggage for each stop. The process of loading up and sheeting over is represented in William Powell Frith's famous painting *The Railway Station*.
It is a vignette of anonymous everyday labour, placed by the artist just
off-centre above and behind the platform of the Great Western terminus
at Paddington, on which passengers of every age, class and position are
depicted to make a sort of *theatrum mundi* of mid-Victorian England. As
it happens, this painting is another product of 1862, our representative
year; it proved to be a popular sensation, carried (by train, we may be sure)
to paying exhibitions round the country and abroad, and reproduced even
more lucratively in print form.

In one key respect, not easily detected in the picture, the carriages
depicted by Frith were quite unlike those of other lines. For Brunel had
chosen to set the rails of his new main line at a markedly greater width
than that used elsewhere: 7ft 0¼in, almost one and a half times as wide as
the 4ft 8½in Stephenson had derived from the colliery waggonways of his
native North East. There were several reasons behind Brunel's adoption of
the broad gauge, as it came to be known, only one of which need concern
us for now. Carriages that ran on standard-gauge lines were necessarily
wider than the tracks, so that their bodies had to be lifted up above the
wheels. Brunel's intention was to make the tracks so wide that his carriages
would be able to sit within the wheels, lowering the centre of gravity of
each vehicle and thus increasing its stability. Without the need to keep
clear of the carriage floor, the wheels could also be made to a much larger
diameter, like those of road carriages. Since large wheels rotate less rapidly
than small ones at any given speed, fast trains could be run without excessive wear on the bearing surfaces of the axles.

So Brunel had reasoned on 15 September 1835, in a letter to the directors of the fledgling company. But when the time came to build all but a
handful of the Great Western's carriages,* he ignored his own arguments
almost completely, placing the wheels below the floor like everybody else.
(He did not forsake the idea of large-diameter wheels, the housings for
which rose up inconveniently from the carriage floors.) What the more
generous clearances associated with the broad gauge undoubtedly did
deliver was an ampler width to the carriage bodies – so much so that many
compartments in first class were subdivided midway, by means of a longitudinal partition and doorway. The set-up was nicely captured by John

---

* On these anomalous 'posting carriages' *see* Chapter 3.

Henry Newman in *Loss and Gain* (1848), in a passage that must have flum-
moxed later generations of readers: the novel's Oxonian hero steps into the
emptier sub-compartment of a London-bound train, noting that the 'far-
ther compartment' is filled by a party of travellers 'talking together with
great volubility and glee'.

Despite these generous dimensions, Brunel did not think it worth
allotting much internal space to the passengers' luggage. Newman's fictional travellers would have watched their trunks hoisted on to the broad,
flat carriage roof, just as on other lines, or indeed on the road vehicles that
would deliver and collect them at each end. It was possible to do this on
the railways because the upper profile of the carriages did not yet reach to
the maximum height of the loading gauge. Not to be confused with the
distance between the rails, this is the term used to describe the standard
dimensions beyond which anything moving on the rails would no longer safely clear the edges of tunnels, buildings and other trains, moving or
stationary. The concept becomes apparent when one looks at almost any
early picture of a train in motion: the locomotive with its chimney tower-
ing up as tall as the loading gauge permitted, and the string of little low
carriages trundling behind.

One common personal object that could not be carried securely on
the roof was the gentleman's hat. These reached their greatest height in the
1840s–60s, as if in sympathy with the soaring chimneys of the locomotives. Too tall to keep on when entering the carriage or standing within,
too bulky to be kept easily on the lap, too fragile and valuable – at least
without some sort of protective box – to risk kicks, treading and dirt by
placing on the floor or in the space beneath the seats: the non-collapsible
'stove-pipe' presented the traveller with quite a challenge. The solution
adopted in many carriages was to stretch taut cords across the ceiling, in
parallel or criss-crossing at right angles, from which hats could be suspended upside-down by the brim. So in each first-class compartment of
1862 we may imagine up to six inverted black hats, juddering and quiver-
ing overhead with the motion of the train.

No special arrangements were needed for the hats of female passengers, for whom any bare-headed public appearance risked an erosion of
respectability. A much greater challenge in negotiating a railway journey
was how to manage the crinoline, which in the same decades expanded to
its most preposterous extent. For all the imagery from Victorian art high
and low, for all the writings by historians of dress, for all the analyses of

feminist critics, it still seems almost beyond belief that these vast encumbrances were once daily wear for half the adult population of the middling and upper classes. That so many women should as a matter of habit and routine have approached and entered the little railway carriages of the day, remained seated for long hours within them, and finally extracted themselves without absolute loss of dignity, composure or sanity, is harder to credit still. As R. S. Surtees put it in 1860, 'to see them attempt the entry of a moderate sized carriage; the utter disproportion of the door to the "object", as it may well be called, that seeks admission!' But this is just one aspect of the trials which the Victorian railway presented to bodies less well-nourished, comfortably dressed and generally healthy than our own, as will become clear when we look at the lower classes of carriage and at the working lives of the railwaymen themselves.

₪

Facilities for even the most expensive travel in the earliest railway years went little further than padded seats and handy hat hangers. Illumination was provided by God's own daylight and the internal climate was governed by the external one. Artificial lighting and heating were the next creature comforts the railways attempted to offer, and by 1862 the privileged traveller would have expected to find both, after a fashion.

Lighting came first. Before the widespread use of electricity, this required the ignition, steady supply and secure confinement of as many small individual flames as were necessary for the task. On the railways this was first achieved by the use of pot-lamps burning rape oil or paraffin, fed by gravity from an upper reservoir, sitting within circular apertures in the carriage roof. In technical terms, the method was neither difficult nor inventive. To protect the lamps from the weather, each was surrounded by an iron cylinder pierced with holes and equipped with a flip-top lid. Refuelling, wick-trimming and cleaning were carried out by removing the entire lamp for attention elsewhere. In early times the lesser classes of carriage were not always provided with covers for the vacated lamp-holes, so that passengers were grateful for their umbrellas in rainy weather.

The Liverpool & Manchester began to lighten the darkness of its first-class passengers in 1834, with one such lamp for each compartment. The Great Western followed in 1842. As the facility spread to other lines, and to second class and levels downward, many railways economised by placing

lamps in a space within or above the partitions, so that a single apparatus could throw light into two compartments. Sometimes lamps appear
to have been left burning during the day, presumably on longer-distance
runs that began or ended outside the hours of daylight. Sir Francis Head
recorded the passengers' experience of entering the London & North
Western's tunnel at Primrose Hill, a few miles out of Euston: 'sudden darkness, visible only by a feeble and hitherto unappreciated lamp, which, like
the pale moon after a fiery sunset, modestly shines over their head'.

Oil lamps had the advantage of using an easily transported fuel, but
in other respects were high maintenance. The radical journalist J. W. Robertson Scott, born in 1866, recalled the once-routine sight at stations of a
railwayman making his way along the roofs of the carriages, catching and
inserting replenished lamps as they were thrown up from a barrow below.
Another man walked along after him to light the fresh lamps and to send
the iron lids crashing down shut afterwards. Dickens, writing in the year
of Scott's birth, describes a still greater feat: the lamp-man 'skipping along
the top of a train, from carriage to carriage, and catching lighted name-
sakes thrown up to him by a coadjutor' – like a shipyard riveter catching
hot rivets (*Mugby Junction*, part 1).

Often these lamp housings had to be located within the railed-off luggage compound on the roof. It was not unknown for a light to fail when
shifting loads or flapping tarpaulins restricted the air supply below, or for a
tarpaulin to catch alight. This was not the only fire risk: pity the passenger
who was once confined in a nocturnal express on the North British Railway, watching the oil dripping steadily past the lamp-flame from a defective reservoir to form a pool in the bottom of the lamp glass, in powerless
dread that the whole thing might suddenly explode. Nor was ordinary
combustion – the 'roof-lamp's oily flame' of Thomas Hardy's poem 'Midnight on the Great Western', published in 1917 – particularly clean. Too
long a wick and the lamp would burn sootily, blackening the glass. Sometimes the wick was jolted out altogether. The penurious North Sunderland
Railway in Northumberland delayed the installation of oil lamps in its carriages until the 1940s, only to remove them again because the vibrations of
travel on its ramshackle tracks so often shook out the flames.

Even when a compartment was favoured with two lamps all to itself,
artificial light was not provided in excess. In dimly lit carriages it might
do little more than allow passengers to find their way in and out of the
compartment and to gather an imprecise sense of who it was they might

be travelling with. To read, and to do so without eye-strain, represented a greater challenge. Some help could be obtained in the form of the pocket reading lamp, usually candle-powered and equipped with a reflector. By 1857 the *Morning Post* could refer to the 'railway reading lamp' as a familiar article. These were lamps specifically adapted for travel by means of hooks for fixing into the upholstery, or rubber suction pads that were supposed to stick securely to the window pane. The *Army & Navy Stores Catalogue* was still offering different types in Edwardian times, together with the special candles that went with them (8½d per box).

A better fuel for carriage lighting was gas. It burnt cleanly, required less maintenance and could be supplied from large reservoirs shared by multiple lamps. The first railways to make standard use of gas carriage lighting were in London, for long the world centre of the technology. One crucial breakthrough was William Sugg's non-corroding steatite burner, invented in 1858, which was at once more durable than older gas fixtures and better at generating light rather than heat. By 1862, London alone used twice as much gas as the whole of Germany.

Early experiments aside, the honour of operating the first gaslit services belongs to the North London Railway, also in 1862. The gas was stored in a large container in the guard's van of each train, from which pipes ran to the individual carriages. It was an enterprising venture for a busy urban and suburban railway that ran for much of its length high up on a viaduct. For the Metropolitan Railway, operating almost entirely in tunnels, adequate lighting was a pressing need from the outset. The opening services in 1863 used gaslit carriages supplied from a sort of giant squeeze-box all along the roofs: an iron-topped wooden housing, within which was a squashy rubber reservoir kept firmly under pressure beneath the weight of a giant trellis made of wood and iron. The passengers' experience was of a clear and welcome increase in light: the *Daily Telegraph* observed the double burners in each first-class compartment, flaming so brightly 'that newspapers might be read with ease' – the point being that Victorian newspapers favoured much smaller and less distinct print than that used in books. Such was Matthew Arnold's 'wonderful Metropolitan Railway which takes you in at Finsbury Circus and puts you out, after you have read for half an hour in an arm chair by the brightest of gas-light, at Victoria.'*

---

* Strictly, the last section of Arnold's journey was by the Metropolitan District Railway, forerunner of the present District Line.

The Metropolitan's coal-gas method did not become generally popular and the company itself gave it up in 1876 in favour of the oil-gas lighting developed by Julius Pintsch in Prussia (one instance among many of technical initiative passing to Germany). This became the standard system used across Britain's railways. Compressed gas was carried in steel cylinders beneath the floor of each carriage, which thus became self-sufficient in supply. The gas could be distilled from oil shale, available in the central belt of Scotland, or increasingly from imported crude oil; the Great Western set up a refinery for the purpose within its mighty works at Swindon in 1893, and the Great Eastern built one at its only slightly smaller works at Stratford, now vanished into the 2012 Olympics site. Within the carriage, each lamp glowed from within a big inverted glass dome, somewhat like those used to show off artificial flowers or taxidermy. The better sort of long-distance carriage sometimes came with a hinged cover of dark-tinted glass fixed alongside for swinging across, to kill the glare in the compartment when trying to sleep at night.

For all that her carriages were the most luxurious on British rails, Queen Victoria had little use or liking for this brightness. When the royal saloon that took her annually to Balmoral was upgraded for gas without consultation, she demanded that the oil lamps be put back. Later, when the same carriage body was refurbished, spliced to another and given a more modern underframe, she shunned the newly provided electric reading lamps in favour of candle-holders. The story is a snapshot of what might be called the mixed economy of Victorian illumination, in which candles, oil and gas all played an everyday part, with electricity an exotic latecomer. Artificial light was a necessity for all, whether in the form of rudimentary street lighting or the candle that lighted both duke and farmhand to bed; in large amounts it was a luxury, laid on extravagantly at gatherings in grand households, or for specially contrived 'illuminations' of public spaces at times of celebration. (The almost complete disappearance during the last century of oil and gas, the broad middle ground of public lighting, would doubtless be almost as surprising from the Victorian point of view as our continuing penchant for candles in electrically lit homes.)

Edwardian trains, and Edwardian lives in general, were more brightly lit than those of the Victorians. That owed less to the advance of electricity than to Carl Auer von Welsbach's development of the improved fluorescent gas mantle in the mid 1890s. Railway carriages adopted this type from circa 1905–6. The curious may still notice these mantles in places where public gas lamps remain in use; strange, pallid, frail-looking little objects, like dwarfish hosiery, made by drying out an open weave of cotton steeped in saturated nitrite salts. The cotton burnt away on first use, leaving a tight, non-flammable mesh which converted a much greater share of the combustion to light rather than heat, and burnt considerably less gas than the old fishtail or flat-flame burners in the process. It is a pardonable mistake to assume that the steady, brilliant, yellowish-white illumination emitted by lamps of this type puts us in touch with the flaringly lit nocturnal world of the mid Victorians.

The mature method of carriage gas lighting allowed forty hours' reserve, with a central control in each vehicle for turning the gas on and off and a bypass system linked to a pilot light that ensured instant ignition of all the lamps. It sounds both splendid and ingenious, and such refinements certainly gave gas lighting a longer run against the electric competition. So they hissed their way well into the mid twentieth century: over a third of carriages in 1935 were still gaslit and one in ten of those taken over when the railways were nationalised in 1948.

Gas had its drawbacks. For all that the experienced traveller might take care to select a well-lit compartment, a steady and continuing supply could not be guaranteed. The infuriatingly erratic gas pressure on the suburban Cheshire Lines trains from Manchester just after the First World War was recalled half a century later by a contributor to *Railway World* magazine. Settled in his compartment with the evening paper, he found that after half a mile the lights often sank to 'a blue glimmer, which would last until the train reached its first stop, when as if by magic the light would flare up again for the duration of the stop and then repeat the process'. Arnold Bennett used this familiar annoyance of travel in his story 'Beginning the New Year' (1907). A man returns after long absence to the novelist's version of his home territory of Stoke-on-Trent – not a seductive place even in its age of prosperity – via the distinctly unbucolic local line, the North Staffordshire Railway. 'The compartment was illuminated by one lamp, and in Bleakridge Tunnel this lamp expired. Everything reminded him of his youth.' (Bennett's own last journey, in the form of ashes from Golders Green crematorium, was made over these same rails in 1931.) In addition, the cleanliness of gas lighting by comparison with oil was often relative: in both cases, condensation and leaked rainwater tended to build up in the bottom of the glass, to be joined there by the disintegrating corpses of moths and other flying insects that had been fatally attracted by the light. The railway author H. C. Casserley remembered from childhood the fascination of this revolting mixture, and its rhythmic slopping action when the train was in motion. Acetylene gas, adopted by some smaller railways in the twentieth century, had a way of freezing in its tanks in hard winters, just when most needed.

More serious was the danger that cylinders of compressed gas presented in case of accident. Oil- or gas-lit, a Victorian railway carriage was effectively a mobile bonfire awaiting ignition. The various materials that provided this potential fuel were noted in their raw state, 'stacked in vast piles' at the Midland Railway's Derby carriage works, in F. S. Williams's *Our Iron Roads* (1883): 'logs of ash, elm, East Indian teak, Honduras mahogany – worth from £15 to £20 a log – red, white and yellow deals from Quebec and Stettin ... and satinwood from Kauri, in New Zealand'.

Sawn, planed, mitred, moulded, nailed and glued together, these timbers became the carriage bodies. The process was essentially one of craft manufacture. Oak or teak were the usual materials for the framing, deal (softwood) for the floors, deal or ash for the long, close-fitting planks that made up the roof. The Midland then required *twenty-five* separate stages of undercoating, painting, rubbing down and varnishing the body, to say nothing of lining-out and lettering. Further painting and varnishing was done within, as well as trimming, lining and upholstery in horsehair, woollen cloth, waxed cloth and linoleum. Taut, waterproofed canvas covered the roof; thick felt layers were used for insulation below the floorboards. When smashed apart and suffused with escaping hydrocarbons, it did not take much input from an unextinguished lamp flame or the coals of a derailed steam locomotive to set these ingredients in a blaze. Especially shocking was the nocturnal collision on the Midland Railway at Hawes Junction in the Pennines in 1910, when wrecked wooden carriages were torched by an entire cylinder of blazing gas, and nine passengers died. Fourteen more were incinerated 'almost without trace' one night three years later, in another collision a few miles north on the same line. Worst of all, in 1915 a triple collision and gas-fuelled fire at Quintinshill in Dumfriesshire killed at least 227, mostly soldiers on their way to Gallipoli.

Electric lighting was much safer, but despite occasional use from 1881 it took over a quarter-century to become firmly established. That was partly because light bulbs that worked reliably on the move were slow to appear. Railway engineers also struggled to find the right balance between dynamo power deriving from the movement of the train and battery power that could keep the lights shining when at rest. Each carriage effectively became a small mobile power station, with its own back-up supply – a roundabout way of generating electricity by burning coal to make steam, as a by-product of dragging a train from A to B. Unlike railway gas lamps, these early electric lights were often elaborately designed, with two or more glass-shaded bulbs branching off each ornate iron stem. Although cheaper to operate, the new technology was more expensive to install, sometimes prohibitively so: it was estimated at £130 per coach versus £34 for gas on the Lancashire & Yorkshire Railway. Also on the financial side, the railways had to consider the capital already sunk into gasworks and plant, for in most cases they made their own gas. The Highland Railway is a case in point: having experimented with both methods to replace its old oil lighting, come down on the side of gas and built a substantial gasworks at Inverness in 1901, the company did not wish to overturn its decision with any undue haste. On top of which were the improvements in gas brilliance already described, which stole a march over the new technology. These were enough for the North British Railway to order in 1908 that its existing electrically lit carriages be returned to gas, but only once all the costly spares had been used up. Shortly after which came the Midland Railway's two fatal Pennine conflagrations, and only then did company after company across the railway network decide to go electric at last.

Electricity had a further advantage: the guard could turn it on when the train passed through tunnels during the day. This was a problem to which gas lighting had no satisfactory solution, short of leaving the lights burning all the time. Other experiments were attempted. In 1880 the London & North Western tried out glow-in-the-dark paint on compartment ceilings, with not much effect beyond some reported alarm among uninformed passengers. One of the steam-hauled Glasgow suburban lines was equipped a few years later with an electric conductor rail, solely to light the carriages as they passed through its underground section; at night, when the carriage gas lamps were lit, the electricity could be turned off. Fully electrified lines were another matter, but there were none of these in Britain before 1890, and very few for decades after that.

A preoccupation with artificial lighting risks overlooking the continued importance of daylight. Rather than enlarging the windows, visibility was improved by raising the central strip of the roof to form a clerestory, with little windows along the sides. Sometimes the lamps were placed in the curved sections of roof on either side, sometimes they were set into the roof of the clerestory itself. The clerestory was the usual form of roof on many lines from the 1870s until the 1900s. It also helped to see off the risky practice of putting luggage on the roof, although this was already in retreat following the substitution of coal for cleaner but costlier coke as locomotive fuel after 1860, with a corresponding increase in fallout from hot cinders. Clerestory openings were nowhere near as large as the side windows, but by allowing light to enter obliquely overhead they could make quite a difference to the middle seats of the compartment, which could be surprisingly dark on a dull day. Rather missing the point, the Great Eastern Railway favoured some of its clerestory windows with 'coloured photochrome transparencies' on the stained-glass principle. A more useful (but never common) refinement was to double-glaze the windows as a precaution against condensation. To sit beneath a single-glazed clerestory in a crowded compartment on a cold day was to risk a steady delivery of drips of less than pure water – another reason to prefer the window seat.

₪

Heating took longer to arrive. To the earliest passengers, not excluding those well-off enough to travel habitually in the inside seats of road coaches, it would not have seemed at all strange that the new trains were unheated. For the whole span of previous human existence, to be transported across Northern Europe during more than half the year was to endure exposure to cold. The only protection against chills, wind or rain was to wrap up well. One extreme case of the technique was the young Brunel on his way across the frozen Pas de Calais in 1829, calling for bundles of hay at each stop to fill the void spaces in his coupé up to neck height, until its human cargo sat 'like three stone Schiedam bottles packed ... for safe carriage'. But that was no way to run a railway.

The first British example of a train that could generate its own heating belonged, like other luxuries, to royalty. The diminutive saloon provided for Queen Victoria by the London & Birmingham Railway in 1843 had a small underfloor boiler fired by oil burners, the heat from which circulated by means of a pipe within the floor cavity. A brass grating allowed the heat to enter the compartment. But the system was ahead of time, and was not repeated even in subsequent royal carriages.

Instead, the solution adopted for royalty downwards was simply to put something hot inside the carriage. Horse-drawn transport provided a precedent: private coaches would sometimes have the chill taken off them by means of a house-brick hot from the hearth, placed in a sand-tray or fireproof box. The railway equivalent was a flat tin or iron box about 2ft long with handles at both ends, filled with hot water and known with disarming candour as a footwarmer. The device made its British début on the long-distance trains of the Great Northern Railway in 1852. It is said to have been a French idea, encountered by the company's chief engineer on a winter holiday. Other British lines followed suit. On some lines the footwarmers were rented for a modest charge from porters or hawkers on the platform, on others they were provided as part of the service, although the recipient might be expected to reward the porter with a tip. The footwarmers spent the journey on the floor of the carriage, sometimes stowed into recesses made for the purpose. Thermal performance improved due to a modification in 1881 by Francis William Webb, the autocratic chief engineer of the London & North Western Railway, again borrowed from France. His containers were sealed permanently and filled with a strong solution of sodium acetate, which released extra heat as it cooled and recrystallised. A brisk shake of the cooling acetate tin would bring a welcome extra pulse of heat. The chemical version was estimated to stay warm three times longer than mere water.

The heat source for both sealed and refillable types was provided at the station. The acetate variety had to be immersed in large wheeled vats of water, the contents kept at a permanent simmer by a small stove. On longer journeys passengers might be issued with a fresh footwarmer, or have the old one recharged. Regular travellers learned to look forward to these stops, the more so when the journey was long and likely to be cold. On the Highland Railway's main line between Perth and Inverness, the magic station names were Blair Atholl and Aviemore. The North British Railway built a boiler house for the purpose at its station at Riccarton Junction in the Southern Uplands, a remote railway hamlet without road access that stood midway on the now defunct Waverley Route from Carlisle to Edinburgh. In such cases, smart work was needed by the porters on the icy platforms to re-equip an entire train within the allowed timetable. Cannier travellers made a point of sitting in the part of the train that would draw up closest to the footwarmer cart on the platform when the train stopped en route.

Availability of footwarmers varied from line to line and from class to class. Initially they were a first-class privilege only. In 1870–71 the Liberal

MP Samuel Plimsoll (originator of the Plimsoll line for shipping) introduced a bill to establish the facility as standard for long-distance travellers in all classes. The bill failed, but individual lines began to comply anyway. Progress was halting; footwarmers were provided to third class on the Lancashire & Yorkshire – hardly the railway with the warmest territory in the British Isles – as late as 1891. Yet they were not especially costly to make: in the same period, the Manchester, Sheffield & Lincolnshire Railway procured them at 8s each.

These personal heaters belong to the great catalogue of artefacts now obscure, but once familiar to the point of banality. The road carriages that met passengers at the station often made use of similar footwarmers, and early motorists found them useful too in their unheated cars. But whatever the host vehicle, the weakness of the method is obvious enough: each heater could store only so much energy, and it dissipated fastest in the coldest weather, just when warmth was most needed. The footwarmer the Rev. Francis Kilvert shared with an army officer from Chippenham to Bath on New Year's Eve, 1874 – seventeen degrees of frost outside – seemed to him to be 'filled with cold water and snow'. As *Punch* lamented:

> Alas! thou art a faithless friend,
> Thy warmth was but dissimulation;
> Thy tepid glow is at an end,
> And I am nowhere near my station!

To be properly cosy, a *Punch* cartoon suggested, get hold of five footwarmers: one for the lap, one for the seat and two tucked behind the back, as well as the one on the floor. Delays or breakdowns risked extra discomfort. Daniel Thomas Holmes's *Literary Tours in the Highlands and Islands* (1909) records a wait through the night for a rescue engine to reach an express stranded at the summit of the fearsome pass of Druimuachdar in Perthshire, where the Highland Railway attained 1,484ft above sea level: 'From end to end of the train resounded the rhythmic beat of cold-footed passengers striving to bring some warmth of blood to their toes.'

As with lighting, the answer lay in a built-in supply. The Glasgow & South Western Railway had a go with heating pipes linked to small boilers placed above the carriage lamps, where most of the heat from combustion immediately and uselessly went, but this thrifty method failed to catch on. The first self-sufficient heating for ordinary passengers came via the United States, in the Pullman cars that were imported and assembled under licence by several companies from 1874. These used an oil-fired system with a circuit of hot-water pipes beneath the carriage floor. Other experiments included a larger boiler carried in the brake van and serving all the coaches; but this simply duplicated the steam-generating function of the locomotive at the other end of the train. Finally, the solution was adopted of tapping a supply of steam at a reduced pressure from the locomotive itself. Transmission between vehicles was via a flexible hose; the radiators found a home in the spaces beneath the seats of each compartment, where the Victorians had been wont to stow their parcels (or, like Paul Bultitude in Frederick Anstey's comic identity-swap novel *Vice Versa* (1882), to hide away when in a tight spot). Early radiators were often of the storage type, filled like Webb's footwarmers with heat-retaining acetate solution through which the steam was piped; these gave way to the more responsive and faster-acting kind containing live steam, suitably shielded to prevent burns and scalds. For the chilled passenger newly entering a compartment, the result was the same: warm seats and a wonderfully soothing heat that welled out from below to suffuse the lower half of the body, where the cold was likely to have done its worst. Add to this the individual radiator controls provided for each compartment in the best Edwardian carriages, and later fitted in all classes as a matter of course, and the transition from mid-Victorian austerities was complete.

So much steam for heating was drawn from the locomotive in winter that formations of carriages on express trains were commonly shortened by one vehicle, to compensate for the loss of haulage power. It was also impossible to distribute the heat evenly through the train. Informed travellers knew that the steam was at its hottest closer to the engine. The common practice of reversing trains for the return journey also meant that the first-class carriages might not be coupled behind the engine every time, turning the tables on those in the more expensive seats. None of this mattered in the summer, during which the heating pipes and valves might be removed for servicing, as on the Great Western, where heating was generously continued until 31 May. This is enough to tell us that the steam that hisses at the platform from the unexpectedly halted train in Edward Thomas's 'Adlestrop' (1914), by some distance the most famous poetic recollection of a British railway journey, can only have been issuing direct from the locomotive itself. ('It was late June. / The steam hissed. Someone cleared his throat.') For the curious, Adlestrop station was opened in 1853 by the Oxford, Worcester & Wolverhampton Railway, later absorbed by the Great Western, and was originally called Addlestrop and Stow Road, to indicate that it was the nearest station to Stow-on-the-Wold in Gloucestershire. It was closed in 1966 – the station yard is now a dump for derelict road vehicles – but the Oxford-to-Worcester route is still in use, and many who cherish Thomas's poem as a token of a vanished England have passed through the site without realising it.

Heating of railway carriages by steam had an amazingly long life in Britain. It outlived the demise of the steam locomotive because of a less than far-sighted decision taken in the 1950s, by which new-built carriages were to be compatible both with steam haulage and with the diesel locomotives that were to succeed it on many lines. The building of carriages that could be heated solely by steam went on as late as 1964, and it was not until the winter of 1969–70 that diesel-hauled, electrically heated services began to spread beyond their first stronghold in BR's Southern Region. Instead, the typical passenger diesel of the period used some of its fuel to fire up a hefty drum-shaped boiler weighing several tons and containing perhaps 800 gallons of water for heating. These heaters also presented the management with grounds for compromise with the railway unions over manning levels, now that a fireman was no longer required to shovel coal alongside the locomotive driver, for it was agreed that operating the boiler should be among the duties of the second man. The faintly absurd set-up of steam-heated trains behind diesel locomotives was not always understood by the travelling public, but its twilight years can be called back to mind by anyone with memories of a big station on a winter's day in the 1970s or early 1980s: mysterious veils of white steam rising up the sides of blue-and-white carriages from beneath the platform level and a pervasive sense of dripping somewhere down below. The last steam-heated trains of this type ran in the winter of 1986–7, nearly two decades after the end of steam haulage in normal service, so it might almost be said that it was Margaret Thatcher rather than Harold Wilson who presided over the last wheezings of the railways' age of steam.

All this was for the future in 1862, when the wise winter traveller still conserved his or her inner warmth as much as possible. That usually meant at least one 'railway rug'. Rugs were another accessory of road travel that made perfect sense on the railway. Their popularity was remarked as early as 1851, in R. S. Surtees' 'Hints to Railway Travellers' for the *New Monthly*

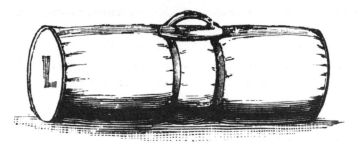

A railway rug in its carrying case, 1882

Magazine (although he urged the superiority of 'a shepherd's plaid or maud' – a wrap – which could double as an article of clothing; Surtees would have had in mind that big checked patterns were also *à la mode* just then, from women's dress to men's trousers and waistcoats). Passengers travelling light could choose to rent a rug; *Baedeker's Great Britain* for 1910 specified sixpence as the standard charge, as also for a pillow. Those who brought their own rug might guard against its unfurling in transit by means of a soft case or by using special straps of leather, with a handle attached. Super-sized rugs could be kept in order with an apparatus comprising a rigid bar with a central handle and a strap at each end. The huge headquarters building of Messrs W. H. Smith at No. 186 Strand, London, had a room entirely given over to rentable rugs and straps, for despatch to the company's bookstalls up and down the country.

Rugs are duly discussed in *The Railway Traveller's Handy Book*, written by Edward Shelton and published anonymously in our year 1862, which addressed itself to the first principles of how to travel by train, 'before the journey, on the journey, and after the journey'. The *Handy Book* makes the railway rug sound a bit like the indispensable towel in Douglas Adams's *Hitch-hiker's Guide to the Galaxy*: 'Not only does it keep the legs warm, but on emergencies it may be made to perform the part of a cloak, a counterpane, a cushion to sit upon, or a wrapper for fragile articles.'

The railway rug provides a quiet running joke in Mary Elizabeth Braddon's novel *Lady Audley's Secret*, one of the literary excitements of the same year. Robert Audley, the young barrister-hero increasingly obsessed with the 'secret' and its solution, is required to hare off from London to all points of the compass, always by train and usually against the clock. We first encounter Robert's rug in summer as he rises from an open-air nap to walk to the station, folding it up to carry over his shoulder. As the days begin to shorten, he travels 'comfortably in a corner of an empty first-class carriage, coiled up in a couple of huge railway rugs'. Later, with snow lying deep, he heads for Southampton on an early morning express, wrapped 'in so many comforters and railway rugs as to appear a perambulating mass of woollen goods rather than a living member of a learned profession'.

Cold was only part of the problem. However skilfully wrought, the joinery of a wooden railway carriage warped or shrank from age, and from the stresses and shocks of motion. That meant plenty of draughts, a source of anxiety as well as mere discomfort at a time when the origins of so many common infections and indispositions were as yet imperfectly understood. The *Handy Book* advised the use on long voyages of a bespoke cap 'made to fit the head, and with lappets to draw over the ears', Sherlock Holmes-fashion. Being without a brim, the cap would support the head without pain, while protecting against earache. For those content with a less than exact fit, it was possible to buy non-bespoke travelling caps at station bookstalls. Another tip in the book was to use one's travelling bag as a footrest to avoid the draught blowing under the carriage doorway. This was usually the worst offender against comfort, especially when the air current carried with it, according to the season, the powdery variety of snow – what might truly be called 'the wrong kind of snow'.

₪

The *Handy Book*'s travelling bag might well contain something to eat and drink, for nothing of that kind could yet be had on the train – there being neither restaurant nor buffet cars in 1862, nor any means of passing through or between carriages. On long-distance journeys, refreshment stops were made at appointed stations instead. The shortcomings of these pit stops – of which there will be more to tell later – encouraged many travellers to take matters into their own hands. R. S. Surtees in 1851 pointed out that the passenger in possession of a food parcel could dine when genuinely hungry, 'instead of when the railway directors think you ought to be'. His recommended bill of fare reads a little like a budget version of the feasts Jorrocks and his fellow sporting men routinely consume in Surtees's own fiction: cold chicken cuts, sliced tongue, bread, biscuits, cakes, with sherry-and-water or brandy-and-water to wash it all down (the injunction *not to forget the salt* is italicised). A more abstemious attitude was implied by the 'new combination' article displayed by W. H. Martin of the Burlington Arcade to the Great Exhibition's visitors: 'a walking stick, whip-stick, or umbrella-stick, containing long cylindrical bottle and wine-glass, and receptacle for biscuits or compressed meat, intended for railway travellers and others'. The *Handy Book* too assumed an appetite less gargantuan than Surtees: 'a few ham and beef sandwiches, together with a little cold wine or brandy and water will answer any purpose'.

Those with no liking for alcohol had to take their own supplies of tea or coffee at ambient temperature, for the vacuum or Thermos flask was not produced commercially until after 1904. Among those who favoured cold tea was the eccentric Andrew Peterson (1813–1906), former Indian Civil Service judge, hypnotist, healer, radical and pioneer of mass-concrete construction, whose 218ft-high folly tower at Sway in the New Forest still bemuses railway travellers between London and Bournemouth. An individualist in small matters as well as large, Peterson insisted on taking his cold tea via a rubber tube from a baby's bottle, to avoid spillages on the train.

One fair criticism of the Victorian railway companies is that they were extremely slow to cater for this market by providing substantial fare that could be carried on to the train and consumed there. Taverns near the principal stopping places along the Liverpool & Manchester route sent out trays of refreshments, including Eccles cakes, brandy and cigars, to tempt passengers in their carriages in the line's early years; but such free-and-easy echoes of the coaching network did not last long. Sometimes there were officially sanctioned vendors on the platform, but overall the railway companies had an ambivalent attitude to these, and the story in general is one of stricter controls, confining trade to the railways' own outlets or those of their licensees.

It took one of these licensed firms, Messrs Spiers and Pond, to show the way. Félix William Spiers and Christopher Pond were two forceful young Londoners who had joined forces out in Australia. Their first enterprise together was to lease a hotel grill-room in Melbourne. They next took over the city's two theatre cafés, importing French waiters and generally doing things properly. An attempt at persuading Dickens to favour Australia with one of his programmes of public readings came to nothing, but the pair did arrange the first All-England cricket tour to the southern hemisphere. The tourists sailed from Liverpool in 1861 (as it happened, on the SS *Great Britain*, the second of Brunel's three mammoth steamships), and proved more than equal to any side the Australians could field against them. Not long after, Spiers and Pond turned their energies back to London, where they took the contract to operate the Metropolitan Railway's refreshment rooms at Farringdon Street station. There was no question of running this business like the take-it-or-leave-it establishments on the platforms of provincial junctions: maximum journey times on the new railway were a mere eighteen minutes, and success depended on attracting extra custom from the non-travelling London public. That meant a serious attention to quality, including the production by the company of all its own biscuits, cakes and ices. The journalist and social critic Henry Mayhew, visiting in 1865, found these better and cheaper than the offerings at other railway refreshment bars; he recorded up to 400 people choosing to dine at Farringdon each day.

By that date the partnership had also taken on the refreshment rooms at the London, Chatham & Dover Railway's Victoria station. Later ventures included theatres and restaurants in the capital (the famous Criterion was Spiers and Pond's), and a steady expansion of railway contracts outside London. These included management agreements with the Midland for the facilities at Leicester and at Trent, a strange junction station opened in 1862 on the floodplain midway between Derby and Nottingham. Trent – named from the river, rather than any nearby settlement – was an interchange only, without public access from outside. Passengers compelled to change trains there were literally a captive market; mention of the name Trent Junction may resurrect memories of ennui or disorientation among cross-country travellers of a certain age (the station closed in 1968). Here, in 1871, Spiers and Pond introduced luncheon baskets, priced at three shillings and containing half a chicken, ham, bread and butter, cheese and a half-pint bottle of claret or stout. The Midland Railway added a two-shilling option when it began selling its own baskets from Derby four years later. The correlation between passengers' budgets and social class is suggested by the rather embarrassing names chosen by the London & North Western Railway for its luncheon baskets, the 'Aristocrat' (five shillings) and the 'Democrat' (two shillings and sixpence). The 'Aristocrat' offered the choice of a pint of claret or half a pint of sherry – enough to get you tolerably drunk, though it must be allowed that Victorian claret was weaker than today's. The plebeian 'Democrat' had a bottle containing ale or stout.

The quality of basket fare was often questionable; jokes were made about the thinness of the sliced ham and the age of the chicken at time

A railway luncheon basket, photographed in 1905

of death. Nevertheless, these services proliferated. The first record of baskets containing hot meals dates from 1884, again on the Midland Railway. Successful operation of the system required the orders to be telegraphed ahead, and the employment of boys to call out the passengers' names at the platform so that their baskets could be claimed. Breakfast baskets and tea baskets (usual charge one shilling) were also available, the latter including bread and butter and a choice of cake, biscuits or chocolate. The term 'basket' may give the wrong picture; after the First World War, the contents increasingly came protected by decoratively printed boxes of waxed cardboard, a forerunner of today's branded fast-food packaging. The basket trade actually peaked earlier still, around 1906, after which custom began to decline in favour of the new restaurant cars. Time was finally called on the basket system in 1941, as a wartime economy. Until then, the cutlery, crockery and non-disposable baskets swelled by many tens of thousands the already gigantic miscellany of reusable or refillable objects that journeyed repeatedly back and forth across the railway network, until breakage, pilfering or obsolescence put an end to their remunerative lives.

Excessive intake of fluids exposed the mid-Victorian passenger to the risk of embarrassment, for the ordinary compartmented carriage did not include a lavatory. This is one subject on which contemporary sources are prudishly silent. *Punch*, for example, was very engaged by the subject of railways and always happy to have fun at their expense, but even in the magazine's rowdy youth there is no equivalent in its caricatures and skits to Honoré Daumier's lithograph of 1843. The colic-stricken old lady pleads with the guard travelling on top of her carriage, only to learn that the company forbids, but that Orléans is only two and a quarter hours away: a reminder from France of how inflexible the ways of the railway seemed to those who grew up with the easy-going customs of road travel.

Necessity, mother of invention, had filled a gap by July 1852, when Messrs Walters' 'celebrated railway convenience for ladies and gentlemen' was first advertised in *The Times*. 'Travelling conveniences' for wearing under everyday dress also feature in department-store catalogues. The publisher Philip Unwin (born 1905) recalled that articles of this kind, made of rubber and strapped to the leg, could be had from shops at the approaches to many stations. Other expedients were possible. John Gloag (born 1896) recorded that women travelling together in an otherwise empty compartment might bring into service from their luggage 'an innocent-looking circular basket, which contained a chamber pot'. Mothers with small children no doubt pressed all sorts of articles into emergency service. The solitary (or companionable) male passenger could improvise at an open carriage window without too much risk of scandal or detection, and doubtless did so often enough, especially at night. Otherwise there was nothing for it but to sit tight and await the next long station stop.

₪

Daumier's guard is shown leaning down from a fixed seat or cabin on the carriage roof. This feature was not unique to French railways. Similar seats, not always protected against the weather, feature on many early views from Britain. Their occupants' duties varied from line to line. A train guard might use the vantage point to keep in visual contact with the locomotive crew on their open footplate, to observe any directions and signals from railwaymen by the lineside and to apply or release the carriage brake accordingly. Another position adopted was on the back of the tender, overlooking the train from against the direction of travel; this was Brunel's choice for the Great Western. Some trains had more than one guard, at a ratio of up to one man per carriage, so that the brakes could be applied to more of the vehicles – this as long as continuous brakes had yet to be brought into use. If the train was carrying mail, a commodity which usually migrated from road to rail the instant a new line opened, there would also be Post Office guards to watch over the mail boxes; and because the habit of carrying the boxes on the carriage roofs was also taken over from the roads, these guards were at first also seated outside and on top. Better arrangements soon suggested themselves, and the guards and their mail moved inside: either to the special vans known as Travelling Post Offices, which were equipped to drop off and pick up mailbags from lineside apparatus while the train was in motion, or to ordinary compartments. In 1848 the Post Office finally accepted that ordinary guards in the employment of the railway could be trusted with the mail. That did not mean the end of roof seats; they were still current as late as 1858, when the Inverness & Aberdeen Junction Railway specified them for its new stock – quite a cruelty, considering the region's climate. But by that time it was more common for the guard to travel in a compartment or dedicated van equipped with a windowed projection on each side, or with a roof rising higher than the ordinary level by means of a vertical glazed section, through which the guard could look out by climbing steps provided within the carriage.

A seat on top had an additional advantage: it allowed the guard to watch for slippages of the luggage riding on the carriage roofs, or for sheetings that were working loose, or for occasions when the lumpy assembly of trunks, packages and coverings trapped a hot cinder from the locomotive and caught fire. In such cases it seems to have been common practice to clamber across the roofs to put things right. The dangers are not hard to see, and they took their toll. One early fatality was a servant of the London & Birmingham Railway, a guard called David Dent (all railway employees were officially 'servants' until 1948, nationalisation year), on 7 July 1838. While Dent was fixing a flapping tarpaulin, his head struck a bridge, knocking him off. The train was moving at thirty miles an hour. Another train then ran him over on the track. The line having opened fully just one month before, Dent may have had only a few weeks in which to master his perilous duties. A railwayman's accidental death was still newsworthy in the 1830s; the *Annual Register* devoted a paragraph to the event, dwelling on the 'frightfully mangled state' of the body, for there was little squeamishness in discussing injuries in early-Victorian Britain. Reports in the

daily papers described the state of Dent's skull, arms and viscera in still
more horrible detail.

Making safe the luggage was not the only dangerous duty that might
be required of the first railway guards. Exactly one month later, on the
same line, Thomas Port fell to his death from a northbound train at Har-
row. His duties as guard included checking the tickets of passengers after
departure, working along the outside of the moving train from compartment to compartment. Gaps between the carriages were negotiated by
stepping across the interval between the footboards. But Port lost his footing and fell beneath the wheels; his legs were crushed; amputation failed
to save him. A servant of the new technology, Port died in time to find a
place within an older and declining tradition, that of the verse epitaph.
The lines carved on his gravestone at Harrow-on-the-Hill may be quoted
in all their artless pathos:

> Bright rose the morn and vig'rous rose poor *Port*:
> Gay on the *train*, he used his wonted sport:
> Ere noon arrived his mangled form they bore,
> With pain distorted and o'erwhelm'd with gore:
> When evening came, to close the fatal day,
> A mutilated corpse the sufferer lay.

The manifestly dangerous practice of checking tickets through the windows of moving trains did not last long. Instead, the job was often done
by means of a special ticket stop, by which long-distance trains were
detained shortly before their termination point so that the tickets could
be systematically examined and collected. Sometimes this was done from
narrow platforms built specially for the purpose, as at Euston and York in
their early years; one of these has survived, against the odds, in the cutting
just outside Liverpool Street station in London. Stops were also made at
ordinary suburban stations such as Finsbury Park (for King's Cross), Preston Park (for Brighton) and Dudley Port (for Birmingham New Street),
places all too familiar to the long-distance passenger into the early twentieth century. The idea of being held for five minutes a mile or two short
of the terminus *on every single journey* will doubtless set the contemporary
traveller's mind twitching with impatience. So it should be remembered
that despite all the time lost, the train remained the swiftest human conveyance yet known. Perhaps the practice can be thought of as equivalent

to the boring but expected modern experience of sitting meekly still after landing at the airport, waiting for the docking bays to engage and the seat-belt lights to switch off at last.

Placing the train crew outside the carriages did not seem startling in the 1830s. The crews of road coaches travelled in the open, as did many of the passengers, coaches commonly having more outside seats than inside ones. This in turn made it perfectly acceptable that the first railways should require passengers travelling at the cheaper rates to journey in the open air. So now we must move out of the compartment for a time, stepping down the social scale from Aristocrat to Democrat, and also back in time from 1862, to the earliest passenger railways.

THE CLASSES IN MOTION

The compartmented coaches of the Liverpool & Manchester were the first of their kind, and influential on the design of thousands more. In the earliest years the company positively encouraged visits to its carriage workshops, 'whether for the purposes of scientific research, or for practical information' – for there was no reason to be nervous of competition, as long as the new lines up and down the country remained isolated from one another. The Liverpool & Manchester's public, timetabled, steam-hauled service is the chief reason it qualifies as the first true railway in the modern sense, despite the prior claims of its famous predecessor the Stockton & Darlington Railway, opened in 1825. The two lines shared the magic name of George Stephenson as engineer and as supplier of locomotives (via Robert Stephenson & Co. of Newcastle, the engine works George set up with his no less gifted son). The different ways in which they chose to convey their human cargoes are worth dwelling on.

The Stockton & Darlington at first owned just one carriage, named *Experiment* – a hint of ambivalence in the title, perhaps. The naming of carriages echoed road practice, and the carriage was indeed fashioned like a single-compartment road coach, for the good reason that the Stockton & Darlington's passengers did not yet travel behind locomotives at all. The chief difference was that *Experiment* had identical ends, so that a horse could pull it either way. After the junketings were done, the core business of the railway as a mineral and goods carrier asserted itself. Access was allowed to anyone who wished to operate trains, effectively on a toll system. These privately run trains took their turn in the intervals between those the company ran using its own locomotives, horses and rolling stock. The young company actually gave up operating passenger trains on its own account for a while, in favour of provision by the horse-drawn carriages of licensed private operators. Only after 1833 did all Stockton & Darlington trains become subject to steam-hauled company operation.

The use of horses to pull passengers along a railway was nothing new for Britain. Mineral and goods lines – railways, tramways (or tramroads), plateways or waggonways, named according to their deployment of various types of iron or timber rails – already had a history more than two centuries long. Informal use by passengers taking rides on their vehicles, perhaps in return for a small fee or tip, was widespread. The next chapter in the story was the operation of an advertised public service, running at fixed times. First in the field was the Swansea & Mumbles Railway, a five-mile mineral line opened in 1806. In the following year the company contracted out the right to run a passenger service by means of road-type coaches, which had wheels with flanged iron tyres. This service lasted only until the late 1820s, when a turnpike road opened alongside: the first instance of a passenger railway killed off by road competition. The sequence of events would not have seemed so strange at the time; as on other horse-drawn railways, passenger traffic represented a useful additional revenue source, but was not intrinsic to the concept. Even the prospectus issued for the Liverpool & Manchester in October 1824 was still cagey about the potential of passenger traffic. Once the Stockton & Darlington had demonstrated the latent demand, the Liverpool & Manchester was emboldened to embrace the concept too, as yet without the additional leap of faith represented by steam haulage. This shyness in teaming locomotives with passenger trains might be compared with the early development of aircraft, which found specialist and military uses in plenty well before anyone had worked out how to make them pay as a means of regular passenger transport.

These early horse-drawn passenger railways should not be dismissed as backward. The principle was sound: iron tyres and iron rails, like canals, allowed a single horse to manage a much greater load than was possible on the roads. The durability of the concept was proved by its revival some decades later in the form of the horse tram, a familiar sight on many British streets in later Victorian times – although it took an American financier, the poignantly named George Francis Train (1829–1904), to re-establish the method. Train's tramcars began running in Birkenhead in 1860, after the failure in the previous year of an attempt (by a Briton) to make a go of a horse-tram service in Liverpool, across the Mersey. In the following year Train demonstrated his trams in London, bringing the capital into line with Paris and with many American cities. So the horse found its place within the new systems of public rail-borne travel, even as it was displaced by the iron horse from heavy and long-distance haulage.

To use horses for railway haulage imposed a limitation on weight, which tended to favour the use of single carriages modelled on those of the roads. The open-topped horse tram demonstrated the principle for later generations; as on the roads, enclosed and exposed passengers all travelled on the same set of wheels. The adoption of steam haulage changed the rules of the game, for a steam locomotive could manage a string of separate carriages – 'a length infinitely extendible', as *The Times*'s man Henry Crabb Robinson put it, with pardonable exaggeration, on his visit to the Liverpool & Manchester in 1833. Now there was an opportunity to build entire vehicles to different standards, of which the second-class carriages were effectively the successors of the outside seats on the roads. Those provided in the company's first years took the form of open wagons fitted with four-a-side benches. For further protection, some carriages sported a lightweight canopy. That much was all that was needed as long as the railways sought only to take over existing traffic from the roads. While the competition lasted – which was rarely long, for coach services usually folded pretty smartly after a railway opened along the route – the passenger could weigh in the balance questions of comfort, economy and speed.

Comfort first. In truth, travelling by train in an open-sided carriage was not always more pleasant, minute for minute, than a coach journey. It entailed exposure to much stronger winds and the risk of stinging rain; effectively, the train created its own wind-chill. 'The cold is great, and [passengers] must have some defence against the wind, through which they pass so rapidly': thus the Duke of Wellington's reported experience of the Liverpool & Manchester. This effect was usually tempered by sitting within an enclosed pen, rather than perching up high, stagecoach fashion. Even then, unwelcome currents of air might whip around the ankles from the holes that were sometimes bored in the floors to allow the escape of rainwater, and for slopping out when cleaning. Open-sided carriages without holes might take on water during heavy rain; a depth of two inches was recorded on the Great Western in 1844.

For extreme exposure, there was little to beat those early railways, which took over the stagecoach habit of placing passengers on the outside of otherwise enclosed coaches. The first steam railway to run out of the capital, the London & Greenwich (opened from 1836 onwards), chose to fix benches across the end walls of its second-class stock, on which passengers could sit with their legs dangling over the track. In its early years the Newcastle & Carlisle offered third-class travel in the form of passenger seats on top of its luggage vans, from which uniformed bands had performed on the railway's opening day in 1835. Anyone who braved an open carriage or outside seat was also exposed to the locomotive exhaust. 'Dust from engine annoying to the eyes & filthy in the carriage: I had dreaded the motion backward.' Thus the young Gladstone in his diary for 13 July 1839, after a journey to Crewe. And not only dust: lighted cinders pattering down from the locomotive exhaust, which might ruin hats and other clothes, or burn the skin directly. One passenger in the early days of the Great Western sent a note of protest to the management, enclosing a cinder 'which fell within my shirt collar in a burning state and caused a large blister to rise'.

As for economy and speed, the train was almost always the winner. The average expense saved was appreciable, though not necessarily enormous; in the 1830s some coaches charged 5d per mile for an inside seat, whereas first-class trains might cost 3½d. But the railways were free of the customary tips or 'vails' payable on the roads at regular stages and at the end of the journey; as recalled in 1858 by R. S. Surtees – famously, an aficionado of fox hunting, but also an enthusiast for railways – 'a man used never to have his hand out of his pocket'. Then there was the time won by travelling faster, which in turn saved on meals, and which on longer journeys might avert the heavy expense of an overnight stay – not to mention the release of valuable extra hours for those who worked for a living.

It was also clear from early on that the railways could unlock a great deal of extra demand by conveying passengers more quickly and cheaply than the roads. The Liverpool & Manchester began by running five daily trains each way; within five years that figure had risen to nine. But even this level of service excluded the poorer classes: those for whom the price of a coach journey remained out of reach, but whose budgets might stretch to a ticket if only the trains could be made to run as cheaply as possible. As a rule, early lines were not built with such people in mind. A few companies actually found it more profitable to raise prices so much that demand

First-, second- and third-class travel, from the *Illustrated London News*, 1846. The first-class carriage has an end compartment of the single-sided coupé type.

began to fall. Even so, the prospect of extra human payloads that could be carried as cheaply and easily as livestock – sometimes, indeed, sharing the same train with livestock – was difficult to resist.

So third-class travel was born. By definition, it offered an inferior service to what was often still an austere second class. Some lines simply provided low-sided open wagons, in which passengers had to stand, lean or balance on their luggage as best they could. The Stockton & Darlington carried passengers on this basis on its Middlesbrough extension in 1835. On the Manchester & Leeds Railway a bar and crossbar were fitted within, making four standing enclosures or pens (the parallel with handling livestock is exact here). Occupants of these vehicles were not even granted the honorific of third class by the company, which used the term 'wagon passengers'. The London & Birmingham was using wagon-type carriages by Christmas Eve, 1838, when the teenaged Alfred Russel Wallace (1823–1913) took one from Berkhamsted to London. His autobiography recalls 'open trucks identical with modern goods trucks, except that they had hinged doors, but with no seats whatever, so that any one tired of standing must sit upon the floor'. Despite mild weather for the season and a speed not over 20 mph, 'the wind was very disagreeable'.

The industry had not finished with Wallace: he went on to work as a railway surveyor, all the while developing his self-education as an entomologist; finally he flourished as an explorer and naturalist, developing independently of Darwin a theory of natural selection. An elder brother, William, preceded Alfred into the business of surveying for railway lines, but with less happy results. In 1846 William was required to travel up to London to appear before a parliamentary committee concerning Brunel's South Wales Railway. Shortly after his return to Glamorganshire he died from congestion of the lungs, an illness which, his brother recorded, had begun with a cold brought on 'by being chilled in a wretched third-class carriage'. At least William died in his bed; in the previous year a wire worker named Jonathan John had fallen down dead just outside Bath station, after enduring a third-class journey in one of Brunel's open-sided carriages. His travelling outfit of two pairs of trousers, two waistcoats, two overcoats and a woollen neckerchief had not been enough to protect him. The coroners' jury found the design of the vehicle partly responsible for his demise.

Even if they might still be lethal in cold weather, the design of third-class carriages was already improving by the mid 1840s. The change was brought about by the Railway Regulation Act of 1844, the credit for which is due to William Gladstone as President of the Board of Trade. The context was growing public concern that the railways were unsafe; the trigger was another journey made on the Great Western on a Christmas Eve, to fatal effect, in the year 1841.

The train in question was the 4.30 a.m. from London to Bristol, which passed through Sonning in Berkshire by means of a cutting. At nearly two miles long, this was the largest earthwork on the line, taking the railway through high ground before the approach to Reading. The cutting was then barely two years old. Heavy rains had made its sides unstable, and the landslip that followed blocked the rails to a depth of nearly four feet. The fall went undetected until the train ran into it. Although the service was officially described as a goods train, the practice had been followed of including a pair of third-class carriages – 'trucks', in the official stock lists – coupled ahead of the wagons. There was no time for either of the train's guards to apply the brake, and on impact the wagons by their own momentum rode up over the derailed passenger trucks and against the engine and tender. The trucks were fitted with planks for seats, protected by sides a mere 2ft high. Some of the occupants were crushed, others thrown out by the impact. Eight were killed outright (of whom six were buried by the company in a communal grave); a ninth later died in hospital. Many more were gravely injured. Building workers made up most of the casualties, returning home for Christmas from employment on the foundations of the new Palace of Westminster; their masters there were the same contractors, Messrs Grissell & Peto, who had built a substantial share of the Great Western's line.

Sonning represented the first major loss of life to passengers on a British railway – an ugly bruise on the public face of the industry. There was no gainsaying that the open carriage was a dismal way to travel (nine and half hours to Bristol in this case, half of that time in winter darkness). Now it was shown to be highly dangerous too. Nor did the working practices of the Great Western emerge with credit. It was not hard to foresee that carriages coupled between the locomotive and heavy wagons would be vulnerable in case of accident. A contributor to the *Mechanics' Magazine*, a journal aimed at skilled artisans, denounced the 'modern mechanical Moloch' for having failed to act on warnings to this effect.

By 1841 these matters were no longer merely a subject for public denunciation. In the 1830s the railways had been left to manage their own safety, but the first Railway Regulation Act (1840) had set up a Railway

Department at the Board of Trade with powers to inspect and approve new lines, and to investigate accidents that resulted in serious injury or worse to members of the public. Such accidents were now to be followed by the publication of an official report, with the power to recommend improved practice.

In the case of the Sonning disaster, the Great Western was exonerated from responsibility for the smash itself, on the grounds that the cutting was not so steep-sided that a landslip could reasonably have been predicted. But the inspector's report did question the safety of several features and practices, and directed that the carriage sides on this and every other line be raised to a minimum of 4ft 6in, both as a safeguard against being jolted out and to protect against 'the cutting winds of the winter'.

This was better than nothing; but there was more going on behind the scenes at the Board of Trade. As Vice-President of the Board in 1841–3, then as President in 1843–5, Gladstone showed a particular interest in taking the railways in hand. He proposed a select parliamentary committee on the subject, steered its deliberations, compiled its reports and masterminded their culmination in the shape of the Railway Regulation Act of 1844. Economic and political historians remember this 'Gladstone Act' especially for its clauses allowing railways to be nationalised after a fixed period, a pet project that came to nothing, but which seemed prophetic in hindsight. Social and railway historians best know the Act for other provisions, especially for that which gave the nation a new coinage: the 'Parliamentary' train.

The Parliamentary got its name because the Act required all future railways with a substantial passenger service to include at least one train in each day's timetable, Sundays not excepted, to be charged at no more than a penny a mile. These cheap trains were to call at every station while maintaining a minimum overall speed of 12 mph. Their carriages were to have seats, and passengers should also be 'protected from the weather', in a manner subject to the Board's approval. That made certain sorts of carriage obsolete immediately; for instance, the Great Western was still running open second-class carriages as well as its horrible thirds. There was also an allowance under the Act of 56lb of luggage per passenger before surcharges were incurred (half a hundredweight, or just over 25kg metrically) – less than the higher classes were routinely allowed, but sufficient for itinerant workers and tradesmen to take their tools or samples with them.

Gladstone sweetened the pill for the companies by exempting these

The experience of second-class travel over 100 miles, from
Angus B. Reach, *The Comic Bradshaw*, 1848

cheap trains from the 5 per cent duty then normally levied on ticket receipts. This exemption also gave existing lines an incentive to run their own Parliamentary-type trains. Such was the take-up that any differences in passenger services between companies founded before and after 1844 soon ceased to be significant.

It is hard to think of any greater single improvement in travelling conditions imposed on unenthusiastic private enterprise by the government of the United Kingdom. In narrow terms, the new rules were a major restraint on free trade, imposing rules and conditions on companies that would rather have done things their own way. On the other hand, the Act also gave a calculated stimulus to capitalism by promoting the free circulation of labour. In addition, the Parliamentary train represented an effective subsidy for the travel of the poorer classes, by the surrender of revenue that would otherwise have come to the Treasury. Only in the daily timetabling of their cheap trains did the companies remain free. The London & Brighton, for instance, initially concentrated them between 6 p.m. and 10 p.m. – deliberately useless to those wanting a cheap day trip to the seaside.

What could not be foreseen in 1844 was the way in which the Board would use the regulation of Parliamentary trains as a hand-hold on the companies, steering them away from dependence on the cheapest and most basic type of covered carriage. These interventions were backed by the power to withhold the remission of duty should any carriage designs be found wanting (timetabled speeds and station stops likewise). The under-sung hero of this story is Major-General Sir Charles Pasley, FRS (1780–1861), the second Inspector-General of Railways. Such military titles would become familiar handles for senior members of the inspectorate even into the 1980s, a tradition that began because the 1840 Act barred from appointment anyone with an existing connection to a railway company. That was enough to rule out practically every civil engineer of note, but not the Corps of Royal Engineers, among whom Pasley cut an outstanding figure: a former child prodigy from a gentry family who could read New Testament Greek by the age of eight; a veteran of Napoleonic battles who survived being bayoneted and then shot through at the Battle of Flushing in 1809; the first head of the School of Military Engineering at Woolwich, and later in charge of instruction at the Engineers' establishment at Chatham, where he added Irish and Welsh to his stock of languages by conversing with rankers under his command; an internationally recognised authority on siege warfare, on the demolition of naval wrecks and on the properties of cement and concrete; an early advocate of decimal weights and measures – the register is so full that Pasley's pages in the *Oxford Dictionary of National Biography* hurry over his railway years in just two sentences.

That Pasley knew little about the new industry when he was appointed proved no handicap. He was able to mug up from the technical literature that was then just beginning to appear, and his diaries record an avid assimilation of knowledge on his journeys over the expanding network. On 28 February 1842, for example, he was in Manchester, watching tickets being printed and numbered by Edmondson's still novel method ('The quickest mode of entering').

The bulk of Pasley's responsibilities concerned the inspection of new lines and the investigation of accidents. His diaries have much less to say about carriage design. Yet it is clear that the 1844 Act opened the way for a culture of arm-twisting, and that this endured well beyond the end of the Inspector-General's term of office in 1846, each intervention offering an opportunity for further improvement. The policy was never officially formulated, and it is difficult to detect any ulterior motives behind it. The bureaucratic instinct to put things in order doubtless contributed, backed by a broader public feeling that the railways deserved more direction and control than they had so far received; but there seems to have been a genuine humanitarian impulse there too.

So the Grand Junction Railway was told brusquely in October 1844 that the open-sided carriages proposed for its Parliamentary trains 'would never do'. The following month, Pasley decreed that the adequate protection for passengers stipulated under the Act meant that carriages should be 'capable of being entirely closed when necessity may require, with provisions for the admission of light and air' (this in response to a submission from the Manchester & Birmingham). In this case the company's proposal had gone to the opposite extreme: a fully enclosed vehicle with unglazed openings that could be made weathertight by means of shutters or blinds, so that passengers could exclude rain and wind only at the cost of sitting in the dark. It was a not uncommon response to the Act, partly suggested by the ease with which existing open-sided carriages could simply be boarded up below the roofline. Tarpaulin hangings, as on the London & South Western, were another way of filling the gap.

The requirement to admit light and air was then circulated to several other companies, as Minute 410. This action took the Department into uncertain territory, for the 1844 Act did not empower it to make legally enforceable regulations. Care was therefore taken not to expose Minute 410 to the glare of the courtroom by taking legal action against companies failing to provide coaches to the standard preferred. Nor was there any need; the Inspectorate's power to refuse the remittance of passenger duty proved enough to secure compliance.

In 1846 it was declared by the Board that lamps were 'absolutely necessary for the safety and comfort of passengers' – though as we have seen, the level of future provision varied a good deal according to class. Glazed windows were an obvious next step. Minute 410 stopped short of insisting on these, as the Lancaster & Carlisle Railway well knew. Its managers hoped to get away with using carriages equipped with slatted or shuttered openings only. The official response gave this short shrift, pointing out that the new route passed through the bleak eastern fells of the Lake Counties, in consideration of which the passengers certainly deserved protection behind glass. A compromise was reached, by which four glass panels would be let into the roof. It is a strange picture: the Parliamentary passengers shuttered within as their train climbed the punishing incline at Shap, deprived of the sight of the Westmorland skyline, or any external view but the clouds visible through the film of rainwater streaming over the skylights above their heads.

This exchange dates from 1846–7. By 1860, the Board of Trade was confident enough to determine the amount of windowing too. Each Parliamentary passenger was now to have a minimum of sixty square inches of window glass, as well as minimum standards of space, at twenty cubic feet per person and sixteen inches' width of seat on which to sit.

None of this meant that open carriages were prohibited as such. Some lines simply redesignated them 'fourth class', others kept them in reserve for cheap excursion traffic. But the passenger-duty rule left little inducement to build new open carriages, and to the ordinary traveller of 1862 the type would already have seemed archaic. Probably the worst excursion stock in regular use by that date was on the ever-thrifty Lancashire & Yorkshire, which carried on using mere open wagons for this traffic as late as 1859. Criticism from the Board in that year spurred the company into fitting temporary roofs to some 200 of these vehicles, which had been built for the conveyance of cattle.

Those who could countenance an occasional trip in an open carriage might yet be daunted by the boxed-in Parliamentary type. One such was Jane Welsh Carlyle (1801–66), wife of the philosopher and critic Thomas Carlyle. In 1835 she had braved a journey on the Liverpool & Manchester, the only rail-borne instalment of a complicated Anglo-Scottish journey. Judging the experience no worse than going by road, she became a confirmed user of second class; but in 1855 she found herself weighing up the attractions of an overnight journey to Scotland under a starry sky. Checking at Euston to see if open-topped thirds could still be had, Jane encountered instead 'a black hole of Calcutta on wheels! Closely roofed in, windows like pigeon holes, and no partitions to separate the twelve breaths of one compartment from all the breaths of all the third-class carriage!'

Jane's 'twelve breaths' – presumably a reference to the risk of contagion while travelling – must refer to individual places within each division of the carriage. Her calculation that passengers should sit in facing rows of six may have been a misunderstanding or exaggeration, five a side being usual. The intended capacity was anyway not easy to tell, for lower classes of carriage came without armrests or headrests to apportion the sitting space. Even five a side was tight, given the overall dimensions. The

Midland Railway's earliest Parliamentary coaches can stand as an example from the more generous end of the spectrum: compartments 6ft 5in wide, which gave just over 15½in for each seat, and 5ft long. The last measurement was reduced in some Great Western stock to a barely endurable 4ft – especially so, given that the railway's broad-gauge carriages were unusually wide. The experience must have been like sitting sideways in a mobile wooden tunnel.

Sitting on mere benches, too, for these third-class seats were not upholstered. That would have seemed less startling in an age when padded furniture was still a status symbol. Church, chapel, school, alehouse, lecture theatre and music hall all made do with timber benches or chairs. Simple wooden seating with removable cushions, rather than upholstered furniture as such, remained the norm in the ordinary home. To guard against jolting and vibration during travel, the traveller was advised to take a supply of padding, whether in the form of thick clothing or cushions of one sort or another. (*The Railway Traveller's Handy Book* recommended the inflatable sort made of *caoutchouc* or India rubber.)

₪

Less comfort, less personal space, visibly cheaper and plainer materials – all these distinctions between first class and the rest remain familiar. The railways also took care to make their first-class carriages look superior externally. Often they were adorned with the company's own heraldry, almost always concocted without the endorsement of the College of Arms, but painted nonetheless with all the care usually lavished on the displays on aristocratic road-coaches – at least until 1870, after which crests and complex lettering could be applied in the form of printed transfers invented by Messrs Tearnes of Birmingham. In his tour of the Crewe workshops in 1849, Sir Francis Head observed one first-class carriage being painted in 'beautiful colours', while another was being stripped out for demotion to second class, with men 'converting large, fashionable, oval windows [another echo of the smart private coach] into vulgar little square ones'. Likewise, older second-class carriages might be stripped down for further use as thirds. The commitment to cleanliness varied too; Head observed that the 'large gang of strong he-housemaids' employed at Euston was divided into dedicated first-class moppers and other men to whose care was allotted everything from second class to horseboxes and luggage trains.

Another difference was the presence of posters and notices pasted within the upper parts of the carriage, an intrusion that first-class was spared. The area available for advertising varied, according to how high the partitions reached. Jane Carlyle remarked on the lack of partitions between compartments in the Euston carriages, and in such cases passengers might sit literally back-to-back on seats of the lowest bench type. The distinction is important, for it made the second- or third-class carriage into a different kind of social space. By means of a bit of head-twisting, every other passenger could be seen (there were normally no more than four or five compartments, even in the longer, six-wheeled type of carriage that prevailed from the 1860s onwards). Above a certain level of background noise, the other passengers could therefore be heard, too.

All this constituted the usual lot of the less well-off when they took the train. Yet the written record of the period is skewed so far towards the elite that there is surprisingly little first-hand record of how people experienced these spaces, or of how they behaved in them. Even the works of Dickens, so curious about the railways, contain no description of a third-class journey; the nearest he came is a 'noises off' reference in 1857, noting third-class excursionists' habit of singing *en masse*.

Some of the most vivid accounts we do have are in the diaries of the Rev. Francis Kilvert (1840–79). As a rural curate in the Welsh borders, Kilvert lacked the tidy income enjoyed by many Anglican clerics; besides, many of his natural sympathies and much of his sense of mission seem to have lain with the common people. Certainly, his railway journeys are often described with a sort of captivated generosity concerning other travellers and their quirks. On a trip from Neath to Brecon on 18 October 1871, he records the singing of some Breconshire people on the way back from the market (group singing, again), reaching him from the next carriage: 'a rich treat ... in perfect time and tune, altogether, the trebles of the women blending exquisitely with the tenors and basses of the men.' In the meantime,

> A strange wild-looking woman was sitting opposite to me with light blue eyes almost starting from her head. She had conceived a mortal dislike to a man who sat in another corner of the carriage and she kept on glancing round over her shoulder at him [i.e., over the backs of the seats] ... 'Do you know him?', she whispered looking stealthily round at her enemy, at the same time pushing me and poking at my leg till I

was bruised and sore. 'Do you know him?' she repeated. 'No', I said extremely amused. 'Who is he?' 'He's wicked man' she said making a horrible face ...

Or on an excursion train to Bath on 18 May 1870, when popular action overcame the lack of lighting:

In the Box tunnel as there was no lamp, the people began to strike foul brimstone matches and hand them to each other all down the carriage ... The carriage was chock full of brimstone fumes, the windows both nearly shut, and by the time we got out of the tunnel I was almost suffocated. Then a gentleman tore a lady's pocket handkerchief in two, seized one fragment, blew his nose with it, and put the rag in his pocket. She then seized his hat from his head, while another lady said that the dogs of Wootton Bassett were much more sociable than the people.

This is the free-and-easy world recalled in 1894 by John Pendleton, who described how the low bench backs 'left the entire vehicle a roaming-place to all the passengers, and fostered indulgence in the game of leap-frog, men climbing over the partitions to get more comfortable seats or gossip with their friends'. Sometimes buskers tried their luck in the carriages too: an east Londoner in 1854 complained of encountering them three times in one week (accordionist, fiddler and singer).

Had Kilvert lived longer, he would have witnessed the eclipse of this type of third-class carriage by the full-compartment version – with upholstered seats into the bargain. The prime mover in this process was no longer the Inspectorate, which by that time was preoccupied with operational safety. Rather, it was the product of competition within the network, on which a choice of routes was increasingly common. One early instance dates from 1858, when the London & North Western began to compete with the Great Northern Railway and its allies for excursion traffic from Manchester to London, cutting fares and 'giving them 15-inch seats, stuffed cushions and backs to lean against' – as an indignant Great Northern shareholder reported. But the crucial decade was the 1870s, the protagonist the Midland Railway.

Under its chairman Sir James Allport, the Midland had opened new main lines to London and Manchester in the 1860s, in each case seeking a share of traffic from well-established rivals, followed in 1876 by a new route to Carlisle. Its trains were not necessarily faster than those of the competition, but they could at least be made more comfortable. The company therefore abolished second class as from 1 January 1875, and did so by effectively upgrading its thirds to a similar standard, with upholstered seats as the most obvious improvement. First-class fares were cut to the former second-class level. That was not all: the Midland had already startled its competitors by decreeing in 1872 that third-class carriages would henceforth run as part of every service, a body blow to the familiar division between the cheap, slow, unsociably timetabled Parliamentary trains and the rest.

Looking back on his term of office, Allport stressed his pride in having opened the full timetable to third class, with what sounds like genuine social concern: 'I felt saddened to see third-class passengers shunted on a siding in cold and bitter weather – a train containing amongst others many lightly clad women and children – for the convenience of allowing the more comfortable and warmly clad passengers to pass them.' Allport's belief that the future of passenger traffic lay with a single, improved class for all but the elite was hardly disinterested: his reforms were enough to win the Midland an extra 4 million passenger journeys a year, although the ultimate consequences for profitability have been questioned by economic historians. His contribution to the public good – comparable in its way to Pasley's – was recognised in 1884 with one of the few knighthoods bestowed on any senior Victorian railwayman. Other lines eventually and grudgingly followed Allport's lead in getting rid of second class, many in 1893, some as late as 1923; the last three-class services lingered on boat trains into the 1950s. But even where three classes were retained, the tendency was for third class to become part of every train, and for standards of accommodation to rise accordingly.

Pressure for improvement often proved irresistible when other lines were at hand for comparison. The Midland provided a service northward from Carlisle to Edinburgh via the lines of its ally the North British Railway, but the carriages supplied by that company were dingy and spartan. Reluctantly, the North British ordered thirty new third-class carriages with cushioned seats and backs in 1879, specifically 'for competitive traffic'. The phrase might have caused some head-shaking among third-class passengers in the company's monopoly areas such as Fife and Kinross, who had to wait rather longer for anything so sybaritic. Even the Lancashire &

Yorkshire Railway – slow in providing footwarmers and lamps, slow in upholstering even its second class – finally equipped its third class with cushions from 1880, covering them in a slippery horsehair cloth to guard against factory grease and lint from the cotton mills on its passengers' clothing. The fabric was remembered without fondness by the younger male generations of York and Lancaster, as the fashion for short trousers spread down the social scale from around 1900. Some things really were tougher Up North.

Wooden seating lingered in certain trains reserved for working men, miners especially. Upholstery was a mixed blessing on services dedicated to carrying men home each day imbued from head to foot with coal dust, as was the case until pithead baths were provided. Most collieries were equipped with these between the 1920s and early 1950s, so that miners no longer had to bathe on arrival at home. Latterly only a few battered trains of uncushioned four-wheelers remained in operation, up and down the Welsh valleys – the last working descendants of Pasley's improved Parliamentary carriage.

Another hangover from nineteenth-century practice that disappeared around the same time was the very name of third class, which was redesignated as second class on 3 June 1956. So things remained until 1987, when the label 'standard class' took its place. The first change recognised an existing reality, the second – like the widely resented decision in the early 1990s that passengers should be called 'customers' – was merely intended to make things sound better. The proportion of lines on which first-class accommodation was provided fell considerably in the meantime, especially on cross-country and suburban lines. In that sense, we are now a little closer to the egalitarian ideal of a single undifferentiated class, an idea that was seriously discussed in the aftermath of the Second World War (the *Daily Mirror* was all in favour), but which never looked likely to prevail.

₪

Other changes were in store for the Victorian passenger. Mirrors were increasingly provided, a valuable resource in a culture of respectable self-presentation. The straightness of ties, hats and partings could be checked, and facial smuts and streaks bestowed by the engine could be eliminated. The mirrors were almost invariably fixed to the partition in the zone between seat and luggage rack, so that they could be looked into directly only by standing up. That was often to invite a curious sliding sensation, familiar to anyone who has journeyed in a compartment of the older type, as the gaze is drawn irresistibly away towards the bright looking-glass landscape unrolling in reverse outside.

In the absence of a mirror, it might be possible to check one's reflection using the glazed pictures that began to appear in carriages in 1884. The Great Eastern Railway set the fashion, with the help of the landscape photographer John Payne Jennings (1843–1926). The images Jennings supplied were relatively small, of various arresting shapes including ovals and rounded-off rectangles, and were typically grouped symmetrically in rows with the titles hand-written below, as on an album page. The subjects included modest places of resort or excursion on the railway's own territory, represented in the artistic-pictorial manner of the day: village streets, lakes amid woods, a hedgerow with a distant figure at a stile.

The next step was into colour: not true colour photography, the early forms of which were not commercially viable, but the Photochrom technique by which a negative image was overlaid with coloured tints from a sequence of lithographic stones. This was a Swiss invention, and was licensed to a London company in the mid 1890s. With their muted greens and tawny browns, glassy-smooth lakes and seas, and skies fading predictably from azure to colourless horizons, these images look hopelessly faked today; but when new they represented a decided advance. The Great Western took the bait almost immediately, becoming the largest single customer for the Photochrom company. Eight men were employed for the sole purpose of taking subjects for its various railway clients (not just for carriages: there was a demand for waiting rooms too), to a total of some 12,000 different subjects. Mounts and frames were supplied as well, and the Photochrom works at Tunbridge Wells cut up twenty-four miles of mouldings annually to make them. Some railways used other methods; the North Eastern favoured photographs printed directly on to oblong pieces of board, which were varnished for protection and slotted into the panelling of the carriage.

Framed advertisements and notices of other kinds proliferated too, especially in the lower classes of carriage. In the railways' own advertisements, the resort, the hotel or the tempting prospect were all stock themes. Early in the new century, maps of the railways' systems began to appear among them, sometimes compressed or distorted to fit the space.* The mid-Victorian passenger was exposed to texts; the late-Victorian and Edwardian passenger journeyed within a little cabinet of images and representations.

It is strange that the pictorial fashion should have started on the Great Eastern, a notoriously hard-up railway with no great reputation for comfort or superfluous display. It may simply have been a personal enthusiasm of the locomotive superintendent, Thomas William Worsdell (after all, this was the line that chose to put pictorial transparencies in the clerestory glazing). But a broader explanation must be sought in the domestic settings of late-Victorian Britain, in which superfluity signified security of possession, a visual vacuum was something to be abhorred, and fringes, knick-knacks and framed images proliferated wherever space allowed. It was as if the enclosure, heating and lighting of the compartment had made it an extension of domestic space, rather than an interior equivalent of the bill-sticker's wall. In some first-class carriages of the North Eastern the photographs were even double-hung, one row of frames above another, as if in an art gallery. Royalty was not immune: the Great Western's royal carriages of 1897 included the usual Photochrom prints, made especially honorific by fluted and gilded frames of sycamore and walnut.

Exempt from the commercial advertisement's cycle of replacement, these pictures might linger for decades, their poised figures ever more obsolete in dress, the odd stain from a cleaner's wet cloth or a luggage-rack mishap gradually darkening in one corner – a metonym for the obsolescence of the carriage itself. This drawback came to the attention of the railways in the mid 1930s, a period of fresh self-consciousness concerning their public image. Thanks to the Grouping of 1923, each of the four new super-companies had a greater territory to celebrate, which the Southern Railway and the London & North Eastern Railway chose to do by means of colour reproductions of views commissioned from professional artists. When the railways were nationalised, this policy became general, with new prints of standardised sizes and coherent themes. It was discovered around this time that the photographs still on display in working carriages included images of Liverpool with horse trams going about their business, the last of which had run in 1903. So here is another instance

---

* A convention taken to its logical end by the individual line-plans between window and roof in the trains of the London Underground, strings pulled from the diagrammatic tangle of the famous map first codified by Harry Beck in 1931.

of the continuities and traditions of the railway, as bewitching to historically minded observers of the mid-twentieth-century scene as they were disgraceful to those charged with its modernisation.

₪

Crucial to the levelling-up of standards was the steady rise in the proportion of travellers who took third-class tickets. The early railway decades showed that it was possible to upgrade the experience of travel for the lowest class considerably without discarding the principle of three-way classification. Yet there was quite a difference between shivering in an open pen and sitting in a glazed compartment, however cramped, with the consolation of a lamp somewhere overhead. Second-class traffic therefore tended to leak away to the improved thirds. By 1874, the last year before the Midland's dual-class service began, 77 per cent of railway journeys were already by third class. Nor was first class immune; on the Great Northern its share fell from 7 per cent to 3.5 per cent of travel between 1872 and 1884, while second class slipped from 25 per cent to 6.5 per cent. By 1913, 96 per cent of all journeys were third-class, accounting for 85 per cent of passenger revenue. It should be stressed too that the ordinary British third-class carriage of the time was greatly superior to the Continental equivalent, where wooden seats were still standard. Baedeker's guide thus assured overseas visitors that it was acceptable for 'a superior class' to go third, especially on longer journeys.

This converging experience of travel is one of the greatest instances of social levelling in our history. It is hard to think of any parallel during the period. Living conditions improved, but housing and areas of residence were still organised and perceived overwhelmingly in class terms. Free and universal education was introduced, but schools remained acutely stratified by type and by cost. Mass literacy was promulgated, but it fostered a market for cheap reading that had little to do with the values of high culture. Class differences in dress became subtler, but could still be read easily enough. The differently priced seats in theatres carried connotations of class, as did the saloon and public bars in pubs. And yet on the trains, all but a shrinking proportion of the well-off sat down together in third class.

Sometimes the point is explicitly made. Here is Rupert Brooke (1887–1915), poet, golden boy, Cambridge graduate and socialist, recording his joyful contemplation of a fellow passenger in a letter of September 1910:

I roam about places – yesterday I did it even in Birmingham! – and sit
in trains and see the essential glory and beauty of all the people I meet.
I can watch a dirty middle-aged tradesman in a railway-carriage for
hours, and love every dirty greasy sulky wrinkle in his weak chin and
every button on his spotted unclean waistcoat.

Yet within four years, during the months between his commission in
the Royal Naval Division and his departure to death in the Dardanelles,
Brooke would be entitled and expected to take a first-class ticket, like any
other officer of His Majesty.

The enduring fascination of the system of classes of travel lies in just
this kind of relationship to broader social attitudes. By 1900 or 1914, Britain was ordered perhaps more consciously than ever before into a hierarchy
of classes in the Marxian or economic sense, and yet its people were much
readier than their grandparents had been to set these divisions aside when
the time came to travel. Things were somewhat different in 1830, when it
was not yet customary to talk of social difference specifically in terms of
class rather than of order, rank or degree. It has even been argued that the
divisions used by the railways helped to establish the concept of class in
the broader, social sense. The railway historian Jack Simmons noted that
the word had never applied to travel by road or by water, for which the
various options were identified by name (inside or outside, cabin or deck
and so on); also, that the terminology of first- and second-class began to
extend to passengers as well as trains from as early as 1837. Nine years later,
Chambers' Edinburgh Journal observed that John Bull was learning to
make more rigid the 'humiliating distinctions' of class by taking cues from
the railway, 'at once his slave and his master'. By that date, with the Parliamentary third class recently added, the suggestion of social self-assessment
at the booking-office window was hard to escape.

Responses to this challenge of self-classification were sometimes
contradictory. When a review of volunteer regiments was held at Brighton in 1862, for example, the London, Brighton & South Coast Railway
announced that any non-officers would *not* be permitted to travel there
first class. In general, however, the companies were as anxious as any theatre
manager that their better-paying customers should not desert the expensive seats. The wrangles after 1844 over carriage design are in part a reflection of this. There were lines such as the Liverpool & Manchester which
had refused to run third-class trains at all, until compelled by Gladstone's

Act, on the grounds that too many of its second-class passengers would defect to them. The Manchester & Leeds reportedly paid sweeps to dump soot in some of its third-class carriages, to teach a lesson to better-off economisers. This was an extreme case, but the basic dilemma remained. Later in the century it was admitted by Sir Edward Watkin, chairman of more than one major railway, that his third-class carriages on the South Eastern were made deliberately uninviting so that passengers would take second-class tickets instead; as late as 1883 he lamented as 'a great public injustice' the Midland's first-and-third model, 'driving together classes who do not naturally wish to associate'.

There was a measure of truth in Watkin's objections. The South Eastern was moved to introduce some third-class carriages around 1873 with iron drainage funnels recessed into the floor, partly so that its cleaners could more easily swill away the spittle deposited by passengers. The clerk whose employers required him to turn up looking spick and span, and whose income stretched to a second-class season ticket, did well to keep away from the reeking and spitting workman travelling third, whose labours required him to get dirty. *Punch* showed a coal-black chimney-sweep appealing to a nonplussed porter concerning his brushes and sack of soot: ''Elp us up with my luggage, mate!' Such collisions help to explain why second class persisted longer on certain suburban lines, especially in London. More broadly, the ad hoc mixing of the classes in response to overcrowding was a standard subject of complaint to the management and the newspapers.

An extra form of social streaming was also practised in the form of super-cheap workmen's trains that ran very early in the morning, in London and several other urban areas. The Metropolitan Railway can claim to have inaugurated these in 1864, when it began running two trains before 6 a.m. each day at a return fare of threepence, reduced later to twopence (roughly a farthing a mile, which really was amazingly cheap). Others were stipulated by Acts of Parliament for new lines into London, and were meant to allow those displaced by demolition to stay within affordable travelling range of their workplaces. The London services also helped to rescue ordinary third-class passengers from the need to compete for carriage-space with the large pieces of timber which some early-travelling workmen habitually took with them, a custom noted in 1906 by the Chairman of the Metropolitan District Railway. By 1914, 1,966 designated trains of this kind were in service each weekday across the network: in effect, a kind of fourth class.

Early running was also meant to discourage the habit of taking the cheapest ticket regardless of the traveller's social class, to the extent that workmen were required by some lines to show particulars of their employment when making the purchase. The practice of budget travel seems to have been particularly tempting to those making regular, short-distance urban and suburban trips. That was what happened on the London & Blackwall, the first railway to serve east London (opened 1840), and on the Glasgow, Paisley & Greenock (opened 1841). Here the merchants who had drawn up grandly at the terminus in their private carriages proved content to take cheap tickets and to travel onwards standing up.

The latter case looks like a communal decision by a particular clique not to spend any more than necessary, and not to mind each other's economies in doing so. Other parts of Victorian Scotland could show similar behaviour. An aggrieved English shareholder of the under-performing North British Railway complained in the early 1850s that passengers north of the border who could afford better too often took third-class tickets instead: 'It will not do for Englishmen to make railways and Scotchmen to travel on them for nothing.' Another anomaly by English standards was the decision of the Great North of Scotland Railway and the forerunner companies of the Highland Railway, long-distance lines that opened their first instalments around the same time, not to bother with second class at all. As a contemporary source put it, in the Highlands 'there are only two ranks of people – a higher rank and a lower rank – the former consisting of a few large tenants ... and the latter consisting of a dense body of small cottars and fishermen'.

That the great lairds would travel first class was not in any question. The same applied to dukes, earls, bishops, senior military officers and sundry other members of the carriage-owning classes. So it is interesting to note that Gladstone recorded two second-class journeys in his diary for 29 January 1850. There is little superfluous detail in this unchatty chronicle, and it may be that Gladstone chose to note the trips as exceptions to his usual habit. Perhaps it is significant that he was then an opposition MP, without a ministerial salary. There may even be a whiff of status anxiety about these *déclassé* journeys. That an element of self-policing entered into the system is suggested by a story told of the neo-medieval architect A. W. N. Pugin (1812–52), who liked to go about in a distinctly bohemian outfit comprising a sailor's jacket, loose trousers, jackboots and broad-brimmed hat. Entering a first-class carriage after disembarking from the

Calais crossing, he was challenged by a fellow passenger: 'Halloa, my man, you have mistaken, I think, your carriage.' 'By Jove, I think you are right; I thought I was in the company of gentlemen.' An apology followed; then, 'The remainder of the journey was most agreeably passed in examining his portfolio filled with sketches just taken in Normandy.' (A 1960s variation on the theme: a guard on the East Coast route recalled being summoned to eject some 'yobboes' from first class, who turned out to be Jimi Hendrix and his entourage, their tickets all in order.)

For those who felt the need to maintain a visible position in society – which included many of the middling sort, as well as the ranks above them – anxieties of this kind were hard to avoid when choosing a ticket. This apprehension seems to have been most pronounced in long-distance journeys, which were also the most expensive. R. S. Surtees's guide to railway travel was aimed especially at the 'numerous and respectable class of country residents' who might be considering a trip to London for the Great Exhibition of 1851, and were concerned to cut a decent figure on the way. So he reassures readers that a second or third may actually be preferable for a summer trip, 'being cooler and less dust-catching' from the absence of upholstery; besides, 'A Tarrier coat and wideawake hat would conceal a timid economist from his best friend.' From fiction, here is Johnny Eames, the young hero of Trollope's *The Small House at Allington* (1864), a clerk in the Income Tax Office, on his way back to London after staying with Lord de Guest, 'taking a first-class ticket, because the earl's groom in livery was in attendance upon him. Had he been alone he would have gone in a cheaper carriage. Very weak in him, was it not? Little also, and mean? My friend, can you say that you would not have done the same ... ?' Nor were Trollope's commercial classes immune, as Mr Moulder in *Orley Farm* (1862) bears witness: 'Hubbles and Grease [Moulder's employers], he said, allowed him respectably, in order that he might go about their business respectably; and he wasn't going to give the firm a bad name by being seen in a second-class carriage, although the difference would go into his own pocket.'

The concern to keep up appearances could weigh heavily in smaller places, where any hint of shifting foundations for apparent wealth was sure to be picked up. A character in one of George Gissing's novels upbraids a visitor for having come innocently down on a second-class ticket: '"In London things don't matter, but here I'm known, you see."'

Single-class railway travel thus remained exceptional. The North

Eastern Railway gave it a brief try after electrifying its suburban lines to Tynemouth in 1904, whereupon usage of first class dropped off so much that the facility was discontinued. But local malcontents immediately mustered a protest meeting under the chairmanship of the Duke of Northumberland – not a man easily ignored in that region – and the superior class was restored. The Tyneside electrics thus remained in conformity with the older of the London Underground lines, which finally did away with their remaining first-class services as a wartime economy in 1941. It is strange to think of the last holders of first-class season tickets stepping over the prone forms of those seeking shelter from the Blitz, as each rush hour of late 1940 faded into evening.

A similar deference to matters of class regardless of real demand appears to explain the rather ridiculous arrangements on some of the tiny, financially straitened lines of the last major phase of railway construction. All three classes could be sampled on the North Sunderland Railway (which duly received complaints in 1944 when wartime circumstances enforced the withdrawal of first class). The Easingwold Railway offered first and second class only for its two-and-a-half miles through the Vale of York, in creaky cast-off carriages bought from larger lines. In 1947, the last full year of operation, just one passenger went first class, contributing 8d to an annual passenger revenue of £18 0s 8d; it is possible that this big spender was actually a ticket-collecting enthusiast snapping up a rarity.

₪

So far, we have been considering the single passenger. That is to disregard what might be called the servant problem. How should Victorian domestic staff travel with their masters and mistresses? Going first class, they would cost their employers more and risk the suggestion of an improper equality of treatment. In third class they might feel themselves hard done by. So the convention arose that they should travel by second, even though this meant that their services could not be called upon between stations. One reason for the popularity of carriages of the 'composite' type with first- and second-class compartments side by side was to permit servants to stay close at hand during the journey (the Liverpool & Manchester discounted one compartment in each of its first-class carriages to allow this).

Another option, for those who could afford it, was to hire a private saloon. Early royal saloons have been mentioned already. These were not actually royal property, but were built by the railway companies for hire by the royal household and for other exceptional uses such as the conveyance of state visitors. Only those companies on the regular routes north to Scotland, west to Windsor and south to the Channel Ports built carriages 'by appointment', but these helped to set a standard for other lines to follow – a way of taking on to the iron road the privileged segregation in travel enjoyed by the owners of private road carriages.

Privately owned railway carriages, it should be added, were almost unknown. Perhaps things would have been different had Victoria and Albert set an example by keeping one, on the model of royal yachts, rather than finding the industry only too happy to come forward. The exceptions prove the rule, for they belonged to George Granville William Sutherland-Leveson-Gower, 3rd Duke of Sutherland (1828–92) and his successors. This fantastically rich duke's seat was Dunrobin Castle in his eponymous Highland county, a partly medieval structure that his no less rich father had tripled in size in 1845–51. The nearest railway station in the latter year was at Aberdeen, some 150 miles away across land. By 1855 the rails had reached Inverness, the last Scottish city to join the network. Construction of a line from there northwards to Dunrobin and beyond, through wild territory with a high quotient of earthworks, bridges and viaducts, was not a project in which capitalists fell over themselves to invest. Nor could a large passenger traffic be expected once the line opened – a situation not helped by the 1st Duke's vigorous clearances of the Highland peasantry in favour of the farming of sheep, whose railway journeys out of the region (in special double-deck wagons) were strictly one-way.

Yet a railway offered many advantages to an improving landowner beyond the convenience of passenger travel, quite apart from its value in this case as a route to the ports for Orkney and Shetland. On his succession in 1861, the new duke therefore set about completing a line to the far north. The new route took until 1874 to finish, by means of four separately constituted and confusingly named railway companies: the Inverness & Ross-Shire, the Sutherland Railway, the Duke of Sutherland's Railway and the Sutherland & Caithness. The second and the last of these depended heavily on ducal investment, and the Duke of Sutherland's Railway had to be paid for entirely by the man himself. As he already owned all the land, the Duke did not even have to wait for the necessary Act before starting work on this particular section. The completed lines were operated by the Highland Railway, with the right of personal running powers

reserved to the Duke. By 1889 Sutherland's investment in railways was calculated at £355,000, including ordinary Highland Railway shares received
in exchange for transferring ownership of his personal railway.

All this to set the scene, and to make it clear that the Duke's private
station and private saloon carriage at Dunrobin were mere baubles by
comparison. The next duke added to these a private locomotive (named
Dunrobin) that was used for personal jaunts over the Highland Railway's
lines: a neat little thing, recently repatriated to Britain from a museum in
Canada. It had a sizeable cab equipped with a comfy back seat so that the
Duke could take his guests for a ride, which made *Dunrobin* certainly the
only locomotive to have carried at various times kings Edward VII and
George V, Kaiser Wilhelm II and King Alfonso XIII of Spain. Two of the
three ducal saloons also still exist, both very smart vehicles, if not especially
large. They are the nearest Britain could show to the private cars of the
American gilded age, objects of competitive display among the Vander-
bilts, Morgans, Harrimans and Fricks, which were frequently equipped to
function as long-distance living quarters and mobile headquarters for the
pursuit of business as well as pleasure. As well as the predictable marquetry
and brocades, furnishings of the grosser sort included gold-plated bathroom plumbing, Venetian glass chandeliers (anchored against swaying by
steel wires) and a green marble fireplace salvaged from a private mansion
(framing electrically lit artificial logs). Cars of this type – American usage
never took to 'carriage' for vehicles that run on rails – were commissioned
well into the twentieth century; Sugar Cane, Marilyn Monroe's character
in Billy Wilder's *Some Like It Hot*, set circa 1929, hopes to find a husband
with 'a yacht, a private railroad car, and his own toothpaste'.

Much of this elaboration would have bemused the traveller in the
British saloon carriage of the 1860s. The saloon had by then established
itself as a facility available for private hire, often at a surprisingly short
notice. Apart from a few one-offs, the first batch was provided for the
Great Western Railway at its opening in 1838. Brunel called these strange,
angular designs 'posting carriages', hoping to evoke the glamour of post-
chaises, the highest-ranking public conveyances on the roads. Their sides
sloped sharply inwards below the windows to make way for huge broad-
gauge wheels, except where the doorway stood upright in the middle of
each long side, and their roofs were topped by the first clerestories to
appear on the railways. Inside were upholstered and cushioned seats, running round each half in a U-shape, with a table placed along the middle.

The intention was to establish a sort of club class, superior to first class and physically distinct from it; 'Extra First Class', as one London newspaper called it. As such, the service lasted barely a year, after which the carriages were kept aside for the use by appointment of private parties.

Having thrown all the volume of the carriage into a single compartment, the next step in saloon design was to subdivide it again, so that the social structure of the household could be respected within the space available. By the 1860s the type was reaching maturity and the best examples offered an enviable degree of self-sufficiency. The main saloon took up the greater part of the interior, with upholstered sofas or benches on two or three sides. A demountable table was commonly provided in the centre. The saloon was entered directly from outside, or via a cross-passage or vestibule – the railway equivalent, perhaps, of the screens passage to the great hall of a medieval house. On the far side of this vestibule, or opening directly from the saloon, was a narrower compartment equipped with facilities that placed the occupants on a level equal with royalty: lavatory and washbasin.* A second-class compartment for servants was also provided, with access either from the far end of the main saloon, or through a door in the other wall of the lavatory compartment. The sense of hierarchy in motion sharpens when one imagines a vigilant paterfamilias in the central seat of the U-shaped arrangement – often the most comfortable place, because the upholstery could be carried up higher there than on the windowed sides. Fill the rest of the seats with wife, children and a few maiden aunts or upper servants – a governess or tutor, perhaps – and we have an image like that of the formal family photograph; except that the personnel are turned inwards as if for mutual scrutiny, at just the right distance to give self-consciousness the edge over intimacy. It is an arrangement that must have made many an unhappy family even unhappier.

Happy or not, the enforced seclusion might be protracted: it was customary for family saloons to be uncoupled and transferred between trains, so that long journeys could be undertaken without having to decant luggage. This is what is meant by the 'special arrangement of Mother's with the G.N.R. [Great Northern] Company', recorded in the diary of Florence Sitwell (1858–1930), maiden aunt of the writers Edith, Osbert and Sacheverell, by which her family party was able to pass all the way from

---

* In 1906 the Great Northern Railway built a saloon with a full-sized bath, but the idea failed to catch on.

A family saloon on the London, Brighton & South
Coast Railway, from *The Graphic*, 1873

Shalford in Surrey, through London and on to Scarborough. The practice did not make a good operational match with express working, so the
saloons tended to be attached to semi-fast trains and the journeys length-
ened in proportion. It was also possible to book a saloon as part of a separate private train, although this cost much more: the standard charge per
mile was five shillings for a one-way journey, exactly sixty times the Parliamentary rate for a single adult. In the railways' early years, private trains of
one kind or another were sometimes rustled up at short notice. This was
the salvation of Mr Isidore, coiffeur to Queen Victoria, when he missed
his train for Windsor in 1843: after explaining his predicament at Paddington, a spare engine and carriage were found in time for him to fulfil
his appointment. The charge was £18 for a journey of as many miles, a sac-
rifice worth making to save Isidore's place, with its annual salary of £200.

This operational responsiveness also favoured the wealthy invalid, for
whom the railways came as a liberation. By reserving one of the better
types of saloon, a long-distance journey that might have been risky or even

fatal by road could now be undertaken in tolerable comfort, with medical attention close to hand. In these cases a bed might be made up on one of the bench seats, or set up in the central space (as could be done, too, for perfectly healthy passengers who were travelling overnight). There was also a specialised sort of saloon designed specifically for invalids, including one on the Great Northern that had an open platform at one end, so that an occupied stretcher or bath-chair could be handled more easily in and out.

Rarer still, and altogether a later phenomenon, were club carriages. These were provided for exclusive use by a select group in return for a supplement on top of the season ticket fee, or a guarantee by the membership to make a minimum purchase of tickets. The first club carriages began running in 1895 on the Lancashire & Yorkshire Railway's Blackpool-to-Manchester route. The carriages really were organised like a club: new members were elected by committee and agreed to abide by club rules, which included the allocation of individual armchair-type seats within the saloon and strict protocols that governed the opening of windows while the train was in motion. Another club was formed fifteen years later for businessmen travelling to Manchester from North Wales. Every day, its two dedicated saloons were attached to the same morning train from Llandudno, returning each afternoon. Tea was served on board and members had their own lockers. A third club train ran to and from Windermere. The set-up is so like the premise of a P. G. Wodehouse story that it is a surprise to learn that gritty Manchester remained the only stronghold of these club trains, which never made the leap southward to the commuterland of the Home Counties.

For those among the wealthiest class who particularly wished to keep apart from strangers, there was yet another way of travelling by train. Passengers of this elevated sort were likely to arrive at the station in their own coaches and often wished to transport these coaches with them on the journey. In such cases the railways were ready with flat wagons, known as carriage trucks, which could be attached to timetabled trains (expresses normally excepted). Horse boxes were also provided, for those wanting to take their teams with them. Suitably secured, the coaches went on their way by train, and their occupants – assuming that they did not install themselves in the railway's own carriages – thus became railway passengers, until the time came to disengage and continue the journey by road.

Besides the extra charge, the traveller was asked to give sufficient notice of the intention to take coach and horses on the journey. Surtees in 1851 advised that a day or two would suffice for this. He had already picked up on the practice in a novel, *Handley Cross* (1843), in which the unstoppable Jorrocks arrives in his own open-topped vehicle, carried on an 'open platform' or flat wagon, together with well-muffled wife and attendants. In the railways' early years, stagecoaches were sometimes piggybacked on flat wagons too, until the direct conveyance of mailbags and boxes by train took over.

There is something unsettling about this arrangement for journeying by carriage and by train at one and the same time, one set of springs shuddering on top of the other: a way of travel at once sequestered and absurdly exposed and conspicuous, as if on a float in a pageant.* Connoisseurs of British eccentricity will recognise the method as among the oddities of the 5th Duke of Portland (1800–79), a pathological recluse whose exalted position allowed him to indulge his protective strategies to an extreme degree. A door with ingoing and outgoing letterboxes served as the Duke's means of communication with the rest of the household at his seat of Welbeck Abbey in Nottinghamshire, where he retreated into a suite of four or five rooms among hundreds. (Other rooms were kept unfurnished, except for the water closets he liked to install in the corners.) He also excavated a suite of underground chambers there, including a chapel and three libraries. To conceal his journeys to the railway station at Worksop, the Duke had another tunnel made as far as the main road. But his onward railway journeys were eccentric, if at all, only for his habit of pulling down the carriage blinds so as to escape observation. In other respects, the railway helped Portland to keep up something of the social profile which the possession of a great title entailed. This required a measure of self-display even for recluses, of which going about in a private coach emblazoned with arms was a normal and accepted component.

Private carriage traffic of this kind could make up a surprisingly large proportion of passenger business in the early years; Sir Charles Pasley's diary for 1845 records a London-to-Birmingham train comprising thirty railway vehicles, among which were nine or ten horseboxes and sufficient flat wagons to carry eleven or twelve gentlemen's coaches. Few readers

---

* The idea perhaps seems slightly less strange to British travellers now that the Eurotunnel shuttle trains have adopted the concept for road vehicles, although their occupants line up within double-deck carriage trucks of the covered kind, with the option of getting out en route.

notice it, but the first description of a railway journey in Dickens's novels – made by the death-haunted senior subject of *Dombey and Son* (1848) in company with the ghastly Major Bagstock, also on the Birmingham train – has as its point of view not a railway compartment, but Mr Dombey's own rail-borne coach.

How the system worked on the Great Western Railway was summarised in its *Time Book* (timetable) for 1863, with a fine sense of upholding class differences:

> Passengers in Private Carriages (not being servants) are required to take first-class tickets, and such passengers may remove during the journey to the Company's First-class carriages if there be sufficient room in them. Servants travelling on private carriages are required to take Second-class tickets and they may remove to Second-class carriages provided there be room. A groom travelling in a horse-box in charge of a horse is allowed to travel at third-class fare.

To travel in such splendid isolation was not without its hazards. The heavy swaying motion proved too much for the stomachs of some, including the Guest family, forced to abandon their carriage in favour of a normal compartment when travelling from Birmingham to Liverpool in 1837. The dust and grime could be as bad as on the roads, and hot cinders were a special hazard. The Countess of Zetland learned as much on a journey from Leeds to London with her maid on the morning of 8 December 1847. Sparks from the engine exhaust set fire to an umbrella on the outside of the countess's coach, from which the flames spread to a trunk on the roof. Shortly after the train left Leicester, the smell of smoke alerted the occupants. The speed at the time was estimated at forty or fifty miles an hour. As the fire took hold, the pair climbed out and sought refuge on the open truck:

> We clung on by the front springs of the carriage, screaming 'fire' incessantly, and waving our handkerchiefs. We passed several policemen [railway servants] on the road, none of whom took any notice of us. No guard appeared. A gentleman in the carriage behind mine saw us, but could render no assistance. My maid seemed in an agony of terror ... I turned away for a moment to wave my handkerchief, and when I looked round again my poor maid was gone. The train went on, the fire of course increasing, and the wind blowing it towards me.

Relief came only when the train stopped at Rugby. An engine sent back to look for the maid accidentally ran her over, leaving her with a fractured skull and 'in an almost hopeless state'.

Lady Zetland's ordeal was related as a cautionary tale by the Irish scientific writer, statistician and busybody Dionysius Lardner in his *Railway Economy* (1850). The book set out to demonstrate that railways were generally safe, while tabulating recent accidents to passengers and staff in lugubrious detail in order to quantify any specific risks. Had he known of any other lethal carriage fires, Lardner would surely have catalogued them too; instead, he noted that railway carriages were much more robustly constructed than those made for the roads, so that anyone who chose to remain within the latter kind while travelling by rail exposed himself to unnecessary peril.

Such strictures were unlikely to have frightened the Duke of Wellington, another habitué of flat-truck travel. Wellington's relationship with railways was complex and often contradictory. In some respects, the Duke was among the best informed statesmen of the time where railways were concerned. On a visit to Lord Londonderry's colliery railway in County Durham in 1827, he was treated to a ride in a specially made rail-mounted landau behind one of George Stephenson's early locomotives (Wellington called it a 'steam elephant'). In those days, barely anyone outside the north-east had even seen such a thing. His term as prime minister included a journey to open the Liverpool & Manchester Railway on 15 September 1830, in an age when such ceremonial duties by a premier were still exceptional. The day was famously marred by the accidental death of William Huskisson, MP for Liverpool and a former ministerial ally of Wellington's Tory grouping. Approaching his carriage to speak to the Duke during a halt midway along the new line, Huskisson failed to keep clear of the *Rocket* as it sped past on the adjacent track, was run over and succumbed to his injuries in the evening. So Huskisson became the first passenger to die in a railway accident, and even after 200 years he remains the most prominent Briton to lose his life in this way. His is also still the best documented railway fatality, falling as it did on a great public occasion, in full view, and in a great age for reportage, memoir and prolific and articulate private correspondence.

Wellington's friend and biographer G. R. Gleig suspected that the sad end of Huskisson lay behind the Duke's aversion to railways; but the tough-minded old soldier had in his time witnessed the deaths and maimings of tens of thousands on the battlefield, among whom were some rather better friends than the late MP for Liverpool. Rather, his enduring dislike of railways seems to have derived jointly from the eclipse of the old coaching system and from the relative lack of privacy when going by train. On the latter point, the fullest denunciation comes in a letter to Angela, Baroness Burdett-Coutts, in 1848:

> It appears to me to be the Vulgarest, most indelicate, most inconvenient, most injurious to Health of any mode of conveyance that I have seen in any part of the World! Mobs of well-dressed Ladies and Gentlemen are collected at every Station, to examine and pry into every Carriage and actions of every Traveller. If an unfortunate Traveller wishes to quit His Carriage, He is followed by one of these well dressed Mobs as a Hunted animal is by the Hounds ...

Less delicately, the Duke wrote elsewhere of the absence on the railway of 'the chance of relief at short distance' – in other words, this national celebrity was followed by gawpers even when attempting to find a lavatory at intermediate stations. As to the end of the coaching network, 'I hope the Gentry of the Country will not allow themselves again to be cheated and bustled, as we were out of the best system and establishment for travelling that existed in any part of the world'. This from one of five letters to Mary, Marchioness of Salisbury over one month in 1850, all of which lament delays, muddles, accidents and incompetence on the railways. When a railway line came close to the Duke's Stratfield Saye House in Hampshire, he tried to insist that any stations should be kept at a minimum of five miles' distance, relenting only at the request of his country neighbours.

Much of this represented a private release of steam; in public life, the Duke recognised that an accommodation had to be made with the iron roads. If nothing else, his duties required him to attend upon the Queen, and when she at last took to the rails in 1843 he could hardly refuse to follow. That meant stepping aboard the luxurious carriage provided by the London & South Western Railway – to the delight of the company's chairman, who had reported ruefully in the previous year: 'Although a special train was always in readiness for His Grace [at Basingstoke, not far from Stratfield Saye], this has not yet been taken advantage of by him.' As a senior soldier Wellington was also convinced of the railways' military potential and lent his support to a plan that circulated in the 1840s by which a continuous strategic line should run along the south coast, to aid in mustering defences against invasion. This interest ran to matters of detail: awaiting a train one day, Wellington beckoned the stationmaster into a third-class carriage and quizzed him on how soldiers were carried by train, 'every point connected with their locomotion and comfort'; fifty questions in five minutes, 'all pertinent and to the purpose'. This happened at Dover, through which Wellington regularly travelled as Lord Warden of the Cinque Ports, a ceremonial post he retained to the end of his life. Many of these journeys were made in an outlandish one-off carriage provided for him by the South Eastern Railway: a composite of first and second class, with the Duke's compartment styled reassuringly like a stagecoach body (had he requested something like one?), and placed so that its floor came down a little below the underframe. The Duke was famously a tall man, and the dropped floor seems to have been there to give him greater headroom.

₪

These documented interests must be set against the persistent legend that paints Wellington as the railways' diehard foe. He is supposed to have disliked them on the grounds that the trains would 'only encourage the lower classes to move about'. Evidence that Wellington actually said or wrote this at all is hard to come by, but the endless recirculation of the tale says something about how the times have been remembered. These were anxious years – the period from 1837 to 1842 in particular was restive and unhappy, as strikes and related violence repeatedly flared up, culminating in the rejection by Parliament of a Chartist reform petition of over 3 million signatures. Viewed from either end of the class spectrum, revolution or civil war seemed perfectly possible by the mid 1840s. It was certainly not yet clear that the freedom of popular movement promised by the railways would serve to reinforce as well as unsettle the established order.

It was the excursion train that did most to expand the possibilities for crowds on the move. The concept was not new: steamboats had already brought discounted group travel within the reach of many, especially along the Thames and the Clyde. The Liverpool & Manchester had been in business for less than two weeks before it started something similar. These first trips were organised by the company itself. Soon, trains were running by arrangement with private groups too, beginning with an excursion between the cities in 1831. Fares might be half the usual rate or less, but high passenger numbers ensured that a profit was made on rolling stock that would otherwise have lain idle.

The 1840s brought true mass transportation, by means of 'monster' trains. Like the lifespans of the patriarchs in the Book of Genesis, some of their statistics beggar belief. Nearly 3,000 people went in sixty-seven carriages from Nottingham to Leicester in August 1840. Four years later, 7,800 excursionists travelled from Leeds to Hull, in 250 carriages pulled by ten locomotives. That was too many for a single train, so the service ran in separate portions, snaking past the eyes of astonished Yorkshire villagers at the close intervals that the rule-of-thumb operating methods of the 1840s allowed.

The famous name associated with early railway excursions is that of Thomas Cook. In later life he even claimed to have pioneered the field, an assertion echoed on Cook's Wikipedia entry at the time of writing. The truth is more complicated, and somewhat stranger. Cook's first excursions were motivated not by profit – his travel business came later – but from his devotion to the Temperance movement. The railway excursion that he organised for 5 July 1841 was meant both as an alternative attraction to the alehouse and as publicity for the abstainers' cause. It carried some 500 sober but happy travellers from Cook's home town of Leicester as far as Loughborough, ten miles to the north. Here lunch, dancing, speeches and other diversions were provided in the private park of a wealthy supporter. Temperance delegations from other towns attended, and the day was judged a triumph – not least by Cook himself, who urged the crowd to give 'One cheer more for Teetotalism and Railwayism!!!' Similar excursions followed as part of a broader social and religious programme which Cook sustained on the profits of his publishing and bookselling activities. Only in 1845 did he strike out with a commercial venture, an excursion to Liverpool and Snowdonia. By that time the South Eastern Railway had already run the first day trip to France, on 14 June 1843. Cook's foreign tours, when they came, were therefore also not as novel as is sometimes stated.

Cook's clientele came from the respectable middle classes. Those whose tastes were rowdier or less moralised made use of excursion trains too. A trip from Lincoln to Thornton Abbey in 1849 ended in intoxication for some passengers, who had reportedly come equipped with 'alcoholic pocket pistols' even though the trip was billed as a Temperance excursion.

For many, drinking en route in like-minded company was part of the holiday fun. F. S. Williams noted that the windows of excursion trains were particularly liable to emit flying bottles, to the peril of railwaymen working along the line. (A poster on the Great Western Railway reminded passengers that 'Empty Bottles may be left in the carriages'; admonition disguised as information.)

Nor were the excursionists' destinations always entirely wholesome. The Bodmin & Wadebridge Railway ran an excursion to the double hanging at Bodmin gaol in August 1840. Special trains brought many of the estimated 100,000 who watched the bungled execution of the multiple murderer John Gleeson Wilson outside Kirkdale gaol in Liverpool on 15 September 1849. To some extent, the railways may even be said to have contributed unwittingly to the decision in 1868 that future executions should be carried out behind prison walls, to put an end to these ghoulish and disorderly sprees.

Another category of train that disappeared in 1868, by prohibition under the Regulation of Railways Act, was the prizefight excursion. The surprise is that these ever happened at all, given that bare-knuckle fights were unlawful in the first place. That did not foil their wild popularity, among the more rackety members of the upper crust as well as with the masses. When the railways came, the sport became at once more furtive and more flagrant. Special trains could supply and whisk away the combatants and the crowds, and it was easier to set up fights in remote places at the limits of county boundaries, between the effective jurisdictions of rival magistracies. Although it was not illegal to attend these events, the readiness with which the railway companies joined in the traffic is startling – as if British Rail had laid on special trains to the ecstasy-fuelled farmland raves of the 1980s.

Take the north–south bout on 9 September 1845 between Ben Caunt, landlord of the Coach and Horses in St Martin's Lane, and Bendigo, 'the Pride of Nottingham'. Bendigo – a version of his middle name, Abednego – had fought the London-based boxer before, and demand for a rematch was high. He came south on a Sunday, to Newport Pagnell in Buckinghamshire, via the London & Birmingham's station at Wolverton. Caunt headed north the day after. He put up at an inn in Stony Stratford, just west of Wolverton. Excursionists from Bendigo's home territory also arrived there and walked towards Newport Pagnell. More came by train the following day. The magistrates watched uneasily, conscious that their jurisdiction stopped a few miles north, at the boundary with Northamptonshire. Finally, the fight was staged, not in the expected place but further west still, at Lillington Lovell (Bendigo won, after ninety-six rounds). And so back to Wolverton, where the station staff refused to open the gates to the mob of returning passengers until their train actually drew in to the platform.

Top of the prizefighting lines in the 1840s–50s was the Eastern Counties Railway. The company was complicit in the attempt to stage a fight in 1842 at Sawbridgeworth, where Essex and Hertfordshire meet, bringing in crowds by timetabled train; combat began on the canal towpath, but the magistrates put a stop to it. There was better sport in 1848 in a lineside field at Fulbourn in Cambridgeshire, attended by 300 who arrived by fast train. Fighting over, the dazed loser was lifted straight into the carriage from which his supporters had watched the action. Prizefighting returned to the same line four years later, in the somewhat farcical to-and-fro match between Orme and Jones. The latter came up from London in a special train full of the better-off contingent of his fans, meeting Orme's party at Newmarket. But the police were on the trail, so the train headed back westwards to start the match at Bourne Bridge (this time using a duplicate route that had been officially abandoned a year earlier, one of the earliest railway closures). The ninth round was in progress when the police arrived and everyone piled on to the train again. It halted next at Warren Heath, just outside Newmarket. Orme and Jones recommenced hitting each other, and had managed another twenty-three rounds when the police caught up with them again. Once more the train set off along the half-derelict line, Orme giving directions from the tender, until Chesterford was reached. But Jones then refused to fight on, saying that he believed that the contest had been declared over and had therefore taken some oranges and brandy, thereby putting himself *hors de combat*.

Orme was the star of yet another Eastern Counties fight special the following year. Once again the excursion train was restricted to those well-off enough to pay a highish fare, and the disorderly poor were not meant to get a look-in. But the news had leaked, and the 'Cheapside' contingent went on ahead by the scheduled early Parliamentary train to the intended destination of Mildenhall Road. The next station after that was Lakenheath, but there the Suffolk police were in attendance. So the excursion steamed straight through the dismayed crowds at Mildenhall Road and a more exclusive fight was staged alongside the line between the two stations. Other boxing matches provoked near-riots at Thames Haven in 1862, when the police refused to send help to tackle a gang who were grabbing match tickets from new arrivals at the station, and at Paddington in 1863. Such incidents were not forgotten when it came to the prohibition of 1868.

Race meetings were a more enduring popular attraction, as well as a more predictable one. The traffic began with the Liverpool & Manchester's trips to the course at Newton-le-Willows, predecessor of the present-day Haydock Park. Sometimes the demand that the railways unlocked was more than they could handle. A matter of days after the London & Southampton Railway opened its line to Kingston upon Thames in 1838, eight excursion trains were run in connection with the Epsom races, a six-mile walk from the station. Not enough: some 5,000 would-be passengers were left milling around the London terminus at Nine Elms in the hope of squeezing on to the last departure. When they were refused the mood turned ugly and the crowd rushed the building and broke its windows. Rowdy hordes of this kind – 'legs', to use the 1830s term for disreputable strangers – were not always welcome at the other end either. At Newmarket, the Jockey Club responded to the influx of railway excursionists by staging the finishes of consecutive races miles apart, so that only the gentry on horseback could keep up with the action. At the other end of East Anglia, in 1874, the restive passengers of a returning Yarmouth races special chose to kill the time before their train left by raiding the surrounding houses for food and drink, and in some cases for crockery too. The dirty plates were thrown out at passing stations as the train made its way home.

Such stand-offs apart, the relationship between railways and racing was generally a matter of happy symbiosis. Attendances at the St Leger showed what could be done for the sport. Before the South Yorkshire Railway opened in 1849, Sheffield people without access to a horse or carriage could only travel the eighteen miles to the Doncaster course on foot – which meant walking all through the night – and then plod back again when the race was over. By 1910 the four-day race meeting brought 1,065 trains to Doncaster from every direction, making their way in and out with the assistance of temporary signal boxes.

The racing world changed rapidly in other ways, as the railways worked their game of unintended consequences. Transportation of racehorses by train began in 1840 and soon became widespread. It was the death-knell for the old structure of half a dozen regional circuits, designed to be walkable by man and horse, which gave way to a more complex programme of nationwide events and overlapping networks. Leading jockeys could ride at more meetings and leading officials too became national figures. The number of meetings increased and the number of horses being raced almost doubled by 1869. These included a great influx of two-year-olds, which were unequal to the strain of racing after a long walk in the old-fashioned way. The telegraph network that accompanied the railways allowed swift transmission of news and information. Snooty Newmarket found a way to make its peace with the crowds: when the station there was rebuilt on a new site in 1902, the Great Eastern Railway provided separate first-class and third-class platforms for race-day specials, something quite exceptional in Britain. As the final instalment of the modern system, open courses with a few paying grandstands were abandoned in favour of fully enclosed spaces controlled by lucrative turnstiles, beginning at Sandown Park in 1875. Even after the transport of horses moved back to the roads, the railways kept the human lifeblood flowing; over sixty long-distance special trains made their way to Aintree for Grand National Day in 1935, and the befuddled evening crowds at Waterloo station in Royal Ascot week must be seen to be believed.

By way of return for so much business, the railways joined the ranks of race sponsors themselves. The London & South Western paid for prizes at courses all down its main line and the Great Western subscribed to the Ascot stakes even though its own lines came no closer than Windsor, several miles off. In Edwardian times the company helped to develop the racecourse and dedicated station on the outskirts of Newbury. The Epsom course received a branch line in 1865 courtesy of the London, Brighton & South Coast Railway, followed in 1901 by a rival branch from the South Eastern Railway to Tattenham Corner – the only terminus on the network to be named after a bend on a racecourse. Football and cricket would in time bring their own fleets of special trains and dedicated stations, but nothing to match the early exertions of the railways to serve the long-established world of the turf.

The crowds flocking to racecourse, boxing ring or gallows might be disorderly but they were not politically conscious, or as a rule even explicitly class-conscious. It is probably true to say that there was a greater sense of solidarity among excursionists who travelled under the banners of Temperance or of the many Mechanics' Institutes and similar associations of mutual help. Above all, there were Sunday schools. For the greater part of the nineteenth century these were concerned less with religious instruction than with the basic education of children who might otherwise never encounter schooling at all. This culture of self-improvement and mutual assistance, sometimes under official encouragement and sometimes proudly independent, has long been identified by historians as one of the reasons political change in Britain took the path of gradual reform rather than violent upheaval.

Even before the railway excursion became the usual thing, Sunday schools in Manchester were making use of canal boats to reach destinations beyond normal walking range. Railway travel allowed these distances to expand hugely, and the numbers on the move to swell in proportion. As the *Sunday School Magazine* had it, 'railways and Sunday schools seem related and both will work wonders in their departments'. Three thousand teachers and pupils went in July 1846 from Macclesfield to Stockport. In the same month, 3,000 children and 500 teachers from the Birmingham Sunday School Union went off to Cheltenham, where they saw the Pump Room and gardens. Also in 1846, 6,125 parents, teachers and children travelled from Norwich to the seaside at Yarmouth, at fares of 3d per child, 1s per adult, together with 500 'ladies and gentlemen' who paid first-class rates. Long before holidaying away from home became more widely affordable, these early experiences must have put the railways in a positive and accessible light for rising generations of young Victorians. For those among the social elite who were nervous of expressions of collective consciousness, such events were reassuring – instances of the exchanges by which the lower classes could improve themselves and acquire some of the prestige and pleasures of respectability.

There was a catch, and it concerned an issue of religious principle: should the Sunday school parties have been travelling on the Sabbath at all? Should *anyone* be travelling then? In late-Georgian times, the custom was widely considered disreputable; readers of Jane Austen's *Persuasion* may remember that habitual Sunday travelling is among the failings of Mr Elliott, who turns out to be morally hollow indeed. The Liverpool & Manchester had established an encouraging precedent in its 1830 timetable, with no Sunday trains between 10 a.m. and 4 p.m. – the 'church interval' – and many other lines followed suit. Even then, some Sunday travelling could be justified from necessity, or pious purpose. Pleasure trips pure and simple were another matter. A summer Sunday excursion on the Newcastle & Carlisle Railway in 1840 provoked the Scottish minister W. C. Burns to denunciations by placard and handbill, placed all across Tyneside:

> A Reward for Sabbath Breaking.
> People taken safely and swiftly to Hell!
> Next Lord's Day, by the Carlisle Railway, for 7s. 6d.
> It is a Pleasure Trip!

Easy to laugh at such things today; the organisers in 1840 were less blasé, putting up bills the following day to reassure people that the excursionists had made a safe return.

The issue of Sunday services came up again during the debates of 1844 over the new Parliamentary trains, when Wellington wrote to Gladstone to urge that these should also be provided on the seventh day. A devout churchman, Gladstone considered Sunday travel to be 'dangerous in its immediate and ultimate results to public morality' (the words are from his letter to Sir Robert Peel in the same year). Not only did it interfere with religious observance on the part of the passenger, travel also violated the day of rest on the part of the worker. Here was a head-on confrontation of social ideals, coming from unexpected quarters: Wellington, the old Tory scornful of the mob, standing up for popular freedom of movement; Gladstone, future apostle of free trade and laissez-faire, still in thrall to the Church-and-State principles of his romantic youth.

Anglican paternalism is nicely illustrated by the responses at Oxford and Cambridge to the coming of the railways. Invigorated by rising numbers and in the grip of a new seriousness of religious purpose, the universities were in no mood to have the running made for them by outsiders. If they could not stop the trains coming, they resolved to do what they could to reduce unsettling influences on their own junior members. As it happened, the Railway Acts in question were both passed during Gladstone's time at the Board of Trade – Oxford's in 1843, that for Cambridge in 1844 – and the two share several special provisions and much identical wording. Donnish anxieties that the trains would carry undergraduates beyond the range of control are very apparent. The universities already had their own policemen or 'bulldogs', who did their best to keep undergraduates away from taverns and loose townswomen; now these policemen could claim the right of entry to the railways too. Officers of each university were empowered to request information from railway servants concerning any of its junior members, as well as those merely 'suspected of being such'. The companies were also instructed to bar from travel for a period of twenty-four hours, on request by an authorised university officer, any member below the rank of Master of Arts, Bachelor of Civil Law or Bachelor of Medicine. As if these controls were not enough, Oxford undergraduates were permitted to travel only to certain approved stations, to steer them away from racecourses and other risky destinations. At Cambridge, academic string-pulling helped to ensure that the station was built well over a mile away from the town proper, to the lasting inconvenience of almost everyone.

The Sunday question also loomed large. Both universities agreed church intervals with the railway companies. At Cambridge, there was an extra provision: the railway would be fined £5 every time it transported a passenger to or from Cambridge, or anywhere within a three-mile radius, between 10 a.m. and 5 p.m. on the Sabbath. Proceeds were to go to Addenbrooke's Hospital, or to another county charity to be decided by the university. It sounds like somebody's pet scheme to do good all round. Whoever framed this clause had not reckoned on the sharpness of the railway's operating department: soon after the line opened, cheap day tickets from Cambridge to London were issued, starting untouchably early at 7 a.m. (which meant that the visitors could make a *really* long day of it). Excursion trains came too, bringing more tourists to mill around the haunts of ancient Sunday peace. Well might the vice-chancellor protest in 1851, with what was presumably an unconscious inflation of equivalence, that Sunday excursions were 'as distasteful to the University Authorities as they must be offensive to Almighty God and to all right-minded Christians'. The position proved impossible to hold; the £5 fines clause, a dead letter long since, was quietly dropped in 1908. By that time Cambridge had become a major junction, with eight lines converging on it.

Despite such victories for popular freedom of movement, the broader effects of Sabbatarianism on railway timetables persisted. Even the Metropolitan Railway observed train-free periods on Sunday mornings until 1909, a change that seems emblematic of the transition from hidebound Victorian to expansive Edwardian London. Gradually, the avoidance of Sunday travelling dwindled to a matter of private conscience – like that of the Rev. Lord Blythswood, who told the annual breakfast of the Lord's Day Observance Society in the same year that in fifty years he had not once set foot in a train on the Sabbath, nor made use of any public conveyance, nor written a letter on a Saturday night when there was a chance that it might be delivered on the day following. Which no doubt went down very well.

Yet Sunday has remained special on Britain's railways, and it is worth asking why. One surprise is that the proportion of mileage which closed on Sundays rose substantially as the nineteenth century progressed. In England and Wales, the 2.6 per cent of the network for which Bradshaw had nothing to show for the seventh day in 1847 had risen by 1914 to almost a quarter. The proportion in Scotland was by that time close to 60 per cent. The difference between the nations had something to do with enduring Sabbatarianism, as the riot at Strome Ferry suggests (*see* Chapter 1). But the chief reason for these train-free days was the same then as now: the lack of sufficient traffic to justify the operating costs. Rural lines were especially liable to reinstate a day of rest. For instance, the Somerset & Dorset began with Sunday running all year through, then tried to make a go of trains on summer Sundays only, then in 1874 gave them up altogether.

Other factors were in play too, some practical and others financial, some in favour of trains and others against. Sunday rails were kept busy with certain sorts of traffic – milk, newspapers, post – which had to be set moving to arrive in time for Monday morning (which also gave passengers an opportunity to travel with the Sunday night mail). On the other hand, the demands of maintenance also made it useful to have a regular day on which the trains were fewer and slower, or did not run at all. Less obviously, selective overtime rates for Sunday working became payable in late-Victorian times, which thus became significantly more expensive.

So familiar has the two-speed weekly timetable become that it often surprises Britons to discover that the Sunday railway timetable on the Continent is not very different from the weekday one. Long-distance and over-night trains can thus run to an uninterrupted rhythm all through the year. Conversely, it is a common misconception that bank holiday timetables in the UK are something like Sunday ones. Christmas excepted, they are not.

Trains or no trains, the increase in permitted Sunday activities is an index of the growth of a more secular culture. Theatre-going is another, for the strict codes of behaviour expected from Nonconformist and Evangelical congregations usually put the stage firmly out of bounds. This began to change in the 1850s, helped by a turn towards more genteel material at the expense of lurid, blood-and-thunder fare. (For the latter, one could do worse than the melodrama of 1863 in which George Stephenson himself kills the villain-seducer beneath the wheels of his own train, having first shunted the heroine to safety in a ballast truck.) Theatres stayed shut on Sundays, then as now; but that did not mean that the theatre companies were at rest too. Thanks to the railway network, the Lord's Day became a sort of nationwide transformation scene, as thespians criss-crossed the country on special trains between weekly engagements, taking their sets and props with them.

Most of these were permanently touring repertoire companies, but a West End hit such as Dion Boucicault's bigamy-and-murder shocker *The Colleen Bawn* (1860) might also be sent around the country. Tours of this kind were sometimes undertaken by companies set up for no other purpose, which would be dissolved after the last journey back to the capital. Even Dickens got in on the act – how could he resist? – using the newly opened Great Northern Railway to take his own company of amateurs up to Knebworth, the Hertfordshire mansion of his fellow novelist Edward Bulwer-Lytton, in 1850. Half a century later, professional theatre trains in England and Wales alone amounted to 142 each Sunday, carrying hundreds of hard-working performers to new digs in time for the curtain to rise on the following Monday night. Henry Irving's famous company was early in the game, venturing on to the rails for a sixteen-week tour in 1882: fifty-four members, with scenery, clothes, musical instruments and lighting sufficient for nine productions. The itinerary proved highly profitable, to the credit of its organiser, one Bram Stoker. (Perhaps the railway logistics recurred to mind when he came to write *Dracula*, the pages of which include the text of a very plausible legal document covering the nocturnal despatch by Great Northern Railway goods train of fifty boxes of vampiric soil.) Irving's rail-borne tours ended only with the great actor's death in 1905, sitting on a chair in the hall of the Midland Railway's hotel at Bradford, after being taken ill at his final curtain.

Among the earliest railway film footage to have survived is a clip of a theatrical train leaving Leeds station in 1896, its carriages followed by flat wagons bearing the mysterious lumpy shapes of tarpaulined sets, the platforms busy with people waving the human cargo on its way. Each train might carry several companies, at least for part of the journey. The *Railway Magazine* recorded that the London & North Western alone managed to convey 112 companies on a single Sunday, 22 October 1911, by means of just nineteen main-line special trains and eleven more on branch routes, as well as ordinary timetabled services. The splitting and shunting involved must have been considerable: one train was composed of six companies, including 'Florodora' on the short hop from Eccles to Preston and 'A Royal Divorce' on the long haul from Hyde to Glasgow.

Railways changed the rules of the game for the established London theatres too. Successful plays stood a better chance of enjoying long runs now that the potential audience included the population of outer suburbia, who could stay until curtain-call and still catch a late train home. With the hope of full houses in mind, producers became readier to invest in expensive sets and effects. Other cities witnessed similar changes. After their suburban lines were electrified in 1904, theatre-goers from well-heeled coastal suburbs could travel into Newcastle on fast early evening trains that hurried through plebeian Byker and Wallsend without stopping, returning no less quickly after the show was over. From a series of local or regional cultures, British theatrical life thus became more national in character, as well as more genteel, under the influence of the railways.

Musical life was also transformed. The National Eisteddfod of Wales was a creature of the railways, without which the Welsh tradition of choral singing could not have developed as it did. For Londoners the lodestar was the reconstructed Crystal Palace, as reopened in 1854 in the southern suburbs. In its newly enlarged form, with the former railway engineer George Grove (he of the monumental *Dictionary of Music and Musicians*) as company secretary, the Crystal Palace hosted orchestral concerts and vast oratorio festivals, fuelled by a national craze for public singing classes: 2,700 people sang at the concert in 1859 that marked the centenary of Handel's death, to a reported audience of 81,000. Some orchestras were thousands strong – the nearest Victorian equivalent to stadium rock. Transporting these throngs to and from London required two stations at the palace, both originally at the ends of branch lines, and both exceptionally large by suburban standards (one is now defunct). The *Musical Times* recorded a morning in 1859 when the trains were delivering passengers at an hourly rate of 12,000, 'for some hours'. Concert-goers who bought programmes discovered the timetables of return services printed helpfully at the back.

The huge gatherings made possible by the railways were not all secular in character. On 7 October 1857, a crowd of 23,654 listened to a sermon at the Crystal Palace by the Baptists' star preacher Charles Spurgeon, who implored divine favour for efforts to suppress the Indian Mutiny. Travelling in north-east Scotland in the 1860s, the French critic Hippolyte Taine encountered an excursion train crammed with workers, farmers and shopkeepers, on their way to a similar revival meeting. So great were the crowds – 20,000 were predicted – that the company had to telegraph for extra carriages. While they waited, the women sang hymns 'with an air of great conviction and serious purpose'. It is fair to say that these mass gatherings were not of the type most feared by the anti-railway reactionaries of the 1830s.

Even the business of death was modified by the railways. The Duke of Wellington himself did not escape. His end came in 1852, at Walmer Castle in Kent. That he should receive a state funeral at St Paul's Cathedral had long been understood. Had Wellington died twenty years earlier his last journey might well have begun by sea, into the mouth of the Thames. Instead, the South Eastern Railway brought up the coffin. Even in death Wellington was a magnet for crowds, so his funeral train was despatched in the middle of the night in order to avoid stirring up too much excitement.

Coffins of less eminent persons were a regular railway cargo. Many main-line stations kept a trolley dedicated to the purpose, and most long-distance travellers, knowingly or not, would have shared a journey with a cadaver at one time or another. When the wife of the Cumbrian merchant and philanthropist George Moore died in London in 1858, the London & North Western took husband and deceased spouse to Carlisle, where Moore slept in the recently built Station Hotel. 'It seemed strange to him, that while lying in his comfortable bed, his dead wife should be lying cold in the railway truck outside, within sight of the hotel windows.' Some lines had special vehicles for the purpose, bluntly titled 'corpse vans'. One of those belonging to the Lancashire & Yorkshire Railway, with occupant, was smashed to bits in a derailment at Hebden Bridge in 1912 (four passengers also died, which ought to be more horrible than the fate of the corpse but somehow isn't, after so many years). The little Festiniog Railway in Snowdonia kept its own black-painted hearse van, adapted from a quarryman's coach and adorned with a cast-iron urn at each corner – this for a line just over fourteen miles long, running on narrow-gauge tracks set at well under half the width of standard gauge.

More discreetly, the railways helped to supply medical schools with bodies for dissection, an increasingly important part of a Victorian doctor's training. These were pauper corpses from the workhouse, available under the notorious rule by which the right to a normal burial was forfeited by those who died in destitution. Trains arriving at Cambridge regularly included these unmentionable consignments, destined for the

Anatomy School in the town, whose own pauper mortality was unequal to the demand.

Then there was the wonderfully titled Necropolis Railway, which operated from 1854 to 1945 from a private station alongside the terminus at Waterloo. Trains comprising hearse wagons and mourners' carriages ran daily to Brookwood cemetery near Woking, the railway operation and the cemetery being parts of the same limited company. A similar but cheaper service started at King's Cross not long afterwards, travelling only to the outer suburbs. Both achieved less custom than was hoped, but the Necropolis company survived into the new century. Its strange neo-Romanesque station was rebuilt in 1902, when two platforms were provided: one for the mourners, the other for loading coffins, discreetly out of view. From 1885 the senior company also helped to foster the exotic novelty of cremation, some of the earliest facilities for which were at Brookwood. This, too, was a symbiotic relationship with the railway. Cremation cost an additional £6, on top of the company's standard charge of £8 10s. At that rate, the investment in furnaces and handling facilities stood no chance of making a decent return without an efficient and dignified method of bringing custom from further afield.

This post-mortem traffic, which ceased officially on British Rail as late as 28 March 1988, reflected differences in wealth no less firmly than the conveyance of living ones. The last journey of Matthew Arnold offers a detailed example of long-distance funereal travel among the upper-middle classes. The poet died suddenly in the street in Liverpool on 15 April 1888, on his way to take a horse-tram to meet some new arrivals at the docks. Two days later Arnold's coffin was driven to Lime Street station, where a clergyman, the unfortunately named J. T. Slugg, was in attendance to receive it. Four porters carried the coffin to the brake van, described as being placed behind a saloon attached to the London train; presumably a family saloon had been engaged to preserve the mourners' privacy. Next day a special train took mourners and coffin from Waterloo to Staines, from where the final stage to Laleham church was, as usual for funerals, by road.

A working-class funeral on such lines was out of the question, for the railways' rates of carriage for an occupied coffin were exacting. When a young actor named William Ryder died of pneumonia while on tour at Middlesbrough in 1899, his friends therefore returned the body to his bereaved family in London by encasing the coffin within a simple crate, scrawled in black chalk with the words 'theatrical properties' and 'this side up'. Carried at the standard goods rate, the cost was 16s 2d; as an acknowledged cadaver, even without the extra weight of the packing case, it would have been around £11. (The ruse was detected, but the Great Northern Railway generously waived the difference.)

₪

We can conclude the examination of class differences by tracing the decline of the Wellingtonian habit of travelling within the rail-borne coach. The last edition of the Great Western's *Time Book* to give details of the procedure appeared on 12 July 1913, although it seems effectively to have died out before then. One late exponent was Mrs Caroline Prodgers (died 1890), who was famous in her day for obsessively taking London cabmen to court for any suspected infringements of the regulations. Hamilton Ellis recorded that her occupied carriage was observed en route at Chesterfield in the 1880s; he claimed that she was the last person to travel in this manner.

For the aristocracy, to travel in one's own vehicle was a tradition centuries old, and difficult for some to forsake. The biographer Samuel Smiles observed that certain grand families continued to use their own coaches even after they began sending the servants and luggage ahead by train – but never for long. 'Railways have taken the starch out of country magnificence', Surtees wrote in 1858; arrival in one's own coach was no longer assumed, and a socially confident visitor might even be dropped off at the gate by the station omnibus. Any diehard who attempted to go long distances on the roads found that chains of coaching inns with fresh horses no longer existed. That meant the gradual acceptance of the railway compartment as a social space common to anyone who could afford to pay, with all the challenges and compromises that came of close confinement with strangers.

JOURNEYING TOGETHER

No one much under the age of fifty will have adult memories of travelling on Britain's railways in separate, non-communicating compartments. To recover a sense of what it was like to share that confined space with strangers, it is best to imagine entering a London-type taxi in which all but one seat has already been taken. The railway compartment was, of course, taller, with full seating on both sides. But in other respects – the rapid, half-involuntary assessment of fellow travellers, the forced intimacy expressed in closeness of gaze, ease of overhearing and exposure to personal odours, the sharing of a limited volume of air (and the control of access to the fresh variety by the passengers closest to the windows), the need to negotiate with the personal space of others when entering or leaving, the psychological advantage enjoyed by those already seated – the cab and the railway compartment have a decided affinity.

For those with an aversion to such circumstances, and the funds to indulge it, the railway companies allowed the reservation of an entire compartment, which then would be kept locked until needed. This was expensive, in inverse proportion to the number of people travelling. Most people with a taste for privacy – which is to say, most people – sought out an empty compartment and hoped that no one would join them there.

Ways of keeping undisturbed possession of a compartment were the occasion for humour. R. S. Surtees advised that a baby (subject to availability) should be held up at the window, it being well established that

'The British Character: Love of Travelling Alone',
cartoon by 'Pont' from *Punch*, 1937

there was nothing like it for keeping grown men away. *Punch* advised trying the same dodge with a doll, breathing on the glass first for verisimilitude. The magazine was still having fun with the dilemma in the 1930s,
when its cartoonist 'Pont', alias Graham Laidler, included 'Love of travelling alone' in his series on The British Character (1937–8): a frowning
businessman has placed his hat, umbrella, gloves, briefcase, parcels etc.
across every free seat of the compartment. The Bishop of Woolwich, in
a sermon to undergraduates in the same decade, recommended the combination of a clerical collar (to deter men) and an unlit cigar (to ward
off women). More extreme measures are recorded on the part of Gerald
Tyrwhitt-Wilson (1883–1950), 14th Lord Berners, composer, author and
playful avant-gardist: by masking his eyes behind black glasses and beck-
oning invitingly from the carriage window at every stop, he was able to
secure the pleasures of solitude.

Undisturbed or not, at least one could hope to get a good seat –
forward-facing and next to the window was the popular choice (cannier
travellers, then as now, might also allow for the quality of the views and

the position and transit of the sun during the journey). To stake a claim, some personal object might be placed on the seat, leaving the traveller free to oversee the loading of luggage, to exchange farewells, or any other activity on the platform. Surtees's guide of 1851 advised that a book or a glove would do the job, but *The Railway Traveller's Handy Book* noted that such light articles were often disregarded by passengers in second and third class, proposing instead the use of a heavy piece of luggage, 'which some persons would be too timid, and others too idle, to remove'.

This seat-marking convention was already current by the end of the 1830s. We know this from the case of Captain Connop's handkerchief, which came to the Old Bailey for trial. Like many petty legal cases, it captures details of custom and circumstance that would otherwise have escaped record. Connop, an army officer on half-pay, was travelling from Paddington station on Boxing Day 1839. Selecting a seat in first class, he placed a silk handkerchief on it before attending to other matters. On his return ten minutes later the place-marker was gone. The nearest person to hand, a carriage cleaner called James Mayhew, denied all knowledge of its fate. Mayhew had been with the Great Western Railway for fourteen of its nineteen months of operational existence, and no complaints had been lodged against him in that time. Things looked rather different after the handkerchief was spotted two hours later, placed high up in the timbers of the roof 'in the urinal of the second class booking office'. A railway policeman was set to watch, hiding in a lavatory cubicle ready to spring out should anyone come to fetch it down. Mayhew then entered. As soon as the policeman emerged, the cleaner dashed into one of the other cubicles and refused to open the door; but the policeman found he could look in 'at the top where there had been glass, but it was broken', and the game was up. (The detail of the broken glass may incidentally be one of the first records of vandalism to a railway station WC.) So ended one early career on the railways.

For many, the best journeys were when others kept away, when no handkerchiefs or seat-markers were necessary, and a whole compartment could be had to oneself. As Hilaire Belloc wrote in 1908, 'The railway gives you seclusion ... in the corner of a third-class going north or west you can be sure of your own company; the best, the most sympathetic, the most brilliant in the world.' With control over the entry of daylight by means of curtains or blinds, and with ventilation also under individual command by means of the window strap, the little sliding grilles set into the carriage sides, and the adjustable dish-shaped vents in the carriage roof, the solitary traveller could fine-tune the railway compartment according to personal inclination. Here were all the privileges of solitary motoring without any of the responsibilities. Humming, scratching, muttering, fiddling, whistling, napping could all be indulged at whim. Nor could any disapproving stare or official reprimand deter the resting of feet on the seat opposite.

This habit was rife by the 1860s, to judge from the experience of the North British Railway. Debating the pros and cons of upholstered seating, the line's locomotive superintendent William Hurst lamented the difficulties of keeping even first-class carriages in decent order when 'the padding is torn to pieces by passengers placing their feet upon it'. (As for a practical floor covering for lower-class carriages, he reluctantly concluded, 'To use sand is out of the question or even straw.') Those susceptible to seat abuse included the very man who – it may be argued – had set in motion the process of upgrading by which third class came to travel on cushions. William Gladstone himself was spotted at Swindon around 1887 by the young writer Ford Madox Ford, who looked across from the carriage alongside to discover the Grand Old Man in a compartment all his own: 'He was sitting reading a memorandum with his feet on the cushions of the opposite seat. His face was expressionless, or rather morose. He was quite alone. He was wearing a black woollen cap with earflaps tied under the chin.' Ford added, 'It struck me that anyone could easily have assassinated him if they had wanted to.'

In practice, discharges of firearms inside trains were mostly limited to suicides. They include the Woolwich linen-draper who shot himself as his train passed through the Blackheath Tunnel of the South Eastern Railway in 1862; a fatal act in one small railway space, in transit through a larger one. A similar fate overtook Silvanus Trevail, premier architect of Victorian Cornwall, in Brownqueen Tunnel in 1903, although he retired to a ladies' lavatory before pulling the trigger – a sign that he was travelling in a newer sort of carriage, with a side corridor. Trevail was among eight railway-carriage suicides reported that year, including one instance of murder-and-suicide and two deaths in which poison was used. Self-inflicted deaths by throat-cutting are also recorded, and the failed suicide by home-made bomb of a nineteen-year-old billiard-marker named Harry Medina, crossed in love, who tried to put an end to himself in a North London Railway compartment between Barnsbury and Highbury in 1899. He escaped with burns and shock, damage to the carriage valued at £6 and

SUICIDE IN A RAILWAY TRAIN

Suicide of a passenger, from the *Illustrated Police News*, 1884

a sentence of one month's hard labour. More recently, the cases of Medina and Trevail were echoed by the bizarre suicide in 2011 of a woman passenger who took a gas canister into a lavatory on a train from Northampton to London and ignited it there.

One qualified exception should be made to the list of solitary and decent activities allowed in the carriage: the smoking of tobacco. The correlation between the railways' attitude to the weed and the customs of wider society is striking. When railways were new, smoking was in decline among the higher ranks. The habit was widely considered eccentric, rather foreign and mildly disgusting, so that a smoker who was a house-guest might have to retreat to the servants' hall or stables. Tobacco was also regarded as a bachelor habit, which men were expected to renounce on marriage – hence its rather 'fast' associations of clubroom and officers' mess, and the air of consolatory or forgivable naughtiness that hovers around the practice in much nineteenth-century writing. No surprise, then, that the Liverpool & Manchester Railway in 1831 used its first by-law to ban smoking in first-class carriages, 'even with the general consent of the Passengers present', on the grounds that the lingering effects would annoy those using the vehicle afterwards. Other lines made similar rules;

the minutes of the Newcastle & North Shields Railway for 1839 record the prohibition, describing tobacco smoke as 'an evil that had caused injury to the best carriages'.

Regulations became stricter as open carriages gave way to closed ones, and bare boards to fabric finishes. In the absence of anyone to keep an eye on passengers between stations, however, it was not difficult to break these rules with impunity. A letter of 1841 from Thomas Carlyle to his wife gloats over the cigars he had just enjoyed on a run up to Derby, in company with the eminent (and presumably complaisant) editor Richard Monckton Milnes MP. The sporty Mr Bouncer, in Cuthbert Bede's *The Adventures of Mr Verdant Green, an Oxford Undergraduate* (1853–7), chooses to forsake the rest of his travelling party and go second class, 'where he could more conveniently indulge in the furtive pleasures of the Virginian weed'. Time was on Bouncer's side: from a historic low point, smoking steadily became more popular from the 1830s onwards, as tobacco was presented in tempting, even fashionable new forms. The cigar was joined by the cheroot, the favoured smoke of East India Company men, and by the cigarette, which came via the troops from the Crimean war, where Russian and Turkish forces alike puffed away on them, and which could be bought in the form of 'Patent Crystal Cigarettes' by 1858. For pipe men there was the briar, an innovation of the 1850s, when it was discovered that the root of the tree-heath or bruyère bush of Corsica could be carved into a robust smoking apparatus. The briar also delivered a cooler smoke than the fragile clay pipe of the working man. Tobacconists even sold 'railway pipes', described as 'adapted for instantaneous concealment'. Matches, including the safety match (invented in 1855), helped the fires along; the ceilings of London & South Western carriages were described in 1866 as covered in scratches where they had been struck.

The railways' response was mixed. Some tried to stand firm, including the Great Western – a little ungratefully, given that nearly £30,000 of share capital in the line and its constituents had been placed by Bristol's tobacco barons, the brothers W. D. and H. O. Wills. Other lines experimented with special carriages, such as the Eastern Counties Railway's first-class saloon of 1846, with its plate-glass-windowed compartment complete with mahogany table and table-lamps. But it was easier simply to designate existing compartments for the habit, as the Eastern Counties began to do in 1854.

The standard penalty for a breach of the smoking ban was a stiff forty shillings, with the additional risk of ejection from the train without refund of fare for those who persisted in the offence. Costs might be added if the matter came to court: in 1862 a magistrate found against two unchivalrous male passengers on the London & South Western who had refused to stop smoking after a polite request from some ladies in their carriage. But in practice a blind eye might be turned, especially if a little inducement changed hands. A *Punch* cartoon of 1858 shows a guard looking into a compartment occupied by three smart travellers, all visibly in breach of regulations: 'There are two things not allowed on this line, gentlemen: smoking, and the servants of the company receiving money.' The pay-off may be guessed. As Robert Audley mused in *Lady Audley's Secret* (1862), 'The Company may make as many bye-laws as they please ... but I shall take the liberty of enjoying my cheroot as long as I've half-a-crown left to give the guard.' Or you could take the rap and pay up: another *Punch* cartoon from these years has a 'fast Etonian' rebuked by a stove-pipe-hatted figure who reveals himself to be the manager of the line, only to receive the cool reply, 'Well, old boy, I must have my smoke, so you may as well take your forty shillings now.' The young Prince of Wales himself was detected in the offence, according to society gossip in the 1860s. Senior personnel did not always escape the suspicion of double standards: an errant passenger brought before Huddersfield magistrates in 1861 was let off partly on the grounds that the companies' officials and directors were habitual and hypocritical smokers on their own trains.

Consistency in the treatment of smoking passengers came with the Railway Regulation Act of 1868. Henceforth, smoking compartments were to be designated on any train comprising more than one carriage of each class – not quite a green light to smoke on every journey, but enough to cover most. Speaking in favour of a less generous provision for smokers was the Radical philosopher John Stuart Mill (1806–73), at that time MP for Westminster, in one of his last interventions in the House of Commons. His best-known work, *On Liberty* (1859), famously makes the case for the freedom of the individual in all actions that are primarily self-regarding, but for Mill there was already so much smouldering tobacco in railway carriages that its consumption had become 'a case of oppression by a majority of a minority'. By October 1868 a newspaper correspondent lamented that carpets were now a misplaced luxury in first class, where what was really needed were ash pans, and that third-class smokers should be equipped with spittoons and sawdust, the latter to be changed four times a day (a reminder that tobacco was chewed as well as burnt). The humorists had a new angle on an old favourite, too. *Judy* magazine, a short-lived competitor to *Punch*, showed a full compartment with just one non-smoker present: 'Passenger (to Guard) "I say, look here, you know, here's somebody not smoking!"'. Even the underground lines of London let in smokers eventually, after some tobacco-free years in which the management invoked an exemption under the 1868 Act.

A crowded smoking compartment was no place for the abstainer. In late March 1875, Francis Kilvert saw his brother Teddy off to London in a Great Western smoking compartment, 'the atmosphere of which I could not have endured for a minute and could hardly bear to stand near the door even'. But there were more smokers all the time: tobacco consumption in Britain rose by some 5 per cent in every year from the 1860s to the end of the century. So the railways were now saddled with increased fire risks, dirt and burns to carriage carpets and upholstery. The companies could at least console themselves with the income from licensing the sale of tobacco at stations, especially after the Wills brothers introduced the 'Bonsack' vending machine from the United States in 1883. Three years later, Wills contracted with Spiers and Pond for exclusive rights of display and sale in its branches, railway refreshment rooms included. Other tobacco companies made similar arrangements. Cheap, universally available, ubiquitously advertised, familiar in every social class, and latterly adopted even by growing numbers of women, the cigarette conquered the railway network as it did the world outside. And so the fumes from millions of Wills's 'Autumn Gold', considered to have been the first brand generally sold by vending machine, made their little contributions to the atmospheric products of combusted coal, coke, oil and gas flavouring the British railway station – the old prohibition of smoking on railway premises, as well as trains, ultimately proving impossible to enforce.

One telling alteration followed, concerning how the carriages were marked. Victorian smoking compartments were indicated as such. The absence of a sign – such as a frosted inscription on the window glass, or the Great Western's big 'S' inside the carriage door – indicated that tobacco should *not* be consumed there. The 1920s began to reverse this convention, so that it was non-smoking spaces that were labelled. The GWR adopted this policy in 1930, when red triangular stickers began to appear on the windows of its non-smokers. Britain's railways thus came into line with the Continental system (by 1899 already 'a smoker's paradise', according to that year's *Railway Magazine*). There were markedly fewer of these refuges, too; Compton Mackenzie's *Sublime Tobacco*, published in 1957 in the author's seventy-fourth year, noted that smoke-free compartments had become as hard to find as the other sort had been in his youth.

By the 1950s 80 per cent of British men and 40 per cent of women had the habit, but the Doll report demonstrating the statistical connection with lung cancer had already been published, and the rest everybody knows. As the habit dwindled, so too did smoking accommodation on trains. Beryl Bainbridge, starting her writer's tour of England at Waterloo station in 1983, found the tables already turned:

> ... I had to walk miles, carrying two suitcases, my handbag, typewriter, notebook and Sunday papers, before finding a carriage which allowed smoking. There's something wrong with British Rail. Anyone with an ounce of sense would put the ciggie coaches nearest to the barrier to avoid passengers pegging out on the platform. After such exertion I was too ill to wrench open the door – the train was about to leave at any moment – so I banged my head against the window and shouted. Several people stared out at me sympathetically before glancing away.

London Underground banned smoking throughout its lines a few years later, spurred on by the disastrous conflagration caused by a discarded cigarette on the escalators at King's Cross in 1987, when thirty-one passengers died. Selected main-line trains lost their smoking sections from around the same time, coming into step with restrictions already in place on many local services. *Bridget Jones's Diary*, a decade later, drew the lesson: 'Realize it is no longer possible for smokers to live in dignity, instead of being forced to sulk in the slimy underbelly of existence ... Maybe privatized rail firms will start running Smoking Trains and villagers will shake their fists and throw stones at them as they pass.'

No such luck: the last service on which smoking was permitted, the King's Cross–Aberdeen sleeper, ran in October 2005. Now, even the most lovingly accurate re-creation on the country's preserved railways cannot bring back the sour smell of wet tobacco ash, smeared thinly in solution with other dirt over the linoleum flooring of a crowded second-class carriage on a rainy winter's day; nor the grey-black deposit of carbonised tobacco particulates inadvertently picked up when the shoulders of coats and jackets rubbed against the tainted condensation on single-glazed carriage windows. These are losses for which few travellers will not be thankful.

One other long-lasting restriction deserves mention here. Dogs did not travel with passengers. Their proper place was the guard's accommodation. The Highland Railway, with its clientele of lairds, sportsmen and shepherds, was among the lines in which a 'boot' for the purpose was provided there. A ticket was required for each dog journey, and in due course dog season tickets were introduced too, in parallel with those devised for humans. Now that there are few guards' compartments on the old model, the practice is easily forgotten. As with smoking, the rule was doubtless waived now and again, especially on lines where staff and regular passengers were on good terms. Or an illicit tip may have changed hands, as anticipated by the complaisant guard of Mr Bouncer's train in *Mr Verdant Green*, after unmistakable sounds are heard coming from a ventilated box on the carriage floor, which the owner professes to be a container for rabbits ('Oh come, sir! What makes rabbits bark?' 'Why, because they've got the pip, poor beggars!').

₪

Behind these restrictions on smoking and on dogs was the idea that behaviour within the railway compartment should be ruled by consideration for fellow passengers. Be that as it may, close confinement with strangers on trains seems to have cast a sort of chill over social relations. In particular, the railway compartment was widely reported to have killed off the convention on the roads by which conversation between passengers was normal and expected. This transformation deserves a closer look.

Coaches on the roads were of two types, mail and stage. As instituted in the 1780s, mail-coaches carried all their passengers inside, usually to a limit of four. After 1803 some extras were permitted to travel outside too. The mails ran to strict timetables and represented the elite of the road. Stagecoaches likewise carried usually just four passengers inside, but on the outside up to ten or eleven, one of whom sat on the 'box' next to the coachman. Spoken exchanges between the coachman and his guard or guards were both usual and essential; conversation between these men and their passengers, and among the passengers themselves, came naturally too. Inside passengers could swap words with those outside by lowering the windows, which were of the same drop-light kind as those adopted for railway carriages. Further exchanges accompanied departures or arrivals of passengers when the coach stopped. At the most basic, simple information, pleasantries and requests went back and forth. For those wanting more, the weather, the state of the passing crops, keeping to time, the mysteries of horse-flesh and the pleasures (or otherwise) of lunching, dining and overnight accommodation were subjects to hand. By these conversations, the communal experience of travel was reinforced. Readers of the *Pickwick Papers* (1836–7) will remember the glamour that hung about the coachman; boys dreamed of taking up the whip, and the seat on the box was coveted.

The railway compartment was different. No longer could the passenger hail the crew from anywhere on board. Driver and fireman were in a world of their own, separated physically from the carriages by the tender of their locomotive and cut off from audible contact by the noise of its working. The guard too was likely to be in another vehicle altogether. The porters who had helped the passengers on to the train were not the same as those who helped them off at the point of arrival. The train moved too fast and too noisily for any bandying of words with traffic passing in the opposite direction, as the coachmen were wont to do, or for calling out to people on foot, on horseback, or working in the fields alongside. Landmarks and other objects of remark slipped by much quicker, and might be barely visible from the further side of the compartment – unlike the broad, slow-moving panoramas shared by the outside passengers on the roads, or those on deck when travelling by water. Conversation was restricted to the occupants of the compartment itself, and the range of subjects within common view diminished too.

What was left? Certainly, the routine exchanges required by courtesy or utility, especially the sometimes delicate consultations on opening or closing the window. 'Don't you think you'd be less liable to cold with that window closed?' an old lady asks Mary Masters, heroine of Trollope's *The American Senator* (1877): a diplomatic way of conveying her own preference. Mary's male companion could hardly refuse to shut the window after that (etiquette required that the opening or closing of windows in mixed company should be done by the male of the party). Open windows were also a trigger for action when the train entered a tunnel. E. Nesbit explains to the young readers of *The Railway Children* (1906) the grown-up custom of standing to hold up the window strap each time the train entered one, so that the engine smoke would not billow in. This too was an action no gentleman could lounge back and leave a member of the opposite sex to perform. A lady's cough was enough to prompt the young F. L. Olmsted, later famous as the co-designer of Central Park in New York, to shut the window of his second-class compartment as the visitor's train headed out of Liverpool Lime Street into rainy Lancashire in 1850. As to the geography of power within the compartment, *The Traveller's Guide to Great Britain and Ireland* (1930) records conventions already generations old: the right to decide whether the window is open or shut 'is vested by custom in the passenger seated next to it, facing the engine', but also that this passenger 'generally takes the sense of the company on the question'. Good form also required that the departing passenger should not leave the door open, and that the window should be pulled up again if it had been lowered in order to reach the outside door-handle (*Baedeker's Great Britain*, 1887).

None of this required much by way of further discourse. Indeed, the sparseness of conversation in railway compartments was so often remarked upon that the difference from the custom of the road must have been real. 'Generally speaking, the occupants of a railway carriage perform the whole of the journey in silence; but if one passenger be more loquaciously inclined than the rest, he is soon silenced by abrupt or tart replies, or by a species of grunt expressive of dissent or dissatisfaction': thus *The Railway Traveller's Handy Book*. The *Penny Illustrated Paper* caught the habitual mood in first class in the same year, 1862:

> Every-body seems to have an idea that he is the only one who is really entitled, by payment and position, to a seat therein, and so is afraid of compromising his dignity by speaking. There is, consequently, no conversation; the heads of the four corner occupants are usually looking out of the windows, and the centre ones looking at each other.

Samuel Sidney's *Rides on Railways* (1851) dared to prefer the 'vulgar and amusing' companionship of third class to the 'dull and genteel' assortment at the other end of the train; this after a starchy outward journey in the company of an Oxford MA, an army officer, a Somerset House clerk and a man who had been visiting a lord, and a cheerful return spent with a tailor, a sailor, a bird-catcher and an ex-convict in greasy velveteens, for whom Reading gaol was the winter resort of choice ('plenty of good vittles, and the cells warmed'). A similar rigidity was observed by American visitors. Nathaniel Hawthorne recorded of first-class carriages in 1852: 'Nothing is to be seen or learnt there; nobody to be seen but civil and silent gentlemen, sitting on their cushioned dignities.' Harriet Beecher Stowe – she of *Uncle Tom's Cabin* (also 1852) – found the railway compartment an analogy for 'that privacy and reserve which is the dearest and most sacred part of an Englishman's nature ... a stranger might travel all through England, from one end to the other and not be on conversing terms with a person in it'.

Observations of these differences worked in both directions. In particular, the contrast with habits on American trains threw the taciturnity of Victorian (and Continental) travel into relief. Here is Dickens, in his *American Notes for General Circulation* (1842), journeying from Boston to Lowell. He explained to British readers that railroad cars over there had single, undivided interiors, 'like shabby omnibuses, but larger'. Each held thirty to fifty passengers, seated two by two in benches either side of a central gangway. The entrance or entrances were at the ends. In the middle was usually a coal stove, which Dickens found made the air 'insufferably close'. Apart from that, the main difference was the freedom of speech: 'Everybody talks to you, or to anybody else who hits his fancy.' The conductor – whose duties usually included the sale of tickets – was himself at liberty to strike up conversation as he strolled up and down the car: actions at once physically impossible and socially unacceptable for his British equivalent, the railway guard. Nor was conversation confined to polite neutralities: Dickens noted especially discussion of politics, banks and cotton, the hard realities of a young and commercial nation. Travelling in the US twenty years later, Anthony Trollope found the same single-class conventions in place – distasteful to him, as representing 'confusion between social and political equality'.

What British visitors apparently failed to discern was the social space from which this habitual jawing and ear-bending derived, a space that predated the railroads, without having been vanquished by them: namely, the riverboat saloon. It was the rivers, not railroads or stagecoaches, that first opened up the interior of North America to settlement and commerce, and anyone travelling long distances sooner or later found themselves afloat on one. The free-and-easy conventions of the riverboat saloon transferred naturally to the railroad, where the capacious interiors likewise allowed the option of moving seats to join in a conversation, or to withdraw with a measure of politeness if the exchanges proved boring or vexatious. Circulation was encouraged further by another American convention recorded by Dickens, even though it cannot always have been respected: if a lady took a fancy to a male passenger's seat, her male companion would make the preference known and the occupant would move elsewhere.

Yet it will not do to think of the early railroad cars of the USA as open to everyone equally. A 'negro car' was included in Dickens's train, 'as a black man never travels with a white one'. The wording is sardonic: at the moral centre of the *American Notes* is the perception that the Republic's high ideals had been warped and corroded by slavery. Railroads played their part in the circulation of enslavement; the negro car of Dickens's train from Fredericksburg to Richmond was carrying a slave woman and her weeping children away from the husband and father, whose master had just sold them off to another. Then there was the writer's shuddering disgust at the native habits of tobacco-chewing and spitting all over the place: the 'flashes of saliva' whizzing past his window between Boston and Worcester made it look 'as though they were ripping open feather-beds inside, and letting the wind dispose of the feathers'. Add to this the shamelessness with which people eager for a glimpse of the celebrity author clustered round his carriage – at Washington, they even let down his windows to look in and discuss his appearance 'with as much indifference as if I were a stuffed figure' – and it is fair to say that Dickens's experience of American railroads was not altogether joyful.

We know a lot about Dickens's British railway journeys too, and those of certain other notables who kept diaries, wrote letters, or otherwise memorialised their lives. In these writings, conversations with strangers are not hard to find. However, it is often unclear whether these interlocutors knew who they were talking to, or whether the presence of a captive celebrity loosened tongues that would otherwise have remained tied. What, for instance, to make of the old man who addressed Dickens on a journey to Birmingham in February 1844? The man 'expressed himself most mournfully as to the ruinous effects and rapid spread of railways, and was most pathetic on the virtues of the slow-going old stage coaches'. Dickens concurred politely with this Wellingtonian tirade, joining in the man's laments at all the jolts, shocks and screeches of their journey. But 'when the speed of the engine was abated, or there was the slightest prolongation of our stay in any station, the old gentleman was up in arms, and his watch was instantly out of his pocket, denouncing the slowness of our progress'. Dickens had some fun with this exchange in the speech that was the purpose of his journey, in which the novelist's general impatience with nostalgia and past-mindedness was ventilated. But whether the old bore was sounding off in the hope of influencing the most popular writer of the day is impossible to say.

Thomas Carlyle (1795–1881) – a much less approachable man – found himself on the rails later in 1843, 'in a somewhat sulphurous condition, not handy to quarrel with'. A fellow passenger in second class

> took it into his head to smile visibly when I laid off my white broad-brim, and suddenly produced out of my pocket my grey glengarry [Scotch bonnet]. He seemed of the mercantile head-clerk species, and had been tempted to his impropriety by a foolish-looking pampered young lady in tiger-skin mantle whom he seemed to have charge of.

Carlyle stared him down: 'the smile instantly died into another expression of emotion'. Was the clerkish man one of his readers, offering misguided tribute? Dickens would have been flattered, but Carlyle only wanted to be left alone.

Then there is Gladstone. Railways run through this statesman's life like a steel thread, shining brightly at the legislation and regulation of the 1840s and the electioneering and speech-making tours of his late years. Sometimes Gladstone's diary records journeys in the unexpected company of other notables – a reminder that the first-class waiting room at a great station was the nearest Victorian equivalent to the airport VIP lounge. Thus 21 June 1855: 'The first three hours in close conversation with Mont-alembert [the French Liberal Catholic historian], whom I was so happy as to have for a fellow traveller.' By that decade Gladstone was on the way to becoming as recognisable a figure as Dickens, or Wellington in his time. So the entry for 9 July 1857 – 'In the train I got from a Newcastle man a good lecture on the Iron Trade' – looks like a case of someone seizing the chance to bend an influential ear.

Putting fame aside, we may take Francis Kilvert, travelling in company with his mother, sister and a maidservant, on a fierce June day four years later:

> The Wiltshire downs and Salisbury Plain were white and glaring with drought and chalk and dust in the scorching blinding sun ... At Heytesbury a young handsome intelligent gentlemanly farmer got into the carriage, a man with a ruddy face, light brown hair, merry blue eyes and a white puggery [a thin scarf wrapped round so as to shade the

neck] on his hat. We fell into talk about the strike and lock-out in the Eastern Counties and the much vexed labour and wages question ...*

These episodes – tersely noted down by the greatest British states-man of the age, or vividly captured by an obscure junior clergyman with no thought of a wider readership – can stand for what must have been countless instances when reserve was laid aside and enjoyable or enrich-ing discussions begun. For in the end, however much the old stagecoach talkativeness dwindled away, it is impossible to credit that a presumption of silence prevailed *without exception* inside the higher classes of railway compartment; that the chatterbox, the monomaniac, the political agitator, the evangelist awaiting his moment, never found a willing ear or a spirited response; that soldier did not speak to soldier, tradesman to tradesman, or undergraduate to undergraduate; that the angler or the hunting man could not detect a fellow sportsman from details of dress or luggage and launch gladly into conversational common ground.

₪

What if you really, truly, did not want a conversation? Surtees in 1851 was ready with the answer: have a newspaper or book to hand, 'in case tiresome people will talk – a purpose for which railway travel was never intended'. The *Handy Book* concurred: 'an excellent weapon against bores ... who can only be silenced by levelling a volume or a journal at their heads'. The author reckoned that at least one passenger in two might be observed tak-ing up a book or a paper (a caveat here, for this author usually ignores third class). Reading at once allowed an escape into a private mental space and signalled to those sharing the compartment that one did not wish to be disturbed. All those books and magazines were so many personal screens, held up in front of the body as if to complement the territory-defining armrests and headrests in the better classes of carriage. In the words of Wolfgang Schivelbusch, whose *The Railway Journey* (1979) remains the most penetrating international study of nineteenth-century railway travel, 'reading becomes a surrogate for the communication that no longer takes place'.

---

* The reference is to an agricultural workers' strike, and not to the former Eastern Counties Railway.

Marking personal space: readers and smokers in
a second-class compartment, 1895

To keep up a measure of civility without a commitment to conversation, printed matter could be exchanged between strangers. This is what Major Grantly and Johnny Eames do in Trollope's *Last Chronicle of Barset* (1867): first *The Times* for the *Daily News*, then *Saturday* for *The Spectator*. Finally, the silence breaks properly, in a discussion of the *Pall Mall Gazette*, of which both men have a copy.

The generosity of this diet of print identifies Trollope's characters as members of the wealthier classes. The same can be said of Gladstone in 1859, filling spare time on a journey in getting by heart the 692 blank-verse lines of Tennyson's newly published *Guinevere*. Likewise, of the Irish nationalist leader Daniel O'Connell, who reportedly hurled his copy of Dickens's *The Old Curiosity Shop* (1841) out of the carriage window in dismay at the death of Little Nell ('He should not have killed her!'). Any railway worker happening on the book in that year would doubtless have found a good home for it: a single instalment of a serially published Dickens novel then required the outlay of a shilling. Even *The Times* cost five-pence, at a time when a station porter might earn not much more than three shillings per day. Surtees's suggestion to his travellers of 1851 that a newspaper could be bartered for another at stations along the way, so that the thrifty traveller might read several for the price of one, underscores the relative costliness of printed matter into the early railway age.

Changes were afoot. Taxes on press advertising were done away with in 1853, taxes on newspapers themselves in 1855, duties on paper in 1861. The Post Office did its bit, enforcing cheaper rates of carriage for books on the reluctant railways in 1853. The market was already there: as early as 1800, three-quarters of the adult male population was accounted literate. A steam-powered press was patented in 1810; the four-cylinder press (as used for *The Times*) arrived in 1828; the rotary press by 1857. Cheap wood-pulp paper, new paper-making machines and letter-founding machines also played a part in bringing costs down. Such was the demand for type in the boom after 1855 that some printers briefly rummaged out their old Georgian 'ſ's to supplement stocks of the familiar modern 's'. *The Times* of 1800 was a luxury item with a daily sale of some 2,500–3,000, each copy hand-stamped to show that duty had been paid; by 1860 it was selling upwards of 55,000. The *Daily Telegraph* in 1856 dropped its price to a penny, which became the expected rate for the mass daily press. By 1880 this paper alone had a circulation of around 300,000. Newspapers were joined by the professional press (*The Lancet*, *The Builder*, etc.), pictorial journals (the *Illustrated London News* started in 1842), women's magazines (four titles in 1846, fifty by 1900), sporting papers and magazines (the forerunner of the *Sporting Life* began in 1859, the first non-horsey periodical, *Athletic News*, in 1875), and by mass-market general journals such as *Answers*, *Titbits* and *Lloyds Weekly*, of which the last claimed a million sales per issue in 1896.

Railways had relatively little to do with making possible this torrent of printed matter – cheap steam presses came about without their direct help, for instance – but everything to do with its distribution and consumption. Newspapers were first carried by the Liverpool & Manchester in 1831. By 1839 they were also on sale at stations. Journals that had been delivered by road swiftly went over to railway distribution whenever a new line opened. At first they were mixed with general parcels traffic, but later in the century they were increasingly likely to be sent by the ton in dedicated newspaper trains, at least in the case of national titles originating in London. Their despatch was tightly choreographed: in order not to miss the late news, Fleet Street would delay printing to the last minute compatible with getting the papers to the station in time for departure in the small hours, so that rival consignments tended to arrive in one rush. Sorting all these papers for onward distribution in advance was out of the question, and much of the job had to be done on trestle tables within the railway vans as the train went on its way. By 1900 Manchester likewise had its own newspaper trains, one of which ran across the Pennines to take the *Manchester Guardian* into the heart of Yorkshire – a significant cultural victory for the red rose over the white.

Local journals flourished too, including a growing list of regional daily papers, little known before 1855. In this case it was the electric telegraph more than the railways that fostered the change. Telegraphy broke the subordinate relationship by which the provincial press served up a belated digest of news that came out physically from the capital in printed form. From the 1860s the railways also made possible a shift of book production away from congested and costly London, in favour of printing firms as far off as Clay's at Bungay in Suffolk, or Butler and Tanner's at Frome in Somerset. Manuscripts and proof pages shuttled back and forth between these works and the publishers' London offices, breaking the ancient link between the intellectual composition and the physical production of books. Some older publishers benefited too: Cambridge University Press in the eighteenth century paid five shillings a ton for the transport of its paper by means of a roundabout water route, as against the two shillings it cost to take the same quantity up the Thames to Oxford. Once the railways had equalised these rates, Cambridge's printing house could compete effectively for business from outside its parent university, on which the best profits were to be made.

By fostering both national and specialist markets for publications, the railways also opened the floodgates to press advertising of every kind, keeping cover prices down. Railway companies themselves added considerably to this acreage of newsprint. Established lines placed regular notices concerning services and traffic, especially small 'non-display' advertisements in local papers. New ventures burnt through piles of money in self-advertisement, and for the associated legal notices. This kind of outlay peaked early with the Railway Mania of the mid 1840s. For a time during 1845, the *Morning Post* came with a supplement devoted entirely to railway matters. In three months of the same year, the Direct London, Holyhead & Porth Dinllaen Railway, a representative Mania project, spent £1,255 18s 8d on self-promotion in the press and still came to nothing.

As to consumption, there was nothing to match the thronged railway station for a captive market. Likewise, for the traveller a newspaper or magazine had advantages over a book: it was generally cheaper, it was not made for consecutive reading from start to finish and it could be discarded without a pang when the journey was done. Writings from the nineteenth century's cultural heights were mistrustful of these trends, as of the rise of a mass readership generally. Those who fear that the electronic media of today are shortening attention spans, blunting the capacity for sustained thought and generally frying the neural pathways might take note of the plan by the egregious Mr Whelpdale in George Gissing's bracingly pessimistic *New Grub Street* (1891) to transform a shallow-minded weekly, *Chat*, into an even more superficial offering, *Chit-Chat*. Aimed at the 'quarter-educated' traveller by train or bus, *Chit-Chat* naturally proves to be a triumph: 'the lightest and frothiest of chit-chatty information – bits of stories, bits of description, bits of scandal, bits of jokes, bits of statistics, bits of foolery. Am I not right? Everything must be very short, two inches at the utmost; their attention can't sustain itself beyond two inches.'

Cultural disdain of Gissing's kind was not new: it echoed arguments over the quality of available reading matter and the direction of popular taste in the earliest decades of railway travel, especially in the matter of books. Here, too, production costs were falling, partly thanks to bigger print runs, partly from mechanisation of the binding process, so that the unit costs of books of comparable types fell by more than half during Victoria's reign.

These changes also promised much to the promoters of moralised and moralising literature. In the eighteenth century this usually had a religious flavour. Streams of more secular or ecumenical material joined the outflow early in the century following: anthologies, uniform 'Library' series, cheap reprints of fiction and wedges of earnestly factual matter aimed at the self-improver and self-educator, such as the dense fortnightly instalments from the Society for the Diffusion of Useful Knowledge. Debate went back and forth higher up the social scale as to the utility or wisdom of spreading information among the lower ranks in this way, but this was beside the point: once mass production had begun, there was no effective means of stopping the circulation of reading material.

The railway bookstall thus became something of a cultural battleground. Unlike the ordinary bookshop, market stall or pedlar's tray, it could be licensed, supervised and controlled, and it played a part too in public perceptions of the soundness of the host company. But the railways themselves were slow to catch on. It took until 1841 for the first recorded bookstall to be set up, at the Fenchurch Street terminus of what was then the London & Blackwall Railway. Before the coming of the stalls, newspapers were simply hawked up and down the platforms. Early interventions from railway management in the running of bookstalls arose from the need to find fresh employment for railwaymen disabled in company service, or sometimes for widows of those fatally injured. The illiterate were not always excluded, so that some stallholders had no idea whether their wares were improving, harmless or disreputable. Nor did the earliest stalls always do a good job with their stock, which was set out 'in amicable jumble with beer-bottles, sandwiches, and jars of sweets', as one writer recalled in 1893. That the merchandise was on display for all to see, from bishop to barrow-boy, also brought home the horrid fact that many readers preferred material with a strong flavour of tripe. As *Punch* later put it:

> I bought from the stall at Victoria
> A horrible sixpenny story, a
> Book of a kind
> It pained me to find
> For sale at our English emporia.

Letters of protest started to appear in the papers. Meanwhile, the business was on the eve of reform.

A well-remembered article in *The Times* in Great Exhibition year catches the point of transition. Its author, Samuel Phillips, describes seeing two young women and a boy travelling first class, all engrossed for three hours by a green-covered volume of Eugène Sue, the French author of shock-horror novels of the underworld. Phillips remembers having seen a pile of such stuff at a station bookstall (just as perverse as if the refreshment rooms should be selling poison, he thought). He then tours the London termini, finding mostly 'unmitigated rubbish'. But Euston proves an exception: rubbish is unavailable there at any price, and the writer's request for something 'highly coloured' is answered by the offer of Kugler's eminently worthy *History of Painting*.

The names of the men who had made the difference at Euston are still familiar: William Henry Smith (1792–1865) and his son and partner, also William Henry (whence their company's original title, W. H. Smith &

Son). As it turns out, *The Times*'s man was friendly with the younger Smith – indeed, newspaper and newsagent were doing very nicely by one another at this period, Smiths paying an annual kickback of £4,000 in return for receiving *The Times*'s earliest copies for onward distribution. Phillips's piece probably therefore exaggerated the differences between the Euston offerings and the rest. (For example, Matthew Arnold spotted his impeccably serious new poem *Empedocles on Etna* on offer at Derby station bookstall in 1853, before Smiths took over there.) Even so, the story of the Smiths' rise is remarkable enough. Smith Snr had set up as a newspaper distributor in coaching days, achieving a near-monopoly of the trade out of London and switching his business to the railways as the network grew. In 1848 the partnership arranged with Mark Huish, the London & North Western Railway's formidable general manager, an exclusive lease on all the bookstalls along that line. A better choice of printed matter replaced the jumbled comestibles, and young men experienced in the book trade were recruited to replace any unsuitable employees. The stock was likewise purged of unrespectable material, for which reason Phillips called the younger W. H. Smith 'the North-Western missionary'. The company's reward was to discover or perhaps to help create a market in genuinely superior reading: Smiths' hot books of 1851 reportedly included Tennyson's latest, *In Memoriam*, books and pamphlets on current theological controversies, and the scientific tracts popular with skilled working men. 'Cheap literature is a paying literature, if judiciously managed': *The Times*'s conclusion shared the optimistic and expansive spirit of the Great Exhibition itself.

Other major lines licensed their stalls to the firm, culminating with the Great Western in 1863. In Scotland, the Smiths' business model was imitated by the Edinburgh bookseller John Menzies, starting with the 'stances' (the old Scots usage) at Perth and Stirling in 1857 and achieving a monopoly on lines north of the border within four years, as well as a wholesale and distribution trade to parallel Smiths' – a duopoly that ended only in 1998, when Menzies' retail chain was sold to its old English rival. Across the Irish Sea, Smiths' business flourished under the management of the English-born Charles Eason, only to be bought out by Eason in 1886. The circumstances of this sale were unusual. Smith Jnr had entered Parliament as the MP for Westminster (having defeated the philosopher and smokers' champion John Stuart Mill) and was subsequently appointed Chief Secretary for Ireland. A Conservative, Smith was opposed alike to Home Rule and the political influence of Catholicism in Ireland; but his business there also did a brisk trade in Catholic prayer books. Accused of hypocrisy, he responded by selling off the Irish division. So Eason's, not Smiths', became the household word for bookselling in Ireland, as it remains today.

For all *The Times*'s high-minded enthusiasm in 1851, price trumped quality in the long run. Stallholders soon found that bargain fiction sold best and, since their income included part of the turnover, what sold best found its way to the front. Smith Jnr – a devout man who in youth had hoped to enter the Church and who steadfastly refused to let his stalls trade on Sundays – was reportedly saddened at the appearance of his company's display at Rugby station, where the essays, poetry and science had been thrust out of sight behind the white of newsprint and the yellow covers of cut-price novels.

Those blocks of yellow were a sign of how the commodity of copyright fiction had changed since *The Times*'s visit in 1851. The old publishing model had fallen apart in the 1840s, when a price war over reprints pushed down the charge to the customer to as low as a shilling. That was the price of Murray's 'Reading for the Rail' series, advertised in 1852 as 'cheap books in large readable type'. Another of the victors was the house of George Routledge, whose green-covered *Railway Library* series likewise made a pitch to fill the empty hours spent in carriages and waiting rooms. Beginning with one of Fenimore Cooper's novels, the series eventually achieved 1,000 titles, non-fiction included, with an especially strong showing by the melodramatic historical tales and society novels of Edward Bulwer-Lytton. This author became a staple of Routledge's list thanks in turn to a cheerful act of piracy: a budget edition of *Uncle Tom's Cabin*, safely beyond the reach of American copyright law. *Uncle Tom* was *the* irresistible novel of the age, selling over half a million in one format or another; Routledge himself claimed to have witnessed six passengers all reading his bootlegged editions in a single compartment. So the money came pouring in, of which £20,000 went on the lease of thirty-five Bulwer-Lytton copyrights in 1854. The deal was as welcome to the foppish and extravagant novelist as it was profitable to Routledge, for Bulwer-Lytton proved to be Smiths' most popular novelist in terms of turnover.

W. H. Smith & Son drew the lesson, entering into alliance with a different publisher, Chapman & Hall, to produce the Select Library of Fiction. These were the first of the so-called 'yellowback novels': reprints priced at two shillings or half a crown, with shiny covers on which stimulating illustrations were commonly displayed. Chapman & Hall's star author was Charles Dickens, and the flourishing railway market had already spurred the firm to bring out a popular serial edition of their man at 1½d a part. To be taken under Smiths' wing, and to have their books distributed and displayed by the fastest-growing network within the market, was better still. The yellowbacks and kindred cheap editions did more than bring literature to an increasingly mobile public: they packaged it in instantly recognisable forms within a developing consumer marketplace.

The 1860s saw a new genre emerge from the ranks of fiction. It was a genre that contemporaries associated both with the demand for railway reading and with the acceleration of habits and experiences that the railway itself was thought to have fostered. These 'sensation' novels are epitomised by Wilkie Collins's *The Moonstone* (1860), Mrs Henry Wood's *East Lynne* (1861) and by a book already mentioned in another connection, *Lady Audley's Secret* by Mary Elizabeth Braddon (1862). The genre took over the best nerve-jangling conventions from the historical and 'Gothic' schools – legal conspiracies, false identities, secret passages, lunacy, poisoning – and transposed them to an explicitly contemporary world. This allowed an exhilarating acceleration of pace, with characters dashing about by train and messages flying still faster by the electric telegraph. There is no better example of this agitation than the mileage covered by the hero of *Lady Audley* as he whizzes along the tracks from the London termini, to Hull, to Liverpool, to Southampton, to rural Yorkshire or Essex; sometimes against the clock, or at night, or to follow a last-minute change of plan. Once, he happens to meet on the platform the bewitching Lady Audley herself – whose 'secret' encompasses insanity, actual and attempted murder and the desertion of her own child; he helps to install her in a compartment with unmistakable displaced eroticism, 'spreading her furs over her knees, and arranging the huge velvet mantle in which her slender little figure was almost hidden'. She is still speaking as the train begins to move, leaving him with a last glimpse of her 'bright defiant smile'. The railways feature too as a material agent as evidence mounts up against the Lady, in the shape of a bonnet box with 'scraps of railway labels and addresses pasted on it'. As in Dickens's writings, railways also figure in the text as quasi-metaphorical invaders of consciousness: another character faints after the sight of a shocking announcement in *The Times* induces the effect of 'a great noise as of half-a-dozen furious steam engines tearing and grinding in his ears'.

Sensation novels were often regarded with suspicion by higher-minded critics. The *Quarterly Review*'s Henry Mansel deplored the creation of a reading public of over-stimulated addicts, fed by railway bookstalls and circulating libraries. An essay of 1880 by Matthew Arnold swiped at 'cheap literature, hideous and ignoble of aspect, like the tawdry novels which flare in the book-shelves of our railway stations'. Ungrateful beneficiaries of these formats included the novelist Ouida, who in 1885 lamented the advance of 'hideous coloured-paper covers, and flaunting colours' at railway bookstalls. Meanwhile her publishers Chatto & Windus were shifting barrowloads of Ouida's own excitable novels of high life in bright two-shilling editions, each with an advertisement for Pears' soap on the back. A few steps downmarket in price and content were the 'rack-marketed' proto-pulp books of the 1880s and 1890s, written for immediate issue under pictorial covers, including detective yarns and the new genres of cowboy stories and science fiction. So it is surprising to find that Henry James, a writer whose depth and seriousness put him at the opposite pole, should have understood the importance of visual appeal, and could even look fondly on it: his 'Essay on London' of 1888 found W. H. Smith & Son's stalls at Euston or Paddington 'a focus of warmth and light in the vast smoky cavern; it gives the idea that literature is a thing of splendor, of a dazzling essence, of infinite gas-lit red and gold. A glamour hangs over the glittering booth, and a tantalizing air of clever new things.'

Gaudy colours should not be confused with scandalous contents. Smiths' railway contracts forbade the sale of obscene, indecent or offensive material, a provision that reflected a consensus among the educated classes. Outright pornography belonged to the nether world, but there was much else that was disreputable without being obscene or illegal; crime was often the focus, and titles such as the *Illustrated Police News* were refused by Smiths. In the mid-Victorian decades, political and religious questions as much as moral or sexual ones might determine where acceptable limits lay: had our traveller of 1862 requested a copy of the *National Reformer*, a radical new paper edited by the atheist and republican MP Charles Bradlaugh, he would have come away from Smiths' stall empty-handed. Distributors and retailers were also wary of anything that might prove libellous, given that the courts had yet to settle the boundaries of liability for damages. But literary history remembers a different episode of exclusion, in a manner which fingered Smiths as an example of high Victorian prudishness: the fuss in 1894 over *Esther Waters*, by the Anglo-Irish novelist George Moore.

Esther Waters was shocking as much for its themes – illegitimacy, illiteracy, gambling and destitution – as for the subversive sympathy of their handling. Yet the novel was a critical success, and even Mr Gladstone commended it in the *Westminster Review*. In practice, Smiths would supply a copy of *Esther Waters* to any customer who ordered one, but the company refused to display such a controversial title for general sale, or to add it to the stocklist of the company's lending libraries. For it was not necessary to buy a book from Smiths in order to read it: the nineteenth century was the great age of the private circulating library, and Smiths had joined the boom in 1860. Its model was the famous business set up by Charles Edward Mudie, which had operated from New Oxford Street in London since 1852. Mudie's standard subscription was a guinea per annum, allowing the loan of one volume at a time. This steep fee restricted membership to the genteel classes: Mudie's list reached a ceiling of 25,000, with branches in provincial cities and elsewhere in London. Material judged morally questionable was excluded, partly to respect subscribers' sensibilities, partly from Mudie's personal inclinations as a Nonconformist lay preacher and writer of hymns. W. H. Smith Jnr appears to have hoped that the senior firm would enter into collaboration, but was rebuffed. Smiths then set up a library of its own, with the same basic subscription rate, and a similar tenderness towards the feelings of their more upsettable members.

Loans from Smiths' had to be returned to the issuing stall, of which there were already 177 across the network by 1861. Patience was required from readers: shortage of space meant that many titles had to be ordered from catalogues and delivered (by train) for collection the following day – a nuisance for those travelling at short notice, but bearable for local subscribers, who came and went at the stalls as they would at any other shop. This customer profile applied to general sales as well: by 1906, 70 per cent of business at Smiths' stalls on one representative line came from non-travellers.

Smiths' bookstalls and the two major libraries together thus had a healthy share of the market. Its managers were bound by personal inclinations as well as by the terms of their licences to keep the stalls free of offensive matter. That was bad luck for George Moore: a *succès de scandale* might be all very well in itself, but any writer who was barred lost a wounding proportion of sales.

The Savoy magazine of 1896 was unlucky too. This was the effective successor to the scandalous quarterly *The Yellow Book*, with which it shared contributors including the sometimes genuinely obscene artist Aubrey Beardsley. The conviction of Oscar Wilde in the year before *The Savoy* was launched put anything with a hint of decadence under the direst suspicion, and Smiths announced after the third issue that the dubious magazine would henceforth be stocked no longer. *The Savoy* limped on for several more numbers, but the loss of access to the railway market shortened its commercial life.

In these circumstances, it is poignant to recall that the dénouement of Wilde's last and finest comedy, *The Importance of Being Earnest*, involves a fateful intersection between railways and fiction-writing. The foundling hero, abandoned as a baby in a handbag in the cloakroom for the Brighton line at Victoria station, learns his true identity only when his former nurse confesses that it was she who had absent-mindedly deposited him there – after which she had gone on her way, pushing the unpublished manuscript of her own three-volume novel ('of more than usually revolting sentimentality') in the pram instead.*

Mudie's Library, spiritual home of the morally unimpeachable three-volume novel, is mentioned in Wilde's play too. But the reference was already out of date, and once again it was the railway market that had triggered the change. For Smiths had never much cared for the venerable three-volume format, which took up excessive shelf-space in the library sections of its stalls, and had recently declared against it in letters sent out to key publishing houses. Mudie's joined Smiths in saying the same thing, for different reasons: increasingly, the shortening gap between first publication and first cheap edition was spoiling the second-hand market for its three-volume cast-offs. So that was the end of the three-volume novel, and Smiths' staff won a little more space on the lending shelves of their booths.

These bookstalls varied greatly in size, but stalls they remained, even at their largest extent: open-fronted timber affairs, at which much of the business depended on requests for items kept behind or under the counter, in racks high up, or securely displayed behind glass. They should not be confused with the walk-in, self-service shops of the later twentieth century. The working routines of these stalls, dependent as they were on cheap boy-labour for fetching, carrying and selling papers, would also be impossible

---

* Perhaps Wilde, the Irishman, remembered a still more explosive incident at the Brighton line cloakroom: in 1884 the structure was demolished by a Fenian bomb, deposited in an innocent-looking Gladstone bag.

in the modern labour market. That these unsophisticated structures could handle such a variety of daily, weekly and monthly publications, books for sale and for loan, stationery and postcards, travellers' rugs and straps and caps, is a tribute to the phenomenal powers of memory and organisation then expected from even quite junior employees. Another difference was the lack of heating; one Smiths clerk who wrote his memoirs recalled a gift of home-knitted mittens from an invalid lady subscriber to his library, who pitied his standing about in the cold all day long.

The working week suddenly became a warmer affair for many of Smiths' employees in 1905. Wrangles over licence levels and rates of return finally reached an impasse in that year, losing the company its pitches on the two biggest railways, Great Western and London & North Western. The 250 vacancies thus created went instead to Messrs Wyman, the Great Western's printing company. Undaunted, Smiths quickly opened new shops and lending libraries as close as possible to the vacated stations: 144 of them in eleven weeks, with more to follow. Suddenly, England had its first high-street bookshop chain.

In a small way, Smiths' exodus helped to loosen the grip railways had established over national life. Yet the enduring strength of the railway market for books should not be underestimated. It was the unimpressive offerings at the bookstall at Exeter station, scanned on the return to London from a weekend as the guest of Agatha Christie and her husband some time before 1934, that inspired the publisher Allen Lane to set up Penguin Books, the greatest British imprint of its time. The instantly recognisable orange-and-white covers of the early Penguins soon had blue-and-white companions in the non-fiction Pelican series, a name selected after Lane overheard a woman at King's Cross station bookstall asking vaguely for 'one of those Pelican books'. The first real Pelicans arrived in 1937, by which time the display at King's Cross would also have included the yellow jackets of Victor Gollancz's books, lettered in various typefaces and font sizes in black and magenta: a house style developed in the 1930s by the gifted typographer Stanley Morison (1889–1967). Gollancz, who detested pictorial book-jackets, wanted his own productions to use the most eye-catching colour possible. The final hue – as if in vindication of the old yellowback bindings – was selected after a reconnaissance tour of the bookstalls of London's railway stations.

Arnold and Gissing assumed that reading was an intrinsically passive activity, and that its proper field was broadly cultural and educational. In

The 'Wryteezy', 1890

this they were quite wrong. Other kinds of railway reading were necessary, often for reasons that had nothing to do with literature or learning. Newspapers remained the primary medium for information of every kind, commercial, legal and political, and in matters local, national and international. This information circulated via sales from railway station stalls, and through reading the contents on the trains themselves. Brokers, agents and farmers on their way to the exchange or the market could arrive better informed as to the going rates and prices achieved, and plan accordingly. Commercial travellers could keep an eye out for new customers, or for evidence of initiatives by rival concerns. Political agents and speakers on their way to meetings could discover what had most recently been said, and by whom, in the civic circles of their destination. Legal and business papers of every kind could be read through too, and noted and prepared for handover. Alaric Tudor, one of Trollope's *The Three Clerks* (1858), is put in his place on a shared railway journey by his colleague Mr Neverbend, who turns up at Paddington with an ostentatiously full despatch box. The contents include 'twenty-six pages of close folio writing' for the attention of Alaric, who had been looking forward to doing nothing very much during the long journey westward. But Trollope himself knew all about making the most of time on trains, as a prolific writer who worked for most of his adult life in the service of the General Post Office. As his *Autobiography* explained, he commissioned 'a little tablet' or portable writing desk:

> and found after a few days' exercise that I could write as quickly in a railway-carriage as I could at my desk. [...] In this way was composed the greater part of *Barchester Towers* and of the novel which succeeded it.* My only objection to the practice came from the appearance of literary ostentation, to which I felt myself to be subject when going to work before four or five fellow-passengers. But I got used to it ...

Another industrious Victorian, the architect George Gilbert Scott (1811–78), wrote most of his autobiography on railway journeys, in five leather-bound notebooks filled with spidery pencillings. This was on top of other written work; as Scott put it, 'pretty well all that I write is the product of my travelling hours'. These hours may be counted in the thousands: the most prolific architect of the age, his working day often included a dash from Westminster office to London terminus before many of the junior staff had even arrived. (A story that may be apocryphal tells of a telegraph message from Scott, sent from some provincial station to his own office: 'Why am I here?')

Many other livelihoods that entailed travelling were at once liberated and disciplined by the possibility of using railway time as an addition to work time. Basic correspondence could be dealt with from a railway seat and posted in letter boxes at stations along the way. These were provided in response to an order by the Post Office in 1849, a few years before the first pillar boxes were set up. The makers of the 'Wryteezy' railway writing desk, advertised in 1890, aimed at this market; strapped on to the forearm, the apparatus was steadied – supposedly – by a cord and hook attached to the luggage rack. A few Edwardian saloons even had little postboxes inside, the emptying and posting onward being looked after by railway staff. Sensing a valuable novelty, the London & North Western briefly introduced a typewriting service for businessmen on its City to City Express between Birmingham and London Broad Street. It serves as a reminder that the

---

* *The Three Clerks*, as it happens, and much also of others subsequent to them.

appropriation of travel time by work, and specifically by those categories of work that involve reading, writing and preparing text, is many generations old, for all that the new facilities offered by smartphones and wireless internet have extended its scope. Also, that this change was made first, and most fully, by the railways.

RISKS AND ANXIETIES

Railways provoked resentment or hostility in many ways, from their violations of natural beauty to their imposition of London time on unwilling towns and cities, from the physical challenges of travelling in their unheated and underlit carriages to their aiding and abetting the advance of trashy printed matter. Those who raised these objections did not necessarily put the railways under a general sign of condemnation: as with the internet in our own century, most people understood that the new technology came with its own risks and drawbacks, even as they enjoyed its benefits. But a deeper note sometimes sounded among the chorus of responses, suggestive of wider disquiet about what was happening to the world and the railways' share in this process.

We have met something of this kind in Thackeray's bittersweet lament for the 'praerailroad world' of his youth, whose apparent solidity had melted under the breath of steam. For a more searching indictment of the railways, the man to go to is John Ruskin (1819–1900). The greatest art critic of the age, as brilliant in the visual analysis of architecture as he was acute in describing the wonders of nature, Ruskin was driven by an implacable sense of moral purpose, rooted equally in profound religious commitment and in enormous and ultimately crushing personal unhappiness. In later life these impulses led him beyond his mission to expound art, history and culture, and into political economy and some highly individual attempts at social reform. By turns prophet, patron, artist, curmudgeon and crank, Ruskin today would seem a remote figure but for the continuing force of his charges against industrial capitalism for its false values, human costs and environmental destructiveness. In this respect, if no other, his closest cousin is that other scourge of his times, Karl Marx.

Ruskin found so much to loathe about railways, and so many ways of saying so, that it is difficult to know where to start. Not that his every reference was hostile – the thirty-nine volumes of his collected works include a level-headed paper on the merits of national ownership of the network, as well as a rhapsodic meditation on the locomotive's 'infinitely complex anatomy of active steel'. But he was ever alert to the penetration of the world by railways, and to any accusation of harm or degradation that could be laid at their door; old enough to have known how things used to be, he felt the change overwhelmingly in terms of loss.

A specimen charge-sheet can be had from Ruskin's *Fors Clavigera*. These 'Letters to the Workmen and Labourers of Great Britain' were issued mostly as monthly pamphlets in the years 1871–8, tackling social and economic questions along with much else, often with conscious hyperbole, paradox and provocation. In these pages the railways do not come off well. There is an exhaustive calendar of accidents and fatalities across the network during one month in 1873, lifted from the *Pall Mall Gazette*; a lament that the railways were severing age-old connections between producer and consumer, exemplified by changing traffic patterns for farmhouse butter; reminders of the vandalistic levelling of the keep of Berwick Castle to make way for the main line to Scotland, and of the invasion of the North Loch site beneath the castle rock at Edinburgh to build Waverley station; and an angry description of the harsh toil of a Worcestershire mother and daughter as they forged iron spikes for fixing rails to sleepers, working from seven till seven, the mother making a mere sixteen pence a day, 'or, for four days' work, the price of a lawyer's letter'.

Injury and death, alienation, destruction, exploitation; the examples could be multiplied and the connections traced outwards from the railways to Ruskin's critique of the social and economic order in which they were embedded. But his condemnation went further still, challenging the assumption that railway travel must be superior to the slower ways it replaced. Ruskin refused to bow to the idol of acceleration: for him, railway speed could only coarsen responses to the beauties of creation and the particularities of place, reducing life to a frenetic and meaningless dashing about. Each halting-place had become merely 'a new arrangement of glass roofing and iron girder'; a true lover of travelling should no more take the train than a devotee of the pleasures of the table should 'concentrate his dinner into a pill'.

Letter 69 of *Fors Clavigera* puts this case in detail. Much of the text recounts a day-long journey into Merionethshire from Ulverston, the main-line station closest to Ruskin's home on Coniston Water, made in the summer of 1876. Here is one of the most vivid and specific accounts of Victorian railway travel which has come down to us. Any such narrative is necessarily coloured by the writer's preoccupations and purposes, and no one should mistake Ruskin's text for pure reportage: there is too much anger in it, and too much pressure behind the words from the private, inadmissible distress which would tip him over into madness within another two years. Even so, it is exceptional in its freedom from the narrative priorities of fictional or satirical writing on the one hand, and the impersonal conventions of travel and guide-book writing on the other.

Things start tolerably enough: Ruskin 'took train first at the Ulverston station', sharing his compartment with a middle-aged man reading a newspaper, and choosing a 'corner' on the side which he knew would give the best views of Morecambe Bay. But at Grange-over-Sands, three stations on, fresh company arrived:

> ... two young coxcombs; who reclined themselves on the opposite cushions. One had a thin stick, with which, in a kind of St Vitus's dance, partly affectation of nonchalance, partly real fever produced by the intolerable idleness of his mind and body, he rapped on the elbow of his seat, poked at the button-holes of the window strap, and switched his boots, or the air, all the way from Grange to the last station before Carnforth, – he and his friend talking yacht and regatta, listlessly.

From his corner seat, Ruskin could observe both the world outside and his companions' indifference to it: 'Not one of the three ever looked out of the windows at sea or shore', where 'the tide lay smooth and silent along the sands; melancholy in absolute pause of motion'.

This first train terminated at Carnforth, where the Furness Railway handed over to the London & North Western. Here Ruskin noted a crowd of third-class passengers for whom no waiting room was provided, huddling into the platform shelter away from the rain. 'Lines of care, of mean hardship, of comfortless submission, of gnawing anxiety, or ill-temper, characterised every face.' When the up train arrived he found a first-class compartment all to himself, but was left wondering 'how long universal suffrage would allow itself to be packed away in heaps, for my convenience'. His solitude ended at Lancaster, where a father and daughter entered the carriage. They too read papers all the way. But as the rain persisted, reducing visibility to 'a mere wilderness of dirty dribblings' on the window glass, even Ruskin was compelled to take up reading for a while.

The next change of train was at Warrington, at the southern edge of Lancashire. Here Ruskin took a cup of tea and slice of bread in the refreshment room of the station, which had been rebuilt eight years before. His gaze was arrested by the painted glass panels in its swing doors: '... two troubadours, in broadly striped blue and yellow breeches, purple jackets, and plumed caps; with golden-hilted swords, and enormous lyres. Both had soft curled moustaches, languishing eyes, open mouths, and faultless legs.' Here was a naïve and blowsy display of bad art, perhaps derived at several removes from the historical fictions and poems of Sir Walter Scott that were Ruskin's favourite after-dinner reading, but appearing here at once out of place and out of time. And it was already a dictum of Ruskin's that a railway station, being 'the very acme of discomfort', was the worst place in which to be confronted by art. The same applied to ornamented architecture, good, bad or indifferent: as his treatise *Seven Lamps of Architecture* (1849) had it, 'Better bury gold in the embankments, than put it in ornaments on the stations.'

Onward from Warrington, by the Chester train; now with 'a middle-class person of commercial-traveller aspect' for company, equipped with a copy of *The Graphic*, an illustrated weekly. As the weather lightened, Ruskin found himself transfixed by 'a landscape more fresh and fair than I have seen for many a day, from any great line of English rail': the sandstone hills of Cheshire, with the estuarine sands of the Dee beyond and the greater hills of Wales on the horizon. But when Ruskin's attention turned back to the compartment, his companion was discovered with legs stretched out to the opposite cushions, boots resting on *The Graphic*, face 'clouded with sullen thought', indifferent to the beauties through which they were passing.

Another change at Chester, and another train, south to Ruabon in Denbighshire. Again Ruskin found himself sharing a compartment, this time with 'two cadaverous sexagenarian spinsters'. The pair had kept the windows all but shut, 'and were breathing the richest compound of the products of their own indigestion' – an unusually explicit reference to the hazards of railway travel in flatulent company. By way of relief, Ruskin pretended anxiety about their progress, first leaning out of the window as the train moved off, then, having cunningly left the window half-open, asking the ladies if they might remove their luggage from the seat 'that I might sit face to the air'. Outmanoeuvred, his companions huddled into the opposite corner 'to make me understand how they suffered from the draught'. Their retaliation was to produce a bag of grapes each and to throw the skins and pips out of Ruskin's open window.

Ruabon brought relief from the malodorous spinsters, at the cost of milder and more routine annoyances: 'a screwing backwards and forwards, for three-quarters of an hour, of carriages which one was expecting every five minutes to get into; and which were puffed and pushed away again the moment one opened a door, with loud calls of "Stand back there."' Then on, through 'puffs of petulant and cross-purposed steam', into the celebrated Vale of Llangollen, now with only a businessman and his inevitable newspaper for company. The man got out at Llangollen, discourteously leaving Ruskin to pull the compartment door shut; whereupon a *paterfamilias* of the lower middle class stayed his hand, and entered the carriage with his four fidgety children, their mother and aunt. The group stayed on as far as Corwen, 'past some of the loveliest brook and glen scenery in the world', although none of the family troubled to look at it. Finally, Ruskin was left alone for the run through to the coast at Barmouth, musing on 'the sense of his total isolation from the thoughts and ways of the present English people'.

'Total isolation', indeed; for all that Ruskin works to keep our sympathies, there are too many detailed imputations of motive and deductions of character on his journey, too many projected personal discontents, for all his conclusions to ring true. An earlier number of *Fors Clavigera* displays the habit of overstatement more blatantly. In it, Ruskin laments the condition of an imagined Coniston peasant who used to walk the twelve miles to market at Ulverston, but who now goes by train, via a branch line opened in 1859. That this new route took the long way round, making a big south-west swerve before returning east-north-east, only added to its offence against the natural order in Ruskin's eyes; and he proceeds to invent a narrative of 'absolute loss and demoralisation' for his puppet-victim, from his 'idle, dusty, stupid' state on the journey, to the waste of a shilling getting drunk on beer at the stations along the way, on top of the two shillings eaten up by the return fare.

No suggestion here that the railway might have liberated the man by allowing him to carry more goods to market, or to come back with more; or that the fatigue and exposure of walking in all weathers might not be morally good in themselves. Nor did Ruskin admit to his readers in 1876 that he had just commissioned his very own road coach, a real old-fashioned brougham made by a London firm, lined out in green and painted with his shield of arms. A happy month was spent dawdling up to Ruskin's Lakeland seat in the new vehicle, using the old coaching highways and arranging horses and a postilion to drive them by telegraphing in advance. It was in this unlikely vehicle that Ruskin arrived on 27 April at Sheffield, to press forward his plan to set up a museum for the benefit of working men. It was probably the same carriage that took him on his drive down to Ulverston station later that year, saving the walk which he so commended to the imaginary Coniston peasant. Sheffield was Ruskin's choice for his museum, incidentally, in part because the noble medieval churches at Lincoln, York, Durham, Selby, Fountains, Bolton and Furness were all within easy reach; the only feasible means of transport there and back may be guessed.

So there is plenty of ammunition with which to shoot down Ruskin as a nostalgic old hypocrite, framing rules for the guidance of lower orders while indulging the caprices of the rich (a month's journey by personal coach) and availing himself of the easy comforts of the age of steam (first-class trains to Wales). Yet *Fors Clavigera* makes some direct hits too. The habit of reading on the move brought into focus a broader sense that the railway passenger had become estranged from the passing landscape. Ruskin was not alone in raising this lament. R. S. Surtees set aside his professional interest as a novelist to grumble that 'a book to prevent people seeing the country [is] quite as essential as a bun to prevent their being hungry' (*Plain or Ringlets*, 1860). Even an artist with Pre-Raphaelite affinities, whose works were championed by Ruskin for their close observation of nature, might succumb to the habit: Ford Madox Brown's diary records a journey to Liverpool in 1856, spent entirely in reading Ralph Waldo Emerson's *English Traits*, hot off the press.

More broadly, rapid travel helped to make banal what had once been intensely felt. Speed itself, so thrilling when the railways were new, became routine, at least as far as the articulate and well-off class of traveller was concerned. As early as 1841, a London journalist referred wearily to 'the dull, monotonous railway'. Uniformity and passivity in travel went together: as Surtees put it in *Mr Facey Romford's Hounds* (1865), 'One journey is very much like another, save that the diagonal shoots across country are distinguished by a greater number of changes.' For *The Magazine of Art* in 1880, the average traveller now ignored the 'hurrygraphs' of the windows, 'framing picture after picture', and turned to them only for ventilation. The irresistible parallel is with air travel: at first glamorously exclusive and dizzyingly fast, but losing its sense of occasion or excitement with repetition, and subject to a similar standardisation of routines and physical settings. Any contemporary account by a Westerner that dwelt on the marvels and novelties of take-off, cruising speed and landing, not to mention the amazing littleness of the world as seen below, would seem merely naïve. Likewise, the breathless accounts of pioneering railway passengers quickly gave way to a sense of passive surrender and efficient despatch; as in Samuel Sidney's *Rides on Railways* (1851), where Coventry is reached in 'a whiz, a whirl, and a whistle'.

By the year 1851, a high level of literary skill was required if the railway experience was to be recreated with any freshness. Dickens knew this better than anyone, and his account in *Household Words* of a trip on the South Eastern Railway's new boat train service for Paris in the same year pulls out all the stops accordingly. Just give in to it all, he suggests: ride the wave of modernity, and you will be none the worse for having your ideas shaken up a bit. The loss of detail and clarity from the passing show, the new man-made landscape of cuttings and tunnels, stations and bridges, telegraph poles and wires – all these should be celebrated, not deplored. It is the sort of writing that once led Ruskin to describe Dickens privately as 'a leader of the steam-whistle party *par excellence*':

> Whizz! Dustheaps, market-gardens, and waste grounds. Rattle! New Cross Station. Shock! There we were at Croydon. Bur-r-r-r! The tunnel ... Bang, bang! A double-barrelled station! Now a wood, now a bridge, now a landscape, now a cutting, now a – Bang! a single-barrelled station – there was a cricket match somewhere with two white tents, and then four flying cows, then turnips – now, the wires of the electric telegraph are all alive, and spin, and blur their edges, and go up and down, and make the intervals between each other most irregular: contracting and expanding in the strangest manner.

These were the same wires that began to transmit the Greenwich time signal to Dover a year later, as described in Chapter 1; another shock to the sense of life lived according to the rhythms of nature. This world of railways and telegraphs was the only one that Ruskin's rail-borne fop, drawling of his yachts and regattas, had ever known; but Ruskin would have remembered how travellers from Lakeland used to make their way south, not via the Furness Railway's iron viaducts across the Kent and Leven estuaries, but by the ancient foot crossing of the shifting sands of Morecambe Bay; waiting not on the columns of Bradshaw's timetable, but on the ever-changing cycles of the tides.

The implications of such changes were immense. If nature was good for you – a view to which most people, then as now, would generally have subscribed in a fuzzy way – then it was hard to escape the suspicion that the railways' challenge to nature came at a price. Ruskin's journey into Wales presents the case chiefly in terms of moral and cultural damage or loss, within a broader critique of the assumptions of progressive capitalism. The majority learned to live with such things, making their own compromises with modernity and its conveniences. But what if railways were also bad for you *physically* – either from the cumulative effects of travel on body or mind or both, or from the brutal facts of injury or death?

₪

Kill passengers directly the railways certainly did, in accidents galore; and any exploration of the impact on health of travel by rail must start here. Death on the rails came in many forms. Trains ran into one another, especially before effective signalling existed to keep a safe interval between them. They ran away down inclines when their brakes or couplings failed. They were derailed by collisions with landslips, fallen objects, stray wagons or livestock, or as a result of a hundred different defects in locomotive, carriages or track. They flew off the rails when going too fast; they were mistakenly switched at high speed into sidings; they toppled from collapsing bridges. Locomotive boilers sometimes exploded like bombs.

As if that were not enough, passengers enlisted the railways in their own unmeaning self-destruction. Some slipped on the platform and fell under moving trains. Others bashed in their skulls against the sides of bridges, tunnels or telegraph poles by leaning too far out from the carriage windows, like the sailor on leave who was found dead and alone in the second-class compartment of a Plymouth mail train in 1862. Some jumped fatally from the carriage in pursuit of dropped parcels or blown-off hats. Others could not resist the same impulse when passing through some conveniently placed station, like the old man on the Norfolk Railway in 1854, who made a mortal leap as a returning excursion train sped past his home platforms at Brundall.

As more trains ran and their speeds increased, the number of significant accidents rose too. Eleven years elapsed between Huskisson's solitary death in 1830 and the disaster at Sonning on the Great Western. By contrast, the worst accident in our representative year 1862 – fifteen dead in a head-on collision in the cutting at Winchburgh, on the Edinburgh & Glasgow Railway – would have evoked responses of dismaying familiarity. The standard history of British railway accidents, L. T. C. Rolt's *Red for Danger* (1955), passes over the Winchburgh smash in a single sentence, reserving full descriptions for two operationally more interesting disasters from the year before: a pile-up and fire in Clayton Tunnel, just outside Brighton (twenty-one dead), and a collision and derailment at Kentish Town in the week following (seventeen dead). According to the *Penny Illustrated Paper*'s summary, seventy passengers altogether met accidental deaths in 1861, thirty-eight in collisions, four in derailments, four because of axle failures or similar mishaps and eighteen getting on or off moving trains.

Passenger fatalities were only part of the story. The *Penny Illustrated Paper* also recorded that seventy-one members of the public were fatally cut down by trains in 1861, of whom seventeen were on level crossings and the rest were trespassing – to say nothing of the railway workers who met similar fates. The popular appetite for affecting circumstances and horrible details ensured that many such deaths received full press attention. A young woman killed at the crossing at Whittlesford in 1847 had her memorial in the *Cambridge Independent Press*: she and a companion stepped across too quickly after a train had passed on the nearer line, failing to notice that another was bearing down in the opposite direction on the line beyond. After the impact, her companion set off down the line, accompanied by some of the station staff. 'The first object that attracted attention was a bonnet, and one of the porters lifting it the head of the poor girl fell out ...'

Matters got worse. The Parliamentary Papers for 1860–64 reported an annual average of fifty-three accidents to trains, freight and goods included. For 1870–74, that figure stood at 145 per annum. By the years

An accident at Warrington on 29 June 1867, from the *Illustrated Police News*. Anxieties about railway travel were both mirrored and exploited by the press, here merging collision and aftermath in a single image

1867–71, the industry was paying compensation for passenger deaths and injuries at an annual average of £324,474, close to 1.8 per cent of the entire revenue from the same traffic.

In a century coming painfully to terms with the causes and consequences of epidemic disease, insanitary living conditions and dangerous working practices, the risk of accidental death while travelling on the railway was statistically trivial. A passenger's odds against being killed on any single journey were calculated with nice exactitude at 6,998,885 to 1 by W. F. Mills, who analysed the Board of Trade figures for 1841–65 in *The Railway Service* (1867). In terms of mishaps per passenger-mile, the railways also became safer with each passing decade, as the rising frequency of accidents lagged behind the growth in traffic on the ever-expanding network. Thus the train-mileage travelled on the network grew by 180 per cent between 1861 and 1888, an increase far larger than that for accidents incurred.

But statistics are one thing, perceptions quite another, and the diminishing intervals between serious mishaps inevitably surrounded the railways with an aura of peril. Lesser incidents were widely reported too, often in multiple; *The Times* for 27 September 1873 rounded up five together, under the weary heading 'Friday's railway accidents'. To this drip-feed of bad news should be added the sense of uneasy self-surrender to a technology of immense and unpredictable power; for the railway passenger was required to submit to a condition of passivity and powerlessness unknown to the pedestrian or equestrian. Even a passenger on a steamship could expect some warning of danger, and could cling to the hope of escape or rescue from a foundering vessel. Things were different for those boxed helplessly within a railway compartment. For many, it was impossible to shake off the unpleasant idea that a trivial equipment failure or a momentary mistake on the part of a distracted or overworked railwayman could bring about violent extinction in a matter of seconds. Any exceptional noise or jolt while travelling triggered its own pulse of fear. For the author of a report published by *The Lancet* in 1862, unease was the prevailing condition of the average railway traveller: '... everyone knows how, if by chance a train stops at some unusual place, or if the pace be slackened, or the whistle sounds its shrill alarm, a head is projected from almost every window, and anxious eyes are on the look-out for signs of danger'.

Sanguine travellers found such alarmism easy to mock. The *Penny Illustrated Paper*'s joky investigation of a second-class compartment in the same year included a representative Old Lady, for whom the buffeting from a train whizzing in the opposite direction is an agony, 'and some time elapses before she can be persuaded that a dreadful accident has not happened and everybody is crushed'. The humorists of *Punch* took a less blasé view, consistently exaggerating the dangers of railway travel and watching keenly for evidence of carelessness or indifference on behalf of the companies and their staff. From the magazine's cartoons, an impressionable reader in a remote, rail-less land might have concluded that a railway journey safely ended was the exception rather than the norm. Two examples: complacent passengers queue at the ticket-office window, manned by a grinning skeleton in a railway uniform cap; no dialogue ('There And (Not) Back!', 1878). A grimly smiling undertaker accosts a passenger on the platform: 'Going by this train, sir? ... Allow me, then, to give you one of my cards' ('Railway Undertaking', 1852).

Another favourite theme was the alleged link between the frequency of accidents and the lack of personal liability of the railway directorate for the resulting losses, injuries or deaths. *Punch* cartoons of 1853 and 1857 ('The Patent Safety Railway Buffer') depicted railway directors strapped to their own locomotives, as if anything less would be insufficient to ruffle their complacency. This attitude reflected the magazine's own radical edge in its early years, under the editorship of Douglas Jerrold, whose boisterous politics and rejection of deference were closer in spirit to the early *Private Eye* than to the later stereotype of middle-aged, pipe-and-slippers humour. The demand that senior figures should accept greater individual responsibility is also a reminder that the separation of ownership, management and everyday operation on the railways was something new (more on this in Chapter 14). Like the method of travel itself, these structures of power and control introduced by the railways were an affront to time-honoured ideas of what was normal and natural.

Punch's cartoons provide a sort of satirical correlative to the steel-engraved depictions of collisions and derailments in the rest of the press, such as the *Illustrated London News*. Accounts of accidents and disasters thus became caught up in the wider circulation of information and imagery which the railways themselves fostered. For the spectacle of a railway disaster had its own unique power. Ships foundered all the time – the *Shipping and Mercantile Gazette* counted 2,029 wrecks for 1861 – but the worse the wreck, the greater the chance that no living soul would remain to tell the tale. Train crashes almost always delivered scenes of stunning disorder, as well as plenty of witnesses and survivors.

It was as well to be prepared, then, and the innovative culture of Victorian capitalism was ready to help. First, the legal position in England and Wales was transformed by the Fatal Accidents Act of 1846, which established the right to claim damages by relatives of those killed as a consequence of the failings of others. The Act opened the way for the Railway Passengers Assurance Company, established in 1849. There was a touch of genius in the way its policies were sold: they could be had at railway booking offices, exactly like any other ticket, which they resembled in shape and size. An element of commission on sales kept the railways happy, and the assurance company also reached an agreement with the Exchequer that tax would be levied only on its premiums – to spare the booking-office clerks the complexities of stamp duty every time an insurance ticket was sold. These were priced at 3d for a first-class journey, initially paying a £3,000 life premium, 2d for second class, paying £500, and a penny for third class, paying £200. (Thus the maximum return per penny was much higher in first class, where the risks of injury or death were substantially less than on the cramped benches of the cheaper carriages.) Lesser premiums were

The old lady is supposed (after a great effort) to have made up her mind to travel, just for once, by one "of those new fangled railways," and the first thing she beholds on arriving at the station, is the above most alarming placard.

Travel insurance as an unwelcome reminder of risk, from *Punch*, 1850.
The handbell, right, rings to announce an imminent departure

paid for injuries. Charges were the same regardless of distance travelled, leaving the passenger to decide whether a particular trip was long enough to justify the outlay.

Success was immediate; in the first nine months of 1850, over 113,000 insurance tickets and policies were sold. Compensation was paid to the first beneficiary a little earlier, on 10 November 1849, when William Good of Dunstable received 7s 6d in respect of an accident north of Preston. Within a few years the company had acquired powers to issue general accident insurance, followed by liability insurance for employers and public bodies.

Its advertisements appeared in Bradshaw's pages well into the twentieth century, under the proud boast 'The oldest Accident Assurance Company in the World'. Which was true enough: all of these policy types were quite new.* So Britain's railways were the midwife at the birth of the entire modern system of insurance against accident and liability. The very concept of insurance must also have been popularised and demystified by the availability of short-term, fuss-free policies that could be had for a few pence.

Precautions of a physical nature were not so tidily arranged. The practice of bodily protection against accident never took off; the 'inflated railway caps' listed in the *Great Exhibition Catalogue* were probably meant for comfort rather than security (and what can they have looked like?). The idea was spoofed by *Punch* in 1876 with a cartoon showing two travellers trussed up in grossly padded safety outfits ('Patent First-Class Costume for the Collision Season'), like fat-suits from a theatrical wardrobe. As often in *Punch*, the image was topical: this issue is dated three days after the Radstock collision on the Somerset & Dorset Joint Railway, then a hard-up and exceptionally badly run line (fifteen dead).

Other, less drastic measures could be taken. Anyone who thought about the matter could work out that neither the very front nor the very back of the train was a promising place in which to sit out a collision ('Never heard of a middle carriage of a train getting smashed up, to speak of,' someone says in F. E. Anstey's *Vice Versa*); indeed, by the end of the century it was common to find the foremost compartment of the train locked out of use. In the event of a collision, the *Railway Traveller's Handy Book* pointed out the advantage of sitting opposite an unoccupied, well-upholstered first-class seat – class distinctions even in catastrophe. The book also noted that hard, sharp-brimmed hats had inflicted 'severe and fatal wounds' on their own wearers in cases of accident, and should therefore be taken off when in motion. Other advice, such as the exact posture to be adopted when jumping from an overturning carriage, presumed a greater presence of mind than most travellers would have been able to muster. More helpfully, the book pointed out that some accidents were preceded by 'a kind of bouncing or leaping of the train', by way of forewarning.

This was the experience of Augustus Hare (1834–1903), the

---

*Close behind the RPAC was the Accidental Death Indemnity Association, also founded in 1849 and renamed the Accidental Death Insurance Company the year after.

biographer, memoirist and travel writer, during a boyhood journey on the
Great Western on 17 June 1845. Hare's party seem to have been using one
of the subdivided compartments of the company's broad-gauge carriages,
as described in Chapter 2. As the train approached Slough, his little cousin
Lucebella asked to be held up to see if the flag was flying above Windsor
Castle.

> At that moment there was a frightful crash, and the carriage dashed
> violently from side to side. In an instant the dust was so intense that
> all became pitch darkness. 'For God's sake put up your feet and press
> backwards; I've been in this before,' cried Lord S., and we did so. In
> the other compartment all the inmates were thrown violently on the
> floor, and jerked upwards with every lurch of the train. If the darkness
> cleared for an instant, I saw Lea's set teeth and livid face opposite
> [Mary Lea, Augustus's nurse] ... After what seemed an endless time,
> the train suddenly stopped with a crash ... Instantly a number of men
> surrounded the carriage. 'There is not an instant to lose, another train
> is upon you, they will not be able to stop it,' – and we were all dragged
> out and up the steep bank of the railway cutting.

Hare's memory of receiving help as soon as the train stopped appears to
corroborate *The Times*'s report that the guards travelling on the outside of
the train escaped serious harm. The paper also noted that the uninjured
passengers included the Great Western's own chief engineer Mr Brunel
and his traffic superintendent Seymour Clarke. There were no fatalities,
nor was the derailment thought worth mention in the Great Western's
official history. The same is true of biographies of Brunel, whose crowded
life included closer brushes with death: tumbling into an uncovered
water tank (1827), almost drowning when the Thames Tunnel excavations
flooded (1828), falling from a fire-damaged ladder into the engine room
of the burning SS *Great Western* (1838), swallowing a sovereign while per-
forming a conjuring trick, then undergoing a tracheotomy before it could
be got out (1843). A non-fatal derailment was small beer.

It is striking too that 'Lord S.' (William Thomas Eardley-Twisleton-
Fiennes, 9th Baron Saye and Sele) had already endured a railway accident,
and knew how to brace his body rather as modern airline passengers are
instructed to do. For the roll-call of deadly accidents was shadowed by
a much longer list of Slough-style mishaps, which in turn shaded into

the daily fusillade of jolts, bangs and shocks inflicted when trains ran less smoothly than they should. The thousands who were caught up in accidents large or small would each have had a tale to tell; in addition, every press report generated its own ripples of anxiety. *The Railway Traveller's Handy Book* could only caution against unnecessary self-vexation by thoughts of catastrophe. The book also pointed out that pestering the guard with nervous questions might bring only 'ambiguous and evasive replies' – possibly making matters worse.

Those nervous of railway travel included the sovereign herself. The intrepid Albert had taken a train at the earliest opportunity, travelling up to London from Slough on the Great Western on 14 November 1839, at the end of his visit to Windsor to initiate the royal courtship. Eager for the full royal warrant, the GWR built a special carriage with furnishings and decorations *à la* Louis quatorze in 1840, the year of the royal wedding. Albert used this vehicle for further travels, as did Victoria's widowed aunt Queen Adelaide. Finally, Albert persuaded his young queen to follow his example, and she took to the rails from Slough to London on 11 June 1842. This endorsement was enormously important; now the court would travel by train too.

Thereafter railways became a routine part of Victoria's life, allowing her to write and conduct business while in motion, and permitting a measure of public display at stations and along the line when the carriage blinds were raised. After Albert's death her progresses became more regular, and tens of thousands of miles were traversed on long-distance runs between Windsor, Deeside (for Balmoral) and Gosport (for sailing to Osborne). But the Queen remained anxious about speed, and a limit of 40 mph was supposed to apply throughout – a rule reminiscent of her neurotic horror of overheated rooms, for which fifteen degrees Celsius was the upper limit. When Victoria suspected that the train was going too fast, she made her feelings known. (Things changed as soon as the reign was over: Victoria's funeral train from Gosport ran very smartly, so much so that her grandson the Kaiser is reported to have sent an equerry to congratulate the driver of the purple-draped locomotive on arrival at London.) In other words, like many ordinary travellers, she never quite lost her mistrust of the railways. Unlike them, she also had the option of writing letters in the following vein – sent from Balmoral to her least favourite prime minister on 3 October 1873 – with the expectation of receiving an unusually considered reply:

The Queen must again bring most seriously & earnestly before Mr
Gladstone & the Cabinet the vy alarming and serious state of the
railways. Every day almost something occurs & every body trembles
for their friends & for every one's life ... There *must* be fewer Trains, –
the speed must be lessened to enable them to be stopped easily in case
of danger & they must keep their time.

Even taking up a novel for distraction risked further shocks. Death in a
railway accident, or under the wheels of a train, was a plot device too useful to waste, lying in wait as a nasty surprise for the susceptible reader in
works by Dickens, Trollope, Gissing, Wilkie Collins, Mrs Humphry Ward,
Elizabeth Gaskell and Mary Elizabeth Braddon ('... masses of shattered
woodwork and iron heaped in direful confusion upon the blood-stained
snow', etc.; *Henry Dunbar*, 1864). Not even Lewis Carroll's Alice escaped:
her railway journey in *Through the Looking-Glass* dissolves in fright and
confusion when the engine and carriage rear up to jump a brook.

Yet the striking fact remains that those killed while travelling on Britain's railways before 1914 included nobody of particular celebrity. Huskisson remained the star name on a thoroughly humdrum bill of mortality.
A list of notable victims from later accidents illustrates the point. Among
the titled classes, no dukes, marquesses, earls or viscounts, only an Irish
peer, the 7th Baron Farnham (1868, Abergele, collision and fire), with Sir
Nicholas Chinnery, 3rd Baronet, and his lady (the same), and also Sir John
Anson, 2nd Baronet (1873, Wigan, derailment). Among the clergy, Archdeacon Freeman of Exeter (1875), William Cureton, canon of Westminster
(1864), the Rev. Theodosius Hathaway, minister of the Floating Church at
Greenwich (1868), and the clerical headmasters of Horncastle and Loughborough grammar schools (1854 and 1862 respectively); but no archbishop
or bishop, or even so much as a dean. Among the professions, Judge William Boteler, 'foremost authority of his day on the Law of Tithe' (1845),
Joseph Carpue, surgeon and anatomist (1846), Thomas Grainger, railway
engineer (1852), William Baly, epidemiologist and Physician Extraordinary
to Queen Victoria (derailment at Wimbledon, 1861). Among figures from
the arts, Robert Brough ARSA, painter of promise, a follower of John Singer
Sargent (1905, Cudworth, collision). Among the upper business classes,
James Gibbs, one of the Great Western's own directors, on his way to a board
meeting (derailment, 1853), Charles Mitchell, publisher of the first British
press directory (1859), and Henry Hoare, banker (Great Eastern Railway,

1866) – though Hoare brought mortal injury on himself, leaning too far out of the window as the train emerged from the Audley End Tunnel.

It is no disrespect to the memory of the dead, or to their sufferings before the end, to point out that these names have not made enduringly large claims on the attention of posterity. Even at the time, it is unlikely that many outside their immediate circles knew who they were – though the death of one of her physicians on a railway journey cannot have helped Queen Victoria's nerves. And even this list is padded out with those who died from lingering injuries, some of whom – Henry Hoare was one – survived for more than a year after injury, thus relieving the railways from legal liability for their deaths.

One famous name has so far been omitted. He was not native-born, nor did he meet his end in Britain, but in a marshalling yard in Canada. Nor was he even human. This was Jumbo the mighty bull elephant, born in the Sudan and killed by a locomotive shunting at St Thomas, Ontario in 1885, after the management at London Zoo had sold him on to Phineas T. Barnum's travelling show. Even Huskisson is now remembered above all for the manner of his death, but Jumbo is remembered for being Jumbo, which in a way is a sign of greater celebrity.

₪

It could have been very different. At the end of *Our Mutual Friend* (1865), Dickens supplied his readers with a 'Postscript, in lieu of a preface', telling of his escape from a 'terribly destructive accident' on the South Eastern Railway on 9 June of that year. He had with him part of the manuscript of the novel, which was retrieved from his carriage, 'soiled, but otherwise unhurt', once he had done what he could to help others. 'I remember with devout thankfulness than I can never be much nearer parting company with my readers for ever than I was then.'

This was no exaggeration: of Dickens's fellow passengers on the 2.38 p.m. boat train from Folkestone, ten failed to survive that day. The accident happened at a low viaduct at Staplehurst in Kent, which was undergoing repairs. These required the removal of the rails at the eastern end, so that the train came off the track just as it began to cross the viaduct. The locomotive and the first two carriages came safely to a halt, but the following seven carriages overturned into the little valley some ten feet below. The novelist was in the last carriage that stayed on the bridge.

The Staplehurst accident came about through a fatal conjunction of lax working practices and simple human error. Before the construction of deep-water harbours, the Channel boat trains ran on flexible schedules determined by the tides. On the day in question the foreman of the repair gang had looked up the wrong page of the timetable and was not expecting the train until two hours later. His mistake in itself should not have caused a crash; the rulebook also required a man with a red flag to be posted 1,000 yards from the obstruction, as well as the placing of fog signals (small detonators, exploded by the wheels of the train) by way of extra warning. But on this occasion the flagman had walked barely more than half the correct distance, which in turn gave the driver only enough time to halve his estimated approaching speed of 50 mph. Even then, all might have been well had the train guards heard his warning whistle and applied the carriage brakes; but they did not.

Dickens's response was heroic. The derailed carriage went onwards for some distance, 'beating the ground as the car of a half emptied balloon might', before tilting over. Finding himself unharmed, he asked his companions to stay calm and made his way out of the window, uncertain at first whether the carriage might topple over to join the others. He next saw two guards running distractedly up and down on the bridge and asked them if they recognised him ('We know you very well, Mr Dickens'). They supplied him with a key to the doors of his carriage, so that he could organise the release of the passengers. He then retrieved a flask of brandy and a travelling hat from his own compartment, filled the hat with water from the stream in the valley bottom and set to work.

What followed is distressing to read. Dickens first encountered a man staggering, with 'such a frightful cut across the skull that I couldn't bear to look at him'. He rinsed the man's face, gave him some water and some brandy to drink and laid him on the grass by the stream, where he said only 'I am gone,' and shortly died. Next, a woman lying with her head against a tree, with a leaden-coloured face, over which blood was running 'in a number of distinct little streams'; Dickens gave her brandy also, but when he next passed she too was dead. A man who had just married was looking for his wife; a witness described how Dickens 'led him to another carriage and gradually prepared him for the sight. No sooner did he see her corpse than he rushed round a field at the top of his speed, his hands above his head, then dropped fainting.' It was easier to help the seventeen-year-old Edward Dickenson (the parallel of surnames is poignant). The

'Among the dying and the dead': Dickens at the Staplehurst
accident in 1865, as imagined by the *Penny Illustrated Paper*

sole survivor from his wrecked carriage, he was sent to convalesce at the
hotel at Charing Cross station, where his rescuer visited him several times.
Never one to do things by halves, Dickens also made the patient one of his
Christmas guests that year.

Much of this detail comes from Dickens's letters, especially that to
Thomas Mitton, his old friend and sometime solicitor. Around twenty-
five more letters survive from the aftermath of the crash, some of them dictated, most of them brief and almost all repeating variations on the phrase
that he had 'worked some hours among the dying and the dead'. Short or
long, Dickens's accounts of the accident are evasive in one essential respect:
he was not journeying alone, but with his mistress of seven years' standing, the actress Ellen Ternan, and her mother. The three were returning
from France, where it appears that Dickens had been maintaining the Ternans in a clandestine ménage near Boulogne. His public image as a happy

family man had been a fiction since 1858, when he separated from his wife Catherine. The Dickens household at Gad's Hill in Kent was kept together after that by Catherine's sister, Georgina Hogarth. All this was handled in the accident letters extremely obliquely: 'Two ladies were my fellow-passengers', as if they had been sharing the compartment by chance. Even the account to Mitton of the words exchanged between the trio when the end seemed near managed to avoid making the relationship explicit.

As if the accident and its aftermath were not enough, the Staplehurst disaster therefore exposed Dickens to other dangers. He had always basked in recognition – even after the smash, he invited as much from the guards of his stricken train – and he enjoyed the privileges of fame, making sure to show his delighted appreciation by way of return. Railway journeys were no exception. On an earlier Channel crossing, a telegraph message was sent ahead to Dover to hold the train until the great man arrived. Later in life, he reportedly returned from Edinburgh via the East Coast main line in a royal saloon, procured after the General Manager of the North British Railway telegraphed to London. When it arrived, the manager obligingly equipped the carriage with bedding and furniture from his own home, ready for its celebrity passenger. Now this fame was suddenly a liability, as Dickens confronted the prospect of public testimony at the inquest, and the risk that his name would become explicitly linked with that of the Ternans. As he made clear to Mitton, he wished neither to speak in public concerning the day's events, nor to turn it into material for publication (which did not stop the *Penny Illustrated Paper*'s artist depicting the wreckage with Dickens centre stage, hat full of water, tending to an insensible young woman). Even before the letter to Mitton was composed, Dickens had written to the stationmaster at Charing Cross in the hope of recovering jewellery lost by Ellen on the day of the accident, one item of which was engraved with her name; valuable articles, no doubt, but – the thought must have crossed his mind – more precious still to a blackmailer. Altogether the accident was a blow on the fault-line of his later life, threatening to shatter it in pieces.

The cover-up succeeded. Dickens escaped having to testify in court, and the relationship with Ellen remained the knowledge of a small and discreet circle. So matters rested until the 1930s, a good time for unfrocking and debagging Victorian heroes, and today the story of Ellen ('Nelly' to Dickens) is central to the understanding of the novelist's later life, work and imagination.

Sometimes missing from this picture is a sense of how utterly this double life depended on the railway. Other men from Dickens's circle who kept mistresses, such as his fellow-novelist Wilkie Collins, maintained separate establishments within walking distance. Dickens, recognisable everywhere, had to be less blatant. The installation of the Ternans in France, within reach of the Channel crossing, made sense within Dickens's manically busy schedule of writing, speeches, readings, theatricals and conviviality only because the train could get him quickly there and back. His description of the fast new service to France in 1851, well before Nelly entered his life, concludes by 'blessing the South Eastern Company for realising the Arabian Nights in these prose days'. Had the little party at the company's Folkestone station fourteen years later happened to choose a carriage further down the train, these words would now seem cruelly inapt. As it was, Dickens's relationship with the South Eastern Railway had to continue – it owned the line to Higham in Kent, the station for Gad's Hill. But the French connection shortly ended, after he rented a cottage for Nelly at Slough early in 1866. Now there were two more railways in the picture: the Great Western, with its main line to the West, and the London & South Western. The pair vied for the traffic from royal Windsor, a shortish walk from Slough; both companies had opened branch lines there as soon as the Queen had allowed.

How Dickens arranged his journeys to spend time with Nelly was reconstructed by the actor Felix Aylmer in *Dickens Incognito* (1959), from cryptic references in a pocket engagement diary for 1867. Outward travel was usually by evening train on the Great Western, direct to Slough. For the return, Windsor station and the South Western were favoured, as if to create the impression that the novelist's business had been somewhere in that town. The route brought Dickens in to London at Waterloo, which was also much closer to his office and apartment off the Strand.

These movements were enmeshed with the other great preoccupation of Dickens's last years: the reading tours. Starting in 1866, he went from city to city across the British Isles (and, once, to the United States), declaiming comic or dramatic episodes from his fiction, always to packed houses. The tours were extremely lucrative, and Dickens relished the connection with his public. That much is clear from the memoirs of George Dolby, the manager of the tours, published in 1885. But the memoirs also show how badly Dickens had been affected by the ordeal at Staplehurst. He was grinding himself down, and it was the railways as much as anything that were responsible.

The two men's first journey together, heading north from Euston, made the situation clear. At first the atmosphere in the compartment was stilted: Dickens, Dolby and a male companion read the newspapers, and not much was said. Things improved after the stop at Bletchley, where Dickens explained that his anxious and nervous state was due to the Staplehurst accident.

> He never, he explained, had travelled since that memorable day [...] without experiencing a nervous dread, to counteract which in some degree he carried in his travelling bag a brandy flask, from which it was his invariable habit, one hour after leaving his starting-point, when travelling by express train, to take a draught ...

Other railway episodes remembered by Dolby were not so bad. They often travelled in style; their private saloon on a trip to Scotland in May 1866 featured baskets of food and tableware, salmon mayonnaise, pressed beef and cherry tart, iced gin punch and coffee made on a spirit lamp. Mishaps that might have tested a less resourceful man were taken by Dickens in his stride. A pipe burst on the locomotive as the train passed through Northumberland; they took a pleasant walk in the woods alongside the line until the relief engine turned up. Once, their carriage caught fire (an overheated axle-box seems indicated) and had to be substituted at Rugby. On the way to Holyhead for the Irish crossing, their train stuck in a snowdrift at Bangor for four freezing hours while the locomotive was dug out. Delays such as these seem not to have put Dickens on edge; rather, it was the routine exposure to express travel, hour after hour, that made him uneasy. On 26 January 1867 he wrote to *The Times* to protest at 'the reckless fury of the driving and the violent rocking of the carriages' on that morning's express from Leicester, which had so disturbed him that he got off at Bedford rather than continue through to St Pancras (letters followed from fellow passengers, three of them in support; another claimed to have been reading one of Dickens's own books all the way 'in greatest comfort'). After going north in the same year, Dickens complained to Dolby of the effects once again, 'constantly referring to the Staplehurst accident, which was ever in his mind'. His nervousness improved after they began to take slower trains instead, but the practice had to be dropped, 'as the delay and the monotony of these journeys were almost worse than the shaking of the expresses'. Touring again in 1868, Staplehurst 'seemed to recur to him with increased horror'.

Dolby also tells of another serious accident, sometimes overlooked by biographers. Leaving Belfast on the midday mail train on 16 January 1869,

> we received a severe jolt which threw us all forward in the carriage. Looking out we observed an enormous piece of iron flying along a side line, tearing up the ground and carrying some telegraph poles with it. The breaks [*sic*] were suddenly applied, a lumbering sound was heard on the roof of the carriage, and the plate-glass windows were bespattered with stones, gravel, and mud ... Possibly having the recollection of the dreadful Staplehurst accident in his mind, Mr Dickens threw himself to the bottom of the carriage, and we all followed his example.

A tyre on the locomotive's driving wheel had fractured, turning instantly to giant pieces of shrapnel. The noise on the carriage roof was caused by the impact of one of these fragments. It happened that the compartment was of the coupé type sometimes provided in the earlier Victorian decades, essentially a half-compartment with a single row of seats facing a generously glazed end wall. Dolby could only wonder how they would have fared if the steel fragment had shot through the glass and into their midst. A few months later, Dickens was taken ill at Preston while on yet another tour, and his doctors ordered a long rest, blaming his condition on the reading circuits and the 'long and frequent railway journeys' that made them possible.

Dolby's fortunes depended on keeping the show on the road. His memoirs stress the novelist's powers of recuperation and his exhilaration in performance, never admitting that the demands of touring were slowly killing him. It is true that Dickens's energy was prodigious; his walking speed was once calculated at 4½ mph. The author Cuthbert Bede recalled talking to him at a railway station: 'During the whole of the time we were pacing up and down the long platform – for he seemed to be one who could not stand still, but must keep moving.' This impatience no doubt helps to explain the reversion to the use of expresses, after the experiment with slower trains. Nor had Dolby known Dickens before the Staplehurst accident. It is in accounts by others, including the man himself, that the depths of his psychic disturbance become clear.

After the burst of activity at the accident scene, Dickens had succumbed to a period of shock, 'weak as if I were recovering from a long illness'. Also, as he put it in a letter later that month, 'I cannot bear railway travelling yet. A perfect conviction, against the senses, that the carriage is down on one side ... comes upon me with anything like speed, and is inexplicably distressing.' Mary ('Mamie') Dickens, who sometimes accompanied her father back to Gad's Hill from London, would witness him

> suddenly fall into a paroxysm of fear, tremble all over, clutch the arms of the railway carriage, large beads of perspiration standing on his face, and suffer agonies of terror. We never spoke to him, but would touch his hand gently now and then. He had, however, apparently no idea of our presence; he saw nothing for a time but that most awful scene.

Yet he pressed on with his divided existence, train after train, between Gad's Hill, London, Slough and the punishing itineraries of touring. Physical symptoms accompanied the nervous complaints: Dickens began to drag one foot while walking. For all his busy-ness this way and that, he never finished another full-scale novel after 1865, and it seems more than coincidence that his death should have come on 9 June 1870, five years to the day after the Staplehurst accident.

Dickens's plight would now be recognised as a textbook instance of trauma, a state of temporary and involuntary possession by memories of the original ordeal. This condition, now familiar under the name of post-traumatic stress disorder, was then not yet understood. Instead, medical science focused on the immediate responses of shock and stress, from which the path to recovery was surer and faster.

That did not prevent Dickens from arriving at a deeper comprehension of his own plight, if his short story of 1866, 'The Signal-Man', is anything to go by. This is usually classified as a ghost story, and so it is – perhaps the finest in the English language. But for all its supernatural elements, the tale also extends his repertoire of haunted and possessed figures, such as Miss Havisham, whose distress is essentially psychological, especially in response to some disappointment or wound. Behind which lies the damage induced by Dickens's own childhood, with its dislocations of place and fortune, culminating in a period as a twelve-year-old worker in a Thamesside blacking factory: a famous episode now, but secret and unmentionable in the author's lifetime. The tale of the signalman is therefore also an acute psychological study, in which the author's possession by a memory of disaster on the railway is displaced on to his own creation – multiplied here to two disasters, for the signalman has been a helpless witness to successive fatal incidents on his stretch of the line, as if to underscore the recurrent nature of traumatic experience.

Those who have yet to discover the story will not find any spoilers here. But there are two further details of 'The Signal-Man' that deserve mention. First, the similarity between its setting – the signal box is buried in a damp and gloomy cutting, hard by the mouth of a railway tunnel – and the situation of Dickens's local station at Higham, deep enough in its cutting to be clothed in shadow when the fields around are sunlit, and with the dark mouth of a long tunnel in close view of the waiting passenger. So 'The Signal-Man' seems to have been written, as it were, out of somewhere close to home; and it seems fitting that the up platform at Higham should have despatched Dickens's own funeral train on its progress to Charing Cross station on 14 June 1870, for the short journey onward to burial in Westminster Abbey. The second point – disguised by the tendency to anthologise it with other ghost stories – is that the tale was one of a set of four narratives with carefully researched and vividly described railway settings, published among the Christmas Stories for 1866 in Dickens's own weekly *All the Year Round*. It is as if the novelist were seeking a deeper understanding of the transport system that had so damaged him, and on which he had yet become so dependent.

The rehearsal of trauma in 'The Signal-Man' ran ahead of medical understanding. Contemporary models of the nervous system presumed an intricate mechanism or apparatus that could be detuned or degraded by loud noises and other shocks; what one influential psychology textbook of the period, Alexander Bain's *The Senses and the Intellect* (1855), called 'a great cost of tear and wear of nerve'. This wear and tear was conceived of as a physical process, akin to other bodily injuries, although much harder to detect. The theory provided a sufficient explanation of any disorders – insomnia, trembling, stammering, numbness, incontinence – which might overtake an apparently unhurt passenger following an accident, often after some delay. But if such symptoms were difficult to diagnose accurately, they were also easy to simulate or exaggerate. Compensation claims of this kind became steadily more common through the 1850s and into the 1860s, alongside straightforward instances of redress for physical injury. Typical were two cases of 1862 arising from the Clayton Tunnel disaster at Brighton the year before: a piano-maker and tuner called Williamson, left unable to work and subject to pains in the head, back and kidneys after 'entire prostration of the nervous system' in the collision, and the taxidermist George Swaysland (*c.* 1814–88) – an authority cited in Darwin's *Origin of Species* – whose palpitations, headaches and general excitability following the crash meant that he could no longer stuff a bird or go out to shoot fresh ones.

Both men won compensation. By that date, indeed, the railways were losing almost every such case that came to court, even as they sought to weed out spurious suits by requiring claimants to submit to examination by doctors of the companies' choosing. In the case of Williamson, medical evidence in support could detect no signs of improvement since the accident, but the 'very eminent surgeon' retained by the London, Brighton & South Coast company reckoned that the patient would probably recover in a few months.

Embarrassed by these public disagreements between its members, and by the still worse implication that medical expertise *pro* and *con* could be had in exchange for a fee, the profession set out to define the condition more precisely, urged on by papers in *The Lancet* and the *British Medical Journal*. The consensus that emerged in the 1860s, set out by J. E. Erichsen of University College Hospital in his *On Railway and Other Injuries of the Nervous System* (1866), was that any otherwise unexplained ailments that followed a railway accident must be due to inflammation of the spine. Erichsen was careful to acknowledge that other kinds of physical shock could have a comparable effect, but the railway question was so dominant that it was the shorthand term 'railway spine' which identified his theory in medical and legal circles. It was generally agreed, too, that railway accidents inflicted shocks to the human frame of a previously unknown level of violence. The only problem was that physiological evidence to fit the theory was simply not there: in railway case after railway case, inflammation of the spine could not be demonstrated. That left the field open to further challenge.

Erichsen returned with a second edition of his book in 1875, arguing now that the spinal cord was impaired after accidental shock not by inflammation but by as yet unidentified changes at molecular level. This version of the hypothesis was by definition harder to disprove, but it was also easy to contest. In the 1880s a railway company surgeon, Herbert Page, set out a different theory. Page took the lack of physical change to the spine as a sign that the primary cause of hurt was the 'great fear and alarm' induced in the victim, without entirely letting go of the idea that the pathological symptoms might arise from physical changes to the nervous system this fear had induced. His position thus came close to convergence with developing theories of hysteria, a long-established way of understanding mental disorders induced by shock, especially in women and in men categorised as excitable or over-imaginative. That line of enquiry had been altogether too much for Erichsen, who refused to countenance the idea that a gentleman of mature years, 'active in mind, accustomed to self-control, addicted to business, and healthy in body', might find himself reduced by mere shock to a condition like that of 'a love-sick girl'. It is a sudden reminder of the assumptions of the age: the primacy of male authority, of age over youth, of the propertied classes over the lower orders. If the disintegration of personality that might occur after a railway accident could be blamed on undetected *physical* injuries, the victim would escape, as it were, with his masculine dignity intact. Much more perturbing was the suggestion that the psyche of the Victorian patriarch might prove no more robust in a calamity than that of a young woman – that physical disorders could be induced in men without physical harm.

By fostering new conceptions of injury on the one hand and new categories of insurance and litigation on the other, the railway network had unwittingly pointed the way towards this fuller perception of the relationship between mind and body. The consequences were for the twentieth century to work out. In terms of medical history, the true heirs of the traumatised survivors of Victorian railway disasters were the legions of shell-shocked patients produced by the First World War, men physically uninjured but lost to their former selves.

Railway accidents were so disturbing because they brought home the powerlessness of the human condition in the face of what had become an indispensable technology. As the *Saturday Review* had it in 1868, 'we are all railway travellers; these trains and collisions, these stations and engines, and all the rest of it, are not only household words, but part of our daily life'. To these fears were now added an insidious new suggestion, that the human frame was unsuited to the hours of jolting and vibration that a railway journey entailed – that something like the effect of a violent smash might be induced cumulatively.

Whiling away train time in 1868, Dickens calculated that the journey from Edinburgh to London subjected each passenger to 30,000 individual shocks to the nerves. (The total presumably allowed for every jolt made when the carriage wheels passed over a joint in the rails; assuming a separate shock from each axle, it is almost certainly a gross underestimate.)

Dickens by that time was hypersensitive; on 9 June 1865 he had crossed the line that divided those who had experienced a railway accident from those merely nervous at the possibility. But he would not have forgotten that his own wife had miscarried on the train between Edinburgh and Glasgow in 1847, losing what would have been their eighth child. The loss was a half-echo of the belief expressed by the drunken midwife Mrs Gamp in *Martin Chuzzlewit* (1844), that fright caused by screeching steam engines could induce premature birth; she claimed to know of a railway guard who was godfather to twenty-six children ('and all on 'um named after the Ingeines as was the cause'). The Gamp theory was hardly medical orthodoxy, but has something of the power of folk belief. A 'true' instance concerned the wife of the illustrator John Leech (1817–64) – the very man who excoriated the railways in many a cartoon for *Punch* and a close member of the Dickens circle in his own right. In 1847 Mrs Leech went into labour on a train from Liverpool, giving birth at the station hotel at Euston soon after arrival there.

Sober medical opinion also found room for the theory that the stress of keeping up with the railway's timetable, as much as the noise and vibration of train travel in itself, was an enemy of health: in the words of the *Journal of Public Health and Sanitary Review* (1855), 'the excitement, anxiety, and nervous shock consequent on the frequent efforts to catch the *last* express; to be in time for the fearfully punctual train'. A publication of 1868 by Dr Alfred Haviland, *'Hurried to Death', or, a few words of advice on the Danger of Hurry and Excitement, especially addressed to Railway Travellers*, had it both ways: not only did railway travel degrade the constitution, so that season-ticket holders on the Brighton line aged much more quickly than non-travellers, it also brought the risk of sudden extinction from rushing to catch the train in the first place. Potential victims included all those last-minute entrants to the compartment, who 'sink exhausted and breathless into their seat with a ghastly smile of self-congratulation, muttering something about their luck in sentences that are broken at every word by their laboured respiration'. Such behaviour risked exposing hidden bodily flaws, illustrated by Haviland with the case of William Searles, fruiterer and fishmonger, thirty-five years old, who travelled regularly from Chelmsford to London on market business; after a successful dash to Shoreditch for his train home, he looked out of the carriage window, 'making a ruckling noise in his throat and nose', then slid down dead. Haviland emphasised that such risks rose sharply when the stomach was full of solid food: his case studies included a jeweller who dropped dead running for a train in 1864, lobster dinner still inside him, cigar burning on the pavement where it fell.

Haviland's evidence was little better than anecdotal, and lacked the medico-legal weight of the investigations into 'railway spine'. Indeed, the impact of railway travel on health was a territory over which many hobby-horses were ridden in contradictory directions – so much so that Wolfgang Schivelbusch's study of the subject found it ultimately 'impossible to consider them as serious scientific investigation'. But this very incoherence indicates the unfocused disquiet the subject aroused, and it was possible to be sceptical of individual theories without escaping the general mood of concern. 'How fast we live!', as the *Church Builder* magazine put it in 1871. It was a familiar sentiment: looking back over the course of his long life, Sir Henry Holland (1788–1873) marvelled at 'the increased *fastness* of living, incident to all classes and occupations of men'; he even thought that people now walked more quickly in London's streets. Surely there was a catch somewhere; surely all this dashing about would have to be paid for one day ...

In parting, it is notable how this pattern of diffused anxiety tends to recur when new activities take hold of the population: bicycling in the late-Victorian decades, when 'bicycle face', 'bicycle hand', 'bicycle foot' and 'cyclist hump' hovered just beyond the fringes of medical diagnosis; or television in the years after the Second World War, when the risks of 'TV Neck', 'TV Crouch', 'TV Dyspepsia' and 'TV Stutter' gave medics and journalists something new to talk about. Mobile phones and computer screens have since generated their own flurries of anxiety. Yet all these perils are now routinely combined by the thousands who cycle in a dash to their local stations to catch the train to work, then pass the time in the carriage by making phone calls and catching old television shows on a tablet computer. Which may suggest that the risks of new technologies will always tend to be exaggerated, partly because danger makes a better story than safety, partly perhaps as a sort of displacement activity to avoid engaging with less far-fetched risks to health, such as those arising (say) from tempting things to eat and drink, or from a failure to take exercise at all.

CRIMES AND
MISDEMEANOURS

Let us for now set aside concerns that the railways were operationally unsafe, or that train travel was damaging to mental or physical health. What did that leave passengers to worry about? The answer is plenty, if fellow passengers were considered not merely as bores, nuisances or seat-hoggers, but as potential sources of peril and harm.

The phenomenon of crime was most conspicuous on the railways not in any red-handed way, but as a form of human spectacle. The reason was simple: trains were the easiest, cheapest and most secure way to transport prisoners over long distances. The railways did not begin the practice of dispersing captives to remote locations; lonely Dartmoor gaol, for instance, began life as a Napoleonic prisoner-of-war camp. Even so, the trend towards fewer, larger and more modern gaols required many prisoners to travel further than they would have done in late-Georgian days, when every county and many large towns maintained their own penal establishments. One decisive event was the Prison Act of 1877, which effectively nationalised the remaining local prisons and initiated the closure of many; all convicts became 'guests of Her Majesty'. The practice of transportation to Australia – scaled down in 1857 and done away with ten years later – also required lengthy cross-country journeys in custody, as did the growing tendency to concentrate prisoners in specialist institutions for women, juveniles, invalids, inebriates, naval and military offenders and so on.

Some railways constructed or adapted special prison vans for this traffic; the London & North Western had one on its books as early as 1850. More usually, prisoners travelled in ordinary carriages, handcuffed and accompanied by their guards. Lady Laura and Lady Vanilla, in Disraeli's novel *Sybil* (1845), find themselves travelling from Birmingham with two intelligent and gentlemanly characters; at Wolverhampton, the plausible pair turn out to be chained together: 'Two of the swell mob, sent to town for picking a pocket at Shrewsbury races.' Disraeli implies a first-class journey, but this looks like artistic licence. More plausible is an item in *Punch* for 1844, noting among the drawbacks of second class the chance of travelling with 'a ragamuffin in handcuffs, with a policeman next [to] him'. Once third-class carriages were roofed and enclosed securely, penal traffic could be handled at the cheaper rate. Among the menagerie of human types squeezed on to the third-class benches in G. A. Sala's account of the 7 a.m. Parliamentary departure from Euston in 1859 is a 'low-browed, bull-necked' man sitting between two guards and striving to pull his coat-cuffs down to conceal a 'pair of neat shining handcuffs'. A later regulation, enshrined as the railways' Rule 166, dictated the use of a reserved compartment for 'prisoners or insane persons' and their escorts.

Government prisoners wore the familiar broad-arrow uniform even when in transit between gaols. They were easy to spot. This exposure to public scrutiny added its own weight of humiliation to the other burdens of punishment – an echo of the stocks and the pillory.

> On November 13th, 1895, I was brought down here from London. From two o'clock until half-past two on that day I had to stand on the centre platform of Clapham Junction in convict dress, and handcuffed, for the world to look at. [...] Of all possible objects I was the most grotesque. When people saw me they laughed. Each train as it came up swelled the audience. Nothing could exceed their amusement. That was, of course, before they knew who I was. As soon as they had been informed they laughed still more. For half an hour I stood there in the grey November rain surrounded by a jeering mob.

Thus Oscar Wilde in *De Profundis*, written after his arrival at Reading gaol and published posthumously in 1905. The half-hour at Clapham Junction occurred during Wilde's transfer from HMP Wandsworth, after his conviction for gross indecency earlier in the same year. His two trials had made him briefly the most notorious man in Britain; Wilde omits to mention that members of the Clapham crowd were spitting as well as jeering at him. But not everyone was so unkind. Thomas Hardy wrote an affecting poem after witnessing a boy play his violin for a handcuffed prisoner and his guard as they awaited a train in Dorset, late in the century; the prisoner begins to sing along 'With grimful glee: / "This life so free / Is the thing for me!"'

By that time the sight of prisoners in charge on the railway was less common, their numbers dwindling as levels of crime and conviction declined astonishingly through the later Victorian and Edwardian period. Sentences to penal servitude in 1914 were at a mere one-fifth of the number fifty years before. The First World War pushed the graph back the other way; for example, the Highland Railway found it necessary to convert some compartments on its naval specials into secure cells for miscreant sailors from Invergordon or Scapa Flow. Sometimes there were as many as thirty-five such prisoners on a single train. For civilian prisoners, the requirement that the broad arrow should be worn in transit was abolished in 1921. When road vehicles took the traffic away from the railways, the imprisoned and convicted effectively vanished from public view altogether.

For desperate or headstrong prisoners, a railway journey raised the prospect of escape. These incidents made good copy, especially when a struggle was involved. The case of Samuel Robinson, editor and proprietor of the *Fifeshire Journal*, offered the press in 1862 the rare chance to turn on one of their own.

Robinson had perpetrated a series of frauds on a local bank. When these came to light, he promptly absconded. Seeking refuge in London, he was arrested thanks to the celebrated Inspector Whicher of Scotland Yard. A report was received that a guest answering to Robinson's description had been observed accidentally breaking a gold pencil case at breakfast in a hotel near King's Cross, where he had registered as 'Mr Chester'; Whicher's men circulated a request for information to the jewellers of London, anticipating that the article might have been sent for repair; the recipient gave notice and the owner of the case was arrested when he came to collect it.

Robinson's journey back to Scotland was made overnight in a locked first-class compartment, escorted by an acquaintance from happier days, Fifeshire's Chief Constable William Bell. But as the train passed north of York not long after 3 a.m., Robinson suddenly exclaimed, 'You may take me to Cupar, but you will never take me there alive,' and threw himself backwards out of the compartment window: unobserved, he had stealthily worked his hand free of the cuffs that joined the two men (some accounts claimed that Bell had nodded off). A desperate half-hour of wrestling followed, the Chief Constable restraining an increasingly bloodied Robinson by the collar as he dangled by the crook of his knees from the window-sill, pleading to be left to fall and die. As the lights of Darlington came into view, Robinson kicked Bell hard in the side and jerked free, bouncing off the footboard and rolling down the embankment to liberty.

The bruised and hatless editor next turned up at a pub in a nearby village, where he sold a shirt-stud to pay his way. Subsistence and lodgings after that were obtained by spinning a line about having been assaulted and robbed, with the promise that he would send postage stamps to reimburse any costs when he 'got home to Brighton'. The authorities finally caught up with Robinson two days later at the village of Stokesley in the north of Yorkshire, thirty-three miles from his place of escape, and sent him on to Scotland for trial. Such was the ferment in Fife by that time that large crowds greeted every train entering Cupar from the south for days after the arrest, until their rogue editor and Chief Constable at last stepped together on to the heavily policed platform.

₪

Quite a few of those who found themselves on the platform in handcuffs got there by misbehaving on the railways in the first place. The network offered enormous opportunities for pilfering, vandalism and fraud. It also extended the operational range for crimes such as housebreaking, by allowing easy transport of tools and swift disappearance with the loot. We are concerned for now only with offences committed within the carriage.

In the first instance, the railway compartment was a great gift to card sharpers, thimble riggers and other con men. Potential victims could be assessed at close range without arousing suspicion, conversations could begin in apparent innocence, routines could be planned to fit the time available before the journey's end. Strictly speaking it was illegal to gamble in public places, although cards were a common enough pastime on trains to leave the way half-open to playing for gain. An exasperated letter of 1854 to *The Times* came from a passenger who had reported a card sharper on the London & North Western; the guard had replied that he could see no harm in it, had no particular orders on the subject (something promptly denied in a letter to the paper from the line's general manager), and that the company even permitted playing boards and packs of cards to be hired out at Euston.

In this case the con artist was acting alone and found no takers; but his routine was the well-worn three-card trick favoured by more organised gangs. Their *modus operandi* was exposed again and again in letters to the press in the 1850s and 1860s, under such signatures as 'Not Swindled' and 'A Lucky Fellow'. The first letter on the subject published in *The Times*, on 30 October 1854, gives the essence of the sting.

The writer was travelling up to London from Dover, in company with his brother, two foreigners and a young English tourist. At Reigate* three smartly dressed men joined them, one of whom was eager to tell the company all about his two brothers serving as officers in the Crimea. 'Always mistrusting suddenly volunteered conversation in public conveyances, I looked at our new companion; he had a brilliant pin in his black satin scarf, and a massive watch guard, but his hands were very coarse and his nails very grubby' – not officer-class material, in other words. Another of the trio then offered cigars round and proposed to demonstrate a card game newly fashionable in the allies' camps at Sebastopol. This appeal to patriotic curiosity was followed by the all too familiar throwing about of two kings and an ace. Satin Scarf promptly guessed which card was the ace, whereupon the third man – a respectable, curate-like figure, also keeping up the pretence that the Reigate passengers were strangers to one another – expressed doubt as to his choice. Satin Scarf vowed that he would bet a sovereign on it and invited the company to match his wager. That was enough to get the foreigners 'fumbling among the five-franc pieces in their leathern bags' and the tourist reaching for his *porte-monnaie*. Asked his own opinion, the writer replied curtly that he would give all three of them into custody as soon as the train reached London Bridge. (They had mistaken their man: a regular traveller on the line, who was known personally to the guard of the train.) A pregnant pause, broken by 'a terrible oath from the curate'; silence from the card man, a huffy display of wounded honour from Satin Scarf, then an hour of 'an amusement quite different from that which they had proposed', as the writer watched the three squirming under the idea of what might await them. In the end, the writer let them go on their way, on

---

* Properly Redhill and Reigate station.

the grounds that no bet had actually been placed; but his letter ended with a warning that such trickery on the railways had reached disturbing levels.

Other correspondents had similar stories to tell. A Mr Cooke of New Cross thought that the description of the Reigate gang matched three men he had encountered in Ireland, where their make-believe gambling had stirred a commercial traveller in the compartment to lay and lose a bet; the gang then got off at different stations to preserve the illusion that they were unacquainted. 'A Traveller' lamented that the swindle was rife on the Midland Railway, where he had witnessed it on a journey from Worcester to Ashchurch that same morning. Informed of what was afoot, the guard's response was that there was nothing he could do.

In the same issue of *The Times* a third-class passenger described how the trick was performed in the cheap seats. He had observed a dubious-looking group travelling from Carlisle to Liverpool. The journey required a change of trains at Preston, at which point the group adopted the pretence of not knowing one another. The carriage was of a primitive type with inward-facing benches for seating and without any lamps. As the light faded one of the group lit a candle, fixed it to the back of a seat and commenced card-play with his accomplice (described as looking like the illustrations of Charley Bates, the Artful Dodger's sidekick in *Oliver Twist*). Others joined the candlelit game and the losses began. At the next stop the writer called the guard in a loud voice, whereupon the sharper snuffed out the candle, bolted through the door on the side away from the platform and 'rushed down the embankment and away into the darkness'.

The card-sharping menace even led indirectly to the deaths of four Ascot race-goers, in June 1864. A gang of sharpers was reported on one of the closely spaced and heavily laden trains returning to London at the end of the day. The men were removed at Egham station only after an altercation, which delayed the departure long enough for the following train to run into the rear carriages before they had cleared the platforms. The three-card trick was an age-old snare for the unwary at the racecourse; this particular gang may simply have been taking their work home with them, so to speak.

Visitors from abroad were especially attractive targets. Newly arrived Americans appear to have been fair game, as were any Irishmen away from their own country – 'as green as the island they come from', according to one Scottish rogue, in the dock for fleecing a traveller on the line from Port Glasgow. Hippolyte Taine found himself on the Dover service in the

1860s with a 'semi-gentleman' who was up to the old game, although it was only the Englishmen who were taken in.

One John Hamilton stands out from the published records for two especially elaborate plots to swindle foreigners. January 1862 brought him before the bench at Southwark on a fraud charge, having won the confidence of a Frenchman he had met at a London hotel. When the visitor returned to Paris, Hamilton went on the train with him. A third man, an accomplice, was of the party. A fourth joined them at Redhill. One of the men held up a gold Spanish coin, which he claimed to have won at cards. Hamilton then produced a deck and suggested a game. Induced to begin gambling by his new friend, the Frenchman lost £580. The two other men got out at Ashford, Hamilton at Folkestone. The victim travelled on to Paris, but later returned to the London hotel. By good luck he encountered Hamilton again and could notify the police.

Hamilton turned up again at Bow Street Magistrates' Court in 1868. A Turkish newspaper proprietor called Ali Suave had fallen into conversation with him at Charing Cross station, in French, on the subject of Parisian hotels. The two men took a compartment together. At the first stop three men joined them and soon the card-play began. Ali held back, but Hamilton joined in the betting, losing heavily. He then turned angrily on Ali with accusations that he had encouraged the venture; grabbing him by the throat, he demanded, 'Pay me your share of the loss.' The others did nothing to help Ali as Hamilton proceeded to rob him of gold, banknotes and a cheque. All four men got out before the train reached Dover, followed by Ali, whose attempts to send a telegraph to stop the cheque foundered on his lack of English. On the Continent he finally found help from a bilingual gentleman, and shortly after returned to London. Accompanied by a police sergeant, Ali tracked Hamilton down at Cannon Street, another terminus with services for the Channel Ports. The prosecution nailed Hamilton as one of a gang who had been travelling up and down the line by means of season tickets, attempting frauds. Passengers with imperfect English who fell in their way were easy targets. Hamilton may even have been one of the well-dressed gang of four who had latched on to a Swiss gentleman at Bletchley in the previous year, helping him into a carriage before suggesting a round of cards, then robbing him with violence when he declined to play. (He escaped further blows by a leap from the moving train.)

The treatment of Ali and of the brave Swiss traveller crossed the line dividing fraud from assault. To be set upon by a fellow passenger, with no immediate help to hand and no safe route of retreat, was a genuine hazard of railway travel. The *Railway Traveller's Handy Book* even advised that hands and arms should be kept 'disposed for defence' when passing through the darkness of a tunnel in a stranger's company. On the other hand, the offence seems never to have been common. The British Newspaper Archive can show relatively few reports for the period, and at least as many legal cases arising from tussles between passengers and railway staff, or the careless slamming of doors on passengers' hands. That attacks on passengers in transit did not happen more often must owe much to high staffing levels: any potential robber knew that he would be observed at the stations by which he entered and left the railway network, and every station stop offered the victim a chance to raise the alarm via a guard or a porter. Theft by stealth was a better bet than open robbery by main force; emptied of their valuables, purses and wallets could be tossed from the carriage window (a practice mentioned in the confessions of one hard case, at Preston in 1851). Still easier game could be found on station platforms and station approaches, where unattended goods and half-distracted persons promised a rich harvest. Among the less predictable offenders was a renegade clergyman with the apposite surname of Holloway, sent down for bag-snatching and bag-swapping at London termini in 1861.

None of these episodes could rival the sensation caused by the Briggs case. Thomas Briggs, a sixty-nine-year-old chief clerk of a Lombard Street bank, was discovered lying on the track between Hackney Wick and Bow on 9 June 1864, on the route of his twenty-minute journey home to Hackney from the terminus at Fenchurch Street. Briggs died without recovering consciousness; that he had been assaulted before falling from the North London Railway's train was established by the parallel discovery of a blood-smeared first-class compartment when the rolling stock was examined at the Hackney end. The compartment also contained a stick, a travelling bag and a flat-crowned beaver hat of unusual design – not Briggs's own. Missing from Briggs's person were his gold watch and its heavy chain.

The watch-chain proved to be the key to the story. After its details were published, a Cheapside jeweller came forward to report that a young man with a German accent had brought in a similar chain some thirty-six hours after the crime, taking in exchange a different chain and a five-shilling ring. The jeweller's name was John Death (he preferred the less arresting pronunciation 'Deeth'), and the little box containing the chain and ring had the name of Death marked within its lid. The watch-chain left in Death's possession turned out to be Briggs's own, and details of the suspect and the exchange were circulated. These caught the attention of a cab driver called James Matthews, eleven days after the murder. He remembered that his daughter had recently been given one of Death's jewellery boxes as a plaything, by a family acquaintance called Franz Muller. The cab driver also remarked on the description of the hat: he had admired Muller's headgear and had asked if the German could get him one like it to wear on his cab run.

Franz Muller was a gunsmith's apprentice from Saxe-Weimar. Failing to prosper in his trade after coming to London, he had instead found work as a jobbing tailor. The trendy hat was doubly significant: he was vain of his appearance and desperate for money to keep up with the flash fashions. Matthews was able to supply a photograph, from which John Death confirmed the identification. But when the police called at Muller's address, his landlord and landlady reported that their 'affectionate and kind' lodger had just emigrated to the United States. Among the possessions left behind was a hatbox from the shop that had supplied the by now notorious beaver hat.

Muller's capture and return proved to be a fraught business. Within twelve hours of the identification of the hatbox, a Scotland Yard inspector was on his way to New York via the Liverpool train and a fast steamship, with the jeweller and the cabman as his witnesses. Muller was travelling under sail and was overtaken. He was arrested as soon as he reached the quay. Briggs's hat and watch, *sans* chain, were in his luggage.

What should have been a straightforward extradition case then became snagged in international politics. The American Civil War was in its fourth year and the British government's perceived partiality to the Confederate side had won few friends in the Unionist north. Muller's defence attorney, an egregious rabble-rouser called Chauncey Schaffer, attempted to turn the proceedings into a patriotism test by means of irrelevant appeals to Anglo-American tensions and grievances. To no avail: Muller was taken back to London for trial, where the German Legal Protection Society paid for his (no less unavailing) defence. He was hanged outside Newgate gaol on 14 November, as a crowd estimated at 50,000 pushed and shoved for a view of what proved to be one of the last public executions in Britain.

This was the first accredited murder of a passenger on Britain's railways, more than three decades after enclosed carriages began running. For a while, public fears of another such outrage pushed aside familiar anxieties over the more substantial dangers of accidental injury or death. As Muller's prosecuting counsel put it, this was 'a crime which affects the life of every man who travels upon the great iron ways of this country'. Those travelling alone faced an uneasy choice: should they keep away from uncertain company, or actively seek safe companionship as a way of warding off any evil-doers? (It must have been a good time for chatty old ladies to make new friends on the train.) Meanwhile the lack of communication between compartments, and between the passengers in the compartments and the crew operating the train, seemed more unsatisfactory than ever, although a long time passed before anything conclusive was done about it. That story is part of the next chapter.

In the end, seventeen years passed before another passenger was murdered by a stranger in a railway carriage. The victim was Mr Gold, a retired Brighton stockbroker, shot, stabbed and thrown dying from the train as it passed through Balcombe Tunnel on the run down from London on 27 June 1881. The perpetrator was a self-aggrandising figure not unlike Muller: born Percy Mapleton, he had adopted the name Arthur Lefroy, and went about claiming to have smart connections in the theatre world.

This time Scotland Yard failed to distinguish itself. Despite having stumbled from the fatal compartment caked in blood and with Gold's gold watch and its broken chain stuffed down the side of his boot, Lefroy managed to postpone his arrest by relating a cock-and-bull story about a mysteriously absconding assailant who had been sharing the compartment and who had attacked both occupants under cover of the darkness of a tunnel. Later, on a visit to his lodgings, Lefroy was able to escape through a back entrance while his shadow Sergeant Holmes (no Sherlock, he) kept the house under useless surveillance from the street. He was finally taken a week or so later in lodgings in Stepney, where theatrical false whiskers and a moustache were found among his effects. Like the runaway Fifeshire editor, his journey back to face justice was widely anticipated and crowds jeered the prisoner and his escort when they changed trains at Haywards Heath – a railway town, where the case had caused dismay. After conviction, Lefroy was hanged at Maidstone Prison. With the newspaperman's appreciation for making the punishment fit the crime, the *Sussex Express* reported that an improved gallows was used, built over a pit, so that the

Scenes from the Balcombe tunnel murder, from the *Illustrated Police News*, 1881

executioner had only to move a lever 'such as those used in shifting the points on railway lines'.

After the Balcombe Tunnel case, there were only three more proven murders of railway passengers in Britain up to 1914. If an unnamed source quoted in 1894 is to be believed, this number was roughly level with Italy, Russia and Turkey, with five, seven and seven murders respectively over thirty years. Germany, Switzerland and the Low Countries recorded no such crimes at all; the most dangerous country was France, with twenty-eight killings, mostly of first-class passengers, of which more than half reportedly remained unsolved.

Murders apart, there were also well-publicised horror stories involving near-fatal assaults by deranged fellow-passengers. A paranoid Irish schoolmaster on his way to London to take an examination in 1863 stabbed a passenger in the head, in the delusion that the man was about to launch an attack of his own. A drunken lunatic travelling with his elderly father between Runcorn and Chester in 1876 pulled a knife on a blameless lithographer sharing their compartment, then grappled with the man for miles in an attempt to throw him from the carriage. During the fracas he bit off his victim's thumb and spat it through the window, having first broken the glass with his own head. Both cases involved long struggles, and both victims would probably have been rescued sooner if the alarm could have been given promptly.

All horrible, and all frightening; but none of these cases had anything like the impact of the murder of Mr Briggs. In journalistic terms, the twists and turns of the story were a dream come true. That the attack occurred in London also had something to do with it, as did the circumstance that the victim was on a routine journey home from work (though at the unorthodox time of 9.50 p.m. on a Saturday, or else the train would have been fuller and safer). Class, too, came into the picture: Briggs was a first-class passenger, his killer came from the precarious fringes of respectability. But the case also channelled something of the spirit of the times, especially the fascination with mystery and detection that created the taste for sensation novels. It was as if art and life had mysteriously converged.

In the absence of another murder following the Briggs case, popular anxieties about railway travel had latched on to an assault of a different kind. Just one week later, the eighteen-year-old Mary Anne Moody, daughter of the curator of Winchester Museum, was followed into a second-class compartment of the 1.10 p.m. departure from Waterloo by a middle-aged man named Henry Nash. He pestered her with personal questions and unsought offers of help with her luggage, to which she made the briefest responses. Another woman then entered the compartment, whereupon Nash appeared to go to sleep, only to perk up again after the extra traveller got out at Surbiton. He then stretched out at full length on the seat opposite Miss Moody, and repeated his questioning on the matter of her age and whether she had always worn spectacles, 'in a very insulting manner'. Again declining to answer, she rose and turned away from him to look out of the window. Next came Nash's hand on her shoulder, moving down to her waist, and the sensation that he was gently lifting her dress. Miss Moody then did a courageous thing: she opened the door, stepped out on to the running board of the moving train and began to edge along it. Her rescuer was a fellow passenger named Stokes, who leant out from the next-door compartment to clasp her against the side of the carriage. In this position she fainted and would have fallen but for the firmness of Stokes's grasp (he was a military bootmaker by trade). Relief arrived after the train had gone some five miles further, some labourers in a field by the line having managed to alert the guard to apply the brakes. At the hearing for Nash's committal, Miss Moody told the court that she understood the dangers of climbing from a moving train, even to the extent of incurring a possible fine – the standard charge in such cases was forty shillings – but 'My character, my welfare, everything that is worth having in this world, is far dearer to me than my life, and therefore I jumped out of the carriage.' Not words likely to win much sympathy for Nash, who received nine months with hard labour.

Press attention tended to be greater when one or both parties came from the prosperous classes. Nash was described as a yeoman of respectable appearance; the Briggs affair likewise offered the spice of a wealthy victim. The *Penny Illustrated Paper* eagerly linked the Moody case with Briggs's murder as 'evidence of the new impunity for crime afforded by our railway system'. In truth it was nothing of the kind, merely an unusually bad case of harassment of a single female passenger. The *Norfolk Chronicle* recorded an early instance, on the Great Eastern Railway in 1851. A Mrs Hicks was travelling in an unlit carriage between Yarmouth and Norwich. In the darkness she felt the hand of a male passenger moving in her direction. Assuming an attempted robbery, she warned him off. Later the groping hand returned, and the approach turned to an attempted kiss. The assailant, a drunk named Robert Ely, then 'behaved in a manner not fit to be stated in print'. Mrs Hicks fainted, and was only rescued by the guard, who handed Ely over to the police. Darkness seems to have encouraged the assault; as the *Pictorial Times* put it in 1845, 'the want of light at night converts the carriage into a den of infamy'. The story is all the more sinister in that the two were not alone: those also in the compartment included another woman passenger, who offered help to get Ely put in charge but did nothing to restrain him, and a male associate of his – evil-minded, or complicit – who told Mrs Hicks not to worry, as the man would not hurt her.

A later case, in 1866, was picked up by the national press. Robert Williams, a Shoreditch cabinet maker, followed a seventeen-year-old servant called Charlotte Martin into a third-class compartment on a Great Eastern train from Brentwood. She refused to answer his pestering questions and rejected his hopeful suggestion that she might wish to kiss him. Once the train was under way he kissed her by force, tried unsuccessfully to undo her frock, then moved to sit opposite her, 'and acted in a most indecent and cowardly manner'. But it happened that the engine driver had noticed Williams's approaches to Miss Martin on the platform, and during the thirteen-minute journey – this in the darkness of a January evening – he left the footplate of his engine three times, climbing along the side to a point from which he could see into the compartment. The suspicion that the driver was a peeping Tom is hard to shake off; either way, once the kissing went on to something worse he called out to Williams to stop. With the driver as witness there was no plausible defence, and the cabinet maker was fined £20 – close to three months' salary for a London artisan, but less swingeing than the custodial sentence for Nash.

All such cases paled beside that of Colonel Valentine Baker and Miss Kate Dickinson, aged twenty-one and 'of very prepossessing appearance' (*The Times*), in 1875. The circumstances matched those of the Moody affair: a single young lady joined in a first-class compartment by an older man, unsought advances culminating in indecent assault, escape by climbing on to the running board of the speeding train, alarm-raising and rescue by the combined efforts of fellow passengers, onlookers and railway staff. Even the route – the London & South Western, between Waterloo and Woking – was the same. The extra ingredient was rank: Baker was colonel of the 10th Hussars, the smartest cavalry regiment of the line, and counted the Prince of Wales among his friends. He was also a reforming soldier of exceptional gifts, with a distinguished record in action and glittering prospects for advancement.

None of this did Baker much good at the Croydon Assizes. The jury heard how he had engaged Miss Dickinson in genteel discussion of the theatre, the Royal Academy and a military ball at Aldershot, before suddenly pulling the window shut at Woking. He then forced her into a corner, murmuring, 'You must kiss me, darling.' His exploring hand had got as far as her stocking when she managed to pull down the window to call for help, before escaping on to the perilously narrow step outside the door, and from there to the platform when the train stopped.

The trial stretched out over seven hours, not so much from its complexity but because of delays caused by noise from the crowds packing the streets outside – a higher turnout than for any murder trial in the county, it was noted – and by several attempts to rush the doors for a glimpse of the prisoner and his accuser. Baker was sentenced to a year's imprisonment for his indecent assault and was heavily fined. Worse, he was dismissed from the army on the Queen's personal intervention, quashing attempts by the broad-minded Prince of Wales to leave a way open for his rehabilitation.

Classified as a 'first-class misdemeanant', Baker was allowed to stay apart from other prisoners. His rooms at Horsemonger Road gaol were specially furnished, wine was permitted and friends could visit between 9 a.m. and 6 p.m. This indulgent treatment did not escape notice in the popular press, and an artist's impression was published showing the heavily moustached ex-colonel relaxing with friends, champagne and cigars. When visitors were away, Baker's prison hours were put to use writing a memoir of his expedition to the frontiers of Persia and Turkestan.

Baker's subsequent history was a matter for marvel; like the wretched Muller, his destiny took an international turn. Rumours had circulated that he was angling for a senior commission under the Czar, but on his release Baker went the other way, giving outstanding service as a general in the Ottoman army in the Russo-Turkish war of 1877–8. Back in London, his old clubs in St James's discreetly re-elected him to membership. Rehabilitation of 'Baker Pasha' continued with his acceptance in 1882 of an invitation to organise and command the army of Egypt, then newly subject to a British protectorate. By 1887 steps were being taken towards his reinstatement as a soldier of the Queen, but Baker died suddenly before he could return to England, and was buried in Cairo. Full military honours were granted for his funeral.

One other detail of the case should be mentioned, as it too anticipates the next chapter. There was an alarm fitted in the carriage, and Miss Dickinson managed to reach it at one point. Nothing happened: the bell that should have connected with her signal failed to ring.

₪

Some of these cases of crime and accident involved locked doors, others did not. The third-class card sharper on the London & North Western scarpered through an unlocked door on the non-platform side and Miss Moody and Miss Dickinson were also able to escape through unlocked doors. On the other hand, it will be remembered that Dickens had to obtain a key from one of the guards before he could release fellow survivors from the tottering carriage at Staplehurst in 1865. And there is another telling detail of the Baker case: the colonel begged Miss Dickinson to come back inside the carriage, promising that he would get out on the opposite side at the next station, but she knew that the pledge was hollow, for the doors on that side had been locked when the train was at Guildford.

This locking or unlocking of doors while the train was in motion was one of the more intractable questions of railway operation. Should passengers be secured within their compartments, to save them from falling out, drunk or sober, or from reckless exits at improper places? Or were the risks associated with imprisoning them so great that they should be trusted to control the doors themselves? In which case, how to ensure that those without the correct class of ticket, or with no ticket at all, did not slip into compartments where they had no right to be?

There were strong arguments on both sides. In his *Railway Economy* (1850), Dionysius Lardner catalogued twenty-seven accidents between 1844 and 1848 involving improper exits from moving trains, eighteen of them fatal, and nineteen more (eleven fatal) in which passengers tried to board trains already in motion. These deaths could have been averted if doors were kept locked. But then there was troubling news from France, which suffered its first major railway disaster at Meudon in 1842, when at least fifty-two people perished; many might have survived if their burning carriages could have been unlocked in time.

This calamity put a brake on the locking of carriage doors across the Channel. It also prompted a withering sequence of letters to the *Morning Chronicle* from the Rev. Sydney Smith, a proponent of what would now be called the libertarian position and a regular traveller on the Great Western. This company in its early years refused to trust its passengers one bit, keeping all its carriage doors firmly fastened. Other lines left the doors unlocked, or secured them down the off-side of the train only, which made the Great Western's policy difficult to defend. Smith wanted the doors on both sides to be unlocked, in case an accident made the unsecured side useless for the purposes of escape. Ridiculing the impulse to save passengers from themselves, he pointed out that 'outside' mail-coach passengers were never tied to the roof in case they fell off, nor sea voyagers locked into their cabins for their own protection.

Shortly afterwards, the Board of Trade ordered the Great Western to keep at least one door unlocked in each compartment, which the company applied to the side that would not normally open on to the platforms. The same practice was in force on five of the twenty-one railways that responded to the Board's circular on the subject; the others did not lock their carriages at all. But the dilemma remained, as mishaps with unlocked doors continued to occur. Some had luckier outcomes than others. In 1844, a two-year-old child in a family party travelling south by express from Liverpool managed to tumble out through an unsecured door on the approach to Crewe, only to be found uninjured by the locomotive and carriage that were sent back to search the lineside. In those days the handle had to be twisted back in a certain way to secure the door after pulling it to, and it was all too easy to forget this requirement, so the child may simply have leant against a door that suddenly yielded.

Or there is the mysterious case of Isabella Lawrence, a factory girl who was found dead on the line near Horsforth, on one of the North Eastern Railway's lines to Leeds, on an October morning in 1854. She had entered an unlit third-class carriage at Leeds on the evening before, and was joined there by Thomas Law, with whom she had been drinking earlier that day. Having arrived too late to buy a ticket, Law had agreed with the guard that his fare should be collected on arrival; but at Horsforth the guard found the compartment empty, with the far door hanging open. Law was traced, arrested and charged. His defence was that he had got off the train well before the point at which the body was found. Law had a good reason for making an early exit; having failed to persuade Isabella to come back to his place, he faced the prospect of paying the fare to Horsforth and back for nothing if he stayed on the train. A railway clerk testified that Law had indeed approached his lineside cabin out of the darkness while the train was held at a junction, and had asked the way back to Leeds. If both men spoke the truth, Isabella must have fallen of her own accord; perhaps Law had left the door swinging behind him, and she in her befuddled state had tumbled out when trying to close it. All the inquest jury could do was to censure the company for running unlit carriages with doors that could not be locked and secured, and to recommend that doors should always be locked on the side *not* in use.

Both arrangements seem to have been in force around 1850, sometimes on the same train, as recorded by Sir Francis Head's detailed description of an arrival at Euston. Some of the station's porters walked alongside the train as it slowed to a halt, holding the doors closed to prevent any hasty exits. Other doors were fastened shut, and those detained inside had time to hail familiar faces among the groups assembled to meet them on the platform while waiting for the porters to release them. F. L. Olmsted described having to call for release in this way at Bromborough on the Birkenhead line in 1850, struggling with his luggage, past ladies' knees, to the platform side – all most unlike the spacious ways of the American saloon car.

The locking mechanism in its developed form was not usually integrated with the door-handles and catches, but was set higher up in the door frame, where it appeared as a hole with an inset spindle, rather like a giant domestic radiator lock. A standard key sufficed for all, allowing a single railwayman to secure or open all the doors of a carriage fairly quickly. Passengers had no business tampering with these locks, although ownership of the keys seems not to have been tightly controlled (given that they were a useful tool to the miscreant, it is a surprise to find the *Army & Navy Stores Catalogue* advertising them for sale, at 9d or 1s, in 1907). Rather, they opened and closed the doors by means of the handle below. This was placed on the outside, so that a window had to be lowered in order to reach it – a safeguard against too-easy opening while the train was in motion.

Opened doors on moving trains were still common enough in the mid 1860s for the Metropolitan Railway to introduce a design with rounded upper corners, profiled so as to keep clear of the incurving tunnel wall if the door began swinging to and fro between stations. The introduction of doors with sprung catches around 1900 eased the problem. Now, to close the door and to secure it became one action, and the vigorous slamming that triggered so many exasperated letters to the press could be justified on grounds of safety. And so the railway added to its repertoire of noises the thudding shut of hundreds of self-closing doors, a sound that reached its peak during the twentieth-century London rush hour. Its counterpart, once familiar from television news clips introducing fare increases or snowbound cancellations, was the decelerating train with doors already held partly open by impatient commuters, many of whom would spring on to the platform even before the train had stopped moving – as irresponsible and irresistible a way of saving time as the Londoner's calculated jump between platform and pavement from a Routemaster bus.

These verbs are in the past tense because trains with automated sliding doors are now the rule, and the diminishing number of carriages with slam doors come equipped with central locking. So now passengers can neither tumble nor jump out between stations, nor slip gratefully away at a more convenient station when an unscheduled stop is made. The verdict in favour of automatic locking was made in 1992, after a report by the Health and Safety Executive concluded that some carriage doors could open accidentally in rare circumstances. The decision put an end to a period in which the toll of falling passengers had been closely monitored by the newspapers, often with the exaggerated implication that No Door Was Safe. Off the record, old railway hands were liable to belittle the risk, or to treat it as an unforeseen consequence of getting foolishly drunk on the train – for many of the victims were thought to have lurched in the general direction of the lavatory only to tumble out through the unsecured door immediately alongside. This critical mistake is no longer possible on trains in normal service, although the doors of the High Speed Trains of the 1970s and 1980s still have windows that will slide down far enough to allow the stricken passenger to be sick out of them.

Lockable doors also helped the railways to address the concerns of female passengers. It was among the duties of porters and guards to help passengers to find a seat, and ladies could expect special attention. An empty compartment could be unlocked on their behalf, and a long-standing regulation required guards to place a single woman, on her request and where possible, in a compartment whose other occupants were also female. Formal designation of ladies-only compartments was an obvious next step, and some companies had already done this by the mid 1840s. Yet the practice never became a legal requirement to match the rule that provided for smokers. Some companies protested that it would seriously complicate their operations if ladies' compartments were to be mandatory. When the Board of Trade investigated the question in 1887, it found that most railways would reserve a compartment for women if requested, but that compartments permanently marked as such tended to be under-used – partly because of fears that predators might home in on them. It was also necessary to stipulate when boys became too old to enter such a compartment; more than one railway played it safe by setting the onset of manhood at nine years.* Ladies' compartments were latterly indicated by a green sticker on the window, easily distinguished from the red stickers for no-smokers and the blue ones for first class. The last few lingered until 1977, casualties of the Sex Discrimination Act passed two years previously – just too early to find advocates from within the radical feminist separatism of the 1980s.

₪

---

* On the railways of India, where ladies' compartments remain, the limit is a more generous twelve years.

From a feminist perspective, it would be easy to take all this as evidence that the Victorian era was a patriarchal nightmare, its public realm an oppressively masculine territory through which unaccompanied women ventured at risk of harassment or worse. By these lights, a woman who initiated anything more than the most distant and formal conversation with a stranger risked placing her own respectability under a cloud. Divulgence of a name or an address was understood on both sides as a form of encouragement; Nash, Williams and Baker all asked, and were rebuffed. Words apart, the very act of gazing freely was a male prerogative, so that a woman who dared to match a male stare risked committing an ambiguous transgression.

In all of these charges there is a measure of truth, but the full story is both more complicated and more interesting. In the first instance, it should never be forgotten that the arrival of the railways came to women, hardly less than to men, as a liberation. To travel cheaply over long distances, alone or in company, was an opportunity open to anyone of either sex who could afford the fare. The assaults described could not have happened if single women had been too afraid to take advantage of this. Charlotte Martin, the victim of the Shoreditch assault, can stand as an example: an orphan, she was making a visit to her sister at the 'industrial' or pauper school out at Brentwood in Essex, a return journey of thirty miles. Railway stations themselves were among the safer public places, staffed by men whose duties required them to attend to the needs of passengers, who were not afraid to intervene to preserve order and prevent annoyances, and who could themselves be reported for any faults or failings.

More unexpected, perhaps, were the ways in which women living on the fringes of the law could turn the confined space of the railway compartment to their own advantage. One well-known instance, barely mentionable at the time, concerned the services initiated in 1866 between the South Eastern Railway's two London termini at Charing Cross and Cannon Street. These ran in an arc across the South Bank, a journey of seven minutes that usefully bypassed the congestion along the Strand and Fleet Street. But Charing Cross was also the West End's epicentre of vice, and before long the company found itself selling tickets to suspicious-looking couples of recent acquaintance, eager to make use of the seven minutes of first-class seclusion offered by its carriages. This unwelcome traffic diminished once an intermediate stop was introduced in 1869, at the present Waterloo East station, and still more as the services themselves dwindled in the 1870s, after the Metropolitan District Railway's shorter and cheaper underground route opened north of the river.

The Charing Cross traffic was a localised affair and a matter for consenting adults. Of broader significance was the possibility of entrapment or blackmail of male passengers by women, playing on the presumption that the man must have been the active party in any encounter. The scam also depended on the victim keeping his loss or humiliation to himself – which was not unlikely, especially if he had been bamboozled by a flirtatious approach, and felt his masculinity devalued by the deception. Even the raffish Wilkie Collins was wary of the risk; as he assured his mother, 'I won't travel alone with a woman – I promise you that.'

The apparent victim of one incident, on the Eastern Counties Railway in 1859, told his story anonymously in a warning letter to the *Braintree and Bocking Advertiser*. At Shoreditch station he had been addressed by a pretty young woman, who said that there was room in her second-class compartment. She then shut the door after his entry, as if to keep others out. He began reading his newspaper, aware that she was gradually edging closer, so that her dress began to press against him – which he admitted to having enjoyed. Nothing was said, nor did he drop the cover of his paper. At a later station another man entered, at which the woman at first seemed displeased. The new passenger seemed to observe them touching. The woman then sprang back, saying that she had been assaulted; at this point it became clear that the new arrival was known to her. At Braintree the train was met by a man claiming to be the woman's brother, who was given a version of events by the other passenger. The men then turned on the letter-writer, roughing him up and ramming down his new hat over his eyes. He was too scrupulous to lay an accusation against the woman, who in turn declared herself too bashful to bring a charge. What was going on? Perhaps the three expected the man to offer money for their silence, but did not want to risk raising the subject first – or the whole thing was just a sadistic lark.

An Old Bailey case of 1866 shows how the blackmail trick could backfire, even when the victim's behaviour fell short of absolute rectitude. Ellen Allen had laid a charge of assault and attempted rape against Alexander Moseley, a twenty-nine-year-old surgeon and dentist of Paddington, married and with children, who had shared her compartment between Watford and Euston. The charge had been thrown out by the magistrates, who heard her claim that Moseley had locked the compartment to prevent her escaping; also, that he had been smoking illicitly during the journey. Moseley then turned the tables on his accuser, who found herself charged with perjury before the higher court. He reported that it was she who had initiated conversation, asking him on the platform if the train was for London. She then followed him into an otherwise empty second-class compartment and began a conversation about her children. After a while, Moseley asked if she minded his smoking his pipe (she did not, although the practice was still forbidden on this line). Moseley then took out a book to read, not wanting to talk more. He admitted to having locked the compartment door at an intermediate stop, but explained that this was to keep out anyone who might object to the tobacco – a dodge he had used for four or five years, ever since he got hold of his own carriage door-key. Moseley also confessed to having given a false name on arrival at Euston, although he supplied the real one when taken in charge to the police station. All of which showed a cavalier attitude to the regulations, not to mention the frankly selfish misuse of a carriage key. But Ellen Allen had a harder case to answer: a former prostitute with a history of bringing false charges, she was described as having been 'molesting gentlemen' at Victoria station over the previous eighteen months. Her perjury and conspiracy at Euston earned her five years' imprisonment.

Another incident at a London terminus, heard at Southwark police court in the year following, looks less clear-cut. The Rev. George Capel of Carshalton was charged with having indecently assaulted a domestic servant, Mary Anne Fraser, as she and her mother made their exit from a third-class South Eastern Railway compartment at London Bridge station. The case hinged on exactly what had happened against or beneath the lady's crinoline as she passed the minister, whose seat was next to the door on the platform side, in a space just 5ft wide between the seat backs. A railway porter who was sitting in the far corner of the compartment reported that he had seen Capel pressing his hand between the accuser's legs. She had then turned round and called him a 'nasty beast'. For the defence, witnesses of both sexes swore that any physical contact was innocent or inadvertent, Capel having merely directed her crinoline away from his person as she passed ('he made no indentation in her dress'). The phrase 'nasty beast', recorded in a press report of a preliminary hearing, prompted another witness to come forward: an elderly man named Richards, who had been accused in similar circumstances at Charing Cross station a few weeks before. In this case, the woman had thrown her crinoline across his knees as she passed him in the compartment. Richards had shadowed his accuser, who had gone to the same address as the complainant in Capel's case: a house in Cecil Court, off St Martin's Lane. Cecil Court was then by no means respectable, and Richards's evidence looks damning; but under cross-examination he could not say categorically that Mary Anne Fraser was the same person who had flung her dress in his direction.

The Capel case aroused considerable press interest, partly because of the accused's clerical status, partly because his surname raised aristocratic echoes. There was confusion about this: 'Capel' was misspelled as 'Keppel' in some early reports, whereupon letters appeared in *The Times* from the (Capell) Earl of Essex at Cassiobury Park, to say that the accused was no connection of *his*, and from the (Keppel) Earl of Albemarle at Quiddenham Hall, to say that the suspect had nothing to do with *him* either. In the end Capel was found not guilty after witnesses on both sides failed to agree on the sequence of events, the words spoken, or the exact positions and postures of the parties.

That relations between the sexes were more diverse and unpredictable than the simple polarity of assault-versus-blackmail might imply is suggested by the Tremlett case of 1875. James Tremlett, a young Royal Marines officer, left London for Chatham, travelling alone. At Woolwich Dockyard station his first-class compartment was entered by a Miss Seraphina Higinbotham, described in the deadpanning newspaper report as 'a lady somewhat over the middle age, and at present walking the London hospitals, with a view to practising as a surgeon and doctor of medicine'. Tremlett sat silently reading. Miss Higinbotham then made her move. Taking off her spectacles, she moved to sit opposite him, looking him full in the face, with the words 'You are a very nice young man!' Snatching his magazine away, she knelt before him and proclaimed that she had surely seen him before. When Tremlett tried to move seats she shuffled after him, holding on to his coat-tails and demanding that he kiss her 'for his mother's sake'. He reluctantly allowed her to kiss him, just the once, but confessed to being alarmed by her advances (the train was passing through a tunnel at the time). Then Miss Higinbotham's tune changed: grabbing at his whiskers, she declared herself a 'lone unprotected female', and warned that he should take care – rather as if she were preparing to lay an accusation against him. Only when she seized his collar did he begin to struggle and cry for help, which duly came from a porter at the train's next stop.

Brought before the magistrates, Miss Higinbotham did not deny the incident; she merely wished (she said) to show her admiration of a handsome young man. She escaped with a warning, but the chairman of the bench made it clear that he took the matter seriously: there were 'many young and inexperienced men travelling by rail, totally unprotected', and army officers in particular might be the subject of blandishments and worse. He therefore requested that the railway companies would designate men-only carriages – a plea that was often echoed whenever the subject of entrapment and blackmail on the rails came round. In view of the near-complete reversal of the usual relations of power between the sexes in Tremlett's compartment, it is also piquant to record what he was reading when Miss Higinbotham snatched his magazine away: an article on the railway misdemeanours of the uncontrollably masculine Colonel Baker.

₪

Somewhere behind all these cases is an obvious truth: that close confinement with another is a matchless incubator of desire. Anyone could guess the drift of one of the music-hall hits of 1863, 'The Charming Young Widow I Met on the Train'.* There was critical disapproval in 1854 when the painter Abraham Solomon showed his canvas *First Class: The Meeting ... and at First Meeting Loved*: a smart young man (travelling with a suggestive rod and line) is getting on rather well with the expensively dressed young lady, while her middle-aged male companion – guardian, uncle or papa – dozes obliviously in the corner seat. Stung, the painter came up with a new version the following year. Now, the young lady is in the corner. From this safer distance she looks on demurely as the young man, reassuringly transformed from free-range angler to army officer, talks earnestly with her sprightly and fully awake guardian. (The painting's title was unchanged, raising the distracting idea that it is the old man with whom the soldier is falling in love, or vice versa.)

Solomon's lapse was a matter of taste as much as of morals, but the two were not easily disentangled in an age when art was expected to have moral force. Artists, dual citizens of polite society and of bohemia, were themselves potentially suspect, especially when it came to their dealings

---

* Apparently a British version of an American song, adapted with a macabre twist: she leaves her admirer in charge of her child, who turns out to be dead.

with female models. A railway episode in the diary of Ford Madox Brown illustrates the point. The context is a journey to Tilbury for the Gravesend ferry, also in 1854:

> Found in the carriage an old acquaintance a certain Miss or Mrs Ashley, who used to sit to me, did not know her at first nor wish to appear to know her ... I was sorry afterwards I was not more civil to her. An awful looking snob in the same carriage went off with her arm in arm & took a boat to some ship – coming back with Lucy [the artist's daughter] in the steamboat to Tilbury my snob sidles up to me, with a considerable smirk on his face he wishes to know who the Lady is, having found her 'very agreeable sort of person'. O ho said I, was you not with her then, no he merely met her in the carriage & saw her speak to me.

In other words, Miss Ashley had drawn attention to her own boldness by addressing Brown, thus encouraging a later approach from the 'snob' (a term then implying social pretension rather than snootiness). For the artist's model, a member of the *demi-monde* almost by definition, with – so Brown tells us – two children born out of wedlock, the opportunity to meet a new gentleman and potential protector may not have been unwelcome; but no respectable woman from the higher classes would have taken a train with such a purpose frankly in mind.

What could not be acknowledged in public, in polite print, or in mixed society circulated in the nether world of pornography. The summit of Victorian literary smut is *My Secret Life* by 'Walter', published in eleven volumes in 1888–94. Opinion remains divided on the authorship of the million-plus words of this obsessive narrative of frigging, whoring and seduction, as well as on the question of how much of it, if any, may be truly autobiographical. The book includes several pick-ups or consummations in railway carriages, from the old flame encountered on a Great Western express (a first-class journey for the narrator in more than one sense) to the comely costermonger's girl who gets into a Metropolitan first-class compartment by mistake. Comfortably seated, secure in his wealth and social class, 'Walter' can assess his quarry at close quarters, undressing female passengers by eye and weighing up the chances of their availability, before finding some pretext to open conversation. The impulse that censorious critics detected behind Abraham Solomon's painting is here made shamelessly explicit.

Another of his tales uses the opening circumstances of the Baker case – by then well over a decade past, but clearly well remembered – and reworks them as a fantasy of mutual gratification. On the platform at Aldershot station he assists a young lady – 'tall, dark-eyed, handsome, and elegantly dressed' – by supplying a stamp for the urgent letter she must post. To follow her into a first-class compartment, with a wink to the guard, is the obvious next step. From the lady's implausibly indiscreet conversation it is soon clear that she is the kept woman of a major, a man temporarily off the scene. Flirtation and chat about theatres turn steadily more physical: 'I got as close to her as the arm between the seats (a fixture) allowed. – My leg met hers, and she didn't move it away. Carelessly I laid my hand on her knee, and, pinching up a bit of the silk dress, admired it.' After which the four-letter words start to kick in; and so on, over many a filthy page, all the way to Waterloo.

The desires 'Walter' gloatingly indulged were treated more decorously in the new medium of cinema. A short film made in 1899, *The Kiss in the Tunnel*, showed the pioneer cinematographer George Albert Smith (1864–1959) and his wife Laura, against a rather terrible painted representation of a railway compartment. We first see them seated, he with his newspaper, she with her book. He looks up, chucks her under the chin a few times, then removes his cigar and hat in order to lean over and kiss her on the cheek. Then he sits down, only to rise again almost at once and kiss her on both cheeks. He knocks his hat back into shape, having sat on it by accident, and both parties resume their reading. The action is topped and tailed by sequences by another film-maker taken from the front of a moving train, first slowly entering a tunnel, then emerging at the other end – an example of the 'phantom ride' genre, popular in the earliest years of moving pictures. The running time is one minute and five seconds.

Not much of a story, then; but at the time, this sequence was sophisticated stuff – to the extent that *The Kiss in the Tunnel* is counted among the earliest narrative edits in the history of moving pictures. It seems a good match: the revolutionary transport technology of the nineteenth century, captured in the first instalment of the supreme story-telling medium of the century about to commence. The film deserves to be better known, especially now that the Institut Lumière's researches have conclusively spiked the old claim that footage of a moving train featured at the first ever public film show, in Paris on 28 December 1895. That celebrated fifty seconds of footage, made by the brothers Lumière on the platform of La Ciotat

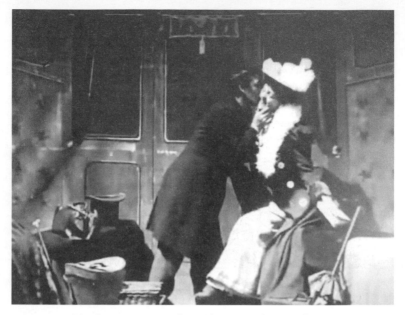

The decisive moment from *The Kiss in the Tunnel*, 1899

station near Marseille, was actually not screened in public until January of the following year (it turns out that the story of panic spreading through its audience as the locomotive loomed ever closer is probably a myth too). Smith's enterprise also anticipated by sixty years the flagrant innuendo in the last frames of Alfred Hitchcock's *North by Northwest*, which cut from Cary Grant's embrace of Eva Marie Saint in a sleeping-car berth to the final, masterful entry of train into tunnel.

As far as Britain's railways are concerned, the sleeping car in its maturity belongs to a later time than the high Victorian decades. The same applies to other innovations that permitted movement and communication within and between the vehicles of passenger trains. All these belong in the next chapters. Before that, here is one last encounter in a railway compartment, representing another sort of hidden history. It comes from the life of Edward Carpenter (1844–1929), free-thinker, socialist and advocate for toleration and understanding of what he called 'the intermediate sex'. A practitioner of the simple life, Carpenter set himself up on a smallholding in the Peak District, near Dore and Totley station. On the train one day in spring 1891, his attention was caught by a smartly dressed working man called George Merrill, twenty-two years his junior. Both men were with groups of friends, but the two managed to exchange 'a few words and a look of recognition'. It was enough: Merrill slipped away from his friends when the train stopped, then followed Carpenter's party until a chance came to speak further. Thus Carpenter met the great love of his life, and his companion for the next thirty years. Let their meeting on the Midland Railway stand as a counterweight to Oscar Wilde's exposure at Clapham Junction a few years later, as a reminder of the opportunities and freedoms the railways made possible.

THE IMPROVED BRITISH
RAILWAY TRAIN

The first chapter attempted to recover the experience of a railway traveller in 1862, so unlike that of today. Leap forward fifty years and the gulf is much less wide. Imagine a passenger arriving at Euston station in 1912 and taking a third-class seat on the afternoon express for Glasgow. The seats are now decently upholstered, the compartment adequately lit and heated according to the season – as already described. Nor is the compartment any longer an isolated cell: a corridor runs along one side, at each end of which is a narrow gangway, corrugated like a giant bellows or concertina, that links the carriage to its neighbour. Within the vestibules next to these gangways are narrow doors, behind which are cubicles each with lavatory and washbasin. The train now requires fewer individual carriages, for they have grown much longer – often with six compartments each. Two or three fixed axles no longer suffice to carry them; instead, their wheels are placed at each end, mounted on pivoting bogies for a smoother ride. Standards of finish and craftsmanship have not slipped: if anything, the materials, liveries and trimmings are still costlier and more substantial. The best Edwardian railway carriages express the spirit of their age just as much as its ocean liners, motor cars and smart hotels.

There is more. Following the corridor from carriage to carriage leads in one direction to a well-appointed saloon in which tables laid with cloths and place-settings await the diner. In the other direction, at the far end of the train, is the much less decorative compartment for the guard, in which is the train's heavy luggage, labelled for correct extraction at the appointed places. Other platforms or sidings outside the station offer glimpses of long-bodied sleeping carriages, amid any number of carriages of the older, corridor-less type that are increasingly restricted to suburban and short-distance services. Thanks to the through corridor, tickets can now be checked en route and the extra stop for their collection just short of the journey's end has been eliminated. The provision of lavatories and dining cars has also put an end to the protracted stops to allow passengers to take refreshments and find physical relief. Everything has speeded up.

Other innovations are not so obvious. Once the train is on its way, the guard no longer has to await a signal from the driver to apply the brakes. Instead, a continuous brake pipe runs through the train, controlled from the locomotive footplate. Should a coupling fail and the train split in two, rupturing the pipe, the brakes will automatically engage in both the stranded and the hauled portions. If the passenger notices some imminent danger, is suddenly taken ill or is menaced by a fellow traveller, the compartment is equipped with a chain to pull, which will ensure an emergency stop.

In truth, the risk of accident would not have pressed heavily on the mind of the average British railway traveller of 1912. By that time, entire years had passed without a single passenger fatality anywhere on the network. The railways of 1912 were safer, better run and altogether more comfortable and reassuring than ever before. But it was not always the companies themselves that forced the pace: many key improvements were pioneered abroad and adopted in Britain only reluctantly, even under duress. The country that had given railways to the world often proved surprisingly unproductive as a breeding-ground for further innovation.

◫

This story can be taken back to Mr Briggs, battered and thrown fatally from his carriage in 1864. Could passengers not be provided with some means of raising the alarm from within their compartments? The question was suddenly urgent. It reopened a wider debate concerning the value and practicality of communication through the whole train.

Twice in the 1850s the railways had been instructed to look into the matter. In 1852 the Board of Trade explored the potential of continuous footboards, rather than the shorter steps then commonly provided along the carriage sides, so that the guard could make his way to every part of the train while it was in motion. This was the current practice in Belgium, but British companies were already dispensing with such external excursions. Some pointed out the risk to their men of colliding with bridges and tunnels. Other objections were that easier access would expose single women to the threat of intruders; also, more prosaically, that bold second-class passengers might use the footboards to sneak into first class once the train was in motion. (Despite all of which, the continuous footboard did later become widespread, helping to give access for cleaning and maintenance, as well as serving passengers with a step up to the door.)

Next, a sub-committee of railway general managers investigated systems of passing signals along the train, including methods already in force abroad. The most common of these involved running a cord all the way from the guard's van to the locomotive, where it was linked to a bell, or sometimes to the engine's whistle. The cord might also operate a bell at the guard's end, so that signals could be sent both ways. To permit passengers to sound the alarm by tugging on the cord through the carriage window might seem an obvious step. But there was a serious objection: with effective signalling still at an embryonic stage, any emergency stop sharply increased the risk of a rear-end collision with a following train. The sub-committee therefore allowed its use by passengers only on condition that its misuse by 'the timid or the reckless' was made a penal offence.

Everything rather fizzled out after that. In 1858 a Parliamentary Select Committee on Railway Accidents urged once more that communication between guard and driver be given the highest priority; but the companies were getting better at deflecting interference from Westminster, and nothing much was done until 1863. In that year, another general managers' sub-committee recommended that the link be made by running the cord *under* the doors on the right-hand side – that is, the side commonly kept locked – where passengers' chances of grabbing at it were slim indeed.

The Briggs affair brought other responses. On the London & South Western, glazed circular openings were cut through the bulkheads between compartments, providing a limited view right through the carriage. This was not a new idea, for similar sight-holes were provided in some French carriages after a comparably shocking murder there in 1860. Although they must have deterred a certain amount of misbehaviour, these 'Muller's lights', as they were grimly nicknamed in England, did not find general favour. Nor did they make it any easier for passengers to pass an alarm to driver or guard. That was what the public urgently wanted, and the Board of Trade spoke for many in July 1864 when it instructed the companies to come up with something.

By this time the objection to emergency stops on a main line no longer had the same force, thanks to advances in protection by signalling. Rather, the sticking point was the lack of any alarm system reliable enough to earn official endorsement. Several were already in use or under trial. Some had switches or buttons in the compartments, wired to a battery-powered electric bell in the guard's compartment. A contraption with an iron speaking-tube running all along the train, linked between the carriages by flexible wire-and-rubber pipes, was quite seriously proposed as an alternative. Most of the devices were also meant to trigger an indicator arm or disc that poked out from the carriage side when the signal was given, so that the guard could track the alarm to its source with a single glance.

Two successive committees of railway managers scrutinised these systems, and found them all wanting. To outsiders, such reservations sounded like temporising. By 1868 the Board of Trade had had enough. Under the Regulation of Railways Act of that year, all trains timetabled to run non-stop for twenty miles or more were required to permit emergency communication between passengers and crew. Which apparatus to endorse was left to the Board of Trade to decide. The Board duly sanctioned an installation devised by the North Eastern Railway's chief engineer, by which a tuggable rope jerked a wheel-mounted bell in the guard's van and banged a gong on the tender of the engine. But the apparatus did not work well in practice, to the extent that the inspectorate had already recommended against it. In 1873 the Board acknowledged these failings too, and quietly withdrew its endorsement.

Left to choose for themselves, the railways came to no collective conclusion. Three of the four main companies in the south of England plumped for electric alarm systems. These had the advantage of allowing the controls to be placed inside the compartment. Making the equipment reliable took some years, however, as the Baker case of 1875 suggests. In court, the train's guard came clean: there was no working connection between the carriages, and not one of the controls actually did anything. The fourth of the southern companies, the London, Chatham & Dover, chose a cord system instead, but spoiled matters by running this along the bottom of its carriages. The alarm could be given only by groping through a hole in the floor beneath the seats. In other regions, passengers had to remember to open the window and grasp upwards for a cord at eaves level on the carriage roof. The existence of all these incompatible systems also made it less likely that an alarm would work at all, because it could not be linked up along the train when rolling stock from different companies ran together. Such were the consequences of laissez-faire.

Some figures for the usage of these early alarms are included in F. S. Williams's *Our Iron Roads* (1883 edition). On the South Eastern Railway, the electric alarm sounded on average about once every three and a half weeks. Of fourteen instances described in detail, only two involved matters of safety, both of a mechanical kind: an open door and an overheated axle. The rest were due to 'curiosity', an impulse that may not have come cheap: the 1868 Act laid down a fine of £5 for improper use, equivalent to 1,200 miles of third-class travel at the normal rate.

₪

There matters largely stood until near the end of the century. The trigger for improvement was a dreadful accident, caused by the unsatisfactory brakes then still in use on many British and Irish lines. The brakes having failed, unsafe methods of signalling and operation made the consequences still worse for the stricken train. Parliament then forced the hand of the reluctant railway industry, and improved braking systems were made mandatory. These brought with them a more reliable method for passengers to operate the alarm. In effect, the lesser hazard of non-communicating compartments was reduced as a by-product of making the network safer overall.

The accident happened in Ulster, on 12 June 1889. An overloaded and underpowered Sunday school excursion train stalled near the summit of the long incline outside Armagh, on the line to Newry. Some 960 people were on board. The crew decided to divide the train in order to proceed. That required the release of the brakes. These were of the 'simple' type, which depended on a continuous supply of vacuum pressure piped from the locomotive in order to stay in place against the wheels. To make safe the rear portion of the train, the men applied the handbrake in the guard's van and wedged stones from the track ballast against the carriage wheels. But when the locomotive began to draw away with the front portion of the train, a fatal jolt was transmitted to the now isolated rear section. The wheels crunched through their restraining stones, and nine carriages and the ineffectually braked van began to roll backwards down the slope. The crew ran after the accelerating carriages for a while, trying to stop the wheels with more stones, but it was useless. Nor could the passengers jump clear: their compartment doors had been locked on both sides, to prevent unauthorised entry. Powerless, the carriages ran back down the incline and into the path of the following train. This was running under the antiquated time-interval method, by which trains using the same line were separated by an intermission calculated to prevent them catching up with each other. As the carriages were smashed or overturned, eighty passengers died, most of them children – the worst toll in any railway accident to that date in the British Isles.

On paper, the Armagh carriages were up-to-date in terms of safety. They had continuous brakes, controlled from the locomotive and effective all the way down to the last vehicle – as if the train were a single organism with a central nervous system. The older method of braking was activated by the guard using levers or chains, and was usually limited to individual vehicles along the train. Sometimes this required a whole posse of guards, positioned at intervals between the locomotive and the guard's van or brake van at the end. To manage an entire train effectively these guards had to work in step with the driver, as he applied or released the brakes of the engine and tender. The weakness of the method is illustrated by Dickens's ill-fated boat train of 1865: the driver saw the emergency signal and braked hard, but the guards remained oblivious until too late. But there is a key distinction between continuous braking and continuous *automatic* braking. The latter kind came instantly into play if the brake pipe was severed or interrupted, as it would be when a train split in two. The brakes at Armagh were of the non-automatic type, requiring a constant input of energy in order to operate; once the rear carriages lost their connection to the vacuum power from the locomotive they could not be reapplied. Automatic brakes worked in precisely the opposite way, remaining clamped against the wheels *except* when released by vacuum pressure to allow the train to move. It is a neat illustration of the fail-safe principle, a term sometimes misused as a synonym for foolproof, but which strictly refers to any system that reverts to a safe position when a fault occurs.

The Board of Trade had been urging the use of automatic brakes for years. The companies could hardly refuse point blank, but often dragged their feet. To complicate matters, there was – inevitably – more than one method available. Most British railways favoured the vacuum principle, by which air was exhausted from reservoirs and pipes along the train. Less widespread were air brakes, which worked by compressing rather than exhausting the air within the system. Much higher forces can be obtained by compressing air above the atmospheric rate than by pumping it out to make a vacuum, so the pipes and reservoirs could be made smaller and lighter. The air brake could also be applied more quickly. It was a better method.

Already common abroad, air brakes had made some progress in Britain by the 1880s. The most popular system was developed from that patented in 1869 by the twenty-five-year-old George Westinghouse of Pittsburgh. Britain was an obvious export market for Westinghouse, not least because of the enormous quantities of rolling stock that were built in its workshops for use overseas. As to the choice of system for home rails, this should have been settled by the trials held on the Midland Railway's lines at Newark in June 1875: a sort of brake Olympics, in which trains belonging to six railway companies demonstrated their stopping distances with roughly equal loads and speeds under eight different braking systems. Westinghouse's automatic air brake was the clear winner.

Yet the Westinghouse air brake found a secure home only in Scotland and in southern, eastern and north-eastern England, where the panting of the little air-pumps attached to the locomotives became part of the background noise at every busy station. Many other railways invested in one or other of the various vacuum-brake systems, after which the expense of conversion to air brakes was forbidding. Even so, the existence of incompatible versions imposed extra costs on any railway sending carriages through to lines on which a rival form prevailed. Such vehicles had to be equipped with two sets of pipes – one to work the brake, the other just passing through – before continuous braking could operate at all. Taking no chances, the royal train in the 1880s was equipped with *three* sets of brakes. The risks were genuine: a derailment of 1887 at Aviemore in the Scottish Highlands, where many trains included through carriages from other parts of Britain, was blamed on a diversity of brakes: every carriage was so equipped, but in such a combination that not one vehicle could be controlled from the locomotive.

All this caused exasperation and mistrust outside the industry. The wrangles over braking also exposed the ways in which vested interests and railway capital had colonised the political realm. The benefits of automatic brakes were widely understood, and moves had been made in

Parliament in 1871 and 1877 to enforce their use; but each time the reform was thwarted by the 'Railway Interest'. This was formally defined as those members of both houses who had seats on the boards of railway companies. There was nothing furtive about the Railway Interest; its members were listed annually under that heading in *Bradshaw's Railway Manual* (sister publication to the famous Guide). The nexus was already strong by the Mania years – there were eighty railway directors in the House of Commons in 1847 – and peaked in 1873, when 132 MPs enjoyed at least one railway directorship. That was almost exactly one in five. Other MPs and peers with railway shareholdings large enough to keep them mindful of sharply increased running costs and capitalisation could be expected to line up behind these well-placed directors.

The railways' defence, articulated inside and outside Westminster, was to claim that they were making good progress with safety improvements, and should be left to get on with the job as their own resources allowed. The Armagh disaster changed all that. A new Railway Regulation Act was pushed through, making automatic brakes compulsory. The Act was a clear break with established relationships between government and railways, by which technical matters had been left for the Board of Trade to determine. Even then, the Act failed to enforce a single system of automatic braking. Instead, the companies had to choose between Westinghouse's air brake and one version or another of the vacuum type. The latter having the head start, the incentive to upgrade to the more efficient system dwindled away.* So it came about that, when Britain's railways were grouped into four companies in 1923, the vacuum brake was endorsed as standard for new locomotive-hauled stock.

There were exceptions, one of which nicely proves the rule. In 1923 the Great Eastern Railway's London suburban lines into Liverpool Street had just been reorganised. Even before the changes they were already the busiest of their kind on any railway system, handling over 107 million passenger journeys a year in 1919; but the strains were showing. Adding to the strain, the average City clerk or typist's working hours after the First World War tended to be shorter than in Edwardian times, accentuating the crush at the evening peak. Then in 1920 the timetable was transformed, increasing capacity by 50 per cent in the crucial evening period, by rethinking every

---

* They did these things differently abroad; the Imperial Railway Office of Bismarck's newly united Germany insisted on air brakes, and got them.

operational detail. Sixteen-coach suburban trains – still four-wheeled, still gaslit, but all equipped with Westinghouse's brake – now set out to climb the incline from Liverpool Street at intervals as short as two and a half minutes, after spending no more than four minutes at the platform after arrival. Each of these movements required the incoming locomotive to be detached and despatched, as well as the prompt appearance of a fresh engine at the opposite end to draw the train out again. Stopping and acceleration times at other stations were kept as brisk as possible too. The result has never been surpassed as the most intensive steam-worked passenger service anywhere in the world. These smart manoeuvres would barely have been possible using the slower-acting vacuum brake.

This was not all. Passengers were steered and signalled through the crush by means of number codes for quick identification of trains across the sea of bobbing hats, and colour codes to indicate the higher classes of compartment within in each train: a blue stripe above the doors for Second, which lingered late on these lines, and a yellow stripe for First. The convention of marking first class with a yellow stripe later spread through the network, persisting even now in some of the flashy liveries of privatisation.

An evening paper soon labelled the new timetable the 'Jazz service', after the latest American musical craze. The inspiration may have been the colour stripes, hence the alternative label of the 'Rainbow service', or (more likely) the accelerated speeds. America was speeding up in other ways too, including the electrification of many of its suburban railway services. The underground lines and several other main-line routes to the London suburbs had already gone electric, but the Great Eastern lacked the money to follow them. So there is a subtext to the 'Jazz' nickname, a whisper that London was no longer the first home of mechanised urban bustle, as it had been in Queen Victoria's time.

By the 1940s no one considered these overcrowded services especially modern any more. As the Second World War drew to its close, a newspaper joked that Goering and Himmler should be punished after capture by being made to ride between Liverpool Street and Romford all day long, for ever. By the end of 1946 it was common for twenty-three people or more to have to cram into each dirty and shabby twelve-seat compartment (squeezing in seven per side, the rest standing). Underframes had to be strengthened after an incident on the Enfield line, when the doors jammed shut because the weight of its sardine-packed passengers had caused the structure of the carriage to deflect out of true. Extra rolling stock could not be drafted in promptly from the rest of the network, because it lacked the necessary Westinghouse brake. Bad coal meant that trains often had to stop to get up steam between stations. In the House of Commons, the service was described as 'a positive disgrace to our civilisation', and compared to something from the time of Dickens or Zola. Things improved at Liverpool Street only after the railways were nationalised, when long-planned electrification began at last.

The advent of single ownership also brought the hoary question of standardised braking back into focus. The obvious reform almost happened in 1955, when air brakes were recommended by two expert committees, but the plan was given up after pressure from the railways' operational side. Air brakes finally became the norm for new passenger stock only in 1967, and many locomotives carried the equipment for both systems well into the 1990s. To the informed eye, the fat, archaic vacuum hoses looped next to the buffers were one more token of the inertia and inefficiency of Britain's railways – weaknesses that may be traced back to the nineteenth-century failure to distinguish between the benefits of unregulated operation and the wastefulness of incompatible systems.

Whatever their other failings, the first generations of automatic brakes at least delivered a better class of passenger alarm. The need for separate communication between passengers and crew effectively disappeared, because the alarm could now be linked directly to the brake. The old usage 'communication cord' somehow survived, even though the new apparatus was more likely to be operated by a handle or a chain. And so matters have largely remained ever since, with the proviso that some alarms now include an intercom connected with the driver. Even the £5 fine for misuse stipulated in the 1868 Act stayed in force until 1977, by which time inflation had made it quite a bargain in the economy of public misdemeanours; it now stands at £200.

₪

The march of sanitation on Britain's railways moved at a slow pace too. The story of the carriage lavatory was outlined by Hamilton Ellis in 1965:

> 1848–50, lavatories in royal saloons … ; 1850–60 (*circa*), lavatories
> in family and invalid saloons; 1873, lavatories in sleeping cars; 1874,

lavatories in Pullman and Pullman-type cars; 1881–2, lavatories in East
Coast first-class coaches with side corridor; 1886, lavatories in M.S.
and L. [Manchester, Sheffield & Lincolnshire] third-class saloons;
1887, lavatories in Midland Railway third-class coaches; 1889, lavatories in second- and third-class coaches with side corridors on East
Coast Route; 1891, lavatories for all classes in complete side-corridor
train on Great Western Railway ...

Saloons of early date, royal or otherwise, with their own lavatories have
already been described. The ultimate outcome for the ordinary passenger
train, with lavatories at the ends of intercommunicating carriages, is familiar. In between came many attempts to crack the problem of how to incorporate the facilities in non-corridor trains. The result was an extraordinary
variety of plans, as diverse internally as the standard, lavatory-free type of
compartment carriage was predictable.

The higher classes of accommodation naturally did best. A representative design was the London & North Western's tri-composite carriage of 1887 – i.e. one with first-, second- and third-class compartments
– in which the two first-class compartments were separated by a pair of
lavatory cubicles, dovetailed together by means of a diagonal partition.
A first/third composite of 1880 on the Manchester, Sheffield & Lincolnshire Railway had just one lavatory, reserved for one of the two first-class
compartments; the other was designated for smoking, as if to imply that
passengers had to choose between different kinds of relief. The more generous standards of the Edwardians can be represented by a tri-composite
carriage built in 1903 by the London & South Western, which can still be
seen in the National Railway Museum at York. Each of its three classes is
represented by two pairs of compartments, separated by pairs of lavatories
with doors opening on opposing sides. In this way every compartment had
exclusive use of its own lavatory.

All these plans had two drawbacks: each lavatory could serve only
one compartment, which was wasteful of space, and each was also a bit too
close to the seating area for comfort. Much better was to have some sort
of transitional space, favouring hygiene and modesty at the same time –
just as houses and offices are not usually designed with lavatories opening
directly into their main living and working spaces. And so the side corridor began to come into its own.

Side-corridor carriages were not a new idea. The principle was first set

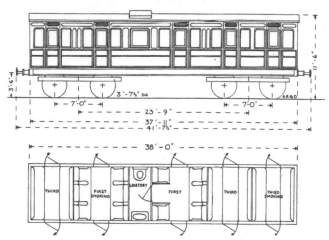

The Manchester, Sheffield & Lincolnshire Railway's composite
carriage of 1880, showing the internal arrangements

out by the German railway engineer Edmund Heusinger von Waldegg in
the wake of the railway murders of the 1860s, but found little immediate
acceptance. How it could work is shown by the Great Northern Railway's
progressive-minded first-class carriage of 1881, with a gentleman's lavatory
cubicle at one end, a ladies' at the other and a corridor alongside the four
compartments in between. Another variant is represented by a composite
design of 1911 for the Great Central Railway, the successor to the Manchester, Sheffield & Lincolnshire company. Each first-class compartment
had its own direct-access cubicle, but the third-class compartments shared
one between two, by means of a short side corridor or vestibule. In this
case each third-class lavatory was held in common between seventeen passenger places, as against seven places in first class.

All these vestibules and lavatories reduced the passenger load of the
carriage. One way to mitigate the loss was to fix a fold-up seat on the
outer face of the lavatory door. Some lines tried this in the 1890s. The
expedient was liable to cause confusion. A correspondent to the *Railway
Magazine* in 1899 recounted his alarm when travelling in a glass-fronted
compartment of the coupé type on the Caledonian line. It happened that
the next carriage also ended in a coupé compartment, in which two passengers were visible. Glancing up from his reading a little later, the correspondent noted that one of the two had apparently vanished. Frightening

possibilities filled his mind, until the missing passenger suddenly reap-peared from within the lavatory compartment that was masked by the middle seat.

The *Railway Magazine*'s man also reported that the company had begun to remove these extra seats, which no one much liked. It is not hard to see why. When the compartment was full, any sortie to the facilities required a polite request that the seat's occupant should stand and make way. And what happened after that? If the displaced passenger sat down again, the visitor would have to tap on the door from the other side to be released. If the displaced person moved instead to the visitor's temporar-ily vacant seat, a sort of *pas de deux* in the space between the knees of other passengers would be necessary before both could get back to their positions. If the displaced passenger proved unwilling to move back, the visitor was left to take a turn on the worst seat in the compartment. Seri-ous embarrassment, one way or the other; much better to wait until the station, if you could manage it.

Lavatory compartments made carriages look different from outside, as little windows of frosted or engraved glass began to appear among the clear-glazed passenger compartments. The Great Central proudly chose a pattern for its lavatory glass comprising the company's own coat of arms and motto ('Forward'). Clear spots within the patterns and frost-ings allowed the passenger to keep an eye on the journey's progress, saving unnecessary panic – for instance, when a signal stop might be mistaken for early arrival at the correct station. In turn, the experienced passenger at the platform could use these windows to help locate a compartment with lavatory access.

The contraptions provided within were comparably diverse. Those in the early saloon carriages, royal ones not excluded, were of the commode or close-stool type. The next step was to make a lavatory with a chute that could discharge directly on to the track. The best of these were of the valve type, in which the basin was kept filled with water. Flushing the lavatory released the water and the waste together. The Midland Railway devel-oped an apparatus that flushed the valve automatically when the lid was closed. It refilled when the lid was lifted again. Cheaper installations made do with a metal pan that emptied by tipping sideways, or a fixed pan with a chute-hole towards the back that could be flushed through after use. The latter type in particular had the drawback of exposing the user to howling draughts from below, especially in colder weather and when the train was moving at speed. The remedy, not always pursued, was to fit a sprung flap at the bottom of the chute or at the back of the pan, to be forced open by the flush. The 1880s brought the washdown closet, in which a fresh discharge of clean water replaced the water and waste in the pan. This became the standard British type. Its chief disadvantage, as most people discover, is that it stops working as soon as the water runs out. The drawbacks of the other kinds will be familiar to many with experience of railway travel overseas.

Gentlemen visiting the facilities in the Great Northern's carriage of 1882 were presented with a choice between a water closet and a urinal. This was uncommon as well as wasteful of space, and the fittings were usually arranged more compactly. Square footage was often saved by the use of fold-down washbasins of nickel plate or some other metal, a type also much used in ships' cabins. These could be fixed to the partition above the lavatory seat. Popular varieties included those patented by James Beresford, which drained through a hopper behind when pushed back upright. The foldaway type gave way in the early twentieth century to fixed basins, which encouraged the use of ceramics (equipped with push-type taps, which could not be left running). Even tiled walls and floors were not unknown. These have been replaced in turn by lighter and more robust fixtures of fibreglass, plastic or stainless steel. Now it is disconcerting to encounter ceramic basins and bowls in preserved railway carriages; the heavy and fragile material seems out of place, as if it had strayed from the immobile world of buildings and mains drainage.

Water for these fixtures had at first to be pumped up from a tank under the floor, by jerking hard on a pivoting handle. Later cisterns were placed higher up, either behind a partition or in the form of a tank under the roof, which also helped give impetus to the flush. The water for the basins was initially not heated, so a single cold tap was all that was needed. Hot water was a refinement of Edwardian times, which our traveller of 1912 would have encountered in the newer sorts of carriages – but only in the colder months, for the warmth came from the same circuit that operated the steam heating according to season. The lack of hot water in summer will be among the railway memories of older readers, not all of whom will have guessed the explanation.

Confusingly for us, washbasins were commonly called 'lavatories' by the Victorians. 'Toilet', a genteelism with transatlantic roots, may have become a familiar British usage in the twentieth century partly because the railways adopted it, according to Hamilton Ellis (who detested the 'silly, mincing' word). Some sort of unisex term was clearly required, especially as railway carriages generally gave up designating cubicles for men or for women shortly after the First World War. At stations, where separate facilities prevailed, the more oblique convention could be used, signposted simply as 'Ladies' or 'Gentlemen'.

Some British railway lavatories are still of the washdown type, although these are fast giving way to the kind in which the waste is collected in an underfloor retention tank for later disposal. These were first used on British Rail in the sleeping cars introduced in 1981, of which more is said in Chapter 8. Since that time, the familiar notices requesting passengers not to flush while at stations have been disappearing from the nation's trains. The more recent kinds are emptied by a startlingly sudden power-vacuum, rather than by flushing through from above. Their ancestry can be traced to the high-speed 'bullet trains' of the Tokaido line in Japan, opened in 1964 – well ahead of the vacuum toilets developed for the US space programme, or those used in airliners since the 1970s.

From the railways' point of view, the best aspect of the old method was its dispersal of the waste naturally; the ballast between the tracks, combined with an element of speed in the discharge and the natural action of the weather, effectively turned the trackbed into something like a linear filter bed. The same could not be said of places where the line ran through a tunnel, although this is probably not something to which many travellers have ever given much thought. But it is impossible to excuse the shameful abuse of the rule against flushing at the station platform, to the extent that membranes of thick black plastic are sometimes now put down between the rails, to make clearing up easier. These open-air latrines may be seen at Paddington, for example (if anyone really wants to). The latest safeguard against the anti-social flusher, introduced in Scotland in 2012, links the toilet mechanism electronically to the train's GPS satellite co-ordinates, so that discharges are made only beyond the station limits. There still remains the hidden burden of cleaning the undersides and wheelsets of the trains, spattered with dried-on filth across every surface and crevice – and doing so without imperilling the health of the workers in the carriage sheds. The faster the train, the worse the effects below the carriage floor. A time-travelling early-Victorian railway engineer might well be nonplussed at what the twenty-first century worker is expected to put up with.

₪

In the matter of carriage wheels, the crucial change between 1862 and 1912 reflected the increasing lengths of carriages. Two or three fixed axles per vehicle were sufficient while wheelbases remained short, but anything longer required wheels that could swivel to follow the curvature of the rails. The lead was taken in the United States, where railroad tracks were often flimsily laid and followed tight serpentine courses. To overcome this problem the pivoting four-wheeled bogie was developed. This in turn favoured longer wheelbases: hence the type of large, open saloon coach which became usual in America in the 1840s. So the two traditions diverged early on, and British carriages (and most Continental ones) stayed small.

In the 1870s things began to change, when some progressive-minded British lines introduced longer carriages with fully pivoting four-wheeled bogies. Their interiors were of conventional form, and most passengers would probably not have noticed the difference in wheel arrangement, however much they may have appreciated the smoother ride. The same could not be said of another innovation of the 1870s, on the Midland Railway. Its manager James Allport toured the North American railroads from coast to coast in 1872. Here he encountered the luxurious new bogie coaches recently introduced by George Mortimer Pullman (1831–97). These 'Palace cars' came in two varieties, open saloons and sleeping cars (of which more in the next chapter). Impressed, Allport invited Pullman to make a presentation to the Midland's next meeting of stockholders in 1873. The American then undertook to send over examples of both types from his works at Detroit in a sort of flat-pack form, for reassembly and operation under contract on the Midland's rails. Central to the deal was that Pullman's company would pay their operating costs over a fixed period, in return for the supplementary fees paid by the passengers on top of the Midland's normal fare. Even the attendants on these trains were provided by Pullman, who initially brought men across the Atlantic for the purpose. Hoping to extend the business model across Britain and beyond, he named his new overseas enterprise the Pullman Palace Car Co. (Europe).

Some of the advanced features of these imported carriages – lavatories, oil-fired heating – have already been mentioned. Names, rather than numbers, were assigned to them, in a possibly unconscious revival of the earliest railway practice: *Midland, Ohio, Enterprise, Victoria*. Especially seductive were the saloons, or parlor cars (in the American usage). Their walnut-lined interiors presented the Briton with a deluxe version of the single spaces that had confronted Dickens and Trollope on their railroad explorations; *The Times*'s man on the trial run in 1874 was reminded of 'a luxuriously appointed yacht'. Instead of bench-type seating, twin rows of velvet-trimmed swivel chairs of spoon-backed profile extended along the main space, which was flooded with light from close-set picture windows, a clerestory and (at night) a generous array of paraffin lamps. For those who preferred more privacy there were also two smaller compartments, each with a pair of swivel chairs and a sofa, reached via a short side corridor. Doors at each end of the car gave on to an open platform like a veranda, sheltered by a projection of the roof. These could be connected with the platforms of other Pullman cars to allow free passage through the moving train.

As with the Westinghouse brake saga, the encounter should have been transformative, an injection of fresh ideas into a hidebound, insular tradition. Certainly there was no shortage of publicity for the new cars; they even popped up in the plot of the Christmas pantomime for 1874 at Covent Garden (it was *Babes in the Wood*). The Pullman company's readiness to supply rolling stock – effectively allowing the railway companies to contract out a service without sharing the financial risk – also had its attractions. Yet the British response was slow, and partial at best. Some resistance was encountered to the idea of paying a supplement, especially on the Midland: affronted letters to *The Times* accused the company of imposing an extra charge for what was a de facto replacement for the old first class, now that the company had done away with second class. And although several lines tried out the new coaches, only a handful took the concept of the premium-rate saloon to heart. In effect, the native tradition of simple pricing by class rather than by supplementary service survived on most trains, and it was as a niche operation that the British spin-off of the Pullman company found its place.

In the forefront of Pullman-friendly routes was the London, Brighton & South Coast; a surprising outcome, perhaps, as its main lines were shorter than most. Improved versions of the early parlor cars made up its 'Southern Belle' service, introduced in 1908 ('The most luxurious train in the world', as the posters had it), which managed the London-to-Brighton run in an hour. The association remained close enough to encourage the Pullman company to relocate in 1928 to a vacant workshop at Preston Park in the outer suburbs of Brighton. When the line was electrified in

1933, the Southern Belle was replaced by an electric version named the Brighton Belle. This ran until 1972, latterly in a rather ramshackle condition, but beloved nonetheless. Its demise was mourned in style; *The Times* reported that the last London service would depart after a performance of Hector Berlioz's cantata *Le chant des chemin de fer*, composed in 1846 for the opening of the Paris–Lille railway and rarely dusted off since (*Que de montagnes effacées! / Que de rivières traversées!*). A coterie of regular travellers had done what they could to retain the service, including the thespian-Brightonians Dame Flora Robson and Lord Olivier; the latter's successful defence of the kipper option on the train's breakfast menu in the 1960s is still remembered in the seaside city.

₪

Olivier's kippers are a reminder that the provision of meals on the railways of Britain also owes much to George Mortimer Pullman. The crucial date was 1879, when one of his parlor cars was adapted for use on the Leeds expresses of the Great Northern Railway. Tables for dining were inserted between the pairs of seats in the middle section, between a little coke-fired kitchen at one end of the car and a smoking saloon at the other, so that gentlemen could withdraw for a cigar after their plates were cleared. The modified vehicle was renamed *Prince of Wales*, as if to hint at the pleasures of good living. The Midland carried out a similar conversion on two of its parlor cars in 1881–2; one was dubbed *Delmonico* after the celebrated New York restaurant company, then in its pomp.

The introduction of kitchen facilities brought into focus the open platforms at the ends of these early Pullman cars. These platforms, whose ancestry lay in the river-saloon prototype, were altogether alien to native traditions of carriage building. To British eyes they may have suggested a rather *déclassé* affinity with horse trams and omnibuses. (The platforms' combination of foreignness and potential peril has since been reinforced for Anglo-Saxons by their many appearances in Westerns, usually as a place to leap for, shoot from or tumble off.) So the platforms of British Pullmans never became a normal means for passengers to move through the train. This in turn explains why one end of *Prince of Wales* could be reserved for a scullery. A further advance in design was required before the ordinary passenger could walk along the train to take a seat in a restaurant car, without having to go out into the open air – and the rain, and the dark

– at every junction between the swaying carriages. Conversely, the dining car was condemned to remain an exceptional luxury unless it could be made to operate more like a restaurant, with multiple sittings if necessary, to make fuller use of an expensive specialist item of rolling stock.

The solution lay in a flexible enclosed gangway between the carriages. This too was an American invention, dating back to the 1850s. The concept crossed the Atlantic in the following decade, at first only as a means of joining together the new royal carriages of the London & North Western. That way, the Queen's attendants could reach her person without the train having to stop (Victoria herself is reported never to have ventured through the gangway while the train was moving). For these carriages, a bellows-type connection was used. An improved connection was developed for Pullman saloon cars in the late 1880s, and this crossed the Atlantic too; it had an enclosed entrance vestibule at the carriage ends, with external doors that opened *inwards* – a peculiar arrangement to British eyes. But there was another way: the end gangway could be combined with the home-grown compartment plan, on condition that a corridor was provided along one side.

So the railways of Britain edged forward to the concept of the passenger train as a continuous internal space, not in one great leap, but by a series of niche-market luxury services and one-off conversions. What looks in retrospect like the point of no return was reached in the early 1890s, when innovative trains appeared on the Great Eastern and Great Western railways.

The Great Eastern came up with a trio of permanently coupled carriages, of which the middle vehicle contained a small dining saloon and a kitchen. At one end was a first- and second-class composite, at the other an all-third-class carriage, both with corridors alongside the compartments. Third-class passengers had to troop through the kitchen to dine, but that was a small price to pay for equal access to these alluring new facilities. The carriages operated on the lines running cross-country to Harwich, which was then flourishing as a port for sailings to the Low Countries. The route carried a healthy traffic from northern England across East Anglia, and the journey was long enough to coincide with one or other of the day's main mealtimes.

These Great Eastern carriages were still of the old-fashioned six-wheeled type. The Great Western's ambitions were grander. After years of complicated co-existence it had finally abandoned Brunel's broad gauge in 1892, converting the last remaining tracks to standard width. Its new corridor train was meant to show that the company was looking to the future. The four carriages were mounted on bogies in the up-to-date manner, which allowed for a greater length – at 50ft each, more than a third longer than the Great Eastern's. Its corridors gave every passenger access to a lavatory, and also a choice between ordinary compartments and a small smoking saloon in each carriage. What they did not yet do was allow the curious or the sociable to go from one carriage to another: the gangway doors were kept locked and were meant purely for the use of the guard. Thus, in effect, were the first-class facilities defended against the third-class intruder. There was some logic to this: with no dining-car service on offer, there was no good reason to go wandering except vulgar curiosity, or a quest for a better class of toilet.

One operational disadvantage of these early carriages was that the end gangways lined up with the corridor, off the central axis. That was helpful to the luggage-laden, who could walk through in a straight line; but it ignored the possibility that a carriage might be reversed by 180 degrees in the course of normal working, so that what had been a right-hand gangway ended up obstructively on the left, or vice versa. The solution was to insert a vestibule or passage at each end of the carriage, connecting to a gangway placed on the centre line. The left-over space thus created alongside became the obvious place to put the lavatory compartment.

Further refinements followed. In particular, the side corridor helped to break the convention that every compartment should have its own external door. Instead, carriages could have doorways opening directly into the vestibules, making a sort of cross-passage at each end. An early example was the sequence of splendidly sleek-sided express carriages built from 1904 for the Great Western, which measured up to 70ft long, a figure not routinely exceeded in Britain until the 1970s. Following the Edwardian fondness for topical nicknames, these became known as 'Dreadnoughts', after the giant Royal Navy battleships of the day. The plan-type represented one further step away from the origins of the railway carriage as a composite of cell-like spaces. Instead, the interior became more like an elongated building, in which a few external doors led to a linear circulation space with internal doors, each opening to the individual 'room' of passenger compartment or lavatory.

Advantages of this arrangement included better protection from draughts, now that each compartment no longer had an external door.

The chief drawback was that entrances and exits were much slower, especially when a train was crowded; worse, the pushiest passengers might elbow their way on board before the slowest or most luggage-laden had a chance to get off. One such incident in 1920, involving a Birmingham football excursion, got so out of hand that carriage doors were broken off in a platform brawl. So a modified plan came into favour in mid century, with doors to a cross-passage halfway along the carriage as well as at the ends.

The standard version of this type, as developed after nationalisation, became the single most numerous design of carriage ever to run on Britain's railways, to a total of 2,168. The last were built in 1963, and the design remained numerous even on some main-line routes out of London into the early 1990s. Borrowing from military usage, this generation of carriages was dubbed the Mark 1, as if to signal a new start. They represented the final eclipse of wood-framed construction, employing steel exclusively for underframe, body and cladding. Joinery for internal use lasted a little longer, and Mark 1s also made much use of veneered panelling, to which were affixed earnest little labels identifying the type of wood and its origin: 'Crown Elm Great Britain', and so on. Less obviously, the carriages were also rather under-insulated, with single-glazed windows and inadequate provision to muffle the greater levels of noise associated with all-steel construction.

A sortie to the buffet car of a train of corridor Mark 1s on a winter's evening was an adventure in microclimates. Warmth and comfort were represented by the compartment, which (if all was well) enjoyed heating and reading lamps that could be controlled by the occupants. The compartment might be made still more private by means of sprung blinds of thick glazed fabric, which could be pulled down over the outside window and also over the tall narrow windows on the corridor side – two next to the seats, one for the window in the sideways-sliding door between. Beyond this threshold was the territory of the draughts, which seemed somehow to come from all directions at once, but with a general impetus in line with the direction of travel. A steady roar of air currents forced an entry through the gaps around the upper windows along the corridor. The draughts were checked a little where swing doors were fixed across the corridor, as when second-class gave way to first within the same carriage, but raged unhindered in the under-lit vestibules at the carriage ends. Here too could be found the narrow doors to the lavatories, not always easily identifiable in the sheer-sided panelling of the carriage wall. Now the draughts were magnified by the input from crevices around the external doors, mingled with the greater inrush through the corridor connection. This was no place to linger, with its chorus of creaks and squeaks emerging from the shapeless and squashy sides and from beneath the steel floor-plate, the point at which the restless differential motions of one carriage against the next became unsettlingly visible.

If the carriage ends were all too dark and solid, the corridors were almost the opposite. Here, overlapping reflections of illuminated compartments in the glass of the windows and corridor windows competed for the brain's attention with the real images of the spaces themselves, and with the sharper, slightly dulled but altogether irresistible glimpses of passengers on the opposing seats presented in the mirrors fixed to the crosswalls of the compartments just ahead. Further disorientation occurred when entering a new carriage that was reversed in relation to the rest, so that the corridor switched from one side to the other – an effect like that of going next door in a mirrored pair of semi-detached houses, and a useful mnemonic and landmark for the swaying journey back to the home compartment. The speeds might be faster, the finishes and fabrics more modern, the light bulbs a little brighter, but the whole experience was in essence the same as that of the traveller on an up-to-date Edwardian train.

All gone now, in Britain at least (the compartmented carriage is still current in parts of the Continent). We are left with variants of the saloon, now stripped of the luxuries and supplements that attended Pullman travel. The single-space interior with its central gangway is so familiar, and so straightforward and logical in its alignment with the corridor connection, that it is surprising how slowly it was adopted as standard. Yet the type was as old as the twentieth century, beginning with two carriage sets built by the Great Western in 1900–1901 for its trains to South Wales. The company hoped to set a trend by providing a kitchen car from which refreshments could be brought to passengers at their seats, to be served on demountable tables. And yet nobody seemed to like the new carriages much, partly because they proved to be unusually cold in winter. There was even a report in 1920 that some passengers encountering the carriages at Paddington had left in a huff to take the rival route via Euston instead, despite having paid in advance for – so they imagined – a reserved first-class compartment. Saloons made more headway on certain electrified suburban routes, and they had a monopoly of London's deep Tube lines from day one, but the side-corridor carriage remained the norm for long-distance railway travel in Britain, with Pullman cars among the occasional exceptions.

Explanations based on national character are out of fashion nowadays, but during most of the twentieth century the idea that Britons were by nature more private and reserved than other races would still have found general assent. This preference for travelling in separate spaces seems to back up the theory. When less than full, a compartment was a place of promising intimacy: somewhere for friends travelling together to exchange confidences, or a neutral enclosure in which strangers might strike up conversation without the self-consciousness that comes with being overheard. The contrast with the American way continued to be remarked. Here are the musings of the hero of Sinclair Lewis's *Dodsworth* (1929), on his first foray to the Old World: '... how strange was the British fashion of having railway compartments instead of an undivided car with a long aisle along which you could observe ankles, magazines, Rotary buttons, clerical collars, and all the details that made travelling interesting'.

By the 1930s Dodsworth would have stood a slightly better chance of enjoying the cavalcade of ankles, thanks to a new generation of carriages intended for excursion trains. On the London & North Eastern, these carriages were explicitly called 'tourist' stock, and were finished in apple-green-and-cream plywood panelling rather than the unpainted teak then still used for the company's other carriages, in costly continuation of Victorian tradition. Travellers in this tourist stock may have welcomed its affinity with the cheery communality of the char-a-banc and motor-coach party. But fun was one thing, everyday travel by privacy-seeking singles and couples quite another. When the LNER set up a committee during the Second World War to consider what future carriage designs should be like, it concluded that compartment stock was 'substantially more popular'. The Southern Railway received similar feedback from a questionnaire handed out in 1945, when it displayed a new prototype main-line coach at Waterloo and Victoria. The Southern passengers' ideal proved to be compartment stock, with individual reading lights, and heating in the lavatories and in the corridors. Warmer corridors mattered at a time when many trains were crammed from one end to the other with standing passengers and servicemen slumped on kitbags. The people got what they wanted: all these features were provided in the new carriages the Southern began to build shortly afterwards.

॥

Not all Southern Railway trains of the period were like this. The company then had as its chief mechanical engineer the gifted but wayward O. V. S. Bulleid, a man who liked to rethink things from first principles – sometimes successfully, sometimes less so. A small-scale example of the former is the coat hanger he designed in the 1920s for the sleeper compartments of his previous employer, the London & North Eastern. Reasoning that the average man began to undress by taking off his jacket and waistcoat, Bulleid provided a separate trouser crossbar, placed above and projecting beyond the curved support for the upper garments. Less successful ideas included the boxy, freakish experimental steam locomotive that Bulleid designed for the state railways of Ireland, where the devoutly Catholic engineer took himself after the Southern Railway lost its independent existence. His Irish engine burnt the native turf instead of imported British coal, but was destined to remain the only one of its kind.

Somewhere between turf burner and coat hanger on the scale of practicality were the two double-decked electric suburban units Bulleid designed in the latter days of the Southern. The aim was to increase rush-hour capacity without having to extend the station platforms to take longer trains. A cross-Channel precedent existed in a class of trains built in 1933 to serve the Parisian suburbs, but these were more like double-decker buses, one saloon sitting straightforwardly above the other. To allow for the more restricted British loading gauge, Bulleid tessellated together L-shaped lower compartments with upper ones of a fat T-shaped section, the crossbar of the T representing the seat level and the space above it, the stem corresponding to the leg-space provided between these seats and the (raised) floor. Access to each upper space was via a narrow staircase tucked into one side of the lower compartment, whose passengers sat with their heads below the seats of those riding above.

A success in terms of increasing seat numbers, the trains had the drawback of slow loading and unloading in the rush hour. The tight clearances meant that the windows at the upper level had to be of the non-opening kind, so the atmosphere within the smoking carriages in particular became taxing. Even so, Bulleid's double-deckers lasted for over twenty years, grinding around the unglamorous Kentish suburbs on the Dartford loop. But no more were built; instead, British Railways quietly set about lengthening platforms and building orthodox new carriages after all.

One of Bulleid's double-decked units at Charing Cross station,
before departure on a demonstration run. The units entered
normal service the following day, 2 November 1949

No less strange were Bulleid's Tavern Cars, another initiative that
appeared just after nationalisation. The concept was the all too literal one
of a pub on wheels, complete with draught as well as bottled beer. Since
each tavern or bar vehicle was coupled alongside a restaurant car, a similar
look was imposed on both. A real pub, the Chequers Inn at Pulborough
in Sussex, was reportedly Bulleid's model. Internally, the bar compartment had a low ceiling of real oaken beams, and oak settles and benches
against panelled or rough-rendered walls. Long and narrow leaded windows were set high up in the carriage sides; artificial illumination came
from miniatures of the carriage-lamp type, beloved of the stereotypical
suburban semi. Only horse brasses and a blazing hearth were missing from
this image of olde-worlde conviviality. The hostelry look worked less well
in the restaurant car, whose first-class customers sat facing each other in
single rows within a timbered interior like that of a giant caravan, or – to
look ahead to the motor showrooms of 1952 – the rear end of a Morris
Traveller. Again, the windows were of the high-set, thin and leaded type,

meant to discourage too much lingering over the tables, but unpopular with those who liked to enjoy the view while dining.

The external decoration ('livery' is hardly the word) was jaw-dropping. Each Tavern Car was tricked out in painted mock-brickwork and black-and-cream timbering, spliced with the standard BR colours of carmine and cream for the non-pub end. As a finishing touch, the half-timbered part displayed a pictorial name panel, according to the formula 'At the sign of the Jolly Tar' (or White Horse, George and Dragon, etc.).

General derision followed, mixed with aesthetic dismay at the nostalgic fakery; now that they were publicly owned, a better lead in matters of design was expected from the railways. In the House of Commons, members queued up to denounce the 'shoddy Tudoresque monstrosity'. Tom Driberg MP read out a letter of protest to *The Times*, signed by the heads of national bodies including the Victoria and Albert Museum, the Royal College of Art, the Council of Industrial Design, the Architectural Association and the Institute of Contemporary Arts. The official response, delivered by the young James Callaghan as Parliamentary Secretary to the Ministry of Transport, was that 'nobody likes these tavern cars except the public' – for the cars were proving to be both well patronised and profitable.* The painted-on brickwork rapidly disappeared and the poky windows of the restaurant cars were soon modified, but the bar interiors managed ten years of service before reconstruction. The guardians of taste had misjudged the popular mood: Bulleid's novelties came as a tonic at a time when catering services on the railways were still struggling to recover the standards enjoyed before the Second World War.

₪

Olde-tyme finishes notwithstanding, Bulleid's combination of bar or buffet with restaurant car was a prescient one, and reflected a general diversification of refreshment on the rails. The usual assumption in the earliest years was that meals would be available only to passengers seated within

---

* Mere coincidence perhaps, but the future Prime Minister also helped Bulleid by signing off his application to build the double-deck units, in the young MP's other role as Chairman of the Treasury Allocation of Materials Committee; *see* Callaghan's foreword of 1984 to the memoirs of Sidney Weighell, leader of the National Union of Railwaymen.

the restaurant car, as in the early Pullman dining saloons. That changed rapidly as the potential of the continuous corridor was realised, and the option was extended to the cheaper classes, without challenging the convention that the courses should always be served to passengers seated at a table. The 1890s and 1900s witnessed a sort of arms race in railway catering, as competing long-distance lines tried to outflank each other in the pleasures and amenities of travel. There could be up to four sittings on an Anglo-Scottish run, regulated by the issue of seating tickets and summoned by calls from the attendants walking up and down the train (no public address systems then). In some cases, separation was preserved by placing the kitchen compartment between dedicated first- and third-class dining carriages or compartments; or the classes could dine together, or come to separate sittings using the same carriage.

Prices were kept strikingly low; managers were commonly undecided as to whether the dining cars were there primarily to make money for the company, or to attract and retain loyal passengers. Menus were often sumptuous, although quantity and quality did not always live up to the billing. For two shillings and sixpence, the London & South Western in 1910 offered four courses at luncheon: *consommé fermière purée parmentier*, boiled turbot in sauce cardinal, roast sirloin with sprouts and potatoes, apple tart and Devonshire cream. Dinner, priced at a shilling higher, comprised six courses, including an entrée of chicken between the fish and meat courses and concluding with cheese. The ingenuity required to prepare and present such meals from a cramped and swaying kitchen without spillage, scalding or breakage may be imagined, and not every railway took the burden directly on itself; the LSWR subcontracted its catering to Messrs Spiers and Pond, pioneers of the railway luncheon basket. Vast complements of crockery, cutlery and glassware were required; the collector John Mander calculated that each dining train on the London, Midland & Scottish Railway needed 1,510 pieces for a full service. In terms of price, there was surprisingly little difference between the restaurant car and the hampers described in Chapter 2; and who would not prefer four kitchen-fresh courses served at table to a flimsy box containing a hunk of elderly pie, an apple and a bottle of beer?

As if to underscore this appeal, catering vehicles were spaces of conspicuous display. The Midland Railway gave out that a new dining car introduced in 1896 had been fitted up by Messrs Gillow, one of the smartest interior decorators of the day, 'regardless of cost'. Third-class examples

The dining saloon of the London & North Western Railway's
American boat train, introduced in 1907 between London
and Liverpool. Passengers sat in moveable armchairs, amidst
fine panelling and imitation neo-classical plasterwork

too were commonly finished to a higher standard than the corresponding ordinary carriages, and sometimes had seating in individual chairs.
Reviewing the stock for the Great Central Railway's new London extension in 1899, *The Graphic* found the third-class dining cars 'so comfortable
in appearance, that one wonders whether there should be any first-class'.
The provision of such well-appointed catering for third-class passengers
was certainly another inducement to give up paying first-class fares.

Half a crown for lunch was beyond the budget of many, even so; yet
it is surprising how slowly the railways took up the idea of serving basic
snacks and liquid refreshment as well as full meals. The Great Central
tested the water in the late 1890s by providing buffet cars on some services
whose hours did not coincide with the main mealtimes of the day. These
were open to passengers of both classes, who were served from an amply
curved mahogany bar, like something from one of the extravagant new
pubs of the period. The buffets should have been an immediate success, but
within a few years they were converted to ordinary restaurant cars instead.
Why they failed is unclear; reasons since suggested include a dislike of mixing with other classes of passenger, disreputable associations of the public

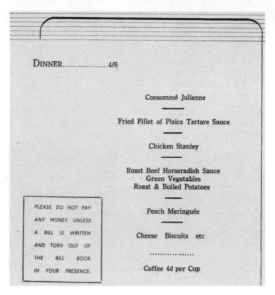

DINNER.................4/6

Consommé Julienne

Fried Fillet of Plaice Tartare Sauce

Chicken Stanley

Roast Beef Horseradish Sauce
Green Vegetables
Roast & Boiled Potatoes

PLEASE DO NOT PAY
ANY MONEY UNLESS
A BILL IS WRITTEN
AND TORN OUT OF
THE BILL BOOK
IN YOUR PRESENCE.

Peach Meringuée

Cheese   Biscuits   etc

....

Coffee 4d per Cup

Third-class dinner menu from a London, Midland &
Scottish Railway restaurant car, 20 May 1939

house and a reluctance to walk along the train to get something to eat, once the custom of having food brought to the seat had established itself.

Only in the 1930s did the buffet concept begin to come into its own. The testing ground was the London & North Eastern's service between Cambridge and King's Cross, beginning with a few low-cost conversions from older carriages. These buffets served simple meals – all cold, apart from the soup – as well as tea, coffee and alcoholic beverages. It was a canny choice: the services proved especially popular with Cambridge University undergraduates, who dubbed them 'beer trains', because you could drink your way to London on them. New buffet cars were promptly built by the LNER for other services, and to accompany the 'tourist' excursion saloons; the other companies followed suit. The interiors on the LNER paraded their modernity, complete with that totem of up-to-dateness, tubular steel furniture – the setting for a quicker and more casual style of living, in an age already impatient with anything that seemed too Victorian. Deeper matters than mere aesthetics were involved here: the dirt-trapping, germ-friendly frills, folds and mouldings of Victorian and Edwardian interiors, railway carriages included, fell under suspicion in an age in which public design increasingly converged with the promotion of public health. A similar spirit moved the Great Western to fit 'Vita glass', transparent to solar ultra-violet light, in its new carriages for the Cornish Riviera Express in 1929, so that passengers could 'commence their sunlight treatment *en route* to their holiday destination'.

So things remained for most of the post-war period, with a choice on long-distance trains between full dining and simpler fare from the buffet. For the ordinary traveller, the balance shifted inexorably away from the restaurant and towards the buffet, and most of the catering vehicles built after the mid 1950s included facilities of the latter type. It was recognised, too, that many passengers wanted to consume alcohol without an accompanying meal. Both were usually consumed within the buffet cars themselves, using washable crockery and glassware, rather than carried back in disposable containers to the ordinary seats; the courtesy of asking a fellow passenger to keep an eye on temporarily abandoned luggage for the duration still prevailed.

In the restaurant cars, the target customer was increasingly the businessman or bureaucrat, travelling at his employer's expense. The change was reflected in the layout of the diesel-powered 'Blue Pullman' trains introduced on selected main lines from 1960. Older Pullmans had seats in single facing pairs on either side of the gangway, suggestive of leisured couples dining *à deux*, but their replacements had off-centre gangways with facing seats grouped two-plus-two on the wider side, so that business meetings could be more easily conducted over lunch. Prices were increasingly set high, not always justified by the quality and choice available. A straw in the wind was the abandonment of croutons with the soup course, after the Pullman company was finally absorbed into the nationalised system in 1962. And as trains became faster and journeys correspondingly more brief, there were fewer services for which the provision of a restaurant vehicle could be warranted at all. In 1969, three-fifths of first-class passengers (and one in five from second class) still took full meals where these were provided, but patronage was shrinking fast. Declining expectations during the 1970s were reflected in the changing make-up of the High Speed Trains (Inter-City 125s). The first batch, put to work in 1976 on the old Great Western main line to Bristol and South Wales, had both restaurant car and buffet, comprising fully one-quarter of the eight passenger-carrying coaches. The later series had a buffet only, or a composite vehicle combining kitchen, buffet counter and a small dining saloon.

Meanwhile food technology was transforming the railway kitchen. In the 1970s microwave ovens were installed, at first used chiefly to speed up cooking times, followed a decade later by the full embrace of the 'cook-chill' meal that could be prepared off-site and reheated for serving on the train. First to adopt the latter was the Euston-to-Manchester service, in 1985. The new menus were launched as 'Cuisine 2000'; an awful name, but also a mark of imminent liberation from the derided Travellers-Fare brand, which had yoked together on-board catering with the much more basic food provided at station cafés and buffet counters. No longer did the kitchen shift begin with heating the oven in readiness for roasting the daily joint; railway catering now came into line with the methods of the airlines, except that certain dishes that were beyond the powers of the microwave to revivify – fried eggs, toast, bacon – were still cooked from fresh. Released from the constraints of fresh preparation, the cook-chill menu was able to welcome back some superior but fiddly dishes that had vanished from railway menus generations before – poached asparagus with Hollandaise sauce, baked salmon with lobster butter – as well as expanding the range with Asian and Mediterranean flavours unknown to the Edwardians. Outwardly, the new methods of preparation were barely apparent: British Rail understood the attractions of silver service, tablecloths, china plates and proper cutlery, measured against the horrible tray-borne, cellophane-wrapped eating experience of the captive airline passenger. And yet the new service was actually symbiotic with the air industry, for the food-supply contracts for Cuisine 2000 were placed with Trust House Forte's airline kitchens based at the airports at Luton and Manchester.

These innovations should have saved the restaurant car, but they did not. Since the privatisation of the railways in 1996–7, the airline model for business travel – standardised meals, included in the ticket price and served to all first-class passengers – has steadily triumphed over the optional system, by which anyone willing to pay for the privilege can walk through the train, take a seat and pick up the menu. In one sense, this is a reversion to the original Pullman model, except that meals designed to be served to all and sundry cannot afford to be ambitious or varied. The last major redoubt of the old, inclusive order was the East Coast main line, including the Great Northern Railway's route from London to Doncaster on which the first British dining cars had been introduced in 1878. Their successors were withdrawn in 2011. A handful of 'Pullman Dining' trains on First Great Western and two services across Wales now keep up the tradition, of which the Welsh contingent cater strictly for first class only.

A similar shrinkage continues on other lines. Now that the custom of taking a seat in the buffet car has died out, its facilities typically consist of a windowless bar-type counter, supplemented by self-service displays of consumables and magazines. On some lines this installation is called the 'shop', dropping any suggestion of a place to eat. The reusable trays once provided for taking away purchases have gone, mostly replaced by the familiar brown paper bags that will join the scatter of plastic glasses, empty drink cans, milk capsules and other travel waste gathered from the carriage at the end of the journey. Even the relatively modest space required for a buffet counter is no longer considered cost-effective on many routes, shrinking the options further towards the standard railway diet of boxed sandwiches, crisps, chocolate bars and floppy Danish pastries, with a premium-priced apple, orange or banana for the health-conscious. All too often, the advice of *The Railway Traveller's Handy Book* rings down the years from 1862: better to take your own choice of something to eat on the train.

Those who failed to dine on a British express train even once – perhaps lacking the nerve, or not realising that standard-class passengers had the right to do so – should kick themselves now. The opportunity to sit for hours in a first-class seat on a budget ticket was undeniably part of the appeal, but it was not the highest pleasure. Nor was the food the primary attraction somehow, although standards in the final years of the service were high; nor did the kindly effects of the wine explain more than part of the magic, though they certainly helped. What made the experience so marvellous was a sort of fusion of all the components, from the soothing and unhurried attentions of the staff to the shifting and fading of the light across the landscape, so that a potentially boring journey became a lovely sequence of anticipated pleasures, separated by space as well as time. The tinkle of the heavy cutlery, occasionally sliding a little across the tablecloth, was calming or amusing rather than irksome. Conversations were struck up between strangers, regular diners as well as infrequent customers, as if united by a sense of gratitude at the sheer unlikeliness of it all – a high achievement of industrial civilisation that deserved to remain for everyone, but which has now gone the way of the airship and the ocean liner. Much of the nostalgia concerning railways is partial, even false; not this.

॥

Most railway journeys past and present have always been of the non-dining kind: short suburban trips, daily commuting runs, modest cross-country jaunts. Here there was less innovation to boast of in the years after 1945. Away from the main lines and fast trains of British Railways, the old order of carriage design continued alongside the (relatively) new. Well into the 1950s, carriages for local services were built on the age-old compartment principle, wasting no space on corridors, gangways or toilets. In no sense was the form considered archaic: even the new electric trains introduced on Tyneside in 1955 were partly compartmented, a form not seen on those lines for half a century previously. But the toll of easy vandalism, as well as long-familiar fears of crime, helped not long afterwards to tip the scales the other way.

Secure from official inspection, compartments had always been easy game to the destructive. The London & South Western was moved to put on display a carriage with slashed seats in 1859, with a warning to the public that cushions might have to be taken away altogether if the nuisance recurred. The press were excited by the case of two drunken first-class passengers who 'completely disembowelled' their compartment on the South Eastern ten years later, especially after one of the gentleman-miscreants fled to the Continent. As for writing and scratching, a letter to the *Railway Record* complained as early as 1847 that some carriages on the London, Brighton & South Coast had been defaced in ways that made them 'totally unfit for a respectable modest female to enter', and F. S. Williams deplored the indecencies inscribed on carriage window panes by 'brainless fops who wear diamond rings'. A dedicated scribbler could get a lot done during a railway journey: the artist Michael Ayrton confessed to having whiled away a night journey to Stoke-on-Trent in 1944 by pencilling the whole interior of an unlit compartment with drawings of cats and fishes, accompanied by his friend, the composer Constant Lambert; the two lay in the luggage racks in order to cover the ceiling.

Pilfering was an attraction too. The Mid-Suffolk Light Railway found that the leather straps of its carriage windows tended to vanish for a new life as strops for sharpening cut-throat razors. Other companies suspected that straps were being taken for boot repairs. When the North Eastern Railway decided to favour its third-class windows with curtains in the 1880s, they were likewise cut off and taken away.

Matters did not improve after nationalisation, confounding those who had hoped that ownership by the people would usher in a new respect for common property. Working at Leicester (Great Central) carriage sheds as a temporary cleaner in the summer vacation of 1953, W. Elgar Dickinson had to contend with 'Much uneaten or half-eaten food ... dumped down toilets, stuffed under seats, wiped on seats, flattened on table-tops, jammed in ashtrays, stamped into floors, flies buzzing with excitement around this bounty or drowning themselves ecstatically in pools of beer, lemonade and vomit.' Light bulbs had been taken out and trodden on for the pleasure of hearing them pop, or left in luggage racks or toilets; soap, paper and handtowels were stolen; ashtrays were unscrewed. On one occasion at Leicester, an entire suite comprising washbowl and toilet fitting had gone missing.

These carriages were from an excursion train, by long tradition especially prone to spoliation, for which the railways tended to reserve their oldest and shabbiest vehicles. But service trains suffered too, and in the later 1950s the situation appears to have worsened. Now the press picked up the subject. The *Manchester Guardian* reported the annual toll on BR's London Midland Region in 1957 under the heading 15,000 MISSING LIGHT BULBS. Some of the damage was blamed on 'Teddy boys', although no age-group was considered especially responsible. Cumulative costs were heavy: in 1960, each repair to a slashed seat was estimated at between £1 and £5, replacement cushions (easily detached and thrown from the carriage windows) at £3 15s upwards, windows at up to £5 each. Worst affected at that time was the Southern Region, where a squad of fifty men was employed every Sunday to patch up the destruction from the night before. These were normal service trains; if the carriages could not be repaired in time, some Monday morning services had to be cancelled. Regardless of the toll inflicted, the maximum fine for damaging railway property remained a mere £5. Nor did the law allow the railways to ban known or suspected train-wreckers from its stations, a sanction limited to violent lunatics or those obviously afflicted by infectious diseases.

Football trains were especially vulnerable. By 1961 the railways were considering the abolition of football specials in the Glasgow area, after a train was sacked by Celtic fans (who also beat up a waiter in the buffet car). What weighed decisively against the idea was the prospect of displacing hordes of drunken rioters on to ordinary service trains. Similar threats to withdraw the excursion service followed in other parts of the network.

Sometimes they were even acted on: midway through the 1963–4 season, Liverpool's clubs temporarily lost their excursion trains after repeated misconduct by 'Mersey Maniacs'. A comic joked on television that his fellow Liverpool supporters could be recognised by the railway carriage doors they wore in their lapels.

When not finding things to break, fans might choose to have fun with the communication cord. The presence of a victorious team on the same train was not necessarily a deterrent. Repeated abuse of the facility caused an exasperated Matt Busby and his squad to go off in search of a road coach at Wolverhampton in the small hours of 5 January 1964, on their return from Manchester United's third-round cup victory over Southampton. By then their train was over three hours late, due partly to a war of nerves between passengers, police and railwaymen at Birmingham New Street ('As station staff ran along the line freeing the brakes, supporters pulled the cords again'). Also taking the train home that night were fans of Manchester City, glumly smashing light bulbs and ripping out tables after a defeat at the railway town of Swindon.

In an attempt to readjust the balance of costs and benefits arising from excursion traffic, an agreement was reached with the National Federation of Football Supporters' Clubs in 1967. Henceforth, those who chartered special trains would be liable for damage up to a sum of £900. That limit was no doubt breached by Tottenham Hotspur on 20 September 1969, after a 5–0 defeat at Derby; supporters on the returning train threw so many carriage fittings on to the track, and pulled the communication cord so often, that they were finally ejected by Bedfordshire police at the quiet wayside stations of Flitwick and Harlington. Here some of the 550 unhappy fans 'went on a stone-throwing spree, terrorising villages, smashing windows, and attacking cars'. Others were last seen walking in the general direction of north London.

In 1973 the railways tried to take the excursion traffic upmarket, by means of the all-first-class League Liner train. This was a dedicated set of carriages that could be hired, staffed and indemnified against damage by interested clubs, who could then sell tickets to their fans at a profitable margin. One carriage was equipped with screens for showing match footage on the primitive videotape of the day. There was a 'Kick-off Disco' vehicle complete with flashing lights and groovy decorations on its windowless walls, to encourage wives and girlfriends to travel with the away fans. But even the twin deterrents of first-class fares and female company did not save the League Liner from vandalistic attack during the three years it lasted in service.

By the 1970s the wrecked British railway carriage had become a stock image for newspapers and television, channelling broader anxieties about the rise of sociopathic behaviour. Levels of destruction were sometimes staggering, both on football trains and on carriages in sidings. A bank holiday excursion returning to Liverpool in August 1975 was evacuated at Crewe after it was set on fire by the occupants, using as fuel the contents of mailbags they had stolen from Leicester station. In an earlier incident, fourteen stationary carriages were assaulted by four youths equipped with a hatchet from an emergency tool kit: 228 windows were destroyed, with 128 compartment mirrors and picture glasses, 86 blinds, 38 window straps, 180 light bulbs and 8 fire extinguishers. At the non-structural level of damage, the railways also had to contend with the new media of marker pen and aerosol paint. The latter was a costly niche product on its first appearance in the 1960s, but in the following decade became widely available as an accessory for car repairs. These new paints and inks allowed graffiti of a scale, ambition and speed altogether beyond the means of pocket knives, chalk, pencil, or water-based ink.

This was no time for building carriages that fostered easy misbehaviour. Many suburban carriages of the 1950s and 1960s were already organised as twin half-size saloons, even if they did not yet feature gangway connections. Suburban electrification was another agent of change. It encouraged the use of carriages equipped with air-operated sliding doors, like those already in use on the London Underground system. The first batch of electric trains introduced on the Liverpool Street lines in 1949 were of this new kind, although another twenty-nine years passed before British Rail built its last slam-door outer suburban trains. In the 1970s it also became standard practice to make a gangway through the whole train, a policy fostered in some areas by the decision to sell tickets on board rather than at lightly used stations. The main exception concerns multiple units (self-propelled, fixed-formation diesels and electrics), some of which lack a connection within the cab end to allow through passage when units run coupled together.

Behind the sliding doors of the new suburban carriage type were large vestibules which served as standing space when the train was full. Dangling from the roof of the 1949 trains were straps for other standing passengers to hold tight, a further instance of the movement away from the idea that a seat should be included in the price of a ticket. This shift has continued, accelerated partly by the need to provide for wheelchair users, but chiefly by the inexorable growth in passenger numbers. Official calculations now include a 'standing allowance', and a policy that short journeys (up to twenty minutes) may be made without the use of a seat – though most able-bodied people who travel regularly by train know that this limit may be exceeded many times over.

So the old, isolated, vandal-friendly passenger enclosures steadily disappeared. The last survivors of the archetypal British carriage belonged to Classes 405 and 415 on the Southern Region suburban electric services: ten compartments in a vehicle 62ft long, each six-foot cell offering six places a side, undifferentiated by armrests or seat divisions. To make an exit from the far side of a full compartment required a cake-walk past twenty-two knees, usually with some deft grabbing at the metal-framed luggage racks that did double duty as handrails. At quieter times this forced intimacy was replaced by solitude, an isolation surely more total than on any other form of public transport. The feeling was heightened when the train halted between stations – held at a red light outside Clapham Junction, perhaps, or pausing on the tight triangle of lines just west of London Bridge – and its thrumming motors fell quiet. The resulting silence soon filled with the tiny creaks and ticks of cooling equipment, and perhaps a muffled phrase or laughter from some conversation in another passenger cell, mysteriously conveyed through the structure of the carriage, before the signal came to move off again. It was better to travel thus in the off-peak daylight hours than at night, beneath the unkindly glow of the bare bulbs (easily unscrewed, for pleasure or for profit), when the entry of any dubious-looking stranger to the compartment might stir the sort of anxieties that Mr Briggs's generation knew all too well.

The corridor compartment type held on rather longer. The electric trains built in 1988–9 for the Bournemouth and Weymouth route – officially Class 442, 'Plastic Pigs' to the railway enthusiast – still included these in first class, because the line's long-distance commuters were known to prefer them. After these trains were withdrawn for modification, the last haunt of the compartment became the four-and-a-half-mile-long Lymington branch in Hampshire, a spur off the same route, on which a few 1960s electric units were retained until May 2010. It was worth paying a little extra to enjoy the comfortable isolation of one of these first-class enclaves; the well-read might indulge a reminiscence of Trollope's

The Claverings (1867), in which Lady Ongar finds herself paying for a first-class ticket for the sponging Mme Gordeloupe when they travel over the same line. By a nice coincidence, the same route also ended up as the last steam-worked branch in Britain, going electric in the centenary year of Trollope's novel.

₪

In terms of the passenger's experience, the passing of the Lymington trains leaves the 1970s slam-door carriages of the Inter-City 125s among the most old-fashioned in the present fleet, the rest of which is equipped almost entirely with automatic doors. It is a curious distinction for these trains, which are perhaps the most admired of the hundreds of types put into service by the nationalised railway. Nor were they meant initially as much more than a ten-year stop-gap, until electrification and trains even faster than 125 mph came along. Their carriages were of the roomy and smooth-running Mark 3 type introduced on the West Coast main line shortly before. They were constructed on the principle of an extremely strong welded-steel shell, following the abandonment in the 1960s of the venerable tradition of building bodies and underframes separately. More noticeable innovations from the user's point of view included automatic doors between the saloons and entrance vestibules, operated by means of tread mats – a blessing to passengers with heavy luggage, as well as an inducement to take food and drink away from the buffet car without the risk of spillage.

What created the image of these High Speed Trains, however, were the streamlined power cars, one at each end. Their lightweight shells of glass-reinforced plastic were styled with exceptional care, thanks to the input of the industrial designer Sir Kenneth Grange (born 1929). Engaged to create a new livery, Grange became so concerned to get the right look for the train that he redesigned the bodyshell of the power cars on his own initiative, testing the models of his prototype aerodynamically by securing nocturnal access to the wind tunnels at Imperial College London. Rather than sacking him, BR had the good sense to endorse the result. In a BBC4 documentary broadcast in 2012, Grange declared the power cars to have been his own favourite project, in a career that included work for Kodak, Kenwood (the restyled Kenwood Chef mixer of the 1960s was his), Wilkinson Sword and many other household names. The 1970s colour scheme has long since given way to others, but the High Speed

Trains endure. With new engines in place, they are presently reckoned good for at least another ten years' service.

Separate power cars represented a break from the usual practice, earlier generations of multiple-unit trains mostly having engines or motors below the carriage floors. This separation was another point in favour of the HSTs, keeping to a minimum the vibrations and noise within the carriage. The double-ended arrangement, as well as the streamlined styling, were in a line of descent from the Blue Pullman diesels of the 1960s, already mentioned. Though these lasted just thirteen years in service, they were the showpieces of the network in their day; *Design* magazine in 1963 called them 'probably the best known trains on BR'. Responses to the rolling stock of the 1950s had often been scathing: critics derided clunky outlines, too many echoes of pre-war conventions, and a general failure to move on from the era of rationing and austerity. In terms of image, cars, coaches and airliners had distanced themselves from all of this as fast as possible; only on the rails did things seem to lag behind. A Design Panel was therefore established in 1956, including consultants from outside the railway industry. Its brief was to ensure that railway equipment should look fit to take its place within 'a great public service', engendering pride and promoting business, and projecting 'the idea of a keen and progressive management'.

These ideals came to fruition with the Blue Pullmans, a leap forward in smartness and technological confidence reminiscent of George Mortimer Pullman's innovations of eighty years before. Their livery was blue and white, the paler colour making a broad horizontal band between the windows – the first version of what became the standard BR livery, suitably adapted, for most of the rest of the century. These windows were double-glazed, and equipped with retractable venetian blinds between the panes in place of curtains. Seats were adjustable, like those on aircraft (also, it was noted, like those on the popular new road coaches lately introduced on the M1), and had built-in ashtrays in the armrests. A visit to the toilet revealed a washbasin with mixer taps. The Blue Pullmans ranked also as the first British trains with full air conditioning, rather than the various earlier forms of pressure ventilation by which heated and filtered air was fed into the carriage. There was a public address system too, another airline-type refinement. Besides these technical advances, the trains were designed throughout with a heightened sense of clarity of outline and the value of 'image', in line with the international business aesthetic then on the ascendant in the West in everything from architecture to adding machines.

Another connection between the Blue Pullmans and the HST can be traced through Grange himself. His early career included a period as an assistant draughtsman to the architect-turned-design consultant Jack Howe (1911–2003), who was the Design Panel's choice to work with the manufacturers of the Blue Pullmans. From here there is a direct line to the architect Walter Gropius, founder of the Bauhaus school of art, who had employed the young Howe during his brief pre-war practice as an exile in Britain, and thence to the fountainhead of socially conscious modernist design in early Weimar Germany. This chain of descent seems apt. The Blue Pullmans were a luxury product, but the Inter-City 125s were for everyone. Here was a genuine challenge to the image of the nationally owned network as a shabby, strike-prone embarrassment. Heavily promoted in poster and television advertising – this was the era of 'The Age of the Train', fronted by the unlamented Jimmy Savile – they were run without charging supplementary fares, unlike the Pullmans. Receipts rose markedly every time they were introduced to a new part of the network. It was quite an achievement to cater for the needs of ordinary second-class folk as well as business travellers, for whom these services represented an attractive alternative to costly domestic air routes. The trains even broke the world speed record for diesel traction on the rails, reaching 148 mph on a test run on the East Coast main line in 1987. By displacing slightly older Mark 2 carriages for use on other lines – 'cascading', in the industry's term – the new trains also permitted a better quality of journey elsewhere on the network, triggering a minor holocaust of the increasingly juddery and corroded Mark 1s from the 1950s and early 1960s.

All in all, it is difficult to think of a more admirable product of 1970s Britain than the High Speed Trains. Here was everything that the mixed economy was supposed to represent, but failed all too often to deliver: innovative world-class design, successful both technically and aesthetically, developed by a state-owned body as part of a strategic national plan; private consultants and manufacturers working fruitfully together; a financial success in operation, without pricing out the ordinary Briton; excellence achieved in the spirit of public service, rather than the delivery of private profit.

Even the royal family were drawn into the story. When testing was complete, the prototype High Speed Train was left spare. For the Silver

Jubilee year of 1977, two of its carriages were refitted as combined sleepers and saloons for the monarch and her consort (a bedroom each, with
single beds, according to the traditions of the royal trains). The discreetly
modern blue-and-gold furnishings were chosen by the royal family under
the guidance of another modernist architect, Sir Hugh Casson (1910–99),
a particular favourite of the Queen and Prince Philip (Casson is reported
once to have said 'I know what Queenie likes'). This was not his first essay
in railway design, for Casson had long been among the circle of consultants favoured by BR's Design Panel. These carriages too remain in service,
the products of a cultural and economic consensus now utterly lost; the
settlement between public and private, capital and labour, that found its
level in the early 1950s but which in the end proved briefer than a single
reign.

₪

To varying degrees, most of the trains now in service are superior in speed
and comfort to those inherited from the great post-war modernisation.
They are also stronger and safer: there will never be another accident like
the Clapham Junction collision of 1988, when thirty-five people died
in crowded slam-door carriages that disintegrated on impact. But the
national picture is a mixed one, with some less alluring designs of passenger train around too. Like the HSTs, these are instructive for what they
reveal about the constraints and assumptions behind the late-twentieth-
century railway. And so we come to the strange story of the Pacers – the
latter-day revenge of the four-wheeled carriage.

   The Pacers originated in the need to replace the fleet of diesel multiple units (DMUs), built between the mid 1950s and early 1960s. These
had displaced steam haulage on passenger routes that were not electrified
and were not thought to justify the use of locomotive-hauled carriages.
By 1963 some 4,000 DMU carriages had been built, from six-car units
for Trans-Pennine services to single cars with a cab at each end for less
busy lines. The immediate effects were often very positive, as passenger
numbers rose sharply. In the first fifteen weeks of the new service between
Leeds and Bradford, for example, an extra 80,000 journeys were made.
People liked the airy, well-lit carriages, especially the novelty of a clear
view along the tracks ahead or behind, through the glazed partition of
the driver's cab. A trip made in a good seat in a DMU was like riding at

A new Trans-Pennine diesel multiple unit on display at Manchester Piccadilly station (formerly Manchester London Road), December 1960. Forward-facing passengers enjoyed fine views through the 'wraparound' cab windows

the front of a road coach, with the extra thrill of strangeness as the shining parallel rails were endlessly eaten up by the train, and the voyeuristic closeness to the driver's back, separated incommunicably behind his glass screen (it was always disappointing when a privacy-loving driver lowered the cab's internal blinds).

So far, so good; but by the mid 1970s these trains were showing their age, and the money to replace all of them with stock of comparable quality was not to be had. Instead, BR cast about for something that came pre-designed, and seized upon the single-decker Leyland National bus. This was a simple and straightforward design, developed jointly by two other nationalised industries, British Leyland and the National Bus Company (then operating as National Express) and built in great numbers from 1972. A railway prototype appeared in 1978, made up of components from the standard bus body mounted on a four-wheel chassis. Even the automatic doors were of the foldaway bus type. Four wheels were considered sufficient because the vehicle weighed under twenty tons, less than two-thirds the average figure for powered DMU vehicles of the first generation. A wheel arrangement that was regarded as old-fashioned a century before was thus resurrected, to bounce and squeal its way along the rails of the modernised network.

This was not the first time that BR had fallen for the four-wheeled railbus concept. Twenty-two of the type had been introduced in 1958, in the hope that they might be the salvation of lightly used lines. Each was designed to operate singly, and each had an engine of only modest power beneath the carriage floor. Those on the Scottish Region earned the nickname 'four-wheel bicycles' on account of their struggles to stick to the timetable. All were gone within ten years, along with most of the lines they served. Not one had managed to produce a surplus of revenue over movement costs, the most basic yardstick of cost assessment.

Second time around, the concept was different, in terms of both manufacturing and operation. The production series consisted of two- or three-car units, for use on more intensively worked lines. The interiors were filled with rows of low-backed, bus-type bench seats. Design and production costs were modest, exploiting the modular system of design and interchangeability of parts that were central to the Leyland National concept. The wheelbase was not a new design either, but an adaptation of a type developed for fast freight wagons by BR's Research and Technical Centre at Derby. Fuel costs were low; initial trials achieved ten miles to the gallon.

In the hope of generating foreign custom, the prototype was sent across the Atlantic for trials by the United States Federal Railroad Administration, together with a second prototype unit. The Americans bought one of these, but decided to stop there. Another prototype was sold to Northern Ireland Railways, with the same result.

Disappointed in its export drive but undeterred from its domestic mission, BR set about developing a two-car prototype, then a first series of twenty two-car units, the Class 141. These had railway-type cabs instead of the broad, low-set windscreens of the bus bodies, so they did at least look like someone's idea of a train when viewed head-on. The 141s entered service on lines around Leeds in 1984, where the first generation of DMUs had enjoyed such success three decades previously. No comparable surge in usage resulted, which was hardly surprising: the new units proved unreliable as well as uncomfortable and had to be expensively modified within a few years.

The mission to the wider world was also resumed. A demonstrator unit spent two years fruitlessly touring the United States. Another made sorties to Belgium and Sweden, with the same outcome. A two-car unit was shipped to Thailand for trials, then to Malaysia, where the authorities decided to buy a rival design from Hungary instead. Finally, the unit went to Indonesia, where it seems to have disappeared from the records. Asia liked the units no more than America, and no orders were placed there either. So the Yorkshire fleet remained alone of their particular kind, working until 1997. The story might have ended there but for the railways of the Islamic Republic of Iran, which bought up most of the redundant units as a job lot a few years later. Until recently, the suburban lines around Tehran were the stamping ground of these fuel-efficient, non-air-conditioned units, a surprising initiative by an oil-rich country with maximum summer temperatures approaching 100 degrees Fahrenheit.

Things moved forward – a little – with the Class 142 (built 1985–7) and their successors. Their bodies were wider, and less obviously bus-like inside. The 'Pacer' name applies properly to these units, a near-meaningless label which served to distinguish them from the sturdier, more expensive and altogether preferable 'Sprinter' DMUs introduced around the same time. One Pacer unit spent some time in Belgium, in yet another doomed attempt to stimulate export trade. Another was singled out for stardom at the transport-themed Expo at Vancouver in 1986, where it operated a shuttle service through the site. There the train managed to attract one remarkable passenger, granddaughter (as it happens) of a cloakroom clerk at Grantham station, but notorious for her aversion to railways at home: Margaret Thatcher. It was almost as if British Rail had contrived an ambush. The Prime Minister was visiting the Expo for its 'British Day', 12 July, where she made a speech laying emphasis on the UK's aspiration to share in the technology of the future. Fine words, in the general sense; but no one can have been much surprised when Vancouver's Pacer came back without having generated a single order.*

The Pacers' habitat consists of provincial and rural lines, especially in the north, the industrial Midlands and South Wales. It is possible to live in south-east England and travel a great deal by rail without once stepping on board one of these noisy, bucking, rattling, cramped and draughty trains,

---

* To be fair, British Rail Engineering Limited successfully exported twelve three-car units of more robust design to the Thai State Railways in the early 1990s.

whose engine note at speed suggests an imminent risk of something bad happening down below. The commuter to Cardiff, Manchester or Leeds may even suspect a metropolitan conspiracy.

Less obvious is a regrettable economy within the standard Mark 3 carriage, concerning the relationship between the seats and the windows. In the days of compartments, each had its own window, or windows, centrally placed; there was no other way. The open carriages that succeeded them retained this alignment between seating bays and windows. Thus the immediate predecessors of the Mark 3 came in two types, seven-windowed for first class, eight-windowed for second, the greater width of each seating bay in first class accounting for the difference. The Mark 3s were long enough to accommodate eight seating bays in first class, each again with its own window, but for the sake of economy the same bodyshell was used for second class as well. With their closer spacings, many second-class seats were therefore out of step with the windows. In the worst cases the hapless passenger was lined up directly with one of the solid piers between them. Those wanting to gaze properly at one of the marvels along the line – Durham Cathedral on its rock, say – were forced into a double manoeuvre: first, squashing back into the seat for a right-angled glimpse through the slot made by the overlap with the window behind, then craning uncomfortably forward to where the next window began.

Forty years on, and the question of an adequate outside view seems to matter to the designers of British railway carriages even less. That is the only possible conclusion to be drawn from the layout of the 'Pendolino' trains, which replaced the Mark 3s on the West Coast main line from 2001. Their seating plans can be inspected on the website of the operating company, Virgin Trains. Seats described as having 'limited/no view' are coloured blue. In standard class there are 449 places, of which almost one-third – 146 seats – are blue. Even first class has a few blue spots, like the dud seats at the outer edges of the circle at the theatre. 'No view' is no exaggeration: some seats truly do adjoin a blank carriage wall. Seats in groups of four are comparatively scarce; by dispensing with tables, more can be squeezed in. The preferred configuration is in long defiles facing the same way, and because seats are now much taller than they were in the 1970s and 1980s, the passenger's view directly in front is of the headrest of the next seat along. It also happens that the tops of the windows of these trains finish unusually low down.

Safety culture explains some of this, including the requirement for

The airline model: inside a Class 370 Pendolino, standard class

ever greater structural resilience at high speeds, especially when crossing in tunnels. That means a higher proportion of solid to void in the carriage sides, in contrast to the less demanding rules applying to those built for slower routes. Some of these, such as the Electrostar commuter units now operating in Essex, Sussex and Kent, have saloons with wonderful near-continuous windows. So now the rule of thumb is, the longer the maximum journey, the worse the likely view.

All of this presents quite a rebuff to anyone who holds to Ruskin's precept that the world is worth looking at. It is poignant that the Pendolinos should operate over the same route used by the great critic to reach London from his Lake District home. The shrinking windows also fall woefully short of the ideals represented by the Design Panel, and the awakening sense in the 1960s that railways should compete against other modes of transport partly by providing a more appealing and distinctive experience. Instead, the Pendolino interior seems to want to converge with the cramped and claustrophobic cabin of the airliner, the dominant mode of long-distance transport for the new century. Visually, perhaps the most obvious difference is that each carriage contains seats facing both ways, sometimes unsettlingly juxtaposed across the aisle. As the rules preventing airline passengers from using mobile phones and wireless devices during flights are relaxed, railway passengers are losing their competitive edge in streaming movies, or spending the journey texting and chattering by mobile phone. Not everyone likes the resulting hubbub, of course – hence the introduction of the 'quiet coach', a new distinction in permitted behaviour between different spaces, now that smoking is forbidden.

Where heavy luggage is concerned, most passengers now have rigid wheeled suitcases of the type designed to withstand the rigours of airport handling. These can be found obstructing the aisles and vestibules of crowded trains, being often too large for the overhead racks – especially so on the Pendolinos, which are not generous in the matter of headroom. The name offers a clue to why the space is so cramped: Pendolino is the Italian word for pendulum, a reference to the hydraulic tilting mechanism attached to the bogies, by which the carriages lean inwards as the train takes curves at speed. This tilting allows a much faster journey, liberating the timetable from many of the speed restrictions on lines built to Victorian standards of curvature. In order to stay within the loading gauge, the carriage sides taper inwards from around waist height.

The tilting principle was developed by British Rail at the same time as the High Speed Train, and embodied in its prototype electric Advanced Passenger Trains of the late 1970s. A maximum operational speed of 155 mph was anticipated, as against the 125 mph service limit of the diesel-powered HSTs. Here, it was hoped, was a world-class design that would permit the modernisation of the network without the vast cost of building new high-speed routes with minimal curves, like those of the Japanese bullet trains and French TGVs (*Trains à grande vitesse*). Yet the début of the APT on the London-to-Glasgow run in 1981 was a dismaying affair. Many of the passengers on the first trial trip – journalists, railwaymen, ministers and civil servants – claimed to have been made nauseous by the tilting motion. Only later was it discovered that a less mathematically exact compensation for the bends was kinder to the human frame, so that passengers felt a slight sensation of tilting to match the visual evidence through the carriage window. Worse, the tilt mechanism failed on some early runs, leaving the carriages stuck humiliatingly on one side. Even the hydro-kinetic brakes that were meant to allow fast deceleration proved liable to freezing. After less than a week of public service, the prototypes were therefore withdrawn for modification.

Trials resumed successfully three years later, by which time the senior management had lost confidence in the commercial case for the service. Unlike the HSTs, the new trains were also operationally hobbled by the placing of their gangway-less power cars in the middle of the train, so that two restaurant-buffet cars had to be provided, one for each group of carriages on either side. Before long the trains were quietly scrapped, not many months after Mrs Thatcher's declaration of faith in the future of British technology at the Vancouver Expo.

The story does not end there. The technology from the tilting mechanism was sold to the railway division of Fiat, who incorporated it in their own tilting-train programme. Thus it came about that the world's first regular public service by tilting train ran between Rome and Milan instead of London and Glasgow. When orders were finally placed for tilting trains to run on the privatised West Coast main line, they went to the French company Alstom, the new owner of Fiat's railway arm. Having effectively exported its own technical lead, Britain had to buy it back from abroad.

So the record of the British passenger railway is altogether mixed. The Pacers illustrate the unevenness of British Rail's own design policy; further back, the braking saga shows that British railways were not always in the forefront of innovation, nor receptive to the best technology from abroad. Yet the system endures, and over the last twenty years its use by passengers has risen in almost every year. The crowding that has prompted more compact arrangements of carriage seating is a sign of this healthy demand. Further evidence of this growth is the rise in the number and frequency of 'interval services' on long-distance routes, by which trains leave at regular intervals throughout the day. In 1838, when the London & Birmingham Railway became the first route to link the capital with another city, there were just a few short trains each day; now, fast trains over the same route leave Euston every twenty minutes during waking hours.

The fate of the Flying Scotsman is a representative story of the modernised railway. Like the naming of locomotives (*see* Chapter 17), bestowing titles on individual services was a special weakness of Britain's railways: the *Railway Magazine* has listed upwards of 260 of them, from The Aberdonian to The Zulu. The one everybody recognises was in informal use for generations before its official adoption in 1927. The name applied to the simultaneous 10 a.m. departures from Edinburgh Waverley and London King's Cross, the two identically named expresses passing each other every weekday somewhere between York and Darlington. In its inter-war heyday this was truly a train to remember. Running non-stop throughout, it was equipped by the end of the 1930s with its own hairdressing salon, cocktail bar and ladies' retiring room, as well as the expected restaurant car. An on-board newsboy plied his wares up and down the corridors, to make up for the lack of intermediate stops at which reading matter could be obtained. Not all of these novelties survived the Second World War, but in the 1950s the crack express was still the obvious choice for St Custard's school excursion in Geoffrey Willans and Ronald Searle's *Molesworth* books ('Now the mity trane rumble over the royal border bridge and soon we are in scotland. we go back to our smoker and lite up our cigs'). But there is no economic case now for a single non-stop run between London and Edinburgh, nor is there anything distinctive about the timings or facilities of any particular service on the route. Too good to discard altogether, the famous name lingers spectrally as the title of the 05.40 departure from Edinburgh, which is hardly the same thing.

The disappearance of prestige services of this kind is part of the price paid for the standardised, accelerated and sometimes rather boring railway network of the twenty-first century. Efficiencies and economies of scale now work against any non-standard practices, excepting the superficial variety presented by the liveries and finishes of the private operating companies. As a sign of how different things were a century ago, consider London & North Western Railway carriage 1513, preserved on the Bluebell Railway in Sussex. Built in 1913, it was one of three observation saloons specially built for the spectacular route between Llandudno and Blaenau Ffestiniog in North Wales. For a surcharge of sixpence, passengers could enjoy the views through its huge windows and glazed ends. The direction of their seats could be reversed, by means of pivoting backs like those used on tramcars, so that everyone could face the optimum direction. It is almost as if John Ruskin himself had been appointed design consultant.

Not that romance is wholly dead on the twenty-first century railway. It survives most fully where sleeping cars still operate – and these deserve a chapter to themselves.

AND SO TO BED

The idea of a sleeping compartment mounted on rails is not, on the face of it, a difficult one to come up with. Yet it took Britain's railways over forty years to do something serious about making it happen.

There were a few early 'bed-carriages', it is true, identifiable by the low boot-like extension at one end; the type survives in the form of Queen Adelaide's conveyance of 1842. Once the outer seat-back had been folded away, the extra volume enclosed by the boot made it possible for the occupant of the end compartment to stretch out at full length, parallel to the direction of travel, by means of a stretcher-like contraption with twin poles that spanned the gap between the seats. After compartments became wider, there was enough space to stretch out across both seats with the aid of these sleeping poles. The device may be compared to the footwarmer, which likewise solved a problem by bringing in extra equipment rather than by rethinking the fundamentals.

They did things differently abroad, where greater distances and protracted journeys stimulated innovation. It was to these models that the managers of Britain's railways looked in the 1870s, when true sleeping carriages were introduced. First in the game was the North British Railway in 1873, for services to London. This followed the French type known as a *lits-salon*, which owed something to the convertible principle of the bed-carriage and rather more to the family saloon. The carriage had two first-class compartments, with a shared lavatory enclosure between – the first lavatories in a British railway carriage built for ordinary service rather than private hire. The main compartments each had three seats along one side only, leaving plenty of room on the lavatory side. When the time came to turn in, the seat backs could be pulled forward and unfolded horizontally, revealing an upholstered reverse side for sleeping on. In addition there was a second-class compartment at one end for the use of servants, who had to manage without access to the lavatory, and a luggage compartment at the other. Despite the ten-shilling charge, bedding was not provided, although passengers (or their servants) could supply their own.

Other lines rapidly provided a few sleeping cars of their own, likewise self-contained and variously subdivided, and sometimes with the novelty of suspended upper berths, bunk-bed-fashion. In most cases clearly designed with family parties in mind, they were available for shared use by solitary travellers too. In Robert Louis Stevenson's short story 'The Rajah's Diamond' (1878), a clergyman flees to Scotland with a snaffled precious stone in his custody, on what is clearly recognisable as a North British sleeper. An adventurer who has designs on the same jewel installs himself in the opposite end of the vehicle. During the night, each man makes a stealthy visit of inspection to the other's space, through the swaying darkness and unlockable sliding doors of the lavatory enclosure.

By the time Stevenson was writing there was another way to go to bed on the train. It is here that George Mortimer Pullman re-enters the story. He had patented a very different type of sleeping car in the USA in 1865, taking the single, shared saloon as his unlikely starting point. By means of upper berths that folded up against the roof, lower berths that were formed by sliding pairs of facing seats forward until they met in the middle, and retractable panels to divide the head and foot of each bed, upper and lower, from the berths to either side, Pullman managed to do the trick. Privacy was ensured by means of thick curtains that could be buttoned together, on the side facing the central aisle. The design saw widespread use. Its memory was kept alive by Hollywood westerns, in which quarrelling passengers would poke their heads out between the curtains, and perhaps throw a boot or two (footwear had to be removed before retiring, as there was nowhere to put it inside the berths).

Three Pullman sleeping cars of this type were among the vehicles shipped over for assembly by the Midland Railway in 1874. A few other railways followed the Midland's lead. Like the Pullman parlor cars, these sleepers were provided with an attendant, and had private 'state rooms' at each end for those desiring greater privacy. Even so, *The Times* considered

Inside one of the Midland Railway's Pullman
sleeping cars, from *The Graphic*, 1874

that the ordinary curtained-off berths were sufficient for complete seclusion. Now there was a way for single, servantless travellers to sleep securely in their own space, with an attendant to hand.

One of the tasks of these Pullman attendants was to enforce the prohibition on smoking in the berths. Portable reading lamps were banned too. These regulations failed to prevent the destruction by fire of the Midland's sleeper *Enterprise* one night in October 1882, en route from St Pancras to Glasgow. The communication cord failed to operate and the engine steamed ahead regardless as the vehicle filled with flames and smoke. Relief came only when a signalman noticed the fire as the train passed and telegraphed a warning ahead. The attendant and three of the passengers escaped, the latter in their nightclothes (which suggests that changing for bed was the custom, at least among male Pullman travellers). When the sleeping car had cooled, the charred remains of a fourth passenger, a Dr John Arthur of Aberdeen, were found inside.

At the inquest the young doctor was described by witnesses as having seemed 'sleepy or gloomy', or else drunk, at earlier stages that evening. After lying down in his berth he had produced a cigar, but the attendant had plucked it from his mouth and snapped the thing in two. Did the doctor then bide his time before lighting up in secret once the curtains were drawn, only to fall into a slumber and set the bedding fatally ablaze? It was plausible.

Then it emerged that Dr Arthur had recently begun dosing himself with chloral in order to sleep, after a bout of tropical dysentery had spoiled his health. When the indignity with the cigar occurred he was already close to nodding off, for the attendant had had to pull off his boots for him. The same attendant also reported that one of the surviving passengers had been detected using an oil-fuelled reading lamp – a much more hazardous article than the usual candle-lit kind – which was 'fixed by two hooks to the curtain' inside his berth. The man with the lamp denied having caused the blaze, blaming the stove in the attendant's cubicle instead. The flames had begun at the opposite end of the carriage, however, and the jury declared the lamp and its owner to be the likely culprits. With so many potential sources of fire around, going to bed on a moving train suddenly seemed less appealing.

The travelling public did not have to wait long for an alternative set-up, for Pullman's type of convertible sleeper was not destined for a protracted life in Britain. On the Continent, as in America, it was different: many journeys were so lengthy that it made sense to install beds in such a way that they could be transformed into seats for daytime use. Few British journeys lasted long enough to make this dual-use type worthwhile. Instead, the home-grown sleeper followed the corridor-compartment model – or, to put it another way, they resembled a long hotel wing with little bedrooms opening off one side of a corridor. Rather than lying along the main axis of the carriage, the traveller slept crosswise to the direction of travel, feet towards the compartment window.

The new type appeared first in the 1890s, on the Great Western and on the East Coast route, and was soon imitated on other lines. Berths might be single or double. The double ones were not necessarily meant for couples; this was an age when strangers were still expected to share a bedroom at inns, and railways were no different. A compartment for the attendant was generally included, and this was bedless. Its occupant sat up all night, to see that all was well and to provide refreshments to his passengers when they awoke. Another common feature was a smoking compartment, so that the sleeping spaces could be kept free of tobacco fumes and perilous smoulderings. By Edwardian times bedding was provided, and some sleeping cars had washbasins in the compartments. Those constructed in 1907–8 for the London & South Western's Plymouth boat trains uniquely had brass bedsteads of domestic type, bedknobs and all.

All these vehicles were first-class only. Third-class passengers had to manage with sleeping upright or stretching out on the seats, as they had always done. The pros and cons of extending sleeper services to all classes were discussed by the joint committees for the West Coast and East Coast routes in the 1900s, but each decided not to pursue the idea because of the anticipated loss of custom to the cheaper berths. Later historians have questioned how far even the first-class service can truly have run at a profit. Edwardian passengers paid a standard supplement of five shillings for the use of a sleeper, the equivalent of the first-class fare for a mere thirty-mile journey. What a truly commercial rate might have looked like is suggested by the charge levied on the sleeping cars between Paris and Marseille, which was about twenty-four times as much. The disparity suggests that British sleeper trains were provided from a commitment to quality of service, for reasons of prestige and also – on the key routes to Scotland, at least – because *not* to have offered them would have lost a considerable share of traffic to the competition. For the passenger, it was a very good deal; the railways shouldered much of the expense of laying on these heavy, costly vehicles, which generated relatively few fares and which could by definition be used only once every twenty-four hours.

None of this finally prevented the extension of the service to third class, which happened in 1928 by mutual agreement on three of the four main British companies (the fourth, the Southern Railway, by then had no sleeping carriages of its own). There was a much greater gulf between the classes in these new carriages than in those for daytime use. Each compartment had four berths, arranged like pairs of bunks. In some early batches the lower beds were convertible to seats during the day, when the upper bunks were folded away: a version of the couchette type, as may still be encountered on the Continent. But this arrangement quickly fell from favour, and later deliveries of third-class sleeper were equipped with beds and beds only.

If the model for the first-class sleeper was the hotel or inn, the thirds had something of the air of a youth hostel (by coincidence, the Youth Hostel Association was founded around the same time, in 1930). The supplements were very much less, at not much more than a third of the first-class rate. Sheets and blankets were not included, but a pillow and a rug could be had on payment of an extra charge. There were no washing facilities in the sleeping spaces, only at the carriage ends. Some compartments on the Great Western lacked doors to the corridor. On the LNER, used soap tablets from first-class sleepers were given new lives in third-class lavatory compartments. Some of these reach-me-down soaps may previously have been rubbed over the bodies of passengers using the shower booths that were provided in the company's new first-class sleeping cars of the 1930s.

This was clearly no way to market the sleeper service to the aspirational traveller of the 1950s. Around the start of Queen Elizabeth's reign, the railways therefore began to provide bedding for both classes. When BR introduced its own standard design of second-class sleeping car – in 1957, just after third class was formally upgraded – they had dual berths with proper beds, and washbasins too. Single berths remained a first-class privilege; *The Times*'s man noted approvingly 'the air of many individual privacies impregnably secured' on a night journey to Inverness in 1956. Other distinctions then still current included a drugget that could be taken from its rack and placed on the floor, and the grandiose display of a passenger list at the carriage door, as if in imitation of an ocean liner ('Two MPs, a peer, a professor, several men with efficient-sounding Scottish names, and a lady with a romantic-sounding French one.') The proportion of listable to non-listable passengers in this period is suggested by the total number of berths within the 380 Mark 1 sleeping cars built for the national network: 1,728 first class, 4,884 second.

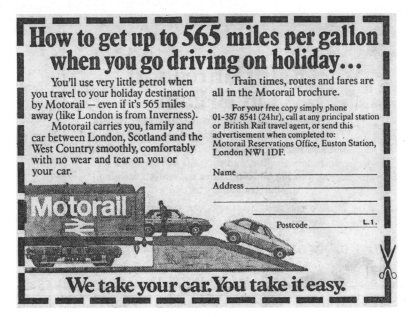

How to get up to 565 miles per gallon when you go driving on holiday...

You'll use very little petrol when you travel to your holiday destination by Motorail — even if it's 565 miles away (like London is from Inverness).

Motorail carries you, family and car between London, Scotland and the West Country smoothly, comfortably with no wear and tear on you or your car.

Train times, routes and fares are all in the Motorail brochure.

For your free copy simply phone 01-387 8541 (24hr), call at any principal station or British Rail travel agent, or send this advertisement when completed to: Motorail Reservations Office, Euston Station, London NW1 1DF.

Name

Address

Postcode   L.1.

We take your car. You take it easy.

Press advertisement for Motorail, 1983

These numbers are a sign of healthy demand in the post-war years. Devon, Cornwall and the major Scottish cities were all connected with London by sleeper, as were many of the ports on the west coast of Britain from which sailings were made to Ireland. Northern English cities such as Manchester, Liverpool and Newcastle were also regarded as sufficiently remote from London to justify sleeping all the way there. Like certain daytime trains, many sleeper services divided into smaller portions for different destinations on the journey down and were reassembled on the return journey. On arrival, passengers were allowed to remain in their berths until a reasonable hour, to allow a full night's sleep. Likewise, berths could be taken and sleep achieved long before the moment of departure on the return journey, so that any thumps and jerks sustained when the carriages were recoupled might pass unnoticed.

These were also the years in which the railways rediscovered the market for transporting passengers along with their road vehicles. Many of these trains likewise ran overnight, and included sleeping cars as well as the necessary flat wagons or vans for the motors. The first of this new wave of trains was a London-to-Perth service in 1955. In 1966 the service was given a smart new name – 'Motorail' – and a new London base, at the under-used station at Kensington Olympia. Cross-country Motorail trains ran too. Even on daytime runs the service was far from cheap, but it had an obvious attraction in the years before the motorway system was ready. It was heavily promoted by BR, with images of Austin Maxis and Vauxhall Vivas trundling out of covered railway vans or speeding into the sunset on flat wagons coupled behind their occupants' carriages. With some success, too: annual loadings around 1970 stood at some 100,000 vehicles.

₪

By the late 1970s the sleeping cars were looking tired. As an interim mea-sure the interiors were updated, with new finishes and furnishings in rest-ful shades of blue. By tradition, the fixtures included an endearing little peg and wall-mounted pad by the bed-head, so that passengers could hang up their watches for easy consultation during the night. Meanwhile the Mark 3 version of the sleeping car was awaited, production of which began in 1981.

This new generation was delayed by a redesign in response to a ter-rible accident to a West Country sleeper train three years previously. Eleven passengers died in their beds, overcome by fumes from a fire that had started in the corridor. The conflagration began after plastic bags full of dirty bedding were piled up against an electric heater, the carriage having been recently converted from the old (and, in this context, safer) method of heating by piped steam. Air circulating through the corridor was directed into the compartments, whose occupants stood little chance against the silent entry of smoke and carbon monoxide in the small hours of the morning. To prevent the recurrence of such horrors, the new sleep-ing cars used fire-retardant materials and advanced smoke-alarm systems. They were also fully air-conditioned, putting an end to the hard choice between stuffiness and the roaring, sleep-defying draughts of an open win-dow in a train travelling at speed. The convention that every compartment should have a chamber pot, tucked away within the base of the washbasin, was quietly abandoned. Another change was that the compartments pro-vided for first- and second-class travellers were physically identical. Each had two berths; payment of a first-class fare secured solitary occupation, the upper bunk being folded away out of use and its demountable access ladder removed. So the classes converged further.

The market for sleeper trains had contracted by the 1970s; just 210 sleeping cars were thought sufficient to replace the 1950s versions. Even this number proved excessive. Shrinking demand for Motorail services resulted in drastic cuts in 1982, when the facilities at Kensington were closed and the network scaled back to a few routes out of London. Ordinary sleeper traffic suffered as daytime express trains ran ever faster, making it easier to get a day's business or visiting done and still be back in good time to sleep at home. Air travel nibbled away at what was left. Sleeping cars to Wales ceased, as business with the Irish ferries dwindled. Losses of other routes followed as privatisation loomed in the 1990s and unprofitable services came under scrutiny. BR found itself with sidings full of sleeping cars that were barely twenty years old, for which there was no obvious use. The lease of ten of them to Danish State Railways in 1988 was a modest but unrepeated coup. Preserved railways queued to pick over the rest, their purchases eventually accounting for nearly one in five of the fleet. These were not acquired to run nocturnally up and down the railways' own short lines, but for stationary use as hostels for visiting volunteers.

What remains on the privatised network is, by past standards, not much. One sleeper train per night goes from London Paddington down to Penzance (the Night Riviera), and two head from London Euston into Scotland (both called the Caledonian Sleeper). The earlier of these Caledonian departures divides into three on arrival at Edinburgh, for onward travel to Aberdeen, to Inverness, and to Fort William, which receives just two carriages. The second Scottish train serves Glasgow and Edinburgh only, splitting in two after crossing the border. In the middle of the night, each of these Caledonian trains passes its counterpart making its way up to London. The Cornish service is the first to arrive in the capital, the Highland one the last (currently at 7.47 a.m., after a journey of eleven hours). Each train also includes ordinary saloon coaches, for those prepared to sit up all night in exchange for a lower fare. Apart from the subdivisions within Scotland, sleeping cars are no longer uncoupled and dropped off at stations along the way, to allow their occupants to continue their slumbers. Plymouth used to be one such stop; now, anyone using the Night Riviera to reach that city must be prepared to get off by 5.43 a.m., or be carried off to Cornwall.

The Cornish and Scottish services have both been periodically threatened, whereupon local MPs, regular users and lovers of the railways in general rise up in well-rehearsed protest, pointing out the wider value of the sleepers to the regions and communities served. It helps that the trains become stopping services as they get further from London, so that modest places such as Ardlui, Inverkeithing and Liskeard all benefit from a direct nightly connection to the capital. On the other side of the equation, the subsidies involved are embarrassingly large. In 2011 it was calculated that each departure of a Caledonian sleeper was underwritten by the taxpayer to the sum of £17,000, out of an annual grant to the service of £21 million. At the close of that year, with the end of the operating franchise period not far off, there was ominous talk of killing off one or other of the Scottish services. Both Westminster and the Scottish government then pledged £50 million each to enhance the future of the service, which was relaunched as a separate franchise in 2015. The Westminster grant was offered first, on condition that matching funds were forthcoming from Holyrood.

This sort of politicking has so far worked to the advantage of the sleepers, which are promised an operational future up to 2029. The victor in the franchise contest held in 2013–14 was the outsourcing company Serco, which is to introduce seventy-two new sleeper carriages with both standard and business-class compartments, the latter with en suite showers and toilets. So distinctions of class are to return in force, reversing sixty years of egalitarian convergence in this particular niche of the transport system. According to Transport Scotland, the service 'will creatively reflect the attributes that visitors say best describe Scotland: a dramatic, human and enduring place'. The carriages that are to embody these Scottish qualities will be built for lease to Serco by the Spanish company CAF, for introduction in 2018. (With a nod to the Scottish tradition of respect for the working man and the engineer, let it be recorded here that the old Mark 3 sleeping cars were designed and built in British Rail's workshops at Derby.)

A similar entanglement of transport and politics spun the saga of the Nightstar sleeper trains, one of the strangest and least-known tales from the network in recent decades. The story began in the mid 1980s, when plans for the Channel Tunnel services were being formulated. Support for the tunnel in Britain was tempered by suspicions beyond London and the south-east that this was a costly vanity project which would bring little benefit to the country at large. Reassurance came in the form of promises to Parliament that international trains would run throughout the country, as well as to Waterloo. Sufficient new trains were ordered to allow for daytime services, and a new service depot was established at Manchester Piccadilly, where the main building was lettered with the hopeful words LE EUROSTAR HABITE ICI. But the long distances involved also meant that some cross-Channel trains would have to run through the night, which is where the Nightstars came in. Besides overnight services from London, trains were to run from all three British nations, with Swansea, Glasgow, Manchester and Plymouth as their starting points, to destinations in France, Holland, Belgium and Germany. Each was to include day saloons as well as sleeping cars, to allow seated travel during waking hours. Catering cars were included too. Work began to build the 139 vehicles that would be needed.

None of this took account of the competition. Just as the bodyshells of the carriages were taking shape, the first low-cost airlines began their remorseless ascent across Europe. What had always been a hazily optimistic business model for the Nightstars and provincial Eurostars now lay in shreds, and the project was halted in 1997. Formal abandonment followed two years later.

In a rerun of the APT débâcle, Britain's railways now found themselves with lots of costly new rolling stock, built or half-built, for which there was no obvious use. To protect them against taggers and pilferers, the carriages were moved from the workshops in Birmingham to secure storage at the Ministry of Defence depot at Kineton in Warwickshire, where they made odd companions for the armed forces' main munitions training school. What was to be done with them all? The obvious answer was to find a home for the trains with one of the operating companies into which the national system had been split – except that the carriages were so heavy, so crammed with current-hungry electrics and safety features needed to qualify for running under the Channel, and altogether so difficult to make compatible with existing stock, that no one wanted them. Meanwhile the Nightstar case became another skirmish in the long battle over public versus private funding for the tunnel route itself, the costs of which had consistently overrun. An exasperated John Prescott, then Deputy Prime Minster, told the House of Commons in 1998: 'Even this week I was asked to find £100 million to pay for specially designed sleeper trains which do not work, have never worked, and are now lying idle in a field.' The best that could be done was for the manufacturers to undertake to buy them back, on condition that a new owner could be found.

Faces were saved in 2000 when a deal was struck with VIA Rail, operators of Canada's passenger trains. The purchase price, at $130 million, was widely considered a bargain. The Nightstars went off from Newport docks, still with their multi-currency cash tills in place in the catering cars. Now, vehicles that were meant to allow the sleeping Glaswegian to pass the sleeping Dortmunder somewhere in the darkened Low Countries make their way across the spacious landscapes between Toronto and Halifax, Nova Scotia.

₪

Meanwhile, we can still travel on the remaining sleeper trains. Can, and should: for there is nothing else like them. It is not simply the singular experience of having a little bedroom on a train – a stranger feeling still, now that ordinary seated compartments have disappeared. Nor is the appeal necessarily much to do with convenience, especially now that the cheap-flight merchants are criss-crossing the skies. There is a certain caravan-like charm in the little space-saving devices of the compartment, such as the fold-down lid to the washbasin that doubles as a sort of window-sill, but that is only a small part of it. It would also be difficult to claim that the sleeping compartments are especially peaceful spaces, with their background roar from the air conditioning, and the mysterious creaks, squeaks and groans when in motion.

No; what makes sleeping and awakening on these trains so special is the promise of magical translation to an utterly different place. Recalling Scottish excursions, the critic and essayist Max Beerbohm (1872–1956) considered that 'nothing is more mysteriously delightful than this joint consciousness of sleep and movement'. The mood of grateful surrender to mechanical power is beautifully caught on celluloid in Powell and Pressburger's *I Know Where I'm Going* (1945): the heroine's night journey to Glasgow is represented not by stock footage of a speeding train, but by a dream-sequence in which a tiny model version glides through mountains made of tartan blankets, as an unseen voice sings a lullaby. Sleep abolishes time; it follows that sleeping through the night on a moving train abolishes distance as well as time. This abolition of time and space was the most astonishing thing about the railways when they were new. To slip into dreams somewhere past Watford or Rugby and to raise the blinds on waking to a view of the stern rocky mass of the Boar of Badenoch at Druimuachdar summit, the highest point on the railway network, is thus to join hands across the decades with the first travellers by rail. So we may feel again as Thomas Carlyle did, of his first nocturnal railway journey of 1839, 'as if some huge steam nightbird had flung you on its back, and were sweeping thro' unknown space with you'.

There is more. Sleeper trains include a lounge car, a sort of joint descendant of the family saloon and the observation car, with leather sofas and moveable armchairs that positively plead with the traveller to gaze out of the big windows. There are no headrests or Pendolino-type blind spots here to block the morning or evening view. Passengers make their way to this saloon, as they formerly did to the dining car when a full menu service was available, or as they might move from cabin to saloon deck on board a ship, with a sense of joining a social space. The peculiar solipsism of railway travel – a solipsism that was observed in the earliest compartments, and which smartphones and tablet computers have made worse than ever – is laid aside. People make eye contact and exchange words. It is discovered that there is value in 'this frail / Travelling coincidence', to quote from Philip Larkin's 'The Whitsun Weddings' (1964), one of the few railway poems in English that can give 'Adlestrop' a run for its money.

Even better: there is a bar at the end of the carriage. Better still: it will serve you an alcoholic drink after 9 p.m., the time at which drinking on trains that run wholly within Scotland became illegal on 20 July 2012, in the interests of public order. Lulled by a whisky – though not by as much of the hard stuff as Larkin was prone to put away – we can fall asleep to the intermittent rhythm of the rails. As for this book, it is time to leave the train, to explore the railway on which it runs.

PART II

DOWN THE LINE

THE PERMANENT WAY

E veryone knows the noise a moving train is supposed to make: a sort of diddly-dum rhythm, four beats close together, repeated over and over. Everyone knows it; and yet the music of wheels on rail joints is unusual now. Modern track uses continuously welded rails (cwr), made by fusing together many shorter lengths that have been rolled separately. Underground passengers were the first in Britain to benefit from the improved ride offered by welded rails, after London Transport adopted the technology in 1937. British Railways followed suit in the late 1950s, and by 1974 continuously welded rails had already been laid on almost a third of track-miles across the network.

Each welded rail may be a mile in length, far too long to be carried on a single train; instead, shorter composite lengths are carried to the site of use, to be welded together as they are laid down. To the passenger in transit these welding points are undetectable, and the use of tapering joints ensures that even the noise made when the train crosses from one continuously welded rail to the next is barely noticeable. Noise reduction is not the only advantage: trains benefit from reduced vibration and friction in terms of maintenance costs, lifespan and lower energy input, and the smoother ride allows much higher permitted speeds.

Whatever its length, each rail will expand and contract according to variations in temperature. The longer the rail, the greater the potential movement, always with the risk of buckling in the hottest weather. Continuously welded rails therefore have to be tensioned as they are laid down, either by mechanical stretching or by heating, before being fixed firmly in place. Any expansion after that is absorbed by the elastic tension within the rail, which remains both taut and firmly anchored to the sleepers. This tension explains the singing noise the rails make when a fast train approaches.

Rails of the traditional type are inert by comparison. With their sleepers, they are laid down in panels of standard length, which in Britain was fixed at 60ft in the second quarter of the twentieth century. Each join is secured by bolting pairs of bars, called fishplates, through holes drilled in the web, the name given to the thinner upright section in the middle of the rail. A gap for expansion is left between adjoining rails, and the holes in the fishplates are elongated so that the greased bolt-heads can slide within them as each rail gently shrinks or grows. The colder the weather, the shorter the rails and the larger the gaps, so that winter trains often make more noise than summer ones; thus the Great Western in the 1930s allowed fully half an inch as its upper limit. The familiar four beats – two close together, a slightly longer gap, then another two closely spaced – are made by the wheels of the twin-axled bogies at the end of each carriage as they cross joint after joint of this type.

The fourfold beat is really a twentieth-century sound, and not the usual rhythm the Victorians knew. As we have seen, most carriages then had four or six wheels, on axles that were more widely spaced. The rails were shorter too – in the first years of the passenger railway, very much shorter. In the form first perfected for waggonways around 1790, this type was no longer than the span between one sleeper and the next. Each rail therefore needed support at the ends only, and from the curved profile of the underside this type acquired the name of fish-bellied rails. Cast-iron manufacture of fish-bellied rails gave way by the 1820s to wrought iron, which was less brittle and crack-prone; the Stockton & Darlington and Liverpool & Manchester both used rails of this material.

The next step was to make longer rails of wrought iron, without the fish-bellied profile. These in turn yielded from the 1860s to rails rolled from steel, which promised to last at least four times longer. Steel rails were also heavier, although at first barely more than half the weight of the thick rails now used on main lines. Lengths have also increased; on the Midland Railway, the progression went from 20ft rails in 1850 to 24ft in 1875, 30ft in 1884, 36ft in 1896 and 45ft a few years after that. Rails of different lengths would therefore have been encountered on

(12)

On the **Steel Rail (12)** look for the gap between
the rails; the chair which holds the rail bolted
to the sleeper; the key—that's the wedge holding
the rail in the chair; and the fishplate which joins
the rails.

How many bolts on the fishplate?........................

.... Score **20**

Track with bullhead rail, as explained in *I-Spy on a Railway Journey*, 1963

most journeys. Altogether, the rails and wheels of the Victorian railway
would have given a less jaunty rhythm, closer to an incessant thumping
or banging, amplified by the basic suspension and noise insulation of the
carriages of the period. The harsh, halting beats of today's four-wheeled
Pacer carriages on jointed track give a sense of how fatiguing the experience must have been.

Jointed rails may still be found all over the modern railway, especially
in sidings and alongside the platforms at stations, where maximum speeds
are low. Much of this is of flat-bottomed outline like that of the welded
rails, with a profile that spreads out below. This is a very old form, and a few
railways adopted the type as early as the 1830s, but it became the national
standard for new running lines only in stages from 1949. The 'bullhead'
form of rail that was near-ubiquitous before then is not hard to spot. It
is more symmetrical in profile from top to bottom, like a swollen letter I
of which the upper cross-stroke is thicker and fatter than that below. As
this lower part is not wide enough to sit upright, the rail depends for its
support on heavy cast-iron chairs that are screwed or bolted to the sleepers. To anchor the rail firmly within these chairs, fat wedge-like fastenings
known as keys – originally of oak or sometimes teak, latterly of folded
sprung steel – are hammered in between the chair and the outer side of
the rail, against the web. Together, the chairs and keys hold the rail with
its upper surface at a slight angle to the horizontal (the standard figure on
straight track is 1 in 20), to offer a continuous surface to marry with the
tapered steel tyres of railway wheels.

Most of the sleepers used in Britain over the years have been of wood. When railways were young, however, sunken stone blocks were used instead. They were drilled with holes for fixing the chairs, and each one sat beneath a single line of rail. Cross ties were often dispensed with in track of this kind; the weight of the blocks themselves was considered enough to stop the rails from spreading. For the horse-drawn routes on which such blocks were first used, there was a clear advantage too in leaving a level pathway down the middle. Stone blocks also had the attractions of durability, outweighing the cheaper initial cost of timber sleepers, and rigidity. The last point is particularly important: engineers around 1830 imagined the railway as a sort of giant horizontal machine, trains and track together, in which hardness and firmness were just as much at a premium as they were within a stationary engine. The London & Greenwich even set its granite sleepers in concrete, to make doubly sure.

This policy was a mistake. Quite soon, it was realised that the shock-absorbing qualities of wood were a positive advantage, reducing wear and tear on the rails and offering a smoother ride. The case was demonstrated in 1837 on the Grand Junction Railway, named because it would connect two early inter-city lines into a single trunk route. These lines were the Liverpool & Manchester and the London & Birmingham, each of which had mostly employed stone sleepers on its tracks. The Grand Junction's engineer Joseph Locke used a mixture of stone and temporary timber sleepers, intending to upgrade the timber sections in due course. Once the differences could be compared, it was the stone blocks that were discarded. Other lines followed suit, which meant that a great many redundant stone blocks of similar size became available. Many were reused within the railway network, with its constant need for materials of every kind. Second-hand sleeper blocks thought to have come from the Liverpool & Manchester turned up during the demolition of a coal depot at Shepherds Bush in 1974, when the railway historian J. B. Atkinson rescued a few at the price of 50p each, payable to British Rail. Perhaps the oddest instance of reuse is still passed by thousands of unwitting railway travellers every day: the prodigious neo-Gothic church of St Walburge, just north of Preston station, built in 1867 using limestone sleeper blocks discarded by the Preston & Longridge Railway in its lower walls.

The drawbacks of rigid running were also discovered by Isambard Kingdom Brunel on the Great Western. Independent-minded as ever, Brunel chose to make his broad-gauge track of a form known as baulk road, in which each rail was supported by continuous longitudinal timbers laid on a compacted bed. Cross timbers were still needed to keep the rails at the correct distance of 7ft 0¼in apart, and these were placed at intervals of 15ft. But Brunel wanted to make his track firmer still, so the cross timbers were anchored by piles driven 15ft into the ground. It did not work. The earth and gravel ballast around the track subsided with time, and the impact of passing trains forced the piles further into the earth at uneven rates. The timber framework also sagged between the points supported by the piles, and the ride became a queasy dipping up and down. So the piles were quietly removed and new broad-gauge routes for the Great Western and its associated lines in the West of England and South Wales did without them. Released from the technological cul-de-sac of the pile, the broad gauge delivered what Brunel had promised, a smoother ride for passengers than stone-sleepered standard-gauge lines. The sounds of travel were different too: the ends of broad-gauge rails were not aligned, doubling the number of joints encountered by the six-wheeled carriages and turning the noise and vibration to an irregular clatter.

The rails on the baulk road were rolled to a distinctive up-and-down section, with horizontal flanges on each side. Holes in these flanges allowed the rail to be fixed to the timbers. The type was known as bridge rail, and versions of it are still used on some railway bridges, where the rails are fixed directly to the structure. On other lines, our traveller of 1862 might also have encountered the Barlow rail, which had a profile like a broad inverted V with the sides curving outwards to a distance of thirteen inches. This width allowed the rails to be buried stably in the ballast without any sleepers at all, and with only iron cross ties to link them. When a train passed in dry weather, these rails tended to throw up a lot of dust; when waterlogged, they were known for squirting out mud.

₪

In another crucial respect, the physical form of the railway in the 1860s was much less diverse than it had been around 1840. In those years, not every railway engineer was yet thinking of how the various lines might be linked in a national system. The Eastern Counties Railway is a case in point. By 1843 its main line from London was open as far as Colchester, to a gauge of 5ft: incompatible with the standard gauge of 4ft 8½in, without offering any compelling advantages over it. When the railway was being planned in 1836, the exact figure must have seemed unimportant; not so by 1843. During the course of one costly and laborious month in the year following, the company therefore converted all its tracks and rolling stock to the standard width. Its neighbour in the East End, the London & Blackwall Railway, did the same in 1849; the original gauge here was 5ft 0½in. North of the border, 'Scotch Gauge' (4ft 6in) was a common choice for horse-drawn mineral railways of the central belt, and the first Scottish passenger railway followed local usage: this was the Garnkirk & Glasgow, opened in 1831. Irish gauges were all over the place too in the early days, ranging from the standard British width to an indulgent 6ft 2in for the first railway built in Ulster. These liberties ended in 1843, when the Board of Trade decreed that Ireland should adopt 5ft 3in as standard. The gauge remains in use, and visitors will notice that Irish tracks have a spacious look by comparison with those in Britain and on the Continent; the difference also explains why there have never been train ferries across the Irish Sea.

A decision on Ireland having been reached, the British nettle stood next in line for grasping. The question was settled by Act in 1846, a decisive early episode of state intervention in the operation of the railways. The Act took account of the deliberations of a Royal Commission that sat during the previous year, to which most of the senior figures within the industry had presented their thoughts. What was under scrutiny by then was not the residue of near-standard gauges, which could be left to the companies to sort out themselves, but the disparity between standard gauge and Brunel's version, fully 2ft 3¾in wider.

Months passed while the country waited to learn how far the Commission's findings would be given legal force. Meanwhile, the pamphlets flew. Some of these came from the pen of the civil servant and design reformer Henry Cole (1808–82), one of those energetic, unclassifiable figures who pops up everywhere in the Victorian world. In 1843 he had commissioned the world's first Christmas card for sale; in 1850 he got the Great Exhibition under way. Helping to settle Brunel's hash was another of Cole's projects. His pamphlet entitled *Inconsistencies of Men of Genius, Exemplified in the Practice and Precept of Isambard Kingdom Brunel, Esq.* was unsparing. Much of its text consisted of self-incriminating material from Brunel's own statements, especially from a sticky interlude in 1838–9 when a faction of Liverpool shareholders in the Great Western had tried to jettison their chief engineer and his clever ideas. Cornered, Brunel had been forced to admit that the broad gauge 'could have no connexion with any other of the main lines'. As Cole put it, 'we have every practical *railway* engineer denouncing the Broad or seven feet Gauge, and only Mr Brunel attempting to defend it'.

He was not far wrong; the consensus against Brunel's gauge was decisive. The engineer enjoyed a few good moments when giving evidence, and even managed to persuade the Commission that trials should be held to show the relative merits of the gauges. The Great Western's trial train easily vindicated Brunel's claims for superior speed and comfort, but that was not really the point; and the outcome was easy to foretell. Under the ensuing Act of 1846, new passenger lines within Britain were to be of standard gauge unless by special exception. The broad gauge was allowed to continue, subject to some lines being converted for joint operation, and to make extensions within its existing territory. Thus the Great Western and its allies in the western lands were spared the immediate disruption and expense of forced conversion.

Brunel was a marvel, and it is impossible to read even a little about him without being delighted at his endless daring, inventiveness and panache. His vitality and intelligence shine from photographs: the quizzical gaze under the thick eyebrows and stovepipe hat, the full mouth that seems about to speak, even through the enormous cigar. By comparison, his admirable contemporaries Robert Stephenson (1803–59) and Joseph Locke (1805–60) seem a little staid. They were certainly less versatile than Brunel, for whom the design of innovative ocean liners, station buildings, docks, gun barrels, workers' suburbs, suspension bridges, water towers and prefabricated hospitals were all in a day's work. When the Great Exhibition opened Brunel walked alone, fourth from the front of the procession, as if representing a one-man aristocracy of genius (in truth, he had been just one among many notables on the organising committees). In his own domain he behaved like a Renaissance prince. No other railway engineer would have made the *beau geste* of taking a ring from his finger to present to the foreman in charge, when the gangs broke through the last rocks in the middle of Box Tunnel between Wiltshire and Somerset. No other engineer entertained the nation's eleven most eminent artists to dinner and commissioned a painting from each. That was in 1847; in Worcestershire four years later, Brunel defied the law of the land by inciting thousands of loyal navvies to set upon the men of a contractor with whom he was in dispute, and got away with it. On his death, huge letters

reading I. K. BRUNEL ENGINEER 1859 were affixed to his new bridge at
Saltash, between Devon and Cornwall, which used up some of the parts
originally intended for Brunel's suspension bridge at Clifton. In another
memorial tribute, leading civil engineers joined forces to ensure that the
Clifton Bridge was completed after all.

Commemorations continue. A London university has been named
after Brunel, he has a near-monarchical total of eight statues in the capital
and points west, and he beat Shakespeare, Darwin and Newton to take
second place, after Churchill, in a BBC poll of the Hundred Greatest Britons in 2002. Like Dickens, he seems somehow to be still with us; an exhibition at the Design Museum in London in 2000 was entitled 'Isambard
Kingdom Brunel: Recent Works'. Brunel's mental processes are accessible
thanks to the copious deposits of drawings and sketches he left on his
favourite squared paper, which are to be housed in a new museum under
construction in Bristol at the time of writing; it will feature a giant replica
of the great engineer's head.

Had the broad gauge been the invention of a committee, or of some
colourless drudge, it surely would not have received so much posthumous
respect. The idea that Brunel was somehow done down in the battle of
the gauges refuses to die entirely, and the Great Western's admirers have
kept up the aura of unfulfilled potential around it. The book of the Design
Museum's exhibition presented the case for and against in the form of
a tennis match, with broad gauge in the lead over standard for most of
the way, only for the 'better engineering solution' to be foiled by outside
intervention in the final set. For L. T. C. Rolt, author of the first modern
biography of Brunel (1957), it was 'the bravest lost cause in engineering
history'; he compared its inventor romantically to a brightly plumaged
bird mobbed by sparrows. There was a political subtext here: Rolt was
writing in the belief that the initiative and individuality of the railways'
era of greatness was being stifled by state ownership. For Brunel also fits
the twentieth century's pervasive myth of the avant-garde, the sense that
the future belonged to a handful of artistic or technical visionaries who
were 'ahead of their time'.

The broad gauge demonstrates the weaknesses of this attitude. Brunel's working method was of the top-down model, impatient with collaboration or delegation, and sometimes impervious to bad news and
inconvenient truths. The engineer compared his Great Western Railway to a language only he could speak, of which 'Every word has to be

Transferring goods from broad-gauge to standard-gauge wagons
at Gloucester, from the *Illustrated London News*, 1847

translated' – as if he had established a happy realm of Esperanto speakers, fully expecting that the rest of the world would decide to learn Esperanto too. Not that his vision was narrow in other ways, for the Great Western was conceived on a global scale. At Bristol it was intended to connect with sailings to the New World by Brunel's own mammoth steamships – by Great Western to take the SS *Great Western*, no less. With international travellers in mind, he even provided a giant hotel close to the city's docks. The railway and the docks did not interconnect at first; passengers and cargoes were conveyed between them through the streets of Bristol. For Brunel, the need for passengers and cargoes to detrain when crossing the frontiers of the broad gauge, and the impossibility of running carriages or goods wagons across those frontiers, were simply part of the due price for its overall superiority.

Not everyone agreed, especially those close to the frontier in the prosperous West Midlands, where the Great Western had expansive plans. The arrangements at Gloucester showed what might result, and it was not a picture that flattered the broad gauge. The cathedral city was reached by standard gauge from Birmingham in 1840, by broad gauge from Bristol in 1844. After 8 July of that year, all rail-borne traffic between the Midlands and the west, human or otherwise, had to be transhipped by means of a badly planned exchange station at Gloucester. The hectic daily round at that station became notorious, partly thanks to negative publicity around the time that the Gauge Commission was sitting. Henry Cole and W. M. Thackeray went down to witness the dashing about and barrowing to and fro, which the novelist then satirised in *Punch* as 'Jeames on the Gauge Question', using one of his cod-cockney personae (Jeames loses his baby because of complications caused by the break of gauge, but learns via the 'elecktricle inwention' of the telegraph that it is safe and well back at Paddington, albeit 'c.r.y.i.n.g.').

This was no mere comical muddle: the break of gauge was a serious restraint on trade and circulation. Brunel had conceived of the Great Western primarily as a passenger route; but on other lines, income from goods traffic was already closing the gap with that obtained from passengers, and freight could not be expected to transport itself between trains at the point of transfer. The *Illustrated London News* quoted a (possibly invented) carrier on the ordeal of a single train-load of mixed goods passing through Gloucester:

> In the hurry the bricks are miscounted, the slates chipped at the edges, the cheeses cracked, the ripe fruit and vegetables crushed and spoiled; the chairs, furniture, and oil cakes, cast iron pots, grates and ovens, all more or less broken; the coals turned into slack, the salt short of weight, sundry bottles of wine deficient, and the fish too late for market.

To reduce the battle of the gauges retrospectively to a technical beauty contest is also to ignore the political and social context. The Gauge Commission happened at the instigation of Richard Cobden, radical MP for the manufacturing town of Stockport. Cobden and his allies won a great victory in these years when the protectionist Corn Laws were repealed, opening the nation's markets to cheaper grain from abroad. There is an affinity between this campaign and the Commission's verdict in favour of standard gauge, because it was better suited to 'the general commercial traffic of the country'.

Nor was the broad gauge quite as far-sighted in practice as Brunel's admirers have suggested. In particular, the great width of the tracks was not carried through proportionately to the loading gauge, so that the spatial advantage over the more generous standard-gauge lines of the next generation was modest at most. In truth, Brunel's choice of gauge was made not so much with a potential future of bigger trains in mind – in his view, the Great Western's wide, squat carriages and large-wheeled locomotives already represented ideal types – but to allow a faster, safer and more stable ride, on trains with a lower centre of gravity than standard gauge could provide. He also failed to anticipate the extent to which the rival gauge could be improved. Better and more durable materials narrowed the gap, as did the adoption of more precise tolerances, and such adjustments as the canting up of the tracks on one side so that trains could take curves more quickly. And so the Great Western's lead in speed and comfort dwindled, and by the end of the century it was the rival London & North Western that was most often cited as having the best permanent way – to use the industry's term for the combination of rails, sleepers, ballast and underlying formation that makes up the running lines.

The story rolls on, for the standard Stephenson gauge has proved amazingly capable of bearing whatever the world has wanted to carry by rail. Continental railways that were built to the British standard gauge used it in conjunction with much roomier loading gauges. Elsewhere even greater clearances were adopted. To British eyes, the trains of North America seem especially gigantic. Thanks to inter-war publicity stunts that sent the latest express locomotives from Stephenson's homeland to tour the New World, it was possible to compare them side by side; photographed next to American locos, the visitors look like dapper little earls in the company of hulking lumberjacks.

In matters of speed, the standard gauge has proved no less accommodating. Those beautiful express locomotives that crossed the Atlantic in the 1920s and 1930s were a legitimate source of national pride, because Britain then still enjoyed the fastest railway timetables in the world. The Great Western's crack train was the Cheltenham Flyer, which achieved an average speed of 81.3 mph over the seventy-seven miles from Swindon to Paddington on 5 June 1932. Such feats of the steam age in its late maturity were left standing by electrification, in which Britain lagged behind; and again by the new generation of dedicated high-speed routes that began with the Japanese bullet trains of the 1960s. Japan's original network was built to a gauge of 3ft 6in (the involvement of British engineers explains the imperial measurements), but standard gauge was adopted for the bullet-train lines. Brunel's supporters referred dismissively to the 'coalwaggon gauge'; in 1964, Japanese passenger trains of mighty weight began operating at speeds of up to 125 mph along tracks whose dimensions and basic principles had indeed been developed to allow wagons of Tyneside coal to run more easily. It is a similar story in Spain: a gauge several inches wider than standard was adopted in the 1840s, but the new high-speed lines added in the 1990s – running now at speeds of over 190 mph – follow the European norm. Standard gauge gets more standard all the time.

₪

Since we have just been kicking Brunel while he is down, this is a good place to discuss the Atmospheric Railway, alias the South Devon Railway. No other project by the great engineer captures his contradictory qualities quite so well. The concept was certainly far-sighted: trains were to run without locomotives, by connecting them via a piston to a heavy tube laid between the rails from which air was constantly exhausted. The vacuum created within the cast-iron pipe drew the train forward. Power to produce this suction came from coke-fired pumping stations spaced along the track. In effect, thinned air took the place of the ropes or cables that were still in use on some passenger routes in the 1840s, usually where gradients were steep. Atmospheric power promised to do the job no less cleanly and quietly, but at much higher speeds and over greater distances. Trains could dispense with the use of heavy locomotives, condemned to carry everywhere their own supplies of fuel and water; track could in turn be made lighter and cheaper. Looking forward, this transfer of the power source from the train to a stationary supplier anticipated the principle of railway electrification.

The atmospheric railway per se was not Brunel's invention. A workable form was patented by two London engineers named William Clegg and Jacob Samuda, who were engaged to install it on the new line to Dalkey in the outskirts of Dublin, opened in 1843. This was a sort of boutique railway, being self-contained, less than two miles long, and devoted entirely to passenger traffic. Trains were relatively light and ran only once an hour. Five minutes' pumping was sufficient to suck each departure up the gradient to Dalkey. It was a steady ascent, so the return journey could be made by gravity. Effectively, here was a vacuum-powered version of a rope-worked incline.

Brunel was not the only senior railway engineer to detect promise in the atmospheric system. The technology was adopted by William Cubitt

Brunel's Atmospheric Railway: reconstruction drawing of a train at
Sprey Point, on the South Devon Railway's seafront section

for the London & Croydon Railway, whose seven-and-a-half-mile route
terminated at London Bridge station. This was not a new railway: the
route had already been open for several years, but its lines were increasingly used by through traffic. What was now attempted was an additional
track for local services. Pumping stations were built at each end of the first
atmospheric section, between Croydon and Forest Hill, about halfway to
the London terminus. Trial services began in 1845.

Local lines like the Dalkey railway and the London & Croydon had
never got Brunel's juices flowing. Reviewing current railway contracts in
his journal for Boxing Day 1835, he dismissed the small jobs with impatience. ('A little go, almost beneath my notice. It will do as a branch.')
These were orthodox, locomotive-hauled lines. More exciting was the
prospect of what the emerging atmospheric technology could be made to
do on a grand scale. The chosen beneficiary was the South Devon Railway,
enacted in July 1844, of which Brunel was chief engineer. The line was to
run for fifty-three miles between Exeter and Plymouth, on a route that
included steep gradients. Brunel believed that the atmospheric system
could take these in its stride, and that he was the man to refine or perfect
its workings in order to achieve this. Questioned about his plans for the

line by the Gauge Commissioners, he promised something 'very superior in general comfort and luxury'.

It was not to be. So many wayward ideas were herded together on the South Devon Railway that even the most brilliant engineer could never have driven them all successfully in one direction. This is not mere hindsight: many at the time said as much, but these dissenters proved no match for Brunel's energetic self-confidence.

The weakest point of this fragile, inflexible and woefully expensive railway was the vacuum pipe itself. As it moved along the pipe, the piston attached to each train opened up a greased leather flap that sealed the slot along the top, which was then pressed shut again behind it. But this flap leaked badly, even without the regular passage of trains. What was meant to be a low-maintenance system therefore came to depend on constant replenishment of the grease. Many sealants were tried: the London & Croydon used a mixture of beeswax and tallow; the South Devon began with lime soap, which proved prone to form a hard skin, followed by a mixture of soap and cod liver oil, which was too easily sucked out by the vacuum. As the leather lost its oils, it became prone to waterlogging and liable to freeze in cold weather. On coastal sections of the line the metal parts of the seal also proved vulnerable, on account of corrosion from salt spray.* So the stationary engines in South Devon had to work three times harder than expected in order to keep the vacuum at working pressure, and the fuel bills shot up.

Rubber seals were tried in the Devon system's last days, but never had the chance to prove themselves. Even if they had stopped the leaks, other difficulties would have remained. In the first place was the extraordinarily difficult matter of how tracks were to merge or divide. Anywhere that trains crossed on the level, the pipes of both lines had to be interrupted. The London & Croydon managed this by means of a flyover, carrying its atmospheric line across the conventional tracks of the original route. Thus the railway flyover was invented, long before the traffic densities and speeds of the time would have justified the expense in a steam-hauled context. But this was a crossover only, not a junction. Braking was also

---

* One tradition places some of the blame on rats chewing holes in the leather. Recent historians have been more sceptical, although anyone who thinks that a greasy leather flap could remain in place at ground level across miles of country without once receiving the attention of inquisitive incisors has surely underestimated the English rat.

difficult, and if an atmospheric train overshot the platforms there was no practical way to reverse using the power in the pipe. Shunting trains into sidings, or adding or removing carriages – everyday operations on railways elsewhere, including Brunel's own – were therefore the preserve of horses, or even of human muscle-power. Heavy trains presented yet another problem: the power from the pumping engines being constant, they could not be made to move as fast as lighter ones. Worse, when a pumping station broke down, there was no back-up system for its stretch of line; by contrast, if a locomotive failed, a spare one could be sent to assist. As Robert Stephenson noted sceptically, 'the perfect operation of the whole is dependent on each individual part'.

In practice, the South Devon Railway barely worked at all in its intended form. Only the easiest graded section of the line, from Exeter to Newton Abbot, was ever operational; it opened with hired locomotive haulage in 1846, went fully atmospheric after much delay as late as 23 February 1848 and reverted to locomotives on 6 September, after a turbulent shareholders' meeting the week before. The London & Croydon had meanwhile given up pumping in 1847. The Dublin operation quietly carried on, until the line was converted from British to Irish standard gauge in 1854.

Thus the South Devon Railway became an everyday broad-gauge line, like the two Cornish companies by which Brunel later carried his trunk route westward to Penzance. The wasted expenditure was calculated at nearly £500,000 – a poor exchange for Brunel's estimated saving of £67,000 in construction costs. The engineer had the delicacy of feeling to waive his fee until the line finally opened all the way to Plymouth. He saddled the company with a line that was cruelly difficult to operate by locomotives, since its gradients were concentrated into sharp climbs in sections where extra pumping power was to have been provided. Today it is hard to credit that the South Devon hills were ever animated by Brunel's quietly gliding trains. It seems like early science fiction, or a retro steampunk fantasy.

₪

Even after the Act of 1846 chopped its ambitions down to size, nearly half a century passed before the broad gauge died. In the meantime, it was perfectly possible for trains of both gauges to share routes provided that mixed-gauge track was laid. The inconveniences of running trains of two different gauges were now internalised within the broad-gauge network itself.

One of the first stretches enabled the Great Western to run trains beyond Gloucester, to Cheltenham. This extension had four rails, the standard-gauge pair being placed symmetrically within the broad ones. However, this was a useless arrangement in terms of bringing standard-gauge vehicles within range of broad-gauge platforms and loading bays. Later mixed lines therefore used three rails, of which that on the platform side was common to both gauges. Even with just three rails, junctions, points and crossovers were of bewildering complexity. Consider what happens when a double-track route divides in two. Each track has a set of points to direct trains the right way, and three of the four rails must cross at least one other rail before the routes swing clear of one another, to a total of six individual intersections. Mixed-gauge track has six rails, five of which make crossings of other rails, to a total of *fifteen* intersections. Only the most masochistic of railway modellers would attempt to reproduce such an installation. Special arrangements were also required when a mixed-gauge line came to a turntable. For these to operate safely, the railway vehicle being turned has to be centrally placed. The three-railed track therefore had to give way to a four-railed section, in which the standard-gauge pair sat exactly between the outer, broad-gauge rails. Altogether, mixed-gauge track was costly to construct and maintain, and for a period in mid century the company was heavily in debt and struggled to pay a dividend at all.

Stage by stage, the Great Western began to give up on the cherished gauge. One milestone came in 1861, when the acquisition of a lesser West Midlands company compelled the extension of mixed-gauge track along the old main line, up to the buffer-stops of Paddington itself. (Brunel had died two years previously; the stock phrase 'after a decent interval of mourning' comes to mind.) In the year following, Queen Victoria made her first journey from Windsor to Scotland on standard-gauge wheels throughout. Another reverse came in 1863, shortly after the first instalment of the Metropolitan Railway opened. The underground line was conceived as a mixed-gauge spin-off of the Great Western, which contracted to operate its services, and its first trains were of broad-gauge type. The Metropolitan's independent-minded management soon fell out with the senior company and went over to standard-gauge operation for a while, using borrowed stock. The broad-gauge rails were removed in 1869, the year in which all the Great Western's routes north of Oxford became standard gauge only. The last new line built entirely to the broad gauge dated from 1877, in the shape of the four-mile Cornish branch to St Ives. By that time only seven of the forty-eight daily departures from Paddington used the broad-gauge rails. It was the main line to Cornwall that held out, like King Arthur making his last stand in the West.

The 1880s saw the Great Western preparing for the inevitable. New broad-gauge carriages were now built with narrower bodies, so that they could be reused on standard-gauge underframes when the day of reckoning came. Convertible wagons were built too, and even some convertible locomotives. The final transformation happened over one weekend in May 1892. By that time only the route between Exeter and Truro and some of the lines branching off it were still broad and broad only, to a total of 171 route-miles. Much of this was of single track, so the option of converting one track at a time was not available. A small army was required to get the job done, and the Great Western set about assembling one from its track workers across the network, to the number of some 4,200. Station waiting rooms, goods sheds and tents provided overnight shelter; the company supplied cooking equipment, and oatmeal to supplement whatever food the men brought with them. They were divided into gangs of twenty, most of whom were allotted just over a mile of line to convert. It was heavy and repetitive work, for which every hour of daylight was needed: the cross timbers were cut short, the rail furthest from the platforms was moved across on its timber baulk and all was fixed and ballasted in place again. Pointwork was more complicated, and to avert delays the replacements were assembled in advance and placed by the track ready for installation.

According to a special timetable, the superseded locomotives, carriages and most of the wagons gathered at the works at Swindon, where fifteen miles of reception sidings had been laid on farmland bought for the purpose. In the other direction, broad-gauge carrier wagons piggybacked standard-gauge locomotives and rolling stock to the places from which services were to resume once the disruption was over. They were soon joined by a stream of adapted broad-gauge vehicles; many of the carriages could be converted at the workshops at Swindon in just half an hour.

It all went like clockwork. Trains resumed as planned on the Monday after, when the first through service pulled in to Penzance four minutes early. Goods services took slightly longer to get back to full strength, the maximum interruption being a little over a week. Rather like the Dunkirk evacuation, what was essentially an episode of defeat became part of the Great Western's sense of its own glorious history. The company can be forgiven: its achievement in 1892 was amazing.

₪

The Great Western's conversion weekend is a reminder of the giant scale of railway construction. Small economies in materials brought big cumulative savings. In its mature form, Brunel's baulk road allowed the use of rails that weighed up to 23lb less per yard than the bullhead type. The difference saved over the double tracks from London to Bristol alone amounted to over 8,500 tons. But the tendency was always to improve the rails by making them heavier, like the trains they supported. To get the best use out of them, rails often had two lives: on the main line first, followed by relocation to a branch line or sidings. In the 1930s, the London, Midland & Scottish Railway allowed an average 21½ years before main-line rails were reused or scrapped; early in that decade it was getting through more than 90,000 tons of rail annually, of an estimated national total of a quarter of a million tons. Rails wore out faster in tunnels, on steep gradients and in places such as Widnes, where heavy industry made the very air chemically corrosive. To support this huge tonnage of rails, the LMS required 2.3 million new cast-iron chairs each year. These were made by the railway itself, at a foundry within its enormous works at Crewe, which was kept in continuous operation; 95 per cent of the metal used was scrap, including the railway's own leavings.

Sleepers were another bulk-order item. Economy in the use of timber was achieved on some lines by making these of half-round section, easily created from split logs; in the 1860s these were still current in many areas. A variant that seems to have disappeared earlier was of triangular profile, the apex being buried downwards in the ballast. But it was the rectangular type that became the norm, to a standard section of 10in by 5in. To be sufficiently resilient, sleepers had to be much wider than the track itself: 9ft was the common Victorian size, reduced in the twentieth century to 8ft 6in. Oak or pitch-pine had the best qualities for the job, but their high cost meant that cheaper imported softwood was usually preferred. These sleepers became a familiar sight at docks around Britain, cut to length and stacked in their millions awaiting despatch.

Softwood timber placed in the ground soon rots. Victorian railway companies varied in their response to this inconvenient fact. At first, some chose to let nature take its course, and replaced their sleepers as needed. Others sought to prolong their lives by artifice. For many years the Great Western favoured a process called kyanising, named after its inventor John Howard Kyan (1774–1850). This involved steeping timber in what Brunel called 'pickle-tanks', using a solution of mercuric chloride – as it happens, the same toxic compound that was prescribed in the treatment of syphilis. More common, and cheaper, was the use of creosote, one of the products distilled from the tar driven off when coal was heated to turn it into coke. The easiest way to apply creosote was by dipping or soaking, but this gave only superficial protection. Much better results came from the use of pressurised cylindrical chambers to impregnate the timbers more deeply: the air inside having been exhausted, the heated solution was pumped in under high pressure, and each sleeper would absorb up to three gallons before the surplus was pumped out again.

Rather than using outside contractors, most companies undertook the preparation of sleepers themselves. By the 1930s the process had largely been mechanised, using adzing and drilling machines to ready the sleepers for the attachment of chairs. Pickling was the next step. At Greenhill depot near Falkirk, 400,000 of the London, Midland & Scottish Railway's annual requirement of 1.25 million sleepers were treated in batches of ten at a time, which worked out at 130 cylinder-loads every working day. Other plants, such as that at Hayes on the Great Western or the Southern Railway's wharfside depot at Redbridge near Southampton, did things on a grander scale. The cylinders here were 75ft or 80ft long and up to 7ft across, enough to take trolley-loads of 600 sleepers at a time. (Manhandling the reeking batches out of these cylinders after treatment was one of the railways' nastier jobs.) In the 1930s the Great Western alone owned some 9,000 miles of track, sidings included; taking the most common spacing of twenty-four sleepers to each 60ft pair of rails as a benchmark, the company therefore had something close to 20 million sleepers on its lines.

The railways' appetite for timber was impossible to sustain at normal levels during wartime, when Continental imports ceased and military needs had priority. The Great Western managed during the Second World War by such makeshifts as the use of paired concrete sleeper blocks in sidings, with a connecting cross tie at intervals. Simple concrete castings

A stack of sleepers at the Great Western Railway's
creosoting depot at Hayes, Middlesex, in 1937

were acceptable for such uses, and the materials to make them did not
have to be imported; they also resisted decay. For main lines, early concrete sleepers were of limited use because they fractured under stress. The
answer was to ensure that their steel reinforcements were tensioned during
casting, turning an inert and crack-prone object into something taut and
resilient. A reliable production method was developed by the Dow-Mac
factory at Tallington in Lincolnshire in 1943–4 (concrete sleepers with
the company's name endlessly repeated in letters cast into the top surface
are still abundant). In 1964 the type became standard for use on ordinary

track with welded rails. Little cushions of cork, rubber or plastic between sleeper and rail help to compensate for the absence of the natural bounce of timber. Concrete sleepers are also both longer-lived and much heavier than the wooden kind, and usually have a different profile, sloping up to a greater thickness under the rails where the stresses are greatest.

Concrete sleepers now prevail on the majority of routes in Britain, although hardwood is still preferred for some of the endlessly varied layouts and dimensions of points and crossings. The standard fixture that holds the rails in place on concrete sleepers is the Pandrol clip, a Norwegian invention shaped a bit like a kinked and partly unbent paperclip, which has the advantage of not working loose under the vibration of traffic. Older sleepers of timber are still out there in numbers as well, and some vintage examples can be seen gently disintegrating on secondary routes and sidings. Ancient rail components linger in sidings too; a Great Northern Railway chair dated 1894 turned up recently among recovered materials sent for recycling. The modern traveller beyond the main lines may also encounter sleepers made of pressed steel, profiled to bite into the ballast, which have become quite common of late. There have even been trials using sleepers made from recycled plastic. Altogether, for those who care to notice these things, there is more variety in the matter of railway track than there was half a century ago.

The third visible element of the permanent way is the ballast. Its task is to hold the track in place and to keep it well drained. Gravel was popular at first, but it was found in time that hard, sharp-edged stones such as granite or basalt that will interlock firmly are best for the job. Over much of the country this was easily obtained. A great deal of limestone was also used, not always of optimum types: in the south-east, the relatively fragile stone known as Kentish rag was pressed into service. Some railways in steel-making districts found that broken-up slag from the blast furnaces had the qualities needed. Other waste products used included spoil from mine workings and ash or clinker from coal fires, including the railways' own; this effectively came free, but was too light to be satisfactory on heavily used lines.

Even the shifting expanses of shingle at Dungeness were plundered for ballast, the South Eastern Railway and its successors taking away trainload after trainload via a branch line that had been built in the vain hope that this weird coastal settlement of lighthouses and cottages might develop into a seaport. Sub-standard ballasting composed of these sea-smoothed flints, with ash and soil mixed in, was a contributory cause of a fatal derailment at Sevenoaks in 1927. After the crash, the penitent Southern Railway went over to using dolerite from Meldon Quarry on the edge of Dartmoor, at the far western end of its territory. Ash, clinker, gravel and other easily compacted materials continued to find uses in goods yards, engine sheds and other areas where there was the need for a smoother surface underfoot. Anyone who has rushed to catch a train across the eerie shingles of Dungeness – where a miniature railway still runs to the end of the headland, on sleepers ballasted by the loose native stones – will appreciate the reasoning behind this.

Heavy modern track needs deeper and more uniform ballasting than the wooden-sleepered type. The railways' hunger for fresh ballast – 3 million tons a year was being laid down in the 1990s – is still redistributing the solid geology of these islands in countless little fragments. Granite is the only material used nowadays, although no longer from the quarry at Meldon, which closed in 2011. Even the hardest granite has a limited useful life: vibration and stress from trains wear away the sharper edges, and the space between the stones begins to clog with the sand-like dust that is produced. Old ballast is unsuitable as the setting for new high-speed track, for it will settle unpredictably; the two must be renewed together. Stiffer recycling targets also mean that old ('spent') ballast is no longer dumped in large quantities, and it finds uses in ready-mixed concrete or as roadstone, so that pieces of stone which once supported the passage of trains now perform the same task for lorries and cars. Modern sleepers are also reprocessed, the ground-up concrete going for new construction, the steel reinforcements for scrap.

Timber sleepers are a different story. When the railway had no further use for them, many others could see the potential of these large, seasoned blocks of wood. Their continuing reuse survived a challenge by the European Union in 2003, when it was declared that carcinogenic creosote residues made softwood sleepers too dangerous to use in places frequented by people; instead, they would all have to be incinerated. A compromise has since been reached, so that creosoted sleepers are still bought and sold, subject to cautions and restrictions; the going retail rate in Britain at the time of writing is around £12–£15. Sleepers are the most common article of what might be called the railway diaspora, instantly recognisable from their shape and size, and from the scars and holes where the chairs were attached at each end. Like any standard-sized unit, sleepers are easy to deploy. They can be built up into timber walls of surprising height by slotting them on top of one another between steel posts, to make outdoor enclosures for coal or discarded tyres, or even modest buildings. Sleepers also make good fences and retaining walls. Huge numbers have disappeared into gardens, to make steps or to frame raised beds (although growing foodstuffs in them is not recommended). Landscape designers value their textured and weathered surfaces, when used as a rustic form of wood-block paving. They turn up along the margins of beaches, marking the boundary between managed land and the natural world; dropped into boggy patches to serve as makeshift bridges, they greet the walker on farm tracks or high up on the fells.

₪

Staying with the railway diaspora, but leaving the tracks behind for the time being, we can return briefly to Dungeness. In the 1920s, the lighthouses there were joined by a huddle of weekend dwellings made from the bodies of redundant railway carriages, many of them bought by railway workers from their employers.* These carriage bodies have become an accepted part of the character of the strange landscape at Dungeness, with its partly demolished nuclear power station, converging power lines and general air of being at the end of things. One of the older carriages has even been reverently encased in a new architect-designed house; re-equipped as a kitchen, the frail relic now sits on the polished floor of a big bare interior behind plate-glass windows facing the shingle and the sea.

It would be mistaken to think of this settlement as unique, for the use of discarded carriage bodies as improvised homes dates back at least to late-Victorian times. One early stronghold was at Shoreham in Sussex, where land by the river mouth was colonised in the 1870s by a cluster for use as net stores by fishermen. Other carriage bodies were then imported for dwellings, and Shoreham's long-vanished Bungalow Town was born. Its denizens were chiefly well-off devotees of the simple life, including theatre folk: H. G. Wells in 1906 referred to 'a certain Bohemian-spirited

---

* Stranded, sold-off bodies of this kind should not be confused with so-called camping coaches, a fondly remembered holiday facility using converted stationary carriages. These were introduced on all four of the big railway companies in the 1930s, and a few lingered until 1971.

class' impatient with 'the dull rigidities of the decorous resorts'. At its most basic, the practice was cheap, too: a smaller carriage body could be had for ten pounds, plus a modest outlay on land and installation. An essay by Max Beerbohm describes an encounter on a Norfolk road with such a vehicle in 1919 (a first-and-third composite, with smoking compartments), being towed by a traction engine to a new, immobile life. Following behind, the writer discovered a colony of carriages already set up amid the dunes, under such names as Spray o' the Sea, The Nest and Brinynook.

None this had any appeal to Beerbohm, who preferred the idea of life in a caravan; as he pointed out, at least you could then be sure that your residence was not the one in which the Balcombe Tunnel murder was committed. But thousands disagreed, and they came increasingly from further down the social scale. The time between the wars was the heyday of shacks and plotlands everywhere, before the Town and Country Planning Act of 1947 made it illegal to set up such settlements without official permission. Cabins and bungalows could be bought in kit form, but how much easier to start with a cheap but sturdy oak-framed carriage body. Encouragement came from articles in magazines such as *The Woodworker*, which showed how they could be adapted. The Sussex coast was especially favoured, partly because its railways had plenty of spare carriages displaced by new electric trains. At Lancing an entire holiday park was cobbled together from carriage bodies with little built-on porches, since boringly replaced by static caravans. Larger homes could be made from two bodies placed side by side under a shared roof, or even raised up to form a second storey, as at Sutton-on-Sea in Lincolnshire. Many owners also chose to add pitched roofs, lean-tos and verandas, and these survivors are not so easy to spot. Some of those at Dungeness give themselves away only by a humped or double-humped outline to the roof.

Carriage bodies were relocated inland too. The Great Western donated one to its Methodist stationmaster at Challow in Berkshire for use as a chapel, whereupon it was re-equipped with pews and two harmoniums. One of the most poetic survivals sits behind a thick roadside hedge at Shirwell in the hills of north Devon, masked in corrugated iron. This carriage was one of a group built by the Great Western to enhance its royal train in the Diamond Jubilee year of 1897. Its social decline began with demotion to ordinary first-class use, followed in 1933 by the sale of its body to a skittle club for £28. Stripped of its compartments and given a new floor, benches and oil lamps, the carriage was ready to receive visiting teams. But many of the finishes and fittings were left gently alone, from gleaming gilded mouldings to the frail silk pulls of the window blinds. In 1984 this royal body became one of the handful to win official protection as a listed structure.

Still more common, though harder to find than they used to be, are the bodies of goods vans. If every wooden-bodied carriage was a chalet in waiting, a goods van made a cheap and sturdy garden shed, or farm store – farmers being one of their steadiest customers. Among them was the Pennine smallholder Hannah Hauxwell, the subject of television documentaries in the 1970s and 1980s. The second of these films, *Too Long a Winter* (1989), ends with the outdoor auction of Hannah's farmstead, including 'the body'; the crowd of sharp-eyed Yorkshire farmers know what the auctioneer is talking about. Without the magic ingredient of home ownership, van bodies were less likely to be looked after in their new locations. The corner of many a field contains one of their rusting skeletons, the planking having rotted away from the lightweight steel frame.

Being smaller than carriages, van bodies could be transported even further from the railway network. One did duty for some years as a bothy, two-thirds of the way along the punishing final stage of the Pennine Way, its only cargo an unappealing stash of dried emergency foodstuffs left behind by walkers about to re-enter the domain of real food. Van bodies have even made it to the rail-less Scottish islands, that empire of outdoor abandonment; one may be seen peacefully disintegrating by the roadside on Hoy, southernmost of the Orkneys. This example came from a standard Southern Railway van, built probably at Ashford in Kent, where many of the Dungeness carriage bodies also originated.

₪

The evolution of railway track towards the continuously welded, concrete-sleepered type has reduced the burden of maintenance on the permanent way. Many procedures have been mechanised, and tasks that once took hundreds of man-hours can now be managed swiftly by means of specialist rail-mounted machinery. Working from the parallel track, the 'Slinger 3' train introduced in 2002 can raise 900ft of old track in a single lift under the charge of a single operator and collect and place the replacement sleepers and rails ready for welding and fixing. Other machines ensure that the tracks are correctly aligned and the ballast repacked ('tamped') under the sleepers, by means of retractable vibrating probes. These tamping machines have a long history, with Switzerland and Austria in the forefront of their development. Even in 1948, when public spending on imports was minimal, British Railways was permitted to buy twelve Matisa tamping machines from Switzerland, as 60,000 permanent-way staff struggled to catch up with wartime arrears of maintenance.

New generations of these self-propelled, ungainly looking, bright yellow or yellow-ended maintenance machines can be seen at rest between duties in sidings and yards up and down the network. Like the combine harvesters that came into general use in the early post-war years, they have displaced a great deal of labour – a valuable saving at a time when shortages among the track gangs led to the recruitment of workers from Italy, as well as the continued use of female labour, as in wartime (nearly 500 women were still busy on the tracks in February 1952). Track of the traditional kind composed of bullhead rails, held in cast-iron chairs by means of wooden keys, demanded careful tending if it was to remain safe for fast, intensive working. Keys needed particular attention: by natural shrinkage these gradually lost their grip, allowing the rails to creep forward in line with the direction of travel of the trains. The remedy was to thump them back in place, or to renew them as necessary. The bolts securing each fishplate were checked for tightness too, and pointwork received especially careful scrutiny. All such joints and points needed regular lubrication, as did the felt pads fixed by the track to smear oil or grease on the wheels of trains as they approached tight curves. Heavier work included levering (or 'slewing') tracks back into their correct alignment, the packing or tamping of the ballast firmly under the sleepers and swapping the position of rails to even out wear. All of this was achieved purely by muscle-power, applied via crowbar, shovel, pick, wrench and hammer.

The larger the railway company, the more complex the organisation required to manage the track. The Engineering Department of the Great Western was divided into eleven territories, each with between 250 and 450 miles of route to look after, within each of which were between 500 and 1,000 track-miles. Every division was composed of separate districts under the charge of a permanent-way inspector, each comprising some ninety miles of track, from main lines to sidings. The work was undertaken by around fourteen gangs per division, composed of a ganger, subganger and a varying number of lengthsmen or platelayers, whose 'length'

worked out at an average two and half miles of route, or six miles of track.*
Awards were often made for the best-kept lengths, as though they were villages. Every day, each ganger or sub-ganger was required to make a walk of
inspection along the entire length. Heavier work required the delivery and
removal of materials by train, and the assembly of larger gangs: the Great
Western allowed twenty-four men in order to lift one standard 60ft rail.
Such trains might include a mess carriage and sometimes even bunks for
overnight stays in remote places.

To help identify locations along the line, the permanent way was (and
still is) divided by posts of timber, cast iron, concrete or inscribed stone,
placed at every quarter-mile. These were made compulsory by statute in
1845. Henry Cole, always quick on the uptake, incorporated them in the
diagrammatic *Railway Charts* which he published for sale to travellers
around this time. The mileposts took many different forms, and it does
not take much railway travelling to spot some of these even now. Where
the fractions of miles are not shown, the posts use may dots, triangles or
bars to indicate how many quarters should be added to the round figure.
The North Eastern Railway's territory can be identified by means of its
rather fierce-looking quarter-mile posts with one, two or three triangular spurs around their cast-iron heads. The zero-point for measurements
may still derive from nineteenth-century boundaries between companies,
which may or may not correspond to the many sequences that start from
London; the latter are helpful tools for the bored or impatient traveller
who wants to monitor progress towards the terminus. Modern-looking
posts may indicate that a line has been recalibrated in kilometres, a policy
adopted on a national basis in 2013.

Track in tunnels was subject to regular inspection and maintenance
too. Rails in a busy tunnel received more wear and needed more attention;
but they were also harder to get at. Every passing train meant a break in the
work, and a retreat to the recesses or refuges provided at intervals along
the tunnel wall. A train passing at speed within the confined space pro-
duces a percussive effect, magnified by its own dimensions: expresses built
to the maximum loading gauge packed the most punch of all, so that a

---

* The term platelayer is a fossil from the early years of railways: the 'plates' were the
L-shaped metal guide rails used to control the flangeless wheels of vehicles on horse-
drawn waggonways. Likewise, the permanent way is so called to distinguish it from the
temporary tracks laid down when railways were under construction.

hardened ganger of 1862 would have been stunned by what his successors routinely endured a century later. The upkeep of drainage within the tunnel, and the need for periodic inspections of the walls and roof, were extra complications. So much water used to drip and dribble into the Midland Railway's Totley Tunnel that it was drawn off and conveyed miles away for use by locomotives, whose condensed exhausts then joined the run-off on the next trip through.

Then there was the smoke. Long and busy tunnels might remain smoke-filled for years on end, the combined exhalations of locomotive after locomotive drifting endlessly from the portals, or welling up from ventilation shafts to the fields or moors above. On a good day, the wind might blow helpfully through; at other times, a crosswind across the tunnel mouths could keep the smoke trapped inside for days. The tunnel inspector W. T. Thornewell, who worked in the Midlands from the 1920s onwards, remembered the environment in the worst of these long man-made burrows, with their 'absence of all normal dimensions':

> All natural light disappears within a few yards and one is swallowed up in complete blackness, surrounded by thick eddying smoke ... The area around our feet illuminated by the handlamps is very small, and the sooty blackness seems to swallow all light above rail level ... On such a day the smoke will eddy back and forth all the time, playing games around our lamps if we lift them to eye level in a fruitless attempt to see more about us.

Men on tunnel duty received an extra allowance, but track work in general was not well paid. Those who undertook it were therefore less likely to spend all their working lives on the railway than staff in more skilled and better-rewarded posts. For the villagers of Bourne near Farnham, a district of Surrey that was distinctly poor in late-Victorian times, the London & South Western Railway's ballast trains were one of the few sources of work of any kind. Up to forty men in the parish toiled at basic rates of between eighteen and twenty-four shillings a week, typically setting off at night, in open trucks and in all weathers. On the southern division of the London & North Western as late as 1908, some rural gangs even went back to the land during harvest time. Strictly this was against regulations, but as their Divisional Engineer tolerantly admitted: 'There is nothing else for them to do after they have finished work at half past five. They are practically living in the middle of the cornfields and harvest fields, and they turn to and help the farmer, and get paid for it.' He reckoned that only about a third of his platelayers were paid more than they had been getting before they joined the permanent staff, but that any shortfall was counterbalanced by the appeal of secure employment on the railway.

The working headquarters of most outdoor lengths was the platelayer's hut. There were thousands of these tiny cabins, mostly built to standard designs, which served the gangs as a place to shelter and to store tools and materials. Derelict examples survive in plenty, especially on the lines of the Southern Railway, which adopted a blockish design in prefabricated concrete, sent out for assembly in panel form from the company's casting factory at Exmouth Junction. By contrast, the pitched-roofed versions on other lines, each with its chimney, narrow door and tiny window, typically looked like a child's drawing of the smallest house in the world (the tinplate Hornby model version even added fictive climbing plants to the fictive brickwork of its walls). There was nothing especially homely about the interiors, however; nor were the huts necessarily given a sufficient allowance of coals. This helps to explain the railwayman's joke about the bad track joint deliberately left in front of the hut, in the hope of shaking some fuel off passing tenders and wagons. A fire meant warmth, and the chance of tea or eggs and bacon. Hot water for washing too, a bucketful of which could be obtained by plunging in a fishplate that had been heated in the grate. This was railway architecture at its most basic; in the nineteenth century the huts were sometimes self-built from old sleepers by the men themselves.

Working on the track was dangerous as well as arduous. Detailed knowledge of train movement – unaccompanied engines, goods trains and empty workings as well as the advertised timetable – was vital. On lightly used routes this was not too difficult, but on busy lines the combination of unpredictable timings and momentary inattention could prove fatal. Many accidents to platelayers resulted from stepping out of the path of one train and into that of another on an adjacent line, which might be invisible and inaudible amid the smoke and noise. Fatigue, bad visibility or harsh weather, rough going under foot – all added to the risks. A full-time lookout equipped with a warning horn was provided only for larger gangs. In the early twentieth century about a hundred platelayers a year were dying on the tracks, representing around a quarter of all accidental deaths on the network. *The Times* for 14 May 1910 recorded the killing of four of a gang of five in just this way on the Great Western main line at Acton and the death of another platelayer on the other side of London on the same afternoon: brief, routine paragraphs, tucked in at the bottom of page twelve.

The coming of fog or heavy snow meant a change in routine. The normal timetable would be suspended and everything slowed down. Signals became invisible at any appreciable distance and even the shifting sounds of passing bridges, trees and cuttings that allowed the driver to gauge his position on a familiar route were muffled or inaudible. The control of moving trains therefore required the creation of louder sounds, obtained by clipping detonators to the rails. Their deployment was not restricted to foggy days: we have met them used as warning signals on the clear summer's day when Dickens's train derailed at Staplehurst. The principle was the same: a flash-bang audible above the clamour of the moving locomotive, to tell the driver to slow down in preparation for a possible stoppage ahead. Further progress was controlled by the flag or lamp of the fogman at his post, who might be favoured by a little cabin and a brazier. Fog made any sortie on to the tracks doubly dangerous, and to reduce the risks a contraption was devised, operable from the trackside or from a signal box, that allowed detonators to be pushed on to the rail rather than being clipped on by hand. The sharp reports of these fog signals were once a familiar note within the railway soundscape; Edwardian toymakers even offered miniature versions with percussion caps, linked to little working signals, for model railways. Heavy snow might demand extra sorties on to the track to check that the point blades could move freely, unless these were favoured with automatic heaters. Platelayers were expected to be on standby for such duties as a matter of routine: at the home matches of Darlington FC in the 1950s, a man would go round with a list of staff required, and anyone who went to the cinema was expected to leave details with the traffic department, so that they could be summoned by flashing their names on the silver screen. Overtime payments were some compensation for the price of the wasted ticket; but it was a hard life.

Mechanisation, low-maintenance materials, the use of special test trains to detect imperfections in the track, the disappearance of fatal smokescreens laid down by steam locomotive chimneys, colour-light signals powerful enough to pierce fog, the use of road vehicles to take gangs to the lineside – all have reduced the exposure of railway workers to risk on the tracks in recent decades. High-visibility fluorescent clothing has played its part too. Trials began on the Glasgow suburban lines in 1964.

It was soon clear that approaching drivers sounded their warnings much faster when the bright vests were worn by trackmen (the term which replaced 'platelayer' around the same time). Even so, it was several more years before lineside safety clothing became mandatory. A British Transport Film short of 1975, *Operation London Bridge*, captures the last years of the old regime. We see the track layouts at London Bridge station being overhauled by a combination of machine and muscle: the younger men with mid-length hair in oil-stained tanktops and flares, or working topless, the older men in suits and pork-pie hats, so that the workteams have a random look, as if they had just been press-ganged from the pubs of Bermondsey Street. Now, anyone who works on lines where trains are running must wear a hard hat and orange fluorescent clothing of a specified chromaticity, with sewn-on reflective strips of specified performance and pattern, all as directed in the latest issue of the Railway Group Standard document GO/RT3279. Orange trousers were added to this compulsory wardrobe in 2008.

₪

The prevalence of safety clothing in Britain, and safety culture in the workplace generally, sometimes attract journalistic ridicule. The truth is that rules and routines on the railways are the culmination of nearly two centuries of learning things the hard way. Some reforms were initiated or enforced by the management (the fluorescent vests), others came about by pressure from the trades unions, others still belong with broader changes to working conditions imposed by Parliament, such as those in the Offices, Shops and Railway Premises Act (1963). This legislation also saw the end of small local track gangs in favour of larger squads based at depots with proper facilities for washing and relief. Safety routines interlock, to guard against cumulative effects: a small one-off risk is a different matter from the same odds faced day in and day out, by many persons in many places. That is why the 1963 Act also required that handrails be provided alongside stairs in places of work, those on the railways included: not to be clutched nervously at every ascent and descent, but to be there for the one time in a thousand when someone stumbles.

Many will remember what happened when the culture of safeguards on Britain's railways was last seriously compromised. The culmination came on 17 October 2000, when a defective rail fractured on a curve just south of Hatfield as a Leeds-bound express passed over it at 115 mph, killing four passengers. By that date the maintenance of the tracks had passed into the hands of private contractors engaged by Railtrack, the privatised infrastructure company. These contractors worked under regimes of incentives and penalties for completing work on time, even as the railways came under growing strain from unexpected increases in traffic. The privatised system created in 1993–6, with its separation of operating companies, rolling stock companies, infrastructure and maintenance, was characterised by displaced or uncertain responsibilities. The changes went against the grain of the existing operation of BR, which had been successfully reorganised not long before into separate business sectors: InterCity (by then no longer hyphenated), Network SouthEast, Regional Railways and Railfreight. These were able to keep tighter control of their operating costs than the old regional divisions had done, while sustaining a close relationship with the engineering and infrastructure side of the network. Privatisation made no serious attempt to engage with the special character of railway operation and engineering; instead, it drew on the one-size-fits-all ideology of the free marketeer, by which every exchange must be monetised, and competition within an agreed legal and financial framework is the universal ideal. Co-operative relationships were thus replaced – deliberately and knowingly – by adversarial ones.

So it came about that the contractors who had detected early faults in the rail at Hatfield were required to compete for the job of replacing it, and another firm won the work instead. The victors then became bogged down in negotiations with Railtrack over how much time they should be allowed for possession of the track in order to set things right. Over at Railtrack, cost-effective management involved a constant quest for ways of minimising the penalty charges it would have to pay the regulator for delays to services arising from necessary maintenance. Meanwhile the suspect rail remained in place, until it shattered. With profit as the benchmark, efficiency had been fatally confused with financial advantage, and financial advantage with genuine economy – for the administrative and legal costs of running a railway in this way can easily be imagined.

Different priorities now took hold at Railtrack. It emerged that the company had shrugged off much of its former knowledge of the system when it was divested of the task of maintaining it. The result was that Railtrack no longer had a coherent picture of the physical state of its own domain. As the company rushed to catch up, faulty rails were identified in frightening numbers all across the network. Emergency speed restrictions were slapped on line after line, to a total of well over a thousand, and travel times on many routes collapsed to those of the 1850s. A month after the accident, trains were taking almost nine hours to reach Newcastle from London. One significant figure within the industry at the time summarised the situation thus:

> The railway as a system, under BR it was totally integrated and one person or group of people were able to balance the system. Performance, safety, efficiency, capacity, growth, it is all one system. I think that privatisation did fragment that system into over 100 different parts. That fragmentation did mean that the accountabilities were diffused and many of the different parts were set up with an economic architecture which by definition pointed them in different directions.

The man thus releasing cat from bag was Gerald Corbett, chief executive at Railtrack, in response to questions from Lord Cullen, who had chaired the enquiry into the railway disaster at Paddington in 1999. Corbett resigned his post shortly afterwards, taking with him a payoff valued at £1.4 million, and Railtrack buckled down to the task of addressing the backlog of repairs to its own sweated assets. This pushed the company's finances deeply into the red, and its share price into a nosedive.

By 2002 the position that Railtrack should still be treated as a profit-making business had become impossible to sustain, and it was taken back into public ownership under the name of Network Rail. While the process was under way, another seven passengers were killed when an express was derailed at Potters Bar, a few miles south of the Hatfield crash. Once again, inadequate maintenance by a private contractor was the cause. Not long afterwards it was announced that Network Rail would itself undertake all routine maintenance of the track. Costs fell sharply as a result. Safety has also benefited: there have been no fatalities to passengers since 2007, and none to employees working on the line since 2009.

Other intrinsic contradictions remain in place. At the most basic level, Network Rail must compensate the operating companies for disruption to the timetable caused by improvements whose only purpose is to support the companies' own services. The privately owned railway also needs much more public money in order to function at all. In the last days of British Rail, the system received a direct annual subsidy of between £1 billion and £1.5 billion. Subsidies since that time have reached as high as £6.3 billion (in 2006–7); the figure for 2013–14 was £5.3 billion, despite the doubling of passenger numbers since privatisation. Much of this money comes nowhere near the operating side of the railway, but is sucked straight out again in dividends, administrative and legal costs, inflated salaries and bonuses. Nor is the system cheap for its users. All of these features are intrinsic, not accidental, parts of the business model under which the railways were privatised – a process that, let it be remembered, was meant to address the supposed scandal of a publicly owned system which required high subsidies in order to operate. It has proved an extremely expensive way of saving money.

More recently, 'deep alliances' – joint management of assets – have been contracted between Network Rail and certain operating companies, beginning in 2012. They represent another reversal of the 1990s structure, the outcomes of which were described by Prime Minister David Cameron in a speech to the Institution of Civil Engineers in March 2012: 'Our railways are crowded and expensive, compared to French, Dutch and Swiss railways, our fares are 30 per cent higher, our running costs 40 per cent higher and our public subsidy is double.'

The latest twist to the story concerns the finances of Network Rail. Its income derives from the access charges that the operating companies pay to use the track. These have never reflected the true costs of maintenance and upgrading, and the shortfall has been piled on in the form of debt, with the government as guarantor. By the end of 2013 Network Rail was spending more on interest charges than on track maintenance and renewal. Shortly afterwards, European directives swung into play, requiring greater transparency in the classification of public borrowing. So the sum – an astonishing £34 billion by August 2014 – will now be accounted part of the national debt. Such is the cumulative result of having rigged the system so that its private constituents can return a guaranteed profit. Mr Gladstone would have seen through this rigmarole very quickly.

SIGNALS AND WIRES

Thanks to the attentions of the platelayers, the typical railway line was a more animated place in former days. A traveller in the 1860s would also have been made aware of another aspect of railway work, represented by a new type of structure that was springing up alongside the lines: the signal box.

Dickens was bang up to date in setting his ghost story of 1866 in one of these boxes. His title, 'The Signal-Man', itself had a new-minted character, for signals developed in the wake of the early railways, not in step with them. At first, responsibility for controlling traffic was shared between the stationmaster or his subordinate who saw off the train, the policemen (as they were known) who stood alongside or patrolled up and down the line, and the pointsmen who switched the trains between routes. Time, not space, was the safeguard: distances between trains were maintained by fixed intervals between departures, regulated by watches or hourglasses supplied to the men. Information and instructions were conveyed by means of hand signals, flags or lamps; drivers and guards kept a constant lookout for trains in front or behind. Even when the telegraph began to thread its wires from station to station, it was some time before these were used consistently to control traffic on the railway.

An integrated system of signalling came about only by stages. It combined inventions that were made separately, and which at first were of limited application. The earliest fixed signals – commonly rotating discs, boards or crossbars – were located at stations and junctions and were effectively the amplified hand-signals of their operators, who stood alongside. Signals that could be worked remotely developed in the late 1840s, beginning with an installation by a practical-minded pointsman on the North British Railway, who rigged up the signals under his control with wires so that he could operate both of them from his cabin. A later advance was to deploy two signals, one to govern possession of the upcoming station, junction or section of track, the other to give advance warning of a stop ahead. These eventually became known as 'home' and 'distant' signals. To allow both departures and arrivals to be regulated, the home type was commonly repeated at the end of a platform (known as a starting signal). The default setting for these early signals was 'clear'; only when the line was obstructed were they turned to show danger.

For ease of working, the levers by which the signals were controlled might be concentrated together, commonly at an open-air platform next to the track. A further efficiency was to operate the points remotely too, a process perfected by the use of heavy jointed rods placed close to the ground. The levers attached to these could then be worked from the same places as those for the signals. An installation of this kind became known as a ground frame.

Early ground frames lacked any mechanism to prevent conflict between different signals, or between what the signals showed and the position of the points ahead. Safe passage therefore depended on the vigilance and memory of the operator. Various attempts were made to address this weakness in the 1840s and 1850s by linking the controls together. The culmination, achieved first in 1860 at Kentish Town Junction on the North London Railway, was to interlock the operation of all points and signals over a given extent of track, grouping the controls within an iron frame in such a way that none could be moved except in the precise order that would ensure safe operation.

Interlocking lever frames were hefty things and required the equivalent of a single-storey building to house them. The operating platform sat on top, usually reached by an external staircase. It was an easy matter to put a roof or canopy over this platform and to enclose it within screens or large-windowed walls. The result was an instantly recognisable new building type, its basic form dictated entirely by function. Early examples were often combined with signal posts, which typically poked up through the roof. Later, as the convention took hold that each signal should stand alongside the point where a train should stop, the physical union between signals and

Inside a signal box at London Bridge, from the *Illustrated London News*,
1866. Lever frame, telegraph instruments and register desk would all have
been familiar to a 'mechanical' signalman a century or more later

box was ended in favour of remote connection by operating wires. A front
balcony was a common feature of the box, less to help signalmen speak to
train crews than to make it easier to clean soot deposits off the windows.

These early boxes were soon linked by telegraph. They communicated
by a coded system of long and short signals that were reproduced by means
of bells, by electro-magnetic deflections of a needle to left or right within
an indicator box, or by the two in combination. Dickens's signalman is
possessed by extra vibrations from the bell of his cabin, which only he can
hear. His is a one-man box, the most common type. At large stations and
junctions the boxes were much bigger, with staff working in shifts round
the clock. Some 13,000 of these cabins, large or small, were required to
operate the network around 1900.

The mature system thus combined three elements, none of which yet
existed on the pioneering railways of the 1830s: the signals themselves, the
boxes that controlled them and the telegraph wires strung out on poles
between. Continuously present, and mostly taller than the trains they
served, all three elements played a part in making the railway more conspicuous in the landscape. In functional terms, they were also standing

reminders of its autonomy, of the self-contained, self-governing character of the ribbons of railway land that had carved up the ancient estates and smallholdings of the kingdom. Even if no trains were running, the alien sound made by the telegraph wires whenever the wind rose proclaimed the existence of the railway; the effect was compared to that of an Aeolian harp. For the passenger looking out to one side, a visual rhythm now accompanied the railway journey: the repeated downstrokes of the poles every fifty or sixty yards, and the incessant sweep and dip of the wires between, calibrating the distance travelled as surely as the staccato noises from the joints in the rail. It is a sight that has disappeared almost completely, as the once-ubiquitous poles bearing wires mounted on little ceramic insulators have made way for multi-core signal cables boxed within trunking along the ground. One of the last strongholds was the line between Ely and Norwich, converted in 2012–13. In their final years the poles here leant at crazy angles, the burden of their multiple crossbars reduced to two or three wires.

Why were there once so many wires strung alongside the tracks? Part of the reason lies with the symbiosis between the railways and the telegraph system, the precursor of the pre-satellite telecommunications network. Most of the early circuits along railways were installed by arrangement with private operating companies, eager to exploit the potential of these long, secure routes under single ownership. By setting up public message offices at railway stations, the telegraph companies also enhanced these buildings as local centres of communication. The earliest commercial electric telegraph anywhere shadowed the Great Western's route almost as soon as it opened: the first stage from Paddington to West Drayton in 1839, an extension to Slough in 1843. Its wires gleamed with the lustre of royal patronage in 1844, when they carried tidings to London of the birth of Prince Alfred, Duke of Edinburgh, at Windsor Castle. One year later, a murderer called John Tawell was caught after fleeing to the capital, when a description was telegraphed from Slough in time for detectives to intercept the train at Paddington. Further publicity came from stunts such as the nine-hour chess match staged by the London & Southampton Railway between adversaries in London and Gosport in 1845. Thackeray's Jeames, awestruck at encountering the invention at Gloucester, caught the general mood; another observer hailed the electric telegraph as 'the railway of thought'.

The potential of telegraphy as an aid to railway working seems obvious, yet the Great Western held aloof from using the technology for its own purposes until the 1850s. It was a similar story elsewhere. When the railways did adopt the telegraph, separate wires and circuits were employed for internal communications, so that these did not conflict with the public, revenue-earning messages. The use of telegraph codes to regulate the passage of the trains themselves took several more years to become widespread, and required extra wires in turn. The later advent of telephony and electricity supply meant that extra wires were again needed, physically heavier than the thin telegraphic kind.

₪

Interspersed with the telegraph poles were the signals themselves. Britain's mechanical semaphore signals all derive ultimately from the founding installation in 1841 at New Cross Gate, on the busy London & Croydon Railway. As standardised in the twentieth century, the two main kinds are instantly recognisable: the home signal with its long arm painted bright red on the approach side (signal red, indeed), with a white vertical bar close to the far end, the distant signal arm a strong yellow with a smart black chevron, echoing the outline of the fishtail cut-out at the outer end. The end of the arm next to the post is pierced with two big openings filled with coloured glass to show red and green for a home signal, yellow and green for a distant. As the arm pivots, one or other of these panes aligns with a lamp housing fixed to the post, so that a coloured light repeats the message of the signal arm in the hours of darkness. The information presented by the pairing of a home and a distant signal on a single post is thus like that of a road traffic light, except that a yellow light on the distant serves to warn that the *next* home signal along the track is presently at danger and may require the train to stop in due course.

Signals of this kind are still surprisingly widespread on secondary lines across Britain. The last mechanical signal box to be built, at Uttoxeter in Staffordshire, opened as recently as 1981, and new semaphores are put up from time to time even now, as at Heckington (Lincolnshire) in 2013. A target for their abolition was announced by Network Rail in the same year, under which the 800 remaining signal boxes and control offices across the country will dwindle to just fourteen. The time-span for this project – 20 per cent of the reduction is not due until after 2026 – suggests that the old order will endure here and there for a good while yet.

Mechanical signs with moving parts no longer play much part in everyday life, so that there is something marvellous about the survival of this Victorian technology into its third century. The twitching of the control wire stretched taut alongside the rails, the shudder of the signal as it hits the clear position, and the gentle diminishing bounce with which it reverts to the level alignment after the train has passed, all brought about by a human being who may be glimpsed at work behind the windows of a neat little building a few feet from the track: these movements are like a polite rebuke by an elder to the callow assumption that nothing much ever gets done without the help of electrons or hydrocarbons. And there is a winning cheerfulness in the smart signal shades of red and yellow, now always of imperishable enamelled metal (painted arms made of timber, like the 'wonderful wooden razors set aloft on great piers, shaving the air' noted by Dickens en route to Carlisle in 1857, were usual until the 1920s).

That the shapes, colours, markings and light codes of signals once differed bewilderingly across the various companies will come as no surprise. Standard colours and markings for signal arms became mandatory as late as 1928.* Even the codes used between adjacent boxes might differ. Uniformity for most of these was imposed in the wake of a suburban misadventure on 10 December 1881. A signalman on the Great Northern at Finsbury Park, prompted by a code received from a North London Railway signalman up the line which meant something completely different on each company, blithely sent four trains into Canonbury Tunnel, one after another. Far from having a clear road, the first train was held at a signal at the other end, and those following bumped into one another in the darkness. No serious casualties resulted, only a great deal of distressed milling about in the murk, until a guard made his way out of the tunnel mouth to warn an approaching fifth train not to join the crush.

One big regional difference remains, a relic of the special tenacity of Great Western traditions: the signals on western lines still drop by forty-five degrees to show a clear road ahead, whereas those in other areas are raised upwards by the same angle. The drooping kind was once preferred across the country, but in their original form they had a serious drawback: should a fault occur, the signal arm might fall to the clear position even when the road ahead was unsafe. The Great Western got round this risk by adding a counterweight, so that gravity pulls the arm back up to the

---

* In the following year the Ministry of Transport turned its attention to road traffic lights, recommending the three-colour code of red, amber and green: a clear echo of railway practice.

danger position. On other lines, the signal drops back to the horizontal after the train has passed. One sublime cinematic instance may be remembered: the climax of *The Ladykillers* (1955). The creepy fake professor played by Alec Guinness, last survivor of a self-destructive gang of bank robbers whose safe house stands above the tracks leading to King's Cross, is felled from behind by the bright red arm of a home signal, falling blindly back to 'danger'.

Semaphore signals and signal boxes belong together in other ways. It was among the signalman's duties to ensure that the lamps for each signal remained lit, so they were normally placed within sight of the box. Signals that faced away from the box had apertures at the back to indicate that the light was still burning. There was also a limit on how far points could be located from the signal box without exceeding the range of control levers and rodding. Until 1892 this limit was habitually set at 150 yards. The distance later increased considerably, but it was not until power-operated points became common that mechanical constraints could be escaped completely. A comparable breakthrough for signals was the invention of the pyrometer, which sent an electrical signal to a 'repeater' display within the box, confirming that the lamp remained lit. Repeaters allowed signals to be spread out much further and still remain within mechanical control by wire. The Southern Railway in the 1930s organised a competition to identify the longest 'pull' on its lines; its upper range at that time included Worgret Junction box in Dorset, where the remotest signal stood almost a mile off (specifically, 1,680 yards). Where semaphore signals survive, however – as along the Cumberland coast, or on the main line through Cornwall – they tend to stand much closer to their parent boxes. The traveller who keeps an eye out for them soon acquires a sense of being handed on from one operating point to the next, traversing long expanses of unsignalled track between.

◻

These clusters of signals make visible another principle of safe operation that was finally enforced after the Armagh disaster of 1889, known as absolute block working. Under this system, the network is divided into 'blocks' or sections of track by means of signals that interlock with the points, each section being permitted to take only one train at a time according to telegraphic indications received. Put another way, no train is

The beginnings of the block system, as illustrated in a children's
book of 1962. The gates represent signal boxes, staffed by boys who
allow only one movement through the section at any time

allowed to enter a section until the train ahead of it has passed through,
having first been accepted by means of an exchange of bell-codes by the
signaller (the gender-neutral, rather military-sounding term now officially
adopted) of the section beyond. Instruments within the box and linked
to the telegraph allow a visual record of the state of traffic to be kept constantly in view. Mechanical and electro-magnetic interconnections make
it physically impossible to change a signal from danger to clear unless the
relevant instrument already shows an unobstructed path, which it can do
only after the next block signal down the line has already been cleared,
which depends in turn on the indicator covering the block after that –
and so on. The *Railway Club Journal* in 1910 summarised the end in view:
'[I]f, at any given junction, a man entirely unacquainted with railway working were to enter the signal box, he might safely be allowed to manipulate

the levers as he chose, in any manner, rational or irrational, without any collision between trains occurring, so long as the signals were obeyed.'

Absolute block put an end to the routine use of the time-interval method, which permitted trains to follow one another at fixed minimum intervals. The Metropolitan Railway, intensively worked in smoky tunnels, had the good sense to install the absolute block system from the line's beginning in 1863. Anyone could see that the system was safer than the alternatives, and the Board of Trade had been urging its adoption on the sometimes reluctant railway companies for years before the Armagh disaster brought matters to a head. Safety did not come cheap: adopting absolute block on the Lancashire & Yorkshire Railway, its chairman complained in 1883, had cost £581,000 and had increased annual operating costs on the company's busy and intricate network by £80,000. Long sections that previously used the time interval had to be chopped into shorter blocks, each with its box, signals and continuing extra outlay on labour. The chairman calculated that all this was enough to knock half a percentage point off his company's dividend.

One alternative was so-called permissive block working, which allowed multiple trains to tailgate one another within a single section, each driver keeping an eye out for the rear lamp of the train in front. The method suited goods lines with steady flows of traffic, such as those serving docks or mining districts, and was sometimes also used where passenger trains moved slowly around busy stations. So the old ways lingered here and there.

The working principle that only one train may occupy a section is still apparent on many single lines. Here the supreme danger is not one train running into the back of another, but a head-on collision between departures that have mistakenly been admitted from opposite ends. Railways of the 1830s and early 1840s were nearly all double-tracked, so the risk did not arise. Telegraphy permitted safe two-way operation over single lines, which were also much cheaper to build. Extra safeguards were provided nonetheless. One method was to require a pilotman to travel with each train. Since he could not be in two places – on two trains – at once, a collision could not occur. To replace the pilotman with a symbolic item such as a wood or metal staff was a straightforward economy. Protection by means of a single staff was awkward, however, because it presumed that trains would pass through consistently in alternate directions, ferrying the staff up and down in unbroken sequence. This was no use when one or more trains had to follow each other, and a method was found to relax the rule in these cases: the driver of the first train (or trains, if there was more than one) was simply shown the staff, as an assurance that the line was under the protection of the box in question, and a ticket was issued for the journey instead. In the 1880s a more sophisticated system was developed by which a supply of tablets or tokens was kept at both ends of a section, secured within instruments that were connected electrically in such a way that only one could be released at a time. A fresh token could be issued at either end only after the first one had been surrendered by the departing train and reinserted in the apparatus.

To save trains having to stop at every box even when the line was clear, the transfer of these tokens or tablets – the fireman handing over one for the section just completed, while accepting another for the section following – was commonly managed by a skilful manoeuvre. The tablets were kept in leather wallets attached to big metal loops that could be slipped over the arm as the train moved past. On the Exmouth branch, as remembered by the poet and railwayman's daughter Patricia Beer (1919–99), the exchange was made 'with dramatic intensity and a fine swinging action while the train was moving quite fast'. In some places the process was eased by the use of fixed receivers and holders alongside the track, which could cope with speeds of up to 60 mph (thrillingly, mailbags used to be picked up and dropped off by comparable methods, but this ceased in 1971). Now that cabs no longer have a crew of two, passengers on single lines are more likely to find that their train stops briefly a little way short of the station platform, or just beyond it, so that the driver can perform the necessary exchanges.

Where no signals or tablets are apparent, there may indeed be none in force. Lightly used branches may operate on the principle that only one train may enter at a time, after which it can run safely up and down as the timetable directs. Or there may be signals of an invisible kind. A method of train control by radio was developed for use on the lines to the far north and north-west of Scotland in the 1970s–80s. Tokens are still exchanged under this system, but of a virtual kind: a driver requests permission by radio, and the signal that is sent in response can be issued to only one train at a time.

₪

Such developments make it yet more extraordinary that the wires, arms and rods invented by Victorian signal engineers are still sending trains safely along substantial parts of the national network. What remains is rudimentary stuff, however, by comparison with the bewildering displays that were once common in the busiest locations. Signals here might stand in groups like ship's masts in harbour, a few arms projecting from each. Or they were combined into enormous gantries spanning multiple tracks, with twenty or more arms and a multitude of the lesser arms and sundry special lights and markings required to cover shunting and reversing in and out of all the various running lines, passing loops and sidings.

All such structures had to incorporate walkways and ladders for tending and replacing the lamps. These had to be placed with care, so that the lamp-man or signalman would not obstruct vital sightlines when about his business. Wicks on quieter lines might be lit and extinguished daily, but it was easier to deploy lamps that contained enough oil to burn for eight days, sufficient to allow a rota of weekly attention. Among the personnel who regularly trudged the lineside were the lamp-men, patiently carrying fresh lamps and fuel to the signals. Even after the most careful trimming, it was not unknown for lamps to blow out in between their visits. Climbing up and down a spindly, shuddering post or gantry on a windy night to rekindle the flame in a 'black light' was not the most popular task on the railway; if a signalman could not be spared from duty, a platelayer might be called out to do the job. Oil was also the usual fuel for the headlamps and tail-lamps carried on the trains themselves, so that the railways continued to depend on the lamp huts and lamp rooms dotted all over the network, even after gaslight or electricity conquered stations and carriages. Dickens's fictional lamp-man in *Mugby Junction* (1866) had a 'greasy little cabin' for the purpose, its walls and bench marked by oily smears and smudges left by shoulders and velveteen trousers. The man himself had even begun to resemble the element of his labours, with a 'peculiarly shining transparent complexion', and hair that stood up so straight that 'the top of his head was not very unlike a lamp-wick'.

Work at a large station or intersection also exacted a busier and more demanding routine from the signalman. This in turn meant better pay: as remembered by one of the men employed at St Helens Junction No. 1 Box in the 1920s, an extra five shillings a week could be earned in the busiest roles on the London & North Western, on top of the basic signalman's wage of £2 10s. His own box had sixty-four levers and the traffic required him to memorise thirty or forty bell-codes – a typical tally on an intensive route – in order to communicate with the boxes on either side.

The largest boxes tended to be very long, and sometimes also very high, without being proportionately deep, all the levers inside being in a single row. Sometimes the gantry principle was adopted for the signal box itself, as at Clapham Junction in 1907, when a weird structure like an elevated bowstring bridge was set up across the tracks at the London end. The operating part was housed in an assembly of little timber cabins on the bridge. Like other boxes on vital routes, it was given a protective steel hat during the Second World War, the framing for which remained in place until the whole contraption was taken down in 1990. Many men might work side by side in boxes of this size, as along a bar in one of the giant urban pubs of the era. The largest box of all, at York Locomotive Yard, required a staff of eight to operate its 297 levers.

Large or small – occasionally very small indeed, like the tiny cabin on the platform at Damems on the preserved Keighley & Worth Valley Railway in Yorkshire, which looks almost like something meant for growing tomatoes in – each signal box carried a nameboard to identify its location. The naming of junctions in particular did not flinch from admitting unglamorous truths: Gas Works Junction, Coke Works Junction, Sheet Stores Junction, Factory Junction. More common were titles taken from nearby settlements, helping the curious traveller to guess at the identities of village churches or country houses visible by the line. Larger stations usually needed more than one box, so their names were distinguished by local features, suffixes of numbers or compass points, or by occasional flights of fancy such as the North Eastern Railway's 'Erimus' at Middlesbrough ('We shall be', adopting the young town's motto) and 'Severus' at York (after the Roman emperor who died there in AD 211). As it happens, the world's largest surviving mechanical box goes by the name of Severn Bridge Junction, and stands a few hundred yards from the platform ends at Shrewsbury: a 35ft-high monster with an original complement of 180 levers, built by the London & North Western in 1903.

₪

The electrified lines that converge at Clapham Junction were typical of the intensively worked suburban lines where colour-light signals made early headway. Colour lights, rather than semaphore arms, were the obvious type to use in the permanently dark tunnels of London's Tube lines, which ran well below the sub-surface routes taken by the Metropolitan Railway and its kindred. One such was that odd anomaly the Waterloo & City Railway, which did not pass into the control of the main underground system until 1994. The line opened in 1898, which means that all-electric signals have Victorian roots. It proved harder to develop lights powerful enough to be legible at a distance under the open sky. By nice symmetry with the Waterloo & City, the first successful installation was raised above the earth-bound world: it belonged to the Liverpool Overhead Railway, an astonishing electric facility that began running in 1893. The only British parallel to the elevated urban railways of New York and Chicago, the Liverpool line ran on an iron and steel viaduct five miles long, along the frontier between the city and its enormous docks. Its colour-light signals were introduced in 1920 and lasted until the entire concern went for scrap in 1956 because there was no money to keep it in repair.

Colour-light signals could be placed anywhere within clear sight of passing trains. Their green, yellow and red lamps abolished the semaphores' cumbersome splitting of the 'distant' and 'home' features between separate signal arms, nor did they depend on the lamp-man for replenishment. They also made extra settings possible. Once again, London suburban routes proved fertile ground for innovation. Holborn Viaduct station received four-aspect lights in 1926, in which the change from red to green was made by two stages, yellow and double yellow. Multiple aspects of this kind allowed more information to be conveyed by fewer signals, and fewer boxes were needed to operate them. The route into central London from New Cross, near where the first semaphores had waved their arms back in 1841, went over to lights of this type shortly after the Holborn Viaduct conversion. The previous arrangements were hideously congested: 'In rush-hour conditions often near to chaos the trains groped their way from one manually-operated box to another: New Cross A and B, North Kent East, Southwark Park, Spa Road, London Bridge A and B, Borough Market, Metropolitan Junction, Union Street, Waterloo A and B, and finally into Charing Cross.' All this in a journey of less than five miles: thirteen signal boxes each endlessly resounding with call-and-response codes for every train passing from one section to the next. The replacement boxes made use of pneumatic or electric power in other ways, as the weighty levers needed to pull signal wires and point rods securely into place gave way to banks of much smaller hand-sized versions.

The four-aspect system has since spread across much of the network, and the quadruple cycle of changes in the wake of each passing train can now be watched from many platforms that command a long straight view of a busy line. One early showpiece for colour lights was the main line between York and Darlington, conversion of which began in the 1930s. Signals were placed every three-quarters of a mile over the thirty miles between York and Northallerton, where the new signal box had sixty-four miles of track under its control. By this date, advanced installations allowed a single switch or button to control all the signals and points on any permutation of route, rather than them having to be changed laboriously one by one.

The freedom in placing colour-light signals also allowed line capacity to be increased by multiplying the number of block sections. Ultimately, line speeds in force determine how short these sections can be; a train travelling at the maximum speed for the route has to be allowed sufficient notice to stop in time. By introducing an extra warning phase, four-aspect signalling therefore allowed capacity to be increased (more sections) without slowing services down.

These changes converged with other technologies. Signalling could be made to work automatically, each train triggering a danger signal as it entered a section and restoring the clear aspect as it left. Liverpool was again the pioneer: the first signals that operated in this fashion were the electrically powered semaphores supplied to the new Overhead Railway in 1893. Track could also be made sensitive to the movements of trains, typically by means of track circuiting. The circuit works by passing a small electric current through one rail, so that the wheels and axles of trains bridge the electrical gap to the other rail. This explains why small lengths of wire may be seen welded from rail to rail across joints of the older type, the bolts and fishplates of which are unreliable as a means of transmitting current. Another method uses sensors to count the axles of trains as they pass. Not only can the track be made sensitive to traffic; trains themselves can be protected against the risk of passing a signal at danger, by means of automatic warning or train protection systems. Most of these work by sounding or displaying an alarm signal within the cab, followed by an automatic application of the brake if the driver fails to override the warning in time. The Great Western began to install its version in Edwardian times, and was always justly proud of it.

These technologies have now been developed into a more

sophisticated system of pan-European train control in which operating instructions and route information are conveyed electronically to displays in the cab. This method has been adopted on the Cambrian Coast route on an experimental basis, although on the Continent its usual application is on high-speed lines. Further advances in technology promise to allow trains to move safely at maximum speed without depending on fixed block sections at all, by means of constant automatic monitoring of their performance and location – the so-called moving block system. A version of this has been in use for two decades on the Docklands Light Railway in London, and more recently on the Jubilee Line of the Underground. As the system spreads to main lines, the signal-free look of the original Liverpool & Manchester will become a reality once more, with electronic monitoring in place of the vigilant eyes of drivers and lineside policemen, at maximum speeds many times greater than those of the 1830s.

₪

Increasingly separated from the need to oversee the tracks, and with the capacity to follow the movements of trains over ever larger areas, signal boxes have become 'power boxes' or 'signalling centres', closer in character to air traffic control towers than to the vigilant cabins of the Victorians. The change of name reflects a genuine enhancement of function, for each of these buildings combines the duties of signal boxes of traditional type with the more strategic responsibilities of the railway control office, as developed early in the twentieth century. Control offices were set up to address a crucial weakness of operation via individual signal boxes, which was the lack of anything like a nerve-centre. Messages and instructions could pass up and down the line briskly enough, but too often reflected decisions made without full knowledge of the wider state of traffic. Telephones allowed a more strategic approach, linking the boxes to centres of shared knowledge and command. These were developed to great effect from the late 1900s on the Midland Railway and the Lancashire & Yorkshire, two lines with heavy goods and mineral traffic, under the influence of recent American practice. This freight moved chiefly in slow consignments in the intervals between the faster services of the passenger timetable, with regular diversions into passing loops, as the long stretches of track parallel with the main running lines are known. The early control offices left passenger services to the management of the signalmen and the disciplines of the public timetable, and used telephones to gather information concerning the state of the remaining traffic. Instructions could then be sent to the boxes to prevent excessive delays to consignments detained in loops and sidings; trains could be rerouted to save mileage or to avoid congestion; they could be terminated in order to send the wagons forward by a later service; relief crews could be directed as required; and so on.

The Lancashire & Yorkshire's system reached its culmination in 1915, when a circular control room opened at Manchester Victoria station. Here was a thoroughly twentieth-century space: a forerunner of every kind of technocratic headquarters, from the ops room of the Battle of Britain to the lair of a Bond villain. The upper wall displayed a huge map of the company's network, with coloured lights representing the locations of trains. Below the map were seventeen desks, one for each sector, each with its own map. Little pegs inserted in holes in these maps, together with tiny hand-written information cards, recorded precisely which train was where. In the middle of the room was a cluster of desks, and here sat 'the chief controller, three deputies, a coal-traffic controller, six controllers for train crews' relief and about three relief controllers'. There was also a control master, to keep the controllers under control.

Control systems of this kind proved their worth during the Second World War, when they helped to allay the convulsive effects of air raids and the constant challenges of congestion. By that time the largest individual signal boxes had effectively assumed some of the functions of sector control offices. The Northallerton power box, opened on the day war broke out in 1939, operated in its first years with the windows bricked up in case of air attack; the combination of telephony, track circuits and automation were already sufficient for it to function without a direct view of the lines a few feet away.

Like control offices, power boxes of the Northallerton type used panel displays studded with little coloured lights to indicate the state of traffic. The position of each train was shown by leaving a bulb unlit, to guard against the risk that a failed bulb might fatally conceal the true situation. Electric panels of this kind are in turn being replaced by electronic information, carried on the screens of visual display units. Like libraries and dealing rooms in the electronic age, the interiors of power boxes and their successors depend on shade rather than floods of sunlight, so that their internal illuminations are easily legible. The latest type is represented by the signalling centre recently installed at Didcot, on the Great Western main line: a long, low, neutral structure, its windows few and small, its working relationship with the railway not at all obvious. As modernisation proceeds, this nondescript building will gradually assume responsibility for nearly all the former Great Western lines in England, so that a journey from Penzance to Paddington will proceed under its guidance and supervision throughout. The size of this intended empire, and those of the thirteen similar buildings from which the integrated national network will be controlled, is recognised by another new name, that of Rail Operating Centre. Like a threatened species, the mechanical signal box will survive in the artificial reserves offered by preserved railways; the electrical and early electronic equipment that followed the mechanical era will quietly disappear.

₪

Anyone curious about these lost technologies will find them documented with inspiring devotion online at www.signalbox.org. Such labours of love reflect the special intimacy between the signalling staff and the systems under their control. A signal box was no place for the woolly minded or the inattentive. Dickens was spot-on: his haunted signalman is thoughtful and self-reliant, a former student of natural philosophy whose life had taken an unexpected turn.

To sign up for duty at a one-man box was therefore to embrace a distinctive way of life, closer in some ways to the isolation of the lighthouse than to the companionship of the footplate or the ready exchanges of the station platform. Physical skill was needed to operate the levers correctly, remembering and judging the force required to overcome the different sprung weights and loads for each. Besides the responsibilities of traffic, the condition of points and signals had to be kept under review; in cold weather, they might require testing hourly to guard against the effects of frost, snow or ice. Each box also maintained a written register of movements within its territory, of which meticulous record-keeping was expected. A desk or flap table for this purpose was usually among the furnishings within the cabin. The space was regarded as the signalman's own territory, even to the extent of allowing unofficial comforts such as an armchair or lengths of carpet to be brought in, but was generally kept clean and uncluttered. Sanitation took the form of an earth closet in the country (until the arrival of the 'portaloo'), or a proper water closet in plumbed-in areas.

The door of every box was marked PRIVATE, and firemen and gangers were expected to knock and ask permission before entering. Visits by firemen were common on lines without track circuiting, where a member of any crew held at a red signal was normally obliged to report to the box 'to remind the signalman of the position of the train' – according to the venerable Rule 55 in the little book of regulations supplied to all railwaymen. The visitor might hope to take away a container of boiling water for tea-making, for each signal box had a little stove for warmth and basic cooking; some coals might be dropped off in return, for the official allowance to each box was not always generous. In remoter locations, coal and water supplies were usually delivered directly from the rails, tokens of the mutual dependency between signalman and train crew.

This was not a job that could be taken on without thorough preparation. At smaller stations, a porter with ambitions might learn the workings of the signal box by assisting at busy times, passing through the intermediate grade of porter-signalman before achieving full status. Larger boxes tended to recruit from among the company's telegraph boys, whose training might include a stint at one of the signalling schools dotted around the network. In 1912 the Lancashire & Yorkshire equipped its school at Manchester Victoria with a splendid model railway for practical demonstrations; amazingly, this was still in use in updated form as late as 1995, after which the National Railway Museum claimed it. Back in the box, a young signalman might be inducted further by learning the ways of the log book and deputising for more senior men. The rigours of the night shift were reserved for fully qualified signalmen. One such stint was described by a Midland Railway signalman at a railwaymen's meeting in November 1886: 148 trains past his box, populated by an estimated 2,000 souls, 3,500 figures written in the book, 1,600 bell beats and dial signals sent, over 500 pulls on the levers. His shift, which was not at all untypical for the time, had lasted thirteen hours.

One of the best depictions of the signalman's way of life comes from an unexpected source. *Border Country* is a novel by the critic Raymond Williams (1921–88), published in 1960. Williams was a key figure in the post-war history of the intellectual left in Britain. His career anticipated the classic route into academia of the grammar-school boys of the 1950s and 1960s, many of whom encountered Williams's own texts along the way, especially *Culture and Society* (1958). His own upbringing was rooted in the working community of railwaymen: his father was a Great Western signalman at Monmouth, in the Welsh Borders. The signal box, not the ivory tower, was the formative vantage point for Williams's world-view.

The fictional Glynmawr signal box in *Border Country* is occupied every day except Christmas. Two of its regulars are single men lodging with the same housekeeper, who looks after their needs within the unsocial hours demanded by weekly changes of shift. The third signalman is the young hero's father, who misses the birth of his son because he is detained in his box – as duty demands – until the last minute of his evening turn. The years pass, and when the boy sets off from the family cottage to catch the train that will take him away to university, his father works the lever to make the distant signal tremble: 'an old game: originally a sign that he should hurry'. The signal is also a signifier: the railway is at home in the landscape, just as its workers belong with the community they serve. Later, the father having become too ill to work, his son goes to clear out his locker at the box, which is now due for closure together with the station it serves.

> On the wide shelf stood the three red fire buckets: the nearest filled with sand, with shreds of tobacco decaying on the moist yellow surface; the next with water, with a faint iridescence of oil. The third was the washing bucket, blue and milky, with a curd of lather round the rim. Beside the washing bucket was a yellow tablet of hard gritted soap, and the two pieces of cotton waste, tangles of multi-coloured threads. The atmosphere of the box began here: a faint, sweet smell of dust, soot, lamp-oil, food [...] He saw the dusty, threadbare red and green flags, and the heavy black megaphone, with its brass lip. He saw the four telephones, and the notice board above the fire-place, with its grimed and yellowing schedules. He saw the high clerk's stool; the open register with its thick, large writing; the round ruler and the white pen. He looked last at the grid, with its twenty-six levers, the shining handles and clips, the distinguishing plates in red, blue, yellow and black, the two check dusters to grip the polished handles; then the line of instruments above: the model indicator signals, the bells mounted in wooden clocks, with swinging notices in the face; the central master-key, with its looped brass chain.

Illicitly, under the approving eye of the duty signalman, the son takes a train through, copying actions he had observed all his life. He remembers to check that the train's red tail lamp is in place, as every signalman must: a safeguard against the rear part having become uncoupled while passing through the section. The duty signalman explains that the best friendships on the railway are not made with colleagues working turn and turn about in the same place, but with those in the boxes to either side, thanks to the possibility of talking free of charge on the telephone in the empty stretches between trains. Communication becomes another form of comradeship.

In the year that Williams's novel was published, a Berkshire teenager named Adrian Vaughan began work as a porter at Challow station in the Vale of the White Horse, on the old Great Western main line. Fascinated by railways since childhood, he was already precociously familiar with signalling routines from unofficial visits to boxes. In a matter of months he had graduated to signalman proper, first at Challow, then at Uffington a few miles down the line. Vaughan has since become one of the eminent British railway writers of his generation, both for works of general history and biography and for three exceptional volumes of memoirs published in the 1980s.*

Like Williams's signalmen, Vaughan's colleagues had a dual loyalty, as deeply rooted in their communities as they were committed to the disciplines of the service. Two of the older hands were active in their parish choirs, and exploited the telephone on night shifts to try out new hymn tunes on their mates. Another used the box to carry on an unofficial barbering service for locals, 'poring over some grizzled old neck, busy with his clippers'. Other regular visitors included the village constable and a beery parish clergyman, after the pubs shut for the night.

Operationally, these boxes still depended on the late-Victorian technology of absolute block. Vaughan celebrates the many ways in which the system fostered a working partnership between train crews and signalmen. When his employment began, the spirit of the Great Western still animated the railway, as though it were a regiment or a college of ancient foundation; senior colleagues persisted in referring to 'the Company', and some even wore their old uniforms and monogrammed badges, quietly tweaking the nose of public ownership. Ancestral loyalties were entrenched higher up, too: taking an examination at the old company's offices at Swindon, Vaughan found his divisional superintendent sitting in a mahogany chair with the carved initials of the Bristol & Exeter

---

* *Signalman's Morning*, 1981; *Signalman's Twilight*, 1983; *Signalman's Nightmare*, 1987.

Railway, with which the Great Western had amalgamated back in 1876. Allegiances and working methods belonged together; most of the trains passing through in 1960 were still hauled by Great Western locomotives, the exhausts 'blossoming like a pure white flower' against the sky.

It could not last: colour lights were coming, with Reading power box set to take control. The mechanical boxes were doomed, along with their village stations. Relations with superiors became edgy after Vaughan and his colleagues began a quixotic private campaign against the new order. Their chief concern was that it would abolish the visual scrutiny of the trains as they passed box after box along the line, each with its signal-man watching for carriage doors ajar, shifted cargoes, red-hot axle-boxes and other hazards that had escaped the train crews' attention. Contact was made with the local MP and a man from the *Daily Mirror*, but the affair blew over without going public; automatic sensors were installed by the trackside to detect hot axle-boxes, so that the train affected could be signalled to stop. Its driver could then ask for advice using one of the telephones installed alongside the new signals. The Berkshire party felt vindicated – a victory for 'the yokel signalmen of Uffington'.

Knowing that the old ways were ultimately doomed, Vaughan com-pares himself variously to a Luddite, a monk turned out of the cloister and a Jacobite after Culloden. This devotion to obsolescent methods was far from unique, nor is it extinct: a BBC2 documentary broadcast in 2013 featured a signaller at Stockport No. 2 Box, for whom the lever frames and bell-codes still in use there represented the 'organic' atmosphere of the 'proper railway', as against the 'sterile' world of the power box. With the passage of time, the technology Dickens represented in the 1860s as subduing men to its own artificial element – the haunted signalman with his nerves twitching to phantom bell-signals, 'Lamps' with his oily skin and wick-like hair – has become aligned with the natural order. Given the choice between eight hours in (say) Arnside box on the brink of Morecambe Bay, watching the same grand cycles of tides and clouds that enchanted Ruskin, and a stint of equal length in front of the power-box panels at Preston (1973, replacing eighty-seven older boxes), we might feel inclined to agree.

Vaughan's memoirs describe how he came to understand that his old working routines were not 'timeless' at all, but represented the fusion of 'a century of Trade Union effort' with 'the security and humanity of old-fashioned railway work'. That fusion brought a less domineering approach to discipline, and less exacting working hours. Williams's novel takes the story back to a harsher time, one generation earlier. *Border Country* stresses the political dimensions of railway labour, especially the challenge to solidarity represented by the General Strike of 1926. Williams's signal-men are divided by the dispute in lasting ways: one man who supported the strike chooses to leave the railway afterwards; another, who took the opposing view, is shunned by one of his fellows, who will communicate with him only by leaving notes. Though himself opposed to the strike, their stationmaster eventually declares the station closed, preventing fur-ther work. After the strike ends he is reassigned elsewhere by the company, like the many railwaymen in real life whose prospects were blighted by having backed the wrong side. All these positions are portrayed with sym-pathy and understanding for the conflicts of loyalty, politics and interests among the men.

This political dimension is important. The signalman's stamina, attention to detail and familiarity with bookkeeping were excellent prepa-rations for union work, and the signalling and telegraphs department was represented disproportionately in the post of branch secretary (one of Vaughan's fellow signalmen among them). Thus the working routines of the signalmen became a factor in the struggle for better conditions across the industry. Sidney Weighell, General Secretary of the National Union of Railwaymen in 1976–83, remembered his signalman father taking the branch typewriter into his box at Northallerton, in the years before the power box there took over, so that he could carry on his union duties in between Sunday trains. These efforts proved more productive than Mr Weighell Snr's repeated attempts to win a council seat for Labour in his Tory home town: he went on to serve on the executive of the NUR, then as secretary and chief negotiator of the LNER Council, representing dis-ciplinary appeals from among 70,000 members.

₪

Masts and wires now stand alongside the tracks at the site of Mr Weighell's Northallerton box, and are being erected through the Vale of the White Horse too; but these no longer have anything to do with signalling and telegraphs. The reason is the spread of overhead electrification, which cov-ers a steadily growing proportion of the network. On such lines the rail-way reasserts its presence within the landscape and against the sky, as in telegraphic days, and the trains travel within an uninterrupted metallic grove of wires, masts and gantries.

A hundred years ago, overhead power installations of this kind were still rare; trams, not trains, made up the vast majority of rail-borne vehicles powered in this way before the First World War, and for many years afterwards. Early systems showed the same localism and indifference to standardisation that we have seen regarding signals, brakes and alarms. Some were also surprisingly short-lived. The London, Brighton & South Coast Railway began running suburban electric trains in 1909, using an overhead supply of alternating current. In the 1920s the Southern Railway decided to get rid of this in favour of an electrified third rail alongside the running lines, on a similar principle to the four-rail system already established on the London Underground. By 1931 all the Southern's wires had been taken down. At the other end of England, the North Eastern Railway's mineral-heavy line between Shildon and Newport (Teesside) was electrified in 1915 with overhead direct current, only to revert to steam haulage twenty years later. Elsewhere in the north, third-rail systems were favoured; the North Eastern chose this method for its Tyneside suburban lines. Thus a single company was willing to deploy two incompatible systems at different ends of its own territory, as if heedless of the prospect that they might ever join up.

Finally, in 1956, British Railways standardised overhead supply for fresh electrification at twenty-five kilovolts of alternating current, at the same frequency used in the National Grid. The Southern Region was exempted, however, and the routes running south from London use the operationally inferior third rail to this day. The system now extends as far west as Weymouth in Dorset, with an odd little satellite line on the Isle of Wight, where superannuated Tube trains work out their final years (standard mainland designs being too large to fit the Island's loading gauge). Until a dedicated new line with overhead wiring was opened, the Channel Tunnel trains crossing Kent had to use the third rail too. In 2012 it was announced that overhead wiring is to be installed on the existing third-rail route between Southampton and Basingstoke, but the enormous costs and relatively modest benefits of converting all the other lines make it difficult to envisage that the larger job will ever be tackled. So these two systems can be expected to endure as long as there is still electricity to run Britain's railways. It is a similar story with the cluster of third-rail lines on Merseyside, incidentally the first place in Britain where a line built for steam locomotion was converted to electricity, back in 1903. But at least the choice of standard overhead system has proved well founded.

This is partly because the power can be conveyed by means of lighter and more efficient overhead line equipment, informally known as 'catenary'. A catenary curve describes the form taken by a cable or chain that is suspended at each end, but the curves of the overhead wires are not as obvious to the eye as the old, hypnotically swooping telegraph wires. In fact, the lowest wires above the tracks – the contact wires, which carry the current for collection – are kept taut by means of insulated weights suspended at each end (or, in more recent installations, by springs). To support each contact wire along its length, thin vertical hangers descend from a second wire immediately above, and it is this upper wire that adopts something like a catenary curve. Keeping the lower wire in tension ensures that a safe and resilient contact can be maintained with the sprung pick-up or pantograph apparatus on the roofs of the trains. The horizontal alignment of the wires is not completely straight: to even out wear to the pick-up on the pantograph, the wire follows a gentle zig-zag course or 'stagger' from mast to mast, so that the contact point slides constantly back and forth across the pick-up surface. Electric flashes, pops and bangs from the pantograph are a sign that this physical connection has been momentarily interrupted, making the current jump directly across the gap.

The weights that keep the contact wires from sagging are easily spotted, hanging in stacks from pulley wheels against the upright support masts. Well before each wire is diverted towards the trackside and its terminating anchor-weight, another wire slants across to take its place in the live catenary over the track, providing a continuous power supply. Thermal expansion applies to wires as well as to rails, so the weighted wires are arranged so that they can move gently up and down over their pulleys, according to the temperature. Each length of wire is also anchored at midpoint, to prevent it from being pushed gradually forward by the pantographs in their direction of travel.

By contrast, the supports for the wires are kept as stable as possible: the masts and gantries require sturdy foundations, and many are anchored additionally by means of diagonal cables. The supports must remain firm against the forces transmitted by trains, which nudge the contact wires upwards so that the whole cat's cradle of wiring stirs visibly up and down in their wake. Part of the load is due to the insulators suspended between the live and the earthed sections of the catenary, each of which is fashioned like a long ridged cylinder or stack of discs. It is not just the contact wire that is alive with current: anyone on a station platform along a route with overhead electrification can observe where these insulators are placed, and work out how much of the steel cage overhead is invisibly charged at twenty-five kilovolts. Most travellers probably never think this far into the matter, for the catenary belongs among those technologies that are at once exposed and somehow invisible. Likewise, the energy it conveys is generated by power stations that are mostly out of sight and miles away, for the benefit of trains that lack the visible and audible drama of steam haulage, running under colour-light signals controlled from drab, bunker-like buildings that turn their backs on the track.

So we go on taking for granted the extraordinary achievement of running the railways safely, at ever faster speeds and closer intervals, on routes mostly designed by long-dead generations for much lighter, slower and less frequent trains. Until something goes wrong, that is; in which case, information may be received that 'signalling problems' are to blame. Many such incidents are not the railways' fault at all, but arise from the vulnerability of grounded signal cables to thieves attracted by their copper content. The annual cost to the railways in terms of delays and repairs peaked at £16 million in 2011–12; steps since taken to regulate the scrap trade have improved matters. It is also fortunate that modern catenary uses steel and aluminium cable rather than copper, and that twenty-five kilovolts make a persuasive deterrent to pilferage. Meanwhile the railways do what they can to keep in repair the walls and fences that mark off their territory, a world like no other.

RAILWAYS AND THE LAND I

The railways did much to change the land, both physically and in the ways it was used and experienced. From the outset, railway building also raised profound issues of ownership and control over space. To understand some of these constraints, we can look first to the United States.

American steam locomotives are not hard to tell from British ones. Even in cartoon form, the transatlantic iron horse is never without a big, angled skirting, sloping out diagonally in front of the buffers. These attachments are known colloquially as cowcatchers, because they served to push aside any large quadruped that strayed on to the track. Candidates for such a collision numbered in the millions, for the railroads that crossed the plains and prairies were not usually fenced in. On lines built after 1850, huge expanses of land alongside the line commonly belonged to the railroad company anyway, having been granted by the federal government as an inducement to start work. The exact route was often left to the engineers on the spot, so that minor obstacles – a rocky outcrop, a patch of bog – could be swerved around. All being well, towns, depots, houses and freight yards might follow. The railroad barons thus grew fat at least as much from their property holdings as from the profits from traffic on the lines themselves.

A British railway was an iron horse of a different colour. Each route was planned with great precision, across land that in almost every case belonged to someone else. Legal preliminaries required the railway's take of this land to be surveyed and mapped precisely, so that ownership of each square foot could be established. Acquisition could then start promptly, as soon as the line received the hoped-for parliamentary assent.

Whether or not their attitude to the coming of the railways was favourable, landowners in Britain were generally wary of the companies themselves. Among their concerns was the risk that a railway might cannily buy up so much land that it could control the best sites for development along the route, just as the American railroad barons would. To guard against this outcome, an Act of 1845 required any railway to sell off unused land above a certain limit within ten years of its completion. This helped to keep British railway landholdings to a limited, if hardly minimal, scale.

Exceptions existed to the usual model. A railway company need not buy land for its line at all. This was common practice for many years in north-east England, where colliery waggonways were laid down on the wayleave principle. A wayleave permitted the right of passage to be licensed by the landowner, without the company having to acquire the ground beneath the tracks. This avoided expensive legislation, since no compulsory purchase was required, and also kept capital costs down during the construction period. On the other hand, wayleave fees could be punitive. The limitations of the practice are shown by the case of the Stanhope & Tyne Railroad, opened in 1834, with a route over thirty miles long. The company found the Bishop of Durham willing to accept a reasonable £25 per annum in return for the right to cross his lands at Stanhope Fell. Further east, it was stung for an equivalent rate of £800 per mile where the route clipped a few fields whose owners had seen the railway coming. Worse, these costs remained fixed regardless of the company's income from traffic, which shortly nosedived. The Stanhope & Tyne sank so far into debt as a result that it had to be dissolved and recapitalised within seven years of opening. Long leases were another alternative to outright purchase, and these too were common in the north-east, although not elsewhere.

At the opposite extreme was the Metropolitan Railway. Originally an urban concern, the company soon pushed a tendril out to Harrow-on-the-Hill and into rural Buckinghamshire beyond. It also managed to secure exceptionally generous clauses allowing development of freehold land along this route. After 1919, the company invoked these to exploit its holdings in such places as Ruislip and Wembley, as no other British railway was able to do. The 'Met' could hardly lose: its estates were developed at a handsome profit, and incoming owner-occupiers provided the line with a continuing reward in the form of new traffic.

Development on such a scale required promotion, and the company proved adept at this. The label 'Metro-land' was first used by its publicity department in the unpromising year 1915. Thereafter, the Metropolitan issued cheap, seductively illustrated yearbooks extolling the rustic charms of the districts which were, in truth, being steadily fenced off and parcelled up, interspersed with advertisements for available houses and plots. Even the door-plates in Metropolitan carriages were inscribed 'Live in Metro-land', in a bold cursive script.

The brand was officially dropped when the Metropolitan was swallowed by the new London Passenger Transport Board in 1933, but English literature has refused to let it die. Evelyn Waugh invented a Viscount Metroland in his first novel, *Decline and Fall* (1928), and married off this tedious self-made peer to the dangerously sexy Margot Beste-Chetwynd. John Betjeman captured the lingering atmosphere of the line in a characteristically bittersweet poem, 'The Metropolitan Railway', and expanded on the subject in what is easily the best of his television films, *Metro-Land* (1973). Julian Barnes dropped the hyphen for his first novel, *Metroland* (1980), whose hero finds himself reclaimed by his native suburbs after youthful excitements fizzle out into a life of comfortable convention.

So a slogan that had an active commercial life of only eighteen years has marvellously outlived its inventors, becoming a period signifier for a certain type of inter-war Home Counties prosperity: domestic cosiness bordering on the twee, with weekends of golf and cocktails and mowing the lawn thrown in, all underwritten by the daily grind to and from the Smoke. Betjeman's film also makes play with the social stratification within Metro-land, which encompassed the regimented streets of Neasden as well as the more expansive semis of Pinner (where the poet, in deadpan mode, commends the thoughtful provision in front of each house of 'a tree, for the dog'), not to mention the outer zones of stockbroker villas and the still unviolated country beyond the Chilterns. Just as in its carriages, the Metropolitan understood that it had to cater to more than one class in order to make the most of its assets.

₪

As a large-scale speculative exercise, Metro-land remained unique in

Britain. In terms of its physical presence, however, the Metropolitan was just like any other line, set apart from the outside world behind walls and fences. The portion of the earth's surface within these limits belonged to the company – exclusively so. The farmland, moor, heath or waste through which Britain's railways ran might be liable to inadvertent trespassing, but it was much harder for an intruder to pretend that he or she had somehow strayed by accident on to the wrong side of the railway's boundaries.

There was more than one explanation for these hard boundaries. Landowners were keen that barriers should be fixed, to prevent livestock straying and to discourage incursions from the railway side. The railways had to keep their tracks clear, and guard themselves against malicious damage or pilfering. The early lineside supervisors were called policemen in recognition that they were there in part to prevent such things happening. An internalised version of this wariness required the men of the Great Northern Railway to carry little brass pass-tokens when walking along their own routes, even for such everyday errands as a porter's journey to take a message to a signal box.

In case of any doubt, the companies set up thousands of trespass notices alongside their crossings and bridges. These were typically of cast iron, often bolted to lengths of old rail for signposts. Their texts often shunned brevity in favour of legal incantation, like the earliest recorded example, dating from around 1845–6:

MIDLAND RAILWAY. 7 VICT. CAP 18 SEC 238 ENACTS "that if any person shall be or travel or pass upon foot upon the Midland Railway without the licence and consent of the Midland Railway Company every person so offending shall forfeit and pay any sum not exceeding ten pounds for every such offence". NOTICE IS THEREFORE HEREBY GIVEN that all persons found trespassing upon this Railway or works thereof will be prosecuted as the Law directs.

J. F. BELL, secretary.

Ten pounds was a lot: the upper limit on most lines was forty shillings.

The basic truth that railway lines were unsafe for public sauntering was manifest as early as 1830, when Huskisson was cut down and killed. Yet the temptation remained irresistible. Country people who had been walking the same unofficial ways across fields and through hedges for generations were reluctant to take the long way round because of some remote and bossy railway by-law, forty-shilling fine or no forty-shilling fine. More than this, the new railway routes often provided a tempting alternative to established public thoroughfares. Their average gradients were usually gentler than on the roads, and their courses straighter and shorter too. Trouble-free crossings of rivers and streams were thrown in for good measure and there were no bogs, quagmires or thick undergrowth to besmirch or hinder the feet.

This pedestrian invasion started early. The Stockton & Darlington Railway began running third-class carriages in 1835 with the specific intention of picking up fares from the many walkers who had forsaken the roads to use its line instead. The habit was shared by those who should have known better, like the workers, no doubt somewhat gone in drink, who were cut down by an express on the main line at Low Gill in Westmorland in 1859, on their way back from the feast to celebrate breaking ground for a new branch line towards Sedbergh. Once completed, this line was habitually invaded as a footpath too, as were other routes through rough fell country. Bridges that spanned obstacles where no road went, and the tracks leading to such bridges, might be especially trespass-prone. The mile-long iron viaduct that opened across the Solway Firth in 1869 proved irresistible to incomers from the Scottish side for an additional reason: the licensing laws there prohibited Sunday drinking. Until the viaduct was dismantled in the 1930s, pubs on the English side received useful extra trade from intrepid Scots travellers.

Anyone who has ever tried to walk along a railway line, licitly or otherwise, sober or otherwise, must decide how to use the sleepers. The standard spacing for these is rather too close for the average stride, but too far apart to tackle two in one step. The Scottish writer Moray McLaren discovered as much, on an unauthorised 1920s crossing of Rannoch Moor – 'a limitless waste of peat and water' – via the track of the West Highland Railway. The complaint came with its own remedy: 'After about a mile or so one gradually begins to alter the natural length [of step] so that it fits the sleepers, and, if the line has been well laid out and the sleepers do not vary, one swings along with a very easy and regular motion.' The trespasser learns to walk like a railwayman.

Smaller strides encounter less difficulty. The young characters of *The Railway Children* (1906), jumping the fence at the bottom of their field to walk the rails for the first time, find the sleepers 'a delightful path to travel by – just far enough apart to serve as ... stepping stones'. That looks like an inducement to trespass – but, like all good children's authors, E. Nesbit watches the moral economy of her story with care. The mother of the family tries to forbid walking on the tracks, but has to admit that she too used to stray across railway fences when she was younger. So she settles for a promise from the children that they will always walk on the right, in order to see any approaching trains directly ahead. Here the reader may pick up a useful fact: then as now, like road traffic, British trains usually travel on the left.* Walking near tunnels remains forbidden, however; and when the Railway Children do break this solemn vow, it is for an emergency sortie to rescue an injured boy who has foolishly run through their local tunnel while following a paper-chase.

All of this may be familiar from the fondly remembered film version of 1970, starring Jenny Agutter and Bernard Cribbins and shot on the Keighley & Worth Valley Railway (actually a single-tracked line whose tunnels are too short to supply the fearful 'black-velvety darkness' of the book). Not included in the film is the sequence following, in which the children go to report the casualty to the signal box, only to find its occupant asleep in the summer heat, 'sitting on a chair leaning back against the wall'. By waking him, they save the man from losing his job. So their triple trespass – on to the line, then through the tunnel and finally into the box (which the children know to be prohibited too) – is justified by circumstance or by outcome.

Edith Nesbit understood very well that railways were dangerous places. One of her friends was killed in 1896 when walking on the line, having apparently failed to hear the guard's shouted warning. There was some suggestion of suicide: the man was a Russian revolutionary, whose life in exile had not been easy. The friendship is a reminder that Nesbit was politically radical, a utopian socialist in the mould of William Morris and a co-founder of the Fabian Society. She also knew how to write in a breezy, up-to-date way ('snarky'; 'like a pig being killed a quarter of a mile off'), as if to show up the fusty moralism of existing books for children. To widen the appeal further, the Railway Children's country is a carefully unspecific amalgam: the hills around are studded with furze (the southerner's word for gorse or whin) and pictures of 'The Beauties of Devon'

---

* This knowledge should be salted away for use when racing for a train at a double-platformed station: the correct side can be identified by thinking of the intended direction of travel, using the course of the sun for reference if needed.

adorn the station waiting room; but there are canals nearby too, and the family's house has a distant view of moorland, hinting at the north or the Midlands. The fictional railway company's name is itself nicely ecumenical: the Great Northern & Southern.

By later standards, however, Nesbit's most famous book is also desperately class-ridden. The children come from a genteel family forced to 'play at being Poor for a bit', before a fairy-tale restoration to their rightful state when father returns from wrongful imprisonment. If sometimes gruff, the railwaymen are always deferential (unlike the ungovernable, semi-criminal barge folk); when the youngsters are caught pinching pram-loads of coal from the station yard, they are let off with a caution ('"Well, you are a brick," said Peter, with enthusiasm. "You're a dear," said Bobbie. "You're a darling," said Phyllis. "That's all right," said the Station Master.') After which, like good Fabians, the three end up more than once rescuing the working men of the railway: not just the dozing signalman, but also in the famous episode in which they save a train from hitting a landslide by waving the girls' torn-up red petticoats as a danger signal. Nesbit's biographer Julia Briggs noted with puzzlement that the Edwardians had long since given up red flannel petticoats, a fashion that peaked in the 1860s–70s; but is it too much to suggest that waving a red flag for the attention of working men by a fine young woman of the upper middle class may have had other connotations in 1906?*

Incursions by children and young people were not always so well-meaning. Pilfering was only part of it. Objects might be placed on the line: not the traditional copper coins left on the rails to be flattened into bright thin circles, but things heavy enough to be lethal. A driver was killed when his engine derailed on a lump of wood left on the Stockton & Darlington's line in 1834, and a sleeper placed on the track near Lewes in 1851 caused a derailment that killed five people. Instances of stone-throwing started on the Great Western almost as soon as the trains began to run. Dickens observed a prohibitory notice against the habit at a bleak Black Country station in 1853. Penalties on detection might be severe: four lads aged

---

* More prosaically, Nesbit was fingered for plagiarism in 2011 when parallels were noted with a forgotten novel, Ada J. Graves's *The House by the Railway* (1896): some middle-class children who have moved to the country save a train from hitting a fallen tree by using red clothing as a danger signal, and are presented with engraved watches as rewards. 'The Red Flag' (the song) was written earlier still, in 1889.

Bobbie still waved the flags.

The landslide episode from *The Railway Children*, 1906

between nine and thirteen who were caught in the act at Leeds in 1875 were each sentenced to a dozen strokes of the birch.

The menace seems to have returned with new force in the 1960s, when the areas worst affected were Manchester and Liverpool, the twin birthplaces of modern passenger railways. Internal documents show that even David Lean's film *Lawrence of Arabia* (1962), with its spectacular train-wrecking sequence, caused disquiet among the railway management at the possibility of evil-minded imitation. Such concerns were not misplaced: in 1965 an evening train to Southend was derailed at Elm Park in Essex by pieces of metal placed maliciously across the tracks, killing the driver and one of the passengers.

The persuasive powers of film were used as a deterrent, culminating in 1977 with the British Transport Film *The Finishing Line*. A sort of nightmare inversion of *The Railway Children*, this twenty-minute short takes us into the imaginings of a T-shirted urchin sitting on a road-bridge parapet, above a cutting on the Hertford loop line. His thoughts come to life in the form of a surreal school sports day held by the trackside, complete with adult supervision, a marquee, brass band and impassive commentary through unseen loudspeakers as the increasingly hideous contests begin. Fence-breaking, stoning of carriages as they pass and races across the double tracks in front of approaching trains all take their toll. Most of the survivors are finally wiped out in the 'great tunnel walk', in which long defiles of youngsters are shown marching off into the mouth of Ponsbourne Tunnel. A speeding train then disappears into the same opening. Cut to the finish, as three bloodied and disorientated children limp out into the daylight, stammering out their names to a complacent race marshal. They are followed by an interminable procession of adults, carrying broken young bodies and laying them silently down between the rails one by one, like a Hertfordshire version of the Battle of Atlanta sequence in David O. Selznick's *Gone with the Wind*.

The British Film Institute now describes *The Finishing Line* as 'among the most audacious public safety films ever made'; but children and parents alike found it too traumatic, and the film was quietly withdrawn from television schedules. Its replacement was the more conventionally preachy *Robbie*, presented by the avuncular Peter Purves from *Blue Peter*, in which a football-loving lad is struck by a train and is lucky to lose no more than his feet.

₪

Absent from the list of trackside sports in *The Finishing Line* is the spraying of graffiti. As late as 1983, London Underground had no dedicated budget for the removal of illicit writing. Shortly afterwards, London began to copy New York, where much of the Subway – trains and stations, but especially the trains – was already covered in bold spray-painted tags. Traditionally the British vandal had been content to mark the insides of carriages only, but the new graffiti culture encouraged large-scale painting, with the highest premium on works that used the carriage sides as a canvas. Coverage of this kind takes time, requiring stealthy entry to depots and sidings where trains can be found unattended and at rest. The hooded trespasser rather than the rogue passenger now became the representative defacer of trains. This helps to explain where the trend took off: not in the gritty urban heartlands, but along the leafy outer reaches of the

Metropolitan and Jubilee lines. The canonical sites for the first UK graffiti artists ('writers', to use the insider term) were Neasden, Uxbridge and Wembley Park, with their spacious depots, easily walked tracksides and none-too-secure fences. Far from the arson-scorched wastes of the Bronx that were the crucible for New York, it was Metro-land – of all places – that nurtured the infant British graffiti scene.

Only a very prim person would be immune to the dynamism and animation of graffiti at its best, or would deny that it can sometimes enliven a drab urban setting. It is the spray can that has changed the game. In 1973, in the first book-length study of vandalism published in Britain, the anarchist writer Colin Ward (1924–2010) hailed aerosol paint as an aesthetic advance 'simply because it imposes a bold, free-flowing line on the user, by comparison with the effect of dripping painting or hesitant chalk ... I would not like the reader to think I am being flippant.'

Ward's indulgence reflected his profound opposition to authoritarianism, and an essentially optimistic view of human nature in which graffiti can be equated with legitimate protest and self-expression. He might have sympathised with one London graffiti writer ('one of da decorators') whose eccentrically spelled manifesto (posted 2004) aspires to the immortality of high art:

> we have produced master piece burners that rolled through the concrete jungle to be destroyed at the hands of the overseer's of order and conformity. Such demonstrations of hate and conformity will ultimatly weave us into myth and legend. This is important for future generations who need a history, stories and masterpieces to strengthen their spirits in the comming darkness ...

A lot of care and attention certainly goes into some of these pieces, especially 'wholecars', in which the entire side of a carriage, windows and all, is painted from end to end with a single design. Thanks to the web, vanished paint schemes that may have lasted only a few hours before the afflicted carriages were sent back to the depot for cleaning have been memorialised for all to see, on sites such as the Digital Jungle UK graffiti archive. Here are a thousand large-scale pieces by practitioners from Agony to Zonk, sprayed on main-line trains as well as those of London Underground, and all dating from the second half of the 1990s, when the scene was especially lively.

The defence that graffiti adds vibrancy to the environment falters when spray paint has blanked out the carriage windows through which that environment must be seen. These collections of graffiti images also show that they are amazingly repetitive in terms of style, and instantly forgettable as a result, for all the defiant hopes of 'da decorator'. And if anyone of an anarchist persuasion still nurses the dream that graffiti might be a harbinger of collective purpose, online forums suggest that rivalry and rancour are the dominant modes of graffiti culture. The creators of ambitious 'pieces' despise taggers, endlessly replicating their drab little marks. Local gangs disparage and detest their neighbours and rivals. Collectively, Londoners hate 'bumpkins' (exponents of graffiti from outside the capital), reserving special venom for upstarts from Brighton. And so on.

Even so, as nobody needs telling, bumpkin versions of London's versions of New York's graffiti are now pervasive up and down the country, along the railways and beyond. Confronted with the derivative sprayings of the track bandits of Droitwich or Spalding, no less than those of west London, the eye slides away and the brain fails to engage. There are phases of visual respite whenever the railway approaches to London are smartened up and the palimpsest of tagging along cuttings and retaining walls disappears under big blocks of dun-coloured paint – after which the taggers creep back as surely as the sea-tide, reclaiming the freshened surfaces to make their scrawls show up all the more clearly. Especially boring are the hurried tags scribbled doggedly on every surface, as if to insinuate the idea that the catenary masts and trackside equipment cabins owe their continuing existence to an adolescent with a knack for fence-climbing and a pocketful of Pentels.

The omnipresence of graffiti culture has another odd effect, in that the elderly survivals from the time when lineside graffiti still communicated in a shared language are now much more likely to hold the attention. There is a certain pathos in the flaking initials of a long-relegated football team, or the declarations of provincial fandom, such as the pot-and-brush-painted slogan BOWIE '77 that lingers beneath a bridge at Maryport station on the Cumberland Coast line, or the marks of extinct tribes at Loughborough on the preserved section of the Great Central Railway:

PUNKS RULE

TED'S ARE BUMERS

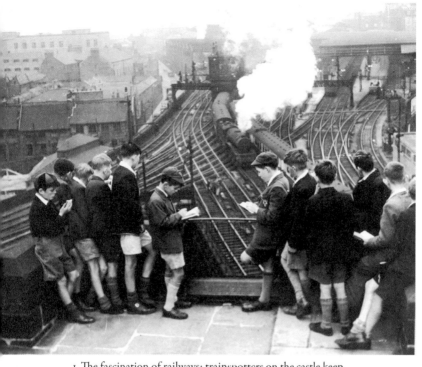

1. The fascination of railways: trainspotters on the castle keep
overlooking Newcastle Central station, 1950

2. Nine examples of the millions of Edmondson ticket types used
on Britain's railways, dating from *c.* 1920 to the 1970s

3. First- and second-class trains on the Liverpool & Manchester
Railway, aquatint after Isaac Shaw, 1831

4. Loading luggage on to the carriage roof: detail of colour print
after William Powell Frith's 'The Railway Station', 1862

5. Abraham Solomon, 'First Class: The Meeting', second version, 1855

6. Interior of a Great Western Railway third-class open carriage, 1938

7. A workmen's train and its passengers at Liverpool Street station, 24 October 1884

8. Smiths' station bookstall at Bude, Cornwall, *c. 1900*

9. The three-card trick, on an Edwardian postcard

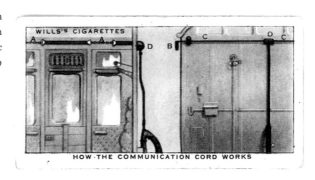

10. The communication cord explained, on a Wills's cigarette card of 1939

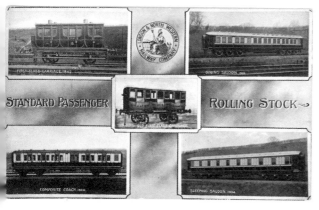

11. Carriages old and new, on a London & North Western Railway postcard of 1904

12. High Speed Train and Advanced Passenger Train prototypes in front of the surviving half of Brunel's station at Swindon, 1975

13. Inside a British Railways Mark 1 sleeper compartment, 1962

14. Remains of a Southern Railway box van on Hoy, Orkney, 2010

LMS **THE PERMANENT WAY**

RELAYING

by Stanhope Forbes R.A.

15. The labour-intensive routines of track maintenance, depicted by Stanhope Forbes on a London, Midland & Scottish Railway poster of 1924

16. Inside the power signal box at Willesden Junction, north London, 1966, showing the display panels

17. The London & North Western Railway's signal gantry at Rugby, *c.* 1897. Each signal is doubled above and below to allow for clear sight-lines past the overbridge for the new Great Central Railway main line, shown under construction behind

18. The mass of steelwork comprising the overhead line equipment at Tamworth, Staffordshire, 2015. The two nearest trains are class 390 'Pendolinos'

19. Crumlin viaduct, Monmouthshire, built 1853–7. The valley below is threaded through with railways at multiple levels, all still in use in this photograph of 1961

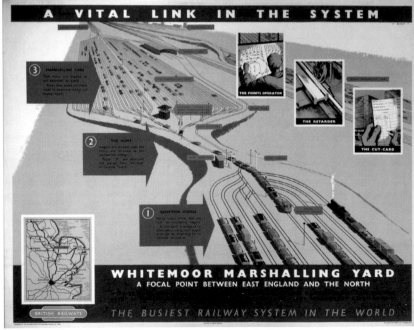

20. Whitemoor marshalling yard explained, on a British Railways poster of *c*. 1950

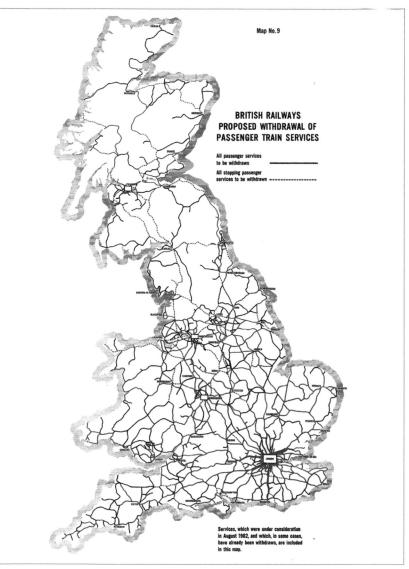

21. The notorious closure map from *Reshaping Britain's Railways*, alias the Beeching Report, 1963

22. Adlestrop station, Gloucestershire, *c.* 1905. The main building of 1853 is on the up platform (right), the platform shelter on the down platform, with the stationmaster's house behind

LONDON.   PADDINGTON, GREAT WESTERN HOTEL.

Colour Photography—The Photochrom Company Limited, 121, Cheapside, London, E.C.

23. The Great Western Hotel at Paddington station, opened 1854, in a Photochrom carriage picture of *c.* 1900

24. Euston station train shed, aquatint after Thomas Talbot Bury, 1837

25. The British Rail corporate image represented in a
model of the rebuilt Tamworth station, 1964

26. Inter-war image-making: London & North Eastern Railway poster of 1932 for the Night Scotsman service, with artwork by Robert Bartlett

27. The seductive liveries of Edwardian locomotives as exemplified in the Caledonian Railway's postcard of no. 50 *Sir James Thompson*, built 1903

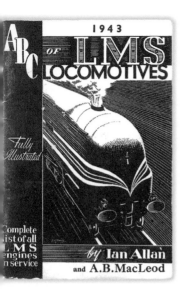
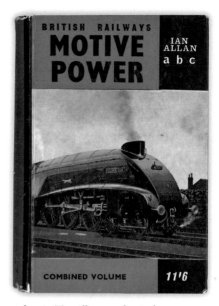

28. Ian Allan ABC guides from 1943 and 1963. They illustrate the rival streamlined designs of the London, Midland & Scottish Railway and London & North Eastern Railway (right), from the mid 1930s

29. Inside 'A' shop at Swindon Works, 1961, showing ex-Great Western locomotives dismantled for overhaul

30. The 'New Approach' to railway photography, exemplified in Colin Gifford's view of Wigan in November 1967. The locomotive is an ex-London, Midland & Scottish Railway class 8F 2–8-0

31. Twenty-first century railway preservation at Ropley on the Mid Hants Railway, 2008. The locomotives have been restored from scrapyard condition, and the engine shed, ash-pit and lattice-post signal (awaiting its semaphore arm) are new structures of traditional appearance

Paddington's celebrated graffiti

Nor has any modern blurt of spray-painted colour come close to the enduring impact of

FAR AWAY IS CLOSE AT HAND IN IMAGES OF ELSEWHERE

as painted neatly on a wall on the approaches to Paddington station in 1974. This haunting declaration piqued the curiosity of thousands of travellers. The *Daily Telegraph*'s columnist Peter Simple attributed the words to the shadowy 'Master of Paddington', the subject of squabbles among imaginary scholars; the poet and commuter Roger Green puzzled over them in his entertaining compendium of railway musings *Notes from Overground* (1984), published under the pseudonym 'Tiresias' (epigraph: 'Man is born free, and is everywhere in trains'). In 2005 the text was revealed to have been the creation of two brothers named Dave and Geoff, working over Christmas when no trains ran. They had taken the first six words from a poem by Robert Graves and adapted the rest from the title of an academic paper by another poet, Ruth Padel. Demolition of the original wall in 1981 failed to suppress this hybrid text, which was promptly recreated further along the line, only to disappear finally around the turn of the century.

'Far Away ...' cost the public nothing. Not so the efforts of the bombers, burners and taggers of the modern graffiti scene. The annual bill for cleaning trains, buildings and lineside structures on the national network now stands at over £3.5 million, while London Underground was reportedly devoting 70,000 man-hours a year to the same task by 2007. The job is made harder by writerly ruses such as mixing brake fluid with the ink of marker pens, so that tags burn their way indelibly into plastic or painted surfaces. Countermeasures that have reduced lasting damage to trains include the adoption of transparent self-adhesive films for carriage bodysides, which can be peeled off and discarded along with any unwanted sprayings, like surgical gloves. Bridge parapets and other perilous locations that enhance the thrill of creating graffiti also inflate the bill for removing it, when safety harnesses and other special precautions may come into play. Then there are the costs of prevention and deterrence, which overlap with the precautions taken against cable thieves: spike-topped palisade fencing of galvanised steel, infra-red security lights, alarms and closed-circuit TV at depots, enhanced lineside patrols and the operation of special 'Q-trains' to spot trespassers and vandals, which work jointly with police teams on the roads along the tracks. Surveillance flights by remote-controlled drones may yet join this list. Prosecution and punishment of offenders, and the maintenance of the National Graffiti Database (part-funded by the British Transport Police), nudge up the bill still further. As surveys of the impact of vandalism have also demonstrated, the final reckoning should include the loss of revenue from those intimidated by edgy, vandalised environments – women and the elderly in particular – who may therefore avoid using the railways at all, especially at night. And that is to speak in terms of money only, without trying to put a price on fear.

₪

The first thing that strikes the Railway Children as they watch a train passing their new home is how *tall* it is in the unfamiliar view from ground level, where it is no longer 'cut in half by platforms'. Railway track, too, seems different when encountered close to. It can be seen by how much the rails stand higher than the sleepers, and how the running surfaces are worn smooth and mirror-bright, making it hard to accept that each dull-sided rail can have been forged from a single ferrous substance. If the line is on a bend adapted for fast running – as the tracks next to station platforms rarely are – the extent of canting inwards against the curve can also be appreciated. Or if the route is straight, flat and long, the tracks may call to mind the definition of parallel lines as those which may be projected infinitely without ever meeting. At close hand the railway appears as it truly is: a linear machine, set apart in its own world and achieving completion only with the passage of a train. Where the tracks are caged within the masts and humming wires of overhead electrification, this sense of latent power is more forceful still. Even when the tracks are visibly clear for miles in either direction, the zone between the rails is still an unsettling place to linger, just as an unloaded gun is an unnerving presence on a table top.

All this may be experienced without any act of trespass, simply by traversing a stile or kissing gate on to one of the hundreds of unstaffed pedestrian crossings up and down the network. Here is the paradox of railway security: the network is at once strictly out of bounds and hopelessly porous. At these crossings the only restraints against turning improperly right or left rather than pressing straight ahead are prudence, common sense and (often) an easily foiled installation of triangular-section timber slats laid down alongside the boardwalk across the tracks, on the principle of a cattle grid. These slats may also be seen at so-called occupation and accommodation crossings, which are gated openings that allow farm traffic to cross the line.

For those not travelling by rail, however, the most familiar way of traversing a railway line is via a level crossing, on the pneumatic tyres of a motor vehicle. In these places it is the railway that is primarily responsible for safety. Here and there, the motorist may even encounter gates that are still swung manually across the road by a crossing-keeper, whose only job is to open and shut them as each train passes. Especially on wider roads, this ritual can be a trial for the impatient: two gates on each side, four separate sorties for the fluorescent-coated keeper before the way is clear. The red warning discs fixed to these gates are incidentally one of the longest-lasting visual conventions on the railway, dating from an order of 1858 (likewise the red lamp displayed on the gates at night).

Other gates may be operated from an adjacent signal box. This type now generally takes the form of electrically operated lifting barriers, painted with the familiar white and red stripes, and with flashing lights and sirens for accompaniment. Already well established on the Continent, the automated version was introduced to Britain in 1952 at an undistinguished station with an ugly name: Warthill, on the line from York to Hull. Crossings of this kind can be operated remotely – helped by the later introduction of closed-circuit TV monitors for surveillance – thus dispensing with a crossing-keeper. They are also much quicker to reopen after a train has passed, sometimes jerking upwards only a few seconds after the last railway vehicle has flashed by.

Lesser roads are often protected by automatic half-barrier crossings. Britain's first example of this Continental invention came into use on

British Railways' first automatic half-barrier
crossing, at Spath in Staffordshire, 1961

5 February 1961 at Spath near Uttoxeter in Staffordshire. This type blocks
the left-hand lane only, by means of stubby barriers without protective
skirtings. At these crossings responsibility for safety is effectively divided,
in that motorists and pedestrians are trusted not to try anything stupid.
Nor do their barriers interlock with the railway's own signals: like the
miniature versions supplied by Hornby, their descent is triggered simply
by the approach of a train.

The investment in the Warthill crossing did nothing to secure the
future of the line in question, which closed in 1965 after having been singled out as a loss-making case study in Dr Beeching's report *The Reshaping of British Railways* (1963). Beeching killed off the passenger service
on the line through Spath too, and in the same year. But lifting barriers
of both types have come to prevail elsewhere, and it is now easy to forget
how common the manually operated kind used to be, especially in flat
landscapes. On lightly used lines they were sometimes worked by the train
crew themselves: the Dornoch branch in Sutherland had six such crossings in a length of less than eight miles, and the guard was allowed three
minutes to shepherd his train across each one. This was no way to run

a speedy railway. Yet as long as labour was cheap, it often suited a railway company to provide a cottage for a crossing-keeper, like a lodge at the gates of a gentleman's park (though rarely so ornate), rather than sinking capital into the construction of a bridge.

Like signalmen, the lives of these crossing-keepers were ruled by the railway timetable, and their movements regulated by the telegraph bell. From an early date they included women, among the first to take a direct part in the operational side of the railway. Some were widows who had taken over the roles of deceased husbands, in which case they were expected to do the same work for less money. The work was not arduous, but the hours were often long. Jane Emerson, who carried on her late husband's duties at a crossing on the outskirts of Carlisle, was released from her duties only at 10.30 p.m. Her working day ended by closing the gates behind the last train, and taking the two gate-lamps into the house for safe keeping. We know these details because they featured in evidence in 1861, when she was found dead after a break-in: another instance of how court cases can preserve glimpses of long-lost working routines.

Even automated level crossings are becoming rarer in our own century. To minimise accidents to road vehicles and pedestrians, Network Rail is replacing crossings of every type by bridges or footbridges where possible, or introducing diversions, or closing pedestrian routes altogether. In 2014 it was reported that 750 crossings of all types had been eliminated over the previous four years alone, equivalent to about 10 per cent of the total. A mere thirty-eight of these were replaced by new footbridges, some rising incongruously amid lonely fields. Closed-circuit filming ensures a national audience for some of the narrow escapes and idiotic dashes on the crossings that remain.

₪

The accommodation crossings that allow farmers to cross the tracks are a reminder of the primal act of invasion committed by the railways. Dead straight or gently curving, their alignments cut across the patchwork of countless fields and estate boundaries. A consortium of Northamptonshire landowners, meeting in 1830 to formulate a response to the impending London & Birmingham Railway, concluded that it would harm their property thus:

1. By destroying the privacy and unity of the farms and cutting off part thereof from the homesteads.

2. By dividing into separate ill-shaped fragments closes which are now convenient in their form, size and quality.

3. By occasioning deep cuttings across the slopes of the hills, and thereby intercepting the supply of water to the wells and grounds below them.

4. By occasioning large embankments across the low lands, and thereby intercepting the natural drainage of the parts above them.

5. By requiring in numerous cases so great a width for slopes in addition to that of the railway itself as to render any communication between the lands separated by it extremely difficult and inconvenient.

All of which was correct on every point – to say nothing of the turmoil during construction, nor of the pollution, noise and visual intrusion that the completed railway might bring. Any or all of these permanent changes might serve to pump up the final sum obtained from the company in exchange for land required. Besides the obvious payments for the change of ownership, these included allowances for 'severance', when the division of fields left pieces that were difficult of access, and often of odd triangular shapes that were harder to plough (the reason fields are normally rectangular). Other losses could follow, for which owners could not always obtain compensation. For instance, property values in coaching towns such as Towcester, where the Northamptonshire elite conferred in 1830, often declined sharply as trade melted away to the railways.

Land in 1830 was still the pre-eminent source of wealth and status, and the ownership of broad acres conveyed powers that would now be considered both corrupt and despotic. A great landowner could expect to play his part in Parliament, as a member of the Lords or by election to the Commons. In the latter case his tenants were expected to vote for him, sometimes on pain of eviction. Or he might control borough seats of the 'rotten' kind, in which a small electorate would reliably vote for the master's candidate. Members of county families also served in a judicial capacity as magistrates, and the counties themselves were administered by their magistrates by means of quarter sessions. On his own terrain the landowner was free to farm as he wished, without interference on matters ranging from his choice of crops to the living conditions and working hours of his labourers. He was the legal owner of his wife's belongings, and enjoyed dictatorial powers over his children until they came of age. Yet his rights of possession could now be challenged by bands of railway speculators, operating through companies that might have no interest in the life of the parishes through which they hoped to pass.

The land itself might be subject to trespass too, as furtive surveyors sought to determine intended routes. Here it is important to distinguish the outline survey, which had to be accurate enough to satisfy scrutiny in Parliament of a line's stated capital requirements, from the much closer survey that followed a successful enactment. There was no point in trying to stop a railway that had effectively passed into law, but that did not mean that every landlord proved to be a pushover when the companies first set out to map their intentions. The hardest fights usually concerned access to the private parks of great estates. George Stephenson discovered as much when the Liverpool & Manchester route was in gestation: 'Bradshaw fires guns through his ground in the course of the night to prevent the surveyors coming on in the dark.' No relation of the Quaker publisher, this was Mr Robert Bradshaw of Worsley Hall: a man with a major interest in the Bridgewater Canal, whose traffic was threatened by the cheaper rates of carriage intended by the railway. Stephenson's answering ruse was to let off some shots in the darkness well away from the intended route, leaving the surveyors to slip in and continue their work after Bradshaw's gamekeepers had gone off to investigate. Another dodge used to expedite the survey involved circulating a false document among Lord Sefton's tenants to say that he had granted permission for the survey (he had not).

Plenty of similar engagements followed, not always so peaceful. Sometimes the surveyors came with navvies for back-up, and the gamekeepers with estate workers, and noses were bloodied and theodolites smashed. Firearms might even be drawn, as at Lord Harborough's estate at Stapleford Park in Leicestershire in 1845. In this instance the pistol-packing surveyor responsible was lucky to spend no more than a weekend in the cells. Lord Harborough won out and the line was routed around his park, but such incidents showed that land ownership no longer meant all that it had done before the railway age.

The surveyor who mapped the railway route and the engineer who subsequently oversaw its design and construction were often united in one individual. This was Brunel's way when determining the Great Western's course from London to Bristol. In person, he entered the domains of land-owners along the way and did his best to charm them into consent (Brunel was expected to write all the letters arising from the survey himself). Trav-elling had to be done on horseback or by means of public stagecoaches, at least until Brunel commissioned a four-horse carriage to his own design. This civilian version of a general's field headquarters was furnished with a drawing board, built-in cupboards for drawings, equipment and cigars, and a seat that could be extended as a couch, for snatching some sleep. It was an exhausting routine: during his visit to South Wales in 1834 to advance the cause of the Taff Vale Railway, Brunel was discovered one morning asleep in his chair, fully clothed, with the ash of a complete cigar fallen on his chest.

Professional roles were transformed by the surge in railway work. There were simply not enough of the right sort of men to go round. Rob-ert Stephenson received cheques in the post from promoters of shaky railway companies, hoping to bribe him to lend his name to their pro-spectuses and thus inspire enough subscriptions to get things moving. Stephenson chose instead to expand his practice by recruiting trusted but essentially self-employed associates, rather like a barrister's chambers. Each newly accepted company was assigned to one of these associates, who were expected to consult with the chief on details and difficulties. For a competent surveyor – especially one with the right combination of physical stamina and finesse in negotiation – the 1840s were a golden age. The young Alfred Russel Wallace and his less fortunate brother (on whom *see* Chapter 3), drawn into railway surveying in the early 1840s, are repre-sentative figures from this time. But as engineers increasingly took over the central task of determining the route, surveyors retreated from their traditional land-measuring roles in order to concentrate on new chal-lenges of valuation and arbitration, often railway-related.

Inevitably, the boom also drew in the incompetent and the unscru-pulous. It was alleged in 1846 that some railway surveyors were buying standard Ordnance Survey maps, making minor changes based on their own observations and charging their employers between 60 and 160 times the purchase price for the result. A few get-rich-quick merchants even set up as tutors in railway surveying, raking in fees for dubious crash courses before quietly disappearing.

Sharp practices of this kind were a spur to the honest majority, encouraging self-regulation and specialisation. The railway companies were thus increasingly able to depend on a group of surveyors who knew how to acquire property smoothly and without over-payment. When the Institution of Surveyors was set up in 1868, no fewer than fifteen of its twenty founding members were specialists of this kind.

The broadcloth-suited eminences of the Institution of Surveyors are not among the most memorable Victorians. Even surveyors themselves would probably be hard-pressed to name any of them today. Railway engineers do rather better: wonderful Brunel with his panache and his cigars, and the steadier but more influential figure of Robert Stephenson and his self-taught father, followed by a few less vivid figures, such as the immensely able Joseph Locke. Then there are the great contractors who marshalled the labour, materials and resources to build the lines, men such as the ex-navvy Joseph Firbank (1819–86) and the admirable Thomas Brassey (1805–70). An ambitious young surveyor from Birkenhead with sidelines in road-making and property development, Brassey took a momentous step in 1835, when he tendered successfully to construct one of the viaducts and ten miles of the route of the Grand Junction Railway. The historical moment was significant. George Stephenson had built the Liverpool & Manchester by means of labour directly employed and supervised by his own team of engineers, but the future lay with the contract system. Each major contractor would usually sub-contract shares of the work in turn, and the sub-contractors commonly appointed gangers who each had the control, and sometimes the direct hire, of the labourers themselves. With variations, this was the method by which most of Britain's railways were built.

Recognising Brassey's qualities, the Grand Junction Railway's engineer Joseph Locke engaged him on his next big project, the London & Southampton. The original chief engineer had just resigned, having entrusted the works to lots of small and under-capitalised contractors – the bane of much early railway building – who were struggling to cope. Locke and Brassey between them did much to turn things round, and their relationship endured. Soon they were collaborating on the first major railway in France, between Paris and Rouen. At home and abroad, working with Locke or without him, Brassey steadily clocked up an astounding 6,500 route-miles of railway. His personal total was equivalent to one-sixth of the British network and one-twentieth of all the lines around the world, including railways on every continent. This one-man multinational kept 100,000 men busy at the peak of his activities. In order to sustain a healthy flow of work he even began to turn his capital over by taking shares in new railway projects himself, like several other big contractors during the busiest railway-building decades. Exceptionally, Brassey entered the business of railway operation too, leasing some self-built lines on completion – the London, Tilbury & Southend was one – and running them at a good profit. At his death, Brassey's British estate alone amounted to £3.2 million: a fortune of ducal proportions.

All this was not achieved merely by shrewd delegation. For relentless hard work and monomaniacal attention to detail, Brassey was your man. His memory and his powers of mental arithmetic were prodigious. He had no time for secretaries, and undertook all correspondence and working records himself. A bag containing letters and writing materials went everywhere with him, even on what were nominally holiday visits to Mr Locke's Scottish grouse moor. In waiting rooms at railway junctions, Brassey would sit writing; in hotels too, into the small hours. His friend Dr Burnett, travelling with Brassey in Italy, once retired at 9 p.m. and came down the following morning to find thirty-one letters written by the contractor and ready for the post. If a reply had taken more than one day to compose, Brassey was known to commence his letter with an apology for his slowness. He also shared the Victorian aptitude for walking long distances very quickly: his brother-in-law recalled how a regular sixteen-mile trudge between Rugby and Nuneaton became part of Brassey's to-and-fro journeyings between his various works in progress, which also included projects in France, the Trent Valley and between Lancaster and Carlisle. His was a very personal business, and – like those of other early railway contractors – it effectively died with its founder.

₪

Brassey was perhaps the closest thing to a railroad baron that the British network produced. As for a British counterpart to the mighty folk heroes of the American frontier, the railway navvy has a very good claim. The archetype is described in Terry Coleman's classic study *The Railway Navvies* (1965). Distinctive in his dress of bright velveteens, impenetrable in his slang, contemptuous of religion and hostile to the conventions of marriage and homemaking, the navvy lived apart from society in temporary shack-towns, until a rumour of better-paid work elsewhere sent him off 'on the tramp' once again. As disciplined in his toil as he was ungovernable in his free hours, as free with his fists as he was thirsty for beer and grog, the navvy introduced to thousands of quiet parishes the near-anarchy of the urban slum. Often there was a tribal element to the navvies' clashes: English against Scots, or English, Scots and Welsh – together, or separately – against the Irish, who were suspected of being ready to work for lower pay. Men even abandoned their old identities, picking up vivid new monikers as they went from place to place: Coleman lists Skeedicks, Moonraker, Mountainpecker, Concertina Cockney, Jimmy-the-new-man, Johnny-come-lately, Beer, Brandy, Fatbuck, Scandalous, Rainbow Ratty and Reeky Hoile, all employed on the Midland Railway's line from Kettering to Manton in the late 1870s. (Reeky Hoile was a Yorkshireman, named from a remark he made when looking down a smoking tunnel-shaft in which a blast had just been set off.) Only when the railway was complete could squire, magistrate and parson resume control, men be known by their true names and modest maidens walk freely abroad once again.

The 1960s were a lively time for labour history. Coleman's book came close on the heels of E. P. Thompson's influential doorstopper of 1963, *The Making of the English Working Class*, with its mission to rescue the forerunners of the modern labour movement from 'the enormous condescension of posterity'. Coleman's hard-drinking, quarrelsome navvies may fall short of Thompson's radical pioneers in terms of solidarity and class consciousness, but the exploitation to which they were subjected evoked some passages of justified anger. For navvies were killed and maimed by the hundred, sometimes from their own reckless haste to get the job done, but also as victims of cynically exploitative contractors. Coleman devotes a chapter to the first Woodhead Tunnel, driven through over three miles of Pennine strata in 1839–45. During this time, up to 1,500 men and their dependants were billeted all year round in squalid dry-stone cabins out on the moors. Even these were provided grudgingly, the men having been expected at first to make do with tents, or even to sleep out in the open. Their sustenance came from rip-off 'tommy shops' run by the contractors or their confederates, which were stocked with inferior produce at inflated prices. The men were paid at irregular and widely spaced intervals, and when the money did arrive nothing was done to deter them from bingeing it all away on tommy-shop beer.

Drunk or sober, the men faced deadly risks at work. One example: the powder charges inserted into the rock prior to blasting had to be rammed into place by means of metal tools called stemmers. The task was safer if these were of copper, which was less likely to make sparks against the rock, but the contractor insisted on using iron, a cheaper and harder-wearing material. The results were predictable: 'William Jackson, miner, No. 5 shaft. He was looking over John Webb's shoulder, while he was stemming a hole charged with powder, when the blast went off, blowing the stemmer through Jackson's head and killed him on the spot.'

The social reformer Edwin Chadwick later compared the chances of death or serious injury among the workforce during the whole course of the job with those at one of Wellington's battles, concluding that a private soldier had a better chance of coming away unscathed from Waterloo or Salamanca than a navvy from Woodhead (where he counted thirty-two fatalities). Pardonable exaggeration, perhaps; but the conditions at the tunnel did result in a broader enquiry by a Parliamentary Select Committee into the human cost of railway construction. As presented in 1846, the Committee's recommendations would have subjected the railways to some of the legal controls already in force at certain other workplaces, including the stipulation that deaths or injuries should be treated as the companies' responsibility unless the victim's carelessness could be proved. Another proposal was that men should be paid weekly and in money, rather than in 'truck' or vouchers for the tommy shops. This moderate, humane and wholly achievable report was then shelved, leaving the contractors free to carry on as before.

Not all contractors were as bad as Thomas Nicholson, the worst of the men in charge at Woodhead. At the other end of the scale was Brassey, who understood the value of a loyal, experienced and well-rewarded workforce. Brassey paid better than others in the business, and banned tommy shops and beer sellers from his sites. His reward was a cohort of super-workers, each capable of lifting twenty tons of spoil a day. From the profits of their labours he subsidised hospital places for men who fell ill, and if a man perished during the course of his work Brassey would assist his dependants. In an age of boom-and-bust, he also tried to arrange his contracts so as to secure steady employment from job to job. Brassey's navvies were even ready to follow their master abroad: half of the work-force on the Paris-to-Rouen contract, to a total of 5,000 men, came from the English side of the Channel. They were paid twice as much as French labourers engaged on the same line, and their unrelenting rate of work was the cause of local astonishment. Here was a reincarnation of the venerable stereotypes of Hogarth's anti-French pictorial satire 'The Roast Beef of

Old England' – 15lb of beef per week being the reported diet of an 1840s navvy in his prime.

Other aspects of Coleman's composite picture have held up less well to historians' scrutiny. For one thing, brawn was not enough on its own to make a railway. Much of the necessary work in railway-making depended on skills learned in the building trade, and bricklayers, masons and carpenters by the thousand laboured alongside the men charged with mere digging and moving spoil. There were temporary brickworks to be built and manned too – Robert Stephenson allowed 20 million bricks to line his tunnel at Kilsby, on the London & Birmingham – and pumping engines to be established so that the shafts and bores for the tunnels could be kept clear. Nor were lawless shanty towns of the Woodhead type a normal adjunct to railway-making. Such settlements were superfluous in places where lodgings could be had with local households, for whom the navvies and artisans were a welcome source of extra income. This certainly applied to urban work, where the concentration of skilled labour on making tunnels, bridges and viaducts was often higher than in open country.

Census returns also demonstrate that many lines were built not by Coleman's sturdy itinerants, but by local labourers, especially in economically stagnant areas where employment was scarce. In south-west England, as many as four navvies in ten were working within ten miles of their birthplace. Youth was no barrier: in an age when unschooled boys were put to work in the fields, there was nothing to stop them trying their hand at the local railway diggings either. Sonning cutting is among the earthworks that were built partly by child labour. The age-old link to the land reasserted its pull in harvest time, when agricultural wages rose high enough to draw the labourers back to the fields. And once the lines were finished, the need for heavy labour did not go away. Many of the local men who had toiled in the gangs that built the railways must have been glad to find settled employment along the new-laid tracks, rather than tramping off to lands unknown in search of fresh navvying. Even the concept of the navvies as a rolling crime-wave has been challenged, if only to point out that their offences were rarely serious enough to land them in the dock at the assize or quarter-session courts, rather than before the magistrate.

Yet the navvy should not be over-domesticated. Regardless of whether anything untoward actually happened, settled populations lived in dread of an outrage of some kind. In some parts of Britain any work on the Sabbath remained taboo. Magistrates at several points along the

Great Western route pounced on some of the offenders and protested to the contractors and committees at the top of the hierarchy. These struggles prefigured the arguments over Sunday trains; it may seem obvious now that the Sabbatarian party were bound to lose, but it would not have felt like that at the time. And there was always the hazard of bad behaviour of the kind that could not be punished in law. Arthur Waugh, father of the novelist Evelyn, recalled in his autobiography a childhood encounter while out walking with his nurse at Chilcompton in Somerset in the 1870s. Here they came upon the works of the Somerset & Dorset Railway's Mendip extension, where 'rough, loud-voiced men' shouted unspecified words at them. Nurse fled, blushing, with her pram. A gang of regular platelayers would not have done this: they knew the risks of being reported and disciplined. The navvies did not care.

₪

The collision of cultures when squire met surveyor or nurse met navvy was real enough. Yet the country before the railways came should not be thought of as a changeless, immemorial place. More than that of many societies, agriculture in Britain was in a state of vigorous evolution long before railways arrived. In some regions the surveyors first came knocking even before the parliamentary enclosure movement had finished parcelling out shared fields and common lands among individual owners. At Cholsey in Berkshire, for example, the Great Western route ran across a common parish field comprising over fifty separately owned strips of land, which entangled the company in some unusually intractable compensation meetings. Enclosure encouraged more highly capitalised forms of farming, and railways in their turn widened the markets for what was produced. The nation's two chief agricultural trades, grain and cattle, were both changed profoundly as a result.

The inland carriage of grain over long distances had been encouraged by the canal network, but the railways helped to foster even stronger regional concentrations of cereal farming, and its dependent industry of malting for the brewers' and distillers' trades. Especially on the eastern side of the country, large warehouses and maltings were constructed alongside many stations. Made redundant by changes in brewing techniques, a good number of the maltings along the commuter routes in Essex and Hertfordshire have been converted to dwellings. Where the housing market is weaker, the abandoned maltings may simply stand derelict, like the astonishing red-brick citadel of the former Bass site at Sleaford in Lincolnshire: an apparition of pigeon-haunted decay six storeys high, stretching block after block for over 1,000ft along the rails.

Distilleries of the railway era have lasted better. Although many of the smaller sites in the Highlands have never had a direct railway connection, those distilleries that were newly established after railways penetrated the region gravitated towards the new routes. Six of the seven Victorian distilleries at Dufftown in Banffshire, the quintessential whisky town, were founded after the little settlement was reached by the Great North of Scotland Railway in 1862. The single malts of Glenfiddich and Balvenie are, in this sense, drinks of the railway age – as is the familiar blended whisky in which Highland malts are combined with cheaper, neutral-tasting Lowland spirits distilled from unmalted grain.

As for the cattle trade, the most immediate change concerned the extinction of the ancient drove routes. These lost their livestock almost instantly when a competing railway opened. Farmers and dealers did not need to be told that a lean and hungry animal that had been walking the dusty roads for days would fetch less at market than a plump one that had made the same journey by train. Jack Simmons cites the case of the Bird-in-Hand inn at Tasburgh in Norfolk, which put up 9,300 beasts in 1845. The following year, there were just twelve. Railways also allowed greater freedom in choosing when to send livestock to market, as prices rose or fell. Besides the sale of beasts for slaughter, there was also a large traffic from upland farms to lowland pasture, where the animals were fattened ready for sale. A cattle dock thus became a common feature at stations. As late as 1962, just before British Railways cut the number of livestock facilities by nine-tenths at a single stroke, the total stood at 2,493, as against circa 4,300 stations open to human passengers. Cattle wagons, and some horse boxes too, were routinely included in market-day trains on certain lines, for the convenience of those who had made purchases in the auction ring.

London, naturally, was the greatest devourer. Sir Francis Head described the 'polished horns, bright eyes, streams of white breath, and healthy black wet noses projecting above the upper rail of their respective wagons' at the Camden Town depot of the London & North Western in 1850. These beasts could well have been of Scottish origin. Dickens, less prone to put a gloss on things, observed the 'dull oxen in their cages, with heads depressed and foam hanging from their mouths', in a night-time vigil at the same railway company's Carlisle station in 1857. There was always plenty of four-legged traffic on the LNWR, which carried much of Ireland's exports of cattle and pigs in addition to its tonnage of Scotch beef on the hoof. Infamously, much of this Irish trade continued during the famine of 1845–9; it is possible that some of Head's bright-eyed cattle at Camden Town had begun their lives amid the stricken peasant cabins of Munster or Connaught. The same railway even used its cattle wagons now and again for the ultra-cheap conveyance of migrant agricultural labour, notably Irish workers – some of them refugees from hunger or eviction – travelling south from Liverpool. The Irish cattle traffic through Holyhead had a long innings: it was the last of its kind on Britain's railways, lingering until 1975.

The rapid migration of existing traffic on to the rails was followed by long-term changes, repeated on other continents, as the railways encouraged livestock farming by giving access to more assured markets. Stimulated by easier transhipment, the number of beef cattle raised in Ireland may have doubled between 1841 and 1851. Cattle-rearing in Wales also increased, as corn-growing declined. This brought a corresponding reduction in farm labour (73,300 workers in 1851, 44,900 in 1871). In this sense, the railways of Wales were agents of rural depopulation.

Dairying depended on the network too. Thanks to its canal connections, Manchester had already developed a modest market for milk, which travelled much less well than butter or cheese. Railways began to augment this flow in 1844. Within two years, between 100 and 150 milk cans of all shapes and sizes were arriving each day, and the average Mancunian was consuming up to an estimated 1.4 pints weekly. By 1869 most of Manchester's supply came by rail. The London story was similar. Here the habit of taking fresh milk was already current, fostered by the practice of keeping dairy cows in odd urban corners. In the absence of pasture, they were fed largely on spent grain supplied by the breweries. The railway trade was stimulated after 1865–6, when most of London's cows perished in the aftermath of a rinderpest epidemic, and took off in earnest in the 1870s. Essex and Suffolk contributed first, then Berkshire, Wiltshire, Dorset, Somerset and counties as far north as Derbyshire joined in. The long-lasting trade name Express Dairies originated in the period, making explicit the railway connection.

Milk trains usually ran through the night to be ready for delivery in the morning, to reduce risk of souring. Standard designs were adopted for the churns, including the once-familiar tall tapering shape (easier to roll along on the edge of the base), with a capacity of ten or seventeen gallons. The 'tall cans' feature in Thomas Hardy's *Tess of the d'Urbervilles* (1892); when Tess Durbeyfield and Angel Clare embark on their fateful drive across the dark Wessex moor together, it is to take a wagonload of churns to the station on behalf of Dairyman Crick, bound for the London market. In the 1920s bulk transportation in glass-lined tank wagons began, despatched from creameries to which the neighbouring farms now consigned their yields for pasteurisation. The last of these trains ran in 1980, by which time only south-west Wales, Devon and Cornwall were still sending milk to London by rail.

Railways also helped to break open the national market for foreign imports. One crucial development was refrigeration, which allowed frozen meat from the New World, Australia and New Zealand to be brought to the British market in the 1870s. The new technology was installed in shipping and in the national network of cold stores that were built to receive the frozen cargoes, but the market for their contents would have been limited had the railways not been ready to carry it briskly onwards in special insulated or refrigerated vans. Fresh meat of domestic origin was conveyed too, a practice at first largely limited to the cooler months. Hampers and canvas bags sufficed to protect these early cargoes, which were placed under tarpaulins in open wagons. The traffic was already vigorous enough by the mid 1860s to justify the construction of a huge underground meat depot beneath the new Smithfield Market in the City of London. Hydraulic lifts delivered the cargo from this four-acre underworld to the market buildings above. The depot was served via the Metropolitan Railway, which happened to be under construction through the area at just the right time. The entry to this cavernous space can still be glimpsed by underground travellers, on the south side of the line between Farringdon and Moorgate stations.

The symbiosis between cattle farming and railways did not end after the distribution of meat. The railway photographer Colin Garratt, growing up in Leicestershire during the 1950s, would time his lunchtime sandwich-eating to avoid the 'smelly bone train' which conveyed raw materials from Leicester cattle market to a glue factory near Market Harborough. Organic waste of other kinds was valuable as well. Manure, animal or human ('night soil'), could be enhanced in value by means of a railway journey. There was a lot of this to go round. Each working horse produced three or four tons of droppings a year, which when made up with straw litter provided twelve tons of good manure. Some of London's night soil found its way up the Great Northern's line through Bedfordshire, where market gardeners at places such as Biggleswade and Sandy used it on their vegetable fields. Trains then took this produce back for sale to the London market. This exchange of muck for food was centuries old; the innovation lay in the distances that could now be covered.

Other cities exported their ordure too. Stable manure from Leeds and Hull was gratefully received by the potato farmers of the Derwent Valley near York, carried via an independent light railway that opened in 1913. The railway's enterprising management then entered into a contract for the output of three entire cavalry regiments based at Catterick Camp, top-quality stuff which it sold on to the farmers at a profit. This happy relationship continued until the regiments abandoned horses in favour of armoured cars.

Even the rotted-down leftovers from making shoddy – cheap recycled cloth – found a profitable path across the network, from the mills of Batley in the west of Yorkshire to the hop fields of Surrey and Kent. The hops thus fertilised were in turn distributed to brewers throughout the country, including those of Burton-on-Trent, where the sulphate-rich water allowed the production of clear and strongly flavoured ales with a reputation that extended far beyond the town's hinterland. Burton ale is recorded as on sale in London as early as 1738, but the arrival of the railway a century later transformed the scale of operations. So lucrative was the traffic that the Midland Railway set aside the entire basement of its huge new London terminus at St Pancras, opened in 1868, for barrels from Burton's breweries. This in turn was merely overspill from the 3.6-million-gallon capacity beer warehouse the Midland had already erected nearby. By 1888 Burton's production of beer was more than twice that of the capital, home of Watneys, Youngs, Whitbread, Charrington and all the rest; by 1900 Burton was producing fifty times as much beer as it had been in 1840. Much of its area by that date was given over to breweries large and small, linked by a bewildering tangle of railway lines that ran ungated across the streets.

Baedeker's guide for 1887 notes that brewery tours at Burton could be had for a shilling, but leisure travel at this drab and reeking town was mostly concerned with getting away. The largest brewery was that of Messrs Bass, builders also of the monster maltings at Sleaford. The Bass works outing to Great Yarmouth in 1893 took fifteen trains to carry the 10,000 workers and their families, together with foremen, clerks, customers, estate workers and so on. A repeat of the trip twenty years later required the first train to depart in darkness at 3.45 a.m., the others following at ten-minute intervals over the next two and a quarter hours.

Thus agriculture and industry, town and country, fell into mutually advantageous roles, with the railway as go-between. Artificial, processed and imported fertilisers – guano, bone meal, nitrates, phosphates – joined or superseded the natural kinds that could be collected at the station yard, allowing marginal land to be brought into cultivation. In certain districts, the railways' ability to deliver produce to distant markets increased the agricultural population, against the general trend. The naturally fertile peat and silt soils of the Isle of Ely, increasingly given over to bulk cultivation of fruit and potatoes, are a case in point. Ruskin might bewail the loss of the age-old face-to-face relationship between buyer and seller in the market square, but that was no use to a farmer trying to shift half a ton of strawberries before they turned to mush – nor to the city dweller with a yearning for seasonal varieties from beyond the daily range of a horse and cart. The rising levels of market-garden traffic of this kind encouraged the Great Eastern to build a tramway-type line in the 1880s along the flat canalside route between Wisbech and Upwell, which was operated by odd-looking steam engines encased in boxy wooden housings. This farmgate branch was well known to a local clergyman, the Rev. W. Awdry, who represented one of its locomotives in *Toby the Tram Engine* (1952), the seventh book in his *Thomas the Tank Engine* series – with the curious result that Chinese factories now turn out model versions of the long-lost engines of this railway backwater to keep the world's toyshops stocked.

Many crops and foodstuffs increasingly became identified with specific parts of the kingdom. Plums and apples in Georgian Britain were locally sourced, but the Edwardians would have expected much of the fruit in the marketplace to have grown in Kent or the Vale of Evesham. Broccoli came from Cornwall, narcissi from the Scilly Isles, rhubarb from Yorkshire. These were true commercial crops: the best in terms of financial return that the soil, climate and logistics of transport allowed the farmer to produce. Even the omnipresent wild rabbit became a dish with a regional bias, thanks to the traffic extracted by the Great Western from Devon and Cornwall. The main artery of supply was the line through the heart of north Devon, between Taunton and Barnstaple. On this bucolic route the nightly 'rabbit special' might convey 400 hampers or twenty tons, comprising up to 15,000 individuals.

Flows of imports established themselves too, and not just of frozen meat: the British taste for Danish bacon and butter began in the railway era, and before 1914 there was a now-forgotten trade in German and Russian eggs via London and the east coast ports. The Empire contributed bananas, especially after Fyffes' rail-served ripening warehouses were established in 1901–2. The banana thereby became the first fruit to join the apple as part of the normal diet of the urban poor. Special trains of heatable vans met each banana boat at the docks, a traffic that lasted into the early 1960s. By that time there were 3,500 such vans, of which some 500 might be required to carry away each fresh boatload from the banana ports of Avonmouth, Barry or Southampton.

Other docks contributed fish, which could now be supplied fresh to inland markets, rather than dried, salted or pickled. Again, railway economies of scale encouraged specialisation: fishing villages might carry on as before, but the heavy traffic came through a few busy ports. Grimsby, a historic town of modest size on the Lincolnshire coast, received shock therapy at the hands of the Manchester, Sheffield & Lincolnshire Railway; its investments there included a six-acre fish dock opened in 1856, complete with a railway-owned fleet of steam trawlers. By 1900 Grimsby was handling a quarter of the rail-borne fish in England and Wales. A good deal of the rest was carried away by the Lancashire & Yorkshire Railway from Fleetwood on the Lancashire coast, giving fresh purpose to a port that was originally established as a passenger interchange between rail and sea. The sale of fried fish and chips is thought to have originated in the industrial Pennines of Lancashire around 1863. As part of the working-class culture in such inland areas, the dish was dependent on the railways, which reduced the price of fresh cod by two-thirds as soon as they began carrying it in the 1840s.

For those who could afford it, the national diet became more varied, but also more processed and more standardised. Modern laments at the loss of the regional traditions of British cuisine tend to overlook the extent to which these had already broken down as urbanisation and industry took hold. Custard powder, shredded suet, jellies, margarine, beef extract, bottled sauces, biscuits, jam, chocolate – all these processed foodstuffs served to diversify a diet that, for the poorest, had shrunk by early-Victorian times to little more than potatoes, bread, sugar and tea, with oats as a staple in Scotland and Ireland. Biscuits were one commodity that came from nowhere to become an everyday indulgence, piggybacking on the national habit of tea-drinking. The greatest producers were Huntley & Palmer, whose enormous factory burgeoned alongside the Great Western's main line on the London side of Reading, just downwind of Oscar Wilde's prison. Adopting factory methods in the 1840s, the firm became the world's largest biscuit maker within thirty years. The railway delivered ingredients and fuel, and carried away its products in their standard 7lb or 10lb tins. For mustard, the market leaders were Colmans of Norwich, who opened a new works at Carrow in the city in 1856, in order to be better connected to the railway. Its bulls-head emblem, still in use, dates from around the same time. Before the biblical dead lion humming with bees was adopted, early tins of Lyle's golden syrup, first marketed in 1885, illustrated its Thameside refinery instead, with the railway connection clearly indicated.

To describe these businesses is not to demonstrate that they would have been unviable in the absence of railways. However, without active use of a railway connection to despatch goods as well as to receive them, it would have been extremely hard for any one company to establish its brands in the national consumer market. Brewing illustrates the point. At the top of the tree was the Bass mega-brewery, with its red-triangle trademark. Much further down were some 150 local brewers who had managed to connect to the railway for their coal, malt and other supplies, but which generated no outward traffic in return. What they produced went out as it had always done – by horse and cart.

RAILWAYS AND THE LAND II

Horses have featured a good deal so far in these pages. This might have surprised some early railway promoters, who argued that the tireless power of steam would cause the demand for equine muscle to dwindle. In 1834 it was even claimed that a million horses would shortly be heading for the knacker's yard. What happened instead was that the making of railways and the keeping of horses flourished interdependently.

This story was outlined by the historian F. M. L. Thompson in 1976 in a celebrated article called 'Nineteenth-century horse sense'. Thompson stressed the ways in which railways promoted all-round mobility, of people and goods alike, and the degree to which this movement still depended on iron-shod hooves. The commercial use of horses actually increased more than fourfold over the period, much faster than the human population. One instance was the explosion in demand for London cabs: around 1,265 just before the first railway opened in the capital, some 11,000 by 1888. Each cab in turn required two horses to stay fully operational. A great deal of their traffic must have come from taking railway fares, including trips to and from the stations of the expanding suburbs.

Then there were the equine establishments of the railways themselves. Heavy draught horses were employed for shunting and marshalling wagons, in places where locomotives would have been too costly, noisy, dirty or dangerous to use. At Newmarket, where steam-powered shunting was prone to cause unacceptable restiveness to the precious thoroughbreds coming to the racecourse, the animals were pulled up and down the sidings in horseboxes by their shire-horse cousins. (This practice lingered until 1967, by which time Newmarket's horses were the last of their kind: mascots of obsolescence, who featured as curiosities in cinema newsreels.) An even larger complement was needed for the collection and delivery of goods. Railway-owned carts carrying general consignments were ubiquitous in cities. Horses pulled the coal merchant's cart that delivered the fuel that was burnt in most inhabited buildings in Britain. Nor did private horse carriers disappear. Thomas Hardy's 'Tranter [carter] Reuben' in *Under the Greenwood Tree* (1872) was no rural fossil: he had the chance of a good working life ahead of him, provided that he could adapt his rounds to the railway timetable. Altogether, it was a fair bet that any rail-borne inland cargo had also been hauled behind a horse at some stage in its passage between producer and consumer, at least until motor vehicles came along.

By 1893 the number of railway-owned horses in Great Britain was calculated at 27,826. Stabling on a prodigious scale was required to accommodate all this horseflesh, like the Mint Stables developed by the Great Western near Paddington station between 1876 and 1911. In its final form this accommodated 665 horses on four storeys, the animals making their way up and down by ramps as in a multistorey car park. Suitably adapted, the building is now part of the adjacent St Mary's Hospital. When the Great Western centralised its resources of fodder in a single depot the outcome was a huge brick edifice, tall as a Lancashire cotton mill, that towered over the sidings at Didcot until the 1970s.

Meanwhile the practice of keeping a horse for personal use became more widespread than ever. The numbers maintained by gentlefolk more than doubled between 1851 and 1901. The overlapping demands of locomotion (a word older than the railways, which effectively pinched it), of exercise and of prestige – all these kept domestic stables occupied in town and country. Riding was considered healthy, and for young men also a distraction from the temptations of vice. The greatest social cachet belonged to racing and fox hunting, both of which did magnificently in the nineteenth century. How racecourses and railways achieved symbiosis has already been described. Fox hunting earns a place here because of the unique way it brought into focus the relationships between railways, the land and those who owned the land.

The hold of fox hunting on the world of the nineteenth-century landed classes is difficult to exaggerate. In consequence the impact of railways on hunting, real and anticipated, is unusually well recorded. At first devotees of the hunt expected nothing but disaster. The railway brought legally enforced violation of ancestral ownership, as England's broad acres were carved up by impassable barriers at the behest of cliques of speculative investors. Worse, these linear tracts of prohibited land were traversed by fast, lethal, horse-frightening machines. The earliest documented response from the hunting side came from 'Nimrod' (Charles James Apperley, 1777–1843), a journalist with the *Sporting Magazine*. In County Durham in 1827, he had encountered 'something, which I could only compare to a *moving hell*' – a pioneer steam locomotive on the Stockton & Darlington – which had unnerved his horse so much that he had to dismount. To the diehard Tory F. P. Delmé Radcliffe (1804–75), Master of the Hertfordshire Hunt Club in 1839, the new technology was 'a monster, which will rend the vitals of those by whom it has been fostered ... the most oppressive monopoly ever inflicted on a free country'. What Radcliffe meant was that anything which tended to weaken the bonds between landowners and their estates was a gift to the forces of subversion. Gloom overtook R. S. Surtees, too: 'in a few years hunting will be a matter of history', he wrote in 1834. Even the coming of cheap rail-borne coal caused him to fret that brushwood would no longer be cut for fuel, so that fox coverts would become tangled and overgrown.

Yet the sport proved much more adaptable than was feared, and not in spite of the railways, but in partnership with them. As with racing, the crucial point was that train travel allowed horses to arrive at the meet fresh and untired. The same was true of the hounds. The railways did not fence the hunts in, so much as set them free. For a growing number of Victorians, hunting the fox now became something that was done at the end of a railway journey.

The first hunt to use railways in this way was the Holderness, in Lincolnshire in 1846. Surtees soon perked up, noting with approval how the railways could also convey orchestras and splendid cakes to enhance hunt balls. Hounds perished beneath locomotive wheels every now and again, it is true. In 1862 this happened at least twice, including the loss of some of Lord Galway's pack to one of the Great Northern's Parliamentary trains, at East Markham in Nottinghamshire. (On the forelock-tugging Great Western, the inside cover of every working timetable even had a notice enjoining employees to watch for 'PACKS OF HOUNDS' in the season.) But such mishaps were a small price to pay.

It was also clear to some landowners from the outset that the broader rewards to be had from the railways – inflated compensation payments for loss of land and amenities, enhanced prices for agricultural produce, the prospect of exploiting coal or mineral deposits – could enhance their preferred way of life. Sometimes these railway-derived premiums went directly to the sport: the landowner and spendthrift George Lane-Fox MP (1793–1848), Master of the Bramham Moor Hunt in Yorkshire, kept afloat partly by selling slices of his land to fourteen different railway companies across England and Ireland. Opposition to new railways from the hunting fraternity gradually dwindled to site-specific skirmishes concerning the choice of route. One well-known case pitted the 5th Earl Fitzwilliam against the Great Northern Railway: the Earl got his surveyor to plot a revised route for its line near Peterborough, where it crossed his estate at Milton Park, 'to prevent the separation of some woods which in a hunting point of view are inseparable'. The aristocracy likewise woke up to the considerable rewards to be had from company chairmanships and directorships, which also allowed them to steer the railways' development to their own advantage. So the same Earl Fitzwilliam who had squared up to the Great Northern in Huntingdonshire duly became chairman of the South Yorkshire Railway. His son and heir later had a private station built on one of its goods lines to allow private parties from the Fitzwilliam estate at Wentworth Woodhouse to travel to Doncaster for the St Leger race meeting.

A parallel change saw the rise of the subscription pack, which released hunts from dependence on the largesse of a single master. Hunts increasingly resembled members' clubs, whose meets were something like paying attractions. Jorrocks, the canny London grocer of Surtees's fictions, takes advantage of the opening of each new line to hunt over fresh country, while carrying on his everyday business: 'hunting one day and selling teas another'. There is much about Jorrocks that is to be taken satirically, but it was certainly true that railway travel allowed wealthy or socially ambitious Londoners to ride with ease alongside the county elites. By the standards of shooting game, a sport that was tightly controlled and dependent on land ownership or invitation for entry, the gates of the hunting field stood wide open. Women began riding to hounds as well, in growing numbers. Hunting became less like mountaineering, the province of the tough and the devil-may-care, and more like skiing, where true devotees mingled with those who had come for the sake of the company, the fashion and the chance of moderate exercise.

For the metropolitan huntsman, a new way of life began. Saved from miles of hacking across country, or from the need to send horses ahead overnight, he and his mount could now hunt in Leicestershire or the New Forest by early morning train and horsebox, and still be back for dinner. Huntsmen were noted at Euston by Samuel Sidney in 1851, waiting for Buckinghamshire trains 'with their pinks just peeping from under their rough jackets'. By the 1860s this tribe of itinerant, non-attached huntsman was numerous. Anthony Trollope was one of them. The sporting press began to include articles on hunting-tourism, with advice on where to go and what to expect. A Londoner could hunt six days a week in season, meets being arranged on different days in different counties; Birmingham and Leeds men could pick and choose too. The journals of the hunting obsessive William Chafy record over 2,822 hunting days, most of which were rail-borne and ended back home in time for tea (thus saving the cost of a night at the inn). Attachments to particular hunts were encouraged by special season tickets, available by the 1850s, which offered repeated journeys at a reduced rate. Rich huntsmen for whom time was at a premium learned to exploit the railways too. Henry Chaplin, a junior minister (in office 1864–71) and master of fox hounds, was known to charter a train to draw up at a point on the track where his stud groom and mount awaited.

Such was the rush to hunt that the number of packs rose markedly, from 99 in 1850 to 137 in 1877. As with racing, some of this growth was sponsored directly by the railway companies: the London, Brighton & South Coast subscribed £25 to the South Downs Hunt in the 1850s. In heavily hunted areas, foxes became scarce; many hunts now tried not to kill their quarry at all. A Devon huntsman claimed that one of his foxes, 'the Bold Dragoon', had been caught and reprieved by a well-trained pack no fewer than thirty-six times. The shortage became so acute that live foxes had to be brought in from Scotland or the Continent. Huntsman, hounds, mount and prey must sometimes have been carried to the meet on the same train.

₪

To understand the railways' impact on the landscape – the subject of huntsmen's early misgivings, and those of the Northamptonshire gentry of 1830 – it is worth considering how their surveyors and engineers approached virgin terrain. Bogs and marshes excepted, it was easy to push

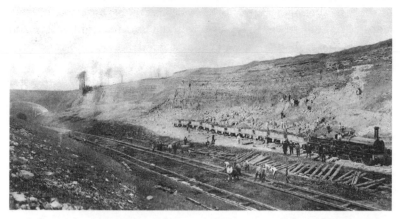

The Great Western Railway's cutting at Harbury, Warwickshire, in the course
of widening in 1884 to reduce the occurrence of landslips. Here the navvies'
task is eased by the use of a locomotive to remove the wagons of spoil

a railway across level ground, nor was a great deal of land needed to do
it. The straighter and more level the line, the simpler it was to operate
too. But much of Britain is gently rolling, hilly, or even mountainous. The
surveyor or engineer confronting such a district had to strike a balance
between the ideally straight and level route – physically achievable perhaps, but prohibitively expensive – and the practicable alternatives, as well
as watching for pitfalls arising from ownership and compensation.

In the first instance, trains are not good at climbing hills. Gradients
along the line were therefore softened by means of cuttings. To even out
the slopes better, spoil taken from the cuttings was transported along the
route and tipped into the depressions, creating embankments. As long as
the subtracted mass did not greatly exceed the deposits required, the engineer would be spared the extra cost of 'putting to spoil' thousands of tons
of surplus rock and soil, which usually had to be done by dumping it in
rampart-like ridges along the cutting edges. The angle of the embankment
sides might also be varied, sometimes going beyond the minimum cut in
order to generate enough spoil to build up the embankments safely. Any
shortfall could be made good by 'side cutting', excavating some blameless
piece of land within range of the route (the Great Western once bought a
whole hill just for this purpose).

This basic equation explains why any longish railway journey is normally neither all cutting, nor all embankment. When a new route is made purely by subtraction, as in the case of underground railways, special measures are required. The English share of spoil from the Channel Tunnel was mostly dumped at the foot of the White Cliffs of Dover, to form a seventy-acre public facility called Samphire Hoe Country Park. The Crossrail route below London, lacking a nearby sea coast, has sent much of its spoil by train and ship to a blank expanse of farmland on the edge of the Essex marshes. In a reversal of the usual Victorian transformation of marginal land into productive use, this is being remodelled into what is described as the largest man-made nature reserve in Europe.

Engineers and surveyors were expected to master the complicated geometrical calculations required to quantify these huge volumes before breaking ground. To make the task easier in the age before electronic calculation, published tables were available. Some of these were compiled by George Parker Bidder (1806–78), a gifted engineer who was also a mathematical prodigy. Bidder's life is another illustration of how the railway industry repeatedly drew out the best from men of talent. The son of a Devon stonemason, he showed enough precocious mathematical skill to be taken on tour by his father as a fairground attraction, the 'Calculating Boy'. In his ninth year the infant was introduced to royalty. To answer Queen Charlotte's request for the square root of 36,372,961 took him eighty seconds.* The astronomer-mathematician Sir John Herschel arranged for the boy to be properly schooled, whereupon Bidder Snr tried unsuccessfully to remove his son to get him back on the touring circuit. Bidder's education continued in the 1820s at Edinburgh University, where he befriended a fellow student named Robert Stephenson. When Stephenson's career as a railway engineer took off, he engaged the assistance of his old friend, beginning with the London & Birmingham Railway project in the 1830s. Bidder proved to be a gifted engineer in his own right: he is credited with designing the first balanced swing bridge, built in 1844 for the Norwich & Brandon Railway. The early skills of the Calculating Boy were not neglected: Bidder had a sideline as an expert witness to Parliament's committees on railway bills, when he was able to trounce rival schemes by exposing and mercilessly quantifying flaws in their engineering data.

Decisions also had to be made concerning the profiles of the cuttings.

---

* It is 6,031.

The steeper the sides, the less spoil had to be removed and the narrower the strip of land that had to be bought in the first place. But if the slopes were made too steep, the risk of landslips increased in proportion. Had Brunel sloped the sides of his Sonning cutting more gently, the fatal accident of 1841 might never have occurred. Brunel was certainly attentive to the challenge of how to give a stable finish to cuttings and embankments, and his notebooks include details of grass species most suited for consolidating earthworks comprised of various soils. The usual method was to set aside the topsoil from when the ground was first broken, so that it could be spread over the finished man-made terrain. As well as grass seed, clover was a common choice for sowing after the job was done, or the original turf was simply kept and re-laid. But the crucial threat came not from superficial slippages in the topsoil, but from more deep-seated collapses.

It was therefore important to understand the nature of the earth and of the underlying geology. Often the true state of affairs below ground emerged only after work began. Seams of clay, shale or sand were all potential weak points. F. S. Williams cited a cutting in northern England, predicted to require the extraction of 50,000 cubic yards, which proved to contain soft earth sitting on a seam of shale. Once the seam was cut the earth slipped and slipped, until the total extraction reached ten times the estimate. Nor did the deposits required to make an embankment always behave as expected. Another engineer's nightmare described by Williams concerned the 100ft-high Intake embankment on the Settle and Carlisle line. Here tipping went on for twelve months before the leading end of the formation could be taken forward at all; the stuff just slipped all over the place. Even after new earthworks had apparently been made secure, it was difficult to predict exactly how these huge gougings and dumpings of loose soil and rock would behave under the action of rain, drought and frost. Fissured clays, of the kind that slipped at Sonning, were especially prone to move without warning.

Chalk was a kinder material. It could be cut both cheaply and steeply and then largely left to itself. At one point where the chalk cliffs of Kent met the sea, at Round Down between Dover and Folkestone, the engineers of the South Eastern Railway simply blew up the unwanted parts, letting the waves take care of the surplus. (As it happens, very near the Samphire Hoe Country Park.) The job was beautifully done. Three shafts were sunk and filled with 18,500lb of gunpowder. The simultaneous detonations were overseen by an officer of the Royal Engineers and watched by crowds who came by excursion train. *The Times* described how the cliff sank with 'a low, faint, indistinct indescribable moaning rumble'. However, the open texture of chalk made it water-absorbent and thus prone to frost damage. In hard frosts, Merstham cutting in Surrey had to be watched night and day in case any great masses of North Downs chalk tumbled on to the tracks.

Drainage was another aspect of the engineer's duties. It was essential that a cutting did not simply fill up with water. The usual safeguard was to make the line on a sufficient slope to allow rainwater and groundwater to run away. On the other hand, the gradients should not be too steep. The steepest part of any line, known as the ruling gradient, determines the minimum power required to operate its trains. The degree to which the engineers succeeded in reducing these ruling gradients can be judged by listening for changes in pitch in the engines or traction motors of a moving train. Keeping an eye on the train speed, and on the rise and fall of the embankment sides as they pass the window, is also instructive. Often the deepest point in the cutting will coincide with a summit in the gradient, where the line crosses a ridge or a watershed, at which point the noise of hard mechanical work will fall off as the train begins coasting on the downward slope. Steam-age travel made these transitions much more noisily explicit.

The conjunction of two gradients at a summit also allowed the water to drain from both ends of the cutting. That was not the end of the matter. As the gentlemen of Northamptonshire had understood in 1830, all this cutting and embanking was immensely disruptive to the established hydrology. The railways therefore had to make arrangements to carry water away from the lines and into existing watercourses, as well as building in their own drainage systems to protect the track itself. To keep the permanent way dry required more than the usual drainage ditch along each side: catchwater ditches might be needed along the tops of the cuttings, and extra drains too within the embankment slopes (commonly composed of rubble-filled diagonal trenches). Embankments demanded drainage ditches at the foot, and plentiful culverts running through the bank itself – or they might act like dams after heavy rain, trapping sheets of water on the higher side. These basic geophysical challenges were no less central to the successful running of the railways than the fast-changing technologies of steam, steel and telegraphy.

On coastal routes, railway embankments also established hard lines between dry land and the tidal zone, often reclaiming a large acreage from the sea. The results can be seen especially well on Ruskin's regular section of the Furness line between Ulverston and Cark and again where the River Kent flows into Morecambe Bay, and on the Cambrian Railways' line along Cardigan Bay, the second of the three greatest seaside routes on the British network (the old South Devon Railway, the site of Brunel's atmospheric debacle, is the third). But the most spectacular instance of the phenomenon in the British Isles is in Ireland, where the embankment of the Londonderry & Coleraine Railway was routed through the silts of Lough Foyle in the 1850s so as to reclaim 22,000 acres from the tide. Over half of this Ulster polder was then enclosed and sold.

₪

A deep cutting is often a sign that the train will shortly enter a tunnel. A depth of some sixty feet was the average point at which it became cheaper to take a railway through the earth, rather than removing the overburden altogether. There were exceptions to the sixty-foot rule. The line to the coast of central Wales crossed the watershed dividing the rivers Severn and Dovey by means of a mighty cutting at Talerddig, 120ft deep, which opened to traffic in 1863. Trains from the coast had to climb for fourteen miles, subject to a ruling gradient of 1 in 52, to reach the precipitous manmade cliffs of gritstone at the summit of this excavation, itself fully three miles long. This remained for some years the deepest railway cutting in the world. Here the decision to make a cutting rather than a tunnel was taken partly because of the need for good building stone for structures elsewhere on the line. This use of cuttings as quarries was common practice, so that the viaducts and stations along many lines seem to belong as profoundly to the land around them as the farms, cottages and boundary walls that are native to the country.

Elsewhere, deep cuttings have sometimes been formed by abolishing existing tunnels, so that a big slice of land above and on each side of the line has been swallowed up by the railway after all. Chevet Tunnel on the old North Midland Railway route to Leeds, one of the nastiest postings recalled by the tunnel inspector W. T. Thornewell (met in Chapter 9), was done away with in the 1920s, in order to widen the line. The resulting excavation, though unequal to Talerddig, is still among the network's deepest, at nearly 100ft.

Perhaps the most drastic of these operations concerned the Lime Street Tunnel in Liverpool, made in 1836 by the Liverpool & Manchester Railway to serve its new terminus in the heart of the city. In 1881 all but a short section of its total length – more than a mile in all – was opened up to the sky by means of sheer-sided cuttings through the solid rock, without closing the line to traffic during the operation. Locomotives could now work more easily along what had originally been a cable-hauled route, at the cost of rending the city's fabric through by a mysterious smoky chasm, bridged at intervals by a dozen pre-existing streets. These cuttings truly are sheer-sided, of tarnished red sandstone adorned with little acid-resistant ferns, and stitched here and there with masonry reinforcement courses that slope up or down according to the bedding planes of the rock. A similar composite of red sandstone and coursed brick infill – the natural patched and mended with the man-made – appears at Chester, where Robert Stephenson shaved away some of the Castle rock to accommodate his line to Holyhead.

All this cutting, blasting and tunnelling of the bedrock had profound consequences for geological knowledge, especially for stratigraphy, the study of sedimentary rocks. In the peak years for railway building geological science was still essentially the preserve of amateurs, and it took time for any central agency for collecting or co-ordinating discoveries to be put in place. The first geological map had been produced in 1815 by the self-taught William Smith (1770–1839), drawing on his observations as a canal surveyor, but the scale and extent of railway excavations exceeded anything undertaken on inland waterways many times over. The first grant to support geological research at railway workings was made by the British Association in 1840, and the decades that followed were busy. Some new routes opened up entire regional geologies: the Caledonian main line through the Scottish lowlands chopped its way into formations that could previously be glimpsed only from scattered local exposures at small quarries and burns.

A few engineers took an enlightened interest themselves. When a petrified forest from the coal measures was exposed by the Manchester & Bolton Railway in the 1840s, the line's engineer John Hawkshaw had a shed built over them and casts and models made. The Geological Society's *Proceedings* for the decade include multiple reports from F. W. Simms, the resident engineer directing the South Eastern Railway's progress through Kent. On occasion Simms took his excavations beyond what was strictly necessary, purely in order to clarify a stratigraphic problem. In 1853 geology even acquired a railway martyr, when the distinguished amateur Hugh Strickland was hit by a train near Retford in Nottinghamshire. On his way back from a meeting of the British Association, Strickland had stopped off to examine the rocky cuttings near the mouth of Clarborough Tunnel. Notebook in hand, he stepped away from the rails to avoid a coal train. An express on the other line then burst from the tunnel, killing him.

Fossil-dealers hung around some railway workings, hopeful of finding saleable specimens, but the big money was in minerals. George and Robert Stephenson made a fine profit from the coal of Snibston Colliery, which they established in 1831 in connection with their work for the Leicester & Swannington Railway. George repeated the venture at Clay Cross in Derbyshire in the 1840s, here with a new ironworks and limeworks for good measure. Fresh ironstone beds of workable quality were exposed in 1857 by the Midland Railway's line from Leicester to Hitchin. Going much deeper, coal deposits were identified in East Kent in 1882, in borings made for the first serious attempt to construct a Channel Tunnel. The tunnel was abandoned unfinished, but the Kent coalfield was mined until 1989.

Where a steep cutting was desirable but the terrain was too unstable to allow it, the tracks were commonly sunk between retaining walls. That applied especially in towns, where land was expensive. When brick was used for these walls, it was often the bluish-purple Staffordshire type, made of dense clays from the coal measures that can be slow-fired at high temperatures to obtain a very hard, water-resistant finish. The railways took avidly to these, and imperishable surfaces of 'Staffordshire blues' still line the approaches to many stations up and down the country, often laid to form blind arched panels for extra strength. There is a characteristic sequence on the long and dispiriting approach to Leicester station from the south, and an even grander sequence in the enormously broad trench by which the railway finds its way out of London from Euston. At Euston, as at the reconstructed Birmingham New Street, these blue brick walls are the last tangible link with the Victorian railway builders.

The contribution made by the various types of nineteenth-century brick and masonry finishes to the visual experience of British railway travel can be appreciated by taking a journey on the Channel Tunnel Rail Link. Here the carriage-window view is repeatedly of surfaces of concrete, especially the finely textured, fair-faced concrete of modern civil engineering, in whose smooth grey surfaces no weed or shrub can find lodging. The same finishes continue through the tunnel and on through the Continental high-speed rail network. It is impressive, if rather boring. On older lines, new technology manifests itself in the form of geosynthetics: ugly black long-life membranes and netting pinned down by steel fixtures, guarding the permanent way against collapses from the cutting sides.

By directing the route to avoid the steeper slopes, a railway company could reduce its outlay on earthworks and tunnels, but at the cost of other drawbacks in the longer term. For one thing, the finished line would be slower to operate (because curves cannot be taken at high speeds and because the line itself became longer), without necessarily being cheaper to maintain, at least to a high standard. An extreme instance is the slow horseshoe curve that takes the West Highland Railway in a loop around Ben Odhar, Ben a Chaistel and Ben Doran, thus avoiding the need for a monster viaduct. The curve is a highlight for those travelling the line for its scenic pleasures, but for Highlanders heading for the shops of Helensburgh or Glasgow it is also a cause of much cumulative delay. A different approach is represented by Brunel's Cornish lines, with their abundant use of viaducts for valley crossings. These may look extravagant, but they came about because the selection of inexpensive routes had kept cuttings to a minimum, which left too little spoil to build grand embankments instead.

It is often possible to distinguish the different approaches to railway building on the sheet of an Ordnance Survey Landranger map. Many lines appear relatively straight, with an irregular border along much of their length composed of the little triangular marks that indicate a cutting (triangles pointing inward) or an embankment (triangles pointing outward). There is a good chance that a line of this type will belong to one of the routes built before the 1860s, when companies were highly capitalised and locomotives less equal to climbing steep gradients. On the London & Birmingham, for example, the curves were rarely of less than a mile in radius. For later branch lines and secondary routes, constructed more cheaply and without fast travel in mind, a gently meandering course was considered acceptable. Now that many such lines have closed, their presence on the modern-day map dwindles with each new edition, having left relatively little in terms of great markings on the earth's surface. In agrarian regions especially, much land has been taken quietly back by the agricultural communities which the railways once served, and which forsook them in the twentieth century in favour of transport by road.

₪

When a deep valley intervened between higher ground, as in hilly Cornwall, there was often no alternative but to throw a multiple-arched viaduct across the gap. There was a precedent in the aqueducts employed by the second wave of canal builders, men such as John Rennie and Thomas Telford, from the 1790s onwards. So when George Stephenson provided viaducts for the Liverpool & Manchester Railway in 1828–30, at Sankey and at Newton-le-Willows, he was merely repeating a form of bridge construction that already existed elsewhere in Britain (the distinction between a bridge and a viaduct, it should be said, is inexact).

The Sankey Viaduct – of nine arches and rising to 60ft – was grand enough to gobble up almost half of Stephenson's budget for bridges along the line. Even so, it was a midget by comparison with the great viaducts that began taking shape in the 1840s. At Welwyn in Hertfordshire, at Balcombe in Sussex, at Stockport, the new trunk lines soared across on multiple-arched structures that would have stupefied any emperor of the Romans. Welwyn has forty arches each up to 98ft high; Balcombe comprises slightly fewer arches and is slightly less lofty, but has extra gracenotes in the form of a cornice, balustrade and little pavilions at each end; Stockport has twenty-two main arches only, but each spans fully 63ft and the overall height is 111ft. Viaducts of this type – round-arched, with uniform right-angled spans, built of brick or stone – continued to appear until the end of the century and few have had to be replaced. The passenger of today looks out over a different landscape, but shares with his counterpart of 1850 or 1900 the experience of lofty isolation as the ground suddenly and marvellously drops away from alongside the moving train.

This resilience is all the more amazing when the vastly increased speed, frequency and weight of the trains that cross these structures are taken into account. Railway engineers knew that their viaducts and bridges would have to stand firm against years of vibrations from fast, heavy loads, unlike bridges built to carry roads or canals, and made their calculations on the safe side. That they so consistently got these right is one of the marvels of railway history. It is almost as if the turnpike roads of Telford's day had proved equal to the thundering traffic of the modern motorway system.

Repeated arches of standard width were well suited to valleys and plains comprising mostly solid ground. Other situations required special measures. The best-known of these stone- or brick-built viaducts is the beautiful double-arched bridge of 1837–9 which carries the Great Western Railway across the Thames at Maidenhead. This was another feather in Brunel's cap. The Thames Commissioners insisted on sufficient clearance for sailing barges, and it would not have been difficult to provide for this by means of a slight gradient on either side. But Brunel had his own ideal to defend, of an exceptionally level railway suited to fast and economical running. So he pushed the technology of brick construction as far as he dared, to a ratio of 5.28:1 between the breadth of each elliptical span and the rise of the arch. No builder in brick anywhere in the world has achieved a flatter arch since. Nor are the spans small: each measures 128ft. The audacious design looked suddenly like a dreadful mistake when one of the arches shifted after its temporary wooden centering was taken away. Partly set mortar was blamed and Brunel ordered repairs. Sceptics waited for a fresh disaster, but it never came, and express trains use the bridge to this day. Aptly, too, it is Maidenhead Bridge that Turner portrayed in his canvas 'Rain, Steam and Speed – the Great Western Railway' (1844), one self-fashioned genius paying homage to another.

Even greater spans of brick and stone were possible. The British maximum was reached as early as 1848, again in the form of a bridge that still stands and still carries trains. It is Glasgow, Paisley, Kilmarnock & Ayr Railway's Ballochmyle Viaduct near Mauchline in Ayrshire, which soars over the flowing Water of Ayr in a single stone arch 181ft wide and 175ft high. Its designer was John Miller (1805–83), who served as engineer to most of the principal lines of central Scotland, making enough money along the way to retire early and buy himself two country estates. Yet no one would call Miller famous, nor is his greatest bridge nearly as well known as it deserves. For posthumous renown, it helps to have a memorable name, and perhaps also to have worked closer to London.

Scotland also witnessed a late flourish of the British arched viaduct. These were the concrete structures built around 1900 for the West Highland Railway's Mallaig extension by the contractor Robert McAlpine ('Concrete Bob'), founder of the construction firm of that name. McAlpine's viaducts were not of the reinforced type with ferrous rods or bars running through, still less of the even stronger pre-stressed or post-tensioned forms. Rather, they were simple mass-concrete castings of the technique the Romans knew (though the Roman world never attempted to make bridges this way). The material was chosen for its cheapness:

McAlpine claimed a saving of 10–30 per cent over masonry construction, once the intractable hardness of the local Highland stones was allowed for. By adopting naturally strong arched profiles, McAlpine's bridges have endured, and some are magnificent: the Glenfinnan Viaduct has twenty-one arches, built on a steady curve; the Borrodale Bridge has a main span 127ft 6in wide. Had large-scale railway building continued across the wilder parts of Britain, there would surely have been more concrete bridges of this type.

Not every prodigious viaduct was of heroic height or span. In towns and cities, where land costs were high and many existing rights of way had to be negotiated, it was often easier to lift up the line on a low viaduct rather than taking it along ground level, or attempting an embankment. This type of urban railway was perfected very early, in the form of the London & Greenwich Railway's route of 1833–6 between London Bridge and Deptford. Here was a single brick-built structure almost four miles long, made up of a mind-numbing 828 arches and with a pedestrian toll-path along one side. The path did not last, and now that the line has been repeatedly widened it is difficult to sense its original appearance from a moving train. The Bermondsey pedestrian may do better: here and there, where a road passes beneath the line, massive Grecian colonnades of cast iron still separate the roadway from the paved walkways on either side, an echo from the last days of Georgian London.

Another achievement of the early railway bridge-builders, a source of wonder in its time, was the skew bridge. For simplicity's sake, most arched bridges are set 'square', that is at right angles to their springing points, like the arched head of a doorway in a straight wall. In other cases, the road, river or other obstacle takes an oblique course and the railway crosses at an angle by means of brick or stone coursing that follows the line of the skew. The form was not invented by the railways, having been achieved by at least one canal builder as far back as the late eighteenth century, but it was hugely multiplied for the new transport network. This in turn speeded up the development of the type.

The railways' earliest skew bridges were of stone and required each course to be cut – expensively – to unique dimensions. Taking no chances, the skew bridge at Rainhill on the Liverpool & Manchester was tested first by means of a timber mock-up erected in a field near the line. In its completed form, the arch of this red sandstone bridge vaults across the railway at a sharp thirty-four degrees. Later in the 1830s, a young engineer

Skew arches were often built at impressively sharp angles,
as at the London, Brighton & South Coast Railway's
viaduct at Westhumble, Surrey, opened in 1867

named Charles Fox (later a key man in the construction of Euston station and the Crystal Palace) developed a cheaper system, by which the
arch courses could be formed of standard-sized bricks. Both methods use
slanted courses that spring from the horizontal abutment of the bridge
at an angle. When viewed from below, this conveys an eloquent sense of
movement, as though of great forces held in check. As skew bridges tend
to be elliptical rather than round-arched, the summit of the arch is often
relatively close overhead and the experience is intensified. If these spaces
belonged to the National Trust, the guidebooks would instruct visitors to
pause and marvel; being public, numerous and grubby, they generally pass
unregarded.

A skew bridge was not essential every time a railway crossed a road
obliquely. As every driver knows, a minor road that approaches a railway
line at an angle will often swerve to the perpendicular at the last minute,
before bending back to its original course on the far side. Sometimes the
road passes under the line, sometimes over (which gives better sightlines).

The road has not always had this kink in it; its old alignment has been tweaked to make the bridge builder's task easier. Buying the extra land required for the small diversion worked out cheaper for the company than making a skew bridge so that the road could keep its straight line.

Most railway bridges are of this simple type, with a single perpendicular span. Huge numbers remain, which makes it easy to forget that bridges were a relatively rare sight before the railways came. Older bridges were almost all bespoke structures, and most were maintained at public expense. Only when the canals arrived were bridges multiplied to standard engineers' designs, and even these fell well short of the railways' needs for crossings over and under. In national terms, it took railways to make bridges truly commonplace.

Other bridges used a material not commonly associated with railways: timber. This amounted to a revival, for the use of timber for bridges carrying heavy loads had effectively been given up on the roads. Timber was abundant and it was cheap. There was a good case for its use as a stop-gap on a new line, to be replaced in more lasting materials when funds permitted. Confronted with a terrain of repeated flat crossings of waterways and broad ditches, several fenland lines adopted this policy. Unfortunately, money was not always available to upgrade their crossings when required. The Board of Trade's inspector in 1855 reprimanded the Eastern Counties Railway for the state of its viaduct across Sir William Beauchamp's Navigation: 'in many parts these timbers could be dug out with a spade like garden mould'. The railway's own engineer resigned two years later, protesting that a safe speed limit of 2 mph should be imposed on one of the worst stretches.

By the standards of Brunel, this was shoddy stuff. His own exploration of timber crossings started in 1839 with a couple on the Great Western main line. One was a skew bridge made of laminated timber arches, conspicuously placed in the middle of Bath. The other was built of ordinary timbers and carried a road across the cutting at Sonning. It had trestle-like uprights, with struts splaying out from the top. Drawings make it look flimsy, but it introduced the basic principle used by Brunel for dozens more bridges and viaducts. By working out a set of standard pinewood sizes and a variety of span types, he was able to make robust timber viaducts of appealing cheapness. Some were built with stone piers for the uprights, others stayed true to the Sonning-style trestle type. From the 1840s to the 1860s these viaducts spread across South Wales and down

Brunel's viaduct at Ivybridge on the South Devon Railway, in a lithograph of 1848. Here the spans alone are of timber, supported on stone piers

through Somerset, Devon and Cornwall. Thirty-four were erected during the 1850s for the Cornwall Railway alone, together carrying the route for about one-tenth of its total length of fifty-three miles. Designs were made on the spare-parts principle, so that worn-out timbers could be replaced piecemeal without having to renew the whole. They could be burdensome to maintain: for years after its opening, the Cornwall Railway employed nine teams of ten men each, working to replace strut after strut as they became unsound.

These bridges must have been nerve-wracking to cross. The Landore Viaduct near Swansea (thirty-seven timber spans on stone and timber piers), an extreme case, looks in illustrations like an enormously long, straightened-out fairground ride. Trains could only proceed across them at a slow pace. A few people today may even remember the experience, as the last timber viaduct on a public line was replaced as late as 1934; it was on the Falmouth branch. Even at this date its successor was made of masonry, laid course by course, as if it were 1834 (or 1134, for that matter), not 1934. That the timber viaducts had a share in prolonging an older, obsolete technology in this way is a pretty paradox.

In Wales it is still possible to take a long wooden ride by train. The bridge in question is the Barmouth Viaduct that carries the Cambrian Railways' line across the half-mile Mawddach estuary. Opened in 1867, it is constructed for most of its course from timber piles and beams, like a gigantic jetty. The line may be the only one in Britain to have survived a closure threat arising from the burrowing action of *Teredo navalis*, or shipworm. That was in 1980, since when the bridge piers have been sheathed in inedible concrete.

₪

Some of Brunel's timber spans were replaced by girders of iron or steel. These had a long ancestry. The potential of iron had been demonstrated most famously at Ironbridge in Shropshire in the 1770s – the first in the world – and the material was taken up before long for plateway bridges and aqueducts. The first iron railway bridge, the Gaunless Bridge of 1825 on the Stockton & Darlington designed by George Stephenson, spaced its trusses just 12ft apart. It was a spindly affair, the ferrous equivalent of a pioneer biplane. The reassembled metalwork now stands outside the National Railway Museum at York, where it looks enigmatic without the heavy stone abutments of the original structure.

The Ironbridge crossing was of cast iron, but the Gaunless Bridge included some wrought-iron members too, in recognition of its different properties. Cast iron, having a large proportion of carbon in its make-up, was strong in compression (good for piers and columns), but weak in tension (unsuitable for struts and ties). Wrought iron, like tools hammered out by a blacksmith, was much more resistant to tension and stress. The further development of iron bridges was steered by these constraints.

Arched bridges of cast iron were built for the railways too. Britain's broadest-spanning example is the 200ft-wide Victoria Bridge at Arley in Worcestershire, constructed for the Severn Valley Railway in 1862 and still in use as part of the preserved line of that name. Its ironwork was supplied by the same Coalbrookdale foundry which had made the mother of all cast-iron bridges, at Ironbridge. By the time the Victoria Bridge opened, another type of cast-iron bridge, using large girders of flat span, had already been and gone. Its drawback was fragility. Robert Stephenson's record was blotted by the failure of one such bridge, across the River Dee at Chester, one evening in 1847. It had three skewed spans, each just short of 100ft and each composed in turn of three castings bolted together. The structure was just six months old when one of the spans failed as a train was crossing it. Five deaths resulted, including the fireman; the driver survived only because he began to accelerate flat out as soon as he sensed something amiss. The investigation found that repeated flexing had weakened a girder, which had fractured in two places; also that the wrought-iron reinforcement rods that were fixed to the cast beams were structurally worse than useless. Witnesses described how they had seen the spans deflect by several inches every time a train crossed.

Far from detecting the frailty of his bridge, Stephenson had inspected it routinely on the very day of the collapse and ordered that an extra layer of ballast be spread across its timber decks as a precaution against fire. The ballast was in place by afternoon, adding an extra nine-ton load on each girder. Had Stephenson been young and with everything still to prove, his engineering career would probably have ended there; as it was, he was lucky to escape a manslaughter charge. Fellow engineers lined up in support of his convenient theory that the disaster had arisen from a derailment.

The Dee affair showed that the immediate future of iron bridge spans lay with wrought iron. Stephenson used the material in two of his most famous bridges, further along the Chester & Holyhead Railway: at Conwy and the Britannia Bridge that crosses the Menai Strait to Anglesey. Both were tubular box-girder bridges, most unlike anything seen on Britain's railways before. The trains ran not on top of each rigid linear box, like the road traffic on a modern example such as the 1990s Skye Bridge, but through the dark tunnel of the interior. For the traveller, the effect at Conwy is as startling as a solar eclipse: instead of the grand views anticipated, the bridge offers only a plunge into 400ft of noise and darkness. (The approach is peculiar enough as it is: trains run right under the ramparts of Edward I's fortified town, the castellations of which are extravagantly imitated on the bridge portals.)

Crossing the Britannia Bridge used to involve a similar journey through darkened iron tubes, raised in this case over 100ft above the water – another case of demands imposed by the need for free navigation below – and extending together for more than 1,500ft. Stephenson was not entirely confident that these flat spans would be self-sufficient, so he carried up the stone piers of his bridge sufficiently high to allow the addition of suspension chains. A consultant engineer then persuaded him that chains were superfluous, and so the bridge never received them. So things stood until 23 May 1970, when some boys set off down the tubes, ostensibly on a quest for birds' eggs. To light their way, they used burning newspapers as torches – not a prudent technique in a 120-year-old structure with a timber roof sealed with tarred hessian. The boys escaped the resulting inferno, in which the white-hot tubes split along their original joins, sagging by twenty-nine inches at the centre. A total loss, Stephenson's spans were reconstructed in steel with arched supports, the Admiralty no longer insisting by this date on clearance sufficient for square-rigged men-o'-war.

Soon after its reopening, a road deck was added along the top of the railway at the Britannia Bridge. This recreated in reversed form the arrangement of another of Stephenson's innovative railway crossings, the High Level Bridge of 1845–9 across the Tyne to Newcastle. Here the railway deck is supported on shallow wrought-iron arches, from which the horizontal road deck is suspended on vertical hangers. It is an efficient as well as an elegant solution – two bridges for the price of one – but the formula was never repeated elsewhere in Britain.

Other rare birds included a type of bridge invented by Brunel which depended on the suspension principle, as used at Chepstow (which has been rebuilt) and most splendidly at the Royal Albert Bridge of 1853–9 at Saltash. The suspension bridge had been brought to something like perfection by Thomas Telford as recently as the 1820s, in the graceful form of the Menai Bridge that still shadows Stephenson's mutilated Britannia Bridge between Caernarvonshire and Anglesey. But the concentrated loads imposed by trains were generally considered to rule out bridges of the springy, flexible suspension type. The Stockton & Darlington built one over the Tees, it is true, but this deflected alarmingly under the weight of coal trains – by as much as twelve inches, Brunel reckoned, when he visited in 1831 – and it was soon replaced by a girder bridge. When Brunel came back to the suspension principle for railways, he reconfigured it by using big iron tubes for rigidity and strength. At Saltash, where high clearances were again demanded by the Admiralty, the iron tubes are of such broad span – two of 455ft, each longer than most cathedrals – that only one pier is needed in mid river. The tubes are arched elliptically between the piers, with vertical hangers supporting the bridge decks, together forming closed suspension spans. The bridge was a success technically, financially and aesthetically, but no one ever built another like it. Like Stephenson's box-girder structures, it belongs to a period of exceptional experiment and diversity, after which things settled down on a more even course.

The main line of development lay with the various types of wrought-iron trussed girder. Some of these were of closely latticed form, others had larger members in criss-cross or zig-zag patterns. Trains ran sometimes on a deck on top of the trusses, sometimes between them, making a flickering blur of the view of river, estuary, road or valley below when travelling at speed. Another common type used the bow-string principle: the upper member of the truss describes an arch, with rigid ties to the lower beam. Others had solid sides of riveted plates.

Flat or flat-bottomed trusses were especially useful in urban settings, where they allowed railways to cross streets with full-height clearances for pedestrians on both sides. This represented an advance on the early type used at Bermondsey, with its three arches for the roadway and pavements. Which is not to say that these dank undersides made for a congenial environment for anyone except the rough sleeper and the feral pigeon. When Morrissey sings 'Under the iron bridge we kissed', the picture is instantly there: the underbelly of the inner-city railway, with its own discouraging smell and its temperature usually a few degrees below that of the streets around. Morrissey's Manchester, with its multitudinous railways snaking towards the city centre across flat terrain, is especially blighted (by contrast, its subterranean approaches make inner Liverpool unusually railway-free). It is strange to read of the wonder such bridges inspired when they were new, whether they took the railway under the road or over it. The 1850 edition of *Black's Picturesque Tourist and Road and Railway Guide Book* catches this sentiment, commending the first mile of the Bolton & Preston Railway with its nine 'much admired' bridges of iron beams. As with skew bridges, a technical achievement that was striking when new has become banal by familiarity and repetition.

Quirks and novelties multiplied in the construction of iron bridges. The crossing of navigable waterways was often the cause, especially in low-lying country. Swing bridges, including the straightforward balanced type pioneered by G. P. Bidder, were far from rare. There were also joint road–rail swing bridges, lifting bridges, rolling lift bridges, telescopic bridges and railway drawbridges. Special arrangements were required each time to allow signalling and telegraphs to be broken and reconnected. At the second Arun Bridge at Ford in Sussex, which carried water and gas pipes as well, railway traffic had to stop for up to forty minutes when the telescopic section was winched open to let a boat pass.

With or without an opening span, a combination of straight trussed girders and bowstring trusses was a good way to take a long bridge (strictly, a viaduct) across a wide expanse of water. That way, the wider bowstring

The first Tay Bridge, photographed in the aftermath
of its collapse in December 1879

trusses could accommodate the deeper flows of the central section, at once
making space for larger vessels and reducing the number of costly piles
that had to be sunk far below the surface. The grandest example is the second Tay Bridge of 1881–7, Britain's longest railway bridge, designed by the
partnership of William Henry Barlow and his son Crawford. For seventy-
one of its eighty-four spans, the passenger has a clear view towards Dundee
on the north shore and Fife on the south side. These outer sections have
trussed girders spanning beneath the carriage. Then the thirteen navigation spans are reached and the prospect is suddenly interrupted by the
rapid uprights and diagonals of the bowstrings, before the straight spans
resume for the final stretch of the elevated two-mile journey.

That is not all. Just downstream of the crossing are the stubs of the
first Tay Bridge, designed by Sir Thomas Bouch, which failed catastrophi-
cally one stormy Sunday night in December 1879, when not much more
than a year old. The collapse took out the navigation spans, which were of
the same length as those of the present bridge. The trussed-girder spans
match too, for the very good reason that the North British Railway reused
what could be salvaged from the old bridge, this time set on broader and
sturdier piers. The sight of the indecently close and prominent stumps,
which the North British chose not to remove, inspires uneasy thoughts
even today, but these are as nothing compared to the thrill of horror when

the collapse occurred. For the spans took with them an entire train with all its passengers and crew: a loss as complete as if a ship had foundered in mid ocean. Nobody on the land even saw it happen, except for one or two who observed the puzzling descent of some lights out on the darkened water – either the fire of the locomotive, or lamps still burning in the falling carriages. Even the number of fatalities was uncertain. Three hundred were rumoured at first, but the final estimate was given as seventy-five, calculated on the basis of the sale of fifty-nine tickets for the journey plus an allowance for any children and railwaymen, who travelled ticket-free. (This total has since been questioned, most recently in 2011 following a local campaign for a permanent memorial to the victims, inscribed with every proven name.) As a catastrophic failure of transport technology at its most ambitious and up-to-date, the episode had something of the impact of the *Titanic* disaster thirty-three years later.

Widely admired when new for its daring and structural economy, Bouch's design proved inadequate in terms of resistance to the winter gales that roared through the firth. On top of that, it was carelessly built. It seems heartless to add to these lethal faults that it was also rather ugly – its successor too. The same goes for many more of the major iron bridges built for the Victorian railways. The most spectacular of these have vanished in their turn, not after structural failure, but because the lines that they served have closed.

Bouch was responsible for two of the biggest examples, at Belah and Deepdale, on the line sponsored by the Stockton & Darlington, which was pushed across the north Pennines in 1857–61. The route's lifeblood was the rich iron ores of the Furness division, required by the ironworks at Middlesbrough, and the coke that flowed in the other direction to fuel the furnaces at Barrow and Millom. This was wild, harsh country: Deepdale Viaduct had a wind gauge which rang a warning bell in extreme weather, so that an extra speed restriction could be imposed. Belah Viaduct was the tallest ever built in England, at 196ft. Beautiful, however, it was not; in photographs, the viaduct has a spindly and temporary look, like something run up from scaffolding. The same applies to the Crumlin Viaduct of 1853–7 across the Ebbw Valley in Monmouthshire, which at 200ft held the British record for height. Its design was sophisticated, as the first large-scale implementation of the Warren triangular girder principle: stresses were distributed in such a way that every member was subject only to tension or compression, rather than sideways forces that might cause bending or shearing. What the viaduct looked like in its final days between closure and demolition is captured in the comedy thriller *Arabesque* (1965), in which Gregory Peck and Sophia Loren are pursued along the triangulated spans by rifle shots from a helicopter containing an armed and dangerous Alan Badel.

The last entry on the roll-call of great railway bridges of Britain introduced a new material, steel, and a new structural principle, that of the balanced cantilever. This is the Forth Bridge, built in 1883–90 in succession to the bridge planned by Bouch, and probably still the most famous railway bridge in the world. Its co-designers were the veteran English engineer John Fowler, born in 1817, and a younger man, Benjamin Baker. Both were knighted on its completion. For good measure, the contractor William Arrol, the resourceful son of a Scottish blacksmith, was knighted too. It was as if the shameful memory of the knighthood conferred on Sir Thomas Bouch a few months before his disgrace could now be purged. Work had actually started on Bouch's own crossing of the Forth, which aimed to revive the long-abandoned suspension type. The fall of the Tay Bridge killed this immediately, but Bouch's workshops were kept, and enlarged for use by his successors. Not everyone admired the mighty new bridge that resulted; William Morris, opposed on Ruskinian principle to building in iron or steel, called it 'that supreme specimen of ugliness'. Baker's response was that his bridge had a visual honesty that was meant to be graceful and comprehensible. He must have been cheered to receive a letter from the eminent architect Alfred Waterhouse, praising the absence of ornament that made the bridge 'a style unto itself', with 'a beauty of its own'.

Waterhouse's sentiments have a modernist ring to them. However, the decline in railway building meant that opportunities to forge a new aesthetic for twentieth-century railway bridges were limited. When large-scale bridge building resumed after 1945, the beneficiaries were the roads, not the railways. Nor was Britain any longer one of the chief sites of innovation. New technologies such as welding and pre-stressed concrete were adopted in time, but often as an exercise in catching up. The emphasis also shifted away from new lines and towards the modernisation of old ones. For the post-war engineer of railway bridges, the hardest challenge was often how to construct and install a crossing on an existing line with the minimum delay to traffic. Increasingly, such bridges were prefabricated in whole or part, so that they could be slid into place sideways and as fast as possible. Sometimes this was done to replace a bridge that had become worn out, or to increase clearances for overhead electrification. But many of the biggest post-war railway bridges – at least until the Channel Tunnel line came along – were needed in order to carry lines under or over the new trunk roads and motorways. One of the railway marvels of 1869 was the new Runcorn Bridge on the London & North Western, a spectacular lattice-girder design, which allowed a more direct route across the Mersey from London and the south. Exactly a hundred years later, *Railway World* magazine proudly reported that British Rail's largest single-span concrete bridge to date had just been inched into place to take the Runcorn-to-Frodsham line over the new M6, a few miles away from the Runcorn Bridge proper. As an engineering exercise this was notable, but this time there was no advantage to the railway – quite the reverse, as the new road route favoured the competition.

₪

Trackbed, verges, cuttings, embankments, buildings: all these components of the network required cumulatively a vast amount of land, much of it taken straight out of fruitful agricultural production. The average area needed to make a single route-mile has been calculated at some eleven acres. Where lines clustered together, the impact could be drastic. By 1911, a section drawn across the Taff Valley at a certain point south of Pontypridd transected railways running at *six* different levels. Other acquisitions of terrain resulted from the common practice by which an extra curve was inserted where two lines branched, to make a triangular junction. The company usually had to buy up the land enclosed, which often became inaccessible. There is an extreme example of this sort of useless purchase at Norwood Junction, in the outer suburbs of South London. Half a dozen lines split and branch and rejoin here, carving up into triangles and segments an area of Surrey otherwise big enough to host a giant housing estate. All around this unofficial nature reserve are the inter-war streets that filled up the district after the railways arrived. By 1873, the landholdings of the companies of England and Wales alone already amounted to 109,762 acres, comfortably more than the entire county of Rutland. A high proportion of this was green, open land.

Presented with the conundrum of what to do with these elongated territories, some railways went in for a bit of farming themselves. Posterity has remembered the agricultural use of railway land chiefly in terms of wartime emergency, when the acreage of land in Britain used for food production rose by an astonishing 80 per cent. In particular, the Dig For Victory campaign encouraged temporary allotments on railway land within easy reach of willing urbanites. Self-seeded, their crops sometimes outlived the war: in the 1970s the nature writer Richard Mabey found 'bizarre horticultural relics' on the Metropolitan's embankments at Neasden and Brent: 'sprawling loganberry bushes, forests of perpetual spinach and one vast and still-sprouting asparagus crown over a yard wide'. That these useful and rewarding plots had to be given up after the end of hostilities says a great deal about the tight control Britain's railways have always exercised over their land.

There were earlier attempts to farm alongside the rails, on a scale beyond that of urban allotments. The most straightforward use of the land was for fodder crops (for obvious reasons, grazing livestock was out of the question). Cutting of the lineside of the Liverpool & Manchester for hay was noted as early as 1837, but the practice seems never to have become general. Lineside fires caused by sparks probably had something to do with this. Even so, there were exceptions. At Eckington in Worcestershire the landowner's settlement with the Bristol & Gloucester Railway allowed him the use of both sides of the embankment, which therefore had lineside fencing along the top of the slope rather than at the bottom. Financial stringency explains the hay-cropping on the Garstang & Knott End Railway in Lancashire, a badly run mid-Victorian branch line that had over-reached itself by needlessly buying enough land to put down double tracks. The railway's staff cultivated the unused strip and local farmers were invited to buy a share of the resulting haystacks. The much grander Great Central Railway achieved a return from its newly made embankment at Eydon in Northamptonshire from 1899: the slopes were sown with lucerne, which was mown by the platelayers and sold to farmers where it lay. The practice was abandoned after a few years, because too many weeds were creeping in. Hay-cropping beside the tracks came back during the Second World War – along the London, Midland & Scottish alone, 440 farmers took up the company's offer in 1940 – but once again it failed to endure.

Other proposals and piecemeal uses came and went, without amounting to much. Seeking to make better lives for the underemployed urban poor by means of farm colonies, General Booth of the Salvation Army lighted on the railway embankment as an overlooked resource. His reform programme, published in 1890 as *In Darkest England, and the Way Out*, hailed them as 'a vast estate, capable of growing fruit enough to supply all the jam that Crosse and Blackwell ever boiled'. Around the same time, F. S. Williams pointed out that the lineside fences of Belgium had been adopted to support espaliered fruit trees, and that the venture promised to have good results. But Britain's railways were never turned into linear fruit farms in this way. Attempts were certainly made – a correspondent to *The Garden* magazine in 1875 described having seen half an acre of a London & North Western embankment planted with strawberries, for example – but the practice seems never to have become general. Neither was anything done to follow up the suggestion of a newspaper correspondent in 1847 that the freshly made, south-facing embankment slopes of Gloucestershire and Kent should be terraced for vines. The world was not yet ready for English railway wine.

Cropping for hay had an obvious advantage, because lineside vegetation had to be controlled anyway. There is nothing stable about the botany of embankments; left untended, the open ground alongside the railways in all but the bleakest parts of Britain will revert to scrub. The botanist Oliver Rackham once suggested that the railways may have helped unwittingly in this process by setting up fences along the boundaries: lodging-places for wind-blown seeds and attractions to perching birds, whose bills and droppings also leave seeds behind.

The truth was often more complicated. Each new railway was required by its founding Act to define its territory by means of a barrier. In towns and in certain upland districts the job might be done by a wall. More common, and much cheaper, was a wooden fence (post-and-wire fences became common only from late-Victorian times). On the railway side of these fences a drainage ditch was commonly dug and a hedge planted. The fence protected the growing hedge from grazing and trampling by livestock, which might otherwise stray on to the line. After the hedge was established there was no need to keep both barriers, so the fence was allowed to drop to bits. But this raised the risk that the farmer might stealthily annexe the little field-strip alongside, so many railways also set up boundary posts to record their true extent.

However the railways' hedges came about, their usefulness as barriers did not apply to trees and bushes growing closer to the track. If an excess of lineside scrub was allowed to build up, it could all too easily be set alight

Barley fields ablaze at Postwick alongside the
Norwich to Yarmouth line, August 1949

by sparks from passing trains. More dangerous still, unchecked growth
could obstruct the driver's view of the signals ahead. The verges therefore
had to be kept clear – a sort of virtual farming, keeping the land in shape
as if for a non-existent crop. A common accessory to the platelayer's hut
was a grindstone, to maintain a sharp edge on the scythes used for the purpose. Another method was to burn the growth off, a task commonly kept
for a dry winter's day. Sometimes the sparks and cinders thrown out by
locomotives did the job accidentally. The process continues along today's
preserved railways, leaving big blackened patches by the line. A journey
during a dry spell may catch one of these fires at work: the crackling orange
flames move frighteningly fast through the tawny grass alongside the track,
pulled by the slipstream of the train, and the sulphurous smell of steam
coal is overlain with a fresher and more acrid vegetable reek.

Inadvertent lineside fires were doubly menacing because they could
spread into the crops and fields beyond, for which the company was liable
to pay compensation. This was not necessarily a bad deal for the farmer, and
suspicions occasionally arose that some such fires were more welcome than
not. Christian Hewison, master of the engine shed at Melton Constable in

Norfolk in the years just after the Second World War, became convinced that the local barley farmers were ploughing their furrows as close to the line as possible in the hope of lucrative conflagrations. On the Masham branch in the Yorkshire Dales, a dishonest farmer was caught out when he put in a fire compensation claim after steam haulage had been replaced by diesel.

A related question concerned farm animals that had escaped on to the track and were killed by trains. If it could be shown that defective fencing was to blame, the railway was again liable to make recompense. This too was a standing inducement to misbehaviour on the part of the cannier sort of hill-farmer. As remembered by Harry Hartley, who inspected the wildest section of the Wensleydale route every day over many years in the 1950s, the cadavers of sheep that had died by other means were regularly placed on the rails, so that a claim could be put in for their value. To even out the score, Hartley sometimes took a spade and buried genuine railway victims before their owners could spot the loss. Some of these casualties resulted from the farmers' habit of fence-breaking so that sheep could graze the lineside; other farmers were bold enough to cut illicit hay from there – little skirmishes that reprised the compensation battles of the railway-building years.

The permanent way could itself give a home to some of the tougher sorts of plants. Fresh ballast was not an encouraging environment, but the steady penetration of wind-blown sediment and earth working up from below gradually made the habitat more inviting.* Steam traction was on the railwaymen's side here, with its constant oily leaks, scalding dribbles and droppings from locomotive ash-pans. The localised ballasting of sleepers with lead-mining waste also kept vegetation at bay, the spoil being so toxic that almost nothing could grow on it. Only in the 1930s did weed-killer come into play, sprayed from the nozzles of slow-moving trains that were steadily extended to cover the whole network by annual rota. Until that time the ballast had to be denuded of growth by the platelayers' hoes and rakes. As with the verges, this was not a matter of mere tidiness. Plant growth across the track and in the gullies along each side rapidly became an obstacle to drainage, and waterlogged track was potentially unstable. In hard frosts, bad drainage might cause further distortion, as groundwater expands by a factor of one-ninth in turning to ice (a cause of many speed restrictions during the severe winter of 1962–3).

---

* Membranes are now laid down to prevent the latter.

Regardless of regular human clearance and accidental burnings, the railways also accelerated the spread of certain wild plants, including non-native species. Especially fostered were plants with wind-borne seeds, which were pulled along the tracks in the wake of passing trains. This seems to have been one of the chief reasons for the advance of rosebay willowherb. In the eighteenth century its tall purple-flowered stems were reportedly scarce outside gardens, but from the middle of the next century willowherb began zipping through Britain, often using the railway network as its conduit. Each plant can produce some 80,000 seeds, which grow well on land that has recently been burnt. The same factors that allowed this 'fireweed' to flourish in the aftermath of the London Blitz also helped it to dominate the lineside.

Clearer still is the claim of Oxford Ragwort to be a railway weed. A hybrid of two Sicilian sub-species, its daisy-like yellow flowers were already to be seen among the specimens of the Oxford Botanical Gardens in Georgian times. From there it spread tentatively until it reached the Great Western's station, on the opposite side of the town. There was no stopping it after that: the ballast approximated beautifully to its dry and stony native habitat, and Oxford Ragwort made its steady way down to Cornwall, across to Kent and up to northern England. The botanist George Claridge Druce (1850–1932) caught the process in action, as he watched seeds from the plant drift into his carriage at Oxford and blow out again at Tilehurst in Berkshire, over twenty miles away. A linear bed of ragwort still flourishes there, in the gap between the slow and fast lines.

Buddleia, a Chinese species introduced in the 1890s, managed the same trick of dispersal even more quickly. It too evolved to grow in dry and stony territory, with tiny seeds that readily germinate in the decaying mortar of old walls. The tapering purple flowers of Buddleia are a well-known favourite of butterflies, sometimes to spectacular effect: in the summer of 2001, trains approaching Norwich passed through swirling clouds of migrant Painted Ladies, attracted by the Buddleia groves around the derelict inner-city station at Trowse. Other alien plants are so invasive that their presence on the lineside constitutes a permanent sump of contamination for the land on either side. Pity the gardens whose fences back on to the route between Brixton and Peckham, which has become a stronghold of one of the most hated of these plants, the near-ineradicable Japanese knotweed. The solid mass of bright green spade-shaped leaves (dry, ugly stalks in winter) stops only where embankment gives way to viaduct, and resumes where the viaduct ends.

These invasions were unknown to the Victorians. Yet the change that would surprise them most concerns not any exotic weed, but something much bigger: the spread of trees along the line. Nineteenth-century photographs of railway routes, or early films, show how their verges were kept strikingly bare (easy to understand why the impulse to farm them repeatedly popped up). Regular mowing of the lineside ceased in 1968. In the absence of livestock to chomp away at any saplings, the trees now have things much more their own way – at least until the slower cycle of felling and removal comes round once more.

Defiles of mature lineside trees, hardy and fast-growing sycamores often dominant among them, change the aspect from the carriage window profoundly. The claim that railways are an unmatched way of seeing the country has, in truth, always been oversold: those elevated perspectives from embankments have to be paid for by viewless stints between the banks of a cutting, and the passenger in a tunnel sees nothing of the unfolding horizons enjoyed by travellers on the roads climbing above. With tree cover, even embankments can no longer guarantee a broad prospect over the land. The effect is strongest on routes without overhead electrification, as this requires a five-metre-wide strip on each side of the line to be kept clear of potentially hazardous vegetation. On a bright day in summer on the Southern lines through Surrey and Hampshire – on the approach to Woking, for example – the sun's rays rake the carriage interior like a stroboscope through the flickering screen of trunks. Where green crowns of lineside vegetation coincide with the window level, distant landmarks and even whole towns may disappear from view almost completely. The Regency mansion of Penrhyn Castle, one of the scenic excitements of the North Wales route, can hardly be glimpsed at all in the high season. On the Uckfield line that rides high through the Sussex Weald, beech-tree branches may brush and rattle against the carriage windows. Cuttings, too, have been transformed into railway dells. Even the electrified approach to gritty Bradford, down the valley of the Wharfe from Shipley, is tree-lined and occluded for much of its length.

Autumn delays attributed to 'leaves on the line', the traditional bane of the Home Counties commuter, are one consequence of this arboreal turn. The hazard is not exclusively railway-grown: even if wholesale lineside clearance were to resume, autumn leaves would still drift down in their billions from trees growing beyond the boundary fences. The slippery paste that results is an intractable problem of railway operation. Special trains are run to blast away the leaf-mush using high-pressure water jets, and leave behind a coating of Sandite (fine sand, aluminium and glue) to help the wheels of following trains to get a grip. On some lines a modified timetable is even introduced for a fixed period each autumn, giving trains slightly longer to travel through the worst-affected areas. The inconvenience is part of the price of living in a leafy, rather than a bleak, part of Britain.

There is another railway landscape which concerns us here; two landscapes, rather. They may be seen whenever towns and cities are approached, especially where the route is unconstrained by cuttings or embankments. One is a landscape of reclamation. Its dwellings are much more recent than those of the streets beyond; in bigger settlements, they may be of the distinctive slab-like type which have their smallest windows towards the line, in order to shield residents from noise. Its open spaces are car parks, its greater monuments are the giant sheds of retail parks and distribution depots. The other landscape is one of dereliction, of abandoned sidings and yards disappearing under shrubs and saplings, of enigmatic structures awaiting demolition or collapse. This second landscape type is often transitional, an extended prelude to the creation of the first. Why did the railways need so much land in the first place? Much of the answer lies with their handling of freight. For an understanding of how this worked, what has disappeared is more important than what little remains.

GOODS AND SERVICES

Seen from a spy plane in the Cold War years, the most conspicuous parts of the British railway system would have been neither its earthworks nor its running lines, still less its bridges or its stations. In terms of individual impact on the land, none of these could rival the great marshalling yards. These were huge enclaves of parallel tracks and reception lines, designed solely for transhipment: trains of wagons came in, were uncoupled, rearranged into new formations, and sent on their way. As the yards did not need to be placed cheek by jowl with sites of production or of consumption, they were mostly established where land was cheap, in the rural intervals and debatable lands between major settlements and industrial sites. Collectively, they represent the last great land grab by the railways on a national scale.

Nearly all of these giant marshalling yards have now closed, and of the handful that remain not one is still operating as originally intended. Yet they were relatively late additions to the network. All but a few were constructed after the Second World War; the latest to open, at Scunthorpe, was not finished until 1971. Some of the abandoned sites have reverted to scrubland, some have become housing estates, retail parks or big-shed distribution centres. Others are still recognisable but largely derelict, such as Tyne Yard (opened in 1963), which stretches along the East Coast main line a few miles south of Gateshead.

To understand why these yards were built is to grasp the ultimately fatal trap the twentieth century set for the railway system it had inherited from the century before. To remain viable – the point cannot be made too forcefully – the railways had to carry freight, huge quantities of it, as well as passengers. They were also obliged by law to take pretty well anything that anyone wanted them to carry. That was all right as far as heavy and regular flows of traffic were concerned, such as the conveyance of coal from pithead to ironworks, dock or quay. But much of the traffic in goods was in much smaller consignments, no more than would fill a single wagon, often less. Each wagonload could not travel singly behind its own locomotive, so the average goods train was composed of wagons or groups of wagons with different starting points and destinations, many of which might have to be uncoupled and recoupled several times over before their journey was done. The marshalling yards were laid down to streamline and accelerate that process.

One of these installations may stand for many. Thornton Yard in Fife opened in 1956, after four years of building. It replaced ten smaller yards or groups of sidings dotted around the coalfields of east and central Fife, abolishing in one stroke an inefficient mass of short local trips back and forth between them. There was even a direct link from a freshly built colliery to the new yard, which had thirty-five classification roads (the separate tracks into which the wagons were sorted) and a total of twenty-six track-miles altogether. The yard had space to hold up to 2,311 wagons, and the total extent of its site from end to end was one and a half miles.

Like most of the later marshalling yards, Thornton was worked on the principle of hump shunting. Each incoming train of wagons was pushed steadily up a single track to the summit of a man-made slope or hump, the couplings having first been undone to separate its wagons or groups of wagons (known as 'cuts') according to their onward destinations. At the summit gravity took command and each wagon or cut began to trundle down the other side. The descending line split in two, each branch then subdividing again and again until the full complement of parallel sorting roads was reached. Here the incoming wagons rolled to a halt, in lines ready for recoupling into trains set for departure. Fast work in switching the points this way and that, overseen remotely from a control tower, ensured that everything ended up where it should. At the 'king points' where the descending line first divided, the interval between passing wagons or cuts might be as little as three seconds.

This exploitation of gravity came with a catch. Wagons could be made to ascend the hump at a standard speed, but the same was not true of their descent. Different weights might accelerate at different rates. Another variable was the state of lubrication of the axles. Strong winds might make a difference to speeds too, as if the wagons were ships at sea. Nor did all wagons have the same distance to travel: some rolled straight down the central roads, others were directed round the curve to the tracks along the outer edges of the yard.

These mixed outcomes would have risked chaos in the reception roads as wagons bashed unpredictably together, except for the presence of bar-like braking devices known as retarders, placed alongside the rails of the downward slope. Powered by compressed air, these were pushed firmly against the wheels of the wagons as they passed. The force employed was variable, in order to slow each consignment sufficiently to prevent over-running or a heavy collision with the buffers of the wagon it would encounter further on. Retarders were not a British invention, but were modelled on Continental practice. At Thornton, for the first time in a British marshalling yard, a secondary set was provided further down the bifurcating track layout, to allow fine-tuning of the momentum of the wagon speeds as they continued on their way. The degree of force applied was derived from a combination of measurements of weight and speed: the former determined by passing the incoming wagons over a weigh-bridge, the latter by means of VHF radar, like a fixed version of the police speed gun. This measurement of speed by radar at Thornton was another new practice for British Railways.

Thornton was hardly small, but in national terms it was only of middle rank among marshalling yards. Bigger installations tended to divide their traffic flows into separate yards, in the 'up' and 'down' directions, and were correspondingly longer and more complex. At Millerhill east of Edinburgh – another yard built in conjunction with a new colliery – the up and down sectors each boasted more classification roads than the whole of Thornton Yard. Others among these double leviathans were Toton Yard in Nottinghamshire (seventy-two classification roads), which handled over 2 million wagons a year in its 1940s heyday, and Whitemoor in the Cambridgeshire fens (eighty-six classification roads), the first in Britain to be built complete with retarders, which could handle 8,000 wagons daily. Work at these yards went on round the clock, aided by the glare of giant lighting masts.

The handling technology continued to evolve after Thornton Yard opened. One weakness of the retarder system was its inability to do anything for wagons that were moving too slowly rather than too fast. By deconstructing the retarder concept into multiple little wheels ('dash pots') installed all over the yard, where they could boost as well as slow down the passing vehicles, every wagon movement could be controlled almost as precisely as if a locomotive were in charge. Tinsley Yard, opened in 1965 between Sheffield and Rotherham, had 23,500 of these miniature power units. Here the unaccompanied wagons glided along their appointed paths with eerie steadiness, amid the strange nagging sounds made when the dash pots engaged with their wheels.

Innovative systems of communication were also developed. Thornton depended on the compilation of 'cut cards' at the point where incoming trains entered the yard. Duplicate copies of these were shot through pneumatic tubes to the inspector's office and the control tower, which was effectively a specialised signal box from which the correct sequence of changes to the points could be set. At Tinsley, the cut cards and pneumatic communication tubes were set aside in favour of a Telex-like system of electronic signals for encoding on punched tape at the control tower. The tape was then fed into a machine, which read the information and set the points automatically.

The railway network sometimes seemed awestruck by what it had created at these automated marshalling yards. Like battleships or nuclear submarines, they had a totemic as well as a practical value: irrefutable evidence that the network was committed to a more efficient future. One new yard or another, with its retarders and control systems, makes its predictable appearance in many of the upbeat British Transport Films of the era. But the full network of automated hump yards never materialised. Too many big yards had already been built for working by older methods, and the publicity films had less to say about these. Some had humps but no retarders; other yards were laid out entirely on the flat, so that wagons had to be pushed into place by a locomotive, or even drawn by a horse. This 'flat' type was described in the 1930s as operating at only one-third of the speed of the hump variety. Non-automated yards were often small, but some were very large indeed. Crewe Basford Hall Yard, where the sidings added up to thirty track-miles and the total of wagons handled reached a peak of 46,000–47,000 per week in the late 1930s, was partly shunted on the flat right up until closure in 1972.

At non-automated yards there was a greater need for manpower on the ground, both to brake the wagons and to direct them along the right road in the first place. Some yards did this by keeping men on duty at the points, as in the earliest days of the railways, to set the route correctly as the shunted wagons rolled towards them. If the yard had a hump, the men would look out for the track numbers that had been briskly chalked on to the front ends of each wagon or cut of wagons before they began rolling downwards. Even an advanced yard such as Tinsley still needed railwaymen to inspect each incoming train from the trackside and uncouple it into wagons and cuts before it was sent over the hump. Manual recoupling was required again before the newly reformed trains could leave the yard. Nor could the automated hump method deal with fragile or dangerous payloads, such as glassware, eggs or munitions. The same ban applied to the glass-lined tank wagons used for the bulk conveyance of milk, and to any outsize loads at risk of shifting, such as heavy castings and forgings. All these wagons had somehow to be got through the yard's mazy tracks separately, whether or not they were destined to rejoin a hump-shunted formation before final departure. That meant yet more uncoupling, shunting and recoupling; more hard and often dangerous work.

₪

To understand the shunter's task, it is helpful to remember the situation of the Victorian railway traveller in the years before continuous brakes. Controlling the movement of a passenger train depended on the co-operation of the locomotive crew and the guard or guards in their vans or brake compartments. The carriages between had no brakes that could be applied or released remotely, whether the train was in motion or at rest. Victorian goods wagons were just the same. Unlike passenger carriages, however, techniques for braking wagons evolved with extreme slowness. Edwardian wagons were braked in just the same way. So were most of those built between the wars, and most of those built by British Railways. As late as the mid 1970s, when the national fleet stood at 240,000 wagons, more than half still had no more than a handbrake to control them. No other railway network with a comparable density of traffic persisted with unbraked wagons for so long.

Most wagons of this type were relatively small and ran on four wheels mounted in a short rigid underframe. The basic forms of open mineral wagon and enclosed box van were fixed as early as the 1850s, although the average weight they could carry roughly doubled in the hundred years after that. Their construction also changed, as steel replaced timber for much or all of the fabric (although box vans mostly stayed loyal to wooden bodies to the very end). Also of pure Victorian descent was the type of brake used. These were operated by a long lever with a horizontal handle at one end, the handle usually being placed next to the right-hand axle-box of each wagon (a left-handed shunter was at a disadvantage here). The lever was held in place within a vertical housing made of two bars, with a toothed ratchet on its inner side. When the lever was disengaged from its housing, the handle could be forced downwards until the brake shoe or shoes pressed against the steel tyres of the wheels. To stop the lever jumping out of the ratchet, the bars of the housing were pierced with holes so that a fixing pin or peg could be passed through. On application, the brakes were said to be 'pinned down'.

Especially in marshalling yards, the task of forcing down the brake handle often had to be done when the wagon was still moving. Men trotted between the tracks alongside these four-wheeled wagons as they rumbled along, judging the right moment each time to grab the brake handle, and the right amount of force with which to push it downwards. The pushing part was normally managed by means of the shunter's brake stick, which could be braced against the underframe to obtain leverage. The greater the excess speed and momentum, the more urgently a wagon needed the shunter's care, and the more demanding the job of catching up in order to slow it down. When a wagon was running much too fast, it could be stopped by placing a slipper brake or 'skid' – a small, curved-up strip of metal – on the rail in front, diffusing the momentum in scorching friction and showers of sparks. Hand signals were used to communicate with the driver of the shunting engine, who would whistle by way of response. At night, the same operations were carried out by means of hand lamps, used both for passing signals to the driver of the shunting engine and for reading wagon numbers and destination labels. So the shunter working in darkness had to juggle with lamp and stick together.

A related tool was the shunter's pole, six feet of ashwood with a steel hook at one end, used for coupling and uncoupling. The standard British wagon coupling took the form of a single short chain of three big, straight-sided links, dangling from a big hook on the buffer beam. Every wagon had one of these chains at each end, but usually only one of them was used to couple on to the next wagon along, leaving the other chain to hang free.

Men of the Lancashire & Yorkshire Railway demonstrate the
hand signals for 'caution', 'all right' and 'danger', *c.* 1910

To couple two wagons together, the shunter first caught the bottom link
in the hook of his pole. He then used the pole as a lever against the top of
the buffers, lifting the link on to, or off, the hook on the buffer beam of the
adjacent wagon. One trick of the job was to use the pole to set the chain
swinging to and fro first, so that the final heft was not quite so demanding
on the muscles. This method of joining vehicles by means of simple chain
links was known as loose coupling.

It was possible to join or detach loose-coupled wagons quite rapidly.
On 4 November 1879, a train was received from Manchester at Pontypool Road Yard, an important centre for traffic in South Wales. It consisted of three wagons each for Swansea, Cardiff and Whitland, two
each for Pontypool, Llanelli, Neath and Neath Abbey and one each for
Aberdare, Aberbeeg, Bridgend, Briton Ferry, Carmarthen, Cefn, Ebbw
Vale, Haverfordwest, Newport and Pontypool (Town). Within thirty
minutes of arrival the complete train had been sorted and all the wagons
for Aberdare, Neath and points beyond were already on their way. The

only unusual thing about the procedure is that a detailed record happens to survive from this particular day.

The shunter's prowess was sometimes displayed in officially sponsored coupling tournaments, a sort of railway equivalent of the village ploughing match. These could be quite elaborate. Fifty-three hopeful shunters competed in the Midland Railway's yard at Spalding in 1890, overseen by timekeepers, a referee, a starter, a treasurer and a managing committee. Victor of the twenty-wagon contest was W. Coulson, who uncoupled his train in one minute and forty-six seconds. Christmas morning at Carnforth in 1925 saw the Furness & Midland sidings busy with sixteen-wagon heats; here the winner was logged at an amazing 66.2 seconds. The mental aspect of the shunter's task was cultivated in some of the railways' staff magazines by means of spatial puzzles using imaginary track layouts, with brisk timings and minimum movements as goals.

Other variations on the job included 'fly shunting', in situations where the locomotive could not be positioned behind the wagons. Instead, the shunting pole was first placed in a position to uncouple the wagons before moving. Then the engine got up a modest speed, the shunter keeping pace alongside. At the right moment the shunter signalled to the driver to slow down and the momentum of the train pushed the wagons together, so that the couplings slackened. Now the pole could be tugged downwards to pull the coupling chain off the hook, releasing the rear portion. The locomotive and any wagons still attached to it then put on a spurt, opening up a gap ahead of the uncoupled wagons rumbling along behind. Once the locomotive and its wagons had cleared the points, the rear portion could be switched to a different track by another waiting railwayman.

All these routines were plainly hazardous, even in the best of conditions. Add the perils of working in darkness, fog or adverse weather, perhaps on uneven ground, struggling with incorrect or muddled instructions, often stiff with fatigue and with hands numb from the cold, and the grimness of the shunter's job is abundantly clear. Yet the practices described represent shunting in what might be called its reformed state. The lot of the mid-Victorian shunter was in many respects worse. Efforts to amend these working practices became caught up in broader struggles, to do with workers' rights of association, hours and pay. Much of the story shows the railway companies at their most flint-hearted.

The simplest reform was the introduction of the shunting pole. A cheap and efficient tool, it was already in use on some lines by 1880 and appears to have become general by around 1900. Prior to that, coupling and uncoupling had to be done at close hand by getting into the space between the buffers. This put the men at risk of injury should the engine begin moving in error, anyone busy with couplings between the rails being invisible from the footplate. Worse still, fly shunting was sometimes managed by taking the shunter for a ride on the wagons, braced above the buffers and waiting for his moment to uncouple by hand, or even by extending a foot. Expedients of this kind were officially discouraged, but when the timetable did not permit the work to be done in the approved manner the men were tacitly expected to ignore inconvenient regulations of this kind.

A more persistent danger arose from where the brake levers were placed. Most early wagons had brakes on one side only, and it was cheaper to build them with a single brake lever on the same side. That was all right as long as the lever faced the working side of the tracks at sidings and depots. However, it was not possible to keep all the brakes facing the same way – especially so with wagons, which were frequently spun this way or that on the little turntables provided in goods yards and depots where space was too tight for full-scale points. The worker on shunting duty might therefore spend his shift repeatedly crossing and re-crossing occupied tracks in pursuit of brake levers. The same single-sided policy applied to the destination labels that were clipped to the wagons' underframes, for inspection when they were shunted and despatched. Every crossing of occupied tracks to attend to a lever or read a label increased the risk of harm to the shunter, against which a six-foot wooden pole was no defence.

Needless to say, the management knew all about these dangers. But whenever changes were proposed that would reduce the risks of harm in return for new investment or higher working costs, the companies preferred to dig in. Their defence of the status quo, regularly rehearsed, was simply that each man was responsible for his own safety, and by extension for that of his colleagues. The case of *Hutchinson* v. *York, Newcastle & Berwick Railway Co.* (1850) confirmed that the companies had the law on their side. This was the case which established the principle that the workforce of a company were all servants alike, in 'common employment'. Confronted with an accident caused by negligence or human error, a company could therefore argue that responsibility lay with one or another of its servants, who might in turn be liable individually for punishment in the courts. In other words, corporate manslaughter did not yet exist as a concept in law. That the men's working conditions could be hazardous or even lethal made no difference: the company could no more be held responsible for any error or oversight – even at the highest managerial level – than the Duke of Devonshire could be called to account for the misdemeanours of his head butler or under-gardener. Only where negligence by the servants of one company had caused death or harm to those of another could questions of corporate responsibility be invoked.

Nor did the Inspectorate from the Board of Trade have much of a hold on operational safety. Having established that certain standards had been met before any new line was permitted to open, the Board left the management to get on with the job, returning only in the case of serious accident. Official accident reports issued by the Board might recommend changes to working methods, but all through the nineteenth century these could not be enforced by law. Within the industry, the idea of direct external regulation was no more welcome than it would have been in Her Majesty's army – an analogy that was often made. As for workers daring to go on strike, this was considered tantamount to mutiny.

This state of affairs began to alter only when the law was changed to permit the existence of truly independent trades unions. The crucial date for the industry was 1872, when the Amalgamated Society of Railway Servants was founded at Derby. Railway unions had been formed or attempted before that time, none of which endured. The ASRS broke the pattern, surviving to become the major constituent of the National Union of Railwaymen (itself now amalgamated with the RMT union). The founding location reflected the patronage of Derby's admirable MP, Michael Thomas Bass (1799–1884), a man who might be called the Nonconformist Conscience incarnate. Moved by a developed sense of natural justice, Bass provided funds to the fledgling union, underwrote its mouthpiece *The Railway Service Gazette* and spoke on its behalf from the Liberal benches in Parliament. As the pre-eminent brewer of Burton-on-Trent his pockets were deep, and his commercial engagement with the railways made him too substantial a figure to dismiss. In the 1870s the Bass company owned 69,954 trucks and despatched half a million barrels of beer by rail every year, most of them via the Midland Railway. (The brewery's reach is indicated by its titanic maltings at Sleaford, and its mass works outings, as described in Chapter 11.) Given time, the railwaymen would doubtless have established a strong union without Bass's help, but his early support was invaluable nevertheless.

The newly formed ASRS began immediately to gather information on casualties. The railways had recently been ordered to submit details of deaths and injuries among the workforce to the Board of Trade, but this coverage was far from accurate. Bass therefore commissioned and published a review, which identified chronic under-reporting: the Lancashire & Yorkshire reported seventy-three injuries during 1872, the ASRS counted 1,387.

However telling, such publicity was of little use without concrete proposals to make things better. The ASRS chose as one of its chief causes the installation of so-called automatic couplings. Already in use on some American lines, these locked into place when two wagons were pushed together, eliminating the need to send a man between the rails. Twice during the 1880s the union sponsored displays of various automatic designs from home and abroad, with other types of improved couplings. In the same year as the second of these shows, a parliamentary bill was introduced to enforce the use of couplings that could be operated without having to stand between the buffers.

These initiatives came to little. Alarmed by the potential costs, railway interests within Parliament lined up to defeat the bill. Even on lines where enthusiasm for the idea was real, there was no broad agreement as to which new coupling system would be best. In effect, this was yet another instance of an all-or-nothing reform faltering from a lack of official support. It was a different story in the USA, where a federal law of 1893 compelled the use of safer automatic couplings. The accident rate to shunters on the railroads halved as a result. (The type may be remembered: they are the big knuckle-like fixtures cowboys and outlaws grapple with in Westerns when someone tries to detach part of a moving train.)

The campaign for safer braking and labelling of wagons did better, but it was a slow business. Things began to look up after the Railway Employment (Prevention of Accidents) Act of 1900, which at last empowered the Board of Trade to impose binding safety measures on the railway companies. The Act addressed some of the other booby traps that the ASRS had long sought to banish from everyday operation. First, any places where shunting was carried on after dark were now to be adequately lit by fixed lamps, not merely the hand lamps carried by the men. Second, any point rodding or signal wires that crossed such areas of outdoor working were to

One of the hazards of shunting, from a British Railways safety booklet, 1961

be properly enclosed as a safeguard against tripping. Action on the matter of wagon brakes took longer: a definitive rule compelling the provision of a lever on both sides of every wagon was not made until 1911. Even then, the companies were allowed up to twenty years' grace to modernise their existing stock. Thus the wagon-chasing, brake-stick-waving shunter of the twentieth-century marshalling yard was in effect working under conditions formalised just before the First World War. It follows that the more intensive handling of wagons in hump-shunted, floodlit yards was feasible only because of changes already forced on a reluctant industry by Parliament, urged on by the railwaymen's own representatives.

₪

What railway safety was like in the years of self-management can be measured by their employee casualty figures. The peak death rate for all ranks combined, at over 700 per annum, came in the mid 1870s. Well into the twentieth century, the number of shunters killed at work remained above 100 a year. Platelayers and gangers also suffered in large numbers, as already described. Senior railwaymen were themselves sometimes numbered among the dead. The Somerset & Dorset lost its locomotive superintendent W. H. French in November 1889: pausing in his own station yard at Highbridge to discuss the quality of the hay loaded into one of the wagons there, he was crushed between the buffers when an oblivious driver began to shunt them. The same month claimed Mr Carter, stationmaster at Reading (South Eastern), 'knocked down and fatally injured by an engine while he was superintending some shunting operations'.

Among train crews, the riskiest occupation was that of goods guard, whose normal duties included a large share of shunting work. In 1906 the annual death rate from accidents among this working grade was 2.7 per 1,000. Put another way, if a thousand goods guards had been recruited in that year and continued working under the same conditions for the full pensionable span of forty-five years, only 885 would have been left alive.* Cumulatively, this survival rate is not much better than that of British Empire service personnel during the six years' duration of the Second World War. The impact of these losses was diluted also because fatalities came in small numbers – a shunter here, two gangers there and so on. Railway work produced no hecatomb headlines to match the pit disasters of the period, or ships lost with all hands. And when a passenger train suffered a serious accident, the fate of the railwaymen inevitably took second place in the public interest to that of their fare-paying charges.

Underlying many fatal errors and misjudgements, whether the harm was self-induced or directed at others, was a regime of long hours. Shifts that would poleaxe all but the fittest and most hardened employee of today were routinely undertaken by the very workers whose fatigue was potentially the most dangerous to others – signalmen, guards and drivers. It was the same story for those whose fatigue was potentially the most dangerous to themselves, notably shunters and platelayers. Viewed in the light of the Factory Acts of 1833 and after, which limited the hours worked in certain industries to twelve and then ten hours daily, the situation was outrageous. But these laws were themselves atypical, for they did not fix a universal standard for every type of workplace. Sailors and dockers (to draw parallels with other kinds of transport work) enjoyed no such protection. Neither did the farm labourers who toiled to bring in the harvest with the new steam-powered traction engines and threshing machines.

---

* In practice, pension rights for all staff were not awarded until 1953. In 1906 barely one worker in five was covered, mostly clerical staff and footplatemen.

Not everybody regarded this situation as acceptable. In 1871, Bass told the House of Commons how things stood for drivers on the Midland Railway. Their standard working day was ten hours long, but he knew of thirty or forty men who were putting in almost double that figure, and one instance of a man who had not left his engine for twenty-nine and a half hours. Meanwhile one of Bass's allies, the journalist James Greenwood (1832–1929), put the frighteners on the readership of the *Daily Telegraph* with his articles on the life of the passenger guard. One piece told of a guard who had gone on shift at 6.35 p.m. on 23 December, finishing at 2 p.m. on Christmas Day, forty-three hours and twenty-five minutes later. On Christmas Eve, the guard was found asleep, standing upright by his own brake wheel. Rather than replace him with a less exhausted guard, a porter was assigned to travel with him and watch over his wakefulness. Greenwood asked how his readers felt about the prospect that their impending Christmas journeys might depend for their safe conclusion on a man 'gaping leaden-eyed and hanging in a state of semi-sensibility over his wheel, only kept from dropping down on to the floor by a friendly "nudging" on the part of the man expressly provided to keep him awake'.

Gruelling feats of endurance were also routinely expected from men out on the tracks. 'Lamps', Dickens's uncomplaining lamp-man at Mugby Junction, worked shifts of 'fourteen, fifteen, eighteen hours a day. Sometimes twenty-four hours at a time'. Such a way of life was no fiction. Altogether, it is a wonder that the network was not clogged with fresh wreckage and corpses every single day.

Much of the history of railway labour from this time onwards therefore concerns the protracted struggle to achieve shorter working hours. The ASRS also did what it could to make the management accept a share of responsibility for accidents caused by negligence. The companies clearly had a vested interest in preventing collisions, derailments and other costly accidents, as they readily pointed out. After the Fatal Accidents Act passed in 1846 they were also liable for deaths or injuries caused to members of the travelling public, where negligence could be shown. But as long as the principle of common employment applied, there was relatively little incentive to invest in reducing casualties among the workforce. Put simply, it worked out cheaper for the companies to regard a proportion of their workers as expendable through injury or death than to spend extra money on keeping them alive and in one piece. To abandon the customary under-staffing that underpinned the practice of hazardously long working hours represented another unwelcome addition to operating costs, at a time when margins were shrinking inexorably.

So things remained until a general reform of the liability laws in 1880. Employees now had the right to compensation in cases of negligence by individual workers, including signalmen and drivers. A loophole remained, in that the companies were permitted to contract out the business of compensation to the provident societies which they themselves sponsored, and which paid out at much lower rates. This was the policy adopted by several big lines, including the London & North Western, a decision that this hard-nosed railway chose to represent as having been accepted willingly by its men. In truth, when open meetings of LNWR workers were held, opinion went strongly the other way. Official pressure to suppress this restiveness followed: name-taking, summonses to the office for warnings and so on, up to the point of dismissal from service. This was no more than the usual response to dissent, for the railway companies expected loyalty from their servants and usually equated internal criticism with insubordination. Parliament alone could amend this situation, and further Acts in 1898 and 1900 finally removed this option of discounted compensation, putting all railway workers on the same legal footing at last.

Why did railwaymen put up with being treated like this for so long? Part of the answer lies in their collective weakness before the 1870s, when the legal position of trades unions was clarified in their favour. Before then, strikers could expect to be sacked, and commonly were. Collective weakness was mirrored by the diverse terms and types of employment: so many independent companies, each with its own practices, pay rates and division of responsibilities. The ASRS campaigned for universal rights, adopting a ten-hour working day as a standard demand in 1887, but there was as yet neither a single negotiating body to represent the companies, nor any consensus in favour of fixing national rates and conditions in the first place. Change happened incrementally, each company managing the pressure for reduced working time in its own way. In practice, the hours worked did not approach those common in other sectors until the 1910s.

By that date the railways had witnessed the most famous of all their labour disputes – famous because it ultimately changed the course of employment law concerning liability for damages arising from a strike. This was the Taff Vale dispute of 1900–1901. The Taff Vale Railway was a smallish but highly profitable line that sweated its men hard, and wanted them to sweat harder. Its workers went on strike after a victimisation case ignited a general sense of grievance arising from unsatisfied claims for better wages. The company won its resulting claim for damages, which exposed striking unions anywhere to the risk of financial ruin, only for the law to be changed six years later in the unions' favour.

That reversal effectively opened the way for the first national railway strike. It was not long in coming. The second half of the 1900s was a time of broad and severe industrial unrest, as prices rose while wages stagnated. Matters came to a head on the railways in 1911. The stoppage was tied up with the wider question of how far the fast-growing unions should be recognised, and ended in their favour, with modest improvements to hours and pay. Two years later, three of the largest unions involved came together as the National Union of Railwaymen. National pay scales, a basic eight-hour day, and an effective forum for negotiations with the railways on a collective basis were finally put in place after the First World War. Yet the practice of punishing key workers for insufficient faithfulness outlasted these changes, as the aftermath of the General Strike showed.

₪

The Taff Vale Case is perhaps less resonant now than it used to be, before the ancestry of the labour movement was displaced from the centre of the history curriculum. That story belonged firmly to the post-war national narrative, in which the mixed economy and a heavily unionised workforce represented both the culmination and the resolution of class conflict. Now that this settlement has been overturned, it is perhaps easier to understand some other perspectives from within the nineteenth-century railway workforce.

Anyone who joined the industry in its first few decades would have encountered a culture in which service on the railway required unquestioning obedience in all matters. As in the army or navy, seniority and authority were not centred in a few, remote superior officers – as the railways liked to call their senior staff – but were embodied and delegated throughout the network. Lateness and other infringements of company rules were punished by fines and stoppages, on the quasi-military model common to the railways and the factory system alike. From early on, the culture was reinforced by the wearing of uniforms by many grades of railway worker, like the Manchester & Leeds's guards noted in 1841 by the spa expert Dr A. B. Granville (1783–1872), 'smart, active-looking fellows, clad in red, and wearing a glazed, round hat, with the name of the railroad in gold letters upon it'. Uniforms – the property of the company, not of the wearer – implied a status something between that of the armed services and the liveried servants of the upper classes. Some lines indeed preferred the term 'livery' for the dress of their traffic staff. On the Great Western, this derived in turn from Sir Robert Peel's new Metropolitan Police: tall hats, and tailcoats with big brass-gilt buttons. Everything about this working culture encouraged acceptance of the principle that dangerous errors committed at work were a matter of personal responsibility, rather than a direct and foreseeable consequence of cost-trimming exploitation directed from the top. Besides, many workers were financially dependent on overtime work, especially when this came to be paid at higher rates, and took all the hours they could get. And the more worn-out by toil a worker became, the less likely that he would have energy or time left over for union agitation.

Individualism of this older kind is the keynote of one of the earliest books by a former railway worker, Michael Reynolds's *Engine-Driving Life, or, Stirring Adventures and Incidents in the Lives of Locomotive Engine-Drivers* (1881). The author had worked on the footplate himself, and set out to explain how a boy recruit might achieve the driver's rank. There was already a customary progression, in which preparing fires and cleaning engines at the running shed were the earliest stages. A boy cleaner might become a junior fireman when he was older and physically stronger, having learnt how locomotives worked from the attentions required to keep them in good order. Reynolds presents this progress in terms of moral as well as physical dangers: ruses, excuses, lies, ill-temper and profanity should all be treated with the same aversion in the running shed as the perilous space between the buffers of engines in steam. At every stage, 'the *elixir vitae* is self-help'. The first ventures out on the line were usually shunting trips, the front line in terms of workforce injuries, and Reynolds explains how the young fireman should draw lessons from finding himself among damaged men each with a cautionary tale to tell: the glass eye, the plate in the head, the false nose and the artificial arm. As a qualified fireman, charged with his share of maintaining the engine, he will himself risk death under its wheels should the driver inattentively set the machine in motion; thus brother has killed brother in the service, and father has killed son. Altogether, 'there is scarcely another calling in life in which hope and death are so blended together' as that of the engine driver.

It is easy to mock a writer who can extol his drivers as 'men who die at the post of duty, in all the pride of manhood', like a jingo journalist; tempting also to dismiss him as a patsy for the bosses, representing hazardous practices as moralised tests of self-preservation. Yet every book published implies an expected readership, and Reynolds's volume (one of several by him on similar subjects) was popular enough to reach three editions; somebody out there wanted to read this stuff. Nor was Reynolds's sense of vocation misplaced: many of those who worked on the footplate kept themselves consciously and proudly apart from the mass of ordinary railwaymen. The division lives on even now in the split between the general union and the Associated Society of Locomotive Engineers and Firemen (ASLEF), which refused to join in the amalgamation of 1913. It is telling that Sidney Weighell and his brother, both footplatemen, should have signed up with the National Union of Railwaymen in the 1930s instead of ASLEF, 'because its craft-union ethic stood for the opposite of the working-class solidarity we had been brought up to believe in'.

That statement alone is enough to temper the idea that the railwaymen ever formed a homogeneous bloc, acting and thinking collectively according to the predictions of the cruder kinds of Marxism. In truth, railway work was always a mixture of the enviable and the deplorable, the paternalistic and the callous. The ingredients and the proportions of this blend varied greatly from company to company, from generation to generation, and from job to job. Some skilled grades and crafts remained aloof from the labouring masses, and watchful against any erosion of their own responsibilities and privileges. The balance between loyalty and discontent within the workforce reflected this diversity.

Even in the earliest days, the casual acceptance of preventable deaths and injuries, and the companies' steadfast refusal to accept liability, were also tempered here and there by some basic welfare measures. Like the better railway contractors, companies might sponsor hospital beds, giving men injured at work a chance to recover properly. Chester Royal Infirmary was subsidised in this way from as early as 1838. After a fatal accident it was customary to meet the expenses of a worker's funeral, and often a payment was made to the man's widow. Permanently disabled men also had a good chance of being found further employment, although this was a privilege to be grateful for rather than a right that could be claimed. The mutilated shunters described by Michael Reynolds are evidence of the practice. Some larger lines took over the production of prosthetics themselves. The

National Railway Museum preserves drawing no. 7629 from the London & North Western's works at Crewe: 'Artificial Leg, General Arrangement and Details'. Skilled carpenters at the Great Western's works at Swindon likewise turned out wooden limbs, wooden feet and wooden hands.

In other corners of the mighty works at Crewe, men busied themselves preparing materials for the LNWR's standard workers' houses, which were built of brick for £350–£400 each, complete with fittings. At the peak the railways owned some 58,000 staff houses, with especially dense concentrations in railway towns such as Crewe (surviving in part), Wolverton (levelled in the 1970s) and Swindon (preserved miraculously almost intact). Rents were stable and moderate, when the house did not come rent-free with the job. Nor do Victorian railways stand out as exceptionally careless or negligent employers by comparison with other highly capitalised industries, such as coal mining or construction. The management certainly wished the men under their control to think themselves fortunate to hold their posts. On their part, the workers would not have signed up in the first place had the railways not offered an attractive combination of secure and decently paid employment, usually with some prospect of promotion. Changes to these attitudes depended on wider shifts in working culture and class consciousness: the railwayman of 1850 and his descendant of 1910 might have the same job to do, but they conceptualised it in different ways.

₪

The long loose-coupled trains assembled by the shunters required considerable skill to operate safely. Responsibilities were split between the locomotive driver and the goods guard, who travelled in a brake van at the back. It was the goods guard's job to help the driver to slow or halt the wagons by braking his own vehicle, which was heavily weighted by means of cast-iron ballast within the underframe, and to release the brakes when required. The trick was to stop short of applying the brakes so tightly that the wheels of the van locked and began to skid, causing damage to tyres and rails. So that the guard could keep watch, the little timber cabin of the brake van was provided with sideways lookouts and a balcony at one or both ends.

There might be up to seventy three-link couplings between brake van and locomotive, sometimes more. Every one of them was subject to the same process of slackening and tightening that made fly shunting possible. The difference in length between a fully extended coupling and one hanging slack between two buffered-up wagons was about a foot. It follows that a very long goods train might vary in length by 70ft or more. The greater the dead weight of the train, the more its couplings were vulnerable to sharp tugs, especially when the engine accelerated too quickly from a standstill. When restarting a train, the driver might therefore choose to 'set back' or reverse a little way first. The total load could then be taken up gradually once the train began to make headway and each coupling was pulled taut again. Only when the whole train was rolling slowly would full power be applied.

The wagons were also subject to a sort of time delay when power or braking was brought into play. Caught between locomotive and brake van, the individual vehicles moved at different speeds according to the degree of slack in the couplings and any time-lag between the application of brakes at one end or the other. Gradients complicated matters further: as the locomotive and leading wagons began to slow down in response to the start of an ascent, the wagons immediately behind were liable to catch up and bunch together, even as the tail end might still be dragging the brake van down a descending stretch of the line, its brakes still firmly on. Thus the entire train stretched and compressed like a caterpillar.

On descending gradients there was also a risk that the wagons would pick up so much momentum that the combined braking power of locomotive and van could no longer control them. The safe negotiation of a steep gradient might therefore entail a stop at the summit to allow the guard to pin down some of the wagon brakes too. This was standard practice at the top of the Lickey incline in Worcestershire, the most demanding gradient on any British main line: two miles at 1 in 38. (Conversely, trains climbing the other way had to be shoved from behind by up to four extra steam locomotives, a practice known as banking.) When the descent was complete the goods train had to stop again while the brakes were released from the trackside, one wagon at a time. On hilly lines the toll on the brake blocks of goods trains was especially severe. Those used on the heaviest engines on the Somerset & Dorset Joint Railway sometimes needed replacement after a single fifty-two-mile trip. Coming down a steep gradient with an unbraked night train, Catherine-wheel sparks flew out from the cast-iron blocks pressing against the hard steel tyres of these engines. The effect was described as lighting up two fields' width on either side.

Those who have known Britain's railways only in the era of smooth continuous brakes would be staggered by the amount of noise this type of train could emit. They got even noisier with the years, as the introduction of more powerful locomotives allowed trainloads to become heavier. In 1906 a veteran goods guard on the LNWR named William Ellison recalled working trains a quarter-century before that were thirty wagons long; the new engines then coming into use could handle up to sixty. Another change concerned the type of buffers used to keep the wagons apart. At first these were simple wooden blocks, called dumb buffers, like those used for generations on the very basic wagons employed on colliery waggonways. As late as Edwardian times there were still plenty of coal trucks of this type thumping against one another, but the majority were already equipped with the familiar round- or oval-headed buffers of forged steel. To absorb the shocks of impact, the sliding shanks of these buffers were held in place by springs or rubber blocks (and later by hydraulic reservoirs) that fitted within the underframe. Arnold Bennett described the sound of one such train in his novel *A Man from the North* (1898): 'The coupling-chains rang with a merry, giant tinkle, and when the engine brought its load of wagons to a standstill, and a smart, metallic bump, bump, bump ran *diminuendo* from wagon to wagon, one might have fancied that some leviathan game was being played.'

Which leaves out the distinctly un-merry squeals after stopping, as the springs within the buffers sought to equalise compression between the wagons, not to mention the loud repetitive clanks when the train moved off again and the couplings were jerked taut one by one. The resulting racket was not limited to industrial areas – audible miles away, the clangour of freight working and shunting was once carried on the wind to villages and suburbs through much of Britain, especially at night – but it was especially characteristic of the communities created or fostered by the industries that depended on the railway and had grown up with it. From another workaday corner of England, D. H. Lawrence used the 'sharp clinking of the trucks' as off-stage mood music for Paul Morel's nocturnal reveries in *Sons and Lovers* (1912), set in Nottingham and its coalfield. From a later generation, the noise echoes through a courtship scene between Albert Finney's belligerent factory worker and his future fiancée in Karel Reisz's film *Saturday Night and Sunday Morning* (1960), based on the novel by Alan Sillitoe.

There were changes in how Britain's railway wagons were worked between Lawrence's time and Sillitoe's. Before the First World War, every company-owned wagon that made its way on to another company's territory had to be returned empty within a set period, or incur a demurrage charge. Any gains from this system in terms of fee income and efficient deployment were more than wiped out by the costs of operational complexity, paperwork and administration. When the railways were placed under the control of a national executive committee during the First World War, all but a few specialised vehicles among the company-owned wagons were therefore pooled for general use. The reform was estimated to have cut by two-thirds the number of wagon journeys that were made empty. The Second World War added to this pool the huge fleets owned by private companies such as collieries and chemical works, to a total of 563,000 wagons. These too had previously to be returned empty to their owners, so that half of their journeys were made without carrying anything.

Private coal trucks were especially abundant, often boldly lettered and even brightly painted under the black dust – railway equivalents of the sign-writer's art on hoardings, gable ends and the bodies of commercial vehicles. The poet Clifford Dyment (1914–71) remembered the cavalcades of these trucks that used to pass along the embankment at the end of his aunt and uncle's garden in Derby: 'Clay Cross, Langley Mill, Sherwood, they filed past, Bolsover, Stanton, Bolsover, Stanton, Hucknall, Hucknall, Hucknall, clattering, clinking empties travelling at speed, Mapperley, Butterley, Staveley, M.R. [Midland Railway], M.R., M.R., Shirebrook, Bulwell, Bulwell, and then the terminal brake van with its porch and cosily smoking chimney.'

Some of these may have been among the same trucks that had made the clinking soundtrack to D. H. Lawrence's early years in the next-door county, for economy required that colliery wagons be kept in use as long as possible. The collieries were charged less when coal was carried in their own wagons, which was another saving; the railways allowed the discount in return for not having to stump up the cost of providing the wagons themselves. Being exempt from the usual demurrage charges, coal trucks often doubled as warehousing on wheels, a practice adopted on a large scale in South Wales. Inland yards with a capacity of 12,000 standing wagons served Newport docks, where space was especially congested. Loaded or empty, colliery wagons spent so much time standing around that the Great Western estimated in 1933 that those on its territory made a journey on average just once a fortnight. The fewer paying journeys made, the less

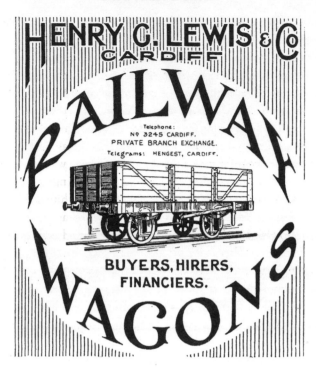

Advertisement by a wagon hire company, 1921, showing a typical coal truck

incentive there was for the coal industry to build and look after its trucks to a high standard. A typical maintenance contract of the 1930s allowed a seven-year outlay of just five guineas per wagon, or less than a halfpenny a day.

This heavy traffic of private wagons was another retrograde feature of the British railway system. The wagons on almost every Continental system, like the passenger carriages, were owned by the operating companies. In Britain, the companies were legally required to accept privately owned wagons unless they were ill-made or in dangerously poor repair. It was not even necessary for a private concern to buy its own stock; wagons were built speculatively, and could be hired from one of the big independent workshops that flourished on the needs of an industrial economy dominated by coal.

These private wagons persisted in using dumb buffers long after their abandonment elsewhere, and clung to the cheap method of lubrication by means of grease rather than oil. The grease needed constant replenishment if the wagons were to run freely, especially to replace what melted and slid out of the axle-boxes in the warmer months. At Netherfield and Colwick station, on one of the Great Northern Railway's routes through the Nottinghamshire coalfield, the weekly summer consumption in Edwardian times was nearly two barrels a week, the equivalent of over half a ton of grease. Often the regreasing was skimped. A visitor to a Yorkshire marshalling yard in the 1930s was shown axle-boxes with grease 'dried almost to the hardness of wood'. It took a lot of pulling to keep wagons of this type on the move; the visitor's guide explained that a full-length coal train running entirely on grease-lubricated axles could not be shifted by a standard locomotive at all. Yet over two-thirds of the private wagons requisitioned in 1939 were of this type, as against just one in a hundred railway-owned wagons by the same date.

When they did get under way, grease-lubricated wagons were restricted to a maximum of 30 mph, or their axles were prone to overheat. That was a respectable upper speed for passenger traffic in the 1830s, but as services became faster it was no longer possible to intersperse passenger and freight trains without clogging up the network. Some goods services could be run during the night, as the London & North Western began to do in 1846, but this was sufficient for only a limited proportion of the fast-growing sector. The usual answer was to provide for overtaking by means of passing loops or long sidings, where slow trains could take temporary refuge. (The modern traveller can deduce their sites from the long flat strips of waste land that suddenly appear and disappear alongside the running lines, often in places remote from any station.) A more thoroughgoing and expensive solution was to double the lines completely, so that fast passenger and slow freight trains could keep out of each other's way. In the 1860s the Midland Railway arranged much of its new route to London in this way, providing platforms for the fast lines only. Despite the existence of dedicated goods routes here and there, rates of progress and times of arrival for goods trains often depended more on decisions taken ad hoc in the area's control office than on any fixed timetable. This extreme slowness was due less to speeds when the trains were moving than to the long periods spent waiting in loops and sidings so that passenger trains could pass. The Great Western calculated in the 1930s that the average speed of goods carried on its routes was less than 10 mph. The LMS and LNER were even slower.

Getting shot of the old colliery wagons altogether was therefore an early priority for the nationalised railways. To replace them, BR raised the payload to sixteen tons and built new standard wagons all of steel, to a total of 200,000, mostly with hand brakes only. A further 9,000 that had been built to help restock the war-ravaged railways of the Continent were repatriated, even as the new Railway Executive was vacillating over plans to push the standard mineral wagon payload up to 24.5 tons (which would have cut the length and dead weight of coal trains in proportion). More capacious types than this had been operating for decades in some areas, but most collieries were equipped only for the smaller versions, as were plenty of the drops, tips, chutes and hoists that received the wagons at depots, factories, wharves and docks. Similar constraints applied to the standard four-wheeled box wagon used for general freight. In this sense, the railways' slow gains in efficient freight handling mirrored the sluggish progress of modernisation through British industry in general. In another sense, these small wooden wagons were simply part of the price of having been first in the field as a railway economy.

The dawn of the 1960s found the operation of freight on British Railways in a thoroughly confused situation. Officially, the future was both bright and clear. Its blueprint was the Modernisation Plan of 1955, which aimed to create a financially self-sufficient system within fifteen years, using diesel and electric traction. Unbraked wagons were to be vanquished by vacuum-braked freight services, streamed through a network of automated marshalling yards. The vacuum brake would allow trains to run much more swiftly, offering a better service to customers and making optimum use of the rolling stock. Faster freight would also lessen conflict with passenger traffic over access to the tracks and allow the abolition of countless loops, refuge sidings and slow lines.

The up-to-date version is celebrated in an instructive British Transport Film of 1957, *Fully Fitted Freight*. This follows the progress of the 4.18 p.m. train of miscellaneous goods from Bristol to Leeds and the onward transit of its cargoes after that. Much of the commentary is spoken in the 'character' mode much favoured by the film unit, as though to establish its distance from the austere intonations of the BBC or the slick facetious tones of cinema newsreels: voices steady, stoical, gently rueful now and again, and peppered with easily grasped workplace jargon. We see the train passing through open country to the stirring chords of Vaughan Williams, as a Bristolian version of the British Transport Voice intones its consignment list:

Seven wagons chocolate ... Fifteen cases Bristol milk sherry ... Twelve cases port ... Six barrels cider ... Ten cases Spanish wine ... Six cases pottery ... Two tons printed matter ... Ten tins tobacco ... Forty cartons footwear ... Fifteen hundredweight cigarettes ... Seven crates machinery ... Two and half tons light castings ... Forty heavy duty chairs ... Thirty revolving office chairs ... Thirty-one wicker chairs ... Eight crates of jam ... Two of marmalade ... Ten of coffee essence ... One ton birdseed ... Two wagons tomatoes ... Fifty-eight stepladders ... Three A-rigs ... Twelve petrol motors ... Nine dynamos ... Seventy-two broomhandles ... and one garden gate.

The final scenes follow some of these goods beyond the railway: budgies receive seed in a Blackpool pet shop, Glaswegians get drunk on Somerset cider, a Highland granny trudges through snow in her Glastonbury-made sheepskin boots.

This method of working had some crucial weaknesses. On the technical side, there was a conflict between the aspiration to phase out loose-coupled trains and the continuing dependence on individually marshalled consignments. From the shunter's point of view, vacuum-braked wagons were much more burdensome to attach and detach, each operation requiring attention to brake pipes as well as couplings. So that the pipes were not jerked apart in transit, these wagons also had to be coupled more closely, like passenger coaches. This was often achieved by means of couplings that screwed together, in place of loose links. Neither brake pipes nor screw couplings could be manhandled using the humble shunting pole. Modernisation therefore brought a revival of the old-fashioned (and less safe) practice of ducking down between the buffers to wrestle pipes and couplings into place when two vehicles were divided or joined. The train filmed in 1957 has to stop at Derby for forty minutes for re-marshalling. 'Any faster, and they'll 'ave all t'passengers sendin' themselves by goods!' says a Derbyshire version of the British Transport Voice; but the camera has already shown that the train includes vans for Carlisle, Preston, Aberdeen and half a dozen more destinations beyond Leeds, all of which will require further re-marshalling somewhere up the line.

Even the commitment to vacuum brakes was double-edged. It was pointless to deploy such wagons if they could not be connected to the locomotive, so they had to be placed at the front of the train, ahead of any unbraked vehicles (for which a brake van was still needed at the tail end).

But this messed up the basic principle of the marshalling yard, that each train could be divided and recombined as required. As a cheaper alternative to full vacuum brakes, many wagons therefore were 'through-piped' instead. That meant fitting them with brake pipes and hoses, but without any connection to the wagon's own brakes, which could still be worked only by a man standing by the track. Many freight trains were composed consequently of a mixture of fully braked and unbraked wagons, piped or unpiped. How fast a freight train could run safely depended on how many of its wagons could be braked from the locomotive, which in turn might depend on where they were in the make-up of the train. BR's system of train operating codes adopted in 1961 reflected these differences: those beginning with three included fast goods braked throughout, class 4 had at least 90 per cent of vehicles vacuum-braked, and so on down to classes 7, 8 and 9, which had no continuous brakes at all. In the same year, the policy of fitting all mineral wagons with vacuum brakes was quietly abandoned. In effect, the Victorian coal train was through to the next round, only now with steel-bodied, oil-lubricated wagons and with diesel rather than steam in charge.

₪

The vacuum-braking of wagons was one aspect of a broader problem. The Modernisation Plan of 1955 was essentially technocratic in nature. It looked for efficient ways to update the tasks the railways had been carrying out for generations. Building one new automated marshalling yard after another was entirely in the spirit of 1955. Meanwhile freight continued to transfer inexorably to the roads. Just as the Modernisation Plan was published, the figure for ton-miles carried by Britain's roads overtook the total going by rail for the first time since the early-Victorian years.

Historians locate the take-off point for British road haulage further back, in the years after the First World War. The early petrol- and steam-driven lorries in service before 1914 had an economic range of about forty miles, which tended to limit them to feeder traffic. Later models were more efficient, and carriers after 1918 could also have their pick of cheap ex-army lorries returning from the front. When the railways were largely immobilised by the General Strike of 1926, it was noted how much traffic managed to get through by road; nothing comparable had happened during the railway strike of 1911. By the 1930s, road hauliers were in contention for door-to-door traffic over distances of up to a hundred miles. Between 1923 and 1939 the number of lorries in use increased eightfold.

Political developments were favourable too. Transport became a department of government in 1919, formalising the emergency arrangements of the war years. From 1920 the new Ministry of Transport could use state funds to maintain and build new roads. The dust clouds raised by Edwardian motorists began to disappear, as the highways acquired impermeable black surfacing (another military spin-off: the technique had been perfected by the Tarmac Co. Ltd when building service roads to the trenches in France). A strategic programme to overhaul the trunk roads began in 1929, with the additional benefit of creating employment during the Depression. Trees and hedges were cut back, curves widened and kinks straightened.

Other advantages to the hauliers were legal rather than physical. Railway companies were required to publish their standard rates of carriage. Any road haulier could look up these charges, which had been subject to government control since 1840, and work out how to undercut them. In practice the railways were permitted to strike individual deals with customers too, and by the 1920s most of their regular traffic flows were covered by these 'exceptional rates'; but any similar business had to be allowed the same rates, on the principle of no undue discrimination. This operational straitjacket was loosened in the 1930s, but altogether it was not hard for the lorry owners to steer fresh business from rail to road. Many larger companies simply bought road vehicles for their own use and waved the railways goodbye.

Lorries also found a ready market among the railways themselves. They were especially useful for small consignments. Victorian working methods required these to be transferred from wagon to wagon as required, which entailed a great deal of sorting and repacking. Collection and delivery were made in short trips by horse-drawn vehicles, often the railways' own. The greater operating range of motor lorries meant that consignments could be carried to the nearest large station, to be placed directly in a wagon destined for long-distance travel. No longer was it necessary to enlist a horse and cart to carry the goods to the local station, for a locomotive-hauled trip that might only cover a few miles before the goods were transhipped to a different wagon for onward despatch. In the 1930s the railways therefore began the systematic abandonment of small goods

Great Western Railway delivery vehicles muster
outside Theale station in Berkshire, *c.* 1930

traffic at most of their lesser stations. The change was pioneered in the old
North Eastern Railway's territory, which by 1938 had cut the service back
to 83 'railhead' stations out of a total of 542. Most of the remainder continued to take wagonload freight, the term for consignments large enough
to require at least one wagon.

Many big customers chose to adapt their distribution systems to this
railhead model by setting up their own warehouses alongside. The railways' own lorries could then distribute their biscuits, feedstuffs, fertilisers
and other goods that tended to be delivered in quantities short of a full
wagonload. At Leeds Hunslet East depot, to take one example from the
mid 1950s, could be found the stockpiles of Kellogg's, Horlicks, Boots and
a new product, Fairy Snow washing powder. After 1928 the railways were
also permitted to undertake direct road carriage from door to door, on the
understanding that this could be more efficient than a three-stage journey
with a railway wagon as the middle instalment. The Big Four companies
even bought heavily into existing haulage firms, with the odd result that
the railways had a stake in the success of their own competitors.

Under the post-war Attlee government it looked briefly as though the tide might be reversed. By 1947 the railways had recovered an estimated 49 per cent of freight traffic by revenue, as against 41 per cent in 1938, and there were aspirations to integrate rail transport and long-distance road haulage (buses, inland water transport and docks too) in a single cost-effective system under the benevolent eye of the British Transport Commission. But these plans were never enforced with any vigour, and were discarded under the Transport Act of 1953. Nor was there any serious intention to reverse the flow of small consignments away from minor stations; as the railways' own policies showed, the only efficient way to handle these by train was through railhead distribution.

It did not help the railways' case that their own goods depots were often chronically outmoded. A single city might have a plethora of separate depots, the legacy of individual companies that mostly lost their identities and competitive *raison d'être* in the Grouping of 1923. Carlisle, an extreme case, ended up with seven general goods depots around the city, served originally by as many different companies. Bristol was no exception: *Fully Fitted Freight* hurries over the embarrassing fact that goods forwarded from the huge depot at Temple Meads (ex-Great Western) have had to come by railway lorry through the streets to the city's other main depot at St Philip's, alias Midland Road (ex-Midland), where they are put back on the rails again. Here they are loaded into box vans, of standard dimensions established decades before: a wooden body somewhat bigger than a large garden shed, mounted on a ten-foot wheelbase and carrying a payload of up to twelve tons. The vans stand at a platform under the open sky as loads are carried in manually through the sliding doors, or brought up on hand barrows, as if this were a house removal. There is a great deal of standing around and conferring over notebooks. Railwaymen in cloth caps, brass-buttoned waistcoats and shapeless jackets amble about. Police guards stand by as vulnerable cargoes – tobacco, alcohol, chocolate – are loaded into several of the wagons, which are then laboriously sealed. It hardly looks like the future of British land transport.

The more interruptions or transhipments required for any railway journey, the higher the chance that a lorry could do the same job more quickly and with lower risks of delay, loss or damage in transit. Already the first instalments of the motorway network were taking shape, a project 'in keeping with the bold, exciting and scientific age in which we live' – to quote the speech made by Ernest Marples (1907–78), Minister of Transport, at the opening ceremony of the M1 in 1959. Marples was quite a character, an able and slippery self-publicist whose reputation never quite escaped the taint of shady dealing (most of his personal fortune came from road building, and it was his own firm that constructed the M1's London extension). Marples also set about knocking the finances of British Railways into a more businesslike shape, setting up an advisory group to re-examine the progress and priorities of the 1955 Modernisation Plan. Wary of the risks of allowing the railways to mark their own homework, Marples made sure that the group was composed mostly of successful private businessmen with some experience of the nationalised industries. Among its members was a jowly, balding man, a former research scientist and fibres specialist whose achievements included a share in the development of Terylene, who had since become technical director of the giant chemicals conglomerate ICI. His name was Dr Richard Beeching (1913–85).

As the Special Advisory Group discovered, the railways' finances were in a horrible state. Integration having been abandoned, the management had pressed on with the project of modernising the network. That the assumptions of 1955 concerning future traffic turned out to be hopelessly optimistic had made no difference. Decisions had been taken on technical merits, without proper regard to capital costs or commercial plausibility. A typical example was the replacement of little-used steam-hauled local trains with diesel multiple units: a high return on outlay might result, but that was not the same as showing a profit. For two North Wales branch lines that were examined the annual return was impressive (23 per cent), but the services still went on losing money. All these losses across the network added up to a deficit that kept growing: £23 million in 1954, £177 million in 1962. It was time to ask hard questions about the future size and shape of the network, and what could feasibly be achieved both for passenger traffic and for freight. That railways had a social value, so that closing stations and withdrawing services would impose hardship or inconvenience, was never in doubt; but the ruling assumption was that no line should run at a loss, unless a reprieve was granted at a ministerial level.

This was the basis on which Beeching was appointed to take charge of the railways in 1961. The ponderous old British Transport Commission was killed off shortly afterwards, and the railways began the year 1963 with a generous write-off of debt and a new controlling body, the British Railways Board, with Beeching as chairman. His report, *The Reshaping of British Railways*, was launched in March 1963 (five days after the Beatles' first LP), priced at one shilling.

The report covered every aspect of the railways, but is remembered above all for its policy of closing lightly used passenger lines and stations. The effects on railway travel were certainly both rapid and drastic. One-third of the 4,300 stations open at the end of 1962 had closed eight years later (by which time Beeching had collected a peerage and gone back to ICI). A great many of these closures hit lesser stations on main lines, served by local trains that tended to get in the way of the more financially rewarding through traffic. Others were on branch or cross-country lines that shut completely, as the network was chopped down from 18,214 miles to 12,098 during the same eight years.

Some of these lines closed with barely a mumble of protest, especially when they duplicated or ran parallel to other routes. Other services on the hit list were keenly contested, and won a reprieve. Some should never have been threatened in the first place, such as the electrified commuter route between Liverpool and Southport with its weekly traffic of 120,000 passengers. It also helped if a line happened to run through plenty of marginal constituencies, because the ultimate decision on closure rested not with the railways' management but with the Minister of Transport. The arrangement was good news for the people of mid Wales, whose railway traversed no fewer than seven marginals on its course between Shropshire and Carmarthenshire. Other remote and beautiful lines that were menaced but have survived include the Far North of Scotland route, the northerly route to the ferry port of Stranraer, the Cumbrian Coast route and the Settle and Carlisle line. Then there were the railways that really should never have closed, and in some cases have since reopened to passengers. Mansfield, Corby, Aberdare, Heysham – all lost their trains, all have now got them back. A final category covers lines that the report meant to retain, but which were killed off after all. So there were no more holiday trains to Swanage or Hunstanton, no more rambles through the Peak District from the old Midland Railway's stations in Dovedale and Wyedale, no more donnish cross-country journeys between the high tables of Oxford and Cambridge (one to weigh in the scales against any accusations of Establishment bias towards Oxbridge).

An under-used, loss-making service is a service nonetheless, and Beeching's vigorous axe-work has left deep scars in the collective memory. That hundreds of stations had already been abolished by his predecessors, that others were closing all over the place even as the doctor went about compiling his report, that dozens more closures were forced through by his successors – none of this can dislodge the association between Beeching's name and the loss of so many lines and stations. As the official historian of British Railways puts it, 'History remembers the Black Death, not the other plagues.' Yet Dr Beeching's prescription for the railways was based on some clear-eyed diagnoses, whatever its detailed failings. Even after the closure of over 3,000 miles of route in the years up to 1961, Beeching could show that half of the network that remained was carrying only marginal levels of traffic: no more than 4 per cent of passenger-miles and 5 per cent of freight ton-miles. One-third of the passenger stations together handled under 1 per cent of total passenger revenue. Goods depots (most of which shared space with passenger stations) numbered 5,000, half of which contributed no more than 3 per cent of revenue for the sector. Critics objected that the traffic surveys were too crude and partial, having been taken over just one week in April 1961, but there was no convincing challenge to the outlines of Beeching's deductions.

Dr Beeching's attitude to freight was rather more complicated. Closing down little-used depots and the lines that served them was the easy part. By the end of 1968 only 912 of the 5,000 total were left, and even these had dwindled to 542 five years later. Sundries depots, of the kind capable of handling the fiddly little consignments celebrated in *Fully Fitted Freight* – garden gates and all – were cut still further, from 950 depots to a target of a mere 100 railheads, from which collections and deliveries were managed by road. The aim was to improve the woeful returns on the sundries trade, for which the average payload was less than one ton per wagon. Seasonal flows of traffic on a larger scale were no longer welcome, because they required keeping too many wagons waiting unproductively in reserve. When the apple-growers of the Cambridgeshire fenland tried in 1964 to arrange transport of their crop from Wisbech, BR could not spare sufficient box vans for the job. Two years earlier, this would have been accounted a serious oversight; now it was a matter of policy. On the other hand, it was clear that bulk flows of year-round traffic – coal for power stations, coke for steelworks, petrochemicals, aggregates – could run at a sound profit, using large wagons with continuous brakes (as with passenger carriages, the vacuum brake was gradually abandoned in favour of air braking, another costly transition).

The power-station traffic was mostly taken over by merry-go-round (MGR) trains composed of air-braked hopper wagons, each carrying twice as much coal as the standard 1950s type. These could be loaded and unloaded automatically while the train crept its way round big looped track layouts at both pithead and power station, eliminating the need for shunting, marshalling or reversing. The MGR system was characteristic of the huge power stations built on rural land by the Central Electricity Generating Board in the 1960s and early 1970s, such as Ratcliffe-on-Soar in the Trent Valley, a few miles south of D. H. Lawrence's truck-haunted native landscape. In place of cheaply built wooden trucks used perhaps once a fortnight, the new hopper wagons could run productively and without a pause for as long as the driver's shift lasted.

Another promising type of traffic was the standard intermodal container, for which BR coined the name Freightliner. Container traffic began to show a profit in 1968, which was also the year in which BR was finally relieved of responsibility for the doomed sundries trade. Containers have since become one of the busiest sectors of the modern rail haulage business, although on a very different basis from the 1960s conception of an alternative to the lorry for inland traffic. Now that the British industrial economy is a shadow of its old self, container trains mostly distribute imported goods from Southampton, Felixstowe, Tilbury and the new Thamesport terminal to inland sites for onward distribution by road. The Felixstowe branch alone now sees twenty-nine container trains in each direction every day. Especially in the Midlands and points north, any imported goods bought from Marks & Spencer, B&Q, or one of the big supermarkets are likely to have come part of the way as rail freight.

But in between the garden gates and the full trainloads were the medium-sized cargoes, and here Beeching could wave neither an axe nor a magic wand. The sector was declining, but remained much too big to write off altogether: as late as 1967, wagonload traffic still accounted for two-thirds of the revenue from freight. It was consignments of this kind – a few wagons a few times a week, coal or oil for the factory boiler-house, batches of breeze blocks or rolled-steel joists for the building industry – that kept the trains rolling in and out of the great marshalling yards. The dilemma for the railways was that the wagonload service could never be made to show a surplus, regardless of how many trains ran, but neither could the existing network be kept up without the income it generated. It was feared that giving up on wagonload traffic completely might tip the system into a downward spiral.

This situation was essentially transitional. As the road network grew, so did its challenge to railway freight in terms of convenience, capacity and speed. The permitted size of the lorries passing endlessly up and down the burgeoning motorway system increased too. Before 1964 they were limited to 24 tons gross weight. The new maximum was 32 tons, a figure subsequently increased to 44 metric tonnes (43.3 imperial tons). Permitted speeds rose too, to 40 mph in 1967, and then to 60 mph on motorways. In the face of such competition, the service offered by the railways had to change drastically.

A determined response finally came when the service was effectively relaunched in 1972, later adopting the brand name Speedlink. The new generation of mixed freight trains ran to fast and reliable timetables, making intensive use of air-braked wagons to guarantee delivery within one working day. Their movements could be tracked by computer technology known as TOPS (Total Operations Processing System), bought in from the Southern Pacific Railroad in the USA to replace the old, ad hoc methods of telegraph codes and telephone calls. Customers were connected directly by means of several hundred private sidings at works and depots, or they could use one of the remaining handful of railhead distribution centres to collect and deliver by road. Each long-distance Speedlink train still had to be made up from small groups of wagons picked up from these sites and broken down again for delivery at the other end – coupled and uncoupled, as ever, by hand. Little groups of these wagons could be seen amid the vast acreage of empty sidings at the few remaining marshalling yards, waiting to be sent on their way, until the service was finally abandoned in 1991. Air brakes, computerisation, accelerated speeds, rationalised distribution – none of these improvements had in the end been enough to make the wagonload service run at a profit.

Histories of British railways have often presented the decline of freight in terms of missed chances, some specific to the service, others deriving from the wider legal and administrative framework. If only the companies had bought out the interests of the colliery owners and set about upgrading their wagon fleets, running speeds and track layouts in earnest. If only all those duplicate routes had not been built, leaving many companies unable to run a profitable service from their share of the divided traffic. If only rival companies had been permitted to amalgamate earlier, to achieve better economies of scale. If only the Big Four companies produced by the merger of 1923 had worked harder and faster to shed some of these surplus assets. If only the railways had made a better fist of developing their own door-to-door collection and delivery services, in conjunction with rail-borne traffic. Above all: if only the railways had been released sooner from the regulatory straitjacket imposed in Victorian times, once it was clear that they were facing genuine and rising competition from the roads. Instead, they were legally defined as 'common carriers' until as late as 1962: obliged to accept traffic regardless of profitability, to treat all customers without undue preference and to publish their standard charges – not to mention the employment of unionised staff on regulated wages and conditions. Just when the government was about to loosen these bonds, in response to a well-argued campaign for 'A Square Deal for the Railways', the Second World War broke out. In peacetime the railways became state-owned and were subjected over several years to an ill-defined project for integrated transport instead.

Yet it is hard to see how things might have turned out differently in the end. At best, more of the heavy industries that had grown up symbiotically with the railways might have escaped closure or decline. As for the trade in sundries, the garden gates, sheepskin boots and other miscellanea of *Fully Fitted Freight* all eventually went over to road haulage because it offered a better and (usually) cheaper service. Even the container trains that carry the imported consumer goods and supermarket foodstuffs of the post-industrial economy will keep running only as long as Network Rail is permitted by its political masters to keep track access charges at a competitive level.

₪

Behind this long tale of decline is a larger story concerning the railways' finances. Back in the 1840s, the bigger companies allotted only around 35 per cent of annual revenue to meeting the costs of operation. By the early 1870s the national figure still stood at a healthy 51 per cent. In other words, almost half of the railways' income was still available for dividends, servicing debts (for the industry depended on borrowing as well as share capital) and investment in new lines, buildings and equipment. From that point onwards, almost everything that happened to the railways served to shrink this surplus. Some of these changes, such as reduced working hours and safer, heavier and better-equipped carriages, have already been described. By the late 1890s the share of revenue taken by operating costs had risen to 57 per cent, by the mid 1900s to 62 per cent.

These shrinking returns were not so apparent externally, as the railways boomed in terms of size and turnover. Between 1870 and 1914 passenger numbers and gross revenue both rose by a factor of four, freight tonnage increased threefold, route mileage grew by half as much again and the total capital invested grew by 150 per cent. Yet the new lines, infrastructure and improved rolling stock no longer delivered the same rates of return that had excited earlier generations of investors. Especially expensive projects included the enormous new stations and goods depots that were required to service the ever-growing cities. John Kellett's classic study of railways and urban change cites the example of Huskisson goods station, built in the 1870s in Liverpool's docks at a cost of £712,527.* If the traffic handled there had been surcharged at a rate to reflect the interest on this investment, the increase would have amounted to a prohibitive 3s 10½d per ton. In effect, the more highly capitalised the railways became, the less capitalist were the attitudes of their directors and managers towards fresh investment. The supreme example was the Great Central Railway, at once a splendid creation in terms of engineering, rolling stock and operation, and a bad dream in terms of outcomes for its investors. In a parallel development, the companies quietly withdrew from competing against one another in favour of pooling resources and revenues and agreeing uniform rates and fares – becoming, in the words of one transport historian, a 'collusive oligopoly'.

This situation was by no means bad news for everyone. Passengers enjoyed faster journeys in better carriages without facing a rise in fares. Industrial customers paid the same predictable rates whether the railway was making or losing money from their custom. Overall, it could be said that the railways were being run in the national interest, rather than as the creature of their own shareholders.

As if to endorse this view of the broader economic benefits of railway transport, an Act was passed in 1896 to encourage construction of so-called light railways in rural areas. A licence from the Board of Trade was sufficient authority to undertake a light railway, which saved the costs of the usual Act of Parliament. They were built to less demanding standards than usual and could draw on grants or loans from the Treasury for the capital costs. The compensation paid to landowners was even adjusted to take account of the benefits the railway was expected to bring. Some 900 extra miles were added to the network by lines of this type up to 1918.

---

* Named after the adjacent docks, rather than in direct commemoration of the Liverpool MP killed on the railway in 1830, which might have been a bit much.

One of the biggest of the new companies served the Isle of Axholme in the agrarian depths of north Lincolnshire, constructed 1903–9. Banners displayed at one of its stations on the opening day caught the mood of having joined the modern world at last: 'Progress and prosperity', 'Patience Rewarded'. Getting a railway connection was like securing mains electricity, radio reception or broadband coverage today: the provision of a basic utility that put the district on a more level footing with everywhere else.

When real competition arrived from the roads, the railways therefore struggled to find a coherent response. Even if they had been free to charge what the market would bear, the government, their business customers and the travelling public would have had none of it. Yet the resulting decline was severe: receipts from freight were £36 million in 1923, falling to £26.5 million in 1932 (an especially bad year). By the late 1930s, operating costs were swallowing 81 per cent of everything the railways could earn.

One of the biggest dilemmas was how to handle the distinction between profitable business and mere turnover. Wagonload freight is one perennial example. And what of those lightly used branch lines: were they sucking financial sap from the healthy trunk, or was it better to regard them as feeders, topping up the traffic on the main lines with enough extra business to make a significant difference to the operating margins? As long as local losses could be subsumed within the company's headline figures, the temptation was to give such lines the benefit of the doubt. No other explanation can account for the longevity of some of the light railways built under the 1896 Act which happened to be swallowed up by the Grouping of 1923. The Mid-Suffolk Light Railway is an extreme case. Planned as a cross-country route to join two lines owned by the Great Eastern Railway, it failed to open all the way despite being built very cheaply indeed – part of the route was laid directly on the Suffolk earth and ballasted roughly over, there were 114 level crossings within eighteen miles to save the expense of bridges, and the terminus building at Laxfield was clad in zinc sheeting printed with a brick pattern, of the kind used for chicken coops. The project even bankrupted its own company chairman before the line opened in 1908; at one point he was reduced to buying jewellery on credit and pawning it the same day. Modest even in the best years, company receipts had almost halved by 1921. Rescued just in time by absorption into the new London & North Eastern Railway, the line somehow bumbled on until 1952.

Other financial handicaps were imposed by the custom of fixed pricing for passengers and freight according to distance carried. The Highland Railway's line through the Grampians to Inverness is a case in point. As constructed in the 1860s, the route came at the town via a big loop to the east, into Morayshire. Twenty years later a rival company proposed an alternative route to Inverness, which the Highland decided to pre-empt by building its own more direct approach. Crossing mountainous territory via the gruelling Slochd summit, and requiring two large viaducts and two deep cuttings, the new line was expensive to construct. Yet when it opened in 1898 the Grampian cut-off attracted no significant business from other railway companies, because Inverness was still served by the Highland alone. Nor did the line unlock substantial new traffic from the empty country along the way. But because the new route was so much shorter, it entailed an appreciable cut in passenger fares and goods tariffs to Inverness – traffic that would have come by rail anyway. Everyone benefited except the Highland Railway itself, which now had to maintain and operate two routes to Inverness instead of one.

Passenger fares on a network with hundreds of companies and thousands of stations were complicated enough, but at least the passengers themselves came in a manageable number of categories: adults, children, workmen, servicemen and so on. By comparison, the permutations for carrying freight were of mind-blowing complexity, especially before 1923. Even the basic categories established by the Railway Clearing House tended as time went by to split types of traffic rather than lumping them together. By 1886 there were 2,753 items on its lists, each classified under one of several rates of carriage. These rates were decided according to the value of the commodity or article (brandy was charged more than coal), its bulk in relation to weight (biscuits were charged more than sugar), ease of handling (outsize loads cost more than handy-sized ones; frozen meat more than fresh), liability to damage in transit and so on.

In parallel with these standard class rates, a separate system of charges was applied to important flows of traffic within the territory of each railway, with a greater margin of negotiation and discretion. For instance, imports and exports were commonly charged at lower rates than inland traffic for many years, to prevent shipowners taking their business to rival rail-served ports. Allowances also had to be made when a customer supplied the wagons and discounts were available too for cargoes carried at the owner's risk. It was cheaper to collect and deliver goods at the station than to send them door-to-door via the railways' own cartage service, and

[55 & 56 Vict.] *Railway Rates and Charges, No. 15* [Ch. liii.]
(*North Eastern Railway, &c.*), *Order Confirmation Act*, 1892.

CLASS 3—*continued.*

A.D. 1892.

North Eastern Railway, &c.

Angelica root.
Aniseed.
Apple rings, in slices, dried.
Apples, dry, or pippins.
Arsenic acid, e.o.h.p.
Awl blades.
Bacon and hams, cured, e.o.h.p.
Baking powder.
Baths.
Bayonets.
Beadings and mouldings, gilt, lacquered, or varnished, packed in boxes.
Bed keys.
Bedsteads, e.o.h.p.
Beehives, made of wood.
Bellows, packed.
Bellows pipes.
Bell ringing (carillon) machinery.
Bells, small.

Bobbins, e.o.h.p.
Bolts, door.
Books, e.o.h.p.
Boothing or stalling.
Boots and shoes, including goloshes and leather cut into boot shapes, in casks, cases, or boxes.
Boracic acid.
Bottle jacks.
Bottles and bottle stoppers, glass, e.o.h.p.
Bowls, wood or iron, e.o.h.p.
Boxes or trunks, tin or sheet iron, packed in crates or cases.
Boxes, safety.
Box or Italian irons.
Braces, except silk, for wearing apparel, in bales, packs, or trusses.
Brands, iron or steel.
Brass work, spun or stamped, packed.

An extract from the North Eastern Railway's classification of goods traffic,
1892. The tables were meant to encompass every transportable commodity,
from agrarian produce to obscure manufactures and exotic imports

cheaper still when the traffic went to or from private sidings instead of
public goods stations. Sometimes the goods were warehoused for a period
by the railway itself, for which another charge was levied. All of this before
the final calculation could be made on the basis of mileage carried, often
with a discount for long-distance consignments. Finally, revenue from
traffic that had been carried on the routes of two or more railway companies had to be shared out to general satisfaction. Small wonder that the
London & North Western was at one point offering *20 million* configurations of charges for the conveyance of goods.

It should not be thought that the railways were indifferent about
economy, especially after the amalgamations of 1923. The initiatives of Sir
Josiah Stamp (1880–1941; later Lord Stamp) as chairman of the London,
Midland & Scottish are especially interesting, because he was the first
outsider in generations to be appointed chief executive of a major British
railway company. Beginning as a boy clerk in the Inland Revenue, Stamp

became a crucial figure in Treasury circles during the First World War and its aftermath. In 1919 he left the Civil Service to direct Nobel Industries Ltd. In 1926, the same year in which the Nobel company was merged with others to form Dr Beeching's future company ICI, Stamp took over at the LMS.

This was the largest of the Big Four companies, and the one most afflicted by old rivalries that had suddenly been internalised. Nonetheless, the new company got some things right from the outset. It transformed the productivity of its workshops and shrank the stock of items purchased from around 30,000 types to 4,400; four kinds of sweeping brush instead of twenty-five, eight varieties of varnish instead of twenty-eight and so on. Stamp's ability to get things done reflected a broader movement of power within railway management, away from the socially elevated board of directors and towards the senior staff. His distinctive contribution, inspired by American methods, was an enthusiasm for statistics as the key to efficiency. The new job offered plenty to get statistical about: in the early 1930s the LMS had 225,000 staff and 8,000 horses and was running 25,000 trains daily using its 9,000 locomotives, 18,700 carriages and 277,000 wagons. It operated twenty-seven hotels, as many docks, harbours and piers, and owned 537 miles of bought-out canals.

One of Stamp's policies was to set targets for locomotive performance, based on systematic records of the maintenance and costs of each engine, as well as the overall rating of the type to which it belonged. Information was collected for eleven different sections of each locomotive, and for seven different sections of their tenders. Data was entered on record cards with holes in the margin, which were punched through to the edge of the card or left whole according to the information recorded. By pushing a rod through a drawerful of cards aligned with one or another of these holes and then lifting it, the cards with relevant details – repair costs to a particular boiler type, say – would drop out ready for scrutiny.

Stamp reassured his shareholders in 1932 that the costs of collecting and processing all this data were justified in terms of strategy and savings. A colder-eyed account of the new statistical culture of the LMS is given by Christian Hewison (born 1909), then a young shedmaster at Walton-on-the-Hill in Liverpool, a joint possession of the LMS and LNER. Hewison's responsibilities lay with the latter company, which placed much greater store by local initiative and delegation. He noted the metaphorical new broom at work on the LMS side, where 'the supervisors always seemed to be devoting so much effort and exertion to organising the organisation that they had no time to run the railway properly ... clerical staff were making work for one another by inventing problems and then sending letters and requesting data in the pretence of seeking solutions'. As for Stamp's beloved locomotive statistics, Hewison reckoned that shrewd LMS men were securing permission for overhauls by fabricating much of the information sent to head office, being careful to represent their engines as slightly more run-down each time.

Mere anecdotal evidence, perhaps; but the dilemma of how to understand what such a gigantic company was doing, let alone how it might be done more efficiently, was real enough – to say nothing of the overlapping distinctions between what was efficient, what was productive and what was profitable. Calculating the balance between costs and returns was a higher form of financial art altogether. Consider the despatch of a crate of machinery from Cornwall to Devon in the 1930s. A road haulier could offer a quotation based on relatively few costs: purchase and maintenance of a vehicle, fuel, a driver's labour, road tax and licence fees, and other overheads represented by his business premises and any other staff. On the railways, costs multiplied in all directions. As well as the outlay represented by the wagon, something had to be allowed for locomotive and brake van too – perhaps more than one of each, if the crate was to be transhipped or the wagon re-marshalled. Locomotives needed coal, water and oil. Drivers, firemen, goods guards and shunters, as well as signalmen, station or depot staff and level-crossing keepers, had to be paid too. Track, signals, bridges, tunnels and cuttings along the way, station or depot buildings at each end – all represented fixed costs, both for construction or renewal and for everyday maintenance. If the crate was despatched door-to-door, the railways' own lorries would be called in, each of which represented costs of purchase, maintenance, fuel, driver, tax and licence, etc. etc. Management and administration were costs in themselves. A sliver of the customer's fee might go towards the railway's subscription to the Railway Clearing House, if the crate happened to pass between the two railways, the Great Western and the Southern, which operated in the south-west after 1923. Another notional slice would be swallowed by the accountant, who was hardly in a position to say whether the carriage of crate-loads between Cornwall and Devon was profitable in itself.

What remained after all these deductions could be paid out as a dividend. In the lean and hungry 1930s only the Great Western managed to keep payments on its ordinary shares above the basic bank rate, at the cost of raiding its own reserves. The other Big Four companies came nowhere near the same level. Yet as long as dividends were still in play, it was possible to sustain the hope that the railways' business model was basically sound. By this view, the solution lay in zealous efficiency at every level and an attentive attitude to passengers' and customers' needs, outflanking the road hauliers whenever possible. The dismaying truth – that the railways' business model was grievously flawed and ultimately doomed – was not uttered publicly from within the industry until Beeching issued his report.

A fresh attempt to confront hard realities was made in 1968, when a new Transport Act at last recognised the principle that public transport, bus as well as rail, was a legitimate object of national subsidy. This was hardly a new idea, as the Light Railway Act of 1896 had made the same case, but it allowed expenditure to be planned more realistically. Local trains and commuter services were now acknowledged to show wider social and economic benefits and underwritten accordingly. In the same spirit, the 1968 Act also introduced the concept of subsidies for rail freight in the form of grants to companies wanting to invest in sidings and handling equipment, although these have not endured. In those sectors of the passenger business that are meant to show a profit, cross-subsidies remain inevitable, as a little thought will show. The journey of the passenger on a nine-tenths-empty Sunday evening train is effectively underwritten by the dozens who will cram into the same carriage the following Monday morning. Even at their simplest, railway economics remain quite complicated.

MANAGING

Whatever their latter-day failings as businesses, it would be wrong to think of the old railway companies as mere victims of gigantism and inertia. The very existence of such large concerns, with all their human and financial convolutions, was itself a novelty; only the army, the Royal Navy and (while it lasted) the East India Company could compare. The industry thus became a kind of forcing house for new methods of management and control, serving in turn as the model for how other large corporations were run. In that sense, every large commercial organisation – and not just those in Britain – is a descendant of the railways.

One crucial development was the formal separation of management and direction. This was not planned from the start, any more than the railways were planned as a single system, but happened in response to the dilemmas presented by their increasing size and complexity. Most businesses prior to the 1830s were run by those who owned them, either directly or through foremen and deputies. Ironworks, mills and the like were essentially family firms or partnerships. Collieries were run by bosses appointed by the landowner. Joint-stock canal and dock companies and turnpike trusts were among the few exceptions, but these were relatively straightforward to look after because the vehicles and boats that used them were privately owned and operated.

Railway companies took the game to a new level. They were owned by shareholders, administered by directors and operated by engineers. Shareholders could not be expected to run the show, although they could be vocal and influential on occasion (as Brunel found in the death throes of his Atmospheric Railway). Directors were not necessarily the best managers either; typically they were local businessmen, or rich and powerful figures appointed with an eye to projecting reassurance or aristocratic lustre. Engineers were at once indispensable to the railways and deficient as its chieftains, partly because their experience of handling commercial issues and a highly varied workforce was often limited, partly because so many problems required non-technical solutions.

In response, the railways gradually established a new class of professional manager. With the passage of time, its membership was drawn overwhelmingly by promotion or recruitment from among their own staff. Programmes were eventually developed to select and train promising employees for service in the higher grades. In due course, the LMS opened a School of Transport at Derby, the railways' first staff college. Such investment in personnel was practically unknown in other British trades and industries. Railway executives were highly respected men, and a few were even lured away to other plum jobs, most notably Sir Felix Pole (1877–1956). Pole joined the Great Western as a telegraph clerk in 1891 and vacated its general manager's chair in 1928 for that of the newly formed Associated Electrical Industries Ltd (AEI). By the same token it was unusual that the LMS chose an outsider, Sir Josiah Stamp, as its chairman. But when the young industry was still finding its feet, the flow of able and experienced men could only run the other way. Senior appointments were made from the navy or army, others from the road-carriage trade. Outstanding among this intake was a former captain in the East India Company's civilian staff, the gifted but domineering Mark Huish (1808–67).

Huish's railway career began in Scotland, until a headhunting mission in 1841 brought him south as secretary and general manager of the Grand Junction Railway. There he set about developing a structure of clearly defined responsibilities under salaried junior managers, with firm rules, disciplinary structures and systems of fines and rewards for the men. When the Grand Junction was merged with other lines to form the new London & North Western company, he retained his senior role. The LNWR was the largest joint-stock company of its time, with a capitalisation of over £29 million in 1851.

There were no business schools to teach the difference between management and direction (or, to put it in military language, between tactics and strategy), and the captain's time at the Grand Junction showed that even the ablest minds within the railway world had yet to determine where that boundary should be drawn. For example, the board minutes from the early 1840s include a claim against the company for a dead horse and another for a quantity of butter valued at 13s 6d. Such minutiae were gradually steered by Huish towards junior committees, leaving the board's members free to take larger views, while their senior officer – Huish, again – co-ordinated the various committees and departments. Scrupulous compilation of reports and tight control of expenditure underpinned all this work.

Huish's own style was the opposite of the light-touch school. In his biographer's words, 'he made strenuous efforts to retain personal control over as many of the company's affairs as possible'. He sat in on many committees, and his grasp of detail allowed him to present monthly reports to the board in such a way that it was hard to resist his recommendations. Meetings often ended with a scratch committee of Huish and a selection of directors sitting on to thrash out matters arising. He also undertook the opening arrangements of new lines, was the company's resident expert on the electrical telegraph and had sole responsibility for its Post Office contracts. These extra duties represented an older way of getting things done, by which the most competent person available would tackle problems ad hoc. They also suited Huish's dictatorial nature. Decisions were made briskly and channels of command were clear. The LNWR had no equivalent figure to the ungovernable engineer-manager Brunel, riding his technological hobby-horses and doing his persuasive best to clear up any messes afterwards.

One challenge faced by every railway concerned the long-term costs of its operations, as infrastructure and other fixed assets began to depreciate at different rates. Huish stands out for his early understanding of what this might entail. In particular, he guarded the company against any illusions arising from short-term prosperity by means of the double-account system, thus keeping a clear picture of assets and liabilities, including any long-term costs that were moving steadily closer. One of his principles was that rolling stock should be maintained from ordinary revenue, being a fairly constant cost, but that big occasional investments should be matched by setting a share aside in a depreciation fund. What he had in mind were such tasks as the need to make good the permanent way on lines that had been profitably open to traffic for several years. When a railway was built on the cheap, early and costly renewals were liable to follow. The board of the little St Andrews Railway in Fife, opened in 1852 with Thomas Bouch as engineer, were dismayed to discover a few years later that the economical Bouch had built bridges from scanty untreated timbers and made the interval between the sleepers a foot wider than specified in the contract. Huish's basic point may seem obvious enough, but many companies in the 1830s and 1840s had done nothing to safeguard their futures in this way, preferring to dish out their surpluses in big dividends instead. One contributory cause of the Railway Mania was the mirage of permanent enrichment from railway shares which these payments helped to induce.

Another creature of the Mania years was George Hudson (1800–71), one of those plausible rogues who rise to the surface of financial bubbles. Hudson used an inherited fortune to build a municipal power base at York, from which he secured election as chairman of the York & North Midland Railway in 1836. Two masterstrokes followed in the early 1840s. The ebullient Hudson was able to persuade the shareholders of eight companies all contending to build a line from York to Newcastle that they should join forces, opening the way to a successful start on the work. Hudson's second coup was to merge his own company with two other medium-sized concerns to form the Midland Railway, which passed under his control too. The Eastern Counties Railway was added to Hudson's managerial empire in 1846, the year he was elected MP for Sunderland. Richer than ever, he bought one estate from a duke and another from an earl.

Then it emerged that the York, Newcastle & Berwick Railway had been buying shares in another of Hudson's companies, and paying a startlingly generous price to do. Worse than that, the vendor was Hudson himself. A lot more secrets came to light after that, none of them good news for the so-called Railway King. Many of the reported figures for revenue, traffic and expenditure on his lines proved to be imaginative fictions. Dividends that should have been paid out of operating profits were routinely diverted from the streams of capital that flooded constantly into the companies' coffers, as instalments became due on partly paid-up shares.

Hudson's misdemeanours stopped just short of criminality, which is another way of saying that railway finance had evolved faster than the law's ability to regulate it. Even so, his exposure left him hugely in debt, and debtors could still be imprisoned under English law at that time. The Railway King would have been a prime candidate for lock and key but for his status as an MP, which brought the privilege of exemption. As soon as each parliamentary session ended, however, Hudson had to remove himself promptly to the Continent to escape arrest. This went on until 1859, when he finally lost his Sunderland seat and retired to France for a while. Tempted back in 1865 by his nomination to contest Whitby for the Tories, he was nabbed at last and detained for three months in England's most grandiose debtors' prison, at York Castle. After coming to terms with his remaining creditors, Hudson went on to enjoy a rehabilitated English afterlife for six more years, to the great satisfaction of his old Yorkshire adherents. His last journey, safely encased in a half-ton triple coffin, was made with the railway companies he had helped to create: leaving London by the Midland route from St Pancras, and on to York by the North Eastern Railway (successor to the York, Newcastle & Berwick), whose general manager and passenger superintendent accompanied the funeral cortège through the city streets to a village burial in the family plot at Scrayingham.

The next financial scandal to rattle confidence in the railways was a smaller affair, its perpetrator obscure by comparison. His name was Lionel Redpath. In 1848 Redpath was appointed registrar of the Great Northern Railway, the very line whose construction Hudson had tried his damnedest to prevent. Redpath had complete personal control of the new company's stock registers. To avoid any impropriety, he was required not to speculate in stocks or shares. The registrar got round this prohibition by creating imaginary stock on his own account. Sometimes he inflated the amounts of genuine transfers, adding an extra figure in the book so that £500 of shares became £1,500 and so on. Sometimes he invented phantom shareholders and assigned holdings to them that were camouflaged as transfers from the previous register. He could feel safe in doing so because the only person who habitually looked at the books was Redpath himself. The ghost shares were then sold on by Redpath to unsuspecting investors, via his unsuspecting brokers. There were 365 such sales, spread over eight years. That was enough for the registrar to clock up fraudulent gains of around £220,000 (roughly 400 times his annual salary). He took a big house in Chester Terrace by Regent's Park and bought a country retreat down at Weybridge. Both properties were lavishly furnished, and it was reported that Mrs Redpath 'had as many dresses as would fill a cart'. Much of the money left over went to good causes, including some showy benefactions; for instance, Redpath donated a rare edition of Milton to the Royal Society's library.

By 1854 the Great Northern's management had spotted that the sum paid out in dividends was mysteriously at odds with the book value of its stock. The registrar was asked to look into the matter. Obfuscating as best he could, Redpath managed to keep his cover intact for two more years. When the story at last emerged it caused a sensation; as with the Hudson case, the public was left wondering how many other railway investments were not what they seemed. As the cell door closed on its disgraced registrar, the Great Northern therefore called in a professional accountant, William Welch Deloitte, to perform a thorough audit. The loss was eventually wiped out by diverting half a year's dividends to buy back company stock, until the quantity in circulation once again matched the true figure. Selling off Redpath's property and goods also helped. The man himself was packed off to penal servitude in Australia.

Deloitte knew his way around railway accounts, having been enlisted in 1849 to assist with the audit of the Great Western. At that time it was still normal practice for the task to be done by representatives from the body of shareholders. As the companies grew larger and more complex, the shortcomings of this method grew increasingly obvious. Although it is not strictly true that the railways' needs created the modern profession of accountancy, they did more than any other industry to transform a practice previously associated most of all with broking and auctioneering. Railways provided a steady stream of work from regular half-yearly auditing, while also allowing new accountancy techniques to be tested and perfected. In that sense, the systems of external auditing now generally in place owe their genesis to the railways' custom. One instance is the requirement under the Regulation of Railways Act (1868) to publish a standardised set of annual accounts. Having established a legal procedure, the same rules were later extended to other big joint-stock companies.

Leading figures in the new profession did much of their most demanding work in the railways' service. Victorian accountants were like barristers or surgeons, dependent on personal reputation and individual appointments. Deloitte (1818–98) was one such man; among the younger generation, the rising star of accountancy was Edwin Waterhouse (1841–1917).

Waterhouse was the youngest brother of the architect Alfred Waterhouse, designer of the London & North Western's mighty hotel that replaced the 1830s frontage buildings at Liverpool Lime Street station. A few years before work started at Liverpool, in 1866, the LNWR appointed Edwin as the public accountant to its own auditors. Despite its vast size, the company still adhered at this time to the system by which the audit was performed by two shareholders elected at the Annual General Meeting on behalf of their fellow investors. One of these shareholder-auditors died in 1873, another in 1882. Waterhouse's status was raised each time, and in the second case he was formally appointed auditor in his own right. In the following year the Midland Railway asked if he would audit its books too; that the Midland and the LNWR were sworn rivals says much for Waterhouse's reputation for integrity. He declined, on the grounds that he was too busy. And no wonder, for Waterhouse had already been signed up by the London, Brighton & South Coast Railway (where he put a stop to the Hudsonian practice of paying dividends out of capital) and the South Eastern Railway. The Metropolitan, Lancashire & Yorkshire and Great Eastern railways were later beneficiaries of his attentions. The fees charged seem extraordinarily low: in 1891–2 the LNWR paid £1,199, the LBSCR just £300. The sums reflect the efficiency of the personal working method of this hard-driven and meticulous Quaker.

As a yardstick of the funds at stake, the railways' total paid-up capital by 1885 amounted to £816 million, as against £495 million invested in all other public companies combined. Railway shares rapidly pushed their way to the top of business at the Stock Exchange, supplanting the government stocks that had sustained most of the trading before the 1830s. The market was so lively that local stock exchanges were set up in the chief cities of England and Scotland, in time for the Railway Mania of the 1840s. Shares became available in less costly units, too. A single share in the Liverpool & Manchester cost £100, but later companies raised their capital in smaller shares, sometimes priced at under £10. For a new line, just 10 per cent of the full sum was usually required as a deposit. The less the outlay, the more potential investors could enter the market, often in the hope of a rapid and profitable onward sale (as the Mania demonstrated only too well).

Waterhouse retired in 1913, but the firm of Price, Waterhouse & Co. continued to dominate railway accounting. It served as joint auditor to three of the Big Four companies, and in the 1930s the company's railway department was engaged by another body from the industry, the Railway Clearing House. This quietly amazing organisation deserves a fuller description, as the privately owned system could never have functioned without it.

Because the first railway companies were conceived as self-contained businesses, no provision was made for through carriage of passengers and goods. As the pioneer lines began to join up to make the beginnings of a national network, this situation began to alter. But it was obvious that something more than a jumble of two-party agreements would be required if the system was to work smoothly. The Railway Clearing House (RCH) was the result. Operational from 1842, it was the brainchild of some leading men of the London & Birmingham Railway, who chose an ordinary house near Euston station as its home. The concept of a central hub for clearing and allotting payment was borrowed from banking and from the coaching trade, for which a similar body already existed charged with parcelling out the proceeds of passenger fares between the different horse owners. This was a simple task compared with the multiple missions of the RCH, even in its earliest years when membership was limited to the nine founding companies. Through booking had to be organised, for horses and private carriages as well as passengers; the proceeds were to be shared out on the basis of mileage travelled; through goods traffic was to be fostered; and any debts between companies were to be settled through the Clearing House itself.

By the time Sir Francis Head visited in 1849 the RCH had moved to a purpose-built new home. Inside was a hall 78ft long, in which 110 clerks worked at thirteen parallel desks. Daily submissions were made from 684 stations on forty-seven participating companies, detailing tickets issued and goods sent or received. Any irregularities were resolved and a monthly division of receipts was calculated and paid. Companies subscribing to the Clearing House were required to use the Edmondson system of numbered and printed tickets, which simplified record-keeping a good deal; but this was only one aspect of the 'astonishing system of minute detail' that Head described. Another concerned the handling of parcels. These were carried by passenger train and had to be accounted for by a different department from that dealing with goods. Eight clerks were engaged exclusively on working out the division of the spoils for each parcel fee; Head noted that a single consignment from London to Edinburgh incurred a four-way split. For a parcel sent as far as Arbroath, seven companies came in for a share. Other clerks dealt with enquiries about lost property, circulating descriptions of untraced items to larger stations. Tides of correspondence flowed in and out each day; five boys were employed just to open incoming letters. Over 50 million items of one kind or another were tracked over the course of a year.

Not all the employees of the Clearing House in 1849 were based in the London office. At every junction between company territories, one of its number-takers stood watch. Unlike the trainspotters of a later age, these number-takers ignored the engines in favour of the carriages and company-owned wagons behind, and also the big white numerals on any tarpaulins that might be covering the wagons, since these too were the property of individual railways. Similar returns were made from each of the 684 participating stations, where the details of any non-native vehicles and tarpaulins were recorded and notified daily. The information was required so that demurrage payments could be calculated when vehicles were not sent back within the permitted period. Even the company-owned ropes that secured the tarpaulins were subject to mileage and demurrage charges.

The existence of the RCH helps to explain how Britain's railway network grew and flourished with a minimum of official external control. The Clearing House did what it could to standardise equipment and operation between companies. Its endorsement of Greenwich Mean Time in 1847 was influential. Another early success concerned the three-link couplings used between wagons. Some versions of these were fully detachable and had a way of ending up in the hands of the local scrap-man. The RCH therefore promoted a standard design that was permanently anchored to the hook of the buffer beam. It was also the RCH which secured the use of standard signal bell-codes. In costly or technically difficult matters such as the choice between brake types or the provision of passenger alarms, however, the RCH failed to give a lead to the stubbornly independent companies on whose subscriptions it depended. Nor did it achieve fast results when it tried to raise the woefully low standards of the private British coal wagon, from the 1880s onwards. The RCH shared the same handicap as the Board of Trade, that it could recommend best practice but could not enforce it.

The bustling organisation portrayed by Sir Francis Head represented the Railway Clearing House in its lusty infancy. By 1883 there were 2,100 clerks, working in much-extended buildings. A major part of these happens to have survived: a very long, very austere block in Eversholt Street north of Euston station, looking like a terrace of giant Georgian houses with mysteriously few front doorways. Within its walls the payments were settled for 2.5 million consignments annually. The comparable figure on the passenger side was 2.75 million – less than might be expected, perhaps,

Sorting tickets at the Railway Clearing House, *c.* 1930

except that most journeys were short-distance affairs that did not cross company boundaries (the proportion that did so has been calculated at around 14 per cent). Another account from the period puts the number of oversize sheets of accounts and statistics that were prepared each month, by hand and in triplicate, at 16,000. The material for these sheets was extracted from the returns received from every participating company, compiled every day for every station on the network, listing all transactions and movements into the territories of other lines.

Another reason the numbers of payments rose proportionately less than the total volume of traffic was the practice of amalgamation. The first nine companies to join the RCH in 1842 ended up within a few decades as constituent parts of four larger companies, including George Hudson's Midland Railway. Other big creations followed, such as the Great Eastern Railway, founded in 1862 by the union of Hudson's hard-up Eastern Counties Railway and four other East Anglian lines, which had been manoeuvring and wrangling with one another ever since the hectic 1840s. The new company had most of East Anglia as its exclusive territory, at least for a while. Another regional bloc was formed by the North Eastern Railway, which steadily took over all the other passenger lines in County Durham, as well as most of those in Northumberland and northern Yorkshire. The Durham contingent included the famous Stockton & Darlington, which disappeared as a separate company in 1863. The process would have gone much further if public and parliamentary opinion had not turned against large-scale amalgamations around the time that the Stockton & Darlington was absorbed, nervous that too many regional monopolies were being created. So when the LNWR and the Lancashire & Yorkshire tried their best to merge in the 1870s, the proposals were twice thrown out by Parliament, and the number-takers continued their vigilant work at Ardwick Junction, Bootle Junction, Bradley Wood Junction and all the other places where the two companies' lines came together.

As if all this were not intricate enough, many lines were jointly owned, and often jointly run as well. Some of the largest joint companies had all the outward signs of separate railways in their own right, with their own headquarters, works, senior staff, uniforms, liveries and rolling stock. The Somerset & Dorset Joint Railway was one such line. Another was the Midland & Great Northern Joint Railway, which originated in an attempt to break the Great Eastern's monopoly of East Anglian traffic by connecting Lincolnshire and Cambridgeshire with new or amalgamated lines running across Norfolk. As competition turned to collaboration, the Midland & Great Northern later went into partnership with the Great Eastern to create the Norfolk & Suffolk Joint Railway – a joint line part-owned by another joint line, truly a case of wheels within wheels. This new joint company constructed two short, physically separate lines to serve Norfolk's fashionable holiday coast, around Cromer and between Yarmouth and Lowestoft. Elsewhere, the Great Eastern and Great Northern embraced one another directly in their own joint concern, the Great Northern & Great Eastern Joint Railway: 123 miles of cross-country route across Cambridgeshire, Lincolnshire and Nottinghamshire, joining the Great Northern's operational headquarters at Doncaster. That railway-dominated town was itself the nodal point for two more joint lines (as well as four big independent companies). An Edwardian holiday party with a good grasp of Bradshaw could have journeyed all the way from Wakefield to Lowestoft without passing over more than three or four miles of route owned wholly by a single concern.* The larger the company, the more likely it was to be entangled in the business of shared ownership: the London & North Western was operating twenty-five separate joint concerns

---

* Great Northern & Great Central Joint to Doncaster, Great Northern & Great Eastern Joint to Spalding, Midland & Great Northern Joint to Gorleston, then Norfolk & Suffolk Joint for the final stretch.

just before the amalgamations of 1923, from the eighty-three-mile web of lines radiating from Shrewsbury, shared with the Great Western, to the little Middlewood Curve, held in common with the North Staffordshire Railway.

On top of these complications, there were also a great many jointly owned stations, which were operated under a plethora of differing agreements up to and including special Acts of Parliament. Like the joint lines themselves, these shared stations had mixed origins: some were the result of friendly co-operation, others reflected a reluctant truce between competitors. Methods of management varied bewilderingly. Some joint stations were subject to periodic transfers back and forth between their owning companies at fixed intervals, others changed hands according to alternating powers of appointment. In some cases the stations were subdivided between owners, either in terms of duties and responsibilities or by separate areas, rather like royal palaces with their distinct courtiers' fiefdoms. Even when ownership was not shared, stations and routes could be opened up to other companies by means of running powers, by which a foreign concern might operate services in return for a fee. For instance, the way to Lowestoft from Wakefield began at the Yorkshire town's Westgate station, joint possession of the Great Northern, Great Central and Midland railways, but trains from the Lancashire & Yorkshire also ran in and out. By 1914 there were some 800 instances of running powers in force across the network. Altogether, in their confounding diversity of ownership, statutes, rights, duties, fees, privileges, exemptions, liveries, uniforms and general paraphernalia, Britain's railways at their zenith call to mind the unreformed societies of ancien régime France or the Holy Roman Empire when compared with the networks of other countries, where joint lines were all but non-existent.

However admirable the Railway Clearing House as a response to the challenges of this interwoven, fragmented, overlapping system, its size and complexity also pointed to the benefits of reducing those divisions. The pooled usage of wagons introduced during the First World War, followed by the amalgamations of 1923, brought this process to its first great climax. Yet there remains something awe-inspiring about the RCH – not so much the scale of its work, which is trifling by the standards of today's digital technology, but the means by which it was carried out. The lost routines of the thousands of anonymous clerks at Eversholt Street – the endless, patient exactions of mental arithmetic in fractions and non-decimal units, even the neat copperplate writing – seem almost beyond the powers of the modern desk-worker. The same goes for the endurance and vigilance of the overworked engine drivers, firemen, shunters, signalmen and others who kept the Victorian network running. Part of the fascination of the railways is their permeation with memories and traces of obsolete working routines, and the human lives and destinies they shaped. The physical record is often patchy, because different aspects of the system have changed and developed at wildly varying speeds. The modernised freight network envisaged by Dr Beeching is already utterly lost; the diffuse and small-scale system which he knocked for six is more remote still. Yet the bridges, tunnels and earthworks that carry the twenty-first-century traveller are still predominantly those the Victorians witnessed taking shape. This confrontation of the modern network with its own embodied past continues where journeys begin and end – at the railway station.

AT THE STATION

This book began with an imagined journey in 1862. It is easy to picture a station of that era, especially one of small to medium size, in terms of its main building. This typically presents a public face to the street or station forecourt, with an entrance to the booking hall somewhere near the middle. On the far side of the booking hall a doorway opens to the platform side. Beyond may be another, parallel platform; perhaps more than one. Thousands of stations were built to this basic form, and hundreds remain in use. But the station house is best understood as only one of a collection of structures, serving different needs and often united by mere juxtaposition rather than integrated design. In this sense a station of the historic kind was a microcosm of the railway itself, a single organism composed of disparate structures, machines and equipment, all with their own distinctive forms and histories.

Some of these structures, such as the mechanical signal box, have already been encountered. Space was found for signal boxes close to the ends of the platforms, or sometimes further off, when track layouts or sight lines favoured a more distant situation. Less commonly, they might be placed on the platform itself, or on a gantry over the platforms, like the North Eastern Railway's wonderfully commanding boxes still to be seen at Hexham and Wylam in the Tyne Valley. But the signal box, as an innovation of the 1860s, was a relative latecomer to the station's family of buildings. The goods shed – no less crucial to the station's economy than the passengers' facilities – was almost always there from the start.

Smaller goods sheds typically enclosed a single siding, with enough space to hold two or three wagons and a platform or loading dock along one side. Wagons could be unloaded securely and under shelter, aided when necessary by a manually operated crane with a swivelling boom. Often there was an awning along one side, to protect the cargoes as they were transferred to or from road vehicles; or the sidings might run alongside the building, with an awning on the rail side too.

The timber-built goods shed at Highworth station in Wiltshire, creaking 'like a yacht in full sail', served as an improvised shelter for John Betjeman and his son as they picnicked there on a blustery day in 1950. This one has long gone, in common with an estimated 90 per cent of goods sheds from the steam age. Many of the survivors have found new uses, especially those built sturdily of brick or stone. Quite a few now house just the sorts of trades – builders' merchants, farm supplies, fuel depots – that depended on the railways' freight service in former times. There is an especially good sequence on the Furness Railway's route along the Cumbrian coast, recognisable by their unusual half-round lunette windows; the one at the bedraggled seaside resort of Seascale now does duty as a sports centre, with a basketball hoop presiding from the inner gable wall.

Like signal boxes, goods sheds tended to stand at a short remove from the main station building, with plenty of space around them so that road vehicles could gather and manoeuvre. Other facilities were installed round about. A weighbridge, commonly accompanied by a little hut-like yard office, allowed road-borne cargoes to be evaluated correctly. A stable building was common too, where a station offered a collection and delivery service, or required horse power for shunting, or both. Coal and the wagons it came in, a major business on almost all railway lines, entailed separate handling to avoid dirtying the other cargoes. At small stations the coal wagons usually had a dedicated siding. The old private-owner wagons might be left standing there until their contents were sold, but as this practice declined the coal merchants increasingly used bunkers instead, rented from the railway and typically made of old sleepers or similar rough timber. Station staff sometimes had to measure the chargeable area of railway land occupied by each trader's deposits; at Rothwell in Yorkshire during the 1950s, this was done on an unannounced day every month to forestall cheating. In the North Eastern Railway's territory the stationmasters themselves were encouraged to trade in coal, on the understanding that everything they could sell represented guaranteed traffic for the railway.

A raised platform for outdoor loading of wagons was another regular feature. Many were equipped with pens where livestock in transit could be held, at a polite distance from passengers' eyes and nostrils. Only rarely was agricultural traffic catered for by means of a private siding away from any station. Loads too large for easy handling within the goods shed might be managed by means of a separate crane that stood out in the open. To ensure that outgoing cargoes did not exceed the loading gauge, a gibbet-like device was usually provided next to the track, from which an arched measuring bar was suspended on chains over the rails. Wagonloads that struck the bar were not safe to convey on to the running lines and would be adjusted. One of these simple devices – confusingly, itself called a loading gauge – somehow lasted long enough to be designated as a historic structure by English Heritage in 2013; it is at Thetford station in the Norfolk Brecklands. Lamps were another fixture, required by the safety rules for outdoor working introduced after 1900 (*see* Chapter 13). Besides what passed through the station yard, high-value consignments were carried by passenger train – typically, parcels, mail and newspapers, but also certain perishables – under the supervision of the guard.

The typical village or small-town station thus helped to make visible the relationships between the railway and its surrounding district; it was almost an epitome of the economic life of the district. Cities and large towns were a different matter. As the amount of freight carried by rail increased, especially from the 1850s onwards, so the option of handling it all through the same buildings and approach roads as those used for the passenger traffic effectively disappeared. Extra land was acquired nearby and the railways began building. Often, this meant building upwards. The result was a new family of hybrid structures, with goods handling below and warehousing above.

One of the earliest depots of this urban monster type is the Great Northern Railway's grain warehouse of 1850–52, just north of King's Cross station. The building has now been adapted as the home of the University of the Arts London, but its mighty slab-sided form remains imposingly clear. The structure stands six storeys high above a basement, which originally contained docks that were served from the adjacent canal. Attached on either side were lofty single-storey transit sheds nearly 600ft long, one for receiving goods discharged from incoming wagons, the other for loading trains ready for departure. Stabling for railway horses occupied part of the basements of these sheds. Horizontal movements at railway level were managed by means of little wagon-sized turntables from which tracks ran off at right angles. The ability to transfer and shuffle wagons easily was essential, because the great marshalling yards did not yet exist; trains had to be laboriously uncoupled and reformed at the depot itself, either within the building or using the tracks nearby. Traversers, which were short sections of track that could be moved laterally, were sometimes used as an alternative to these miniature turntables.

Vertical circulation of goods at the King's Cross granary was by hydraulic lifts and hoists. Hydraulic power is one of the great forgotten factors in technological history. It was developed a little later than locomotive-hauled railways and was avidly taken up in dockyards and inner-city warehouse districts. Power was transmitted by means of water mains conveyed in iron pipes, which were maintained at a constant high pressure. At first the force was procured by pumping the water up to a tank in a lofty tower. Grimsby docks has the outstanding example of this type of structure, erected shortly after the granary at King's Cross was commissioned; it rises 309ft high and finishes marvellously with battlements and machicolations that have a wholly deliberate look of medieval Tuscany. There would have been many more such towers, smokeless cousins of the mill chimneys of Yorkshire and Lancashire, but for the invention of the hydraulic accumulator, by which a much shorter column of water was kept under heavy weights within a giant cylinder. When pressurised water was drawn off from the mains, fresh supplies were pumped into the cylinder to replenish the losses. The power source for the pumps – the electricity to recharge the batteries, as it were – was steam from coal-fired boilers. Hydraulic mains could extend surprisingly far; by 1900 several cities were favoured with public networks with whom businesses could sign up for a connection.

Railway companies arranged their own hydraulic supplies for major London installations, and made good use of it at some split-level termini. The Midland Railway deployed a hydraulic lift to lower wagons loaded with Burton ale from the station deck at St Pancras for emptying and storage in the cool undercroft below, where passengers now muster for Eurostar trains to the Continent. London's meat market at Smithfield likewise communicated with its basement storey by hydraulic lift, although here the railway entered below street level, via the sub-surface lines of the Metropolitan Railway. Hydraulic capstans and other equipment also allowed wagons to be moved around quickly and easily on the level, without

The approach to St Pancras station in London, *c.* 1930, seen from the
summit of the train shed. In front of the central signal box is the hydraulic
lift for lowering beer wagons into the station undercroft. Giant railway
goods depots lie ahead and on either side, beyond the edges of the image

risking the entry of smoky, spark-spewing locomotives to the realm of
unprotected cargoes and timber floors.

There are striking parallels between hydraulic power and the

Atmospheric Railway essayed by Brunel and others. As developed in the 1840s, each anticipated the modern use of steam-generated electricity to operate machinery cleanly and at some distance from the source of power. The founding genius of the hydraulic method was another of the great Victorian engineers, William, 1st Lord Armstrong (1810–1900). Hydraulic equipment from Armstrong's Tyneside works was duly incorporated in the goods depot Brunel built in 1851–6 on the vacated site of his first, short-lived passenger station at Paddington.

₪

The demotion of the first railway site at Paddington to the goods department was far from unique. Quite often, the original station buildings were kept too. Among them was the London & Southampton's London terminus at Nine Elms, opened in 1838, which closed to passengers after a mere ten years in favour of a bigger and more conveniently placed new station at Waterloo. The old facility then put in over a century of service as a goods depot, incongruously combined at first with occasional use by that creature of habit Queen Victoria, who had grown accustomed to travelling from there to Windsor and did not want to change. In the 1950s the British Transport Commission earmarked the old terminus for use as a national railway museum. It was not to be; in 1963 the train shed and its fine early-Victorian frontage building that Betjeman had admired, 'classic, stuccoed and deserted, amid the gasworks, goods yards and factories', were razed to the ground.

Outside London, these *déclassé* passenger stations have survived rather better. A nondescript storage depot at Selby in Yorkshire turns out to be the Leeds & Selby Railway's terminus, built at the amazingly early date of 1834 and dedicated from the outset to handling goods and passengers side by side. The goods lines ran right through the building via sliding doors, to finish at staithes or jetties on the River Ouse. Rapid relegation also protected the Curzon Street terminus of the London & Birmingham Railway, constructed in 1838 to designs by the architect Philip Hardwick. This is the Ionic-porticoed counterpart to Hardwick's lamented Greek Doric 'arch' or propylaeum at Euston in London, destroyed with the rest of the old station in its 1960s rebuilding. The Birmingham site and its building may yet come back into passenger use, if the proposed HS2 route goes ahead. Meanwhile Hardwick's building sits boarded up on waste ground, in full view of the tracks to its successor station at New Street. Then there is Durham's first station, a terminus built in 1844 at Gilesgate, north-east of the old city, which lasted only thirteen years in its original use before the goods department took over. The modern traveller uses its replacement, set at the northern end of the fine viaduct that crosses the western edge of the old city. (This helps in turn to explain why the railway approaches to Durham are so modest and tidy, having escaped major colonisation for goods traffic.) Now the old buildings are shared between a Travelodge hotel and a restaurant chain, which has hung mock-Victorian lamps from the plain iron arcades and roof bracing above where the wagons once stood.

More extraordinary still, the original Manchester terminus of the Liverpool & Manchester Railway, opened in 1830 and deserted by passenger trains fourteen years later, still exists in something close to its original form: both the buildings for travellers (of which more later) and the three-storey warehouse that stands parallel to them on the opposite side of the tracks. In order to clear the River Irwell for navigation, George Stephenson had to carry his new railway into Manchester on a viaduct. As a result the tracks at the station were at first-floor level, so the goods building ended up with one storey for warehousing at a level above the railway and another storey below. The structure has been interpreted as a sort of railway elaboration of a building type developed for canal-served warehouses, with sidings in place of a dock. In that sense, the warehouse at Liverpool Road (as the Manchester station is known) already demonstrates an understanding of how specialist buildings could be reshaped to suit the railway's needs.

Buildings of more than one storey were also a response to the constraints of urban land. When the Great Northern constructed a new general goods depot for Manchester at Deansgate in 1898, it took the type to fresh heights. As at King's Cross, there was a canal-served basement storey, for Manchester was threaded through with canals well before the railways came, and their relationship was often as much symbiotic as competitive. Two storeys were given over to rail-to-road transhipment, one at ground level, the other served by a viaduct, with ramps as well as lifts to connect them. Above were two storeys of warehousing. At the top of the building, the legend GREAT NORTHERN RAILWAY COMPANY'S GOODS WAREHOUSE may still be read, picked out in imperishable white brick just below the cornice. Despite the contribution of the canal network,

Manchester had surrendered 7.3 per cent of land in its central area to the various public railway companies by 1900, even without including independent enclaves such as the city's big locomotive-building works.

₪

As might be expected, the buildings of Manchester's primeval station at Liverpool Road have something of an improvised air. The passengers' part takes the form of a two-storey range of stuccoed buildings, appearing like a pair of near-twin terraced houses. These sit alongside an older and plainer house, constructed in 1808–9 for the master of a nearby dye works. This dwelling was included with the property bought in order to build the station, and the company decided to retain it as the residence of its 'station agent', as stationmasters on the line were known. This was by no means the only instance of making an existing structure do duty at a railway station, especially in the railways' infancy. In its early years the Stockton & Darlington did not bother with buildings at all, but followed the stagecoach practice of selling tickets at inns. Other stations operated at various times from a handily placed gentry house (Red Hall at Bourn, Lincolnshire), redundant theatre buildings from a pleasure garden (Norwich), the poop of an old Dutch trading ship (Hartlepool) and even an enormous hollow oak tree (Moreton-on-Lugg in Herefordshire). Nor did the Liverpool & Manchester at first feel the need to build anything at its intermediate stations. Trains simply stopped at acknowledged places, usually a level crossing. A policeman – of the railway variety – would be on hand to halt the approaching train for the benefit of any passengers, by raising a red flag or showing a lamp. It did not matter that there were no platforms; for that matter, the main stations at Manchester and Liverpool did not have platforms when they opened either. Passengers climbed up into the carriages, as they would do at a coaching inn.

In other respects, the station at Liverpool Road established some enduring principles. At the most basic, the building combined the functions of the sale of tickets, a place to wait and the point of departure for the train itself. It also controlled access to the railway side, by the simple fact of its elevation above street level. There was no way up to the trains except through the building and the staircases it contained. As one bumptious early account had it, 'a moment ago we were in the midst ... of a busy multitude ... anon we find ourselves, as it were insensibly, translated to another equally sublunary scene, from which to discern the self-same beings of a previous companionship still plying the self-same stern activity ...'

Wherever there are stations on an urban railway that is raised up on a viaduct, the experience may be repeated; Manchester and inner London, especially to north, east and south, have some of the highest concentrations, and Liverpool's Overhead Railway, while it lasted, was entirely of this kind. All these are the children of Manchester Liverpool Road and all offer the same amplified sensation of having left the world outside the railway behind, even before entering the carriage to begin a journey.

Another notable feature of Liverpool Road station was its strict class separation. First- and second-class passengers each had separate entrances, separate booking halls and staircases and separate waiting rooms at rail level. The arrangement was reflected in the design of the frontage, with its division into two not quite equal elements, and the greater architectural emphasis on the doorway of the first-class part. (There was no need to provide for third-class passengers, because the company did not carry them until impelled by Gladstone's Railway Act of 1844.) Station design soon retreated from this extreme segregation, and communal entrances, circulation routes, platforms, and (usually) booking facilities – but not waiting rooms – were provided at all but a few stations.

Stations without platforms were usual in the 1830s. The consequences may still be seen along the Newcastle & Carlisle Railway, the first line to provide station buildings at the stops along the way. The earliest of these date from 1835–6. Several were placed at a distance from the running lines, sometimes at a skewed angle, and were separated from them by a siding. When platforms came to be added, they were sometimes treated as detached structures placed some way from the buildings, with steps or ramps for access. The results are apparent at stations such as Haydon Bridge and Bardon Mill, where the platform levels roughly correspond to those of the older buildings' window sills.

Railway platforms are such commonplace things that it may require a visit to lines beyond Britain or Ireland to stimulate any thoughts about them. Platforms in these islands now have a standard height of 915mm, the metric equivalent of 3ft. On most of the Continent the historic dimension has been not much more than half that, sometimes rather less. Because the British railway loading gauge is less generous than those abroad, its carriage floor levels also tend to be lower. So the British traveller must take only a step or two up in order to enter the train. By contrast, passengers on most other European lines, and those on other continents, are usually faced with a steep climb up to the carriage door.

The curious traveller may notice other distinctive features of the British railway platform. If its trackside face is a simple vertical surface of brick or masonry, the structure is of relatively early date. By the early twentieth century, the Board of Trade's regulations for new platforms included an overhang at the top. This was safer, for it allowed railwaymen more space to manoeuvre when wrestling with couplings and brake pipes down at buffer level. The overhang rule in turn encouraged the use of materials other than stone or brick. The Great Western introduced concrete platform-edge slabs in standard 6ft lengths, which were cast at its depot in Taunton. Or the whole platform might be assembled as a framed structure using timber, or the more durable twentieth-century material of reinforced concrete. The Southern Railway preferred concrete, despatched in prefabricated sections from its factory at Exmouth Junction. To step from a third-rail electric train on to a concrete platform of the 1930s, with its slight but distinctive ring underfoot, is to experience what might be called the Southern's *terroir*, if railways were wines.

Older platforms are more likely to have been built lower than the standard three-foot height. Where the shortfall is pronounced, these low platforms may have acquired a 'Harrington hump'. The title – which sounds unsettlingly like an aristocratic deformity – commemorates the first of these lightweight modular additions, installed at the Cumbrian station of that name in 2008. Sitting on top of the existing platform surface, with shallow ramps for access at each end, the humps or decks allow wheelchair users and other passengers with impaired mobility to use the trains more easily. Until their humps arrive, other low-platformed stations must make do with the next best thing, in the form of chunky, yellow-painted blocks of steps that can be moved to line up with the train doorways. Partly raised platform surfaces are also being created on the London Underground to give wheelchair users a more level entry to its trains, and here the raised areas are solid rather than of the Harringtonian kind.

Ramps of a different type terminate the ends of most railway platforms. Their gradient was standardised by the Board of Trade at one in eight. A platform ending with a straight drop protected by railings is almost certainly of no great age; it may be among the modern network's many prefabricated steel structures installed ('delivered') by Corus Infrastructure Services since 2002, often as extensions to allow the use of longer trains. Ramped ends were formerly necessary in part because the everyday routines of a station involved a great deal of barrowing and transference of packages, luggage and equipment between platforms. To make the crossing easier, boardwalks were laid over the ballast and sleepers. Passengers, too, were routinely expected to cross the running lines by means of these walkways.

There were obvious drawbacks to traversing the lines in this way, and several ways of avoiding it. Sometimes the requirement for dual or multiple platforms was done away with by handling all the services on a double-tracked line by means of a single platform. At these stations the trackwork was arranged so that trains using the far line could cross over and back again, like ships drawing up at a quay. The practice survives at Maryport in Cumberland, and something like it still happens at Cambridge. Here the original platform is not far short of a third of a mile long and can handle two full-length trains at once. Another variant was the double one-sided station employed by Brunel at Slough, Reading and elsewhere. These consisted of two single platforms placed alongside the same track, one for up services and the other for down, each with its own buildings. Any passenger changing trains – for example, to take the Windsor branch after arriving at Slough from the west – had to leave one station and walk a short distance along the road to reach its next-door neighbour. It was not one of Brunel's most robust or influential ideas, and all these stations have been rebuilt with multiple platforms instead.

₪

As trains grew faster and more frequent, the permissive attitude to passengers walking across the tracks became untenable. Instead, the footbridge joined the family of structures that, variously selected and combined, made up the railway station. A snapshot of the process is given by the deaths of two passengers who were struck by a train while changing platforms at Nuneaton station in 1868. In his accident report, the Board of Trade's inspector noted that these platforms were so low that people did not even stick to the designated crossings, but stepped down wherever they pleased. He concluded that a footbridge was the only safe alternative at Nuneaton, where movements by trains and locomotives already numbered 143 each day.

Railway footbridges seem to have proliferated from around the time

A covered footbridge typical of the Great Western Railway, photographed
at Langport East station in Somerset shortly after its opening in 1908.
The train is one of the company's self-propelled steam railmotors

of the Nuneaton report. These structures are so familiar that it is easy to
forget how outlandish the type must once have seemed. Outside railway
territory, any pedestrian using a bridge would expect to share it with road
vehicles. These required a crossing on the level, or by means of an arched
rise that was made as shallow as possible. Bridges carrying railways or
canals needed decks that were more level still. There were also the little
humped footbridges on the canals, but these did not rise very high. Now
the railways introduced passengers to another new kind of spatial experience, a parallel to the dislocating sense of having to climb the stairs at a
station in order to travel on an elevated line, or the still weirder descent
below ground level to take the underground trains of the new Metropolitan Railway.

Timber or iron construction was preferred for footbridges, sometimes on piers of brick or stone. Large railways tended to develop their
own standard designs, especially for the basic single-span form used at
stations with two facing platforms. Trains along the Newcastle & Carlisle route still pass under seven footbridges of the North Eastern Railway's graceful type in which arches brace the span over the tracks, all now
repainted in versions of the old company's red-brown and buff colours.

The Great Western distinguished itself by providing canopies for many of its footbridges, as may still be seen at such stations as Chippenham, St Austell and Stratford, where the sheltered area extends uninterrupted from platform to facing platform. Twentieth-century railway engineers often turned to prefabricated concrete, including the concrete-loving Southern Railway in the years after 1923. The glum results, kindred to the Southern's concrete platforms and platelayer's huts, survive all over its former lines, as in the leafy suburban streets of Mortlake and East Sheen. The company also experimented with making thrifty footbridges from old rails bent into shape, of which Wokingham has an example. Until money for such improvements could be found, passengers were liable to encounter annoyances like that at Sidcup station, where the only permitted route between platforms was via the road approach, under the railway bridge and back up the other side.

Older footbridges in their original state are becoming less common. Many are falling victim to overhead electrification, which requires higher clearances. Footbridges alongside level crossings, where the contact wire is suspended at almost one metre above the standard height to allow sufficient headroom for lorries, are the tallest of all. Other footbridges are being modified or replaced by new installations with lifts accessible to all – counterparts of the Harrington hump. The results are not necessarily any worse in aesthetic terms, although they sometimes kill the historic atmosphere at stations that have kept a good collection of older buildings. Considered more broadly, the railways' commitment to equality of access is a logical successor to the national peculiarity of tall platforms. It has always been easier to get on and off trains in the British Isles than elsewhere, and it is getting easier still.

Footbridges at stations, being simpler and cheaper to construct, are generally more common than subways below the line. Where a station was built on a viaduct or undercroft, however, it was not difficult to contrive a passage through the arches or vaults and up steps to the platform on the far side. Subways at stations that sit closer to ground level are often a sign of reconstruction in the late nineteenth century or after; Blackburn, Huddersfield and Ely are instances from the 1880s. Because people require less headroom than trains, there are commonly fewer steps to negotiate (or less walking up and down ramps) at an underpass than on a footbridge. Sometimes the overhead clearances come down uncomfortably low where the tracks pass overhead, as until recently at Canterbury West.

Less claustrophobic examples include the broad concourse-like subways at Cardiff Central station, rebuilt by the Great Western in the 1930s, and the 30ft-wide subway at Bristol Temple Meads, as renovated around the same time. Both these projects were made possible by cheap government loans, introduced during the Great Depression to stimulate employment and demand – another twist in the convoluted relationship between the State and the private railway companies.

Among the smaller stations to be enlarged under the loans scheme was Carnforth in north Lancashire, which acquired a new platform served by a ramped subway. The renovated station was among those inspected by the film director David Lean (1908–91) while looking for a location to shoot the 'Milford Junction' scenes of *Brief Encounter* in 1945. To allow for nocturnal filming, the station had to be somewhere safely beyond the wartime blackout zone. Carnforth was selected partly because Lean thought that his female lead Celia Johnson would look more dignified and 'swan-like' going up and down ramps rather than steps. Life now imitates art at Carnforth, where the refreshment room has been restored to its 1940s state – although the interior scenes in which the hero and heroine meet and fall in love were actually filmed on set at Denham Studios in Buckinghamshire.

Big stations such as the rebuilt Cardiff mostly have platforms of the island type, with railway lines on both sides. The same principle was also used at stations with only two running lines, where the tracks part and rejoin on either side of the platform, like twin streams of a river. An island platform could be reached from beneath or above, depending on the level of the line. One common arrangement was to place the station buildings above the platform and parallel with the access road, bridge-fashion. The road could then be carried conveniently across the railway line without interruption by a level crossing. The Great Central Railway adopted this model for the lesser stations on its London extension, of which two Leicestershire examples (Rothley and Quorn & Woodhouse) have been impeccably preserved. Travellers will be vaguely aware of passing through large versions of bridge-type stations because of the dark interval when the train approaches or leaves the platforms, an interval too short to be accounted for by a full-scale tunnel and too long for a simple road bridge. Leicester and Nottingham are outstanding examples, both rebuilt by the Midland Railway around the turn of the twentieth century. Going still deeper, some Tube stations in London may be interpreted as dug-out versions of the bridge type: a long staircase descending from a street-level building, with platforms on either side at the bottom. The arrangement is explicit when trains in both directions draw up at a narrow island platform placed within a single broad chamber. This nerve-racking arrangement now survives only at Clapham North and Clapham Common on the Northern Line.

To get adequate circulation into the body of a very large station, it was sometimes necessary to provide both subways and footbridges. Clapham again provides an example: its sprawling Junction station, joint offspring of the London, Brighton & South Coast and London & South Western railways, already had both kinds of access by 1900. In that year, two porters were cut down by a train as they transferred luggage across the tracks. They could use neither subway nor footbridge, because these were insufficiently wide to take barrows without impeding the flow of passengers. The following day the station's platform staff petitioned the Board of Trade to make their lives safer ('Our lives are nothing but a series of thrilling adventures and hairbreadth escapes'). Before long the station was reconstructed with a splendid new footbridge, broad enough to entrain a regiment, and equipped with luggage lifts that eliminated the need for porters to convey trunks and milk churns across the running lines. The footbridge also included an extra station building and booking hall at one end, thus making Clapham Junction into a hybrid of the bridge and subway types of station.

These categories, and combinations of categories, could be multiplied almost endlessly. There are through stations that include bay platforms that finish with buffers at one end, as at a terminus; stations where lines cross at different levels, as at Willesden Junction and Tamworth; stations built as separate enclaves by different companies that have since been knocked through, as at London Victoria; and multiple combinations of these types and features. But enough has been said to show that stations should not be understood simply as pieces of architecture, rather than as diverse facilities within the greater system that is the railway itself.

₪

When railways still carried goods and parcels, the phrase 'at the station' carried associations of trade, delivery and despatch that have now largely been lost. Another casualty of recent decades is the expectation that there will be anyone on duty there at all. Even the sale of tickets depends less and less on face-to-face transactions. The first great reduction in everyday sales was due to the season ticket, which has a history almost as long as that of the passenger railway itself. Initially these were offered only to first- and second-class travellers, saving them the chore of queueing to buy a daily ticket. Next, tickets became available from machines at some stations, or from the guard or conductor after boarding the train. Now they can be booked online in advance, at any time and from anywhere in the world. Fewer and fewer travellers turn up at the station with the purchase of a fresh ticket in mind.

Machines for selling railway tickets go back a long way in Britain. They were already in place at a few busy stations before 1914, but made slow progress until after the Second World War, when British Railways began to install machines that could print tickets on demand. The first London terminus to achieve full mechanisation of its ticket-issuing equipment was Euston, in 1960 (which was just after the decision to demolish the entire station and start again). Later machines were networked electronically, so that centralised records could be kept. Portable ticket machines for use on trains were also developed. These methods have now converged, and a growing proportion of the tickets bought on board are issued using the same software system, called AVANTIX, which is used for online and station sales. It may surprise many to learn that AVANTIX belongs to the transport division of the French multinational company Atos, better known in the UK as the beneficiary of lucrative outsourcing contracts for IT services to public bodies and the assessment of disabled people for fitness to work.

The de-staffing of stations is among the economies that distinguish the modern network from the essentially Victorian model that Dr Beeching set about hacking into shape. Yet Beeching himself failed to grasp the potential of liberating the issue of tickets from the fixed points represented by station booking offices. The curious story of the East Suffolk line shows what might have been achieved had matters turned out differently.

The East Suffolk line runs between Ipswich and Lowestoft, with no great centres of population or traffic in between, and was accordingly earmarked for oblivion in Beeching's report. Its saviour was the manager of BR's Eastern Region, Gerard ('Gerry') Fiennes (1906–85; properly Twisleton-Wykeham-Fiennes). Fiennes directed that intermediate stations should be largely de-staffed – which was easily done once goods and sundries traffic was given up – and fares collected on the trains instead, using portable ticket machines. The idea was hardly new; for example, the little Keighley & Worth Valley line had adopted on-board ticket sales back in 1955. With no lineside goods depots, the trackwork could be simplified accordingly and the line run as a 'basic railway'. Later, the removal of semaphore signals and signal boxes (replaced here with early radio-operated signalling) allowed the East Suffolk line to operate still more cheaply. By that time, the gifted railwayman who reformed the route had got himself sacked, having been excessively candid about the shortcomings of railway management in his book *I Tried to Run a Railway* (1967).

Friends of the railways have argued that Fiennes's basic model might have brought other lines on Beeching's hit list within acceptable financial limits, had they been given the chance. Something similar was indeed tried elsewhere, but without the same cutbacks of station staff and goods facilities. These were the lines on which the puny four-wheeled railbuses described in Chapter 7 took over loss-making passenger services from the late 1950s onwards. As these trains had conductor-guards who sold tickets, it was also possible to add new stopping places in the hope of attracting extra custom: little unstaffed platforms known as halts, the nearest railway equivalent to a bus stop, where trains called only on request. So the names of a few extra rural stations flickered briefly on the railway map – and there cannot be many surviving habitués of Trouble House Halt (1959–64, named from a pub on the Tetbury branch), or Ballifurth Farm Halt (1959–65, Speyside line) – before their lines closed altogether.

An earlier wave of halt building had come in the years after 1900, stimulated by the invention of the steam railmotor. A precursor of the diesel railbus, this was powered by a midget four-wheeled locomotive enclosed within one end of the carriage. A Great Western railmotor has recently been restored, reviving after a gap of more than sixty years the compelling sight and sound of a single, self-propelled steam carriage hissing and panting its way along the rails. The powered end is betrayed by the exhaust plume from the carriage roof, and by the little wheels and motion (the collective term for the coupling and connecting rods and cylinder valve gear) busily working below. Like tramcars, railmotors could be driven from either end, which saved time and labour when reversing. Their passenger sections were designed on the tramcar principle too, as a single open compartment. The Great Western's featured tram-type seats with hinged backs, which could be pushed either way so as to face the direction of travel.

Encouraged by the potential of the railmotor, the Great Western became especially keen on halts. At first the company tried to keep a distinction between stations proper and these new stopping places, which were classified either as mere halts (sometimes spelled 'haltes') or as 'platforms'. 'Halts' might be no more than an area of timber decking alongside the track, to which retractable steps could be lowered from the carriage door. The waiting area might be lit, or it might not. A 'platform' was more likely to be of regulation height, but had only a cabin-like shelter by way of a building. One of these platform-grade facilities has survived, complete with two of the Great Western's distinctive pagoda-like shelters: it is Denham Golf Club station, in the Buckinghamshire commuter belt, not far from the site of the studio where *Brief Encounter* was made.

Now that so many stations have been de-staffed, the crucial distinction is between those where timetabled services always stop and those that are served only on request. An element of unpredictability has thus entered many railway journeys. Approaching Dyffryn Ardudwy, Corkickle, Scotscalder or scores of little-frequented stations like them, the driver must scan the platform for waiting passengers, unless the conductor-guard has already advised that someone already on the train wants to get off there. The same routine is followed after dark, when it may take the driver a little longer to obtain a clear view. Changes in the pitch of the engine as a request station comes into visual range betray any necessary slackening of speed. Those waiting at the platform must be careful too: however vile the weather, it is no good huddling invisibly within the shelter on the assumption that the longed-for train will definitely stop.

Denham's corrugated-iron-clad shelters, now protected by listing, are the last of their kind on the national network. Until a few years ago, Great Western pagodas could also be seen at Appleford station (née Appleford Halt) in Oxfordshire. Now Appleford is equipped with the Paragon Anti-Vandal Shelter, made by Macemain & Amstad of Corby. Developed in response to a brief from Railtrack in 1998, the shelter consists of a prefabricated stainless-steel frame, infilled with 'vision strips' of toughened glass and panels of powder-coated aluminium. Some versions have close-fitting roofs, others have canopy-type roofs raised on struts above the tops of the enclosing panels; most have a gap of several inches between the platform surface and the lower edge of the panels. If you have recently perched on a slim metal seat fixture while waiting for a train within a shiny, draughty, practically indestructible platform shelter, it is probably one of Macemain & Amstad's Paragons.

Platform shelters of this basic open-fronted type have always been common. They sprang into existence in the 1830s, as soon as buildings began to be provided at stations with more than one platform. Sometimes the old shelter survives in use even after the station building proper has been levelled as redundant; or there may be modern shelters only. Unattended public buildings accessible round the clock are sitting ducks for vandals, and in the worst-affected areas BR's response was necessarily drastic. The blighted Welsh valleys were particularly hard-hit; twenty-seven stations in that region lost their historic buildings in 1971–5 in favour of grim shelters of brick or concrete, which were described as 'neater and cheaper to maintain'.

Elsewhere – especially on rural lines – redundant station buildings have often found new purposes. In a few fortunate places, the passenger can actually enjoy better facilities in sold-off station buildings than they ever offered in their railway-owned prime. Taking the East Suffolk line from Lowestoft to Ipswich, after a nod to the freshly installed Paragon Anti-Vandal Shelters at Beccles, the modern traveller will find a 'traditional butchery and smokehouse' in the old station at Melton, and a café in the old waiting room at Woodbridge, which has become a bed-and-breakfast guesthouse. Other survivors on the route include Darsham station, now a youth centre run by the Woodcraft Folk, who were founded in 1924 as a co-operative and anti-militarist alternative to Baden-Powell's Scout movement. Here, at least, the 'basic railway' has turned out to be not so basic after all.

₪

Detached from their platforms, these East Suffolk stations would look like big, plain, somewhat under-windowed mid-Victorian houses, at least when viewed from the road approach. This is hardly a coincidence, for they also functioned as the residence of the stationmaster. To be master of such a station (or a member of the household) was to live 'over the shop' – literally so, in buildings where the domestic section was entirely upstairs. For example, the intermediate stations for the Birmingham, Wolverhampton & Dudley Railway, opened in 1854, each had three bedrooms, with parlour, kitchen and WC. This appears to have been a typical level of provision.

Despite the modesty of his accommodation, the rural stationmaster's life has often been regarded wistfully, especially in retrospect. Here,

Needham Market station in Suffolk, built for the Ipswich & Bury Railway in the late 1840s. It housed both stationmaster and head porter, in separate wings

perhaps, was the closest commercial equivalent of the parson's way of life: social recognition and respect, distinctive dress, a loyal and hard-working porter or two in place of a verger, a reliable weekly rhythm of duties and a house to go with the job. Sir John Betjeman, lover of churches and of railways alike, is reported to have named his ideal job as stationmaster at Blake Hall in Essex. This was a characteristic joke. Blake Hall was on the Great Eastern Railway's branch from Epping to Ongar, opened in 1865, which had been annexed to the London Underground network when that line was electrified in the 1950s. Set deep amid fields, with barely another house in sight, the lonely platform and station building at Blake Hall was the least-used station on the Underground map; just before closure in 1981, it was said to have only six passengers a day. So the stationmaster would have had plenty of time for pottering about, and to tend the roses round his door – for Blake Hall was among those stations with two-storey living quarters rather than a mere upstairs flat, in this case with frontage and entrance facing sideways behind the platform. Now it is a private house, and the Ongar branch has closed too, although preservationists are reviving it.

Stations of similar design to Blake Hall, open or closed, can be found all over East Anglia. In 1865 the Great Eastern adopted a standardised vocabulary for its buildings. There was nothing new in this policy, for most railway companies had a reasonably consistent approach to architectural design. Sometimes their stations were designed by outside architects, sometimes by the company's own engineers. The Newcastle & Carlisle chose a professional Newcastle architect, Benjamin Green (1813–58), for its pioneering lineside buildings. These used a simplified version of the English Tudor style, by that date already current as a fashionable alternative to classical design for country houses, and likewise for lodges, gatehouses and other small dwellings on gentlemen's estates. So these station houses were intended to appear at home in a well-ordered landscape, considered politically and socially as well as in aesthetic terms. The same style was chosen by the Liverpool & Manchester when it bowed to the need for buildings at intermediate stations, as may still be seen at Earlestown in Newton-le-Willows. Neo-Tudor station architecture reached an early peak in the mid 1840s on the line between Northampton and Peterborough, on which the architect John Livock played a series of pretty stone-built variations on themes of clustered chimneys and shaped or decorated gables. Examples survive at Oundle and at Wansford, the latter now part of a preserved railway.

Blake Hall and its kindred stations represented an altogether different approach. By reducing the task of design to a series of permutations from a small set of elements, the Great Eastern was able to do without the costly input of a professional architect in favour of a simpler procedure within the office of the company's chief engineer. The Ongar branch was among its earliest routes to have stations designed on the new model. There were about thirty of these in all, plain buildings of brick with hipped roofs, composed in a lopsided way: a two-storeyed residential side, attached to a single-storey section housing the public facilities. The standard provision of rooms – three bedrooms, parlour, kitchen – was the same as at the Birmingham, Wolverhampton & Dudley's stations of the 1850s.

The humorist and broadcaster Paul Jennings (1918–89), investigating the aftermath of the Beeching cuts in the late 1960s, found a retired stationmaster named Mr Purdie still living in his 1865-built home at Linton in Cambridgeshire. The station house had 14ft-high ceilings, an 'elegant curved staircase', and rusting rails as yet unlifted next to the empty platform. Following the same defunct route into Suffolk, Jennings visited the boarded-up and doomed Haverhill station, with its garden of 'straggly rosebeds and vague asters'. Here he imagined a lost world of

> formal stationmaster's teas, given every other Tuesday afternoon for the staff and friends, the stationmaster's wife presiding, the young porters clumsy with the delicate cups and too bashful to ask for sugar,

in the long sunlit Edwardian summer. There are thirty-seven minutes
before the next train is due. Larks sing in the cloudless blue sky ...

It is a charming picture, and the stationmaster's garden makes a pretty
backdrop. Station gardens proper – those in the public areas along the
platforms, rather than in the station house's private ground – were already
well established by Edwardian times. A memorable example that has survived is the topiary display at Ropley station in Hampshire, now part of
a preserved line. The Great Eastern had its own nursery from which trees
and shrubs could be supplied to stations. Sometimes a station's name was
picked out in bedding plants, or (less demandingly) in whitewashed stones
or gravel. Kinross station in the 1950s had an 'impressionistic' model of
Loch Leven in its platform garden, romantically including a version of the
castle in which Mary Stuart had been held captive.

Plants and seeds might be informally exchanged with railwaymen at
other stations, but there was healthy rivalry too, encouraged by official
rewards for the best displays. Scottish companies appear to have taken the
lead in offering incentives, both for floral displays and for general neatness and tidiness, with recorded instances starting in the mid 1850s. Such
prizes could be substantial; Mr Watt, stationmaster at Bannockburn,
received £3 in 1861 for the all-round best station on the Scottish Central
Railway. England caught up after a while: the Midland Railway, often a
leader in aesthetic matters, began to award cash prizes for station gardens
in 1884. Over in Wales, a one-armed stationmaster-gardener is recorded
on the Cambrian Railways in the 1890s. Having made a 'beautiful garden'
at Tylwch in Montgomeryshire, he was moved to Pontdolgoch station in
the same county, where the *Western Mail*'s correspondent reported his
creation of 'another paradise'.

Sharp horticultural practice was not unknown. Hatfield station was
reportedly once victorious in the 1940s after borrowing potted plants
from a nearby nursery, burying them up to the rims in the flower beds,
then taking them back as soon as the inspector had gone. Long-term
champion stations included Midsomer Norton on the Somerset & Dorset Joint Railway, favoured by a long earthen bank with a south-easterly
aspect behind its down platform, which scooped its regional first prize
every year between 1953 and 1960. It happens that Midsomer Norton is
yet another station now in the hands of preservationists. The very name
conveys a sense of rural ease, a West Country idyll in which passengers

and railwaymen join in unhurried fellowship; a good place to linger on a
bench amid floral scents and the sound of bees, the calm 'broken only by
the crunching of a porter's feet on the gravel, the soft country accent of the
stationmaster and the crash bang of a milk can somewhere at the back of
the platform' (Betjeman again).

₪

Yet it would be misleading to think of the average stationmaster's life as a
pretext for competitive gardening. At all but the smallest stations he was
a busy man, at least until road competition and the advent of railhead
goods depots began eating away the local trade that had been so carefully
built up. Even in the years just after 1945, Mr Purdie at Linton had enough
business to require two clerks and two porters, and a freight turnover of
£80,000 a year (the present-day equivalent of close to £5 million).

With activity came responsibility. The stationmaster's authority
extended to all employees attached to his station, and to the railwaymen working trains through the area within its control. Their collective task was to ensure safe and punctual operation. The stationmaster's
other duties, as enumerated in the LMS rulebook, included the security
and protection of buildings and property, reporting any observations
of neglect of duty, the proper distribution and exhibition of timetables,
notices, rules, by-laws and staff lists, and unannounced supervisory visits
to the local signal boxes. Every day, the station and other premises were to
be inspected for cleanness and neatness, closets and urinals not excepted.
Orders and instructions received were to be complied with and books
kept up to date. Economy in the use of stores items was to be enforced.
Complaints received from the public were to be notified promptly. Other
rules directed the stationmaster concerning the inspection of defective
rolling stock, the correct setting of clocks, the supply of detonators, the
onward reporting of defective points and signals, the supervision of work
to clear obstructions on the line and much else besides.

Some of these tasks would arise only rarely, or not at all; but the primacy of paperwork was a universal law. Its central role in a stationmaster's
routine was recorded in an article by J. Thornton Burge in *The Railway
and Travel Monthly* for July 1912. Burge's post was on the London & South
Western Railway at Templecombe in Somerset, on the main line to Exeter.
Templecombe was not a large station – it had just two through platforms

– but it was busy, being at a junction with the Somerset & Dorset Joint Railway. Burge's working day began at 7.45 a.m., when he would find between fifty and a hundred letters waiting for attention and response. Some came from head office, others from his own staff, others still from fellow stationmasters; the contents might cover anything from special workings and traders' complaints to making advance arrangements to look after a child travelling alone. Templecombe was kept open round the clock, so there was also the night inspector's report to be read, as well as those from the yard foreman and the signalman. The accounts and returns for passenger and freight business required regular attention as well.

All this work had to be fitted around the running of trains and the supervision of the station's normal routines, as well as any out-of-the-ordinary events or crises. Burge confessed that it would be helpful not to have to wear his uniform at such times, to avoid the risk of being buttonholed by passengers and traders with minor enquiries or petty grumbles. Off duty, Burge was expected to remain within range of his workplace, on call in case any serious matters came up.

Even the lower steps on the ladder to a stationmastership could be an arduous place for anyone who hoped to keep a healthy work–life balance. The memoirs of Henry Edward Hawker, one of the first railwaymen to publish an autobiography (in 1919), tell how he and his fellow clerks would work late at the Great Western's Taunton goods depot for four or five nights a week, each evening representing half a crown of overtime. In these circumstances, going blithely home on time for day after day would not have been a good career move. On many lines the goods department offered better prospects for advancement than the passenger side, and so it turned out for Hawker, who was eventually promoted to stationmaster at the little Newent station in the Forest of Dean. Here he found himself in a tight spot on one occasion while sitting down to the task of registering the month's issue of tickets. Heat rising from his desk lamp cracked a wall-mounted lamp immediately above it, the fuel ran down and both lamps went up in oily flames. Unassisted, Hawker managed to save his station from burning down. In the accident's aftermath he even secured the replacement of its oil lamps with gas ones. The episode captures something of the lonely clerical procedures of the average stationmaster, a slave to the lamp, bending meticulously once again over some recurrent task.

Not everyone who took charge of a station was suited to these exacting routines. Among the early drop-outs was Branwell Brontë, brother of the famous novelist sisters, who was an unlikely recruit to the service of the Manchester & Leeds Railway in 1840. From his first posting at Sowerby Bridge, Branwell was promoted to clerk-in-charge at the nearby Luddendenfoot station, on a starting salary of £130 per annum. ('Clerk-in-charge' was this railway's term for stationmaster, the counterpart of the 'station agent' on the Liverpool & Manchester.) But Luddendenfoot did not make Branwell happy, for he aspired to the life of an educated gentleman with artistic gifts. His lonely, boring hours on duty were diversified by making sketches of his colleagues and composing verses of a Byronic rather than Betjemanian kind:

> The desk that held my Ledger book
> Beneath the thundering rattle shook
> Of Engines passing by;
>
> The bustle of the approaching train
> Was all I hoped to rouse the brain
> Or startle apathy.

As soon as the day's last train had gone, Branwell headed uphill to the inn, where there was a circulating library and the prospect of lively conversation. Then he began slipping away before the last train, leaving the porter to issue tickets and keep the books without supervision. When the annual audit came, the accounts at Luddendenfoot were short by £11 1s 7d, and Branwell's ledgers were found to have been scribbled all over with his drawings and caricatures. Both clerk-in-charge and porter were promptly sacked and the missing sum deducted from the amount due in arrears on Branwell's salary.

Writing years after his friend Branwell's early death, the railway engineer Francis Henry Grundy recalled the station building at Luddendenfoot as 'a rude wooden hut'. This was actually just a makeshift; construction of a permanent building started only after the sackings. As he could not live at the hut, Branwell had taken lodgings nearby during his year with the Manchester & Leeds. The practice was not unusual. Sometimes, a stationmaster with a large family was given an allowance towards renting a house rather than living at his place of work. Besides, many station buildings did not include a residence for the stationmaster, even when it would have been easy to provide one. H. E. Hawker's Newent station was one example, being a modest, single-storeyed affair. Instead, the Great Western liked to build tied houses near its stations, sometimes (as surviving within sight of the main line at Didcot) with a clear hierarchy of size and importance. Even the little station at Adlestrop was provided with a standard Great Western house for accompaniment, as the railway author Chris Leigh discovered on a visit of inspection just before its closure in 1966.

₪

What of Adlestrop station itself? Here Leigh found one of the familiar pagoda-type shelters on the down platform, confronting a small cabin-like building that dated back to the line's origin as the Oxford, Worcester & Wolverhampton Railway in the 1850s. This simple weatherboarded structure, one of a now extinct sequence designed by the OW&W's engineer John Fowler, represents the more basic end of the station architecture spectrum. It housed a booking hall with an office on one side and a waiting room on the other, all fitting into a structure barely 30ft long and without any pretensions to architectural display. An awning along the platform front provided a small area of shelter. At the back was a small projecting room for a lavatory.

A fully functioning station could get by with even less than this. The tiny two-room structure still to be seen at Damems on the Keighley & Worth Valley Railway (companion to the midget signal box there) is sometimes cited as the smallest in England; a local joke had it that the building was taken indoors when it rained. Here the little booking hall and waiting room are one and the same space. But the ensemble at Adlestrop was more representative of the average everyday functions.

The passenger of 1862 could expect to buy a ticket at a little window within the station building, at an opening in the wall or screen separating booking hall and office. It was not so everywhere in the earliest years of railway travel; for instance in the booking hall of the short-lived first station at Paddington, where the booking clerk stood behind a counter, as in a shop. The fifteen-year-old Richard 'Dickie' Doyle (1824–83), later a professional illustrator whose work adorned *Punch* and Dickens's Christmas Books, drew himself buying a ticket here in his illustrated diary for 1840: 'What an important thing that was, actually paying down ninepence each and taking up a piece of buff paper.' These were the big paper tickets in use before Thomas Edmondson's small cardboard ones established themselves. The Edmondson system was not easy to set up on a flat and open surface, with its tubes of numbered tickets, contraption for date-stamping and countertop bowls for holding cash; but these could all be fitted nicely around the ticket clerk's window – a fact which must have encouraged the division of space between the public area and the clerk's domain. The French term *guichet* was (and is) sometimes borrowed for these openings, which allowed a very limited view of the room behind – 'that sacred inner temple behind the little window where the tickets are sold', which so fascinated the Railway Children. Where booking hall and office remain in their original relationship, the little windows have generally been enlarged or replaced with screens of security glass, but the principle of strict and secure separation remains.

The Railway Children would no doubt have lingered at the window for a chat, but at a busy station the passenger understood that he or she was expected to submit to brisker protocols. As *The Railway Traveller's Handy Book* put it, there was a right way and a wrong way to order a ticket. 'Bath – first-class – return' represented the right way. The reverse is exemplified by the elderly lady who wants to go to Putney. She asks what all the possible fares are, forgetting to specify single or return. The matter decided, she begins to search within her clothing for her purse, producing in succession 'pocket-handkerchief, smelling bottle, a pair of mittens, spectacle-case, a fan, and an Abernethy biscuit', before her fingers at last close on it. Then the long fumbling with small change, in a foredoomed attempt to avoid breaking into a sovereign – and so on. At least the old lady did not have to remember her PIN number.

The modern traveller expects to buy a ticket before beginning to await the train. Things were not always so straightforward in earlier times. For one thing, the booking office was not staffed continuously, but opened and closed as the timetable required. The *Handy Book* tells us that opening time was usually around a quarter of an hour before the train was due. The author's advice was to find a carriage seat and get any luggage stowed first, *before* buying a ticket – advice that was sound only when a train began its journey at the station, rather than passing through.

Access to the platform might be intermittent too, depending on the *modus operandi*. At some stations in the early years of Britain's railways, passengers were required to stay in the waiting room or booking office, or even outside the doors, until their train was imminent. This was one point on which practice soon came to diverge from certain Continental systems. By 1856, when the French engineer Auguste Perdonnet (1801–67) published the first edition of his treatise on railways, he was struck by the freedom granted to British travellers to move freely around the platforms; all the better, he thought, to allow them to become familiar with the loco-motives and thus to lose their fear – 'et c'est ainsi que les chemins de fer deviennent populaires'.* In France, as the journalist Blanchard Jerrold observed in 1865, you would be locked up in the waiting room instead, 'with your nose against the window', until the train came.

Perdonnet glosses over the distinction between those who were pre-paring to travel and those who had merely come to say their farewells, assist with boarding, greet a new arrival or just to watch the passing show. Whether such people should be allowed on the platform at all and, if so, under what circumstances, are questions the railways of Great Brit-ain have never conclusively settled. The central problem has always been the risk that some people might try to sneak a free ride. Before tickets could be checked on board trains, there was also a chance that passengers might award themselves an illicit upgrade to a higher class of carriage. This was one reason the Great Western preferred to lock its passengers in their compartments, tickets being inspected as the seats were taken. In 1842, when the Board of Trade directed the company to keep the doors unlocked during the journey for safety reasons, the company promptly set up ticket barriers instead. Passengers now showed their tickets as they left the station.

At first, these new rules were implemented so strictly that non-trav-elling members of the public were barred from the platform altogether. The result was a popular outcry. As a correspondent to the *Bath Chronicle* put it, 'No "little last attentions" can now be paid at parting – no friendly smile and welcome nod of recognition can now greet the arrival of the stranger at the Station – no faithful old domestic can now pounce on the well-known carpet bag ...' Within a few weeks, the Great Western relaxed its rules to allow friends, companions and servants to meet or see off its fare-paying passengers, at the discretion of its staff.

Similar tussles recurred as the passenger-only policy was taken up and dropped again elsewhere. One objection to 'closed' stations was that the discretionary power to admit or exclude individuals was being used

---

* 'and this is how the railways are becoming popular'.

in arbitrary ways. A traveller on the Eastern Union Railway in 1850 protested to the local paper that he had lately been refused entry at Ipswich when seeing two children on to a train, even though he had been allowed through when doing just the same two weeks before. Norwich's main station closed its platforms to the public in 1858 unless they had first got hold of a platform ticket, but the staff were said to issue these only grudgingly, or else the tickets could not always be got hold of quickly enough to make it through the barriers in time to meet the train – and so on.

The earliest platform tickets or passes are described as things of paper, which were issued on a discretionary basis. These arrangements appear to have changed shortly after 1900, when platform tickets went on general sale, at a standard price of one penny. Because they could be issued from machines, the new type also released the station visitor from the need to queue at a ticket window. Platform tickets now brought in a worthwhile income, while reducing the numbers of motley non-travellers milling obstructively around the platforms. By placing a ticket collector at the platform barrier, a watch could also be kept for pilferers, loiterers, drunks and other undesirables, with or without a penny ticket. The practice of halting main-line trains at lesser stations or special ticket-platforms shortly before their final destination, so that tickets could be checked and collected, began to fall out of favour at the same time; instead, tickets were examined when passing through the platform barrier and sometimes also during the journey, when the train was of corridor type. Respectable London commuters were spared inspection at first, the murmured phrase 'season ticket' being enough to pass muster, but in 1917 the duty of display was imposed on them too, as part of a clampdown on fraudulent wartime travel. So the establishment of barriers and platform tickets accelerated the flow of passengers in some areas, even as they slowed it down in others.

Platform tickets were commonly marked as valid for one hour only, and sometimes were specific to a particular platform. At first they were of cardboard, of the standard Edmondson shape and size. Even London Underground stations sold them. Extra-long souvenir tickets could be bought at Llanfair station on Anglesey, spelled out in all its tourist-pleasing fullness as Llanfairpwllgwyngyllgogerychwyrndrobwllllantysiliogogogoch. By the 1970s the standard type in the slot machines took the form of paper slips torn from a perforated coil, like bus tickets. The venerable penny charge remained inflation-resistant until 1958, when British Railways doubled the price to 2d, and the *Railway Magazine* lamented

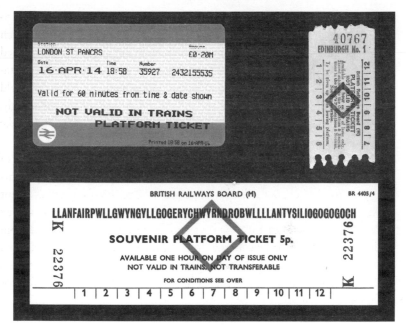

Platform tickets, new and old style, with the popular souvenir
ticket formerly available at one North Welsh station

that 'one of the last penny facilities' had gone from British life. By 'D-day',
alias 15 February 1971, when the currency went decimal, the cost had
increased to 5d, converted as 2p. On the Sunday prior to the great event,
a man from *The Times* accompanied Lord Fiske of the Decimal Currency
Board to the newly rebuilt Euston station, where he bought a platform
ticket with the unfamiliar new copper coins, as well as two ordinary tickets to Kilburn and a cup of British Rail tea.

The choice of purchases for Lord Fiske's public relations exercise
shows that the platform ticket was still an everyday item in 1971. No one
would make that claim nowadays; and yet platform tickets are not quite
dead. The price in 2014 – at the dwindling number of stations where
they can still be had – is 20p. But the once-familiar slot machines have
gone, and the tickets must once again be obtained by queuing at a staffed
ticket window (there is now apparently no option to buy a ticket to 'platform' in the ticket machines' software displays). Barriers between the
platform and the outside world are more likely than ever to be electronic

and automatic, and the tickets which operate them are less and less likely to have been bought by a face-to-face transaction rather than printed out from a machine. As these automatic ticket machines can be placed anywhere around the station – even, as at the renovated Paddington, facing the street outside – the booking hall or ticket office is of dwindling importance in the life of a major station. So the communal experience of railway travel has diminished slightly, even as its inconveniences and delays are reduced. The recent edict that has closed the ticket offices of the London Underground network suggests where this process might ultimately lead.

₪

Even before platform tickets began to disappear, the railways had lost the once-standard custom of ringing a bell to give notice when a train was due or about to depart. Five minutes was the standard interval for this. The practice explains why some inns and pubs built within easy reach of stations were named The Railway Bell, the sounding of which must have prompted some hasty drinking-up within. Before electric bells were available the instrument was rung by hand, like 'the shining bell, who lived in a little tray on stilts by himself', noted by Dickens at Carlisle in 1857.

Max Beerbohm had fun with the railway bell in the opening scene of his Oxford novel *Zuleika Dobson* (1911), which is set amid 'the grey eternal walls of that antique station, which ... does yet whisper to the tourist the last enchantments of the Middle Age'. Fans of Matthew Arnold may have spotted the subverted quotation from his *Essays in Criticism* (1865), and perhaps the banal echo of Oxford's much-romanticised choir of church bells. They may also have called to mind the Great Western's distinctly unimpressive buildings at Oxford, a collection of single-storeyed weatherboarded structures, like Adlestrop writ large, which somehow managed to escape rebuilding until 1972. Facilities at a station as sizeable and busy as Oxford were more likely to reflect the division of travellers by class; and sure enough, the bell in *Zuleika Dobson* finds the Warden of Judas College standing at the doorway of the first-class waiting room.*

---

* The Warden is not travelling himself, but awaits the arrival of his bewitching niece Zuleika; so he must have bought a platform ticket.

Stations with more than one class of waiting room are now rare. First-class waiting rooms still exist at some main-line stations, relabelled 'lounges' in imitation of airports, but these are so few, and often so tucked away, that most standard-class passengers probably fail to notice them. Oxford certainly manages without one, as do all but two of the stations – namely, Paddington and Cardiff – now served by the trains of First Great Western, operational heirs to the old GWR. Yet the designers of stations in the nineteenth century commonly went to great lengths to ensure that the different classes could wait, as well as travel, in separate enclosures. There was even a sumptuous super-class of royal and ducal waiting rooms, at such stations as Windsor, Wolferton (for Sandringham), Ballater (for Balmoral) and Redmile (for the Duke of Rutland's Belvoir Castle, Leicestershire).

The complexity that could result is illustrated by the stations built in the 1840s by the York architect George Townsend Andrews (1804–55), who had the good luck to form an alliance with his fellow citizen George Hudson. Even stations as modest as Andrews's Richmond or Tadcaster were equipped with three separate waiting rooms, each with its own entrance from the platform side. The third room was not, as might be guessed, for third-class passengers – as yet, dedicated third-class waiting rooms were provided only at a few city stations – but for the exclusive use of ladies. This was no Hudsonian quirk: a ladies' waiting room was then a common feature of any station of appreciable size. Where just two waiting rooms were provided, the division was as likely to be by sex as by class. So the formal segregation of male and (unaccompanied) female passengers that never quite took hold in the railway carriage was nonetheless a central principle of station planning.

There were variants galore. Sometimes, first class was divided into separate waiting rooms for gentlemen and ladies, and a general waiting room served for all the rest. Waiting rooms might be duplicated where there was no easy connection between the platforms; Andrews's station at Malton had three waiting rooms on one side and two on the other. These conventions help to explain the characteristic planning of medium-to-large station architecture in Britain, with sequences of relatively small, individually heated apartments stretching along the platforms. Behind many of those mysterious doorways, now bricked up or used only by station staff, the separate classes and sexes once waited for their trains. It was different on the Continent and in America, where a single big hall often combined the functions of concourse and shared waiting room.

With class divisions came graduated standards of furnishing and finish. What the traveller actually encountered nevertheless seems to have differed wildly from station to station. Carpeted floors were not unknown, if not especially practical. In 1858 the North British Railway board addressed the question of whether to order a new carpet for the first-class waiting room at Berwick, in which case the old one would be passed on to the waiting room for second class. Other decorative grace notes are recorded. At the Midland Railway's terminus at Bath, opened in 1869, the ladies' first-class waiting room featured a blue, white and gold chandelier and the gentlemen's had a marble chimneypiece painted with flowers. Elsewhere things were not so alluring. At Leuchars in Fife in 1866, the gentlemen's and ladies' rooms were both so grim that some passengers chose instead to seek refuge in empty carriages kept in an adjacent shed. Big towns did not necessarily do better. A member of the Portsmouth Chamber of Commerce expressed dismay in 1894 at the facilities offered by the London & South Western to the town. In the first-class waiting room were 'an old table and one or two wooden chairs. The walls were decorated with advertisements inviting people to go elsewhere.' As for second class, the room was

> the worst kind of place he had ever seen. One end of it was the way from the ticket office to the platform, so that it was always open, and people must suffer from cold. The furniture consisted of an old oblong table and a couple of wooden settees, which could scarcely be found in any public house in the country.

Such complaints have a way of showing up in the records where satisfaction leaves no trace. Even so, there is much to suggest that the average waiting-room experience was closer to Portsmouth-type privation than to Bathonian luxury. Among the malcontents was Anthony Trollope, whose work for the Post Office required him to linger for a connecting train at many a remote junction. By the time he wrote *The Belton Estate* (1866), waiting-room hours were obviously getting to him quite badly: 'Everything is hideous, dirty, and disagreeable, and the mind wanders away, to wonder why station-masters do not more frequently commit suicide.' In an address to the Society of Civil and Mechanical Engineers in 1886, the architect Alfred Cole Adams (1844/5–1909) described a typical interior at a lesser station in more sober detail: 'Bare floor, bare table, bare wooden chairs ... eternal varnished or grained woodwork, French-grey walls, and

dead-white ceilings.' For visual diversion, there was nothing except advertisements, mostly the company's own.

Cole's remedies included the introduction of warmer tints, painted
or stencilled dadoes and friezes, simple wallpapers and picture rods, from
which 'the better class of framed and glazed advertisements', or photos of
local attractions and interesting places, might be hung. Whether or not
these suggestions had any direct result, the railways did at least take up
the idea of pictorial decorations (counterparts to the framed pictures in
their carriages). John Betjeman evoked the results in a radio talk in 1940.
He asked his listeners to imagine a waiting room on a wet evening, as it
might be encountered at a hundred junctions: 'the vast interior, the black
horsehair benches and chairs, the mahogany table, the grate with its winking fire, the large framed photographs of yellowing views of crowded
esplanades and ivy-mantled ruins, the framed advertisement for the company's hotel at "Strathmacgregor"'. Betjeman suggested vaguely that this
ensemble might date back to eighty years before, but the framed views fix
it firmly in the late-Victorian or Edwardian era.

The winking fire is a significant detail too. Complaining letters from
travellers to the Victorian press often mention the failure to heat waiting
rooms adequately, if at all. On a chilly night, cosy first-class must have had
rather less appeal than fireless second-and-general, and vice versa. How
effectively the station staff were able to police the use of waiting rooms,
especially at busy junctions, must be open to question. Ladies' waiting
rooms, barred to male travellers of every class, were a different matter.
These in turn open the way – literally and figuratively – to the diverting
subject of station lavatories.

The plan of Adlestrop station indicates a little projection opening
off the waiting room, coyly identified as the 'ladies room'. This linkage of
waiting room and ladies' lavatory was common, yet far from ideal. Cole
Adams's lecture drew attention to what everybody knew: that it was
embarrassing to cross the waiting room to use the facilities under the eyes
of fellow passengers, especially when the company was mixed (just like the
awkward conjunctions of lavatories and compartments in some carriages
of the period). Yet the plan-type continued in use. The smaller stations on
the Great Central's London extension of the 1890s adopted it, for example, and the results can still be visited on the preserved section of the line,
at Rothley and at Quorn & Woodhouse in Leicestershire.

Male passengers were provided for at these Great Central stations by means of a separate building further down the platform, robust enough in construction to recall the popular simile of the brick shithouse. There is a particularly large, glass-roofed example at Loughborough, a full-scale town station that has been lovingly preserved in its 1950s state. The result is intensely atmospheric, a sort of distillation of the drab urban existence in the Midlands or the north portrayed by the angry young novelists and realist film-makers of the day. It could stand in for the station at Strad-houghton, fictional home town of the hapless hero of Keith Waterhouse's *Billy Liar* (1958). The final scene of that novel finds Billy and his suitcase in the waiting room after midnight, planning to escape to a new life in London but already losing his nerve, with a vomiting drunk and three elderly prostitutes for company. In a similar downbeat spirit, the Lough-borough toilets displayed until recently a 1950s poster from the Ministry of Health warning of the perils of venereal disease.

These Great Central lavatories had cubicles as well as urinals. This was enough to mark them as superior to a small station such as Adlestrop, where the male facilities comprised a urinal only, likewise placed some way from the station building. Again, similar arrangements may be seen on preserved railways. One of the most rugged was at Oxenhope, termi-nus of the Keighley & Worth Valley line. Its stalls were squeezed into an awkward corner at one end of the main building, sheltered by an angled roof or canopy with a wide gap below it and lit by a single lamp on an iron overthrow. They were replaced in 2013 by a conventional toilet block, reportedly after complaints by visitors whose notions of a trip back in time were not quite so all-embracing. Other stations featured door-less urinals of cast iron, often incorporating finely patterned openwork panels reminiscent of the *mashrabiya* lattices of Islamic architecture, and manufactured in most cases by such Glasgow firms as Walter Macfarlane & Co., or the Sun Foundry of George Smith & Co. There is a good Macfarlane's specimen at the East Anglian Railway Museum at Chappel and Wakes Colne station in Essex, embossed on its inner sides with the customary injunction PLEASE ADJUST YOUR DRESS BEFORE LEAVING.

The situation for the modern traveller on the national network is sometimes better, sometimes worse. Station lavatories now have cubicles for both sexes, sometimes for those with impaired mobility too, and gen-tlemen are no longer banished to separate structures on the platform. The awkward conjunction of ladies' lavatory cubicle and general waiting room has become rare; March station in Cambridgeshire is among the survivors in 2015. But fewer stations now have lavatories at all, just as fewer have waiting rooms rather than mere shelters. In which case, calls of nature must be answered on the train, and not at the station: a complete reversal of the arrangements that confronted travellers in the past.

₪

The absence of lavatories on long-distance trains was easier to bear thanks to the nineteenth-century institution of the refreshment stop. A fixed interval was allowed, so that passengers could eat and drink something, and (although this was not spelled out) relieve themselves too. Even more than the patrons of today's motorway service stations, travellers at these stops were a captive clientele. The railways could have milked them directly, but mostly chose instead to contract out the service to private caterers. These deals were sealed by guarantees that all trains would stop at the station in question, or at least that specified trains would stop in sufficient numbers to make the trade worthwhile.

The best-known of these agreements concerned the Great Western's station at Swindon. It was a painful case of a self-inflicted wound. Seeking to reduce its direct costs, the company granted a ninety-nine-year lease of the refreshment rooms in lieu of payment to the contractors who built Swindon station, with an agreed ten-minute stop by all timetabled passenger trains. The builders first subcontracted the service to a Cheltenham hotelier, then in 1848 sold the lease outright for £20,000, which was already around £5,000 more than the construction costs of the entire station. Eager to accelerate its crack trains, the Great Western had meanwhile begun to chafe at the ten-minute-stop agreement. When the company tried to curtail these stops their caterers went to law, and won. The company then had to sit by for half a century, watching the lease change hands for sums of up to £70,000. Finally, in 1895, it swallowed hard and bought back – for £100,000 – what had been carelessly granted away. The restaurant cars the Great Western began running at just this time reduced the value of this non-investment still further, but at least the company was at last free to give itself permission to end the compulsory stop.

Swindon's refreshment rooms were grandly conceived; as usual, Brunel wanted to outshine everyone else. There were first- and second-class rooms on both up and down platforms. The finishes in first class evoked the civilised luxury of the fashionable clubs of Pall Mall, with columns and pilasters in the imitation marble known as scagliola, a ceiling of ornate plasterwork, and walls painted in the manner of Italian Renaissance palaces. Second class was sober by comparison, but the overall level of decoration and comfort far exceeded that of the ordinary waiting rooms. The rooms were smart enough to be borrowed at least once for a county ball.

This mismatch occurred on other lines too. It was as if the delivery of food and drink made the companies eager to emulate the best rooms of the hotels and inns beyond their territories. Refreshment rooms at city stations sometimes developed a life of their own, competing with the businesses in the streets around them, on the model of Messrs Spiers and Pond's establishment for the Metropolitan Railway (*see* Chapter 2). Photographs of the better sorts of facility from the early twentieth century show a decorous tea-room environment of upholstered furniture and spindly coat stands, lightened by tablecloths and floral displays.

John Betjeman's *Metro-Land* film of 1973 opens in one of the latest and most genteel of these spaces, the panelled Chiltern Court restaurant. This was an addition of 1911–13 to the Metropolitan's Baker Street station. Spiers and Pond, then still flourishing, were the caterers. The space survives, subsumed in a giant block of 1920s mansion flats; it now trades as the Metropolitan Bar, one of J. D. Wetherspoon's pubs. Another London survivor is harder to recognise as such. Visitors to the branch of Foyle's bookshop at Waterloo, opened in 2014, find themselves in what was the Windsor Bar. Two curvaceous little cashiers' booths are still in place by the entrance, converted to display cabinets (the bar itself, formerly equipped with an American soda fountain, has vanished). Now, the best place to experience the mingling of travellers and townies is probably the gleaming faience-lined refreshment room that was created at Newcastle Central station in 1893, now restored after a period of eclipse behind false ceilings and neutral paint. Honourable mention might also be made of the restaurant of 1909 at the Lancashire & Yorkshire Railway's Manchester Victoria station, although its present furnishings are unworthy of the thick Edwardian plasterwork and hovering coloured-glass dome overhead.

These surroundings often belied the brusque exchanges that occurred in railway refreshment rooms, especially those of the Swindon type that depended for custom on brief passenger stops. The flurries at Swindon were far from unique. Passengers on the London & Birmingham Railway were likewise allowed just ten minutes at its midway stop at Wolverton in

Buckinghamshire, and periods of five to ten minutes are described as the general rule in *The Railway Traveller's Handy Book*. Anglo-Scottish travellers were allowed more time, having further to go, but even the customary stops for dining at York, Normanton or Preston were no more than twenty to thirty minutes long.

Refreshment stops on fast stagecoach journeys had been hurried too, but at least the numbers involved were not great. Railways introduced a new problem: how to serve a crowd of hungry and thirsty travellers in a limited space and time. The solution – to require them to line up at the counter of a long bar – may sound self-evident, but in the 1840s this was still a relatively unusual way of serving food and drink. At that period customers in the average public house were attended to at their seats by waiters or pot-boys, and the 'bar' referred more often than not to an office-like space rather than a room with a public counter. Kings of these railway bars were Brunel's installations at Swindon, with their long U-shaped counters projecting into the middle of the first- and second-class interiors, together making a shared central enclosure for the staff.

Even the longest bar could not make up for rushed service or for having to eat and drink against the clock. A newspaper report in 1879 castigated

> the rush out and search for the buffet as soon as the panting loco-
> motive draws up to the platform; the crush and confusion when the
> buffet at length was found; the frantic attempts to gulp scalding soups
> or hot coffee; the cries oft-repeated for fowl, or tongue, or ham, and
> the frequent fruitlessness of the demand; enough, in short, to chafe
> the patience of a saint, and impair the digestion of an ostrich.

To make matters worse, the quality of fare was often low. The rot seems to have set in almost straight away. A comment from 1841: 'Be very careful what you eat at Wolverton. Avoid pork-pies especially.' Brunel himself sent a famously sarcastic letter to the first lessee at Swindon, wondering why the man should buy such bad roasted corn: 'I did not believe you had such a thing as coffee in the place; I am certain that I never tasted any.' For the *Sheffield Daily Telegraph* in 1865,

> Railway tea is liquid nausea, whether you get it in the common room
> or are served with it in the first-class room, out of a silver urn; and
> railway coffee is (except at King's Cross, where it is really good) made

with a slight suspicion of coffee, just as if *a* coffee berry had *bathed* in it early in the day.

Sandwiches, too. For Trollope, the railway sandwich was 'that whited sepulchre, fair enough outside, but so meagre, poor, and spiritless within, such a thing of shreds and parings, such a dab of food, telling us that the poor bone whence it was scraped had been made utterly bare before it was sent into the kitchen for the soup pot' (*He Knew He Was Right*, 1869). Other staples of railway catering were skewered by Dickens, in his journalist's persona of the Uncommercial Traveller: 'brown hot water stiffened with flour', 'shining brown pasties, composed of unknown animals within, and offering to my view the device of an indigestible star-fish in leaden pie-crust without'. On a shopping visit to a Birmingham silversmith during his last reading tour, Dickens spotted some 'old friends', dilapidated tea urns from the London & North Western; after inspecting their interiors, he could only wonder at the harm caused by the contents, 'produced under the active agency of hot water, and a mixture of decomposed lead, copper, and a few other deadly poisons'.

Customer service did nothing to make up for these shortcomings. The counters were frequently staffed by well-groomed, unmarried young women, who had no time for *politesse* and still less for flirtation. According to Sir Francis Head, the contingent at Wolverton were officially discouraged from conversing even with one another, let alone with the imploring faces across the counter; 'But they may sometimes attempt to appeal to the generosity in travellers' natures, when milk has turned or soup be over-peppered, with the hundred-thousandth part of a smile.' Head also reassured readers that the girls were of unsullied reputation, although he did allow that four of them had managed to make 'excellent marriages'.

Head's was an unusually sympathetic treatment, written in co-operation with the railway company and certainly skewed in its favour. For the *Pall Mall Gazette* in 1868, the normal attitude behind the counter was mere 'supercilious complacency'. This exposure to female beauty, haughtiness and inaccessibility, combined with the hurried eating and drinking of nasty, overpriced produce, made the refreshment-room experience especially indigestible for male travellers, from whom the surviving accounts overwhelmingly come. Why, asked Dickens in *Household Words* in 1856, did these attractive women, with their 'glossy hair and neat attire', always treat him with scorn?

The canonical text among these protests is Dickens's much-anthologised account of the facilities at Mugby (i.e. Rugby) Junction. In his other *Mugby* tales of Christmas 1866, he displayed understanding and admiration for railway workers – the industrious 'Lamps' in his oily hut and the haunted, doomed Signalman. Entering Mugby's fictionalised refreshment room, Dickens left these sympathies at the door in favour of a gleeful settling of scores. The trigger was an incident at Rugby on his reading tour earlier that year. As his companion prepared to supply the correct change, Dickens had reached for the sugar and milk, only for them to be snatched away 'with the remark, made in shrill and shrewish tones, "You sha'n't have any milk and sugar 'till you two fellows have paid for your coffee"'. To make things worse, the contretemps brought much laughter from a 'boy in buttons', another employee of the rooms.

Dickens made this youth our insolent guide to the facilities at Mugby, where the staff maintain a 'proudly independent footing' and offer as little help as possible. He explains how the serving girls are marshalled by Our Missis and spend their time between trains bandolining their hair. When the telegraphic signal announces the imminent arrival of a train carrying 'the Beast', alias the travelling public, 'you should see their noses all a-going up with scorn, as if it was a part of the working of the same Cooke and Wheatstone electrical machinery'. We learn of Our Missis's research trip to France, from which she returned with 'Orrors to reveal': cleanliness and tastefulness everywhere, soup without flour in it and the outrageous sale of baskets each containing a tasty cold lunch for one.

Satirical drubbings of this kind seem to diminish after 1870. For one thing, there was more choice for travellers after Spiers and Pond introduced luncheon baskets to British rails. The company's growing empire of leases – 211 buffets and refreshment rooms on seventeen different lines by 1888 – was another force for improvement. Perhaps the Food and Drugs Act of 1875, which criminalised the practice of adulteration, also made things better. Yet the failure of the railways and their chosen contractors to do better from the start remains slightly mysterious. For they had supplanted the old coaching inns for more than just the provision of snacks: the companies themselves were also hoteliers on the grandest scale, and most of their hotels were incorporated within the station buildings.

Railway hotels represent the supreme instance of adding a commercial service to the basic necessities of travel. That there would be a demand to stay
overnight close to many of the new railway stations was anticipated almost
straight away, and local entrepreneurs jumped at the chance. Many self-
styled Railway Hotels belonged in this private, independent category, as
did the multitudes of Railway (or Station) Inns, Railway (or Station) Taverns and the odd Railway Bell. The type is still a familiar sight, especially
in the form of a mid-Victorian building that is noticeably older than the
houses and commercial architecture that have grown up around it. Other
early hotels began as private undertakings but were later bought up by the
railways, like the big Midland Hotel that was built across the road from
Derby station in 1841.

By that year the railways had already made their first venture into
the trade, in the spectacular form of the hotel erected in front of the London & Birmingham's new terminus at Euston – two hotels rather, because
the facilities were divided into large matching blocks. Each was operated
independently at first, although the blocks were later combined, and then
linked by building a cross-range that obscured the view of the station's
mighty Doric entrance. The split arrangement favoured symmetrical
grandeur over convenience and was not repeated. Other early one-offs
included Brunel's facilities at Swindon, where the hotel rooms were appor-
tioned between the two upper storeys over the pair of refreshment rooms,
with a covered bridge across the tracks by way of access. One half of this
odd Siamese-twin building survives, looking neutral and nondescript now
that its counterpart has been demolished and the resplendent refreshment-room interiors destroyed.

Not until G. T. Andrews's station at Hull was built in 1847–51 were
the functions combined in a way that allowed the hotel to make a grand
architectural display towards the station approach. This arrangement
arrived in London with the second Paddington station, where the Great
Western Royal Hotel, a grandiose design in a mid-seventeenth-century
French style, opened its doors in 1854. It was an instant success, justifying
the company's outlay of £59,500 (furnishings included) and encouraging
others to follow. A terminus was especially suited to the type of grand fron-
tal composition employed at Paddington, and London had several other
examples, of which the South Eastern Railway's Charing Cross (opened
1865) and the Midland's St Pancras (opened 1873, completed 1877) are the
best preserved.

The Midland Grand Hotel at St Pancras was designed by Sir George Gilbert Scott (1811–78), the pre-eminent architect of his time. Costing £437,335, it was the apotheosis of the British station hotel, just as the train shed immediately behind it (of which more later) remains the most daring and spectacular in the country. Its grandiose scale is amplified by Scott's use of a modern Gothic Revival style, in which boldly patterned arches derived from medieval Italy are mixed with motifs from France, England and the Low Countries, culminating in a magnificently spiky skyline of pinnacles and towers. The torch then passed to Edinburgh, where the flagship hotels of the rival Caledonian and North British companies squared up to one another from opposite ends of Princes Street. The Caledonian Hotel of 1897–1903 has survived the closure and demolition of the terminus it served, which the buildings enclosed by means of angled wings that stretch back from a symmetrical, eight-storeyed entrance front. The North British Hotel, opened in 1902 and now pretentiously renamed the Balmoral Hotel, trumps this display with its soaring four-square mass and thoroughly municipal clock tower, placed just north of Waverley station. The architectural historian Charles McKean regarded the Edinburgh hotels as a representation of the 'approximate draw' between the two greatest Scottish companies. Likewise, the Midland Grand at St Pancras was a spectacular gesture of rivalry towards the adjacent King's Cross station and the underwhelming Great Northern Hotel that stood awkwardly – and, until recent renovations, unconnectedly – alongside its parent terminus.

It would be a mistake to regard these hotels simply as trophy buildings. They were expected to run at a profit, and generally did. They offered a valuable service to passengers, with calibrated sizes and standards of rooms to suit different means. They also set new standards of comfort and display by which existing hotels were found wanting – another instance of how the railways' financial muscle allowed them to make the running. Almost every large British city felt the impact: by 1914 only Plymouth, Portsmouth, Bristol, Cardiff and Dundee were without a railway hotel, and Glasgow, Liverpool, Manchester and Edinburgh all had more than one. More subtly, railway hotels helped to foster the growth of civic life, because their public rooms offered neutral ground for meetings and celebrations. That could not be said of the older type of private hotel, with their individual proprietors and known political alignments. The function rooms at some London hotels were especially busy with political conventions, shareholder meetings, annual dinners and the like, and the Great Eastern Hotel at Liverpool Street even found room for two Masonic temples within. This ecumenical attitude extended to the Communist Party of Great Britain, founded in 1920 in the hotel at the former South Eastern Railway's City terminus at Cannon Street.

By the time that the British communists came together, the railways had taken the management of their hotels into their own hands. The Midland proved to be a particularly enthusiastic hotelier, mirroring its achievements in raising standards of comfort within its carriages. Its hotels were latterly managed by Sir William Towle (1849–1929), from offices within the top storey of the Midland Grand's west tower. Towle sought to fill gaps in the company's hotel network, which at Manchester and Liverpool meant building close to its existing stations, rather than integrating hotel and station together. The Midland Hotel in Manchester, opened in 1903, fell only slightly short of its Edinburgh cousins in its scale and degree of architectural embellishment. Advertised in Bradshaw's back pages as 'The most complete hotel in the world', the hotel used an early form of air conditioning by means of linen filters to protect its guests from Manchester's thickened atmosphere. Its 'tropical' level of warmth was noted by J. B. Priestley in his state-of-the-nation travelogue *English Journey* (1934).

The next great Midland project was the Adelphi Hotel in Liverpool, opened in 1914. By that date the hospitable Midland had accounted for 41 per cent of the total of £5,758,836 expended on building England's railway hotels. Elegantly plain where the Manchester hotel was busy and ornate, the huge Adelphi would have been even larger, but falling levels of transatlantic custom and shortages of capital after the First World War kept these plans on the shelf. Sir William Towle had retired by then, leaving his sons to take over the hotel and catering division.

One of these sons, Arthur Towle, found himself at the head of the largest hotel business in Europe once the Midland became a constituent of the London, Midland & Scottish Railway in the amalgamations of 1923. Arthur Towle's greatest project in the LMS period was the Queen's Hotel at Leeds City station, built in 1936–8. However luxuriously appointed, station hotels had to contend with the dirt and round-the-clock commotion generated by trains, and the architect responded accordingly. The hotel's multi-phase air conditioning used both oil and cotton-wool filters, delivering a supply Towle described as 'clean and pure as the air of St Moritz'. Guest rooms were centrally heated and noise levels were kept low by the use of double glazing, rubber-cushioned doors and soundproofed flooring. Every bedroom also had its own bathroom; sixty years before, the five storeys of bedrooms at the Midland Grand had made do with just nine shared bathrooms between them, plus movable hip-baths for those guests who wished, at the extra charge of one shilling, to take a hot bath in their own room.

Leeds was the last great flourish of the British railway hotel, reflecting the shift in expectations away from high ceilings and ornate public rooms, towards private comfort and convenience. As such, it was almost in a class of its own. Complete replacement of an older railway hotel was rare, the work at Leeds happening only because of a general reconstruction project in which two existing stations were merged. In London especially, railway hotels between the wars slipped down the ranks of smartness. When the Midland Grand opened, its best rooms were the most expensive in London, but lavish new establishments such as the Dorchester, the Savoy and the Ritz all overtook it. The *Travellers' Guide* for 1930 records that average charges at railway hotels began at 7s 6d for a room, 4s 6d for lunch and 6s 6d for dinner, all no more than half the equivalent rates at 'First Class Hotels'. Outside London, railway hotels still had few rivals as superior places to stay and socialise until the 1960s, although they have not always escaped contagion from the relative decline of their host cities. The Adelphi, in retreat from the palmy days of the Atlantic crossing, is one instance of diminished prestige. A BBC fly-on-the-wall series in 1997, full of mishaps and bickering senior staff, did nothing to change this perception.

Among the railway hotels that retained their lustre best were those which served tourists rather than travellers. Some of these were not at stations at all, nor were they necessarily even built as hotels. The Great Western was early into the field, leasing Tregenna Castle near St Ives for hotel use in 1878. Cultivating tourist traffic to the outermost end of Cornwall had an obvious value to the company, which shortly afterwards coined the advertising phrase 'Cornish Riviera' and produced a rather spurious poster in which the outline of the Duchy was mirrored by that of Italy, under the slogan SEE YOUR OWN COUNTRY FIRST. Railway hotels in northern destinations began earlier still, including one built at Poulton-le-Sands in Lancashire as part of an archetypal railway-dependent plan to develop a bathing resort there. Under the more familiar name of Morecambe, this town grew into one of England's busiest seaside attractions, and Arthur Towle decided in due course to invest in a replacement hotel for the LMS.

The new building of 1933–4, now restored after near-terminal neglect, projected a thoroughly modern image thanks to the white, streamlined design provided by the flamboyant society architect Oliver Hill.

The east coast of Scotland was especially well provided with railway-owned resort hotels, which differed from the urban kind in that they did not necessarily stay open all year round. The popularity of Scottish hotels reflected the rising enthusiasm for golf, and at resorts such as Dornoch (Sutherland), Gleneagles (Perthshire) and Cruden Bay (Aberdeenshire), new courses and new hotels were created together. Gleneagles and its course have become internationally famous, but the Great North of Scotland Railway's Cruden Bay Hotel failed to flourish, hampered by a shorter than average season and by the lack of a direct railway connection. After closure in 1932 the building continued in use for several more years on account of its well-equipped laundry, served by the little mile-long electric tramway that connected with Cruden Bay station, on which the bedsheets and napery of the LNER's Northern Division were shuttled up and down.

The final addition to the ranks of railway hotels belongs in this Scottish golfing group. It is the Old Course Hotel at St Andrews, built in 1967–8 to the designs of a New Orleans architectural practice whose best-known work is the exactly contemporary Louisiana Superdome. The hotel was the creation of British Transport Hotels Ltd, a wholly owned subsidiary of British Railways, from which it enjoyed a high degree of autonomy. Certainly, the Old Course Hotel was not planned in any close relationship to the rail network, opening its doors less than a year before the branch line to St Andrews closed to passengers. Like its older railway-owned siblings, the Old Course Hotel was sold off in 1983–4. Today it belongs in the Leading Hotels of the World (LHW) group, whose website keeps silent about the hotel's origins as a venture by the nationalised railway – an ancestry that now seems as remote as the lost societies of the Eastern Bloc.

₪

Station hotels were places of architectural display because they had to appear worthy of the well-off traveller's patronage. Hence the Great Northern Hotel at King's Cross, the least ostentatious of London's terminus hotels, adopted a version of the Italianate classical manner then in favour for the terraces of Pimlico and Belgravia. But the most distinctive structures developed to serve railway stations had little to do with conventions handed down from architectural styles of the past. These were the train sheds, all-over enclosures large or small, which sheltered platforms, passengers and traffic alike – the fullest development of the various structures by which stations offered outdoor protection from the weather.

Even small stations commonly provided a sheltered area alongside the platform. One influential type was developed on the London & Brighton Railway, for which the architect David Mocatta devised a symmetrical plan for thirteen lineside stations built in 1839–41 (all now destroyed). These had a central, open-fronted waiting area towards the platform, enclosed by projecting rooms or simple screen walls on either side. The roof slope of the main building was carried down over the sheltered space. A similar configuration was still recommended for small stations by Alfred Cole Adams in 1886. But the type had a weakness, for its compact, self-contained form left an exposed gap between the train and the building. Better coverage could be provided by means of an awning or canopy that stood proud of the station walls, even if it could not always protect the platform right up to its edge. At Adlestrop, for instance, the timber canopy stuck out for just over 6ft from the eaves of the little station building, offering about 166 square feet of protection from the Gloucestershire skies.

Brunel was especially attentive to the value of shelter. For his smaller stations, he developed two standard types that could offer protection on all four sides. The more elegant kind, now best represented by the little station at Culham in the old county of Berkshire, juts out generously on deep brackets from a level close to the base of the main roof-slope. Another version exploits the hipped roof of the main building as the sheltering medium, achieved by means of a steroidal exaggeration to the eaves. Among the few survivors is Charlbury in the well-set Oxfordshire Cotswolds, where regular travellers once fought off a proposal by British Rail to replace the coal fire in their waiting room with an electric one. Kindred designs are widespread on other, non-Brunellian lines. Exemplary sequences remain at the late nineteenth-century timber-built stations of Glasgow's Cathcart Circle, where the canopies are glazed, and on the island platforms of the West Highland Railway route to Fort William and Mallaig.

To cover a still larger area it was necessary to give canopies and awnings a structural life of their own, so that they could extend down the

Twyford station in 1852, showing the expansive platform canopy designed by
Brunel. The track is of his broad-gauge type, with continuous longitudinal
timbers under each rail and cross timbers spaced at wide intervals

platforms. Sometimes these canopies are supported by a wall backing on
to the platform, especially where a station sits in a cutting or somewhere
built-up. When island platforms are present, the canopies necessarily
stand free. Depending on the date, these linear umbrellas may be of timber, iron or steel, concrete, glass or some less heavy and brittle translucent
covering, variously combined. From the late 1850s until around 1920 canopies of timber were usually finished with shaped vertical slats known as
valancing, a cheap form of ornament (because the ends could be machine-
cut) which also served to direct the run-off of rainwater. Or the boards
might be pierced higher up, leaving the bottom edge straight or arranged
in gently arching profiles. There used to be a specially good set at Christ's
Hospital station in Sussex, as rebuilt in 1902 by the London, Brighton &
South Coast Railway; the architectural critic Ian Nairn commended its
'taut and suave loping rhythm'. Other ex-LBSCR stations, including Bat-
tersea Park, preserve the type. Valancing also serves to break and diffuse
the sun's rays at the edge of the canopy's shadow – a minor but appreciable
enhancement of the experience of travel, which is lost every time a canopy
is trimmed, or replaced with something straight-edged and utilitarian.

Most medium-sized British stations, many smaller ones and quite
a few of the largest were given individual platform canopies. The seaside resorts of Kent and Sussex still have them in plenty, as does the old
Midland Railway main line (Nottingham, Derby and Leicester stations

included), and hosts of multi-platformed suburban stations on the main lines from London. Their epitome is Clapham Junction, where the seventeen numbered platforms are sheltered by eight open-sided canopies, of wildly varying age, length and design – essential components of this giant station that nowhere quite presents itself as a giant building.

If a station were to achieve architectural grandeur rather than mere extent, a train shed was essential. 'Shed' has an odd ring in this context, suggesting a small improvised enclosure rather than a giant marvel of engineering. As it happens, the first example – built at the Liverpool end of the Liverpool & Manchester in 1831 – was indeed a makeshift. Here the station's single platform originally had a straightforward flat canopy on iron columns. To make the train shed, the canopy was extended all the way across the tracks to a supporting wall on the far side, by means of an open-ended roof of simple timber trusses. In this form the station served passengers for just five years, until handsome municipal funding secured a grander and better-placed new terminus at Lime Street.

Despite the obvious fire risk, timber-roofed train sheds were far from being a false start. Brunel and his followers adopted the type for many small-to-medium stations, of which the best remaining example is at Frome in Somerset, opened in 1850. Thurso, the northernmost station in Britain, and its sister station at Wick, on the other end of the two-pronged termination of the Highland Railway's Far North line, are other examples. But for anything more ambitious, the future ultimately lay with iron.

The crucial building for the introduction of iron to station buildings was the train shed opened in 1837 at Robert Stephenson's terminus at Euston, an early work by the brilliant engineer-entrepreneur Charles Fox (1810–74). In its first form this had three parallel spans of lightweight wrought-iron trusses. Each truss was braced by spindly tie rods and hangers below the roof slope, which were carried on two arcades of slim cast-iron arches set on no less slim columns. Roofing was by slates secured with copper wire. The basic form was a development of fireproof iron roofs already in use at some of the workshops, warehouses and mills of the new industrial economy. By far the best place to see this primal type of iron train shed is Dublin, where several of the termini built in the 1840s have escaped rebuilding. The finest British survivor is at Scarborough, where the 1840s parts were designed by G. T. Andrews for George Hudson's York & North Midland Railway; these were brought back to something like their original form in the 1970s, when enlargements were chopped away.

King's Cross station, photographed in 1898

Trusses of this type could be made to span up to 80ft, although at Fox's Euston the figure was less than half that. As traffic levels increased, and railway construction became more ambitious and assured, station designers turned instead to arched trusses in order to span much greater distances. Arches also supplied an increase in overall height, and thus an enhanced potential for ventilation – a valuable asset by the 1860s, as smoky coal replaced cleaner coke as the usual locomotive fuel.

Among the best-known early arched train sheds is the Great Northern's terminus at King's Cross, opened in 1852. This has twin arched spans each measuring 105ft across. The double volumes are expressed with beautiful clarity in the arched windows of the severely plain end wall. These double volumes also suited the way the station originally functioned: just one platform each sufficed for departing and arriving trains, and the rest of the enclosure served for the storage and shunting of rolling stock. Structurally, however, there was a catch: the trusses were of laminated timber rather than iron. The material proved structurally unstable, and in less than two decades the Great Northern began replacing the timber arches with wrought-iron ones. As a result of these alterations, it is Brunel's second station at Paddington, opened in 1854 with an iron-framed train shed from the outset, that is now the earliest London terminus in something close to its original form. Paddington is also memorable for its unique plan, with a central span of roughly equivalent width to one of the King's Cross arches, and lesser spans on each side. (A fourth span is an addition from the 1910s.) The triple form raises spatial echoes of the nave and aisles of a great church, and these echoes are amplified at Paddington by a bewitching arrangement of double transepts, also arched, each of which cuts through the triple arches of the main axis.

Brunel was not the first to enlist wrought iron to make an arched train shed. Earlier by a few years were two showpieces from the northern heartlands of the railways, at Newcastle and at Liverpool. Newcastle Central station was provided with a three-span structure, built in 1849–50 and later enlarged with a fourth span, Paddington-fashion. Newcastle has a spatial magic all its own, because the train shed follows an even curve with a radius of 800ft. Liverpool's train shed was a replacement for the timber installation provided at the first Lime Street station of 1836, which was a mere 55ft wide. Its successor of 1849 managed 153ft 6in in a single span. This soon proved too small as well, so the London & North Western Railway pulled down the train shed in 1869 and put up a still more spectacular arched roof, 212ft across. Even this did not make Lime Street big enough, so an additional span measuring 191ft was erected alongside in 1879. Yet Lime Street pales beside the greatest of the iron train sheds, the pointed-arched volume designed by the engineer William Henry Barlow (1812–1902) for the Midland Railway at St Pancras and finished in 1867. A worthy companion for Scott's Midland Grand Hotel, it measures 246ft 6in across – a world record for a clear-span enclosure, not bested for nearly thirty years afterwards – and rises 102ft to the peak of the arch, making it the tallest as well as the widest train shed ever built in Britain.

Even after the engineers' arms race had peaked at St Pancras, arched train sheds continued to rise outside London. The Midland and its allied companies provided Manchester with a 210ft-span example in 1880, long since devoid of trains and now in use as the Manchester Central Convention Complex. The Glasgow & South Western Railway's St Enoch terminus of 1876–9 at Scotland's second city, now destroyed, was only slightly less wide. Both designs depended in many details on St Pancras. Likewise, the parallel arched spans of Newcastle Central were echoed by the North Eastern Railway's rebuildings of York, Darlington and Hull stations from the 1870s onwards. The York train shed even adopted the

The curved train shed at Newcastle Central station, in a lithograph of *c.* 1850

gently curved plan of Newcastle, although it lacks the minimal lightness of the prototype.

But there was a halfway house between arching grandeur and the workaday platform-canopy type, and the future belonged to it. For it had never been essential to raise giant arches in order to provide all-over coverage at a large station, given the potential of the simpler and cheaper up-and-down roofs of the kind pioneered at Euston. The lesson is pointed up by stations in France, where pitched-roofed enclosures were pushed to extraordinary widths by introducing extra colonnades to support each sloping side at midpoint. By this method, the Gare du Nord of 1861–5 in Paris includes a single span of 238ft. Late-Victorian stations in Britain preferred instead to support small-scale ridge-and-furrow roofs on colonnades of straight horizontal girders. The 40ft-high roof of the Great Central's underwhelming Marylebone station (1899), the last terminus built in Victorian London, is of this type. A slightly higher ridge-and-furrow roof covers the platform acreage at the North British Railway's rebuilt Edinburgh Waverley station in its sunken site between the Old Town and New Town, completed shortly after Marylebone opened.

These are spacious and efficient structures, in a neutral, boring sort of way. Only at Waterloo, where the station that had grown by muddled increments was almost completely rebuilt in 1901–22, did the type achieve a level of grandeur to challenge its arching London cousins. Here the train-shed roof runs aslant across a wedge-shaped enclosure covering more than twenty acres, with ridges at an altitude of 60ft. The concourse is generously wide and curves gently along its 770ft length, and the entire space is flooded with light that even the murk of steam locomotion could not overcome. Although its external architecture is feeble by comparison, Waterloo remains the closest thing on the British railway network to the great early-twentieth-century stations of the Continent, where the fusion of civic pride and public investment gave cities such as Milan, Leipzig and Helsinki a new image of railway travel.

What the future holds for Waterloo is not yet clear. As the final British development of its type, the train shed was recommended for listing by English Heritage in 2010, only to be turned down by the minister in charge. The decision has left the Victory Arch, a combined war memorial and grand entrance that stands at the far end of the concourse buildings, as the one part of the complex with statutory protection. Painful echoes from Euston in the 1960s begin to reverberate at this point. Almost everyone agreed back then that the Euston Arch was at once a treasured London landmark, a masterpiece of design and a key building from the dawn of the railway age. The only problem was that neither the railways nor the London County Council could stump up the funds necessary to reconstruct the arch on a different site when rebuilding began. A last-ditch deputation of architects and architectural historians (Sir Hugh Casson and Nikolaus Pevsner among them) attended on Prime Minister Harold Macmillan in 1961 with a plea for clemency. Macmillan said that he would consider the matter, then did nothing. Official records show that his previous meeting concerned likely death rates among the nation's children in the event of a nuclear holocaust; perhaps he may be forgiven a little for having failed to ride to the rescue. But the naughty thought also occurs that if the Euston Arch had been dedicated to the victims of war, it would still be standing today. Instead, it was levelled in 1962–3, for the want of a sum described by the Victorian Society as 'rather less than the Treasury ungrudgingly paid out around the same time for two indifferent Renoirs, which no one was threatening to destroy'.

The lack of protection for Waterloo raises the spectre of a future cash-in on the 'air rights' to the space over its platforms, and possibly over the concourse too. In the days of steam these areas had to be kept open and spacious to allow sufficient ventilation, but diesel and electric traction are not so demanding. The consequences were first felt in the United States around the turn of the twentieth century, when electrification released valuable tracts of inner-city real estate for redevelopment. This explains why New York's Grand Central Station, as rebuilt in 1903–13, has grandeur only in its upper levels of circulation; the trains themselves are confined to a gloomy basement. Air rights – the concept, if not yet the name – in due course determined the form of the 1960s station at Birmingham New Street, which had lost its marvellous 1850s arched roof after wartime bomb damage.* The Euston end of the old London & Birmingham was also reconstructed with a broad building on top, although this station is much less cramped than the 1960s New Street. Euston's platforms are prefaced by a great circulation hall that was one of the more underrated public spaces of 1960s London; an intrusive shopping deck is under construction across one side at the time of writing.

After that the capital had to wait until the 1980s, when deep-plan office blocks were contrived over the platforms at Cannon Street, Charing Cross, half of Liverpool Street and the Brighton side of Victoria station. None of these projects involved the destruction of an admired train shed (Cannon Street, like Birmingham, having lost its fine arched roof in the aftermath of the Second World War), but the glum darkened spaces are none the better for that. As for the future shape of Euston, dependent as it is on the outcome of the HS2 scheme for a new high-speed route to the Midlands and points north, all bets are off at the time of writing.

It would be wrong to suggest that post-war railway architecture amounted to little more than opportunistic plonking of buildings over tracks. In addition, much had happened to the look of the network between the last Edwardian initiatives and the convulsions of the 1960s. Most of these changes were not architectural, but concerned the ways in which information was conveyed to the passenger, and the overall image that the railways sought to present. The narrative begins in visual disorder, culminates in a systematised national aesthetic and dissolves into bittiness once more, especially after privatisation. It all begins on the railway platform.

---

* Since rebuilt again, allowing merciful daylight to flood the concourse for the first time in half a century.

INFORMATION AND IMAGE

B ack to Edward Thomas's 'Adlestrop' one last time:

> The steam hissed. Someone cleared his throat.
> No one left and no one came
> On the bare platform. What I saw
> Was Adlestrop – only the name ...

'What I saw': Thomas knew where he was thanks to the station signs.* Adlestrop's were lettered in the standard Great Western pattern of fat capitals on a contrastingly dark board. The name has outlived the station it served: rescued after closure in 1966, one of these 9ft-long signs now shares the village bus shelter with a salvaged Great Western bench and a plaque inscribed with the text of the poem that picked out station and village from rural obscurity, an ugly-sounding place made beautiful by association.

The oldest surviving photograph of a British railway station, taken at Linlithgow in the mid 1840s by David Octavius Hill and Robert Adamson, already appears to show a nameboard under the eaves of the platform shelter. Nameboards are routinely captured at lesser stations as

---

* Scholarly scrutiny of Thomas's notebooks has shown that the poem combines impressions and details from more than one station and journey; but that hardly matters here.

the photographic record becomes fuller in the 1850s and 1860s (big city stations seem to have done without for longer; the platforms at Paddington, for instance, stayed anonymous until 1933). Early-Victorian railways favoured dark lettering on a light ground, giving way to light on dark towards the end of the century. The usual form employed by that period used cut-out or cast letters of a standard pattern fixed to a backboard. Assembly, painting and repainting of the nameboard could thus be done on a semi-skilled basis, without calling on the services of a signwriter – quite a contrast with the ornate lettering displayed on locomotives and carriages. Still more durable were the enamelled metal nameboards that became the preferred type in the twentieth century.

Nameboards came in many sizes. The largest were often placed close to the platform ends, sometimes (as on the Midland Railway) in the form of double boards set at an angle to one another, so that they could be read more easily from a moving train. On a smaller scale, cast or enamelled metal nameplates were fixed to the backs of many station benches. Names might also be emblazoned on backlit transparencies gummed inside the glass panels of station gas lamps and in the windows of waiting rooms. British Railways liked to put up big enamelled name signs on station frontages too. The commitment to make station identities readily visible from the train was well advised. Dim artificial lighting by gas or oil made it all too easy for passengers to get out at the wrong station. Worse, unlocked carriage doors offered no barrier to an injurious exit at a signal stop between stations, or the fatal misidentification of a bridge parapet with a waiting platform.

Besides these visual cues, the porters at each station would shout out its name. The practice was familiar enough by the 1840s for the poet Arthur Hugh Clough (1819–61) to borrow it for a simile:

> I was as one that sleeps on the railway; one, who dreaming
> Hears thro' his dream the name of his home shouted out; hears and
>   hears not ...

These shouts were not always very clear. As Baedeker's guide had it, 'the way in which the porters call [the names] out, laying all the stress on the last syllable, is seldom of much assistance'. Baedeker's warning glossed over the diversities of regional speech, which made things still harder. Cuthbert Bede described in the 1850s how County Durham porters announced

Ferry Hill ('Faweyill') and Fence Houses ('Fensoosen'), and joked that 'Change here for Doom' (Durham) might cause alarm to uncomprehending southern travellers.

Different arrangements came into force at large stations with the arrival of public address systems, which allowed a single, King's-English voice to ring out over the vernacular cries of the railwaymen. The Great Western's first such loudspeakers were installed at Paddington in 1936. (The 'refeened' pronunciation of one company announcer later made a private joke for John Betjeman and his wife, regular travellers through Berkshire from Paddington, for whom Didcot became 'Deedcoate'.) Announcements at termini at least had no need to remind hearers where they were, but they did have to convey masses of information of every other kind, supplementing or correcting whatever could be shown on the station's fixed destination boards. The grandest of these visual displays were things of wonder, the passengers' nearest equivalent to the giant, multi-armed signal gantries that guarded the station approaches. Early destination boards were built of wood, and displayed information on demountable panels or swivelling lettered bars, manipulated by a specialist staff who moved constantly around the internal passageways. One of the last survivors – in daily use, amazingly, up to 1985 – was the installation above the gracefully shaped oval booking office at Glasgow Central. This Edwardian structure has been converted to shops, with a bar in the old destination-board storey above, from which drinkers can look over the passing show on the concourse.

By the time that modernisation overtook Glasgow Central, the standard type of destination board in use elsewhere on the network was operated electrically, and was made up of thin, hinged slats that dropped down vertically from a rotating spindle. Each slat could be lettered on both sides, and the characters were typically split along the middle so that every panel in the display comprised one slat above another, together spelling out the name. Before more advanced electronics took over, the boards were controlled by punch cards, as at Charing Cross in the late 1960s. The riffling clatter of their slats, endlessly updating the display of arrivals and departures at busy concourses, has been silenced in its turn, and various types of electronic screen now keep the passenger up to date. Paddington was again in the technological forefront, in the experimental form of a 27-inch television screen linked to a teleprinter, installed in 1962. Its successors can now display any text, including such vital details as last-minute changes of platform, and so there is less need for station announcements to be made at all.

The electronic revolution has also transformed these announcements themselves. Instead of the scratchy push-button tapes of elocution-stiffened voices that were the newest thing fifty years ago, eerily affectless announcements are now assembled automatically from digitised words and syllables. Minor stations are quieter still, with no loudspeakers to make up for the abolition of the old Rule 130, which required guards to call out the names at every stop (together with connecting services at junctions). Besides, the introduction of public address systems on the trains themselves has made the task largely redundant. Routine announcements can now be triggered automatically by GPS signals as the train goes on its way, although the method is not faultless, as anyone learns who has ever gazed out over a radiant West Country landscape while the speakers calmly advise of the imminent approach of Clapham Junction or Wimbledon. For the technologically advanced (or technologically dependent), all the relevant information can be downloaded live from Network Rail, and supplemented by text-message alerts and Twitter feeds from the various operating companies. In effect, the personalised, hand-held destination board is now within the reach of any traveller with a smartphone.

₪

All the nameboards, nameplates and transparencies that bedecked Victorian stations could not prevent complaints that the railways were making a bad job of letting passengers know where they were. The root of the problem was the lack of clarity caused by competition from other notices. Some of these were the railways' own – all those directions to waiting rooms, refreshment rooms and telegraph offices – but the principal distractions were caused by advertising. As one American visitor noted in 1885, it could be difficult to pick out a station name amid the insignia of whiskies, soaps and mustards. Worse, advertisements were often placed on any available surface without regard for overall effect. The resulting visual chaos, captured in photographs, comes as a reminder that railway space was ultimately summoned into being by the imperatives of capital. Station buildings might adopt prestigious historical styles, staff might dress in smart uniforms imitative of the police or armed forces, carriages and locomotives might be painted with as much exquisite care as the conveyances

RAILWAY PUZZLE
To find the name of the station.

Advertising takes over, as depicted by *Punch* in 1883

of the elite – but all these displays of prestige had to coexist with endless insistent messages on behalf of Messrs Pears ('Good morning! Have you used Pears' soap?'), Beecham's Pills ('Worth a Guinea a Box'), Dr Williams ('Pink Pills for Pale People') and the thousand other branded goods of the consumer economy.

The railways took some time to wake up to the potential of income from advertising. The Great Exhibition of 1851 was an early watershed, when schematic images of products such as Brogden's watch-chains and Heal's bedsteads began to appear on poster hoardings to catch the eyes of railway pilgrims to London. As with refreshment rooms and bookstalls, railway companies preferred to farm out display space to agents, prominent among whom was the empire-building W. H. Smith Jnr. A typical contract, such as the one arranged with the Chester & Holyhead Railway in 1855, gave Smiths sole rights of display on walls and fences, in waiting rooms and booking halls. Smiths was responsible for providing poster frames and canvassing for business; on its part, the railway company retained the right of approval over what was shown. Outsourced advertisements of this kind should be distinguished from the railways' own notices, timetables and the like, which were customarily stuck up on dedicated boards headed with the company's initials. So the situation remained, until the railways began to take the advertising business into their own hands in the twentieth century.

Paper posters were joined by bright, imperishable signs of enamelled metal. The initial patent for these was granted in 1859 to Benjamin Baugh, manager of Salt's enamel works in Birmingham. Enamelled signs were best suited to branded products, which sold year in and year out. Once fixed, they could be left for years on gable ends, retaining walls, bridge parapets and such-like locations that bill-stickers could not easily reach, as well as on platform fences and other spots with straightforward access. Advertisements of this kind provided the household words used by E. Nesbit's Railway Children for their thoroughly modern version of charades, played in an empty waiting room (answers: Fox's umbrellas and the ubiquitous blot that advertised the Blue Black Writing Fluid patented back in 1837 by Dr Henry Stephens – mimed by Peter, face blackened with coal dust, in a 'spidery attitude').

What was good fun to the Railway Children was distressing to many grown-up members of their class. For Arnold Bennett, writing slightly later, there was no allure in a 'dirty platform, in a *milieu* of advertisements of soap, boots and aperients'. Railway space was especially receptive to the formula which took a name or emblem, boldly presented, and repeated it to death – what the *Saturday Review* in 1907 called 'The dreary drip of constant iteration.' At Rugby station, for instance, a frieze of enamelled advertisements for Hudson's soap, with its emblem of light flooding from a lamp, ran below the first-floor windows on the platform side. Other product names that may seem comforting and dependable in retrospect – Reckitt's Blue, Brasso, Pratt's Motor Spirit, Mazawattee Tea – were merely banal in their day. Especially insistent were the little enamelled panels fixed to the risers of station staircases, such as the 'IRON JELLOIDS, IRON JELLOIDS, IRON JELLOIDS' remembered by Betjeman, 'in blue on an orange ground, insisting, as one ascends, on the weakness of one's heart and its need for the stamina which those pills supply'.

The railways' increasingly active publicity departments joined in the display. Many of their productions are now regarded as classics of commercial art, as advertising moved away from 'informative' text-based formats and into 'creative' pictorial modes. The best-known is the beaming Jolly Fisherman created by John Hassall for the Great Northern Railway in 1908 ('Skegness is *so* bracing'), since adopted as a sort of mascot by the grateful Lincolnshire resort. Not everyone at the time was so apprecia-tive, however. 'No. 251, bigger boilered than ever, leers at us from every hoarding!' – thus the response of one viewer to another Great Northern poster, showing a prototype express locomotive. And for every colourful Jolly Fisherman, the traveller could expect as many commonplace banners for commercial hotels, or depressing palliatives for anaemia or halitosis, stuck all too often anywhere and everywhere.

It was not always necessary to take the train to be exposed to this advertising binge, for some of the railways' urban displays were grossly intrusive. In Aberdeen, for example, where the showpiece of Union Ter-race Gardens was (and is) bounded on one side by the Denburn railway cutting, drab and sooty commercial displays lingered until a civic pogrom after the Second World War. Worse, the potential of the railways' passing audience stimulated freelance advertising within sight of the line, so that visual pollution followed the physical pollution caused by the smoke and noise of the trains. Station approaches were obvious targets, but rural set-tings by busy lines did not escape. George Gissing's novel *In the Year of Jubilee* (1894) features an advertising agent called Luckworth Crewe (the surname surely no coincidence) who brags of a garden by the 'South West-ern Railway' where he managed to put up an advertising board, 'as ugly as they make 'em ... a certain particular place, where the trains slow, and folks have time to read the advertisement and meditate on it'. Four years later, Max Beerbohm deplored the 'texts about pills and soaps' that were spread-ing through English meadows.

A few were concerned enough to fight back. In 1895 the Board of Trade floated the idea of a minimum distance between station signs and advertisements, to create an area of visual calm that would allow the names to stand out better. A Society for Controlling the Abuses of Public Adver-tising (SCAPA) had been set up two years before. William Morris, the poet Robert Bridges and the artist Holman Hunt were among SCAPA's found-ing members, and Rudyard Kipling later lent his support. The railways must have seemed a hopeless lost cause, but the society and its allies had suc-cesses elsewhere, fighting off schemes for illuminated signs on Edinburgh's Princes Street (Bovril) and the White Cliffs of Dover (Quaker Oats). An Act followed in 1907 allowing by-laws to regulate hoardings and protect amenities from invasive advertising for the first time, and by 1936 the vari-ous local and national restrictions in force were counted at over 250.

The railways began to take notice too. This is especially a London story, starting on the deep lines of the Tube. The key figure was Frank Pick (1878–1941), who was appointed Traffic Development Officer of the amalgamated underground railways in 1909. He made an immediate impact, banishing advertisements for commercial clients from station exteriors, so that they appeared only on platforms and internal passages. Rather than spreading haphazardly, advertisements were also placed within carefully defined poster grids and kept at a clear distance from the station nameboards, so that they enhanced rather than disrupted the architectural outlines. Pick raised the visual standard of his own company's advertising by commissioning bold pictorial posters, including early patronage of the brilliant modernist artist E. McKnight Kauffer. The posters were meant to help turn round the company's fortunes by encouraging leisure travel and exploration, and they appear to have had some success.

An up-to-date image was also fostered by the station signs themselves. Pick sharpened up the recently invented circle-and-crossbar design used on the nameboards, later registering the new version as a trademark. From 1916 these signs were lettered with a display typeface which Pick commissioned from the calligrapher Edward Johnston (1872–1944), who broke with convention by omitting the serifs, producing an effect of graceful, stripped-down clarity. No one had seen anything like it in the public realm before. Versions of the emblematic circle-and-crossbar signs and a gently tweaked variant of Johnston's sans serif face are famously still in use today across the Underground network.

Pick did not – could not – stop there, for passenger traffic continued to grow apace. Wholly new Underground lines were required, and many existing stations needed reconstruction. His mainstay for much of this work was the architect Charles Holden (1875–1960), a fellow northerner, with whom he shared a profound belief in the social value of rational design. They had much to do. Holden was responsible for the renovation of Piccadilly Circus in 1926–8, replacing lifts with escalators and making a sub-surface concourse big enough to cope with the growth in annual passenger numbers from 1.5 million to 25 million since the station opened in 1906. Suburban extensions to the Northern and Piccadilly lines allowed Holden and Pick to pursue an increasingly spare architectural language for the many new stations along the way. Those built for the Northern Line (Morden, Balham, Tooting Bec, etc.) were hailed by the *Architectural Review* in 1929 as 'prophetic beacons of the new age amid a drab wilderness of Victorian edification'.

Another milestone was the takeover in 1933 of the old Metropolitan Railway, which was subsumed into the newly founded London Passenger Transport Board. An internal report for the Metropolitan in 1927 had criticised the jumble of shapes and sizes, posters and enamelled plates on its routes. Now its network could be brought in line with Pick's paternalistic vision of public design, which ultimately harnessed architecture, rolling stock, buses, trams and trolleybuses, street furniture, signage, ticketing and advertising to a single programme of integrated transport for the growing capital. Overall, Pick took municipal transport and made of it what would now be called a brand. London Transport was duly acclaimed as the best organisation of its kind anywhere and foreign visitors came to inspect and learn from it, as they had once come to see the achievements of the Stephensons and Brunel.

₪

The Big Four companies could only look on in envy. Here was a transport authority with a rising demand for travel, empowered to integrate bus, tram and trolleybus services so that they complemented rather than undermined those of its trains, all backed by ready access to government loans, and largely free from the shackles of common-carrier goods obligations. None of the main lines could match these advantages, but they could at least have a go at imitating London's strong visual identity – as far as their budgets allowed.

The Southern Railway managed most in terms of new architecture, as it rebuilt stations and even added a few branches to its electrified suburban routes. New Southern stations of the 1930s echoed Holden's blockish lines and plain surfaces, but ventured into Art Deco styling here and there; Surbiton, for example, with its ridged, Odeonesque clock tower, or Horsham, described by the architectural critic Gavin Stamp as 'a good example of the application of the wireless-set aesthetic'. The London, Midland & Scottish proved less excitable when providing its newly electrified Wirral route with modernist brick-and-concrete stations in 1938. The series culminated in a showpiece building at the seaside suburb of Hoylake, with a cylindrical booking hall and a broad outswept canopy to shelter passengers as they arrived on the road side – the commuter's equivalent of the contemporary Midland Hotel at Morecambe. These were just a handful of the company's 2,500-odd stations, however. For the rest, the cash-strapped LMS could offer only superficial modernity in the shape of new 'Hawkseye' name-boards, clearly in debt to London Underground's circle-and-crossbar, with the novelty of little pieces of glass embedded in the surface to help them show up better at night. The Southern's target-style nameboards of the period were even more blatantly derived from those of Frank Pick's empire, rendered in the company colour of green.

The other two companies avoided this imitative flattery. The Great Western left its station signage largely alone, but began to adorn loco-motives, carriages, bench-ends and printed publicity with a little roundel containing angular versions of the august letters GWR. Guardians of taste hated this 'shirt-button' logo; Betjeman called it a 'new and hideous monogram in distorted lettering designed to save space'. It was certainly at odds with the time-honoured slab-serif lettering that had been used on the Great Western's locomotives ever since Brunel's day.

The London & North Eastern came up with a little monogram too, its initials squeezed into a pointed vesica piscis or fish-like shape; but its main initiative was the adoption in 1929 of another classic modern type-face. This was the celebrated Gill Sans, then barely a year old. Its creator was Eric Gill (1882–1940), a former pupil of Edward Johnston who had developed into another luminary of the Arts and Crafts movement, mov-ing with ease between the roles of sculptor, letter-cutter, calligrapher and graphic artist. By a happy chance, Gill's first love had been railways. As a child growing up by the line in late-Victorian Brighton, he had made draw-ing after drawing of bridges, tunnels, signals and locomotives, concentrat-ing finally on the last in a mission to capture on paper 'their character, their meaning'. As the LNER extended its use of Gill Sans from posters and publicity to liveries and signage, these dormant enthusiasms revived. The culmination was a public relations event at King's Cross in 1932, when the stockinged and beret-wearing artist fixed his own newly painted head-board inscribed FLYING SCOTSMAN to the front of the waiting express. He then travelled part of the way on the footplate – 'something like riding on an enormously heavy solid-tyred bicycle' – a treat he had requested as part of his fee.* Along the way, the Flying Scotsman would have passed many of the superlative posters commissioned by the LNER, which had

---

* Consciously or not, Gill was following in the path of the great typographer and first patron of Gill Sans, Stanley Morison of the Monotype Corporation; a lifelong railway-lover, Morison had himself wangled a footplate trip on the Flying Scotsman in 1929.

[1] A FAMOUS TRAIN HALTS DURING A "LAND-CRUISE" AND DIS-PLAYS ITS NAME-PLATE, PAINTED ON THE MODEL OF "MONOTYPE" GILL SANS 231

WHEREVER **L.N.E.** USES LETTERING IT STANDARDIZES

GILL SANS:

[2] A NEW STATION IN COURSE OF CONSTRUCTION. NOTE LETTERING ON GLASS AND [BELOW] IN RELIEF AS PART OF A NEW BUILDING [3]

[4] ALL THE VEHICLES USED BY THE LINE HAVE BEEN RE-LETTERED. DINING CAR MENUS, LABELS AND NOTICES, HUGE POSTERS AND EVEN THE LITTLE MATCH-BOOK BELOW [5] SPEAK IN THE CLEARLY "RECOGNIZABLE VOICE" OF GILL SANS.

ALL THIS LETTERING IS DONE ON THE MODEL PROVIDED BY PRINTS OF 72 POINT "MONOTYPE" GILL SANS TITLING SERIES 231

THE MATCH-BOOK IS SET IN 262, 275, AND 110 ITALIC

The London & North Eastern Railway's systematic use of Gill Sans, from the *Monotype Recorder*, 1933

absorbed the graphic lessons of the London Underground better than any other main-line railway. What it did not have was money for many new buildings; unlike in Frank Pick's London, good design was no more than a top-dressing for an ageing, investment-starved network.

What did the nationalised railway make of this rather mixed legacy? Alas, not much. Gill Sans was favoured for signage and posters, mostly of a heavier weight than the slim form preferred by the LNER, and as often as not with some coarsening of Gill's lissom lines (the angled leg of the upper-case Rs is one giveaway). Applied to locomotives, the bald legend BRITISH RAILWAYS seemed drab and prosaic after the shaded lettering and crests of the old companies, as if to cause deliberate affront to established loyalties. The Archdeacon of Lincoln wrote a letter of protest on the matter to *The Times*, which responded with a half-serious editorial endorsing his suggestion that locomotives need no longer be inscribed at all, now that they all belonged to one body. The BR livery crest that succeeded this blunt lettering not long afterwards won few plaudits either, with its malnourished, 1920s-looking lion straddling a spoked wheel. Nor were the new 'totem' signs for stations universally admired. These suggested an Underground circle-and-crossbar rolled flat, so that the name-bar had rounded ends and the backing was flattened at top and bottom. Comparisons were drawn with a schematised hot dog. This pudgy emblem also appeared on notices and stationery, lettered with British Railways' name.

One concession to territorial feeling was the use of colour coding for the new station signs, to represent the regions into which the network was divided. These were based on the old Big Four empires, with a few differences. Western Region signs were chocolate brown, a colour used on the Great Western's old brown-and-cream signage, building paintwork and carriage livery. Southern Region signs were green, like the old Southern Railway's signs, carriages and express locomotives. The London Midland Region had maroon signs, again reminiscent of the carriage and locomotive liveries of its LMS predecessor. The rest were more complicated. Scotland was now a region in itself, with the former LMS and LNER sectors uniformly re-signed in a fetching Scottish-bluebell blue. The English domain of the LNER was split into the Eastern Region, whose signs were a much deeper blue, and the North Eastern Region, where a rather nasty tangerine colour prevailed. Not only station signs, but station paintwork, seats, timetables, cap badges and other miscellanea were also colour-coded across the regions.

All these shades belonged firmly within the mid-century palette, as lately recycled and commodified ad nauseam with the slogan KEEP CALM AND CARRY ON and its variants. By the time Dr Beeching arrived, these Attlee-era station signs were looking distinctly dated, as were most of the liveries of the trains serving them, the 1951 generation of staff uniforms – in fact, almost everything that represented the public face of the railway. The Design Panel that had been set up in 1956 was already doing its bit to improve matters, with the Blue Pullman trains of 1960 (*see* Chapter 7) and Glasgow's new suburban electric trains among its showpieces. Regional colour-coding had been relaxed and was now kept to a minimum when stations were replaced (not yet a large group: as late as 1961 the nationalised railway's tally of rebuilt stations had still not reached the hundred mark). Selected older stations were facelifted according to the Design Panel's Code of Practice booklet, with fluorescent lighting, new waiting-room interiors and smartly designed benches, litter bins and other essentials. Timetables for all regions were issued to a new standard design, replacing various superannuated Bradshaw-esque settings with lucid tabulations in Gill Sans – a strange destiny for this late product of the Arts and Crafts movement, with its roots in the teachings of John Ruskin. A public exhibition at the Design Centre in 1963 showed off BR's new uniforms, the first on the railways to incorporate some man-made fibres. They were based on research into Continental practice as well as contemporary trends in menswear; *Design* magazine was not alone in detecting a 'perceptible Germanic influence' in the neat peaked caps and Wehrmacht-grey colours (although this was officially denied).

1964 was the culminating year. In April, Beeching announced in the *Financial Times* that an entirely new corporate image was impending: '... powerful enough to symbolise the service it stands for, a distinctive name style and logotype for the title of the undertaking, with subsidiary letter forms for secondary and subsidiary purposes, and distinctive house colours for use throughout the system'. The ghost of Frank Pick must have raised a cheer; here, at last, was the plus side of Dr Beeching's new railway, a modern network able to look its Swiss or West German equivalents in the (sans serif) face.

What this corporate image would be like emerged in stages over the next two years. In June 1964 a blue-liveried prototype train dubbed XP64 began running between King's Cross and Leeds, its new-built diesel locomotive adorned with an unfamiliar emblem rather like a two-way arrow. It was then announced that this mysterious emblem – derided by some for its suggestion of coming-or-going indecision, or for looking like a bit of barbed wire – was to be the universal symbol of British Rail, as British Railways was renamed at the start of 1965. Later, it was decreed that all passenger trains would be painted in a slightly darker version of the XP64 blue shade (all-over Rail Blue for local services, Rail Blue with a light grey band around the windows for main line trains). Carriages in the old regional colours would no longer appear. By a further ruling, locomotives and multiple units were to have full yellow ends, for easy visibility out on the line – the equivalent of the red buffer beams sported by BR's fast-vanishing steam engines. What railway enthusiasts call the 'Blue Period' was on its way.

The double arrow was the creation of Gerry Barney, then a twenty-one-year-old employee at the Design Research Unit. By the 1960s the DRU was the favourite port of call for any large organisation seeking to transform its corporate image. A private consultancy, it had been co-founded in the 1940s by an unlikely triumvirate comprising the anarchist poet-critic Herbert Read, an ad-man named Marcus Brumwell and the Russian-born architect and industrial designer Misha Black (1910–77). Its central place in the history of British public design is often overlooked, despite a client list that included the Festival of Britain, shipping companies, breweries, airlines and even the post-Pick London Underground, for whom the DRU acted as consultants on the Victoria Line. Misha Black in particular became quite a power in the land, combining his DRU work with a professorial chair of industrial design at the Royal College of Art.

The Design Research Unit was not the only outside body helping to transform old British Railways into new British Rail. A system of universal signage was also introduced, finally doing away with regional colour-coding. The signs were lettered in the Rail Alphabet, a sans serif typeface designed by Richard 'Jock' Kinneir and Margaret Calvert. After a spell at the DRU, Kinneir had set up his own design practice in 1956. One early commission was the signage for the new Gatwick Airport. Soon after, he was appointed chief designer to the Advisory Committee on Traffic Signs on Motorways, with Calvert as his assistant. Breaking with tradition, Kinneir recommended mixed-case rather than wholly upper-case lettering, arguing that this was at once easier for the motorist to read and more in tune with the spirit of post-war Britain, which had 'moved on from the Victorian concept of empire'. The resulting road signs were lettered in Kinneir and Calvert's new Transport font, beginning with white texts on a blue or green ground for motorways and A-roads, then from 1963 on minor roads, in black on white. BR's version was a slightly weightier development of this Transport font, with closer spacing between the letters.

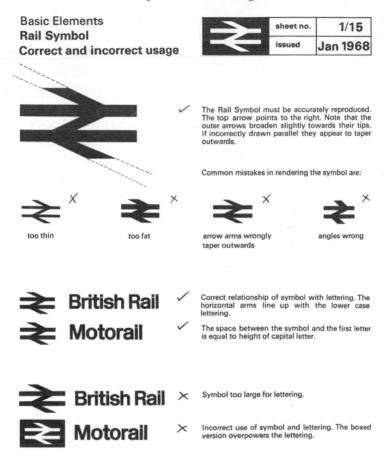

Basic Elements
Rail Symbol
Correct and incorrect usage

sheet no.	1/15
issued	Jan 1968

✓ The Rail Symbol must be accurately reproduced. The top arrow points to the right. Note that the outer arrows broaden slightly towards their tips. If incorrectly drawn parallel they appear to taper outwards.

Common mistakes in rendering the symbol are:

✗ too thin ✗ too fat ✗ arrow arms wrongly taper outwards ✗ angles wrong

British Rail ✓ Correct relationship of symbol with lettering. The horizontal arms line up with the lower case lettering.

Motorail ✓ The space between the symbol and the first letter is equal to height of capital letter.

British Rail ✗ Symbol too large for lettering.

Motorail ✗ Incorrect use of symbol and lettering. The boxed version overpowers the lettering.

The correct proportions of the British Rail symbol,
from BR's Corporate Identity Manual, 1968

When used on station signs, it likewise appeared in black on white. The new mixed-case signs were rarely large, and there were no direct equivalents of the old super-sized signs at the platform ends. Passengers hurtling through stations now had to rely on other landmarks to work out their location. The railways' ferry services – renamed Sealink in 1970 – were brought into line too. So that the top arrow would always appear to point towards the bows, a mirror image of the standard BR symbol was used on the port side of their red funnels. Across the sea, BR's Transport font was adopted in 1971 by the Danish State Railways – a reversal of the usual direction of flow of modernist public design.

New signage was just one aspect of a continuing campaign of rationalisation. Also in the management's cross hairs were the plonked-down-anywhere assemblages of kiosks and stalls that cluttered up larger stations – what the architect Donald Insall in 1967 called the 'self-righteous little platform "buildings", each with its individual anxiety to appear respectable and weather-worthy'. The resulting jumble is captured in the opening minutes of the Beatles' film *A Hard Day's Night* (1964): the Fab Four elude screaming fans by dodging behind poster hoardings and into telephone boxes and photo booths, intercut with shots of their long-suffering manager as he grapples with a plastic-wrapped purchase from a giant milk-vending machine. (The departure station is meant to be Liverpool Lime Street, but London's underused Marylebone terminus did duty for both ends of the fictional journey.)

Overall, the aims of BR's station campaign were essentially positive and humane: clarity, ease and visual restfulness for the traveller, improved morale for the staff. The renovations were also meant to reveal and celebrate the lines of historic station buildings. However, the impact was sometimes vandalistic by the standards of present-day conservation, as decorative details were shaved off or rendered over. New railway architecture was not always inspiring either. The best sequences belonged to the all-too-rare electrification programmes of the period, as on the West Coast main line or the Lea Valley route in Hertfordshire. The firm modernist lines, expansive glazing and generous circulation spaces at stations such as Coventry, Stafford and Broxbourne still convey this sense of purposeful progress. The worst included the bleak platform shelters already described, but also some fully staffed buildings. Among the more dispiriting were those of the Southern Region after 1965. For smaller reconstruction jobs, the region adopted an off-the-peg steel-framed system known as CLASP – an acronym of Consortium of Local Authorities Special Programme – which had been developed for schools in Hertfordshire in the 1950s. These boxy, flat-roofed CLASP stations varied in size and facilities, but the effect was of interchangeable uniformity, done on a shoestring and without specific railway character. Other rebuilt stations had speculative office blocks attached; even proud Swindon sprouted a twelve-storey office slab. No wonder that the railway enthusiasts' press in the 1970s began to celebrate the survival of station signs, benches and other details from the days of the old companies – anything to distract from the homogeneous, cool-blooded paternalism of BR's corporate image.

Jump forward forty years and British Rail has gone; but maps and road signs still use Gerry Barney's double arrow on a red panel to indicate a station on the national network. On arrival at the station, however, the typography of Kinneir and Calvert rarely shows its face on the platform unaccompanied. One common formula adds a lower band of solid colour, to show off the name and logo of the present operating company, invariably in a clashing font – as with First Great Western, First Capital Connect, Arriva and others. The three Southern lines and the new company called London Midland (not to be confused with the old London Midland Region) have all plumped instead for light lettering on a dark ground. Some companies have been unable to resist selling space on their station signs to advertisers, whose messages appear on a parallel board below the name. The results can be unintentionally comic, as at Cambridge, 'Home of Anglia Ruskin University'; or at Clapham Junction, 'The home of James Pendleton Estate Agents, a passion for excellence'; or at little-regarded Brimsdown on the Lea Valley line, 'Home of The Brimsdown Business Area' (where else, indeed?).

As these company franchises come and go, so their signage and logos change with them. Variant signs introduced during BR's own 1980s restructuring into sectors rather than regions, such as those for Network SouthEast (with added bright blue, white and red stripes, like toothpaste), have already gone the way of the Big Four. A few stations have customised signage; the old British Railways upper-case lettering and colours of circa 1950 are even creeping back here and there, as at Barnstaple or at King's Lynn. The latter even has an electronic ticket machine incongruously emblazoned with the British Railways totem, officially superseded half a century before. But for true staying power, there is still nothing to match the impeccable signage of the London Underground and its affiliate known as London Overground (with an orange crossbar in place of the Underground's red), which has been steadily taking over selected main-line suburban routes since 2007.* Only in the control of advertising

---

* Unlike its older sibling, London Overground is currently managed as a joint venture between MTR of Hong Kong and Deutsche Bahn, the German state railway network, of which the German government is the majority owner – for there are no barriers to foreign state-owned railways joining in the subsidy-feast offered by Britain's privatised railways.

has the Underground suffered a relapse, so that vexing little commercial messages on top of some automatic ticket barriers now distract the eye, and enamelled metal strips have resumed their place on the risers of the staircases, now directing passengers towards sustenance from McDonald's rather than Iron Jelloids.

₪

Stations in the twenty-first century, large or small, are emphatically not what they were sixty or even thirty years ago. So many functions and facilities have fallen away that it is difficult even to imagine them all – the post, parcels and newspapers, the small consignments and the wagonload freight, the livestock and horseboxes, the special excursions and school trains, troop trains and football specials, the railway-owned hotels, the domestic quarters; all gone. Much else that was once familiar has vanished with them. Clattering strings of BRUTE trolleys – another acronym, from British Rail Universal Trolley Equipment – no longer weave their way through crowded concourses behind little electric tractors. The end came for these soon after 1999, when the railways' Red Star parcels service was bought out.* Porters have long gone, too. Even passenger-operated luggage trolleys with their refundable pound-coin locks are becoming scarce, as the wheeled suitcase continues on its mission of global domination.

What we have instead is retail. Passengers with money to spend and minutes to fill are an asset, measurable in terms of footfall and 'dwell time'. No longer portals through which goods pass, stations have more than ever become places to sell things. This includes food and drink, of course; and the old functions of refreshment room, waiting room and sales kiosk may now be handily combined in one interior, as at Preston or Darlington. But this is basic stuff compared with more recent developments. Mini-supermarkets, such as Marks & Spencer's station branches at Sheffield and Oxford, now allow the traveller to select an evening meal before boarding. The remodelled St Pancras, with its giant retail concourse at basement level, even offers a 'Sourced Market' selling local and seasonal produce. Whenever a city station is renovated, the area allotted to retail is sure to go up. All those redundant parcels offices, long-forgotten waiting rooms,

---

* So passengers are no longer baffled by platform-end signs inscribed 'Brutes not to be left unattended beyond this point'.

porters' rest rooms, lamp rooms and telegraph offices can be put to profitable use once more.

One instance of the new model is Liverpool Street, which was reconstructed in 1985–91 as part of a much larger office development, complete with its own malls and upper-level shopping deck. Martin Amis put the new version, 'a flowing atrium of boutiques and croissant stalls and limitless cappuccino', into his novel *The Information* (1995): 'Trains no longer dominated it with their train culture of industrial burdens dumbly and filthily borne. Trains now crept in round the back, sorry they were so late, hoping they could still be of use to the proud, strolling, cappuccino-quaffing shopkeepers.' And why not? The old Liverpool Street was a dirty, baffling place, little changed from the days when the steam-hauled Jazz trains still plied their trade. The 1991 incarnation with its all-electric trains is bright and convenient, and has even extended the best part of the Victorian train shed in a carefully matching design, while sweeping away the bottlenecks and confusions caused by the original, piecemeal construction process. The old railway ambience may have gone, but cappuccino and croissants smell better than diesel fumes, and polished terrazzo flooring and white-enamelled steel have more appeal than sooty brick and the brownish, magnetised dust from cast-iron brake blocks that formerly clung to every metal surface. After all, railways never set out to be 'atmospheric', but to perform a valuable and profitable service; they can survive and flourish only by adaptation, for they belong to the future as well as the past.

Our journey could end here, as we leave the station via its concourse-cum-retail zone and go out into the world which the railways did so much to remake, by accident or by design. Except that there are other kinds of station – now numbering in their hundreds across Britain, including some mentioned in earlier chapters – where the hand of time is stayed, obsolescence is treasured or counterfeited and the staff are probably unwaged volunteers. How on earth did this happen?

ENTHUSIASM

One hundred years after our imagined journey of 1862, Dr Richard Beeching and his wife joined a special train from London to the Bluebell Railway in Sussex. On arrival, Beeching opened a halt on the newly preserved line, inaugurating its third annual season. At a press conference held in a 'swaying guard's van' he praised the little railway, but added, 'We are preserving a bit too much of British Railways. Our job is not to preserve.'

The Bluebell Railway was something quite new: a section of the former national network, rescued by voluntary efforts and run as a visitor attraction, with a mission to maintain in working order a portion of the railways of times past. A good few historic locomotives and carriages had already been rescued, starting with the decision in early-Victorian times that pioneer locomotives such as *Rocket* were worth keeping for posterity. Two other passenger lines had already been preserved under the aegis of volunteer societies; but these were self-contained narrow-gauge routes in the holiday region of North Wales, with quaintness and scenic drama on their side. The Bluebell set out to operate a standard-gauge line using old rolling stock, to make what was called a 'live' museum. It was both a forerunner of many industrial museums that followed, in which obsolete processes and equipment are animated by expert demonstration, and a new kind of leisure attraction that could be enjoyed without engaging with any didactic purpose.

The Bluebell's line comprised the middle chunk of a little-regarded late-Victorian railway, built to fill a gap between existing routes to East Grinstead and Lewes, and opened in 1882. By 1955 the line was moribund; few services still ran and the timetable had been fossilised to allow for the loading of milk churns that in reality had long since gone over to the roads. Trains stopped running in that year, only for a local resident to discover a procedural flaw that forced BR to reopen the line pending a second, legally watertight closure. In the meantime, three students came up with a visionary plan to save part of the route by means of a preservation society, which rapidly attracted support. The locally current 'Bluebell' nickname was eagerly embraced.

Life imitated art at the Bluebell, in the celluloid form of *The Titfield Thunderbolt*, an Ealing Comedy of 1953. The plot concerns an obscure branch line condemned by British Railways, only to be resurrected by the squire and the railway-loving vicar of Titfield. Financial help comes from a rich resident who can get happily plastered outside pub opening hours, once the little railway acquires its own buffet car. (The bibulous investor is played by Stanley Holloway, whose comic banter featured in the refreshment room scenes of *Brief Encounter*.) Among the co-stars is *Thunderbolt*, actually the Liverpool & Manchester's fantastically antiquated goods locomotive *Lion*, built in 1838 and lent for filming by Liverpool Museum. The real-life railways helped too, making available for filming a recently closed country line near Bath.

Titfield's screenwriter T. E. B. Clarke took his inspiration from the Talyllyn Railway, the first of the Welsh narrow-gauge lines to be preserved. Ignored alike by the 1923 Grouping and post-war nationalisation, the line had struggled on in a state of grass-grown dereliction until 1950, when the Talyllyn Railway Preservation Society stepped in. At its head was L. T. C. Rolt (1910–74), the future heroising biographer of Brunel, a man with a developed mistrust of corporatism and statism. With other enthusiasts, Rolt had already helped to kick off the revival of England's moribund canals through the Inland Waterways Association, founded in 1946.

Clearly, something was in the air. Transport systems that had once epitomised modernity and change became identified with altogether different qualities in their decline. Rural railways now represented localism, tradition and a society of face-to-face relationships. Like several other Ealing Comedies, *The Titfield Thunderbolt* is a fantasy in which community values and amateurism are permitted to triumph over the impersonal forces of government and bureaucracy. Its politics are finely balanced: the heartless party is the nationalised British Transport Commission, but the valiant railway's local rival and enemy is the brash operator of a private bus service.

Rolt was far from alone in the early 1950s in his affection towards the old companies. Kindred spirits included the resident of Birch Grove, a country house a few miles away from the Bluebell route, one Harold Macmillan MP. Railways had been good to Macmillan: he served as a Great Western director in the 1930s–40s, receiving a gold pass for a lifetime's free travel as part of his compensation for loss of office at the end of 1947. Missing the Great Western's traditions, Macmillan wrote in 1952 to the incoming transport minister Lord Leathers to urge that its name and colours be revived for BR's Western Region: 'The regimental system is a great one with the British and it is always a mistake to destroy tradition.' Macmillan and his wife were also early visitors to the reopened Bluebell line, even before Dr and Mrs Beeching made the trip. When the Bluebell rescued a London, Brighton & South Coast Railway tank locomotive in 1962 and repainted it with its original name *Birch Grove*, Macmillan's Edwardian nostalgia must have been gratified indeed. But none of this prevented him from setting Marples and Beeching loose with the axe, or giving the coup de grâce to the Euston Arch.

This sequence of events is significant, because it shows that the impulse to preserve steam-hauled railways preceded the ravages of Beeching's report. The choice of candidates for rescue widened hugely after that, and by the early 1970s some half-dozen defunct lines had been reopened for steam-hauled services, mostly by volunteer initiative. Many others have followed, and now there are well over a hundred preserved lines across the UK, standard or narrow gauge, as well as museums and other preservation sites wholly or partly devoted to historic trains. No other country has anything like as many.

This was not just playing at trains; almost every job of work on the national network has to be undertaken sooner or later on its preserved counterparts, from track maintenance to locomotive overhauls. Invaluable help came from professional railwaymen, either in retirement or visiting at weekends and holiday time. The Talyllyn drew on the expertise of the shedmaster from Norwich locomotive depot, who described the week he spent in the little railway's repair workshops as 'one of the most enjoyable holidays of his life'. Trains on the Bluebell in its first years were driven by retired veterans from the main lines.

That so many were willing to devote their free hours to unpaid work on these railways was the source of some wonderment, even among railway enthusiasts themselves. One of the first attempts to make sociological sense of it all came in 1969, in an article by Derek Hanson in *Railway World* magazine. Hanson placed the preservation movement in the context of contemporary debates about the nature of the affluent society, in which a combination of rising incomes and disposable leisure time made it possible for the first time to 'pay for the privilege of voluntary labour'. Volunteering thus became a form of emancipation from 'the commercial pressures of capitalist society'. Warming to his theme, Hanson identified an affinity between the weekend track gangs lugging sleepers about on the Bluebell Railway and the rebellious students of '68 with their chants of 'Marx, Mao, Marcuse!'

A lively correspondence followed, and quantities of cold water were poured on some of Hanson's suggestions. It was pointed out that railway enthusiasts were more often lower-middle than working class, and unlikely to succumb to Maoism. Also, that their attitudes were generally backward-looking and indulgent towards the old system of private railway companies, and that this defiant industrial nostalgia à la L. T. C. Rolt was poor preparation for the future, which in 1969 was widely imagined as an idyll of technocratic leisure funded by constant economic growth. One letter noted matter-of-factly that railway work had merely joined other activities, such as gardening, photography and music, which some people did for a living and others chose to pursue unpaid in their spare hours.

Unmentioned in 1969 – perhaps taken for granted – were the broader historical pre-conditions for volunteering: the victories of trades unions in shortening working hours on and off the railways, the advent of paid holidays and state pensions and the improvements in public health that enabled a growing number of Britons to pass into retirement in good enough shape to lend a hand on the line. The motorways and improved trunk roads that had done such harm to BR's ordinary business also had the opposite effect on its preserved offshoots, fostering leisure travel and widening the hinterland from which volunteers could be drawn. More broadly, by the late 1960s the inheritance of the Victorian and Edwardian past was valued more highly than it had been even ten years before. As city after city was violated by ring roads, concrete shopping centres and office-block slabs, the qualities of what had been so heedlessly lost began to glow again in the popular consciousness. Planning laws were changed to reflect this mood. The Civic Amenities Act of 1967 allowed local authorities to designate 'conservation areas', within which ordinary but non-listed buildings received a measure of protection. In effect, most preserved railways were private, linear conservation areas, with a mission to protect any structures and paraphernalia that could enhance the sense of the past.

All of this is necessary explanation for the preserved railway cult, but falls short of being sufficient. Inland waterways partly excepted, no other shrinking or obsolescent technology called forth such battalions of volunteers to keep bits of it in working order. Copies of the *Railway Magazine*, *Trains Illustrated* and *Railway World* were stock items on newsagents' shelves, but no one founded hobby magazines called *Jute Mill Enthusiast*, *Glue-boiler's World* or *Hydraulic Accumulators Pictorial*. Why this should have been the case can best be understood by tracing the story back beyond the twentieth century, to the last years of Queen Victoria.

₪

As we have seen, railways were received with excitement and wonder when they were new, followed by a complex mixture of dependence and mistrust. Some imaginative minds were repelled by them; others found much to admire. Railways generated technical and financial literature too, but these served a strictly practical purpose, and the lavish pictorial folios devoted to some early lines had no successors after the 1840s. The existence of a broader interest is suggested by books such as Michael Reynolds's engine-driving manifestos, or F. S. Williams's *Our Iron Roads*, which went through seven editions between 1852 and 1888. Williams understood how to draw out the romance and excitement inherent in the railways; how, in the words of the modern economic historian John Kellett, 'the apparatus of transport is invested with infinitely more glamour than that of production'. But the Victorians consumed books about many subjects, and it is unsafe to infer from a handful of successful titles that railways were high up the list.

By the 1890s this was beginning to change, for reasons that are still not entirely clear. The end of the broad gauge in 1892 was widely remarked, provoking reflections on the passage of time since the Great Western's 'brave days of old', as *The Times* put it. The first description of a rural branch line in terms of time-bound tradition, as identified in Ian Carter's exhaustive study of railways in literature, came as early as 1893: it is Arthur

Quiller-Couch's 'Cuckoo Valley Railway', a thinly disguised travel sketch of the archaic Bodmin & Wadebridge Railway in Cornwall, opened in 1834. A copy of the earliest surviving edition of Bradshaw fetched £25 at Sotheby's in 1901. All these details suggest an emerging perception of the railways as a subject of historic interest.

Looking forward, national attention was caught by the so-called Race to the North of summer 1895, in which the East Coast and West Coast companies vied to run the fastest through service from London to Aberdeen. The 'race' was partly a protracted stunt, but it also showed excitingly that locomotives could run for long distances much faster than the timetable required. It is tempting to link the contest to the advent of railway anthropomorphism in English literature, in the shape of Rudyard Kipling's story '.007' (1898). Long before *Thomas the Tank Engine*, Kipling's locomotives talked, felt pain and experienced pride, shame and boastfulness. His rolling stock could converse too, and was much less silly than the Rev. W. Awdry's.

Railways exercised a disproportionate pull over many other clergymen besides Wilbert Awdry (1911–97). This, too, is not easily explained. One early devotee was the Rev. Victor Whitechurch (1868–1933), author of *Thrilling Stories of the Railway* (1912), featuring the vegetarian railway detective Thorpe Hazell. Another sign of interest among the professional classes was the establishment in 1899 of the Railway Club, the world's first railway enthusiasts' society, complete with a London clubroom and library. Aristocratic interest was rarer, but not unknown. The Dukes of Sutherland with their private train are too rarefied to count, leaving 'Dozey' Collier, third Lord Monkswell (1875–1964), as the best candidate. Monkswell seized any opportunity to mount a locomotive footplate, and sounded off on railway matters in the Lords over many decades. The General Strike found him in his element, acting as a volunteer signalman at Marylebone.

The Railway Club shut its doors in 2008, leaving the *Railway Magazine* (founded 1897) as the oldest survivor from the dawn of organised enthusiasm. Like the club, the magazine was the first of its kind anywhere. Its opening issue straddled the gap between enthusiasm and older sorts of writing, mixing stodgy analysis of railway share performances with livelier material such as an illustrated interview with the Great Western's general manager. The magazine soon clocked up monthly sales of 25,000, under its tetchy and opinionated editor G. A. Sekon (properly Nokes, with the letters reversed). Sekon liked to use the now-extinct terms 'railwayac' and

First issue of the *Railway Magazine*, 1897. The locomotive is one of the
Great Northern Railway's admired 'single drivers', introduced in 1870

'locomotivac' for followers of the railways, and signalled his own membership of the emerging tribe by naming both his house and his son after Brunel.

As they woke up to the benefits of cultivating a public image, the railways began to encourage outside interest as well. The roots of this consciousness can be traced back to competition for passenger traffic, in which the Midland's upgrading of third class in the 1870s was an early gambit. The companies' seductive publicity posters were among the later products of this policy, as well as such things as the stylish books, jigsaws, board games and other paraphernalia mass-produced by the Great Western between the wars. Stressing its seniority, the London & North Western took to calling itself the 'Premier Line' and churned out thousands of postcards depicting its locomotives and carriages alongside their forerunners from Liverpool & Manchester days. The display of real railway antiques at certain busy stations – *Locomotion* itself at Darlington from 1892, an archaic Furness Railway engine at Barrow and a Bodmin & Wadebridge carriage at Waterloo from early in the new century – made the same point in a different way. That railways were a British invention, a legitimate source of national pride in a nationalistic age, added to their appeal. By Edwardian times, too, the nation's trains were at their all-time peak of visual allure, with richly elaborate liveries for both locomotives and carriages – the *Railway Magazine* in 1899 noted the 'lighter and more artistic shades' coming into vogue for the latter – and high standards of cleanliness and finish. No other country lavished so much trouble and expense on the appearance of its trains. Another attraction was the diversity of the network, with its plethora of separate companies (*Bradshaw's Railway Manual* for 1894 lists 277 of them across the British Isles), multifarious private manufacturers of locomotives and rolling stock and industrial systems and feeder lines of every type.

This proliferation of types and variants was in inverse proportion to economy. As the locomotive historian W. A. Tuplin tartly put it, 'The efforts of a score of design staffs of different railways, independently feeling their way to what was essentially a common goal, produced designs in profusion to the delight of any interested observer who was not at the same time a railway shareholder.' Amplifying this delight, locomotives designed for home rails were more fully aestheticised than almost anywhere else. The utilitarian pipes, valves, boxes and handrails that disfigured the silhouettes of so many American or Italian engines were less

conspicuous on their British equivalents, tucked away out of sight or integrated with the main outlines of the machine. Particular care was taken
with the profile of the chimney (never, ever, to be called a 'funnel'). In
the words of J. G. Robinson, Chief Mechanical Engineer of the Great
Central Railway, 'A chimney to a locomotive is like a hat to a man; the
finishing touch.' In a similar spirit, the young Hamilton Ellis (born 1909)
daydreamed about 'the *faultless engine*', made up of all his favourite bits of
existing ones. Only after nationalisation was this tradition of tidy styling
wholeheartedly given up in favour of rugged accessibility for the working parts. One diehard Great Westernite was moved to denounce British
Railways' 'hideous Americanised progeny' in a letter to *Trains Illustrated*.
Even this transition was slow and partial: the first new standard locomotive did not emerge until 1951, and one Great Western design was still in
production five years after that. Amazingly, in 1949–51 BR built itself a
batch of twenty-eight small shunting engines to a pure North Eastern
Railway design dating back to 1898.

Locomotive naming, like the naming of particular timetabled trains
(*see* Chapter 7), was another national indulgence. Railways elsewhere
often began with named engines – *Der Adler*, the first locomotive in Germany, *Tom Thumb* in the United States – before adopting prosaic systems
of numbering as their stocks grew. Most Victorian railways in the UK
took a similar course, but not all: the Great Western used names without numbers for its broad-gauge engines right to the end, the London &
North Western applied both names and numbers to its express locomotives. Some of this name-giving had a scattergun quality; the LNWR's
Prince of Wales class, built from 1911 onwards, included *Czar of Russia*,
Witch, *John Ruskin* (safely dead by then) and *Gallipoli*. The Great Western
sharpened the focus by introducing themed names for certain classes: cities, saints, even flowers. But the true heyday commenced with the trend
in the 1920s for enlisting locomotive naming to the conscious pursuit of
better public relations.

The newly constituted Southern Railway made the first move. Hoping to foster West Country tourism, the company transformed its existing
N15 class into 'King Arthurs' – a late echo of the dying fall of Victorian chi-
valric ideals, like the clear-browed young knights depicted in war memorial
windows of the period. So E736 became *Excalibur*, E742 *Camelot*, E750
Morgan le Fay and so on. As more locomotives rolled into service, obscure
corners of Arthurian legend were scoured for material, yielding names

unvoiced even at the most fanciful Victorian christenings: *Sir Ontzlake, Sir Galagars, Sir Dodinas le Savage.* A later class was named after public schools, a valuable source of Southern traffic, except that the roll-call had to be extended well beyond the railway's own territory in order to forestall a loss of social tone or academic standards. The Great Western likewise ended up with some names from outside its own domain, as it compiled long feudal catalogues of castles, abbeys, halls, granges and manors for its large passenger engines (stretching the point further, it also roped in *Albert Hall* and a couple of Oxford colleges).

Over on the London, Midland & Scottish, military and imperial themes weighed more heavily, with classes named after regiments, naval ships and British imperial possessions. Once bestowed, these names were taken seriously: LMS locomotives were sometimes specially rostered to pull their namesake regiments' troop trains, and some of those with Scottish names were reallocated to be nearer their home territories. By contrast, names on the London & North Eastern had a happy insouciance. Many of its largest express engines were named after racehorses, some nicely resonant (*Sun Chariot, Velocity, Dick Turpin*), others mystifying to the uninitiated (*Sugar Palm, Hornet's Beauty, Pretty Polly*). Mindful of both ends of the social spectrum, the LNER honoured other kinds of sporting traffic by naming locomotive types after football clubs and foxhunts, with little brass footballs or foxes incorporated into the nameplate designs. A private enthusiasm of the chief engineer accounts for the decision that many of the company's most charismatic type, the streamlined A4 Pacifics introduced in 1935, should receive the names of wild birds. One consequence, in the words of the historian John Walton, was that 'the world speed record holder [4468 *Mallard*, 126 miles per hour, 3 July 1938] was named after the commonest and most everyday species of duck'.

So ingrained did the custom of affixing names to new passenger locomotives become that it continued during the darkest years of the Second World War. O. V. S. Bulleid's new locomotives for the Southern were given big showy plates with names of Merchant Navy lines, West Country locations, or squadrons and other subjects associated with the Battle of Britain. The irresponsible LNER even began naming its B1 class, introduced in 1942, after species of antelope (advance, *Bongo* and *Puku*), reaching a total of forty-one before running out.

Nationalisation did not change the picture immediately, as fresh castles, country houses and long-defunct racehorses were commemorated on new examples of existing designs. This disjunction between locomotive naming and the new world of socialist public ownership was pointed out in 1949 in a book by the railways' most eminent clerical devotee, the Rev. Eric Treacy (1907–78), distinguished railway photographer and future Bishop of Wakefield. Treacy asked how a trade unionist driver might feel about driving an engine 'bearing the name of an aristocratic parasite whose very existence was a threat to the emancipation of the working class'. Around the same time, an LNER-type locomotive was named *W. P. Allen* after a former leader of ASLEF, the enginemen's union – but even this gesture was double-edged, for Allen had crossed over to take up the role of chief negotiator with the railway unions on matters of pay. When BR introduced its own express locomotives in 1951, their names were very much business-as-usual: *Britannia* for the first of the class, the rest largely shared between canonical British authors, stout-hearted monarchs, princes and generals, and a selection of dormant names from the Great Western's broad-gauge days. When a powerful prototype locomotive was rolled out three years later, it was christened *Duke of Gloucester*, after the Queen's second-oldest uncle.

₪

Politics aside, locomotive names were an effective way of attracting public attention. The special glamour of 'namers' also helped to foster the pursuit that still dominates perceptions of railways as a hobby interest: trainspotting.

The story of trainspotting follows a long arc. There is a slow and shadowy Victorian lead-in, then a steeper ascent through the 1920s and 1930s to a golden age in the 1950s. A steady and apparently terminal decline follows the end of steam in the 1960s, increasingly accompanied by popular abuse.

The practice of noting down details of passing trains goes back a long way. The *Great Western Railway Magazine* in 1935 reproduced pages from the notebook of a fourteen-year-old Londoner living at Westbourne Park in 1861, in which engine names and other information about trains to and from Paddington were neatly recorded. The most surprising detail is that the observer, Fanny Johnson, was female. She has since been claimed as the earliest known trainspotter, but a challenge can be made on behalf of a 'young Berkshire diarist' living further along the Great Western main line, who wrote on 7 May 1840: 'In the evening went up to the railway. Saw a new engine started today, the Tiger. I have seen altogether nine engines, running on the railway. The Morning Star, Evening Star, Dog Star, Ajax, Atlas, Planet, Mars, Firefly, & Tiger.'

In regions where engines went unnamed, mere numbers had to do. In *The Railway Children*, the station porter Perks tells the boy Peter that he knows of a 'young gent' who used to write down every engine number he saw. So Peter begins to do the same, on a yellow envelope supplied by Perks:

379
663

at which he 'felt that this was the beginning of what would be a most interesting collection'.

Number-collecting could turn out to be the first stirring of something more serious. Around the year 1920, A. C. Perryman joined his fellow pupils in monitoring the London, Brighton & South Coast line, which passed close to the school. In 1924 he was caned for disturbing the class by exclaiming when an engine in the new Southern Railway livery ran past the window. Four years later, he entered the company's service as a premium apprentice at its Brighton works. Schoolboy enthusiasm had to be kept under wraps here, but Perryman discovered a kindred spirit in the workshops: a senior chargeman who slipped wordlessly out of the building each day to watch the 5.05 p.m. departure go by, hauled by a 'King Arthur'.

To make the most of collecting engine numbers, it was necessary to know what there was to see. Published details of engines in service appeared sporadically, starting with a list of Great Western 'namers' in 1869, but for a long time these were neither comprehensive nor regular enough to keep the observer up to date. The first published compendium was produced in 1935 by the Railway Correspondence and Travel Society as a supplement to its members' magazine, under the ponderous title *The Locomotive Stock as at 31 December, 1934 of the Main Line Companies of Great Britain (and Ireland) including alterations to stock during 1934*. These booklets were unsatisfactory for spotters' record-keeping, however, as they summarised continuously numbered classes in blocks, in the form (for example) '5000–5499'. Few spotters of the 1930s and early 1940s would ever have seen a copy, and most kept hand-written lists instead. One labour-saving dodge popular with Birmingham observers was to draw paper grids of ten squares by ten, numbered graph-wise along two sides, which could be infilled square by square as new engines were noted.

There was a publishing opportunity here, and the man who seized it prospered as a result. He was Ian Allan (1922–2015), a young official on the Southern, whose duties included answering letters of enquiry concerning the company's new locomotives. Allan's suggestion in 1942 that the Southern should issue its own engine list was approved by his superiors, who left him to arrange publication himself. Allan called his booklet *An ABC of Southern Locomotives*. *ABC*s for the three other major companies followed, with steeply rising print runs: 2,000 for the first Southern edition, a total of 145,000 for all four railways five years later. Every engine number was shown and could be individually underlined (for some reason, ticking off the numbers never caught on). More remarkable still, their first printings appeared when railway traffic was a matter of national security, and photographing trains was explicitly forbidden. A hardback combined edition, known to spotters as the 'Combine', appeared in 1948; a single, simplified booklet listing every locomotive together with its home allocation, known as the *Locoshed Book*, followed in 1950.

These books could be kept up to date by consulting Allan's monthly magazine, *Trains Illustrated*, which supplied details of new, withdrawn and reallocated engines. He also founded a Locospotters' Club, entry fee and member's badge one shilling. ('Do you know a Real Spotter when you see one? All genuine spotters wear this badge' …) By 1952 Real Spotters could buy club notepaper, envelopes and Christmas cards, cycle pennants, ties and special locospotters' pencils. The club required its members to vow never to interfere with railway equipment, cause a nuisance to staff or trespass on railway land. Over a quarter of a million enthusiasts eventually signed up.

The spotters' code notwithstanding, not everyone felt kindly towards the craze. Crowds of school-capped youths on the platform ends of favoured stations were sometimes a hindrance to the smooth and safe operation of the railway. Certain stations chose to ban spotters altogether, beginning in 1948 with Tamworth in Staffordshire. Two main lines cross at different levels at Tamworth, and on busy days some 250 youths might gather to watch the passing show. When not scribbling down numbers, they also reportedly 'ran across the metals [tracks] in front of trains, rode on slow-moving vehicles, threw stones, interfered with signal wires, and got in the way of passengers'. Banished, spotters gathered instead in a nearby field, blessed with good vantage points across the angle between the lines.

Episodes such as the Tamworth ban helped to draw the craze to the attention of outsiders. Newspaper reports begin around 1946. Journalists took a while to decide on phraseology; 'taking train numbers', 'collecting locomotive numbers', 'engine-numbering' were all in use, as well as 'trainspotting'. The snappier formula is also less accurate, given that the objects of scrutiny were locomotives rather than the trains they pulled, and the aim was to identify them individually rather than merely to spot what kind they were. It may be that the coinage carried an echo of 'plane-spotting', the colloquial term for aircraft recognition during the Second World War, when observers on rooftops and other vantage points watched for Luftwaffe intruders. Plane-spotting was an adult and purposeful business, so any half-conscious associations with number-taking on the rails could only have been flattering. Some fans certainly embraced the term with pride, like the eight boys aged between eleven and fourteen who came together as the North Hull Estate Train Spotters' Club in 1948.

Accounts of this subculture as seen from outside include a piece from the *Manchester Guardian* in 1951. A reporter went to Crewe, one of the stations that later closed its gates to spotters. He found the platforms pullulating with hundreds of them, drawn from a wide social range. The 'almost drug-like fascination' of the locomotives was noted. One aficionado, a seventeen-year-old clerk, had travelled from Wakefield with enough food to survive for two days, and nowhere to stay overnight but a waiting room or the open platform. The ticket had swallowed almost half his weekly wage. Two other teenagers had cycled all the way from Bristol. Despite this zeal, the spotters struggled to explain why number-taking had such an allure. 'Well, what else is there to do?' was the commonest response. Playing in the street was the main alternative cited. The interviewer left none the wiser.

Had he dug deeper, the *Manchester Guardian*'s man might have learned more about the compulsive aspects of spotting. Steam locomotives were strongly territorial creatures: each had a home shed where maintenance and light repairs were carried out and its own roster of regular duties. The average spotter could expect to see the same engines on his patch over and over again. Visitors from further afield were a cause for excitement, especially if they belonged to unfamiliar classes – like exotic migrants dropping in to a birdwatcher's back garden. Thanks to the immense operational flexibility of the pre-Beeching railway, excursions, cup ties, summer holiday traffic and diversions for engineering work could all pay dividends, bringing 'rare' locomotives from distant sheds. Anywhere like Crewe, a hub station with a constant passage of trains from all directions, became a destination of exhilarated pilgrimage. Time spent away from home, on holidays or visiting family, offered the chance to encounter new types and numbers. If the journey was made by train, so much the better.

Besides, steam locomotives were exciting. This is easier to appreciate today than in 1951, when every train in almost every region outside London and the south-east had one at its head. No other land-bound machine can match the impact of a powerful engine working hard. The sharp propulsive beat of the exhaust, synchronised in sight and sound as the wheels and rods revolve, the smell of coal-smoke combined with steam mixed with its own fine suspension of hot oil, the penetrating shriek or hoot of the whistle, the orange-red glow of the firebox within the cab and the sparks hurtling from the chimney when working in darkness – all these are sublime. Even little shunters have a bustling charm of their own, as the Rev. W. Awdry well knew.

Nationalisation made the hobby at once more challenging and easier to follow. Great Britain became a single hunting ground, as a unified system of numbering succeeded the overlapping lists of the Big Four. Locomotive exchanges were announced, to allow the relative strengths of different designs to be assessed on unfamiliar lines. Engine sheds themselves were gradually reclassified under a single, orderly set of codes. Locomotives wandered more easily beyond the boundaries that had divided the Big Four, echoing the promiscuous improvisations of the war years. Outlandish transfers were reported; in autumn 1948 a pint-sized shunting engine from the Burton brewery lines (ex-LMS) was sent to the former LNER fastness of Northumberland, to work the North Sunderland branch while its own pint-sized engine was away for repair.

Locomotives in 1948 were also bewilderingly, inexhaustibly varied. Despite years of striving for standardisation by the Big Four, there was still great diversity when their holdings passed into public ownership. British Railways' dowry of over 20,000 engines included all manner of archaic, specialised or experimental designs, originating from over fifty different companies. Among the prodigies was a ten-driving-wheeled monster built by the Midland Railway solely to assist trains up the Lickey incline by pushing from behind. Among the veterans were three London & South Western suburban tank engines of a design originating in 1863, which survived in Cornish exile, working china clay trains on a mineral line connected to the venerable Bodmin & Wadebridge. Even these were not the oldest on the network, an honour that fell to a North London Railway tank engine that had first turned a wheel in 1858; rebuilt with a small rotary crane grafted on to the back, it was confined exclusively to the old company's works at Bow.

Few schoolboy spotters could hope to encounter all these exotica, but the prospect was alluring, like the blank spaces left for rare stamps in an album. For all-round variety, London enthusiasts had the easiest time of it, with fourteen termini to choose from. Such was the devotion to spotting in the capital that a viewing gallery was built in the 1950s on the slope of the cutting at Finsbury Park, next to the Great Northern main line. Hard-hit cases might even take up Underground spotting, as Ian Allan published lists of its trains too, as well as London's buses, trams and trolleybuses, the coastal shipping fleets and many other subjects besides. A businessman rather than a hobbyist at heart, trainspotting's first and only tycoon used his *ABC* profits to found an enduring commercial empire that at various times has taken in printing, a travel agency, miniature railway operation, Masonic regalia, organic garden supplies, garages and hotels.

One axiom the *Manchester Guardian* got right was that spotting 'inculcates a strict regard for truth'. No one at Crewe would tick off what he hadn't seen, and the boys were shocked that the reporter even raised the suggestion. In reality, he didn't know the half of it. Trainspotting, especially of steam locomotives, was apt to raise intense metaphysical conundrums concerning perception and identity. How much of a locomotive's presence was it necessary to witness before it could be ticked off? Did a glimpse of the wheels or buffers count, or even the plume of its exhaust? What about a good view of the tender, but not of the locomotive to which it belonged? Some held that it was enough just to hear and smell an engine, a heresy W. Elgar Dickinson overheard being contested by juvenile spotters on a railway journey in the 1950s.

Workshops and scrapyards posed still more complex dilemmas. A steam locomotive is essentially a kit of parts, which are at once widely interchangeable and liable to replacement at varying rates. By convention, the identity of each locomotive – its mortal soul – is constituted by the main frames, which sit under the boiler and hold the axles of the driving wheels in place. A spotter visiting a steam-age railway works might encounter all of the following temptations to swell his list: a collection of parts from a single dismantled locomotive, unmistakably numbered, but with the frames nowhere in sight; a line of new locomotives under construction, each more complete than its neighbour, and ending with a pair of virgin frames that were still being welded or riveted together; some redundant frames that had just been cut in two; an entire defunct locomotive broken up into a big pile of bits. In spotters' argot, how many of these could honestly be 'copped' without risking the accusation of 'fudging'?*

Trips to locomotive works and engine sheds were essential for any spotter who wanted to fill his *ABC*. Steam locomotives were less efficient than diesels and electrics not only on account of their squanderous use of fuel – converting perhaps 7 per cent of the energy from combustion into useful work – but because they spent relatively little time actually working trains. The rest of their hours were given over to taking on fuel and water, getting up steam, being cleaned after use, undergoing repair or overhaul, or just being kept in reserve in case of need – like the London, Tilbury & Southend tank engines that spent seven profitless years stored at a Carlisle engine shed, easy game for visiting spotters, before they were finally condemned in 1955. The British convention of reduced services on Sundays was another factor, as spotters well knew: the morning of the Sabbath was an ideal time to visit an engine shed, where locomotives simmered in rows awaiting the start of the weekday timetable.

As the hobby continued to develop, comprehensive coverage could be procured by joining one of the 'shed-bashing' coach tours arranged by railway societies, which followed gruelling whistle-stop schedules in order to scour as much territory as possible. Looking back, the film editor Ian Krause reckoned that his local railway club 'covered every slum-clearance area in England in a year' during the late 1950s. Its excursions sometimes dragged on into the small hours of morning, with spotters stumbling around darkened sheds by electric torchlight.

---

* Even the axiom about frames sometimes faltered. Preservationists restoring Great Western no. 4983 *Albert Hall* discovered in 1998 that its frames belonged to 4965 *Rood Ashton Hall*, identities having been swapped during overhaul. In acknowledgement of this divided self, the locomotive has run in recent years with different name- and number-plates on each side.

Older railway enthusiasts looked down on this kind of number-chasing. It seemed a mark of immaturity in the young, and of a narrow or obsessive outlook in those old enough to know better. This was to miss the point. For successive generations in the 1940s–60s, spotting was the usual entry-level activity from which any broader interest in railways developed, a desire to join the workforce not excluded. This allure was knowingly exploited as early as 1946 in *The Railwaymen*, a short recruitment film made for the Ministry of Transport and Central Office of Information. The last scene shows a kindly old railwayman urging a schoolboy to head for home after a long day on the platforms, before furtively whipping out his own notebook to take the number of an approaching express. By 1956, the back cover of the 'Combine' featured an advertisement headed BRITISH RAILWAYS HAVE A MESSAGE FOR BOYS ABOUT TO LEAVE SCHOOL. Wherever they ended up working, spotters collectively generated traffic and revenue in their own right, as pocket money and paper-round income was poured into travel and platform tickets.

Special excursions were another channel through which railway enthusiasts repaid their debt to the network. The foundation year was 1938, when Great Northern Railway No. 1 was brought out of retirement at York Railway Museum. Built in 1870, it was the sole survivor of a fabled class that starred in the Race to the North of 1895 (one of which was the 'cover star' of the first *Railway Magazine*). Its single axle of enormous eight-foot driving wheels gave No. 1 a wonderfully obsolete look by the 1930s, a railway equivalent of Grandpa's penny-farthing bicycle. Yet its general outlines were elegant, with 'the perfect balance of the thorough-bred', in the words of Hamilton Ellis. For authenticity, No. 1's special train was made up of antique six-wheel carriages (though this time they only went as far as Cambridge or Peterborough).

British Railways also favoured special trains, many of which were organised by railway societies. Some of these toured remote or little-used lines, others offered haulage by out-of-the-ordinary locomotives; sometimes the two attractions were combined. Often there was also a valedictory element, a last chance to travel behind this class or that, or to traverse a route whose closure was imminent. As the replacement of steam accelerated in the later 1950s, followed by Dr Beeching's unflinching amputations, it became barely possible even for the most keenly focused enthusiast to keep up. In 1962 alone, 2,924 steam locomotives were earmarked for disposal by BR, equivalent to the rate of one every three hours. The photo-spreads in the *Railway Magazine* for August 1964 (to take an issue at random) include the following headings: 'Scottish Branch Closures', 'Welsh Holocaust Continued', 'East Anglian Deceased Diesel Services', 'Condemned!' Another photo shows a well turned-out special train taking the Home Counties Railway Society over the scenic Somerset & Dorset Joint line, on which Beeching had already pronounced sentence.

Most of the trains depicted in this issue have woefully grimy and unkempt steam locomotives in charge. It is noticeable too how shabby and under-used many stations appear, with weed-grown platforms, peeling paintwork, gap-toothed valancing and empty sidings. There was no point in directing care or money towards assets, wheeled or otherwise, that were scheduled for imminent disposal. Besides, manpower to keep up the labour-intensive routines imposed by steam power was in desperately short supply. In the prosperous sixties, few wanted to begin their working life on an engine cleaner's scanty wage. For most of the existing footplatemen, a white collar and a comfortable seat in an enclosed cab – diesel or electric – could not come too soon. A vignette from Scotland, 1966: enthusiast (to driver of one of the last A4 streamliners): 'Nice to see one of these on the train'. Driver: 'Should be scrapped.'

For devotees, all this happened far too quickly. In 1955 it was officially anticipated that steam might not finally expire until 1990. The last steam locomotive built for BR, 92220 *Evening Star* (another revived Great Western name), was turned out from Swindon works as late as March 1960. Expected to work well into the 1970s, *Evening Star* managed only five years before redesignation as a museum piece. BR's last ordinary steam-hauled trains ran three years later, on Sunday, 4 August 1968 (the equivalent date in West Germany, where modernisation was less convulsive, was 26 October 1977). What was billed as the final steam train of all ran a week after that: a valedictory trip for enthusiasts, remembered as the 'Fifteen Guinea Special' because the ticket prices were widely regarded as a rip-off. By nice symmetry, its route included the original Liverpool & Manchester line, main-line steam having retreated in its last months to the very region where it began 138 years before. Crowds of the ticketless crammed station platforms to watch. Others lined the route, just as people had done three years before to pay their respects at the passing of Sir Winston Churchill, Britain's last great railway-borne funeral.

It was not simply the extinction of steam that left a void: an entire working world had disappeared too. In 1962 Britain was still a land of well-staffed country stations served by steam-hauled carriages of pre-war design, with goods yards equipped to handle wagons full of anything from coal to cattle. By 1968 there were no such stations or trains left, many of the lines they served had gone, and the surviving network had adopted new uniforms, liveries and typography which all seemed to spurn the inheritance of the past. These years were the enthusiasts' equivalent of the Dissolution of the Monasteries (missing only the martyrdoms), an onslaught that has been dissected, mourned and memorialised within the subculture ever since.

Any outsider curious to know what steam-age trainspotting was like can read all about it in veterans' memoirs. This is a relatively recent publishing genre. The British Library's oldest item with the key word in the title, beating Irvine Welsh's grim novel of Edinburgh junkie life by three years, is *30 Years of Trainspotting*, by John Stretton (1990). Unlike Welsh's book, no one could accuse *30 Years of Trainspotting* of having a misleading title. In its pages we learn that 1962 was Stretton's peak year, with 3,198 'cops', and that by the end of 1963 his loco tally stood at 14,565, of which 11,666 were steam. A little autobiographical detail is included too, including the author's love of the guitar sounds of Duane Eddy, but the text really takes second place to the photographs, whose subjects may easily be guessed.

Anyone hoping for a more reflective account had to wait for Nicholas Whittaker's *Platform Souls* (1995). Whittaker took up spotting in 1964, aged eleven. There was then still plenty of steam around his home town of Burton-on-Trent, but it was fading fast. Spotters hailing from Liverpool or Manchester were envied, even though they seemed 'thinner, paler, and not as tall as the rest of us', as if from too much exposure to smoke and steam. Aware that his objects of devotion were on borrowed time, Whittaker staged a magnificently futile protest in 1966, standing with a friend on the already disused platform of Horninglow station as the line's last ever freight train came through. They waved a home-made banner lettered UP WITH STEAM at the diesel in charge and were captured on film by the man from the *Burton Mail*.

For Whittaker and his friends, spotting was but one adolescent pursuit among several, taking its turn with football, music and (a little later) girls. Musical references in particular have become a touchstone of the 1960s 'spot-lit' genre – blatantly so in the case of Phil Mathison's *Shed Bashing with the Beatles* (2006). The stock props of 1950s recollections tend to be more tangible: gabardines, school caps and blazers, duffel bags (or old gas-mask holders), egg sandwiches, Tizer (or R. White's lemonade). These half-generational differences count for less than the similarities, especially the memoirs' emphasis on the rewards of friendship. Spotting was a good way for adolescent males to fill their empty hours together. It was democratically cheap, requiring minimal equipment: notebook, pencil, *ABC*. Like birdwatching, the payback came from a mixture of application, observation and luck; it encouraged both co-operation and good-natured rivalry. Spotters did not usually form gangs, defend territory or set out to beat each other up. They also developed an early taste for independence and a working knowledge of cheap public transport. For a gaggle of unsupervised twelve- and thirteen-year-olds to cross an unfamiliar city, locate an engine shed and joyfully swarm all over forty or fifty examples of British heavy engineering was – to borrow an expression from a later time – empowering. If the visit was a stolen one, via a back gate or hole in the wall, so much the better.

A decade after the end of steam, this subculture was still in a fairly healthy state. Diesel depots were used to incursions by spotters, and some allowed them in on the nod. Ian Allan's booklets could be found not only at station kiosks, but in ordinary bookshops too. There was even a rival brand, Platform 5 Publications. Their purchasers haunted the platform ends, even as their fathers had. But the contingents were thinning; and as they thinned, the proportion of spotters who might on first inspection come up to scratch in the pursuit of football, music or girls steadily fell. The residue of spotters were (and are) highly conspicuous on their platform ends, and could be (and are) jeered and gestured at from the safety of a carriage seat: dowdy-looking misfits to the public eye, pointlessly engaged in a project with no cultural, aesthetic or monetary value.

By 1987 the hobby's image problem was being debated in the pages of *Rail Enthusiast*, upstart junior cousin to the *Railway Magazine* and *Railway World*. One apparently genuine letter prescribed wardrobe makeovers, even to the extent of red-framed specs ('Get trendy, get trainspotting!'). But it was no use. *Viz* comic, that bellwether of 1980s popular culture, introduced a new character in the same year, 'Timothy Potter, Trainspotter'. Bespectacled, acne-dappled and dressed as if by his mother, myopic Timothy is too hopeless even to cut it as a number-collector. After various punishing mishaps, he decides to go home and spot phone numbers instead ('there are lots of them in the telephone directory').

This was not a case of an outsider picking on the hobby, for Chris Donald, the comic's founder and editor, was himself an ex-practitioner. Profits from *Viz* allowed him to buy three large ex-North Eastern Railway country stations in Northumberland, one of which he restored and lived in, complete with an imported brake van in the old goods yard. But other mockers were circling around the dwindling tribe. 1988 is the earliest citation for the *Oxford English Dictionary*'s secondary definition of trainspotter, '(freq. *depreciative*): a person who enthusiastically or obsessively studies the minutiae of any subject; a collector of trivial information'. The related term 'anorak' is cited from four years earlier and defined thus: '(*derogatory*): a boring, studious or socially inept young person (caricatured as typically wearing an anorak), *esp.* one who pursues an unfashionable and solitary interest with obsessive dedication'.* In 1994 Stephen Dinsdale's one-man show *Anorak of Fire* enjoyed a long run, introducing West End audiences to the character of Gus Gascoigne, trainspotter. With his thermos flask, chunky glasses, fur-lined hood and woolly hat, and his credulous stories about a legendary super-spotter with the power to see an elusive locomotive 'even when it wasn't there', Gus was an amiable but predictably ludicrous figure. Such people were to be pitied or despised; not to do so was to miss out a little on the consolations of normality. Bill Bryson, in *Notes from a Small Island* (1996), dismissed the entire railway-loving tribe: 'they are irrational, argumentative, dangerously fussy and often ... have an irritating little Michael Fish moustache that makes you want to stick out two forked fingers and pop them in the eyes'.

₪

People who have come within the orbit of railway enthusiasm will recognise Bryson's sketch, without necessarily sharing his impulse to violence. But most railway enthusiasts were not and are not like this. A good many were never trainspotters at all, a term that has been stretched by outsiders – as with 'twitchers' (chasers of rarities) for birdwatchers – to cover a much broader range of interests. Seen from within, with a lover's eye, the

---

* The *OED* also finds room for 'gricer', the fraternity's half-mocking, half-affectionate term for its own hard core, thought to derive from an obscure joke shared by some members of Manchester Locomotive Society while on a ramble across a grouse moor in 1938.

view across the railway network is one of breadth, rather than narrowness: an inexhaustible panorama of connectedness, extending together through time and space. For Eric Lomax, whose cruel destiny it was to be tortured by the Japanese as a slave labourer on the Burma–Siam railway, the revelation came in a moment, on 12 September 1932. Crossing a footbridge at Portobello goods yard in Edinburgh, he saw below him

> a shiny heavy web of iron and wood, dead straight parallel lines of metal suddenly curving and merging smoothly into other sets of tracks; ladders fixed to the earth, climbing into the distance. They were spread out and branched off beyond the bridge; close up I could see the worn silver of the rail surface and the dark steel of the chairs and the wood of the cross-sleepers. In the dusk the tracks looked like lines of mercury on the oil-stained timber and gravel.

The thirteen-year-old Lomax became possessed by this 'animated, mechanical, mysterious paradise'. Exploring the tangled lines around the Scottish capital, he 'felt like Darwin on the Galapagos'. Number-taking was for lightweights; Lomax's railway was 'a scholarly passion, a "subject" as valid as mathematics or French, and I took it just as seriously as any specialist'.

A common response to this sense that railways *mattered* was to record them photographically. For the broadest portrait of life and work on the railways, the best source is usually the material taken for record or publicity purposes by the companies themselves, or (in the twentieth century) by news agencies. Here will be found everything from new infrastructure to long-obsolete working practices, captured with equipment of professional standards and taken with all the advantages of privileged access. But this is not to deny the impact of the conventional three-quarter view of a steam-hauled train in full cry, with a fine plume of exhaust to supply the effect of frozen movement. The best of these photographs convey a strong sense of place, locating the railway in its landscape or townscape, or simply in the self-contained world of ballasted track, signal gantries and sooty retaining walls. For railway initiates, the wind-bleached eastern fells of Cumberland and Westmorland will always be associated with the camerawork of the Rev. Eric Treacy, while the lusher landscapes of east Somerset and inland Dorset are inseparable from the name of Ivo Peters (1915–89), who recorded the steeply graded Somerset & Dorset Joint Railway – the southern railway enthusiast's *Anglia perdita* – in its late heyday and last decline. Scotland had its own masters: W. J. V. Anderson in the Highlands, Derek Cross in the Ayrshire coalfields and the wilds of Dumfries and Galloway. Examples could be multiplied.

Other cameras were attracted not from any devotion to the steam-age railway as such, but because of the formal, incidental or atmospheric opportunities it offered. The Anglo-German modernist photographer Bill Brandt (1904–83) captured the smoke-laden railway ambience of northern English cities as early as the 1930s. In contrast to Brandt's gathering darkness, Eric de Maré (1910–2002) and Edwin Smith (1912–71) engaged more explicitly with the heroic presence of railway architecture and the human paraphernalia of station platforms.

All these strains came together in the work of some younger railway photographers, just in time for the last years of steam. The representative figure in this movement was Colin Gifford (born 1936), a graphic designer and former art student who joined Ian Allan's publishing operation in the early 1960s. Gifford's day job included the restyling of Allan's *ABC*s and magazines to have a more modern look. Much of his spare time was spent in pursuit of a corresponding modernist aesthetic in railway imagery, with the Swiss photographer Jean-Michel Hartmann's anthology *Magie du Rail* (1959) as his chief inspiration. Gifford's pictorial manifesto, *Decline of Steam*, appeared in 1965, priced by Ian Allan at a luxurious three guineas. Pattern, silhouette and mood were now legitimate subjects too; compositions ranged from crepuscular landscapes animated by the white plume of a distant train to still-lifes of piled-up brake lamps. Readers expecting the usual enthusiasts' diet of hyper-specific information had to make do with minimal captions, bunched provocatively at the back of the book.

Railway World magazine soon began to present other examples of the so-called New Approach, including four-page selections under the heading 'Take Four' (the modern-jazz echo was presumably deliberate). Colour film and advanced equipment played a part too, like the telephoto lenses associated with the work of Paul Riley, hell-raiser, part-time folk roadie and leading light of the Midland Neverers Association. Named from their objective of going ticketless when travelling by train, the Neverers paid their quixotic dues to BR by acting as voluntary engine cleaners, working through the night with ladders and oily rags so that boilers and cabsides would have the right kind of dull shine in photographs taken on the following day. The last year of steam was a frantic time, as the few remaining services through the northern fells were chased by car-loads of devotees with tripods and light meters, overtaking and snapping the same trains again and again. The most dedicated photographers watched for the dawn, sleeping in their vehicles, in sodden tents, or dossing illicitly in platelayers' huts.

Riley's luck ran out in 1976, at the Severn Valley Railway's Victoria Bridge. Awaiting another master shot, he stretched out on the parapet to sleep. Somehow he then rolled off the edge, falling to his death. By that time the bohemian-modernist moment of British railway photography had passed, leaving some outstanding images among its outpourings of grainy greys and velvety blacks. Work by Gifford and his fellow icono-clasts will be searched for in vain in the national collection at the Victoria & Albert Museum – perhaps to be a self-identified 'railway photographer' is an automatic disqualification – but five of Gifford's train portraits were honoured by the Royal Mail on a stamp issue in 1994.

Other kinds of recording grew in popularity too. Film was increas-ingly affordable, although simultaneous sound recording was beyond the means of most. Unaccompanied sound was cheaper, and enthusiasts crammed the leading carriages of steam-hauled trains to hold their micro-phones out of the window, or waited by the lineside to immortalise the passing of steam, in both senses of the phrase.

The top player in this game was the eminent sound recordist Peter Handford (1919–2007). Handford's other location work ranges from the authentic din of battle, captured in the aftermath of D-Day, to a share in many acclaimed post-war films, including works directed by Hitchcock, Tony Richardson and Joseph Losey. Karel Reisz's *Saturday Night and Sun-day Morning*, with its episode of background shunting noises (*see* Chapter 13), is another on the list. All this would have been quite enough for most people, except that Handford's dearest love was trains. Having founded his own record company, Transacord, he tested the railway market in 1955 with two 78 rpm pressings. They were well received. He also gave up full-time employment in favour of freelancing, to allow more time to capture the soundscapes of the railway. Earnings from work on Jack Clay-ton's *Room at the Top* (1959) allowed Handford to buy one of the earliest stereo tape recorders. The first Transacord 12-inch LPs appeared in 1960, one of which covered the ever-popular Somerset & Dorset. Later discs were issued through the esoteric Argo company, best remembered for its spoken-word output and its coverage of British jazz.

an ARGO TRANSACORD recording argo

TRAINS ON THE NARROW GAUGE

A Transacord 7-inch single from 1965. The sleeve shows the Talyllyn
Railway in North Wales, the first line to be rescued and run by volunteers

Railway sales in all Transacord formats peaked at 40,000 per year
in the 1960s, 7-inch singles included. Their sleeve notes are a genre in
their own right, sometimes raising incongruous echoes of opera-scene
summaries:

> A branch line train from Audley End and Saffron Walden is approach-
> ing Bartlow, a rural junction on the Cambridge–Haverhill line,* on an
> April afternoon in 1956; a 'G5' class 0–4–4 Tank engine, No. 67279,
> heads the two coach push and pull train down the gradient, round a
> curve and squeaks to a stop at the branch line platform where a small

---

* For the posthumous fate of this route *see* Chapter 15.

boy greets his friend, the engine driver; the driver exchanges local
gossip with the porter, while the engine brake pump sighs impatiently.

In his New York home, the poet W. H. Auden used to listen to British
railway recordings to assuage occasional feelings of homesickness. Perhaps
the sounds also called to mind the verses he had contributed to one of
the earliest and finest of all British railway documentaries, the GPO Film
Unit's visionary *Night Mail* (1936).

₪

A less tangible form of recording was train timing. Equipped with a stop-
watch, the train-timer calculates the range of speeds achieved over the
course of a journey by watching the lineside for mileposts and other landmarks. The performance of the locomotive or multiple unit – it is usually a locomotive – is then assessed against the challenges posed by load,
gradients, signal stops, speed restrictions and other variables such as slippery rails and coal quality. Comparisons can thus be made with the performance of other types over the same route, past and present. The hobby
should not be confused with the railways' own scientific investigations
of locomotive efficiency, for which special recording carriages and static
testing plants were brought into play, allowing calculations of the crucial ratio between power output and fuel consumed (a factor most train-
timers ignored). The appeal of train-timing may be compared instead to
the speculative rivalries and statistical number-crunching associated with
certain sports, especially cricket. In truth, many railway enthusiasts find
it boring, flipping through the Practice & Performance pages of the *Railway Magazine* ('The world's longest-running railway series, established in
1901') with a mere glance at the pictures.

The obverse of this fetish for detail is a fascination with the roles of
driver and fireman, whose names and sheds are sometimes published in
train-timers' accounts. Here is the adult quantification of boyhood rever-
ence, of the kind which inspired the seven-year-old Adrian Vaughan to
buy cups of tea from the refreshment room at Reading station and carry
them solemnly to the drivers of trains waiting at the platforms. Outside
interest in what the engineman's job was actually like was satisfied first by
reportage pieces, then by a growing number of published accounts from
the workers themselves.

The 1950s fell somewhere between, as witness Patrick Ransome-Wallis's *Men of the Footplate* (1954). Its pages present the railway autobiographies of four drivers, one from each of the old companies. All had long service behind them, a reminder that express driving was then no job for a youngster; as often as not, the object of boyish hero-worship was 'a solid man in his early sixties', in the words of one footplateman-author. Unfortunately, Ransome-Wallis's quartet all come out sounding exactly the same, as if ventriloquized (and did driver Albert Young of Camden shed *really* say 'I feel indeed a gay sense of pride and well-being as we speed along'?). Following official direction, Ransome-Wallis also suppressed any political content. Nothing here, then, to deter 'boys about to leave school'.

Less mediated accounts have more to offer. One of the earliest took the form of the introduction to Frank McKenna's *A Glossary of Railwaymen's Talk*, published as its Pamphlet No. 1 by the History Workshop movement in 1970. Founded by the Marxist historian Raphael Samuel, and drawing strength from the recent achievements of academic labour history, the movement aimed to encourage working people to record and understand their own lives in terms of 'history from below'. McKenna (1929–2013) was an early luminary: a former driver and ASLEF official, he had taken up a place under Samuel at Ruskin College in Oxford, named in honour of the great critic, where those who have missed out on formal education receive a second chance to study.* Released from railway service, and with steam now a memory, he was free to chronicle its hardships and penances.

Starting at Carlisle Kingmoor shed in 1946, McKenna was set to work cleaning engines that had accumulated up to a year's worth of grease, impacted with coal dust and soot. Novice cleaners had the worst of it, taking on the moving parts; senior hands were given the boiler; the head cleaner was usually an ex-footplateman demoted on account of failing eyesight or fading health. No laundry would accept their filthy overalls, which were used for as long as possible before being thrown away. Hand-me-downs from the footplate were sought after, because cleaners still had to provide these outfits themselves. Promotion to fireman brought the new challenge of keeping upright on a jolting, swaying footplate; as McKenna discovered, 'Everything on a locomotive hurts'. When running fast, speech was impossible, so that driver and fireman communicated by

---

* McKenna's major publication, *The Railway Workers 1840–1970*, dates from 1980.

sign language instead. Hot days were something else again, when 'a curtain of sweat runs continuously from your head'. McKenna was honest, too, about occasional tensions between English, Scottish and Welsh enginemen, racial prejudice towards West Indian newcomers at the London sheds and the mixed responses of his colleagues to his youthful communist idealism: older men thought him precocious or disloyal while most of his peers found 'the professor' too clever by half.

If all this is a long way from the blandly reassuring accounts proffered by Ransome-Wallis, McKenna's testament is atypical too of the coming wave of railway memoirs aimed primarily at enthusiasts. Ottley's mighty *Bibliography of British Railway History*, second supplement (1998), lists 103 'biographical and autobiographical memoirs of railwaymen' published between 1981 and 1996 alone, and even this total omits masses of material in periodicals. Many of Ottley's authors are former steam-age footplatemen, sometimes writing with the help of a 'ghost', but managers, inspectors, shed- and stationmasters, mechanical engineers, signalmen (Adrian Vaughan among them), clerks, porters, shunters, guards, carriage painters, boilersmiths, fitters, gangers and storesmen are also represented. By the standards of Ruskin College, these memoirs are often tinted from the rosy end of the spectrum, or otherwise deficient in critical-historical thinking. But this is to miss the broader point: without the existence of an informed lay readership, few railwaymen's working lives would have ever been written or published in the first place. The result is a historical resource without parallel in British industry.

₪

Just as the flow of memoirs swelled after the end of steam, so did the impulse to collect railway artefacts. Closures and modernisation generated mighty streams of redundant material, most of which was junked, scrapped or burnt. So much was simply left lying around that the boundary between legitimate rescue and pilfering was not always clear. Aboveboard purchases were made locally, by individual arrangement with collectors; for a long time, even locomotive nameplates could be had at scrap prices.

BR soon woke up to the idea that certain types of redundant asset had a substantial resale value. Six hundred collectors turned up for an auction held at Stoke-on-Trent in 1964, where barrows, seats, signs and lamp-posts were all on offer. In 1969, just after steam's Year Zero, a weird shop called Collectors' Corner opened in a dowdy warehouse near Euston station, selling pretty well any portable or detachable object with a railway provenance. Brass buttons from porters' uniforms were a penny each; big stuff such as station signs was piled up in the front yard. The wider fashion in the 1960s–70s for using bygones as household furnishings must also have encouraged the collecting trend, these being the years in which middle-class kitchen walls were first adorned with rusting or replicated enamelled advertisements, and Victorian rubbish dumps were dug out to retrieve their glass bottles and stoneware jars. Michael Palin's exploration of the British railway network in a BBC2 travelogue of 1980, which began with confessions of boyhood spotting and ended with his purchase and removal of the enormous 1950s nameboards from Kyle of Lochalsh station, was (in more than one sense) a sign of the times.

The custom of marking company property ensured that there was plenty to keep Collectors' Corner stocked. John Mander's *Collecting Railwayana* (1988) takes in signs, station furniture, buckets, scuttles, pokers, tongs, kettles, brushes, wheelbarrows, clocks, watches, weighing machines, horse brasses and tackle, parcel and newspaper stamps, sacks, tarpaulins, posters, carriage pictures, paperwork and documents (everything from engineering drawings to goods invoices), postcards and other publicity material, rulebooks, timetables, tickets and passes, luggage labels, pencils, pen nibs, inkwells, table- and silverware, cutlery, menus, saucepans, hot water bottles, chamber pots, lavatory fittings, lavatory paper ('An LNER roll survives in the Rogers collection'), soap tablets, towels, uniforms (including badges and buttons), pay tokens, truncheons, whistles, first-aid kit, signal arms and finials, signal block instruments and tablets, cast-iron toe-plates from signal-box steps, mileposts, gradient posts, detonator cans, oil cans, lamps (indoor and out), locks, keys, locomotive whistles and every kind of nameplate, numberplate and lettered board from locomotives and trains themselves. Even this list omits esoterica such as railway telegraph insulators, of which the founding study is W. Keith Neal's *Searching for Railway Telegraph Insulators* (1982).

Not all these categories have much of a following, admittedly; but the combined market in railway collectables was valued at £3 million per year by 2001. Much of this trade is taken up by posters, tickets, station signs and nameplates. Posters stand out because they have a broad, non-specialist appeal as accomplished works of commercial art; there is even a sizeable holding at the Yale Center for British Art in Connecticut. But in terms of market value, a medium-rare or medium-tatty poster will easily be overtaken by a choice station sign. British Railways' totem-style signs of the 1950s are especially sought after, reaching a record price of £12,700 for Paddington in 2009. Locomotive nameplates rank highest of all, topped by the £60,000 paid for *Golden Fleece*, from a sister locomotive to *Mallard*, in 2004.

Nameplates from diesel or electric traction are sought after too, and have been known to fetch over £20,000, although the market for more recent examples is weaker. BR and its successor companies must share the blame here. Things started to go awry in the 1980s, when names began to be applied to butter up valued customers (*The Coal Merchants' Association of Scotland, Hartlepool Pipe Mill*), swiftly followed by any sort of good cause, ephemeral or otherwise (*Capital Radio's Help a London Child, Mum in a Million 1997 Doreen Scanlon*), then by tongue-in-cheek facetiousness, like the diesels named by Virgin Rail after marionettes from Gerry Anderson's sci-fi TV series *Thunderbirds*. To make matters worse, identities were repeatedly exchanged, so that *Royal Observer Corps* was demobbed as *Dave Berry* and *Gwynedd Dunwoody* took on a new gender-swap identity as *Sir Peter Hendy CBE*. Names were also extended to mere multiple units, usually in flimsier physical forms than the traditional cast metal plates. But just as there are enthusiasts who collect LNER lavatory paper, so others will doubtless be ready to give pride of place over the mantelpiece to the plates from *Brains*, *Victim Support* or *Penny the Pendolino*.*

₪

As if spotting, photographing, filming, recording, writing about or collecting artefacts from the railways were not enough, they could also be copied in miniature. Toy trains arrived on the scene quickly enough and clockwork versions followed, first recorded in 1867. Toys and models are not the same thing, however; most toy trains were 'no more like the original than a perambulator is like a steam roller', as the *Railway Magazine* sniffed in 1904. Model railways properly so called are just that, a scaled-down version of some prototype existing in the real world, past or present. Interest in

---

* Two 'Thunderbird' nameplates, *Tin Tin* and *Parker*, indeed fetched over £4,000 at a charity auction in January 2014.

models – toys for grown-ups – grew up side by side with amateur fascination with railways themselves. So the twentieth century witnessed a proliferation of railway models large and small, mass-produced or hand-made, British or imported, and powered by low-voltage current or live steam as well as clockwork. At their smallest, T-gauge trains shrink the prototype to the barely feasible scale of 1:450; at the upper end, modelling shades into model engineering, using many of the same techniques as the full-size version.

It is therefore not easy to say where the line between big model and small train should be drawn. The upper limit is generally accepted as the 15-inch gauge, as pioneered from the 1870s by Sir Arthur Heywood, Bart (1849–1916), in his own landscaped grounds at Duffield Bank in Derbyshire. Heywood intended his 'minimum-gauge' railway to serve as a prototype for lightweight lines everywhere, and designed a Lilliputian sleeping carriage (for four) and dining car (seating eight; oil-fired stove included) to demonstrate his case. The 1st Duke of Westminster was sufficiently impressed to equip his Cheshire seat at Eaton Hall with a Heywood-designed line, but this failed to set an aristocratic trend and the main use of the minimum gauge proved to be for so-called miniature railways intended as passenger attractions. For instance, a 15-inch-gauge line was provided to carry visitors round and round the Liverpool Garden Festival, an initiative of 1984 that was meant to bring regeneration to derelict post-industrial land. But the engines and rolling stock at Liverpool were borrowed from two established and permanent railways, the Ravenglass & Eskdale in Cumberland and the Romney, Hythe & Dymchurch in Kent. These lines manage to have it both ways. Many of their engines are one-third-size versions of 1920s main-line designs and all barely reach chest height on an average adult standing alongside at the platform; but each provides a public service for most of the year, over a combined length of over twenty miles. The Romney line even runs a school train, under contract with the local authority (Sir Arthur Heywood would be proud).

The model scale at which things get especially interesting is O gauge, calibrated at 1:43.5, or 7mm to the imperial foot. At this level, and doubly so at the more common OO gauge (1:76 scale, or 4mm to the foot), it becomes much easier to model a surrounding section of the world beyond the railway. A train set becomes a 'layout', a microcosm of some real or invented location. Decisions must be made about what sort of world this slice of life will represent, in historical time as well as geographical space.

Where these decisions can lead is illustrated by the extreme case of Pendon Parva, the 4mm-scale layout displayed in the Pendon Museum at Long Wittenham in Berkshire (now Oxfordshire). The model may be described as an imaginary portrait of a real place, for it aims to represent a typical parish in the Vale of White Horse in Berkshire as it might have been around 1930. Its founder was a lanky young Australian, Roye England (1908–95), who found himself bewitched equally by the region and by the Great Western Railway that carried him through it, on his first visit in 1925. Concerned that its rural ways were being overtaken by change and decay, he set out to create a permanent record in three dimensions.

Roye England's first instalment, a meticulously detailed model of a pub, took him five years in the 1930s. Other volunteers joined the project, and when *Country Life* magazine visited in 1965 the diorama had grown to include a railway, animated by impeccably correct Great Western models (no box-fresh Hornby products here), of just the right types for the region in the years in question. The same attention to detail was extended to every element, including the use of prepared human hair on the roofs of Pendon's cottages to represent traditional Berkshire thatching.

These guidelines still govern the present, greatly expanded incarnation of Pendon Parva. The museum's website in 2014 carried a film taken from the front of a moving model locomotive – like the 'phantom rides' that entranced early cinema-goers – as it traverses the entire layout. Proceeding at a proportionately sedate speed, this uncannily realistic journey lasts over two minutes, its only false note the presence of the museum's ceiling and viewing gallery in place of a Berkshire sky and horizon. Another film explains the profusion of model pigsties and allotments in the context of rural poverty and self-reliance, in which pig-killings were staggered to ensure mutually beneficial bartering between neighbours. 'Railway modelling' is ultimately too narrow a term for this extraordinary project, which enlists social and architectural history to create a vessel for the collective memories of an entire community.

If Pendon Parva still sounds a little too sepia-tinted for some, different approaches can be found elsewhere. One of the best showcases is the London Festival of Railway Modelling, held each year in the echoing Victorian halls of Alexandra Palace. Among its regular performers is the Model Railway Club's portable Copenhagen Fields layout, over 300 square feet in extent, which represents a huge chunk of north London in the inter-war years. The chosen scale is 2 mm to the foot (1:152): small enough to allow room for all the cuttings, tunnels and viaducts of this thoroughly drab district in a drab epoch, with a cunning diminution to 1:450 to create the illusion of perspective distance for streets and buildings furthest from the viewer. Other layouts tackle the modern scene in all its aesthetic banality, with big-box retail sheds, multistorey car parks and plenty of scaled-down graffiti for verisimilitude. Accessories to be had from the many specialist stalls catering to modellers' needs include miniature tramps and street drinkers, cast in 4mm scale and ready painted.

Portable or not, layouts of this type require a commitment to slow and patient progress, and usually also a dependence on collaboration and shared decision-making. Construction of model stations and platforms must be co-ordinated with the members who wire the tracks and make the signals work. Purists may even attempt to replicate the block system, so that a large club layout resounds with the tinging of tiny bells, as messages pass wordlessly back and forth between operators who stand a few feet away from one another. This imperative to get the details right also inspires a mission to record things that would otherwise pass away: model railway magazines are full of meticulous scale drawings of buildings, lineside equipment and rolling stock. Pendon is merely an extreme case of how modelling can feed back into a sense of history, as its devotees attempt to create as close a version as possible of what the ordinary civilian past was like.

₪

In most of these activities there is a tension between the broader picture and the tiny details, between knowledge and information. If pure information is your thing, railways certainly offer a hobby in which you will never risk running short. Consider this enticement, in the Lancashire & Yorkshire Railway Society's journal: 'This issue of *LYR Focus* is the first of two [!] volumes which study the development and retrenchment of the mile of track from Rose Grove West Junction to Gannow Junction.' The society's website reports the intention that the journal will 'build up' over the years into a history of the LYR.

Yet it is difficult to see how a series of small-scale magazine articles could ever take the place of a coherent and usable history, of the kind represented by John Marshall's three-volume Lancashire & Yorkshire survey of 1969–72, or the still more impressive three-part history of the Great Central published in 1959–65 by George Dow (1907–87). The career of this remarkable railwayman-scholar encompassed periods as a senior pub-lic relations officer, the direction of policy on posters and carriage pictures, and the management of the Birmingham and Stoke divisions. He was also a co-founder of the Historical Model Railway Society, and the author of other definitive studies ranging from railway heraldry to Midland Railway carriages. Dow thus made, wrote and modelled railway history in a single lifespan; he combined a gift for detail as well as outline, and was himself a latter-day actor in the world he described.

The perception that George Dow's generation had passed, and that the railway landscape was being viewed through ever-smaller pinholes, led to a celebrated controversy in 1993. The occasion was an after-dinner speech at the National Railway Museum by Sir Neil Cossons, then direc-tor of the Science Museum. Notwithstanding his hallowed surroundings, Cossons charged the assembled historians and preservationists for hav-ing allowed their subject to retreat into mere antiquarianism: a harmless hobby of photo-gazing, number-listing, fact-grinding and relic-trading, with about as much social or intellectual value as the keeping of cats. Enthusiasts who missed the chance to take offence in person at the dinner were soon able to read Cossons's restatement of his case in *Steam Railway* magazine: 'Railway history is not highly regarded or even recognised in the broad spectrum of historical studies and there is no obvious advance-ment of knowledge, or interpretation to a wider audience.'

The historical landscape looks a little different two decades on, in part because of the foundation shortly afterwards of the Institute of Rail-way Studies, a postgraduate body set up as a joint venture between the Museum and the University of York. On the other hand, railway publish-ing – the written and pictorial record – remains scattered, undirected and diverse. It is conditioned variously by publishers' sense of what the market wants, the programmes of societies such as that devoted to the Lancashire & Yorkshire (there are many others) and the efforts of any number of indi-viduals. Few write in the expectation of financial reward, even fewer for academic recognition.

Yet Cossons's speech missed a vital point: that this lack of intellectual policing can be a source of strength as well as weakness. When the aca-demically rigorous *Journal of Transport History* turned to railway autobi-ographies in 2002, in a thoughtful article by Tim Strangleman, the verdict was sympathetic rather than dismissive. He noted how often these written lives were embedded in narratives of social existence, both in terms of the interpenetration of family and workplace and in the wider communities of railway towns and districts. Railway authors were also able to convey an acute sense of the challenges and disciplines of skilled work, and the self-conscious differences between skilled trades – engine driving among them – and the unskilled or semi-skilled sectors. Whether or not they wrote out of a sense of political engagement, some were also motivated by a desire to make a stand against oblivion. Ron Spedding, for example, wanted to show that his working world – Shildon Wagon Works in County Durham, where 3,000 worked in the 1950s – was more than 'a collection of buildings occupied and worked by nameless robots'.

₪

This mission to redeem the past culminates with preserved railways, another item on Cossons's charge-sheet at York. He dared to ask the hard question of what it was that preserved railways were actually preserving. Were they truly 'live museums' – repositories for historic objects, displayed and operated in authentic contexts – or had they merely become another sector of the tourist industry, evoking an ill-defined sense of pastness within a well-packaged day out? The highest goal, he suggested, should be 'to preserve and operate a railway to absolutely authentic historical and technical standards, in terms of real estate, locomotives and rolling stock, and methods of operation'.

Few preserved railways have come anywhere near to fulfilling this demand. Nonetheless, they have grown hugely in numbers and diversity since the early 1970s, where we left their story. In 2013 over 9 million passenger journeys were made on them. Among the hundred-plus concerns currently in operation are a few classic branch lines, still with a connection to the national network. Others are isolated lengths that run between stations accessible only by road, or offer only a short ride up and down a length of track from a single base. Some are narrow-gauge lines laid out along old standard-gauge routes, operating as straightforward commercial attractions. Even the most historically minded lines have to make compromises in order to keep going. Visitors expect to find facilities which historic buildings cannot always supply, as the demise of the Keighley & Worth Valley's grim urinal at Oxenhope shows. Wheelchair access is another challenge. Maintenance and repairs that would in times past have been done at distant workshops must now be tackled on the line itself, either in purpose-built sheds (old goods sheds, even if they survive, are not really big enough), or in the open air. The practice of giving track-space to individual owners means that almost every preserved line has sidings chock-full of rolling stock awaiting attention, often in extreme decay. The cumulative effect can resemble that of the yard of an old-fashioned farmer who can't bear to throw anything away.

The process of repair in turn complicates the mission to preserve, as worn-out or decayed parts are endlessly replaced. As a result, any locomotive or vehicle contains less and less historic material after each trip to the workshops. Nor are historic materials and techniques always used, even when modern safety standards have not overtaken them. What was once riveted may now be welded, what was veneered may now be laminated, what was leather may now be vinyl. Those enterprising enough to undertake the resurrection of older, timber-built carriages often end up dismantling any fabric that can be rescued for reassembly, rather as aviation enthusiasts recreate airworthy Spitfires using tangled remains from crash sites and huge quantities of money. On the Bluebell Railway, the body framework of London, Brighton & South Coast third-class carriage no. 949 has been reformed using pieces of Africa utile wood, the original Brazilian mahogany being no longer available. On completion it will join LBSCR first-class carriage no. 661, formerly used as a holiday cottage called Wind Demon at Bracklesham Bay, Sussex (no. 949 was a farm outbuilding in Surrey). The compartments of no. 661 are convincingly plush, with studded upholstery and braided seams, but all this fabric is new. Having lost their wheelbases when sold out of use, both vehicles now run on salvaged post-war underframes.

A more recent movement aims to recreate locomotive types that slipped through the preservationists' net in the 1960s. The new express locomotive completed in 2008, 60163 *Tornado*, represents the lost A1 Pacific class, otherwise consigned to the smelting furnaces in the 1960s. Other lost locomotive types are taking shape with the help of existing spare bits, obtained from dismantling a few of the 213 ex-BR locomotives that were retrieved over many years from a scrap merchant's stock at Barry in South Wales. Old spotters' debates about which engine is really which have been resurrected, as cylinders, frames, boilers and wheel-sets are parted and spliced to achieve the best-looking match. Like the Bluebell's Victorian carriages, these locomotives will be at once old and new, authentic and imitative – specimens of 'living history', as anatomised by

Raphael Samuel in *Theatres of Memory* (1994), who recognised its ability to galvanise mass interest in ways that were inaccessible to academic practice. Visitors who learn about these restorers' compromises are thus more likely to admire than to deplore them.

More broadly, preserved railways are so compelling because they offer a closer relationship between appearance and reality than other kinds of 'living history'. No one actually gets killed, maimed or taken prisoner when Civil War re-enactment societies take to the battlefield; the costumed chambermaids at Hampton Court are not really awaiting the pleasure of an absent queen; no one toils in the mine or has their teeth drilled in the dentist's parlour at the North of England Open-Air Museum at Beamish; but the visitor to a steam railway buys a real ticket at the booking hall, is shepherded by a real guard on to a real train and travels according to a timetable on real track behind a real locomotive and its crew, under the control of signals worked from a real signal box. Playing at trains is a serious game: from boiler repairs to brakes, exacting standards and procedures must be respected, or the Railway Inspectorate will want to know why.

Passengers are themselves co-opted into these disciplines. They are trusted not to lean dangerously far out of the unbarred, drop-down windows, or to open the doors between stations. In return, they are granted freedoms forbidden to visitors to most historic houses: to sprawl on the seats, to manipulate the blinds or curtains, to fiddle with the heating controls and light switches (where applicable), to visit the historic lavatory (ditto), with its archaic paper-holder, sink-plug and cake of hard soap. For most, the journey itself is both real and unreal: real in that it carries them through space and time from A to B and back again, unreal in that the experience is itself the goal of the journey, so that the time spent at station B is nicely taken care of by its café, shop and museum, before the timetabled return to station A.

The status of the railways' labour likewise challenges the usual categories. A survey in 2003 found that 90 per cent of workers on preserved lines were volunteers, but the proportion varies a lot from place to place. A well-established line such as the Severn Valley Railway, with its sixteen-mile route and heavy engineering workshops, can muster the equivalent of seventy-eight full-time staff, with up to 200 volunteers on duty on an especially busy day. By no means are all of them paid-up railway enthusiasts. Women may be drawn in because of their husbands' interests, retired people may find the railway a grateful recipient of their professional knowledge or physical skills. Paid staff may themselves have begun as volunteers.

Like a 1:1 scale model railway club layout, the steam railway has thus become a giant communal enterprise carried on down the generations, a sort of post-industrial folk performance. Too easily dismissed as nostalgic wallowing, each railway in practice brings together a coalition of forward-looking goals and projects, especially where plans exist to extend a route and bring more stations into use. It is a curious outcome for a form of technology that the Victorians experienced, and sometimes denounced, as the wrecker of established social relationships. Even the rites of death have been incorporated: the West Somerset Railway is one of several railways that offer a service by which cremated ashes are tipped into the firebox of a moving train, to be sucked through the boiler tubes and blasted out of the chimney.

Those who never visit will at least encounter preserved railways on film or television. The Bluebell was first in the game, with a short location sequence in *The Innocents* (Jack Clayton again, 1961): a version of Henry James's late-Victorian novella *The Turn of the Screw*, with Deborah Kerr as the haunted governess. The real breakthrough came with the celluloid version of *The Railway Children* in 1970, in which the Keighley & Worth Valley Railway's trains performed to marvellous effect. So many visitors came to the line as a result that an extra passing loop had to be built to increase capacity. This surge was a one-off event, but the film's enduring popularity and family appeal helped to fix the steam-age railway in the popular idea of the past.

A symbiotic relationship is now well established. The host railway receives its fee, and perhaps some helpful publicity. In return, the film company can use ready-made locations with on-site facilities, complete with props. All those enamelled signs, platform scales, milk churns and trolleys piled high with old suitcases, the clichés of many a preserved line, create instant atmosphere when framed in the camera lens. Exclusive occupation for filming is another attraction, as long as the high season is avoided. As viewers of period dramas may dimly be aware, their characters' meetings and tear-stained partings on railway platforms occur suspiciously often in the colder months, amid evocative clouds of steam. The Bluebell does all this especially well, dressing its stations with well-chosen signage, posters and accessories from different periods, late-Victorian to 1950s.

Other railways make use of diesel as well as steam, hosting locomotives and multiple units built under the Modernisation Plan of 1955, or more recently still (there is even a Pacer Preservation Society). These may display the blue-and-yellow corporate colours of the 1960s–80s, or some of the more hectic liveries of the sectors and private operators that followed. The boundary between preserved and non-preserved modern traction has become porous on the privatised railway, as operators hire or buy back locomotives for revenue-earning use on the national network. Types that were banished to preserved lines or museums three decades ago have suddenly reappeared earning a crust on short-term contracts, like the fifty-year-old Deltic express diesel that was summoned to haul freight in Northumberland in 2011. Diesel power in bygone or passably contemporary-looking livery can be a useful resource to the film-maker too. The preservationists who have rescued the Ongar branch, John Betjeman's old fantasy retreat, promote it online as 'Railway for Hire', conveniently close to London, with clips to show it in both late twentieth-century and contemporary roles.

A diesel muttering at the front of the train may disappoint many visitors, but an inclusive policy also helps to draw in younger generations of preservationists whose railway memories begin in the 1970s or later. For a sector that depends on volunteer labour, this is important. Soon no one under retirement age will have adult memories of main-line steam. Most of the volunteers who grin out from the photo pages of 1960s and 1970s railway magazines are young men; most of those working on a typical line today are middle-aged, or older. The need to look to rising generations for future volunteers partly explains the emphasis on education and outreach on some lines, some of which – the Bluebell is one – now incorporate museum displays that would pass the Cossons test of expert interpretation to a wider audience. Many more lines operate children's services of some sort, typically 'Santa Specials' in which a gift from Father Christmas is included with the ticket, or Thomas the Tank Engine trips. If the railway can afford the stinging licence fee to the company that owns the rights to Awdry's creations, a bright blue shunting locomotive may lurk somewhere round the back of the engine shed, with an eager face painted or clipped on to its smokebox door. Main-line engines have too much prestige to be much Awdrified in this fashion, but the boom in all things Harry Potter has generated another invented livery, applied to a Great Western 'Hall' that currently masquerades as *Hogwarts Castle*.

Amid the clamour of competing attractions for children's free time

and parents' money, these initiatives seem unlikely to recruit many youngsters to the ranks. Reversing the relationship between fiction and reality,
so that real trains imitate fictional appearances in children's books, is a
double-edged policy; earlier generations became fascinated by railways
not because they were child-friendly, but because they belonged unmistakably to the adult world. Meanwhile, prices paid for locomotive nameplates
suggest that a crucial demographic peak may already have passed: at the
time of writing, seven of the top ten were clustered in the years 2002–6.
After half a century of growth, the middle decade of the twenty-first century may mark the start of the inexorable decline of railway preservation.

₪

We can end where this book began, with a railway journey. One barrier to
'authentic' operation on preserved lines is their speed limit, generally fixed
at a sedate 25 mph. It is possible to travel much faster behind steam by
booking a ticket for one of the special trains that run on the national network, to a total of several hundred every year. Depending on the engine's
driving wheel diameter, these are permitted to touch up to 90 mph. *Tornado* is in the top group for speed, with wheels that measure a generous
6ft 8in across.

The carriages too are like nothing else now in ordinary service. Varnished wood will greet the eye inside many of them, indicating a construction date in the 1960s or earlier. Dining may be available en route,
for those willing to pay. Dining or not, passengers can expect to be the
centre of attention. A steam-hauled express arrives like a visitant from
another world, a sort of industrial unicorn or dragon. At each stop, magnetised crowds gravitate to the locomotive, milling around with vague
smiles while taking bad photographs in which backs and heads figure
prominently. Bystanders all along the way stop to gaze at the train's passing, or hurry to the lineside to catch a glimpse in time, as if to confirm the
unlikely evidence of their own ears. Others – the clusters of men hunched
over tripods on platform ends and overbridges – may have travelled a long
way just for this encounter. Fields and hedges offer the still stranger sight
of lone photographers perching on their stepladders, awaiting the decisive
moment.

The living world joins in the commotion. At the unfamiliar sounds
of cylinder-beat and steam-whistle, horses and cattle hasten away across

their fields, alarmed but unharmed. Startled flocks of birds rise into the air, passing in and out of the clouds of exhaust for mile after mile. Made vivid again, here is something that transcends Nature, an amazing work of man; what H. G. Wells, writing in 1901, proposed as the best symbol for the century that had just passed, 'a steam engine running upon a railway'.

SOURCES

Some standard works used for this book are cited only occasionally below but have been consulted extensively. These include the indispensable *Oxford Companion to British Railway History* edited by Jack Simmons and Gordon Biddle (1997), the fifteen-volume *Regional History of the Railways of Great Britain* (1960–89), *Britain's Historic Railway Buildings* by Gordon Biddle (2003), Ian Allan's *ABC* guides, the *Oxford Dictionary of National Biography* and the English, Scottish and Welsh series of the *Pevsner Architectural Guides*. For brevity, I have excluded in the following list some references, from novels especially, for which the source is identified within the text. Citations within the notes are abbreviated as indicated below.

'A Tourist': *The Railway Companion, Describing an Excursion along the Liverpool Line ... By A Tourist* (1833)

Ackroyd: Peter Ackroyd, *Charles Dickens* (1990)

Acworth: W. M. Acworth, *The Railways of England* (1900)

Adams: Charles Francis Adams Jnr, *Notes on Railroad Accidents* (1879)

Addyman and Fawcett: John Addyman and Bill Fawcett, *The High Level Bridge and Newcastle Central Station* (1999)

Aitken: Jonathan Aitken, *Margaret Thatcher* (2013)

Alderman: Geoffrey Alderman, *The Railway Interest* (1973)

Alford: B. W. E. Alford, *W.D. & H.O. Wills and the Development of the United Kingdom Tobacco Industry, 1786–1965* (1973)

Allen 1: Cecil J. Allen, *The Great Eastern Railway* (1975)

Allen 2: Cecil J. Allen, *The North Eastern Railway* (1964)

Allen 3: Cecil J. Allen, *Titled Trains of Great Britain* (1946)

Allen and Woolstenholmes: D. Allen and C. J. Woolstenholmes, *A Pictorial Survey of Railway Signalling* (1991)

Altick: Richard Altick, *The Presence of the Present: Topics of the Day in the Victorian Novel* (1991)

Ambler: R. W. Ambler (ed.), *The History and Practice of Britain's Railways: A New Research Agenda* (1999)

Anderson and Fox: Roy Anderson and Gregory Fox, *A Pictorial Record of LMS Architecture* (1981)

Andrews: Cecil Bruyn Andrews, *The Railway Age* (1938)

Arnold: Matthew Arnold, *Complete Prose Works: English Literature and Irish Politics*, ed. R. H. Super (1973)

Arnold and McCartney: A. J. Arnold and S. McCartney, 'Rates of Return, Concentration Levels and Strategic Change in the British Railway Industry, 1830–1912', *JTH* 26/1 (2005), 41–60

Atkinson: J. B. Atkinson, *The West London Joint Railways* (1984)

Atmore: Henry Atmore, 'Railway Interests and the "Rope of Air"', *British Journal for the History of Science* 37/3 (2004), 245–79

Atthill and Nock: Robin Atthill and O. S. Nock, *The Somerset & Dorset Railway* (1970)

ATYR: *All The Year Round*

Ayrton: Michael Ayrton, *Golden Sections* (1957)

Bagwell 1: Philip S. Bagwell, *The Railway Clearing House in the British Economy* (1968)

Bagwell 2: Philip S. Bagwell, *The Railwaymen: The History of the National Union of Railwaymen* (1963)

Bagwell 3: Philip S. Bagwell, 'The Sad State of British Railways: The Rise and Fall of Railtrack, 1992–2002', *JTH* 25/2 (2004), 111–24

Bagwell and Lyth: Philip Bagwell and Peter Lyth, *Transport in Britain: From Canal Lock to Gridlock* (2002)

Bainbridge: Beryl Bainbridge, *English Journey* (1984)

Baker: Anne Baker, *A Question of Honour: The Life of Lieutenant General Valentine Baker Pasha* (1996)

Banks: Chris Banks, *British Railways Locomotives, 1948* (1990)

Barker: Nicolas Barker, *Stanley Morison* (1972)

Barnum: P. T. Barnum, *Life of P. T. Barnum, Written by Himself* (1888)

Barringer: Tim Barringer, *Men at Work: Art and Labour in Victorian Britain* (2005)

Barson: Susie Barson, '"A Little Grit and Ginger"', in Holder and Parissien, 47–73

Baxter: Alan Baxter & Associates, *Great Western Main Line Route Structures Gazetteer* (2012)

BDP: *Birmingham Daily Post*

Bede: Cuthbert Bede, *The Adventures of Mr Verdant Green* (1853–7)

Beebe: Lucius Beebe, *Mansions on Rails: The Folklore of the Private Railway Car* (1959)

Beeching: *The Reshaping of British Railways* (The Beeching Report) (1963)

Beer: Patricia Beer, *Mrs Beer's House* (1968)

Beerbohm 1: Max Beerbohm, *And Even Now* (1924)

Beerbohm 2: Max Beerbohm, *More* (1898)

Beerbohm 3: Max Beerbohm, *Yet Again* (1909)

Belloc: Hilaire Belloc, *On Nothing and Kindred Subjects* (1908)

Bennett: Arnold Bennett, 'The Death of Simon Fuge', in *The Grim Smile of the Five Towns* (1907)

Betjeman 1: John Betjeman, *First and Last Loves* (1952)

Betjeman 2: John Betjeman, *Trains and Buttered Toast: Selected Radio Talks*, ed. Stephen Games (2006)

Bewley: Marian Bewley, *The British Building Industry* (1966)

Bills and Knight: Mark Bills and Vivien Knight, *William Powell Frith* (2006)

Binding: John Binding, *Brunel's Cornish Viaducts* (1993)

Bonavia: Michael R. Bonavia, *A History of the LNER* (1983)

Booth: William Booth, *In Darkest England, and the Way Out* (1890)

'Bourne': 'George Bourne', *Change in the Village* (1955)

Boyes: Grahame Boyes, 'The British Road Haulage Industry since 1954', *Railway and Canal Historical Society Journal* 34 (2002–4), 514–24

Brailsford: Dennis Brailsford, *British Sport: A Social History* (1992)

Bray: Maurice I. Bray, *Railway Tickets, Timetables & Handbills* (1986)

Brendon: Piers Brendon, *Thomas Cook* (1991)

Briggs: Julia Briggs, *A Woman of Passion: The Life of E. Nesbit, 1858–1924* (1987)

Brindle: Steven Brindle, *Paddington Station: Its History and Architecture* (2004)

Brodie et al.: Allan Brodie, Jane Croom and James O. Davies, *English Prisons: An Architectural History* (2002)

Brogden: W. A. Brogden, *Aberdeen: An Illustrated Architectural Guide* (1986)

Brooke 1: David Brooke, 'The "Lawless" Navvy: A Study of the Crime Associated with Railway Building', *JTH* 10/2 (1989), 145–65

Brooke 2: David Brooke, 'The Railway Navvy – A Reassessment', *Construction History* 5 (1989), 35–45

Brown, F. A. S.: F. A. S. Brown, *Nigel Gresley: Locomotive Engineer* (1961)

Brown, F. M.: *The Diary of Ford Madox Brown*, ed. Virginia Surtees (1981)

Bryan: Tim Bryan, *The Great Western Railway: A Celebration* (2010)

Bryson: Bill Bryson, *Notes from a Small Island* (1996)

Buchanan: R. Angus Buchanan, *Brunel: The Life and Times of Isambard Kingdom Brunel* (2002)

Burghclere: *A Great Man's Friendship: Letters of the Duke of Wellington to Mary, Marchioness of Salisbury*, ed. Lady Burghclere (1927)

Burton: Anthony Burton, *The Railway Builders* (1992)

Byatt: A. S. Byatt, *The Children's Book* (2009)

Cannadine 1: David Cannadine, *Aspects of Aristocracy* (1994)

Cannadine 2: David Cannadine, *Class in Britain* (1998)

Carlson: Robert E. Carlson, *The Liverpool and Manchester Railway Project, 1821–1831* (1969)

Carr: Raymond Carr, *English Fox Hunting: A History* (1976)

Carter, I. 1: Ian Carter, *British Railway Enthusiasm* (2008)

Carter, I. 2: Ian Carter, *Railways and Culture in Britain* (2001)

Carter, O.: Oliver Carter, *An Illustrated History of British Railway Hotels* (1990)

Casserley 1: H. C. Casserley, *The Lickey Incline* (1976)

Casserley 2: H. C. Casserley, *Railways Between the Wars* (1971)

Catt: A. R. Catt, *The East Kent Railway* (1970)

Cattell and Falconer: John Cattell and Keith Falconer, *Swindon: The Legacy of a Railway Town* (1995)

Chapman: W. G. Chapman, *Track Topics* (1939)

Chesney: Kellow Chesney, *The Victorian Underworld* (1974)

Clarke: J. M. Clarke, *The Brookwood Necropolis Railway* (2006)

CLC: *The Collected Letters of Thomas and Jane Welsh Carlyle* (1970–)

Clifford: David Clifford, *Isambard Kingdom Brunel: 'The finest work in England': The Construction of the Great Western Railway* (2006)

Clough: Arthur Hugh Clough, *The Bothie of Tober-na-Vuolich* (1848)

Cohen, D.: Deborah Cohen, *Household Gods: The British and their Possessions* (2006)

Cohen, M. N.: Morton N. Cohen, *Lewis Carroll* (1995)

Cole 1: Henry Cole, *Fifty Years of Public Work of Sir Henry Cole, K.C.B.* (1884)

Cole 2: Henry Cole, *Inconsistencies of Men of Genius ...* (1846)

Coleman: Terry Coleman, *The Railway Navvies* (1968)

Comfort: Nicholas Comfort, *The Mid-Suffolk Light Railway* (1997)

Connor: J. E. Connor, *Liverpool Street to Chingford* (2002)

Cooper: B. K. Cooper, *British Rail Handbook* (1981)

Davies: John Davies, *A History of Wales* (1994)

Davis: D. J. Davis (ed.), *Encyclopaedia of Cremation* (2005)

Day-Lewis: Sean Day-Lewis, *Bulleid: Last Giant of Steam* (1964)

Dendy Marshall: C. F. Dendy Marshall, *A History of the Southern Railway*, rev. R. W. Kidner (1963)

Derbyshire: Nick Derbyshire, 'The Liverpool Street Station Story', in Peter Burman and Michael Stratton (eds), *Conserving the Railway Heritage* (1997), 175–85

Dickens Jnr: Charles Dickens, Jnr, 'The City of Honest Imposture', *ATYR* 8 Apr. 1871

Dickens, C.: Charles Dickens, *American Notes for General Circulation* (1842; Lowell edn, 1883)

Dickens, M.: Mamie Dickens, *The World's Workers: Charles Dickens* (1885)

Dickinson, P. 1: Peter Dickinson, *Lord Berners* (2008)

Dickinson, P. 2: Peter Dickinson, *Still Nodding: A History of the Class 142* (2010)

Dickinson, W. E.: W. Elgar Dickinson, *A Friend in Steam* (2007)

DN: *Daily News*

Dolby: George Dolby, *Charles Dickens as I Knew Him* (1885)

Donaghy: Thomas J. Donaghy, *Liverpool and Manchester Railway Operations* (1972)

Dorsey: E. B. Dorsey, *English and American Railroads Compared* (1887)

Dow: George Dow, *Great Central* (1959–65)

Doyle: Richard Doyle, *Richard Doyle's Journal*, ed. Christopher Wheeler (1980)

Dyment: Clifford Dyment, *The Railway Game* (1963)

Edelstein: Teri J. Edelstein (ed.), *Art For All: British Posters for Transport* (2010)

Edgar and Sinton: Stuart Edgar and John M. Sinton, *The Solway Junction Railway* (1990)

Eley: Harold W. Eley, *Advertising Media* (1932)

Ellenborough: Lord Ellenborough, *A Political Diary*, ed. Lord Colchester (1881)

Elliott: Blanche B. Elliott, *A History of English Advertising* (1962)

Ellis, C.: Chris Ellis, *The Hornby Book of Model Railways* (2008)

Ellis, C. H. 1: C. Hamilton Ellis, *The Beauty of Old Trains* (1952)

Ellis, C. H. 2: C. Hamilton Ellis, *The London, Brighton & South Coast Railway* (1960)

Ellis, C. H. 3: C. Hamilton Ellis, *The Lore of Steam* (1984)

Ellis, C. H. 4: C. Hamilton Ellis, *The Midland Railway* (1974)

Ellis, C. H. 5: C. Hamilton Ellis, *Railway Carriages in the British Isles* (1965)

Ellis, C. H. 6: C. Hamilton Ellis, *The Royal Trains* (1975)

Ellis, C. H. 7: C. Hamilton Ellis, *The Trains We Loved* (1971)

Ellis and Morse: Chris Ellis and Greg Morse, *Steaming Through Britain: A History of the Nation's Railways* (2010)

Ellman: Richard Ellman, *Oscar Wilde* (1988)

Essery: Bob Essery, *Railway Signalling and Track Plans* (2007)

Fairman: J. R. Fairman, *Making Tracks* (1988)

Faith: Nicholas Faith, *The World the Railways Made* (1990)

Faulkner: J. N. Faulkner, *Rail Centres: Clapham Junction* (1991)

Fawcett: Bill Fawcett, *George Townsend Andrews of York, 'The Railway Architect'* (2011)

Fellows: Reginald B. Fellows, *Railways to Cambridge* (1948)

Ferneyhough: Frank Ferneyhough, *Liverpool & Manchester Railway* (1980)

Ferrey: Benjamin Ferrey, *Recollections of A. W. N. Pugin* (1861)

Fielding, H.: Helen Fielding, *Bridget Jones's Diary* (1996)

Fielding, K. J.: K. J. Fielding (ed.), *The Speeches of Charles Dickens* (1988)

Fitzgerald: R. S. Fitzgerald, *Liverpool Road Station, Manchester* (1980)

Flanders: Judith Flanders, *Consuming Passions: Leisure and Pleasure in Victorian Britain* (2006)

Ford: Ford Madox Ford, *Memories and Impressions*, ed. M. Killigrew (1979)

Forman: Charles Forman, *Industrial Town: Self-portrait of St Helens in the 1920s* (1978)

Forster: John Forster, *The Life of Charles Dickens* (1875)

Foster: Roy Foster, *Modern Ireland* (1988)

Franks: D. L. Franks, 'Earl Fitzwilliam's Private Railway Station', *Forward: Journal of the Great Central Railway Society* 25 (1980)

Freeman 1: Michael Freeman, *Railways and the Victorian Imagination* (1999)

Freeman 2: Michael Freeman, *Victorians and the Prehistoric* (2004)

Frith: W. P. Frith, *John Leech: His Life and Work* (1891)

Garfield 1: Simon Garfield, *The Last Journey of William Huskisson* (2002)

Garfield 2: Simon Garfield (ed.), *Our Hidden Lives: The Remarkable Diaries of Post-war Britain* (2004)

Garratt, C.: Colin Garratt, *The Last Days of British Steam Railways* (1985)

Garratt, P.: Peter Garratt, *Victorian Empiricism: Self, Knowledge and Reality in Ruskin, Bain, Lewes* (2010)

Gash: Norman Gash, *Robert Surtees and Early Victorian Society* (1993)

Gasson: Harold Gasson, *Firing Days: Reminiscences of a Great Western Fireman* (1973)

GD: *The Gladstone Diaries*, ed. M. R. D. Foot and H. C. G. Matthew (1968–90)

Gerin: Winifred Gerin, *Branwell Brontë* (1961)

Gill: Eric Gill, *Autobiography* (1940)

Girouard: Mark Girouard, *Victorian Pubs* (1975)

Glancey: Jonathan Glancey, *John Betjeman on Trains* (2006)

Gleig: G. R. Gleig: *The Life of Arthur, Duke of Wellington* (1889)

Gloag: John Gloag, *Victorian Comfort* (1961)

Gordon: W. J. Gordon, *Our Home Railways* (1910)

Gourvish 1: T. R. Gourvish, *British Rail, 1974–97* (2002)

Gourvish 2: T. R. Gourvish, *British Railways, 1948–73* (1986)

Gourvish 3: T. R. Gourvish, *Mark Huish and the London & North Western Railway* (1972)

Gourvish and O'Day: T. R. Gourvish and Alan O'Day (eds), *Later Victorian Britain* (1988)

Granville: A. B. Granville, *Spas of England* (1841)

Green: Oliver Green, *Underground Art* (1990)

Gregory: Adrian Gregory, 'To the Jerusalem Express: Wartime Commuters and Anti-Semitism', in Matthew Beaumont and Michael Freeman (eds), *The Railway and Modernity: Time, Space and the Machine Ensemble* (2007), 177–90

Griffin: Emma Griffin, *Blood Sport* (2007)

Griffiths: Major Arthur Griffiths, *Mysteries of Police and Crime* (1901)

Grinling: Charles H. Grinling, *History of the Great Northern Railway* (1903)

Grundy: Francis Henry Grundy, *Pictures of the Past* (1879)

Guise and Brook: Barry Guise and Pam Brook, *The Midland Hotel: Morecambe's White Hope* (2007)

Hardy: R. H. N. Hardy, *Beeching: Champion of the Railway?* (1989)

Hare: Augustus Hare, *The Story of My Life* (1896)

Haresnape 1: Brian Haresnape, *British Rail, 1948–1983: A Journey by Design* (1983)

Haresnape 2: Brian Haresnape, *Design for Steam, 1830–1960* (1981)

Harrington 1: Ralph Harrington, 'The Railway Accident: Trains, Trauma and Technological Crisis in Nineteenth-century Britain', 1999 (www.york.ac.uk/inst/irs/irshome/papers/rlyacc.htm)

Harrington 2: Ralph Harrington, 'The Railway Journey and the Neuroses of Modernity', in Richard Wrigley and George Revill (eds), *Pathologies of Travel* (2000)

Harris, J.: Jose Harris, *Private Lives, Public Spirit: Britain, 1870–1914* (1993)

Harris, K.: Ken Harris, *Jane's World Railways, 2008–2009*

Harris, M. 1: Michael Harris, *Preserved Railway Coaches* (1976)

Harris, M. 2: Michael Harris, 'Rolling Stock, the Railway User, and Competition', in A. K. B. Evans and J. V. Gough (eds), *The Impact of the Railway on Society in Britain* (2003)

Harris, S. A.: S. A. Harris, 'Introduction of Oxford Ragwort, *Senecio squalidus* L. (Asteraceae) to the United Kingdom', *Watsonia* 24 (2002), 31–43

Hart: Gwen Hart, *A History of Cheltenham* (1965)

Hartley: K. E. Hartley, *The Easingwold Railway* (1970)

Haviland: Alfred Haviland, *'Hurried to Death'* (1868)

Hawker: H. E. Hawker, *Notes of My Life* (1919)

Hawkins and Reeve: Chris Hawkins and George Reeve, *Southern Nouveau: An Essay in Concrete* (1987)

Haworth: Victoria Haworth, *Robert Stephenson* (2004)

Hawthorne: Nathaniel Hawthorne, *The English Notebooks*, ed. R. Stewart (1962)

Head: Sir F. B. Head, *Stokers and Pokers: Or, the London and North-Western Railway* (1850)

Headley and Meulenkamp: Gwyn Headley and Wim Meulenkamp, *Follies* (1990)

Hebron: Chris de Winter Hebron, *Dining at Speed* (2004)

Hendry: Dr R. Preston Hendry and R. Powell Hendry, *The North Western at Work* (1990)

Hewison: Christian H. Hewison, *From Shedmaster to the Railway Inspectorate* (1981)

Hill: T. W. Hill, 'The Staplehurst Railway Accident', *The Dickensian* 38 (1942), 147–52

Hilton: Tim Hilton, *John Ruskin* (2002)

Hoare: Philip Hoare, *England's Lost Eden* (2005)

Holder and Parissien: Julian Holder and Steven Parissien (eds), *The Architecture of British Transport in the Twentieth Century* (2004)

Holland, H.: Henry Holland, *Recollections of Past Life* (1872)

Holland, J.: Julian Holland (ed.), *Steam Railway: The Glorious Years* (1996)

Holmes: David Holmes, *Station Master's Reflections* (1992)

Holroyd: Michael Holroyd, *A Strange Eventful History* (2008)

Hoole: K. Hoole, *The North Eastern Electrics* (1961)

Howse: Derek Howse, *Greenwich Time and the Longitude* (1997)

Huggins: Mike Huggins, *Horseracing and the British, 1919–1939* (2003)

Huggins and Tolson: Mike Huggins and John Tolson, 'The Railways and Sport in Victorian Britain: A Critical Reassessment', *JTH* 22/2 (2001), 99–115

Hunt and Krause: John Hunt and Ian Krause, *On and Off the Beaten Track* (1976)

Hunter and Thorne: Michael Hunter and Robert Thorne, *Change at King's Cross* (1990)

Hurren: Elizabeth Hurren, *Dying for Victorian Medicine: English Anatomy and its Trade in the Dead Poor* (2012)

HW: *Household Words*

ILN: *Illustrated London News*

Itkowitz: David Itkowitz, *Peculiar Privilege: A Social History of English Foxhunting* (1977)

Jack: Ian Jack, *The Crash that Stopped Britain* (2001)

Jackson, A. 1: Alan A. Jackson, *London's Metropolitan Railway* (1986)

Jackson, A. 2: Alan A. Jackson, *London's Termini* (1972)

Jackson, D.: Dick Jackson, *Great North Memories: The LNER Era* (1993)

Jeaffreson and Pole: John Cordy Jeaffreson and William Pole, *The Life of Robert Stephenson F.R.S.* (1864)

Jennings: Paul Jennings, *Just A Few Lines* (1969)

Jerrold: Clare Jerrold, *The Married Life of Queen Victoria* (1913)

Joby: R. S. Joby, *The Railwaymen* (1984)

Johnson and Long: John Johnson and Robert A. Long, *British Railways Engineering, 1948–80* (1981)

Jones, E.: Edgar Jones, *True and Fair: A History of Price Waterhouse* (1995)

Jones, W.: William Jones, 'The Cardiff Valleys Division', *Railway World Annual, 1976* (1976), 36–55

JTH: Journal of Transport History

Keiller: Patrick Keiller, 'Phantom Rides: The Railway and Early Film', in Matthew Beaumont and Michael Freeman (eds), *The Railway and Modernity: Time, Space and the Machine Ensemble* (2007), 69–84

Kellett 1: John Kellett, *Railways and Victorian Cities* (1969)

Kellett 2: John Kellett, 'Writing on Victorian Railways: An Essay in Nostalgia', *Victorian Studies* 13/1 (1969), 90–96

Kennedy and Treuherz: Ian Kennedy and Julian Treuherz, *The Railway: Art in the Age of Steam* (2008)

Kidner 1: R. W. Kidner, *The Dartford Loop Line* (1966)

Kidner 2: R. W. Kidner, *The Railways of Purbeck* (1973)

Kilvert: *Kilvert's Diary*, ed. William Plomer (1969)

Kingsford: P. W. Kingsford, *Victorian Railwaymen* (1970)

Kirby: M. W. Kirby, 'Railway Development and the Role of the State', in Ambler, 21–35

Lang: Cecil Y. Lang (ed.), *The Letters of Matthew Arnold* (1997–8)

Laqueur: Thomas Walter Laqueur, *Religion and Respectability: Sunday Schools and Working Class Culture, 1780–1850* (1976)

Lardner: Dionysus Lardner, *Railway Economy* (1850)

Legg: Stuart Legg (ed.), *The Railway Book* (1952)

Leigh 1: Chris Leigh, *GWR Country Stations* (1981)

Leigh 2: Chris Leigh, *A Railway Modeller's Picture Library* (1995)

Lewis: Jeremy Lewis, *Penguin Special: The Life and Times of Allen Lane* (2005)

Lewis and Gagg: P. R. Lewis and Colin Gagg, 'Aesthetics versus Function: The Fall of the Dee Bridge', *Interdisciplinary Science Reviews* 29/2 (2004), 177–91

Lloyd and Insall: David Lloyd and Donald Insall, *Railway Station Architecture* (1967)

Lomax: Eric Lomax, *The Railway Man* (1995)

Mabey 1: Richard Mabey, *Flora Britannica* (1996)

Mabey 2: Richard Mabey, *A Good Parcel of English Soil* (2013)

MacDermot: E. T. MacDermot, *History of the Great Western Railway* (1927–31)

Macfarlane: Charles Macfarlane, *Reminiscences of a Literary Life* (1917)

Mackenzie: Charles Mackenzie, *Itinerary of the Great Northern Railway* (1852)

Maggs 1: Colin Maggs, *Highbridge in its Heyday* (1973)

Maggs 2: Colin Maggs, *The Weston, Clevedon and Portishead Railway* (1964)

Mander: John Mander, *Collecting Railwayana* (1988)

Mann: F. A. W. Mann, *Railway Bridge Construction* (1972)

Manser: Jose Manser, *Hugh Casson: A Biography* (2000)

Marshall: John Marshall, *The Lancashire & Yorkshire Railway* (1969–72)

Matus: Jill L. Matus, 'Trauma, Memory and Railway Disaster: The Dickensian Connection', *Victorian Studies* 43 (2001), 413–37

Maxwell: Sir Herbert Maxwell, *Life and Times of the Right Honourable William Henry Smith M.P.* (1893)

McCulloch: J. R. McCulloch, *Dictionary of Commerce* (1834)

McKean: Charles McKean, *Battle for the North: The Tay and Forth Bridges and the 19th-Century Railway Wars* (2006)

McKenna: Frank McKenna, *A Glossary of Railwaymen's Talk* (1970)

McKitterick: David McKitterick, *A History of Cambridge University Press* (1992–8)

McNeil: Ian McNeil, *Hydraulic Power* (1972)

Meacham: Standish Meacham, *A Life Apart: The English Working Class, 1890–1914* (1977)

Meeks: Carroll L. V. Meeks, *The Railroad Station* (1956)

Melville: Jennifer Melville, *Robert Brough ARSA* (1995)

Milne and Laing: Alistair M. Milne and Austen Laing, *The Obligation to Carry* (1956)

Minnis: John Minnis, *Britain's Lost Railways* (2011)

Moody: G. T. Moody, *Southern Electric* (1968)

Moran 1: Joe Moran, *On Roads* (2009)

Moran 2: Joe Moran, *Queuing for Beginners* (2007)

Morgan: Brian Morgan (ed.), *The Railway-Lover's Companion* (1963)

Morley: John Morley, *The Life of William Ewart Gladstone* (1903)

Morrison and Minnis: Kathryn A. Morrison and John Minnis, *Carscapes* (2012)

MP: *Morning Post*

MPRB: *Mr Punch's Railway Book* (n.d.)

MR: *Modern Railways*

Murray: Nicholas Murray, *A Life of Matthew Arnold* (1996)

Nairn and Pevsner: Ian Nairn and Nikolaus Pevsner, *The Buildings of England: Sussex* (1965)

Nevett: T. R. Nevett, *Advertising in Britain: A History* (1982)

Newby: Howard Newby, 'Antiquarianism or Analysis? The Future of Railway History', in Ambler, 1–5

Newton: Fiona Newton, 'Off The Rails', *Context* 124 (May 2012)

Nock: O. S. Nock, *The Great Northern Railway* (1958)

Norman: Oscar E. Norman, *The Romance of the Gas Industry* (1922)

Norton: Greg Norton, *Landscapes under the Luggage Rack* (2001)

O'Dea: William T. O'Dea, *The Social History of Lighting* (1958)

O'Gorman: Francis O'Gorman (ed.), *The Cambridge Companion to Victorian Culture* (2010)

Oates: G. Oates, *The Axholme Joint Railway* (1961)

Olmsted: F. L. Olmsted, *Walks and Talks of an American Farmer in England* (1852)

Paar and Grey: Henry Paar and Adrian Grey, *The Life and Times of the Great Eastern Railway* (1991)

Palmer and Buckland: Beth Palmer and Adeline Buckland (eds), *A Return to the Common Reader: Print Culture and the Novel, 1850–1900* (2011)

Parissien: Steven Parissien, *Station to Station* (1997)

Parris 1: Henry Parris, *Government and Railways* (1965)

Parris 2: Henry Parris, 'Pasley's Diary: A Neglected Source of Railway History', *JTH* 6 (1963), 14–23

Peacock: Thomas B. Peacock, *Great Western Suburban Services* (1970)

Pearson: Geoffrey Pearson, *Hooligan: A History of Respectable Fears* (1983)

Pendleton: John Pendleton, *Our Railways* (1894)

Perkin: Harold Perkin, *The Age of the Railway* (1970)

Perryman: A. C. Perryman, *Life at Brighton Loco Works* (1972)

Pettigrew: Terence Pettigrew, *Trevor Howard: A Personal Biography* (2001)

Pevsner et al.: Nikolaus Pevsner, John Harris and Nicholas Antram, *The Buildings of England: Lincolnshire* (1989)

PIP: *Penny Illustrated Paper*

PMG: *Pall Mall Gazette*

Powers 1: Alan Powers, 'Conservation: The Heroic Period', *Twentieth Century Architecture* 7 (2004), 9–18

Powers 2: Alan Powers, *Front Cover* (2001)

Priestley: J. B. Priestley, *English Journey* (1934)

Pritchard: Arthur J. Pritchard, *Historical Notes on the Railways of South East Monmouthshire* (1962)

Pryor: Francis Pryor, *The Making of the British Landscape* (2010)

Quick: M. E. Quick, *The Wrong Sort of Fish Oil: The Trials, Tribulations (and Triumphs) of the Early Railway Passenger* (2012)

Quinn: Tom Quinn, *Tales of the Old Railwaymen* (1998)

Rackham: Oliver Rackham, *Trees and Woodland in the British Landscape* (2001)

Ransom: P. J. G. Ransom, *The Victorian Railway and How it Evolved* (1990)

Ransome-Wallis: Patrick Ransome-Wallis, *Men of the Footplate* (1954)

Rappaport: Helen Rappaport, *Queen Victoria: A Biographical Companion* (2003)

Raven: James Raven, *The Business of Books* (2007)

Reading: S. J. Reading, *The Derwent Valley Light Railway* (1967)

Redford and Chaloner: Arthur Redford and W. H. Chaloner (eds), *Labour Migration in England, 1800–1850* (1976)

Reynolds: Michael Reynolds, *Engine-Driving Life* (1881)

RHR: *The Regional History of the Railways of Great Britain* (1960–89)

Richards: J. M. Richards, *Memoirs of an Unjust Fella* (1980)

Richards and Mackenzie: Jeffrey Richards and John M. Mackenzie, *The Railway Station: A Social History* (1986)

Richter: Amy G. Richter, *Home on the Rails: Women, the Railroad, and the Rise of Public Domesticity* (2005)

Riley: R. C. Riley, *Great Western Album* (1966)

RM: *Railway Magazine*

RMM: *Railway Magazine Miscellany, 1897–1919*, ed. Henry Maxwell (1958)

Robbins 1: Michael Robbins, 'The Missing Doctor: An "If" of Victorian History', *Journal of the Royal Society of Medicine* 90 (Mar. 1997), 163–5

Robbins 2: Michael Robbins, *The North London Railway* (1953)

Robbins 3: Michael Robbins, *Points and Signals: A Railway Historian at Work* (1967)

Robertson: Kevin Robertson, *Britain's Railways in Wartime* (2008)

Robinson: Henry Crabb Robinson, *Diary, Reminiscences and Correspondence* (1869)

Roden: Andrew Roden, *Great Western Railway: A History*

Rolt 1: L. T. C. Rolt, *George and Robert Stephenson: The Railway Revolution* (1978)

Rolt 2: L. T. C. Rolt, *Isambard Kingdom Brunel* (1970)

Rolt 3: L. T. C. Rolt, *Railway Adventure* (1962)

Rolt 4: L. T. C. Rolt, *Red for Danger* (1966)

Rooney and Pye: David Rooney and James Pye, '"Greenwich Observatory Time for the public benefit": Standard Time and Victorian Networks of Regulation', *British Journal for the History of Science* 42/1 (152), Mar. 2009, 5–30

Ross: David Ross, *The Highland Railway* (2005)

Rowbotham: Sheila Rowbotham, *Edward Carpenter* (2008)

RTHB: [Edward Shelton], *The Railway Traveller's Handy Book* (1862; ed. Jack Simmons, 1971)

Rush and Price: R. W. Rush and M. Price, *The Garstang & Knott End Railway* (1964)

Ruskin 1: John Ruskin, *Fors Clavigera* (1871)

Ruskin 2: John Ruskin, *Modern Painters* (1856)

Ruskin 3: John Ruskin, *The Seven Lamps of Architecture* (1849)

Ruskin 4: John Ruskin, *The Stones of Venice* (1853)

Saint: Andrew Saint, *Architect and Engineer* (2007)

Sala: G. A. Sala, *Twice Around the Clock* (1859)

Schivelbusch: Wolfgang Schivelbusch, *The Railway Journey: Trains and Travel in the 19th Century* (1979)

Scott, G. G.: George Gilbert Scott, *Personal and Professional Recollections*, ed. Gavin Stamp (1995)

Scott, J. W. R.: J. W. Robertson Scott: *The Day before Yesterday* (1951)

Sellwood and Sellwood: Arthur and Mary Sellwood, *The Victorian Railway Murders* (1979)

Semmens: Peter Semmens, *A History of the Great Western Railway* (1985)

Shannon: Richard Shannon, *Gladstone: God and Politics* (2007)

Sidney: Samuel Sidney, *Rides on Railways* (1851)

Signalling Study Group: Signalling Study Group, *The Signal Box: A Pictorial History* (1986)

Simmons 1: Jack Simmons, *The Railway in England and Wales, 1830–1914* (1978)

Simmons 2: Jack Simmons, *The Railway in Town and Country, 1830–1914* (1986)

Simmons 3: Jack Simmons, 'Railways, Hotels and Tourism in Great Britain, 1839–1914', *Journal of Contemporary History* 19 (1984)

Simmons 4: Jack Simmons, *St Pancras Station*, rev. Robert Thorne (2012)

Simmons 5: Jack Simmons, *The Victorian Railway* (1991)

Simmons and Biddle: Jack Simmons and Gordon Biddle (eds), *Oxford Companion to British Railway History* (1997)

Sitwell: Osbert Sitwell, *Left Hand Right Hand!* (1947)

Skempton: A. W. Skempton, 'Embankments and Cuttings on the Early Railways', *Construction History* 11 (1995), 33–49

Smiles 1: Samuel Smiles, *George Moore, Merchant and Philanthropist* (1878)

Smiles 2: Samuel Smiles, *Lives of the Engineers: George and Robert Stephenson* (1879)

Smith, D. N.: David Norman Smith, *The Railway and its Passengers* (1988)

Smith, G. R.: G. Royde Smith, *The History of Bradshaw* (1939)

Smith, M.: Martin Smith, *British Railway Bridges and Viaducts* (1994)

Smithers: Mark Smithers, *Sir Arthur Heywood and the Fifteen Inch Gauge Railway* (1995)

Spedding: Ron Spedding, *Shildon Wagon Works: A Working Man's Life* (1988)

Spence: Jeoffry Spence, *Victorian and Edwardian Railways from Old Photographs* (1975)

Spencer: Colin Spencer, *British Food: An Extraordinary Thousand Years of History* (2002)

Spender: Stephen Spender (ed.), *W. H. Auden: A Tribute by his Friends* (1975)

Spiers: R. G. Spiers, *Spiers and Pond* (2008)

Stamp 1: Gavin Stamp, 'Early Twentieth-Century Stations', in Holder and Parissien, 23–46

Stamp 2: Gavin Stamp, 'What Did We Do for the Victorians?', in Rosemary Hill, Colin Cunningham and Aileen Reed (eds), *Victorians Revalued* (2010), 7–26

Stein: M. A. Stein, 'Priestley v. Fowler (1837) and the Emerging Tort of Negligence', *Boston College Law Review* 44.3.3 (2003)

Storey: Graham Storey (ed.), *The Letters of Charles Dickens*, xi (1999)

Stowe: Harriet Beecher Stowe, *Sunny Memories of Foreign Lands* (1854)

Strangleman: Tim Strangleman, 'Constructing the Past: Railway History from Below or a Study in Nostalgia', *JTH* 23/2 (2002), 147–58

Stretton: John Stretton, *Thirty Years of Trainspotting* (1990)

Sturgis: Matthew Sturgis, *Aubrey Beardsley* (1998)

Surtees 1: R. S. Surtees, *Ask Mamma* (1858)

Surtees 2: R. S. Surtees, *Handley Cross* (1843)

Surtees 3: R. S. Surtees, 'Hints to Railway Travellers and Country Visitors to London', 1851, in *Town and Country Papers*, ed. E. D. Cuming (1929)

Surtees 4: R. S. Surtees, *Plain or Ringlets* (1860)

Sutherland: John Sutherland, *The Longman Companion to Victorian Fiction* (2009)

Taine: Hippolyte Taine, *Taine's Notes on England*, tr. Edward Hyams (1959)

Taylor, J. B.: Jenny Bourn Taylor, introduction to *Lady Audley's Secret*, Penguin edn (1998)

Taylor, M.: Maxwell Taylor, *Going by Train* (1962)

Taylor, S.: Sheila Taylor (ed.), *The Moving Metropolis* (2001)

Thomas, E.: Edward Thomas, *The Annotated Collected Poems*, ed. Edna Longley (2008)

Thomas, J. 1: John Thomas, *The North British Railway* (1969–75)

Thomas, J. 2: John Thomas, *The West Highland Railway* (1970)

Thomas, R. H. G. 1: R. H. G. Thomas, *The Liverpool & Manchester Railway* (1980)

Thomas, R. H. G. 2: R. H. G. Thomas, *London's First Railway: The London & Greenwich* (1986)

Thompson 1: F. M. L. Thompson, *Chartered Surveyors: The Growth of a Profession* (1968)

Thompson 2: F. M. L. Thompson, *English Landed Society in the Nineteenth Century* (1963)

Thompson 3: F. M. L. Thompson, 'Nineteenth-century Horse Sense', *Economic History Review* series 2, 29 (1976), 60–81

Thornewell: W. T. Thornewell, 'Tunnels – The Inside Story', *Railway World Annual, 1976*, 112–17

Thorpe: D. R. Thorpe, *Supermac: The Life of Harold Macmillan* (2011)

Timbs: John Timbs, *Wellingtoniana; Anecdotes, Maxims, and Characteristics of the Duke of Wellington* (1852)

Tomalin: Claire Tomalin, *The Invisible Woman: The Story of Nelly Ternan and Charles Dickens* (1990)

Tomlinson: W. W. Tomlinson, *The North Eastern Railway* (1915)

Trollope: Anthony Trollope, *North America* (1862)

Tuplin: W. A. Tuplin, *British Steam Since 1900* (1971)

Turner: John Howard Turner, *The London, Brighton and South Coast Railway*, ii (1978)

Turnock: David Turnock, *Railways in the British Isles: Landscape, Land Use and Society* (1990)

Tyrrell: S. J. Tyrrell, *A Countryman's Tale* (1973)

Unwin: Philip Unwin, *Travelling by Train in the Edwardian Age* (1979)

Vallance: H. A. Vallance, *The Highland Railway*, rev. C. R. Clinker (1971)

Vamplew: Wray Vamplew, *The Turf: A Social and Economic History of Horse Racing* (1976)

Vaughan 1: Adrian Vaughan, *Grub, Water and Relief: Tales of the Great Western, 1835–1892* (1985)

Vaughan 2: Adrian Vaughan, *Isambard Kingdom Brunel: Engineering Knight Errant* (1991)

Vaughan 3: Adrian Vaughan, *A Pictorial Record of Great Western Architecture* (1977)

Vaughan 4: Adrian Vaughan, *Signalman's Morning* with *Signalman's Twilight* (1984)

VCH: Victoria County Histories

Votolato: Gregory Votolato, *Transport Design: A Travel History* (2007)

Walker: Charles Walker, *Thomas Brassey: Railway Builder* (1969)

Wallace: Alfred Russel Wallace, *My Life* (1908)

'Walter': 'Walter', *My Secret Life* (1888)

Walton: John K. Walton, 'Power, Speed and Glamour: The Naming of Express Steam Locomotives in Inter-war Britain', *JTH* 26/2 (2005), 1–19

Ward: Colin Ward (ed.), *Vandalism* (1973)

Waugh: Arthur Waugh, *One Man's Road* (1931)

Way: R. Barnard Way, *Mixed Traffic* (1937)

Weighell: Sidney Weighell, *A Hundred Years of Railway Weighells* (1984)

Wellington: Gerald, Duke of Wellington, *Wellington and his Friends* (1965)

Wells: H. G. Wells, *Anticipations* (1901)

Western: R. G. Western, *The Lowgill Branch* (1971)

Whitehouse and St John Thomas: Patrick Whitehouse and David St John Thomas, *The Great Western Railway* (1984)

Whittaker: Nicholas Whittaker, *Platform Souls: The Trainspotter as Twentieth-Century Hero* (1995)

Whittle: G. Whittle, *The Railways of Consett and North-East Durham* (1971)

Wikeley and Middleton: Nigel Wikeley and John Middleton, *Railway Stations: Southern Region* (1971)

Willans: Geoffrey Willans, *Molesworth*, Penguin edn (1999)

Willes: Margaret Willes, *Reading Matters: Five Centuries of Discovering Books* (2008)

Williams 1: F. S. Williams, *The Midland Railway: Its Rise and Progress* (1876)

Williams 2: F. S. Williams, *Our Iron Roads* (1883)

Williamson: J. W. Williamson, *A British Railway behind the Scenes* (1933)

Wilson, A. N. 1: A. N. Wilson, *Betjeman* (2006)

Wilson, A. N. 2: A. N. Wilson, *The Victorians* (2002)

Wilson, C.: Charles Wilson, *First With The News: The History of W. H. Smith* (1985)

Wolmar 1: Christian Wolmar, *Blood, Iron and Gold: How Railways Transformed the World* (2009)

Wolmar 2: Christian Wolmar, *Fire and Steam: A New History of the Railways in Britain* (2007)

Wolmar 3: Christian Wolmar, *The Subterranean Railway* (2004)

Wooler: Neil Wooler, *Dinner in the Diner: The History of Railway Catering* (1987)

Worsley: Giles Worsley, *The British Stable* (2004)

Wright: A. Wright, *The North Sunderland Railway* (1988)

NOTES

Introduction

p. 4 *'crossing the Border'*: W. H. Auden, 'Night Mail' (1936).

Chapter 1: The Time of the Railways

p. 9 *More miles of canals*: Faith, 16.

p. 9 Railway Times: Nock, 2.

p. 11 *In certain towns*: Robbins 3, 211.

p. 12 *Matthew Arnold*: Murray, 123.

p. 12 *Wordsworth composed*: Morley, i, 269n.

p. 13 *Dr Arnold*: Simmons 5, 364.

p. 13 *'come down today'*; *'by the new rail'*: Lang, ii, 89; 217.

p. 15 *'perfectly legitimate words'*: 'Deprivations of English', *ATYR*, 17 Jan. 1863.

p. 15 *Bradshaw*: Smith, G. R.; *RM*, Oct. 2001, 38–9.

p. 16 *'B is the Bradshaw'*: *MPRB*, 38.

p. 16 *'Do not buy a Bradshaw'*: Surtees 3, 234.

p. 16 Guida di Bragia: Cohen, M. N., 11.

p. 17 *'Thirty years ago'*: *The Times*, 12 Jan. 1850.

p. 17 *Coggeshall*: Paar and Grey, 42.

p. 17 *A story from Devon*: Betjeman 2, 37.

p. 17 *Richard Altick*: Altick, 192.

p. 18 *the railway kept to standard time*: Howse, 92–110.

p. 20 *Royal Observatory at Greenwich*: Rooney and Pye.

p. 21 *'like a little Bradshaw'*: 'An Unsettled Neighbourhood', *HW*, 11 Nov. 1854.

p. 21 *Sunday fish trains*: Thomas, J. 2, 107.

p. 21 *Thackeray*: *Cornhill Magazine*, Oct. 1860, 504.

p. 22 *Leicester & Swannington Railway, Edmondson*: Bray, 16, 21–3.

p. 23 *Sheffield, Ashton-under-Lyne & Manchester*: Dow, i, 34.

p. 24 *F. S. Williams*: Bray, 24.

p. 24 *stock of the London, Midland & Scottish*: Williamson, 113.

p. 24 *450,000 tickets every day*: Robertson, 104.

p. 24 *tearing of return tickets in half*: RW, Dec. 1969, 517–19.

Chapter 2: Seating, Lighting, Heating, Eating

p. 27–8 *black-and-yellow livery; these half-lunette windows; just 4ft 6in*: Ellis, C. H. 1, 22–3; 14; 17.

p. 29 *'padding it, and petting it'*: Head, 107.

p. 29 *Rachel Whinyates*: Hart, 234.

p. 29 *Richard Mansell*: Ellis, C. H. 5, 48.

p. 30 *cromet references*: RMM, 16; Betjeman 2, 126; Ellis, C. H. 5, 155; *Taunton Courier*, 25 June 1845.

p. 31 *Frith*: Bills and Knight, 19.

p. 31 *So Brunel had reasoned*: Vaughan 2, 54.

p. 32 *taut cords across the ceiling*: Ellis, C. H. 5, 75.

p. 33 *'to see them attempt'*: Surtees 4, ch. 20.

p. 33 *pot-lamps*: Ellis, C. H. 5, 201–6.

p. 34 *'sudden darkness'*: Head, 41.

p. 34 *Robertson Scott*: Scott, J. W. R., 99–100.

p. 34 *confined in a nocturnal express*: Thomas, J. 1, ii, 65.

p. 34 *North Sunderland Railway*: Wright, 26.

p. 35 *'railway reading lamp'*: MP, 9 Oct. 1857.

p. 35 Army & Navy Stores Catalogue: *Army & Navy Stores Catalogue*, 1907 edn, 260.

p. 35 *non-corroding steatite burner*: O'Dea, 55.

p. 35 *first gaslit services*: Robbins 2, 24.

p. 35 *Metropolitan Railway*: Ellis, C. H. 5, 77; Lang, iii, 323.

p. 36 *Julius Pintsch*: Ellis, C. H. 5, 202; Peacock, 41.

p. 36 *Queen Victoria*: Ellis, C. H. 6, 68.

p. 36 *Carl Auer von Welsbach*: Norman, 54–7; Ellis, C. H. 5, 205.

p. 37 *carriages in 1935*: Peacock, 41.

p. 37 *erratic gas pressure*: RW, June 1969, 272.

p. 38 *H. C. Casserley*: Casserley 2, 105.

p. 38 *Acetylene gas*: Comfort, 115.

p. 38 *'stacked in vast piles'*: Williams 2, 365, 369.

p. 38 *Hawes Junction*: Rolt 4, 210–14.

p. 39 *£130 per coach*: Marshall, iii, 114.

p. 39 *gasworks at Inverness*: Ross, 181.

p. 39 *carriages be returned to gas*: Thomas, J. 1, ii, 212.

p. 39–40 *Other experiments were tried; 'coloured photochrome transparencies'*: Ellis, C. H. 5, 203–4; 168.

p. 40 *'three stone Schiedam bottles'*: Macfarlane, 282.

p. 41 *made its British début*: *Liverpool Mercury*, 13 Jan. 1852.

p. 41 *sodium acetate*: *Graphic*, 3 Dec. 1881.

p. 41 *look forward to these stops*: Ross, 180; Thomas, J. 1, i, 105.

p. 42 *MP Samuel Plimsoll*: *Nottinghamshire Guardian*, 18 Feb. 1870.

p. 42 *progress was halting*: Marshall, iii, 103; Dow, ii, 264.

p. 42 *'filled with cold water and snow'*: Kilvert, iii, 128.

p. 42 Punch: *Punch*, 19 Mar. 1892; *MPRB*, 109.

p. 43 *Pullman cars*: Ellis, C. H. 5, 92.

p. 43 *continued until 31 May*: Whitehouse and St John Thomas, 127.

p. 44 *new-built carriages*: Gourvish 2, 251.

p. 44 *diesel-hauled, electrically heated services*: *RW*, Dec. 1969, 518.

p. 45 *'shepherd's plaid or maud'*: Surtees 3, 235.

p. 45 *huge headquarters building*: Wilson, C., 156.

p. 45 Handy Book: *RTHB*, 61.

p. 46 *'instead of when the railway directors'*: Surtees 3, 234.

p. 47 *'new combination' article*: *Great Exhibition Catalogue* (1851), 3.16.

p. 47 *Andrew Peterson*: Hoare, 351–2.

p. 47 *trays of refreshments*: Thomas, R. H. G. 1, 194–5.

p. 47 *Spiers and Pond*: Spiers, 25, 31–5, 94–7.

p. 48 *Farringdon Street station*: Wolmar 3, 58.

p. 48 *luncheon baskets*: Wooler, 99–105.

p. 50 *'Travelling conveniences'*: Unwin, 51; *Army & Navy Stores Catalogue* (1907), 549.

p. 50 *'an innocent-looking circular basket'*: Gloag, 159.

p. 51 *Inverness & Aberdeen Junction Railway*: Vallance, 160.

p. 51 *David Dent*: *Annual Register* (1838), 7 July.

p. 52 *a special ticket stop*: Quick, 173–4.

Chapter 3: The Classes in Motion

p. 54 *'whether for the purposes of scientific research'*: Donaghy, 63.

p. 54 Experiment: Wolmar 2, 16–17.

p. 55 *Even the prospectus*: *English Historical Documents, 1783–1832* (1959), 639.

p. 55 *George Francis Train*: Ellis and Morse, 20.

p. 56 *'infinitely extendible'*: Robinson, ii, 184.

p. 56 *took the form of open wagons*: Donaghy, 61.

p. 56 *'The cold is great'*: Ellenborough, ii, 370.

p. 56 *holes ... bored in the floors*: Ellis, C. H. 5, 39, 64.

p. 56 *a depth of two inches*: Quick, 79.

p. 57 *London & Greenwich*: Ellis, C. H. 5, 20.

p. 57 *uniformed bands*: *Newcastle Journal*, 14 Mar. 1835.

p. 57 *'Dust from engine'*: *GD*, ii, 614.

p. 57 *'fell within my shirt collar'*: Vaughan 1, 67.

p. 57 *'a man used never to have'*: Surtees 1, ch. 58.

p. 59 *Middlesbrough extension*: Tomlinson, 400.

p. 59 *Manchester & Leeds*: Marshall, iii, 24.

p. 59 *Alfred Russel Wallace*: Wallace, i, 72, 129.

p. 59 *Jonathan John*: *Bath Chronicle*, 20 Mar. 1845.

p. 60 *Sonning*: Rolt 4, 36–8; Quick, 81.

p. 60 *'modern mechanical Moloch'*: *Mechanics' Magazine*, Jan. 1842, 5–8.

p. 61 *minimum of 4ft 6in*: Board of Trade, *Accident Returns*, 25 Dec. 1841, 79.

p. 61 *Gladstone showed a particular interest*: Parris 1, 92–9; Kirby, 26–7.

p. 63 *Pasley*: Parris 2; Parris 1, 95–9, 118–19, 143–4, 200n.

p. 65 *Jane Welsh Carlyle*: *CLC*, xxx, 26.

p. 66 *Midland Railway's earliest Parliamentary coaches*: Ellis, C. H. 5, 37.

p. 66 *Sir Francis Head*: Head, 107, 50.

p. 67 *Dickens*: 'The Lazy Tour of Two Idle Apprentices', *HW*, 3 Oct. 1857.

p. 67 *Rev. Francis Kilvert*: Kilvert, ii, 70–71; i, 139.

p. 68 *John Pendleton*: Pendleton, i, 190.

p. 68 *east London traveller*: *The Times*, 2 Nov. 1854.

p. 68 *'15-inch seats'*: Grinling, 164.

p. 69 *Allport stressed his pride*: Williams 1, 205.

p. 69 *'for competitive traffic'*: Thomas, J. 1, i, 195.

p. 70 *slippery horsehair cloth*: Marshall, iii, 105; Ellis, C. H. 7, p. 35.

p. 70 *up and down the Welsh valleys*: Riley, 77.

p. 71 *single undifferentiated class*: Garfield 2, 221.

p. 71 *glazed pictures*: Norton, 10–20.

p. 72 *domestic settings of late-Victorian Britain*: Cohen, D., 89–144.

p. 72 *colour reproductions of views*: Norton, 21–36.

p. 73 *Nor was first class immune*: Grinling, 371; Smith, D. N., 19.

p. 73 *Baedeker's guide*: *Baedeker's Great Britain* (1887), xix.

p. 73 *Rupert Brooke*: quoted Byatt, 606–7.

p. 74 *broader social attitudes*: Cannadine 2, 60, 85–6.

p. 74 *Jack Simmons*: Simmons 5, 359–60; *Chambers' Edinburgh Journal*, 26 Sept. 1846.

p. 74 *review of volunteer regiments*: *MP*, 9 Nov. 1862.

p. 75 *paid sweeps to dump soot*: Acworth, 44.

p. 75 *Sir Edward Watkin*: Smith, D. N., 62.

p. 75 *iron drainage funnels*: Ellis, C. H. 5, 75.

p. 75 *coal-black chimney-sweep*: *MPRB*, 52.

p. 76 *super-cheap workmen's trains*: Wolmar 3, 54–6; Smith, D. N., 101–7.

p. 76 *large pieces of timber*: Simon Abernethy, 'Thinking Allowed', BBC Radio 4, 28 Jan. 2013.

p. 76 *Glasgow, Paisley & Greenock*: Gourvish 3, 65.

p. 76 *An aggrieved English shareholder*: Thomas, J. 1, i, 55.

p. 76 *'there are only two ranks of people'*: Ross, 178.

p. 76 *two second-class journeys*: *GD*, iv, 181.

p. 76 *neo-medieval architect*: Ferrey, 98.

p. 77 *Hendrix and his entourage*: Quinn, 86.

p. 77 *'being cooler and less dust-catching'*: Surtees 3, 229.

p. 77 *one of George Gissing's novels*: George Gissing, *Demos* (1886), ch. 14.

p. 78 *lines to Tynemouth*: Hoole, 12.

p. 78 *All three classes*: Wright (1967 edn), 15, 22.

p. 78 *one passenger went first class*: Hartley, 30.

p. 79 *Duke of Sutherland*: Vallance, 28–32, 148.

p. 80 *the American gilded age*: Beebe, *passim*.

p. 80–1 *'posting carriages'; next step in saloon design*: Ellis, C. H. 5, 25–6; 132–6.

p. 81 *saloon with a full-sized bath*: Brown, F. A. S., 25.

p. 81 *Florence Sitwell*: Sitwell, 148.

p. 82 *Mr Isidore*: Jerrold, 323–4.

p. 83 *club carriages*: Allen 3, 39–40, 125–6.

p. 84 *take coach and horses*: Surtees 3, 233.

p. 84 *5th Duke of Portland*: Headley and Meulenkamp, 301–2.

p. 84 *Sir Charles Pasley*: Parris 2, 15.

p. 85 Time Book *(timetable) for 1863*: Peacock, 34.

p. 85 *Guest family*: Gash, 355.

p. 85 *Countess of Zetland*: *The Times*, 9 Dec. 1847; Quick, 204; Lardner, 294–5.

p. 86 *accidental death of William Huskisson*: Garfield 1, 156–88.

p. 86 *biographer G. R. Gleig*: Gleig, 354.

p. 87 *letter to Angela, Baroness Burdett-Coutts*: Wellington, 266–7.

p. 87 *'the chance of relief'*: Simmons 5, 17.

p. 87 *'I hope the Gentry'*: Burghclere, 112.

p. 87 *Stratfield Saye House*: Simmons 2, 308.

p. 87 *'in readiness for His Grace'*: *RHR*, ii (1982 edn), 115.

p. 88 *'all pertinent and to the purpose'*: Timbs, 77.

p. 88 *an outlandish one-off carriage*: Ellis, C. H. 5, 32.

p. 88 *the excursion train*: Simmons 5, 272–3; Quick, 104–6.

p. 89 *Thomas Cook*: Brendon, 6ff.

p. 89 *first day trip to France*: *Back Track*, May 1998, 242.

p. 89 *Lincoln to Thornton Abbey*: *Hull Packet*, 13 July 1849.

p. 90 *flying bottles*: Williams 2, 401.

p. 90 *'Empty Bottles may be left'*: poster, Great Western Society museum, Didcot.

p. 90 *double hanging at Bodmin*: *Back Track*, May 1998, 242.

p. 90 *outside Kirkdale gaol; bare-knuckle fights; north–south bout*: Chesney, 356; 315–19; 325–7.

p. 91 *top of the prizefighting lines*: Paar and Grey, 32–6.

p. 92 *Race meetings*: Vamplew, 29–31.

p. 92 *'legs'*: Gash, 383.

p. 92 *Yarmouth races special*: Paar and Grey, 38.

p. 92 *St Leger*: Vamplew, 30; Gordon, ii, 72–4.

p. 93 *overlapping local networks*: Vamplew, 32–9; Huggins and Tolson.

p. 93 *Snooty Newmarket*: Paar and Grey, 42.

p. 93 *Grand National Day*: Huggins, 127.

p. 93 *race sponsors and supporters*: Brailsford, 85.

p. 94 *Sunday schools*: Laqueur, 178–9.

p. 94 *travelling on the Sabbath*: Simmons 5, 282–4.

p. 95 *denunciations by placard*: Tomlinson, 73–4.

p. 95 *letter to Sir Robert Peel*: Shannon, 43.

p. 95 *Officers of the universities*: Fellows, 11–12.

p. 96 *Even the Metropolitan Railway*: Jackson, A. 1, 31.

p. 96 *Rev. Lord Blythswood*: RMM, 138.

p. 97 *mileage which closed on Sundays*: Simmons 5, 286.

p. 97 *Somerset & Dorset*: Atthill and Nock, 172–3.

p. 97 *melodrama of 1863*: Flanders, 331.

p. 98 *a West End hit*: O'Gorman, 50.

p. 98 *Dickens got in on the act*: Ackroyd, 610.

p. 98 *professional theatre trains*: Flanders, 367.

p. 98 *Bram Stoker; Irving's rail-borne tours*: Holroyd, 138; 367–8.

p. 98 *112 companies on a single Sunday*: RMM, 169–70.

p. 99 *theatre-goers from well-heeled coastal suburbs*: Hoole, 12.

p. 99 *National Eisteddfod*: Davies, 409.

p. 99 *reconstructed Crystal Palace*: O'Gorman, 104–6.

p. 99 *Charles Spurgeon*: Reynolds's Newspaper, 11 Oct. 1857.

p. 99 *Hippolyte Taine*: Taine, 281.

p. 100 *George Moore*: Smiles 1, 199–200.

p. 100 *Lancashire & Yorkshire's corpse vans*: Board of Trade, *Accident Returns*, 21 July 1912, 24–35.

p. 100 *bodies for dissection*: Hurren, 189–90.

p. 101 *Necropolis Railway*: Clarke; Davis, 400.

p. 101 *similar but cheaper service*: Quick, 101.

p. 101 *ceased officially on British Rail*: Clarke, 155.

p. 101 *last journey of Matthew Arnold*: Murray, 349–50.

p. 101 *young actor named William Ryder*: Liverpool Daily Post, 6 May 1899.

p. 102 *Great Western's* Time Book: Peacock, 34.

p. 102 *Mrs Caroline Prodgers*: Ellis, C. H. 3, 70; *Derby Daily Telegraph*, 16 Oct. 1924.

p. 102 *Samuel Smiles*: Smiles 2, 273.

p. 102 *taken the starch out*: Gash, 385.

Chapter 4: Journeying Together

p. 103 *a baby (subject to availability)*: Gash, 373.

p. 104 *breathing on the glass*: Punch, 15 Nov. 1856.

p. 104 *'Love of travelling alone'*: Punch, 4 Aug. 1937.

p. 104 *Bishop of Woolwich*: Western Gazette, 25 May 1934.

p. 104 *Lord Berners*: Dickinson, P. 1, 33.

p. 105 *a heavy piece of luggage*: RTHB, 55.

p. 105 *Connop's handkerchief*: Proceedings of the Central Criminal Court, 6 Jan. 1840, 338–9.

p. 105 *'The railway gives you seclusion'*: Belloc, 78.

p. 106 *'the padding is torn to pieces'*: Thomas, J. 1, i, 149.

p. 106 *the Grand Old Man*: Ford, 70–71.

p. 106 *Woolwich linen-draper*: PIP, 26 Apr. 1862.

p. 106 *Silvanus Trevail*: Cornishman, 12 Nov. 1903.

p. 106 *Harry Medina*: Illustrated Police News, 2 Dec. 1899.

p. 107 *bizarre suicide in 2011*: Daily Mail, 14 Apr. 2011.

p. 107 *ban smoking in first-class*: Carlson, 242.

p. 108 *Newcastle & North Shields Railway*: Tomlinson, 425.

p. 108 *A letter of 1841*: CLC, xiii, 78–9.

p. 108 *fashionable new forms*: Wilson, A. N. 2, 197–8.

p. 108 *the briar*: Alford, 111.

p. 108 *'railway pipes'; covered in scratches*: Quick, 169, 171–2.

p. 108 *nearly £30,000 of share capital*: Alford, 87–8.

p. 108 *first-class saloon of 1846*: ILN, 12 Sept. 1846.

p. 108 *Eastern Counties*: Paar and Grey, 71.

p. 109 *two unchivalrous male passengers*: PIP, 7 June 1862.

p. 109 *cartoon of 1858*: Punch, 23 Oct. 1858.

p. 109 *'fast Etonian'*: Punch, 28 Sept. 1861.

p. 109 *The young Prince of Wales*: Ellis, C. H. 6, 35.

p. 109 *Huddersfield magistrates*: Harris, 49.

p. 109 *John Stuart Mill*: Hansard 193, 24 July 1868, col. 1736.

p. 109 *By October 1868*: RW, Jan. 1969, 38.

p. 110 *Judy magazine*: Judy, 2 Dec. 1868.

p. 110 *Great Western smoking compartment*: Kilvert, iii, 159.

p. 110 *Wills brothers*: Wilson, A. N. 2, 198.

p. 110 *red triangular stickers*: Harris, 55.

p. 111 *I had to walk miles*: Bainbridge, 9.

p. 111 *Realize it is no longer possible*: Fielding, H., 216.

p. 111 *King's Cross–Aberdeen sleeper*: Wolmar 2, 48.

p. 112 *clientele of lairds*: Vallance, 160.

p. 112 *Coaches on the roads*: Bagwell and Lyth, 40.

p. 112 *The railway compartment was different*: Schivelbusch, 15–16.

p. 114 *F. L. Olmsted*: Olmsted, 85.

p. 114 *Every-body seems to have an idea*: PIP, 22 Mar. 1862.

p. 114 *'vulgar and amusing'*: Sidney, 8.

p. 114 *Nathaniel Hawthorne*: Hawthorne, 153.

p. 115 *Harriet Beecher Stowe*: Stowe, i, 42–3.

p. 115 *from Boston to Lowell*: Dickens, C., 642–3.

p. 115 *'social and political equality'*: Trollope, i, 30.

p. 115 *the riverboat saloon*: Schivelbusch, 111–14.

p. 116 *'negro car'*: Dickens, C., 642, 712.

p. 116 *'flashes of saliva'*: Forster, i, 318–19.

p. 116 *'stuffed figure'*: Dickens, C., 693.

p. 116 *'expressed himself most mournfully'*: Fielding, K. J., 62.

p. 117 *Thomas Carlyle*: *CLC*, xvi, 308.

p. 117 *Gladstone*: *GD*, v, 59, 236, 431.

p. 117 *Francis Kilvert*: Kilvert, iii, 34.

p. 119 Guinevere: *GD*, v, 431.

p. 119 *Little Nell*: Ackroyd, 319.

p. 120 *a newspaper could be bartered*: Surtees 3, 234.

p. 120 *Taxes on press advertising*: Elliott, 170.

p. 120 *The Post Office did its bit*: Bagwell 1, 92.

p. 120 *steam-powered press*: Nevett, 40–41.

p. 120 *their old Georgian 'f's*: Flanders, 147–9.

p. 120 The Times *of 1800*: Nevett, 41.

p. 120 *Newspapers were joined*: ibid., 43, 78; Flanders, 153.

p. 120 *Their despatch was tightly choreographed*: Acworth, 87–8.

p. 121 *Manchester too*: *Manchester Guardian*, 20 Oct. 1900.

p. 121 *Local journals; shift of book production*: Simmons 5, 240; 242–3.

p. 121 *older publishers benefited too*: McKitterick, ii, 11.

p. 121 *'non-display' advertisements*: Smith, D. N., 161.

p. 121 *Railway Mania*: Elliott, 169; Nevett, 30.

p. 122 *production costs were falling*: Raven, 329.

p. 123 *Fenchurch Street*: Wilson, C., 101.

p. 123 *disabled in company service; 'amicable jumble'*: Maxwell, i, 48.

p. 123 *'I bought from the stall'*: *Punch*, 1 Aug. 1891.

p. 123 *well-remembered article*: *The Times*, 9 Aug. 1851; Freeman 1, 88–9.

p. 124 *annual kickback*: Wilson, C., 176.

p. 124 Empedocles on Etna: Simmons 5, 247.

p. 124 *the Smiths' rise*: Maxwell, i, 50–56.

p. 124 *John Menzies*: Simmons 5, 246.

p. 124 *Charles Eason*: *Dictionary of Irish Biography*.

p. 125 *cut-price novels*: Maxwell, 86.

p. 125 *Murray's 'Reading for the Rail'*: Mackenzie, advertisement.

p. 125 *George Routledge*: Willes, 204–5.

p. 125 *Bulwer-Lytton*: Sutherland, 553.

p. 125 *'yellowback novels'*: Maxwell, i, 85–6.

p. 127 *Henry Mansel*: Taylor, J. B., xiii.

p. 127 *'cheap literature'*: Arnold, 126.

p. 127 *Ouida*: Palmer and Buckland, 48.

p. 127 *'rack-marketed' proto-pulp books*: Sutherland, 527.

p. 127 *Henry James; much else that was disreputable; Esther Waters*: Wilson, C., 88; 166, 375; 365–8.

p. 128 *private circulating library*: Flanders, 184–6; Wilson, C., 355–60.

p. 128 *the issuing stall*: Willes, 203.

p. 128 The Savoy: Sturgis, 192.

p. 129n *Fenian bomb*: Jackson, A. 2, 294–5.

p. 129–30 *morally unimpeachable three-volume novel*; *home-knitted mittens*: Wilson, C., 363; 281.

p. 130 *Wrangles over licence levels*: Willes, 252.

p. 130 *Penguin Books*: Lewis, 87, 112.

p. 130 *Victor Gollancz's books*: Powers 2, 22.

p. 132 *George Gilbert Scott*: Scott, G. G., f, k.

p. 132 *an order by the Post Office*: Quick, 52.

p. 132 *'Wryteezy'*: ILN, 4 Jan. 1890, 11.

p. 132 *typewriting service*: RM, Nov. 2011, 24.

Chapter 5: Risks and Anxieties

p. 135 *his every reference*: Hilton, 365.

p. 135 *railways do not come off well*: Ruskin 1, letters 35 (Nov. 1873), 69 (Sept. 1876), 77 (May 1877), 33 (Sept. 1873) and 80 (Aug. 1877).

p. 135 *'a new arrangement of glass roofing'*: Ruskin 4, ii, ch. 1.

p. 136 *'concentrate his dinner'*: Ruskin 2, iii, ch. 17.24.

p. 137 *'Better bury gold'*: Ruskin 3, ch. 4.21.

p. 138 *An earlier number*: Ruskin 1, letter 44 (Aug. 1874).

p. 139 *his very own road coach*: Hilton, 615–16.

p. 139 *Sheffield was Ruskin's choice*: Barringer, 235–7.

p. 139 *Ford Madox Brown's diary*: Brown, F. M., 188.

p. 139 *'the dull, monotonous railway'*: The Odd Fellow, 8 May 1841.

p. 140 *'hurrygraphs'*: Harrington 2, 243–59.

p. 140 *new boat train service*: 'A Flight', HW, 30 Aug. 1851.

p. 140 *'a leader of the steam-whistle party'*: Hilton, 475.

p. 141 *sailor on leave*: PIP, 4 Jan. 1862.

p. 142 *old man on the Norfolk Railway*: Paar and Grey, 62–4.

p. 142 *Winchburgh smash*: Rolt 4, 64, 51–8.

p. 142 *accidental deaths in 1861*: PIP, 17 May 1862.

p. 142 *the crossing at Whittlesford*: Cambridge Independent Press, 23 Jan. 1847.

p. 143 *average of £324,474*: Simmons 5, 279.

p. 143 *W. F. Mills*: Fielding, K. J., 362n.

p. 144 The Lancet *in 1862*: quoted Schivelbusch, 203.

p. 144 *representative Old Lady*: PIP, 22 Nov. 1862.

p. 144 Punch: *Punch*, 14 Sept. 1878; 18 Sept. 1852; 23 Mar. 1853; 18 July 1857.

p. 145 *Railway Passengers Assurance*: www.aviva.com/about-us/heritage/companies/railway-passengers-assurance-company.

p. 147 *'inflated railway caps'*: Great Exhibition Catalogue (1851), 3.20.

p. 147 *'Patent First-Class Costume'*: Punch, 19 Aug. 1876.

p. 147 *Radstock collision*: Rolt 4, 147–53.

p. 147 *In the event of a collision*: *RTHB*, 81–2.

p. 147 *Augustus Hare*: Hare, i, 153.

p. 148 The Times's *report*: *The Times*, 16 June 1845.

p. 149 *The intrepid Albert*: MacDermot, i, 659–60.

p. 149 *the GWR built a special carriage*; *routine part of Victoria's life*: Ellis, C. H. 6, 4–7; 62–5.

p. 149 *overheated rooms*: Rappaport, 150.

p. 149 *Victoria's funeral train*: Ellis, C. H. 6, 81.

p. 149 *sent from Balmoral*: Andrews, 114–15.

p. 150 *notable victims*: *Oxford Dictionary of National Biography*; G. E. Cokayne et al., *The Complete Peerage* (1910–59); John Venn, *Alumni Cantabrigienses* (1940–54). Also Rolt 4, 162 (Anson); Robbins 1 (Baly); Melville, 7 (Brough); MacDermot, i, 648 (Gibbs); *Cambridge Independent Press*, 1 Apr. 1865 and 21 Apr. 1866 (Hoare).

p. 151 *Jumbo*: Barnum, 344.

p. 152 *The Staplehurst accident*: Hill.

p. 152 *Dickens's response was heroic*: Ackroyd, 958–60.

p. 152–3 *Edward Dickenson*; *Dickens's letters*: Storey, 61n; 56–7 (Thomas Mitton), etc.

p. 153–4 *Ellen Ternan*; *sent ahead to Dover*: Ackroyd, 794, 912; 683.

p. 154 *in a royal saloon*: Dolby, 356.

p. 154 Penny Illustrated Paper's *artist*: *PIP*, 24 June 1865.

p. 154 *jewellery lost by Ellen*: Ackroyd, 962.

p. 155 *fast new service to France*: 'A Flight', *HW*, 30 Aug. 1851.

p. 155 *cottage for Nelly*: Tomalin, 167–8.

p. 156 *The two men's first journey*; *trip to Scotland*; *in his stride*: Dolby, 11; 33; 29, 35, 73.

p. 156 *'reckless fury of the driving'*: Storey, 306–7.

p. 156–7 *'ever in his mind'*; *Leaving Belfast*: Dolby, 67–8, 353; 366–9.

p. 157 *his doctors*; *Cuthbert Bede recalled*: Ackroyd, 1044; 837.

p. 157 *a period of shock*: Forster, ii, 376.

p. 158 *'suddenly fall into a paroxysm'*: Dickens, M., 115–16.

p. 158 *textbook instance of trauma*: Matus.

p. 159 *Alexander Bain*: Garratt, P., 199.

p. 159 *explanation of any disorders*: Schivelbusch, 138–9.

p. 159 *two cases of 1862*: *The Times*, 27 Mar. 1862.

p. 160 *Embarrassed by these public disagreements*: Harrington 1, 34–40.

p. 160 *J. E. Erichsen*; *Herbert Page*: Schivelbusch, 140–41; 141–3.

p. 161 *30,000 individual shocks*: Dolby, 353.

p. 162 *miscarried on the train*: Ackroyd, 539.

p. 162 *Mrs Leech went into labour*: Frith, i, 235–6.

p. 162 *'the excitement, anxiety, and nervous shock'*: Schivelbusch, 203.

p. 162 *Alfred Haviland*: Haviland, 22, 9, 50–52.

p. 163 *'impossible to consider them'*: Schivelbusch, 202.

p. 163 *Sir Henry Holland*: Holland, H., 268.

p. 163 *'bicycle face'*: Pearson, 66.

p. 163 *'TV Neck'*: Moran 2, 177.

Chapter 6: Crimes and Misdemeanours

p. 164 *larger and more modern gaols; Prison Act of 1877*: Brodie et al., 120–44; 145–7.

p. 164 *special prison vans*: Lardner, 113.

p. 165 *'ragamuffin in handcuffs'*: Punch, 7 Dec. 1844.

p. 165 *'low-browed, bull-necked man'*: Sala, 63.

p. 165 *half-hour at Clapham Junction*: Ellman, 495–6.

p. 166 *Thomas Hardy*: Hardy, 'At the Railway Station, Upways', ll. 12–14.

p. 166 *penal servitude in 1914*: Harris, J., 209.

p. 166 *cells for miscreant sailors*: Vallance, 109–10.

p. 166 *abolished in 1921*: Brodie et al., 173.

p. 166 *Samuel Robinson*: PIP, 1 Mar. 1862, *Dundee Courier and Argus*, 20 Feb. and 19 Apr. 1862, *Dundee Advertiser*, 24 Feb. 1862, *DN*, 19 Feb. 1862, *Caledonian Mercury*, 20 Feb. 1862, *BDP*, 21 Feb. 1862, *Standard*, 22 Feb. 1862, *Leeds Mercury*, 19 Feb. 1862.

p. 167 *An exasperated letter*: The Times 1 and 2 Nov. 1854.

p. 168 *'Not Swindled' and 'A Lucky Fellow'*: The Times, 23 Jan. 1865, 2 Nov. 1854.

p. 169 *four Ascot race-goers*: The Times, 8 June 1864.

p. 169 *one Scottish rogue*: The Times, 5 Dec. 1865.

p. 169 *Hippolyte Taine*: Taine, 289.

p. 170 *John Hamilton*: PIP, 11 Jan. 1862.

p. 170 *Hamilton turned up again*: The Times, 16 Apr. 1868.

p. 170 *a Swiss gentleman at Bletchley*: The Times, 14 May 1867.

p. 171 *'disposed for defence'*: RTHB, 74–5.

p. 171 *one hard case*: Preston Guardian, 18 Jan. 1851.

p. 171 *Henry Holloway*: PIP, 4 Jan. 1862.

p. 171–3 *Thomas Briggs; hanged outside Newgate gaol; Mr Gold*: Sellwood and Sellwood, 11–52; 57–66; 73–116.

p. 174 *unnamed source*: Pendleton, ii, 13.

p. 174 *paranoid Irish schoolmaster; drunken lunatic*: Adams, 32–4; 38–9.

p. 175 *Mary Anne Moody*: The Times, 12 and 16 June 1864.

p. 176 *'evidence of the new impunity'*: PIP, 23 July 1864.

p. 176 *Mrs Hicks*: Norfolk Chronicle, 26 Apr. 1851.

p. 176 *'the want of light'*: Pictorial Times, 13 Sept. 1845.

p. 176 *Robert Williams*: The Times, 22 Jan. 1866.

p. 177 *Colonel Valentine Baker*: The Times, 19 June 1875; Baker, 77–82.

p. 177 *Croydon Assizes*: Bradford Observer, 3 Aug. 1875; BDP, 5 Aug. 1875.

p. 178 *'first-class misdemeanant'*: Derby Mercury, 11 Aug. 1875; Nottinghamshire Guardian, 15 Oct. 1875.

p. 178 *Baker's subsequent history*: Baker, 99–174.

p. 178 *an alarm fitted in the carriage*: DN, 25 June 1875.

p. 179 *twenty-seven accidents*: Lardner, 333–5.

p. 178 *Rev. Sydney Smith*: Vaughan 1, 66–70.

p. 178 *the Board's circular*: *Yorkshire Gazette*, 2 June 1842.

p. 179 *a two-year-old child*: *London Standard*, 11 Sept. 1844.

p. 180 *Isabella Lawrence*: *The Times*, 20 and 25 Oct. 1854; *DN*, 21 Oct. 1854.

p. 180 *an arrival at Euston*: Head, 45, 48.

p. 180 *having to call for release*: Olmsted, 86.

p. 181 *Opened doors on moving trains*: Ellis, C. H. 5, 76.

p. 181 *doors with sprung catches*: Paar and Grey, 157.

p. 181 *automatic locking*: *RM*, June 2012, 60.

p. 182 *ladies-only compartments*: Simmons 5, 334.

p. 182 *the limit of manhood*: Comfort, 36; Maggs 2, 47.

p. 182 *The last few lingered until 1977*: *The Times*, 11 Mar. 1977; Mike Horne, machorne.
blogspot.com/2013/06/ladies-only.html.

p. 183 *epicentre of vice*: Jackson, A. 2, 177.

p. 184 *Wilkie Collins*: Simmons 1, 230n.

p. 184 *a warning letter*: Paar and Grey, 66.

p. 184 *Old Bailey case of 1866*: *Proceedings of the Central Criminal Court*, 9 July 1866,
249–56.

p. 185 *The Rev. George Capel*: *DN*, 18 Apr. 1867; *Reynolds's Newspaper*, 21 Apr. 1867; *The
Times*, 23, 25 and 27 Apr. 1867; *PMG*, 24 Apr. 1867.

p. 186 *the Tremlett case*: *Nottinghamshire Guardian*, 8 Oct. 1875.

p. 187 *'The Charming Young Widow'*: O'Gorman, 40; Richter, 23.

p. 187 *Abraham Solomon*: Kennedy and Treuherz, 84–8.

p. 188 *'Found in the carriage'*: Brown. F. M., 95.

p. 188 *summit of Victorian literary smut*: 'Walter', viii, ch. 4; ix, ch. 13; vii, ch. 2.

p. 189 A Kiss in the Tunnel: Keiller, 79–80.

p. 190 *Edward Carpenter*: Rowbotham, 179–80.

Chapter 7: The Improved British Railway Train

p. 193 *a single passenger fatality*: Simmons 1, 232.

p. 193–4 *continuous footboards*; *systems of passing signals*; *nothing much was done*: Bagwell
1, 192; 193; 194.

p. 194 *glazed circular openings*: *Observer*, 24 July 1864.

p. 195 *in use or under trial*: Ellis, C. H. 5, 20, 199–200.

p. 195 *duly sanctioned an installation*: Bagwell 1, 195.

p. 195 *the Baker case*: *DN*, 26 June 1875.

p. 195 *groping through a hole*: Ellis, C. H. 5, 200.

p. 196 *usage of these early alarms*: Williams 2, 450.

p. 196 *Ulster, on 12 June 1889*: Rolt 4, 187–93.

p. 197 *older method of braking*: Ellis, C. H. 5, 193–5.

p. 198 *George Westinghouse*: Bagwell 1, 216–17.

p. 198 *brake Olympics*: Ellis, C. H. 5, 196–7.

p. 198 three *sets of brakes*: Gordon, i, 174.

p. 198 *derailment of 1887 at Aviemore*: Bagwell 1, 218.

p. 199 *132 MPs*: Alderman, 232.

p. 199 *suburban lines into Liverpool Street*: Allen 1, 184–7.

p. 200 *'Jazz service'*: Connor, viii.

p. 200 *these overcrowded services*: Hewison, 80–82.

p. 200 *incident on the Enfield line*: Brown, F. A. S., 111.

p. 201 *'a positive disgrace'*: Hansard 432, 22 Jan. 1947, col. 301.

p. 201 *question of standardised braking*: Gourvish 2, 157.

p. 201–2 *story of the carriage lavatory*; *tri-composite carriage of 1887*: Ellis, C. H. 5, 215–16; 125.

p. 202 *first/third composite of 1880*: Dow, ii, 400.

p. 203 *von Waldegg*: Schivelbusch, 91.

p. 203 *first-class carriage of 1881*: Ellis, C. H. 5, 119–20.

p. 203 *composite design of 1911*: Dow, iii, 409.

p. 203 *glass-fronted compartment of the coupé type*: RMM, 45.

p. 204 *pattern for its lavatory glass*: Dickinson, W. E., 20.

p. 204 *contraptions provided within*: Ellis, C. H. 5, 211–17.

p. 206 *gave up designating cubicles*: Harris, M. 2, 48.

p. 206 *underfloor retention tank*: Haresnape 1, 178.

p. 206 *safeguard against the anti-social flusher*: RM, Oct. 2012, 81.

p. 207 *fully pivoting four-wheeled bogies*; *George Mortimer Pullman*: Ellis, C. H. 5, 68; 89–104.

p. 208 Babes in the Wood: *The Times*, 28 Dec. 1874.

p. 208 *Affronted letters*: *The Times*, 27 Jan. and 1 Feb. 1875.

p. 208 *'Southern Belle'*: Allen 3, 73–5.

p. 209 *mourned in style*: *The Times*, 21 Feb. 1972.

p. 209 *provision of meals*: Wooler, 32–7.

p. 210 *flexible enclosed gangway*: Ellis, C. H. 5, 100–1, 106–10.

p. 210 *trio of permanently coupled carriages*: Allen 1, 70.

p. 211 *new corridor train*: Ellis, C. H. 5, 154.

p. 211 *a sort of cross-passage*: Harris, M. 2, 53–6.

p. 212 *the Mark 1*: Haresnape 1, 69, 74.

p. 213 *for its trains to South Wales*: Ellis, C. H. 5, 155.

p. 213 *left in a huff*: Harris, M. 2, 52.

p. 214 *'tourist' stock*: Brown, F. A. S., 159.

p. 214 *'substantially more popular'*: Harris, M. 2, 56.

p. 215 *coat hanger*; *burnt the native turf*: Day-Lewis, 85; 273–7.

p. 215 *double-decked electric suburban units*: Moody, 142, 145.

p. 216 *Bulleid's Tavern Cars*: Haresnape 2, 162; Hebron, 91–2.

p. 216 *A real pub*: Haresnape 1, 162.

p. 217 *members queued up*: Hansard 466, 27 June 1949, cc. 935–46.

p. 217n *the future Prime Minister also helped Bulleid*: Weighell, 9.

p. 218 *up to four sittings; meals were often sumptuous*: Hebron, 51; 54–6.

p. 218 *1,510 pieces*: Mander, 46.

p. 218 *spaces of conspicuous display*: Ellis, C. H. 4, 100; Dow, ii, 272–4; *Graphic*, 18 Mar. 1899.

p. 219 *The Great Central tested the water*: Hebron, 57–8.

p. 220 *between Cambridge and King's Cross*: Brown, F. A. S., 159.

p. 220 *frills, folds and mouldings*: Votolato, 43–4.

p. 221 *'Vita glass'*: Bryan, 51.

p. 221 *'Blue Pullman' trains*: Haresnape 1, 106–9.

p. 221 *abandonment of croutons*: *RW*, Jan. 1969, 337.

p. 221 *three-fifths of first-class passengers*: *RW* 338.

p. 221–2 *make-up of the High Speed Trains; 'Cuisine 2000'*: Hebron, 107; 109–11.

p. 224 *electric trains introduced on Tyneside*: Hoole, 17.

p. 224 *'completely disembowelled'*: *PMG*, 22 Nov. 1870.

p. 224 *writing and scratching*: Turner, 21; Williams 2, 376.

p. 224 *pencilling the whole interior*: Ayrton, 128–9.

p. 224 *leather straps*: Comfort, 118.

p. 224 *third-class windows with curtains*: Smith, D. N., 17.

p. 225 *'Much uneaten or half-eaten food'*: Dickinson, W. E., 205.

p. 225 *15,000 MISSING LIGHT BULBS*: *Manchester Guardian*, 11 Dec. 1957.

p. 225 *Cumulative costs*: *The Times*, 30 May 1960.

p. 225 *known or suspected train-wreckers*: *Guardian*, 25 May 1961.

p. 225 *football specials in the Glasgow area*: *Sunday Times*, 3 Sept. 1961.

p. 226 *'Mersey Maniacs'*: *The Times*, 7 and 28 Jan. 1964; *Guardian*, 13 Jan. 1964.

p. 226 *Matt Busby and his squad*: *Guardian*, 6 Jan. 1964.

p. 226 *National Federation of Football Supporters' Clubs*: Ward, 236.

p. 226 *Tottenham Hotspur*: *The Times*, 22 Sept. 1969.

p. 226 *League Liner*: *The Times*, 24 Jan. 1973; *RM*, June 2014, 26–7.

p. 227 *Levels of destruction*: *The Times*, 1 Sept. 1975; Ward, 48, 220–21.

p. 228 *'standing allowance'*: Network Rail, 'Passenger Capacity Summary', period 2014–19 (ref. SBPT231), 1.

p. 228 *last haunt of the compartment*: *RM*, July 2010, 8.

p. 229 *Inter-City 125s*: Haresnape 1, 158–60.

p. 229 *Sir Kenneth Grange*: *Building Design*, 12 Aug. 2011.

p. 229 *In a BBC4 documentary*: *The Inter-City 125*, BBC4, 13 Sept. 2012.

p. 230 *'probably the best known trains'*: *Design*, Mar. 1963, 59.

p. 230 *Design Panel*: Haresnape 1, 92.

p. 231 *Jack Howe*: Obituary, *Independent*, 16 Dec. 2003.

p. 231 *Receipts rose markedly*: Wolmar 2, 293–4.

p. 231 *Silver Jubilee year*: *MR*, Aug. 1977, 306.

p. 232 *Sir Hugh Casson*: Haresnape 1, 94, 107, 160; Manser, 288.

p. 232 *The Pacers originated*: Dickinson, P. 2, 10.

p. 232 *an extra 80,000 journeys*: *RHR*, viii (1984 edn), 23.

p. 233 *Leyland National bus*: Dickinson, P. 2, 11–13.

p. 234 *'four-wheel bicycles'*: *Railway Observer* 79/967 (Sept. 2009), 524.

p. 234 *surplus of revenue*: Gourvish 2, 209.

p. 234–5 *production series; mission to the wider world; Class 142*: Dickinson, P. 2, 10, 17, 26–8; 21–4; 26–8.

p. 235 *cloakroom clerk*: Aitken, 12.

p. 235 *'British Day'*: www.margaretthatcher.org/document/1064521.

p. 236 *a regrettable economy*: Cooper, 161.

p. 238 *Advanced Passenger Trains*: ibid., 127–30; Gourvish 1, 218–23.

p. 239 *Flying Scotsman*: *RM*, Nov. 2011, 33; Harris, M. 2, 54.

p. 240 *Molesworth*: Willans, 369.

p. 240 *three observation saloons*: Ellis, C. H. 5, 247.

Chapter 8: And so to Bed

p. 241 *'bed-carriages'; French type known as a* lits-salon; *George Mortimer Pullman*: Ellis, C. H. 5, 22–4; 82–4; 90–96.

p. 244 *destruction by fire of the Midland's sleeper*: *RM*, Feb. 1964, 251–5; also *The Times*, 30 Oct. and 1 and 2 Nov. 1882; *Aberdeen Weekly Journal*, 1 Nov. 1882; *Freeman's Journal*, 8 Nov. 1882; *MP*, 9 Nov. 1882.

p. 245 *The new type*: Ellis, C. H. 5, 139–43.

p. 245 *Plymouth boat trains*: Spence, pl. 96.

p. 245 *pros and cons of extending sleeper services*: Harris, M. 2, 51.

p. 245 *historians have questioned*: Simmons 5, 83–4.

p. 246 *extension of the service to third class*: Smith, D. N., 69.

p. 246 *shower booths*: Harris, M. 1, 160.

p. 246 *some compartments on the Great Western*: *Back Track*, Feb. 2015, 109.

p. 246 *second-class sleeping car*: Haresnape 1, 91.

p. 246 *'many individual privacies'*: *The Times*, 5 June 1956.

p. 248 *'Motorail'*: Atkinson, 123–4.

p. 248 *endearing little peg*: Haresnape 1, 151.

p. 248 *accident to a West Country sleeper*: Department of Transport, *Report on the Fire that occurred in a Sleeping-Car Train on 6th July 1978 at Taunton*.

p. 248 *the new sleeping cars*: Haresnape 1, 178.

p. 250 *the sum of £17,000*: *Independent*, 21 Nov. 2011.

p. 250 *pledged £50 million each*: *RM*, Aug. 2012, 9.

p. 250 *victor in the franchise contest*: *RM*, Oct. 2013, 75; June 2014, 6.

p. 250 *'will creatively reflect'*: www.transportscotland.gov.uk/news/exciting-new-sleeper-contract-unveiled, 28 May 2014.

p. 250 *Nightstar sleeper trains*: Gourvish 1, 327–8.

p. 251 *John Prescott*: Hansard 313, 3 June 1998, col. 367.

p. 251 *faces were saved*: *RM*, Oct. 2001, 42–3.

p. 252 *Recalling Scottish excursions*: Beerbohm 3, 130.

p. 253 *'huge steam nightbird'*: *CLC*, xi, 182–3.

p. 253 *illegal on 20 July 2012*: *RM*, Aug. 2012, 9.

Chapter 9: The Permanent Way

p. 257 *welded rails*: Fairman, 31.

p. 257 *British Railways followed suit*: Gourvish 2, 277, 512.

p. 258 *fully half an inch*: Chapman, 124.

p. 258 *fish-bellied rails*: Ellis and Morse, 19.

p. 258 *rails rolled from steel*: Simmons 1, 148–9.

p. 258 *Lengths have also increased*: Essery, 9.

p. 259 *'bullhead' form*: Ransom, 219–20.

p. 260 *sunken stone blocks*: Simmons 1, 146–7.

p. 260 *granite sleepers in concrete*: Thomas, R. H. G. 2, 40.

p. 260 *Joseph Locke*: Ransom, 219.

p. 260 *depot at Shepherds Bush*: Atkinson, 119.

p. 261 *baulk road*: MacDermot, i, 47–9, 72–80.

p. 261 *doubling the number of joints*: Bryan, 45.

p. 261 *bridge rail*: Simmons 1, 146.

p. 261 *Barlow rail*: Ransom, 224.

p. 261 *Eastern Counties Railway*; *London & Blackwall*: Allen 1, 12; 9.

p. 262 *Irish gauges*: Gordon, i, 57–8.

p. 262 *Royal Commission*: Rolt 2, 199–203.

p. 262 *Henry Cole*: Cole 2, 3–4.

p. 263 *Act of 1846*: Simmons 5, 81.

p. 263 *Brunel was a marvel*: Vaughan 2, 229, 201; Rolt 2, 182, 207–8.

p. 264 *in the form of a tennis match*: Vic Stephens, in *Isambard Kingdom Brunel: Recent Works (Art Catalogue)*, ed. A. Hudson and E. Kentley (2000), 53–5.

p. 264 *'the bravest lost cause'*: Rolt 2, 410, 164.

p. 264 *'Every word has to be translated'*: Vaughan 2, 87.

p. 265 *sailings to the New World*: Buchanan, 57–9.

p. 265 *arrangements at Gloucester*: Cole 1, i, 77–82; ii, 150–57.

p. 266 *ordeal of a single train-load*: *ILN*, 6 June 1846.

p. 266 *spatial advantage*: Chapman, 237.

p. 267 *the best permanent way*: Simmons 1, 151.

p. 268 *South Devon Railway*: Vaughan 2, 170–81.

p. 268 *A workable form*: Atmore.

p. 269 *London & Croydon Railway*: Ellis, C. H. 2, 27–30.

p. 269 *journal for Boxing Day 1835*: Vaughan 2, 56–7.

p. 270 *coastal sections of the line*: Roden, 58.

p. 271 *'the perfect operation of the whole'*: Jeaffreson and Pole, i, 327.

p. 272 *placed symmetrically*: MacDermot, i, 327.

p. 272 *came to a turntable*: Rolt 2 (1957 edn), 209.

p. 272 *struggled to pay a dividend*; *the buffer-stops of Paddington*: Brindle, 52–3.

p. 272 *first journey from Windsor to Scotland*: Roden, 91.

p. 272 *spin-off of the Great Western*: Jackson, A. 1, 27–35.

p. 273 *branch to St Ives*: Chapman, 37.

p. 273 *forty-eight daily departures*: Brindle, 59.

p. 273 *The final transformation*: MacDermot, ii, 376–81.

p. 274 *23lb less per yard*: Simmons 1, 146.

p. 274 *London, Midland & Scottish Railway*: Williamson, 84–5, 206.

p. 274 *Economy in the use of timber*: Dow, ii, 45; Essery, 9.

p. 274 *standard section*: Williamson, 86.

p. 275 *a process called kyanizing*: Vaughan 2, 214.

p. 275 *use of creosote*: Fairman, 20–21; Essery, 119.

p. 275 *Pickling was the next step*: Williamson, 87; Fairman, 21.

p. 275 *some 9,000 miles of track*: Chapman, 11.

p. 275 *paired concrete sleeper blocks*: Semmens, iii, 29.

p. 276 *Dow-Mac factory*: Bewley, 89.

p. 276 *In 1964 the type became standard*; *Pandrol clip*: Fairman, 17; 18.

p. 277 *Great Northern Railway chair*: RM, May 2012, 47–9.

p. 277 *recycled plastic*: Daily Telegraph, 4 May 2009.

p. 277 *Kentish rag*: RW, Sept. 1969, 395.

p. 277 *broken-up slag*: Williamson, 90–92.

p. 277 *Sub-standard ballasting*: RW, Oct. 1969, 440.

p. 278 *Stiffer recycling targets*: RailwayPeople.com, rail news, 6 July 2011.

p. 278 *challenge by the European Union*: Daily Telegraph, 15 Feb. 2003; www.europa.eu/rapid/press-release_IP-11–925_en.htm, 26 July 2011.

p. 279 *huddle of weekend dwellings*: Building Design, 26 Sept. 2008, 10–13.

p. 279 *One early stronghold*: Newton, 27–30.

p. 280 *encounter on a Norfolk road*: Beerbohm 1, 257–64.

p. 280 *heyday of shacks and plotlands*: Newton, 27–8.

p. 280 *for use as a chapel*: Vaughan 4, 223.

p. 281 *'Slinger 3'*: Railway Gazette, 1 May 2003.

p. 282 *twelve Matisa tamping machines*; *shortages among the track gangs*: Gourvish 2, 667n; 86.

p. 282 *careful tending*; *Engineering Department of the Great Western*: Chapman, 127–31; 137–9.

p. 283 *a mess carriage*: Joby, 119.

p. 283 *diagrammatic* Railway Charts: Cole 1, ii, 147–8.

p. 284 *Totley Tunnel*: Anderson and Fox, pl. 495.

p. 284 *tunnel inspector*: Thornewell.

p. 284 *villagers of Bourne*: 'Bourne', 53, 147.

p. 284 *On the southern division*: Hendry, 130–38.

p. 285 *casting factory at Exmouth Junction*: Hawkins and Reeve, 2–7.

p. 285 *bad track joint*: Weighell, 180.

p. 285 *sometimes self-built*: Cheshire Observer, 24 June 1876.

p. 285 *full-time lookout*: Bagwell 2, 109–10.

p. 286 *when Dickens's train derailed*: Hill, 149.

p. 286 *a little cabin*: Essery, 43.

p. 286 *a contraption was devised*: Marshall, ii, 242.

p. 286 *miniature versions with percussion caps*: *Army & Navy Stores Catalogue* (1907), 1040–42.

p. 286 *expected to be on standby*: Weighell, 184.

p. 286 *High-visibility fluorescent clothing*: *MR*, June 1964, 373.

p. 287 *Railway Group Standard GO/RT3279*: Issue 6, Aug. 2008, www.rgsonline.co.uk.

p. 287 *a defective rail fractured*: Jack, 8–13.

p. 288 *privatised system created in 1993–6*; *separate business sectors*: Wolmar 2, 304–10; 296–9.

p. 288 *faults in the rail at Hatfield*: Bagwell 3, 117–19.

p. 289 *'The railway as a system'*: Jack, 77.

p. 289 *payoff valued at £1.4 million*: *Guardian*, 23 June 2001.

p. 289 *Network Rail*: Bagwell 3, 119–21.

p. 290 *'deep alliances'*: *RM*, Apr. 2012, 10.

p. 290 *David Cameron*: *Guardian*, 20 Mar. 2012.

p. 290 *£34 billion*: *Financial Times*, 12 Aug. 2014.

Chapter 10: Signals and Wires

p. 292 *practical-minded pointsman*: Ransom, 162.

p. 292 *starting signal*: Essery, 52.

p. 292 *Kentish Town Junction*: Ransom, 163.

p. 294 *Aeolian harp*: Head, 126.

p. 294 *between Ely and Norwich*: *RM*, Nov. 2012, 10.

p. 294 *earliest commercial electric telegraph*; *nine-hour chess match*: Ransom, 142; 154.

p. 294 *'railway of thought'*: Steven Roberts, distantwriting.co.uk/ electrictelegraphcompany.html.

p. 295 *codes to regulate the passage*: Ransom, 157.

p. 295 *As standardised*: Bonavia, i, 57.

p. 295 *Heckington (Lincolnshire)*: *Rail*, 26 June 2013.

p. 295 *target for their abolition*: *RM*, July 2013, 35–40.

p. 296 *'wonderful wooden razors'*: 'The Lazy Tour of Two Idle Apprentices', *HW*, 3 Oct. 1857.

p. 296n *road traffic lights*: Morrison and Minnis, 334.

p. 296 *misadventure on 10 December 1881*: Nock, 109.

p. 296 *on western lines*: MacDermot, iii, 492–3.

p. 297 *how far points could be located*; *pyrometer*: Essery, 93; 64.

p. 297 *the longest 'pull'*: Kidner 2, 7.

p. 298 Railway Club Journal: quoted Essery, 66.

p. 299 *Metropolitan Railway*: Simmons 1, 218.

p. 299 *had cost £581,000*: Marshall, ii, 242.

p. 299 *symbolic item*: Essery, 88–90.

p. 300 *On the Exmouth branch*: Beer, 161.

p. 300 *train control by radio*: Allen and Woolstenholmes, 52–3.

p. 301 *walkways and ladders*: Essery, 44.

p. 301 *burn for eight days*: Quinn, 46.

p. 301 *St Helens Junction*: Forman, 96.

p. 302 *gantry principle*: Faulkner, 17, 26.

p. 302 *'Erimus'*: Signalling Study Group, 63–4.

p. 303 *hideously congested*: Kidner 1, 13.

p. 305 *pan-European train control*: *RM*, Sept. 2013, 18–23.

p. 305 *railway control office*: Simmons 1, 233.

p. 306 *at Manchester Victoria station*: Marshall, ii, 245.

p. 306 *Northallerton power box*: Signalling Study Group, 200.

p. 306 *installed at Didcot*: *RM*, Sept. 2008, 77.

p. 308 *school at Manchester Victoria*: Marshall, ii, 243.

p. 308 *Midland Railway signalman*: Bagwell 2, 430.

p. 310 *Adrian Vaughan*: Vaughan 4, 121–52, 188, 245, 345–52.

p. 311 *Stockport No. 2 Box*: *The Railway*, BBC2, 5 Mar. 2013.

p. 311 *Vaughan's memoirs*: Vaughan 4, 176.

p. 312 *Sidney Weighell*: Weighell, 34–41, 190.

p. 313 *suburban electric trains*: Dendy Marshall, i, 241; ii, 409–10.

p. 313 *At the other end of England*: Allen 2, 204–6.

p. 313 *between Southampton and Basingstoke*: *RM*, Jan. 2012, 12.

p. 314 *more efficient overhead line equipment*: Cooper, 79–86.

p. 315 *delays and repairs*: *Guardian*, 15 Apr. 2013.

Chapter 11: Railways and the Land I

p. 316 *lines built after 1850*: Wolmar 1, 131–50.

p. 316 *Legal preliminaries*: Burton, 25–6.

p. 317 *Stanhope & Tyne*: Whittle, 16–17, 26–7.

p. 317 *Metropolitan Railway*: Jackson, A. 1, 134–42, 238–41, 289–93.

p. 319 *little brass pass-tokens*: Dickinson, W. E., 82.

p. 319 *legal incantation*: Mander, 128.

p. 320 *Stockton & Darlington Railway*: Smith, D. N., 17.

p. 320 *cut down by an express*: Western, 24–5.

p. 320 *across the Solway Firth*: Edgar and Sinton, 53.

p. 320 *Moray McLaren*: quoted Legg, 175.

p. 321 *One of her friends*: Briggs, 184.

p. 322 and n. *red flannel petticoats*: ibid., 33; *Daily Mail*, 20 Mar. 2011.

p. 322 *Objects might be placed on the line*: Quick, 221; Rolt 4, 133.

p. 322 *stone-throwing*: Clifford, 206; Dickens, 'Fire and Snow', *HW*, 21 Jan. 1854; *PIP*, 10 July 1875.

p. 323 *The menace seems to have returned*: *Guardian*, 31 May 1963; Ward, 251; Ministry of Transport, *Railway Accident Report 29th March 1965*; *Guardian*, 9 Apr. 1965.

p. 323 The Finishing Line: British Film Institute, www.screenonline.org.uk/film/id/1077210.

p. 324 *no dedicated budget*: *Los Angeles Times*, 12 June 1988.

p. 325 *Neasden, Uxbridge and Wembley Park*: www.rockingthecity.com.

p. 325 *aerosol paint*: Ward, 305.

p. 325 *we have produced*: www.route79.com/journal/archives/000138.html.

p. 325 *Digital Jungle UK graffiti archive*: www.graffiti.org/dj/index_dj.html.

p. 327 FAR AWAY IS CLOSE AT HAND: *The Times*, 16 Apr. 2005.

p. 327 *The annual bill*: *Guardian*, 20 Jan. 2007.

p. 328 *remote-controlled drones*: *Daily Telegraph*, 27 May 2013.

p. 329 *red warning discs*: Essery, 83.

p. 329 *Warthill*: Leigh 2, 61.

p. 329 *automatic half-barrier crossings*: *Trains Illustrated*, Apr. 1961, 195–6.

p. 330 *Dornoch branch*: *RM*, Jan. 1958, 104.

p. 331 *Jane Emerson*: *PIP*, 30 Nov. 1861.

p. 331 *750 crossings*: *RM*, Feb. 2014, 6.

p. 331–2 *Northamptonshire landowners*; *'severance'*: Simmons 2, 300; 305.

p. 333 *'Bradshaw fires guns'*: Burton, 28–9.

p. 333 *Lord Sefton's tenants*: Ferneyhough, 17.

p. 333 *Firearms might even be drawn*: Burton, 30–31.

p. 333 *This was Brunel's way*: Vaughan 2, 49–50.

p. 334 *asleep in his chair*: Rolt 2, 131.

p. 334 *Robert Stephenson*: Michael Bailey, lecture to the Victorian Society, London, 22 Feb. 2012.

p. 334 *engineers increasingly took over*; *the incompetent and the unscrupulous*: Thompson 1, 113; 110–11.

p. 335 *Institution of Surveyors*: Gourvish and O'Day, 32.

p. 335 *a momentous step*; *Brassey's qualities*; *relentless hard work*: Walker, 16; 19–20, 36–9, 77, 118; 23–5.

p. 337 *vivid new monikers*; *the first Woodhead Tunnel*; *the Committee's recommendations*: Coleman, 154; 115–38; 149–50.

p. 338 *Brassey paid better*: Walker, 30–32, 42–3.

p. 339 *Coleman's composite picture*: Burton, 128, 162, 175; Brooke 2.

p. 339 *four navvies in ten*: Burton, 133.

p. 339 *child labour*: Clifford, 49.

p. 339 *rolling crime-wave*: Brooke 1.

p. 339 *work on the Sabbath*: Clifford, 51–2.

p. 340 *'rough, loud-voiced men'*: Waugh, 28.

p. 340 *At Cholsey*: Clifford, 190–91.

p. 340 *maltings*: Simmons 2, 327.

p. 341 *distilleries at Dufftown*: Turnock, 138.

p. 341 *Bird-in-Hand inn*: Simmons 2, 328.

p. 341 *'polished horns, bright eyes'*: Head, 76.

p. 341 *'dull oxen'*: 'The Lazy Tour of Two Idle Apprentices', *HW*, 10 Oct. 1857.

p. 342 *Ireland's exports*: Foster, 336.

p. 342 *migrant agricultural labour*: Redford and Chaloner, 189–90.

p. 342 *Cattle-rearing in Wales*: Davies, 410.

p. 342 *began to augment this flow*: Spencer, 250.

p. 342 *rinderpest epidemic*: Wilson, A. N. 2, 428.

p. 342 *Milk trains*: *RM*, Mar. 1959, 155–7.

p. 343 *frozen meat*: Spencer, 282.

p. 343 *'smelly bone train'*: Garratt, C., 46.

p. 344 *Each working horse*: Thompson 3, 77.

p. 344 *London's night soil*: Pryor, 558.

p. 344 *manure from Leeds and Hull*: Reading, 26.

p. 344 *leftovers from making shoddy*: Dickens Jnr.

p. 344 *Burton ale*: Simmons 4, 33–7; Hunter and Thorne, 51; VCH, *County of Stafford*, ix (2003), 65–8.

p. 344 *brewery tours*: Baedeker's *Great Britain* (1887), 183.

p. 344 *Bass works outing*: Smith, D. N., 118; Paar and Grey, 39.

p. 345 *Isle of Ely*: Pryor, 574.

p. 346 *'rabbit special'*: Semmens, iii, 38.

p. 346 *heatable vans*: Taylor, M., 72.

p. 346 *six-acre fish dock*: Dow, i, 171–3.

p. 346 *fish and chips*; *more processed and more standardised*: Spencer, 264; 284–5.

Chapter 12: Railways and the Land II

p. 348 *knacker's yard*: noted by McCulloch, 654.

p. 348 *F. M. L. Thompson*: *see* note to p. 344

p. 349 *number of railway-owned horses*: Worsley, 233.

p. 349 *Mint Stables*: Brindle, 143–6.

p. 349 *resources of fodder*: Vaughan 3, 370.

p. 350 *'Nimrod'*: Itkowitz, 13.

p. 350 *Delmé Radcliffe*: Carr, 107.

p. 350 *Gloom overtook R. S. Surtees*; *the Holderness*: Itkowitz, 13; 53.

p. 350 *Lord Galway's pack*: *PIP*, 29 Mar. 1862.

p. 350 *'PACKS OF HOUNDS'*: Semmens, iii, 94.

p. 351 *George Lane-Fox MP*: Cannadine 1, 57.

p. 351 *5th Earl Fitzwilliam*: Thompson 2, 259.

p. 351 *private station*: Franks, 4.

p. 351 *Jorrocks*: Surtees 2, ch. 3.

p. 351 *Women began riding*: Itkowitz, 53.

p. 352 *Huntsmen were noted at Euston*: Sidney, 10.

p. 352 *By the 1860s*: Carr, 106–10.

p. 352 *number of packs*: Itkowitz, 53.

p. 352 *'the Bold Dragoon'*: Griffin, 137.

p. 353 *To even out the slopes*: Williams 2, 109, 134.

p. 354 *Samphire Hoe*: www.samphirehoe.com/uk/samphire-hoe/creation.

p. 354 *Crossrail route*: *Guardian*, 17 Sept. 2012.

p. 354 *'Calculating Boy'*: *MP*, 3 Apr. 1815.

p. 354 *Edinburgh University*: Rolt 1, 92, 229.

p. 355 *details of grass species*: Rolt 2, 149.

p. 355 *a cutting in northern England*; *Intake embankment*: Williams 2, 115; 134.

p. 355 *fissured clays*: Skempton, 43–4.

p. 355 *Round Down*: Dendy Marshall, ii, 293; *RHRGB*, ii (1982 edn), 30; Quick, 126.

p. 356–7 *Merstham cutting*; *Lough Foyle*: Williams 2, 110; 135.

p. 357 *A depth of some sixty feet*: Head, 27.

p. 357 *Chevet Tunnel*: Thornewell, 112.

p. 358 *stratigraphy*; *A few engineers*: Freeman 2, 34–43; 44–9.

p. 359 *George and Robert Stephenson*: Rolt 1, 209–10, 289.

p. 359 *ironstone beds*: Perkin, 130.

p. 359 *East Kent*: Catt, 4–5.

p. 360 *horseshoe curve*: Thomas, J. 2, 57.

p. 360 *London & Birmingham*: Burton, 66.

p. 361 *at Sankey*: Turnock, 64.

p. 361 *multiple-arched structures*: Smith, M., 30–31, 57–8.

p. 362 *Maidenhead*: Rolt 2, 171–2.

p. 362 *Ballochmyle Viaduct*: Smith, M., 45.

p. 362 *concrete structures*: Thomas, J. 2, 95–101.

p. 364 *a cheaper method*: Haworth, 71.

p. 365 *The Board of Trade's inspector*: Paar and Grey, 4.

p. 365 *exploration of timber crossings*: Simmons 1, 158.

p. 365 *standard pinewood sizes*: Burton, 178.

p. 366 *Cornwall Railway*: Smith, M., 88–90.

p. 366 *Landore Viaduct*: Vaughan 2, 151.

p. 366–7 *Barmouth Viaduct*; *Victoria Bridge*: Smith, M., 97–9; 82–3.

p. 367 *Robert Stephenson's record*: Lewis and Gagg.

p. 368 *tubular box-girder bridges*: Smith, M., 40–41, 49–52.

p. 369 *High Level Bridge*: Addyman and Fawcett, 39–49.

p. 369 *suspension principle*: Smith, M., 61–3, 70–72.

p. 369 *this deflected alarmingly*: Rolt 2, 70.

p. 370 *Arun Bridge*: Smith, M., 38.

p. 371 *the first Tay Bridge*: McKean, 1–3, 167–77.

p. 372 *Belah and Deepdale*: Smith, M., 80–82.

p. 372 *warning bell*: Weighell, 63.

p. 372 *Crumlin Viaduct*: Smith, M., 64–6.

p. 373 *Not everyone admired*: McKean, 299–300.

p. 374 *post-war railway bridges*: Mann, 1.

p. 374 *Runcorn Bridge*: Smith, M., 101–3; *RW*, Oct. 1969, 426.

p. 374 *across the Taff Valley*: Jones, W., 47.

p. 374 *109,762 acres*: Simmons 2, 301.

p. 375 *'bizarre horticultural relics'*: Mabey 2, 60.

p. 375 *Cutting of the lineside*: *Sheffield Independent*, 1 July 1837.

p. 375 *Financial stringency*: Rush and Price, 46.

p. 375 *embankment at Eydon*: Tyrrell, 115.

p. 375 *440 farmers*: *Lichfield Mercury*, 11 July 1941.

p. 375 *General Booth*: Booth, 126.

p. 376 *fences of Belgium*: Williams 2, 137.

p. 376 *a correspondent to* The Garden: *BDP*, 4 June 1875.

p. 376 *terraced for vines*: *Hampshire Telegraph*, 10 July 1847.

p. 376 *railways may have helped unwittingly*: Rackham, 176.

p. 378 *lucrative conflagrations*: Hewison, 72.

p. 378 *Masham branch*; *Harry Hartley*: Weighell, 169; 178.

p. 378 *weedkiller*: Johnson and Long, 353.

p. 378 *groundwater expands*: *RM*, Nov. 1963, 11–12.

p. 379 *rosebay willowherb*: Mabey 1, 235–6.

p. 379 *Oxford Ragwort*: Harris, S. A.; Mabey 1, 376–7.

p. 380 *Regular mowing*: Johnson and Long, 353.

Chapter 13: Goods and Services

p. 382 *relatively late additions*: *RM*, Nov. 2013, 36–40.

p. 383 *Thornton Yard*: *RM*, Feb. 1958, 129–33.

p. 385 *'dash pots'*: *RM*, Dec. 2013, 46–7; British Transport Films, *Freight and a City* (1966).

p. 385 *'flat' type*: Williamson, 134.

p. 385 *Crewe Basford Hall Yard*: *RW*, Dec. 1973, 504–7.

p. 386 *240,000 wagons*: Gourvish 2, 435.

p. 386 *fixed as early as the 1850s*: Simmons 1, 203–5.

p. 387 *slipper brake or 'skid'*: *RW*, July 1979, 352–3.

p. 388 *set the chain swinging*: Vaughan 4, 60.

p. 388 *4 November 1879*: Pritchard, 34–5.

p. 389 *Fifty-three hopeful shunters*: *RW*, Mar. 1969, 136.

p. 389 *at Carnforth*: *RM*, Aug. 2009, vii.

p. 389 *The mental aspect*; *'fly shunting'*: Vaughan 4, 109; 109–10.

p. 389–90 *shunting pole*; *brake levers*: Bagwell 2, 105; 107–8.

p. 390 *'common employment'*: Stein.

p. 391 *Amalgamated Society of Railway Servants*; *information on casualties*; *automatic couplings*: Bagwell 2, 47–8; 99; 103–7.

p. 392 *Things began to look up*: ibid., 107–10; Hewison, 129.

p. 393 *Senior railwaymen*: *Western Gazette*, 8 Nov. 1889; *Sheffield Evening Telegraph*, 27 Nov. 1889.

p. 394 *2.7 per 1,000; Not everybody regarded; provident societies*: Bagwell 2, 94; 47–8; 119–20.

p. 396 *Taff Vale dispute*: Wolmar 2, 200–201.

p. 397 *Matters came to a head*: Meacham, 214–15.

p. 397 *unquestioning obedience*: Kingsford, 13–34.

p. 397 *Manchester & Leeds's guards*: Granville, i, 392.

p. 398 *On the Great Western*: MacDermot, i, 674–6.

p. 398 *Individualism of this older kind; 'men who die at the post of duty'*: Reynolds, 5–7, 19, 25, 35; vi.

p. 399 *ASLEF*: Weighell, 29.

p. 399 *Chester Royal Infirmary*: VCH, *County of Chester*, ii (2005), 51.

p. 400 *Skilled carpenters*: Perkin, 96.

p. 400 *standard workers' houses*: Anderson and Fox, pl. 689.

p. 401 *Lickey incline*: Casserley 1, 39.

p. 401 *Catherine-wheel sparks*: Maggs 1, 36.

p. 402 *William Ellison*: Hendry, 112.

p. 402 *how these wagons were worked*: Williamson, 150; Gourvish 2, 3–5; Bagwell 1, 278–9.

p. 403 *cavalcades of these trucks*: Dyment, 210–11.

p. 403 *warehousing on wheels*: Williamson 129; Semmens, i, 52–3.

p. 403 *Loaded or empty*: Semmens, ii, 27–30.

p. 404 *heavy traffic of private wagons*: Simmons 1, 206–9.

p. 404 *Netherfield and Colwick*: Hendry, 129.

p. 405 *visitor to a Yorkshire marshalling yard*: Way, 75.

p. 405 *a maximum of 30 mph*: Roden, 195.

p. 405 *during the night*: Gourvish 3, 132.

p. 405 *platforms for the fast lines only*: Simmons 1, 210.

p. 405 *less than 10 mph*: Semmens, ii, 27.

p. 406–7 *standard wagons all of steel; Modernisation Plan of 1955; commitment to vacuum brakes*: Gourvish 2, 86; 256–66; 291.

p. 409 *the new Ministry of Transport*: Pryor, 644.

p. 409 *military spin-off*: Moran 1, 9.

p. 409 *Any road haulier*: Wolmar 2, 229–30.

p. 409 *found a ready market*: *RW*, Jan. 1981, 6–12.

p. 410 *Leeds Hunslet East*: Holmes, 35.

p. 410 *post-war Attlee government*: Gourvish 2, 92–6, 137.

p. 411 *Ernest Marples*: Moran 1, 26–7, 40.

p. 412–13 *an advisory group; two North Wales branch lines; One-third of the 4,300 stations*: Gourvish 2, 300–309; 278; 401.

p. 413 *between Liverpool and Southport*: *MR*, Mar. 1965, 149.

p. 414 *'History remembers the Black Death'*: Gourvish 2, 436.

p. 414 *some clear-eyed diagnoses*: Beeching, 10–11.

p. 414 *Dr Beeching's attitude to freight*: Gourvish 2, 426–9.

p. 414 *less than one ton per wagon*: Hardy, 81.

p. 414 *apple-growers*: *MR*, Dec. 1964, 420.

p. 414–5 *merry-go-round (MGR) trains*; *Freightliner*: Gourvish 2, 489–90; 492–3.

p. 415 *The Felixstowe branch*: *MR*, Nov. 2011, 16.

p. 415 *wagonload traffic*: Gourvish 2, 493.

p. 416 *size of the lorries*: Boyes.

p. 416 *Speedlink*; *TOPS*; *abandoned in 1991*: Gourvish 1, 94; 93–4; 284–5.

p. 417 *'A Square Deal'*: Bagwell and Lyth, 82.

p. 417 *around 35 per cent*: Gourvish 3, 156.

p. 417 *By the early 1870s*: Gourvish 2, 1.

p. 417 *size and turnover*: Arnold and McCartney, 56.

p. 418 *Huskisson goods station*: Kellett 1, 85.

p. 418 *'collusive oligopoly'*: Milne and Laing, 27.

p. 419 *Isle of Axholme*: Oates, 7.

p. 419 *the resulting decline*: Bonavia, i, 49.

p. 419 *81 per cent*: Gourvish 2, 2.

p. 419 *Mid-Suffolk Light Railway*: Comfort, 17, 27, 37, 73.

p. 420 *line through the Grampians*: Vallance, 37–8.

p. 420–1 *2,753 items*; 20 million: Kirby, 31; 32.

p. 422 *stock of items purchased*; *enthusiasm for statistics*: Williamson, 181; 5, 184–7.

p. 422 *colder-eyed account*: Hewison, 31–5.

p. 423 *paid out as a dividend*: Semmens, ii, 92.

Chapter 14: Managing

p. 426 *new class of professional manager*: Robbins 3, 147–60.

p. 426–7 *Huish's railway career*; *management and direction*; *Huish's own style*: Gourvish 3, 50–54; 61–4; 110–16, 257.

p. 427 *double-account system*: Jones, E., 52.

p. 428 *St Andrews Railway*: *RHR*, xv, 129.

p. 428 *George Hudson*: Wolmar 2, 97–103.

p. 429 *His last journey*: *York Herald*, 23 Dec. 1871, 10.

p. 429 *Lionel Redpath*: Robbins 3, 139–43; Griffiths, iii, 352–3.

p. 429 *'as many dresses'*: *Manchester Times*, 22 Nov. 1856.

p. 430 *William Welch Deloitte*: Jones, E., 52.

p. 430 *modern profession of accountancy*: Gourvish and O'Day, 31.

p. 430 *Edwin Waterhouse*: Jones, E., 50–55, 81.

p. 431 *total paid-up capital*: Perkin, 177.

p. 431 *joint auditor*: Jones, E., 134–5.

p. 432 *Sir Francis Head*: Head, 136–43.

p. 433 *demurrage charges*; *three-link couplings*: Bagwell 1, 72–3, 189–90.

p. 433 *the private British coal wagon*: Simmons 1, 208.

p. 433 *2,100 clerks*: Williams 2, 310–12.

p. 433 *around 14 per cent*: Smith, D. N., 58.

p. 434 *number of oversize sheets*: Bray, 207.

p. 435 *public and parliamentary opinion*: Kirby, 29.

p. 435 *Norfolk & Suffolk Joint Railway*: Allen 1, 64–5.

p. 435 *twenty-five separate joint concerns*: Simmons and Biddle, 240–41.

Chapter 15: At the Station

p. 439 *'a yacht in full sail'*: Betjeman 2, 278.

p. 439 *an estimated 90 per cent*: information from John Minnis, Historic England.

p. 439 *at Rothwell in Yorkshire*: Holmes, 9.

p. 440 *grain warehouse*: Hunter and Thorne, 94–100.

p. 441 *hydraulic accumulator*; *Hydraulic mains*: McNeil, 67–9, 98–108.

p. 441 *loaded with Burton ale*: Simmons 4, 37.

p. 443 *from Armstrong's Tyneside works*: Brindle, 130–31.

p. 443 *Nine Elms*: Richards and Mackenzie, 163; Betjeman 1, 78.

p. 444 *Durham's first station*: Fawcett, 145–7.

p. 444 *original Manchester terminus*: Fitzgerald, pp. 33–6.

p. 445 *Manchester had surrendered*: Kellett 1, 290.

p. 445 *stations operated at various times*: Pevsner et al., 175; Allen 1, 29; Simmons 5, 31; Walker, 121.

p. 445 *acknowledged places*: Thomas, R. G. H. 1, 128.

p. 445 *station at Liverpool Road*: Fitzgerald, 53–8; 'A Tourist', 28.

p. 446 *Railway platforms*: Essery, 70.

p. 447 *concrete platform-edge slabs*: Chapman, 248.

p. 447 *'Harrington hump'*: *RM*, Aug. 2009, 78.

p. 447 *one in eight*: Essery, 70.

p. 447 *Corus Infrastructure Services*: Corus brochure, 2008.

p. 448 *'one-sided' station*: Vaughan 3, 21, 146.

p. 448 *changing platforms at Nuneaton*: *Leeds Mercury*, 11 Apr. 1868.

p. 450 *Sidcup station*: Kidner 1, 15.

p. 451 *cheap government loans*: Semmens, ii, 33, 41.

p. 451 *Carnforth was selected*: Pettigrew, 72.

p. 452 *Clapham again provides*: Faulkner, 23.

p. 453 *The first London terminus*: Jackson, A. 2, 38.

p. 453 *East Suffolk line*: *MR*, Mar. 1964, 162; Gourvish 2, 435.

p. 454 *Keighley & Worth Valley line*: *Trains Illustrated*, Feb. 1956, 48.

p. 454 *got himself sacked*: Wolmar 2, 285.

p. 455 *keen on halts*: Peacock, 58–62.

p. 455 *Paragon Anti-Vandal Shelter*: www.macemainamstad.com/products/shelters/paragon-anti-vandal-shelter.

p. 456 *'neater and cheaper'*: Minnis, 26.

p. 456 *Birmingham, Wolverhampton & Dudley*: Simmons 5, 66.

p. 457 *stationmaster at Blake Hall*: Glancey, 4.

p. 457 *Stations of similar design*: National Heritage List 141233, Clare Station.

p. 458 *aftermath of the Beeching cuts*: Jennings, 37–9.

p. 459 *its own nursery*: Simmons 5, 260.

p. 459 *Kinross station*: Dickinson, W. E., 119.

p. 459 *Scottish companies*: *MP*, 12 Oct. 1853; *Stirling Observer*, 10 Oct. 1861.

p. 459 *prizes for station gardens*: *London Standard*, 21 July 1884.

p. 459 *one-armed stationmaster-gardener*: *Western Mail*, 2 Sept. 1893.

p. 459 *Sharp horticultural practice*: Quinn, 42–3.

p. 459 *Midsomer Norton*: Atthill and Nock, 111.

p. 460 *'broken only by the crunching'*: Betjeman 2, 125.

p. 460 *Mr Purdie at Linton*: Jennings, 37.

p. 460 *J. Thornton Burge*: David Turner, 'The Man with a Gold Cap', turniprail.blogspot.co.uk, 16 May 2011.

p. 461 *Henry Edward Hawker*: Hawker, 106–7, 118–19.

p. 461 *Among the early drop-outs*: Gerin, 179–81, 187–94, 203.

p. 462 *'rude wooden hut'*: Grundy, 75.

p. 463 *station at Adlestrop*: Leigh 1, 120–24; Leigh 2, 198.

p. 463 *Damems*: *RHR*, viii (1984 edn), 115.

p. 463 *first station at Paddington*: Doyle, 45.

p. 464 *a right way and a wrong way*: *RTHB*, 57–8.

p. 464 *Access to the platform*: Quick, 44.

p. 465 *Auguste Perdonnet*: Schivelbusch, 211.

p. 465 *'with your nose against the window'*: *MP*, 8 Nov. 1865.

p. 465 *set up ticket barriers*: *Bucks Herald*, 11 June 1842.

p. 465 *popular outcry*: *Bath Chronicle*, 30 June 1842.

p. 466 *traveller on the Eastern Union*: *Ipswich Journal*, 27 July 1850.

p. 466 *Norwich's main station*: *Norfolk Chronicle*, 16 and 23 Oct. 1858.

p. 466 *standard price of one penny*: Mander, 176.

p. 466 *fraudulent wartime travel*: Gregory, 180–81.

p. 466 *valid for one hour*: Bray, 199.

p. 466 *Extra-long souvenir tickets*: *RM*, June 1962, 504.

p. 467 *'one of the last penny facilities'*: *RM*, Feb. 1958, 73.

p. 467 *Lord Fiske*: *The Times*, 15 Feb. 1971.

p. 468 *'the shining bell'*: 'The Lazy Tour of Two Idle Apprentices', *HW*, 3 Oct. 1857.

p. 468 *unimpressive buildings at Oxford*: Vaughan 3, 81–8.

p. 469 *George Townsend Andrews*; *station at Malton*: Fawcett, 167, 172–3; 148.

p. 469 *a single big hall*: Meeks, 78–9.

p. 470 *Carpeted floors*: Thomas, J. 1, i, 174.

p. 470 *terminus at Bath*: *Bath Chronicle*, 5 Aug. 1869.

p. 470 *Leuchars*: *Fife Herald*, 15 Feb. 1866.

p. 470 *Portsmouth Chamber of Commerce*: *Portsmouth Evening News*, 22 June 1894.

p. 470 *Alfred Cole Adams*: *Building News*, 12 Feb. 1886.

p. 471 *a radio talk in 1940*: Betjeman 2, 123.

p. 473 *Great Western's station at Swindon*: MacDermot, i, 152–6, 643–4; ii, 407–9.

p. 473 *The finishes in first class*: Cattell and Falconer, 38–40; Quick, 58.

p. 474 *Windsor Bar*: Minnis, 182–3.

p. 474 *faience-lined refreshment room*: Addyman and Fawcett, 105.

p. 474 *midway stop at Wolverton*: *Black's Picturesque Tourist and Road and Railway Guide Book* (1850), 202.

p. 475 *Anglo-Scottish travellers*: Simmons 5, 354.

p. 475 *waiters or pot-boys*: Girouard, 25–42.

p. 475 *newspaper report in 1879*: *Portsmouth Evening News*, 5 Apr. 1879.

p. 475 *'Be very careful'*: *The Odd Fellow*, 24 Apr. 1841.

p. 475 *such bad roasted corn*: Rolt 2, 186–7.

p. 475 *'Railway tea is liquid nausea'*: *Sheffield Daily Telegraph*, 28 Oct. 1865.

p. 476 *'brown hot water'*: *ATYR*, 24 Mar. 1860.

p. 476 *dilapidated tea urns*: Dolby, 438.

p. 476 *the contingent at Wolverton*: Head, 87–9.

p. 476 *'supercilious complacency'*: *PMG*, 5 Oct. 1868.

p. 476 *'glossy hair and neat attire'*: 'Why?', *HW*, 1 Mar. 1856.

p. 477 *an incident at Rugby*: Dolby, 29–31.

p. 477 *growing empire of leases*: *PMG*, 11 June 1888.

p. 478 *two hotels rather*: Simmons 3, 202.

p. 478 *Brunel's facilities at Swindon*: Baxter, 381–2.

p. 478 *station at Hull*: Fawcett, 139–42.

p. 478 *Great Western Royal Hotel*: Simmons 3, 203.

p. 479 *Midland Grand Hotel*: Simmons 4, 54–75.

p. 479 *'approximate draw'*: McKean, 323–8.

p. 479 *Almost every large British city*: Simmons 3, 205.

p. 480 *Communist Party of Great Britain*: Jackson, A. 2, 176.

p. 480 *Sir William Towle*: Carter, O., 86–7.

p. 480 *'tropical' level of warmth*: Priestley, 255.

p. 480 *total of £5,758,836*: Simmons 3, 206.

p. 480 *Queen's Hotel*: *Yorkshire Post and Leeds Intelligencer*, 27 July 1937.

p. 481 *early into the field*: Simmons 3, 205, 215.

p. 481 *Morecambe*: Guise and Brook, 2–8, 16–46.

p. 482 *enthusiasm for golf*: Simmons 3, 206.

p. 482 *Cruden Bay*: Jackson, D., 39.

p. 482 *Old Course Hotel*: Gourvish 2, 524.

p. 483 *thirteen lineside stations*: Minnis, 16.

p. 483 *two standard types*: Leigh 1, 15, 20–23.

p. 484 *'taut and suave'*: Nairn and Pevsner, 188.

p. 485 *built at the Liverpool end*: Saint, 108.

p. 485 *primal type of iron train shed*: Fawcett, 113–14, 133–5.

p. 486 *King's Cross*: Hunter and Thorne, 60–64.

p. 487 *St Enoch terminus*: Minnis, 64–5.

p. 488 *Gare du Nord*: Saint, 121–3.

p. 488 *Only at Waterloo*: Jackson, A. 2, 229–40.

p. 489 *Painful echoes from Euston*: Richards, 216–17.

p. 489 *his previous meeting*: Tristram Hunt, *Britain in their Sites*, BBC Radio 4, 31 May 2009.

p. 489 *'two indifferent Renoirs'*: Stamp 2, 10.

p. 490 *electrification released valuable tracts*: Parissien, 147–8, 155–62.

Chapter 16: Information and Image

p. 491n *scholarly scrutiny*: Thomas, E., 176–7.

p. 492 *anonymous until 1933*: *Western Morning News*, 8 Sept. 1933.

p. 492 *fatal misidentification*: Quick, 46.

p. 492 *Arthur Hugh Clough*: Clough, vi,11. 60–61.

p. 492 *Baedeker's guide*: *Baedeker's Great Britain* (1887), xx.

p. 492 *Cuthbert Bede*: Bede, 3, ch. 1.

p. 493 *first such loudspeakers*: Semmens, ii, 43.

p. 493 *'Deedcoate'*: Wilson, A. N. 1, 163.

p. 493 *punch cards*: *RW*, Sept. 1969, 413.

p. 493 *27-inch television screen*: *RM*, Feb. 1962, 136.

p. 494 *American visitor*: Dorsey, 16.

p. 495 *schematic images*: Maxwell, i, 72.

p. 495 *Chester & Holyhead; Benjamin Baugh*: Nevett, 122; 92.

p. 496 *best suited to branded products*: Eley, 129.

p. 496 *'dirty platform'*: Bennett.

p. 496 *'The dreary drip'*: Nevett, 91–2.

p. 496 *'IRON JELLOIDS'*: quoted Morgan, 243.

p. 496 *Jolly Fisherman*: Edelstein, 73.

p. 497 *'No. 251'*: Nock, 117.

p. 497 *Union Terrace Gardens*: Brogden, 89.

p. 497 *'pills and soaps'*: Beerbohm 2, 243.

p. 497 *area of visual calm*: *MP*, 28 Nov. 1895.

p. 497 *SCAPA*: Nevett, 117–18, 127–8.

p. 498 *Frank Pick*: Green, 9; Taylor, S., 184–5.

p. 498 *Charles Holden*: Barson, 54–6.

p. 499 *internal report for the Metropolitan*: Wilson, C., 316.

p. 499 *New Southern stations*: Stamp 1, 31–4.

p. 499 *Wirral route*: Anderson and Fox, pls 295–303.

p. 500 *'Hawkseye' nameboards*: Stamp 1, 38.

p. 500 *'shirt-button' logo*: Semmens, ii, 26.

p. 500 *'new and hideous monogram'*: Betjeman 2, 126.

p. 500 *Gill's first love*: Gill, 73–4.

p. 500 *the great typographer*: Barker, 268.

p. 500 *'something like riding'*: Legg, 172.

p. 502 *Archdeacon of Lincoln*: *The Times*, 11 and 16 June 1948.

p. 502 *colour coding*: Haresnape 2, 168.

p. 503 *Regional colour-coding had been relaxed*: *Trains Illustrated*, June 1961, 352.

p. 503 *tally of rebuilt stations*; *older stations were facelifted*: *MR*, Oct. 1962, 249; 252–5.

p. 503 *Timetables for all regions*: *Design*, Mar. 1963, 21.

p. 503 *BR's new uniforms*: ibid., 64–5; *The Times*, 25 Feb. 1964.

p. 503 *entirely new corporate image*: Haresnape 1, 121.

p. 503 *XP64*: *RM*, Nov. 1964, 350.

p. 504 *The double arrow*: www.testpressing.org/2011/08/
british-rail-logo-design-research-unit-gerry-barney.

p. 504 *Richard 'Jock' Kinneir*: Moran 1, 62–8; Haresnape 1, 119–22.

p. 506 *Danish State Railways*: *MR*, May 1979, 198.

p. 506 *'self-righteous little platform "buildings"'*: Lloyd and Insall, 48.

p. 506 *CLASP stations*: Wikeley and Middleton, 131–7; *RW*, Feb. 1970, 86.

p. 507n *London Overground*: Harris, K., 497.

p. 508 *BRUTE trolleys*: Gourvish 2, 561.

p. 509 *Liverpool Street*: Derbyshire.

Chapter 17: Enthusiasm

p. 510 *Dr Richard Beeching*: *Guardian*, 2 Apr. 1962.

p. 510 *The Bluebell's line*: *RM*, Apr. 1962, 223–30.

p. 511 Titfield Thunderbolt: Carter, I. 2, 255.

p. 511 *Talyllyn Railway*: Rolt 3, 49–53.

p. 512 *Harold Macmillan M.P.*: Thorpe, 666.

p. 512 *'The regimental system'*: Gourvish 2, 571.

p. 512 *shedmaster from Norwich*: Rolt 3, 115–16.

p. 513 *article by Derek Hanson*: *RW*, May 1969, 244–6.

p. 513 *A lively correspondence*: *RW*, Sept. 1969, 416; Nov. 1969, 511.

p. 513 *the Victorian and Edwardian past*: Powers 1.

p. 514 *'the apparatus of transport'*: Kellett 2, 93.

p. 514 *'brave days of old'*: *The Times*, 20 May 1892.

p. 515 *'Cuckoo Valley Railway'*: Carter, I., 252–3.

p. 515 *earliest surviving edition*: Smith, G. R., 35.

p. 515 *Race to the North*: McKean, 308–16.

p. 515 *Rev. Victor Whitechurch*: Carter, I., 182.

p. 515 *Lord Monkswell*: Obituary, *The Times*, 16 Jan. 1964.

p. 515 *G. A. Sekon*: *RM*, Mar. 2010, 35–6.

p. 517 *books, jigsaws, board games*: Whitehouse and St John Thomas, 145–54.

p. 517 *'Premier Line'*: Ellis, C. H. 7, 20.

p. 517 *'lighter and more artistic shades'*: *RMM*, 45.

p. 517 *'The efforts of a score'*: Tuplin, preface.

p. 518 *'A chimney to a locomotive'*: Dow, iii, 124.

p. 518 *'the* faultless engine': Ellis, C. H. 1, 19.

p. 518 *'hideous Americanised progeny'*: quoted *MR*, Aug. 1977, 332.

p. 518–20 *Hoping to foster West Country tourism*; *'world speed record holder'*; *'bearing the name'*: Walton, 11; 12; 5.

p. 520 *fourteen-year-old Londoner*: *RM*, Aug. 2014, 48–9.

p. 520 *'young Berkshire diarist'*: Clifford, 206.

p. 521 *A. C. Perryman*: Perryman, 8–10, 13, 32.

p. 521 *details of engines in service*: *RM*, Aug. 2014, 49–52.

p. 522 *One labour-saving dodge*: information from Mr Martin Bradley.

p. 522 *Ian Allan*: Carter, I. 1, 32–3, 60–62.

p. 522 *Real Spotters could buy*: flyer in *Trains Illustrated*, Dec. 1952.

p. 522 *Tamworth*: *Manchester Guardian*, 14 May 1948.

p. 523 *North Hull Estate Train Spotters' Club*: *Hull Daily Mail*, 29 Nov. 1948.

p. 523 *A reporter went to Crewe*: *Manchester Guardian*, 7 Aug. 1951.

p. 524 *Outlandish transfers*: Banks, 130.

p. 525 *a viewing gallery*: *RM*, Mar. 2009, 56.

p. 525 *enduring commercial empire*: www.ianallan.com/group.

p. 525 *to hear and smell an engine*: Dickinson, W. E., 161.

p. 526 *squanderous use of fuel*: Hewison, 93.

p. 526 *'every slum-clearance area'*: Hunt and Krause, 5.

p. 527 *Great Northern Railway No. 1*: Casserley 2, 124–5.

p. 527 *'perfect balance'*: Ellis, C. H. 1, 66.

p. 527 *2,924 steam locomotives*: Ellis and Morse, 135.

p. 528 *A vignette from Scotland*: *Steam World*, Oct. 2007, 12.

p. 528 *steam might not finally expire*: Johnson and Long, 528.

p. 529 *3,198 'cops'*: Stretton, 30, 47.

p. 529 *Whittaker took up spotting*: Whittaker, 58, 77.

p. 530 *'Get trendy'*: *Rail Enthusiast*, Mar. 1987, 40.

p. 530 *'Timothy Potter, Trainspotter'*: *Viz*, 25 Aug. 1987.

p. 531 *Chris Donald*: *Independent*, 8 Jan. 1995.

p. 531n *'gricer'*: *RM*, Aug. 2014, 52.

p. 531 *'they are irrational'*: Bryson, 261.

p. 532 *'a shiny heavy web', etc.*: Lomax, 13–14, 19–20.

p. 533 *New Approach*: *RW*, June 1966, 250–53; Jan. 1967, 24–7.

p. 533 *Paul Riley*: Holland, J., 72 –80.

p. 534 *Peter Handford*: Neil Innes, *A Life In Cans*, BBC Radio 4, 19 Dec. 2007.

p. 535 *'A branch line train'*: *L.N.E.R.: Sounds of the Steam Age*, ASV Transacord ATR 7010.

p. 536 *W. H. Auden*: Spender, 110.

p. 536 *the seven-year-old Adrian Vaughan*: Vaughan 4, 5.

p. 537 *'a solid man'*: Gasson, 32.

p. 537 *driver Albert Young*: Ransome-Wallis, 65.

p. 537 *Frank McKenna*: Obituary, *Guardian*, 30 Oct. 2013.

p. 537 *Starting at Carlisle Kingmoor*: McKenna, 1–9, 18–21.

p. 538 *Six hundred collectors*: *Guardian*, 6 June 1964.

p. 539 *Collectors' Corner*: *The Times*, 22 Dec. 1969.

p. 539 *Michael Palin's exploration*: *Great Railway Journeys of the World: Confessions of a Trainspotter*, BBC2, 27 Oct. 1980.

p. 539 *£3 million per year*: *RM*, Nov. 2001, ii.

p. 540 *£12,700 for Paddington*: *Railways Illustrated*, Aug. 2009, 86.

p. 540 Golden Fleece: www.railwayanapage.com/top_50.htm.

p. 540n *Two 'Thunderbird' nameplates*: *RM*, Feb. 2014, 11.

p. 540 *clockwork versions*: Ellis, C., 10.

p. 540 *'no more like the original'*: *RMM*, 97.

p. 541 *Sir Arthur Heywood*: Smithers, 7–15, 44–6, 56–62.

p. 542 *Pendon Parva*: *Country Life*, 25 Nov. 1965, 1422–4.

p. 542 *Copenhagen Fields*: www.themodelrailwayclub.org/about-us/layouts/28-copenhagen-fields.

p. 543 *Lancashire & Yorkshire Railway Society*: *LYR Focus* 67 (2008); www.lyrs.org.uk/lyr_resources/pubs-focus.html.

p. 543 *George Dow*: Obituary, *British Railway Journal* 16 (1987), 308.

p. 544 *celebrated controversy in 1993*: Newby.

p. 544 *railway autobiographies*: Strangleman.

p. 545 *'a collection of buildings'*: Spedding, 72.

p. 545 *over 9 million passenger journeys*: *RM*, Apr. 2014, 6.

p. 547 *90 per cent of workers*: Carter, I. 1, 127.

p. 547 *Severn Valley Railway*: *Shropshire Star*, 1 Dec. 2012.

p. 548 *The real breakthrough*: *The Golden Age of Steam Railways*, BBC4, 28 May 2013.

p. 549 *fifty-year-old Deltic*: *RM*, June 2011, 9.

p. 550 *prices paid for locomotive nameplates*: www.railwayanapage.com/top_50.htm.

p. 550 *'a steam engine'*: Wells, 4.

PICTURE CREDITS

Colour Plates

1. Photo: Daily Herald Archive/Science & Society Picture Library/Getty Images
2, 9, 10, 11, 14, 25, 27, 28, 31. Author's collection
3, 5, 7, 12, 15, 17, 20, 21, 24, 26. Photos: © NRM/Pictorial Collection/Science & Society Picture Library – All rights reserved
4. Photo: Fine Art Images/Heritage Images/Getty Images
6. Photo: Science & Society Picture Library/Getty Images
8. Photo: Ray Boyd/Bude-past-and-present.org.uk
13. Photo: © NRM/British Transport Films/Science & Society Picture Library
16. Photo by courtesy of Mike Musson, WarwickshireRailways.com
18. Photo: Dave Hewitt
19. Photo: T. B. Owen/Colour-Rail
22. Photo: John Alsop Collection
23. Photo: Greg Norden Collection/Travellingartgallery.com
29. Photo: Colour-Rail.com
30. Photo: © Colin T Gifford/Getty Images

Text Illustrations

10, 12, 28, 62, 104, 107, 131, 143, 146, 174, 219, 220, 247, 265, 293, 298, 323, 364, 366, 393, 404, 421, 457, 467, 488, 495. Author's collection
45. Engraving, S. F. A. Caulfeild, *The Dictionary of Needlework*, ii, 1882
49, 388, 410. Photos: © National Railway Museum/Science & Society Picture Library – All rights reserved

ACKNOWLEDGEMENTS

This book is dedicated in memory of Peter Carson, editor and friend, whose wise and gentle guidance shaped the early and middle stages of the writing. I hope that the finished version would have pleased him no less. Andrew Franklin and Penny Daniel at Profile steered the book smoothly through to completion, with invaluable contributions from Cecilia Mackay as illustrations researcher, Peter Dyer as designer, and Trevor Horwood as copy editor. Thanks are also due to Claire Beaumont, Diana Broccardo, Anna-Marie Fitzgerald, Cecily Gayford, Drew Jerrison and Niamh Murray at Profile, to my agent Peter Straus, and to my employers, Yale University Press, who kindly granted two priceless months of writing leave.

The text was read in draft by Colin Divall, John Minnis, Paul Russenberger, Robert Thorne and Gavin Watson, all of whom generously suggested corrections and improvements. John Minnis also helped materially with the illustrations, as too did John Alsop, Mike Ashworth, Alyx Elliott, Mike Musson and Nigel Rees. Guidance on particular themes was received from Steven Brindle, Eric Latusek, James Mackay, James McConnachie, Clare Pettitt, Rob Smith, Malcolm Tucker and David Turner. Conversations with Claire Armitstead, Michael Bailey, Nicolas Barker, my father Martin Bradley, Tim Brearley, Richard Butler, Mike Chrimes, David Edgerton, Dave Farmer, Andy Foster, Andrew Grantham, Elain Harwood, Chris Holland, Tristram Hunt, the late Charles McKean, David McKie, Andrew Martin, Charles O'Brien, Hubert Pragnell, Andrew Saint, John

Seaton, Gavin Stamp, Peter van Zeller, Sarah Whittingham, Peter Worsley and Andrew Wilson also stimulated the writing, as did exchanges with railwaymen and ex-railwaymen up and down the country.

Final thanks go to my parents for having indulged my adolescent interest in railways, and to my wife Clara Farmer for her supreme patience with the demands of writing the book over so many holidays, evenings and weekends.

₪

This paperback edition incorporates several corrections kindly sent in by readers, and gratefully received.

INDEX